Fanny and Joshua

The Enigmatic Lives of Frances Caroline Adams and Joshua Lawrence Chamberlain

Diane Monroe Smith

Thomas Publications
Gettysburg, PA 17325

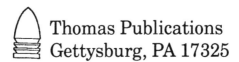

Fanny and Joshua

The Enigmatic Lives of
Frances Caroline Adams
and
Joshua Lawrence Chamberlain

Published by:
THOMAS PUBLICATIONS
P.O. Box 3031
Gettysburg, PA 17325

Publisher — Cataloging-in-Publication Data
Smith, Diane Monroe.
Fanny and Joshua: The Enigmatic Lives of Frances Caroline Adams and Joshua Chamberlain / Diane Monroe Smith
416 pp. 15.25 x 22.9 cm.
Includes index, bibliography.
ISBN 1-57747-046-X

1. Chamberlain, Joshua Lawrence, 1828-1914. 2. History — United States — Biography 3. History — United States —Maine I. Title
E467.1 .C45 LCC 98-88579

Printed in the United States of America

Cover design by Ryan C. Stouch

Cover photos: Joshua L. Chamberlain courtesy of the Pejepscot Historical Society, Fanny Chamberlain courtesy of Bowdoin College.

For my dear Ned

Contents

Preface

There are those students of the 19th century and the American Civil War who say that they need no introduction to Joshua Lawrence Chamberlain, but as Edmund Wilson observed in the introduction to his extraordinary study of Civil War literature, *Patriotic Gore*, it seems that everyone spoke "in character" during the 19th century. Certainly the official reports of Gen. Chamberlain, and the lectures and papers of the professor, governor, and college president are "in character," as that of soldier, statesman, and academic. We gain more insight to Chamberlain the man in his writing on the Civil War, moving reflections that offer catharsis for the brutality and slaughter, and immortalize those who made the sacrifice that was laid on the altar of country. But one must hear his words to those he loved—his family, his dearest friends, and most of all, to his much loved wife to come nearer to encountering "Lawrence," as they saw him and as he saw himself.

As opposed to the selfish, willful woman portrayed in previous Chamberlain biographies, Frances Adams Chamberlain was a talented and dutiful woman, whose caring nature and idealism were so much in harmony with Chamberlain's, that she became his love, helpmate, and confidante. To come to know Fanny and to explore the dynamics of their relationship with each other, their families and friends, is to meet Chamberlain on new ground. For all that Joshua Lawrence Chamberlain has been lionized, he had dreams, fears, triumphs and failures as do we all.

This effort to approach Chamberlain as son, husband, father and friend has meant a eight year search, and the examination of thousands of pages of correspondence and archival material, scattered at archives, historical societies and academic institutions all over the country. Though some of these sources have been investigated by previous Chamberlain biographers, few pursued the material that they did not see as specifically relative to the "Hero of Little Round Top." Ironically, pursuing such sources has uncovered new material on Chamberlain, the soldier, as well as that which throws revealing light on the lives of Fanny and Lawrence Chamberlain.

My research journey has been an unqualified joy, for this dynamic man and woman, inspired by a lifelong search for knowledge, spiritual truth and fulfillment, not only embraced classical studies, but also explored all that was new in the arts and intellectual pursuits of their day. With the Chamberlains' wide interests came the responsibility of considering many aspects of the society and culture of the 1800s and early 1900s—the music, art, literature, philosophy, theology, and politics—for most of all I wanted to avoid viewing this 19th century husband and wife with 20th century eyes.

Fanny and Lawrence Chamberlain experienced the joy and pain that all of us meet with in our lives. But they also experienced tragedy and trials that few of us will know. To borrow the sentiments of Franz Schubert, one of Chamberlain's favorite composers, songs of love would become songs of sorrow many times during their lives. Yet in this remarkable relationship, the saddest strains could and did return to the music of love.

Acknowledgements

It is the most pleasant of duties to thank those whose knowledge and generous goodwill made this work possible: Julia Oemig, for her guidance and friendship; Erik Jorgensen, and the staff and volunteers at Pejepscot Historical Society for their encouragement and invaluable assistance; Tom Desjardin, for his kind support and unerring common sense; John and Margaret Pullen, for their inspiration and thoughtful advice; Sue Wennrich, Molly Larson, and the staff of the Bangor Public Library—my ideal of those who make a library the home of knowledge and learning; Mildred Jones, historian for the First Parish Church in Brunswick, whose "viking" determination made the Rev. George Adams' diaries available for research; Sylvia Sherman and Jeff Brown at the Maine State Archives, for "knowing their stuff," and for their cheerful dedication; the late Dr. George Files, for sharing his great insight on medicine and life; Clifton Davis, Librarian, Bangor Theological Seminary, for his valuable assistance and patient efforts to enlighten me on 19th century theology and life at the seminary; William W. Erwin, Jr., Senior Reference Librarian, Special Collections Library, Duke University, for introducing me to Chamberlain's "Charge at Fort Hell" and Gen. Thomas Munford's manuscript; Susan Ravdin, Special Collections, and Sherrie S. Bergman, director of the Longfellow-Hawthorne Library at Bowdoin College, for making it possible for me to study their large holding of Chamberlain archival material; Wendy Thomas, Schlesinger Library at Radcliffe College, for her assistance in obtaining a mountain of material from their extensive Chamberlain-Adams collection; the staff of the Department of Manuscripts and Archives at Yale University Library, for their unfailing assistance;

Jennifer Topa, Massachusetts Historical Society, for her kind help and for introducing me to the Ashur Adams correspondence; Muriel Sanford and staff at Special Collections, and Mel Johnson, Fogler Library, University of Maine at Orono, for all their able assistance; Anne Rogers, Washington Memorial Library, Macon, Ga. and Nancy Davis Bray at Georgia College Library, Milledgeville, Ga. for information on 19th century Milledgeville, Georgia; Rosamond Allen and Jackie Beard, for their thoughtful interest in this project; The Rev. James C. Hoge and Duncan MacRae, for providing valuable insights on Homosassa and Ocala, Florida of the late 1800s; arrell Smoker, GNMP Library, for his "beyond the call of duty" willingness to assist me; Phyllis Scribner, First Congregational Church of Brewer, for her kindness and her great appreciation for history; Donald Winslow, Laselle College, Newtonville, Ma., for his generous assistance on Laselle's history; Judge Herbert Silsby II, for sharing his great knowledge of local history and his insights on 19th century law; Don Troiani and Paul Loane, for making the letters of their collections available to researchers; Earle Shettleworth, Maine Historic Preservation Commission; Bedford and Janet Hayes, and Jim Frasca for allowing photographs from their collections to be published here; Special appreciation to Charles and Peggy Pearce for their outstanding contributions to Civil War scholarship, and to Darrell Beauchamp, archivist at Navarro College, Corsicana, Texas; Bob and Dennis Lawrence and the Gettysburg Discussion Group, for providing access to an amazing collective knowledge so generously shared, for a great number of thought provoking discussions, and for supplying many a good laugh. I would especially like to acknowledge the esteemed members John Gross, and Bill and Jim Cameron for their help. I extend special appreciation in the "Information, Inspiration and Friendship Department" to John McNulty, Claire Fitzmaurice and Bob Singleton. A special thank you to Sally Thomas, my editor, and all the kind folks at Thomas Publications for their help in navigating the perilous seas of publishing. I also wish to express my sincere gratitude to all the many scholars whose works are cited in this book. On the firm foundation of their hard work, this work was begun. Most of all, I thank my husband (and first editor) Ned, and my sons Rob and Alex, for their patient and loving support and their unflagging interest and confidence in my work.

Fanny and Joshua

CHAPTER

1

The Minister's Daughter

In the summer of 1850, twenty-four year old Frances Adams pursued her passion for all that is beautiful. "Fanny," as she was called by friends and family, was living in Portland, Maine's largest city, once lovingly described by one of its sons, the poet Longfellow, for its shady, tree-lined avenues and its busy harbor, with the "sheen of the far-surrounding seas and islands...." She had made the short journey to Portland on the new rail line from her childhood home in Brunswick, Maine, having set off for that city shortly after the death of her much-loved adoptive mother, Sarah Folsom Adams. Here Fanny hoped to establish herself as a painter and musician in Portland's thriving art community. Establishing a painting room, as an artist's studio was then called, she declared her determination to enter a profession in which few women of that time achieved recognition. She also continued her study of music with the English-born Prof. Frederick N. Crouch, who had recently arrived in Maine. Crouch, trained in the choirs of St. Paul's and Westminster Abbey, had won international fame singing the "Irish" ballad he had composed, "Kathleen Mavourneen," a song of love and sad parting.[1]

Fanny's circle of friends came to include artists, writers, composers and poets, but Benjamin Paul Akers, a talented and rising young sculptor, became her closest friend. Akers shared Fanny's love of the arts and literature, and he charmed both Fanny and her adoptive father, the Rev. George Adams. Fanny's father, himself a lover of the arts, approved of her friendship with Akers, whom he consulted regarding the monument for his wife's grave, but Fanny's relationship with Akers cooled when she began to see beyond his considerable talent and charm to a man of irresponsible character. In the early days of their relationship, Fanny had seen him as not only a gifted sculptor, but as a "noble, good, & pure" man. Yet she would be disappointed by Akers' apparent willingness to adopt the uninhibited bohemian lifestyle of the 19th century artiste. Perhaps Fanny's judgment saved her from the fate of the woman who would become Paul Akers' wife several years later. In her memoirs, Elizabeth Taylor Akers wrote bitterly of a trip they made to Europe, a seemingly compulsory pilgrimage for every serious artist of the time. Though yet to be married, Akers took charge of Elizabeth's money and went through her hard-earned savings so recklessly that they soon found themselves stranded on the Continent.[2]

Maine Historical Society

Benjamin Paul Akers

Fanny in later years described her relationship with Akers as a friendship, not love, grounded on their mutual love of art, but Anna Davis, Fanny's adopted sister, acknowledged the disillusionment Fanny experienced during that period. Anna, recovering from a broken relationship of her own in early 1852, commented to Fanny, "I don't think much of *the men—* and I *know you* do not—." Fanny was about to begin a relationship with another man who, though no artist, had what she saw as an inner beauty that would touch her heart as no other had. He was the man she would marry and with whom she would spend the rest of her life.[3]

Fanny, born Caroline Frances Adams in 1825, was the seventh and last child of Ashur Adams and his third wife, Amelia Wyllys Adams. It was a family proud of their lineage, for they were cousins, though distant, to the John Adams family of Boston and were descendants of Miles Standish. Amelia, called Emily by her family, was a descendant of the Wyllys family, the early governors of Connecticut. Yet if the biography of Ashur's elder brother, Eliashib Adams, is to be considered, Fanny's birth father grew up a poor and sickly youth on a rundown farm in Canterbury, Connecticut. Though they were impoverished, Ashur attended the Andover Academy's Latin School and in later life was a Boston banker and broker. But Ashur Adams and his family, at their home in rural Jamaica Plain just outside the city, lived in perpetual genteel poverty, frequently teetering on the brink of economic disaster.[4]

Despite their limited means, Ashur Adams placed great value on education and the arts, and music and art flowed from the Adams' home, as well as a good deal of laughter. Though an acumen for financial success seemed to elude all members of this household, artistic talent and keen wit were two outstanding attributes of her Boston siblings. Fanny's eldest brother, George Wyllys Adams, a talented writer and artist, never seemed to make his talents pay. After shamelessly failing to apply himself at Brown, to which his family struggled to send him, he contracted tuberculosis in the 1830s and the family gamely pinched pennies to send him to southern Europe, in hopes that the mild climate would save his life. Though feeble, George enjoyed the trip immensely, his infrequent letters replete with the humorous observations of a rather cynical "innocent abroad." He did recover his health, but for all that, he never seemed to become a contributing member to the family's strained income.

Fanny's brother Sam emulated George, and often was described as an incorrigible during his attempts at higher learning. Family letters over the years are filled with news of Sam, who, Micawber-like, was perpetually starting on a new job or career, with his family's forlorn hopes that each new venture would bring success. These two brothers were engaging, charming—but often irresponsible and a considerable strain on the family finances. Two of Fanny's four sisters, Catherine and Julia, however, were made of different stuff. Educated and talented in music and art, Catherine and Julia proved themselves breadwinners by selling their art and teaching their skills, but the earnings of working women then, even very determined ones, were so meager that the family struggled from year to year.[5]

Fanny's birth in 1825 no doubt disconcerted her aging father, a man often enfeebled with illness. Beyond being another small mouth to feed, Frances, as her family called her when she was little, periodically displayed the symptoms of an unnamed, painful affliction in her eyes, seemingly one that ran in the family. Their inability to meet their youngest daughter's needs left her parents feeling dismayed and rather desperate. As Ashur would explain to Fanny many years later, "I had met with a sad reverse of fortune, and knew not how to provide for my family; [I] was therefore induced to part with my little pet (altho' with great reluctance) in the hope that she would fare better in her new home than in her old one."[6]

By the time Fanny was four years old, it was decided that she would go to live with her childless cousin, the Reverend George Adams and his wife, Sarah Ann Folsom Adams of Brunswick, Maine, as their daughter. Rev. Adams was the son of Ashur's elder brother, the stern and unsmiling Eliashib of Bangor, Maine. Eliashib Adams, by his own description had spent the first part of his life saving his Connecticut parents and siblings, including the sickly Ashur, from financial ruin, and the rest of his existence building from scratch a life and home for his own family in Bangor. A deeply religious man, he worked his way out of poverty, despite the hardship of having his wife become mentally unbalanced. Young George, when deprived of his mother's care, was sent away to school, and Eliashib eventually managed to send his eldest son to Yale. After college, George taught for several years in Portsmouth, New Hampshire, where he met his future wife, teacher Sarah Ann Folsom. Some six or seven years older than George, Sarah was the daughter of a prominent ship's master, Nathaniel Folsom. George left Portsmouth to attend Andover Theological Seminary, returning shortly after his graduation in 1826 to marry Sarah, or "Ann," as she was called by her family. When young Fanny came to Brunswick, Maine, around 1829, the handsome man who became Fanny's adoptive father was now the Reverend George Adams, the dedicated and much respected minister of the Congregationalist First Parish Church of Brunswick.[7]

The Adams were delighted with their new little daughter. Mrs. Adams, a kindly woman quite unconcerned with the style of her own simple dresses, indulged herself when dressing her little girl. A contemporary would remember four year old Fanny outfitted in a beautiful scarlet dress trimmed with black velvet with a charming little hat to match. In their longing for children of their own, George and Ann also adopted Anna Davis, a little girl near Fanny's age, the granddaughter of Dr. John Delamanter, a faculty member of Bowdoin's medical school. Their little daughters brought joy and life to the quiet minister's home, though Rev. Adams admitted that, with all this new bustle in the house, it was a challenge to summon the concentration he needed to write his weekly sermons. Surely little Frances missed the music and laughter of her Boston family in those first weeks and months in her new home. But as time passed, Fanny loved George and Ann Adams as father and mother. As her parents, they would guide and mold her young character.[8]

Brunswick was not a typical small town in 19th century Maine. It followed the calendar of agrarian pursuits and the tides of the seafarers, while its shore echoed with the hammers of the shipbuilder. But it also boasted of the first bastion of higher education in Maine, that red brick sanctuary of learning, Bowdoin College. This combination of influences provided a happy and intellectually stimulating climate for Fanny. The professors and students of Bowdoin came from all over the young United States and, in keeping with Bowdoin's staunch affiliation with Congregationalism, many of the faculty belonged to Rev. Adams' church, while the First Parish Church services were mandatory for Bowdoin students.

Though Bowdoin provided an erudite atmosphere, it would not provide Fanny with an opportunity for higher education. This institution, like most others in the country, educated men only, and few indeed were the women who would claim a college education in the first half of the 1800s. While enjoying the society of the college faculty, Rev. Adams and his family hardly held themselves aloof from the working classes of Brunswick. Picnic excursions and the town-wide celebrations that launched Brunswick's ships were as much a part of the Adams' family life as college lectures and teas, though no event surpassed the annual commencement at Bowdoin. Each summer, all households filled with company who came to attend the speeches and ceremonies.[9]

George Adams ministered to sailor and scholar alike. Though among the elite who served as a Bowdoin overseer, when the fire alarms of the town rang, he took his place on the bucket lines with the other men of the town. Many in Brunswick looked to Rev. Adams for moral leadership. Fanny's childhood home saw a constant stream of visitors from both town and college, who came to seek her father's advice and opinions. Though the conversations were often theological in nature, Rev. Adams, well read and actively interested in the affairs and politics of the day, was an influential man in Brunswick. Fanny, a lively and bright child, took in much of the religious debate and exchange going on around her. When no more than twelve years old, Fanny wrote a letter home to her adoptive parents that shows her to be a precocious observer of the adults around her. Describing her journey to Bangor, Maine to visit Rev. Adams' family, she reported her amusement at the orations of a Freewill Baptist minister who regaled his fellow passengers with religious opinion and sang Methodist hymns. Fanny also alerted her father that an acquaintance of his was injudiciously relating to others Rev. Adams' observation that there was no piety in the Episcopal Church. Revealed, too, in this letter, is the promise of a piquant wittiness that would be a beguiling part of Fanny's personality as an adult. Explaining to her father why he should write her a long letter, though she has written him a short one, she quipped that her letter, though brief, contained "a great deal of valuable information." Sending love to her mother, Fanny reported that she could have guessed that her mother's message to her would be for her to mind her books.

Mrs. Adams and her sister, Deborah Folsom, who had come to live in the Adams' household, were former teachers, and Fanny received her early education at home. And as she came into her teenage years, her life and education expanded to include visits with her Boston family.[10]

Fanny did not visit or establish a regular correspondence with her birth family until she was twelve years old, the Boston Adams' silence seemingly indicating a complete surrender of their youngest member to the Brunswick family. In a poignant letter from her birth mother to twelve year old Fanny, Emily Adams answered her daughter's inquiry about what date she had been born. Birthdays did not receive the sort of observance that we give them today, but it is, nonetheless, touching to see evidence of a growing desire on young Fanny's part to know of her beginnings.[11]

Fanny enjoyed an affectionate correspondence with her birth family in the 1840s, and received warm assurances from her birth mother, Emily Adams, of her Boston family's love for her. Emily, a religious and affectionate woman, encouraged Fanny to realize her deep obligations to her adoptive parents and to be a dutiful and obedient daughter to them. Emily emphasized her daughter's indebtedness to Rev. and Mrs. Adams, and she expressed her enthusiasm for Fanny's study of music and art, asserting that these skills might provide a livelihood in the future, if need be.

When Fanny was thirteen, she began spending time at Ashur Adams' home in Jamaica Plain, just outside Boston, studying art and music with her talented sister, Catherine Adams Lombard. Though married, no mention is made of the whereabouts of her husband, Daniel Lombard, and Catherine earned a modest income for herself and her two daughters by painting and teaching art. Catherine, at least fifteen years Fanny's senior, would, in the years to come, be quick to take offense if any praise of Fanny's talents implied that they outshone her own, leaving one to wonder if she resented the opportunities that Fanny enjoyed with her Brunswick family. Fanny's sister Charlotte cautioned her younger sibling to be discreet when discussing art and music with Catherine. Fanny's letters to and from Charlotte Adams display a special bond that sprang up between the two half-sisters, though Charlotte was eight years Fanny's senior. Charlotte followed news of Fanny's activities with great interest, never failing to tease her little sister over some new enthusiasm or a new flame, and Charlotte took it upon herself to write to Fanny with their own news and questions on the Boston family's behalf.[12]

During one of Fanny's first visits to her birth family's home, Charlotte Adams traveled to Brunswick to spend time at the home of Fanny's adoptive parents. Fanny's eldest half-sister, Mary, did her best to convince the thirteen year old Fanny that Rev. Adams had decided to keep Charlotte in place of her. Fanny wrote to her father that she had assured Mary "that if all the people in Boston should tell me so, I should not believe it." This was a sad way of teasing a young girl who knew very well what it was like to be "given away," but Mary's dark sense of humor may be explained by her recurring periods of debilitating depression.

Fanny's roguish brother, George Wyllys, expressed an amused fondness for his little sister, as did Samuel, the only one of Fanny's siblings who was born from the marriage of Ashur and Emily. Sam would take pains to stay in touch with his younger sister over the years, despite his ramblings and the undisciplined nature of his life.[13]

As Fanny entered womanhood, she finished her education in Brunswick's high school. A paper that Fanny wrote as an eighteen year old school girl in a favorite teacher's class reveals a lively and witty scholar. In her assignment to use verbs ending in "fy," she incorporated an apology for indulging in laughter in Mr. Pike's class: "This is to certify, notify, exemplify, testify, and signify my obedient disposition; and I hope that it will gratify, satisfy, beautify, and edify my teacher, and pacify, modify, mollify, and nullify his feelings of dissatisfaction toward me.... Please do not to exclaim 'O fie!,' when reading this paper." Though Fanny was a student at Alfred Pike's Brunswick High School in 1843, in that same year she also began teaching drawing and painting at the school, as she would in a number of Brunswick schools in the 1840s.[14]

The Adams family provided numerous opportunities for Fanny to develop the artistic talents they recognized in their daughter, for Rev. Adams held the arts in great esteem. He recorded a favored quotation from Jean Paul in his 1842 diary: "The world of art must be the highest, the most ideal, wherein every pang dissolves into a greater pleasure, and where we resemble men on mountain tops; the storm which bursts heavily on the real life and world below is to us but a cooling shower." Fanny would go beyond the superficial training in the decorative arts that society encouraged for young ladies, studying painting with Maine's premier portrait artist, Jeremiah Hardy. And in music as well, Fanny sought and obtained excellent training.

Perhaps it was during the daily prayer and hymn in their home that Rev. and Mrs. Adams first noticed that little Frances could sing and had a love of music. Here, too, it is no surprise that Rev. Adams encouraged Fanny's talents. Another citation in his diary offered a quote from Luther: "Next to theology it is to *music* that I give the highest place and the greatest honor."

Fanny received instruction from the Portland organist, Henry S. Edwards, then considered the best in the state. And occasionally when Fanny's father traveled to New England cities for religious conferences, she accompanied him. On one trip, they heard the celebrated singer, Jenny Lind, and on others Fanny had the sublime pleasures of visiting the art galleries and museums of Boston and New York. This willingness to provide extraordinary opportunities for a young woman provoked comment from family and friends, and may account, in part, for the perception that Fanny was their "pet."[15]

Though proud of their talented daughter, Rev. and Mrs. Adams instilled in Fanny a sense of modesty concerning her abilities and accomplishments, and Fanny displayed an earnest desire to please her Brunswick family and meet their expectations. In her letters to Brunswick while studying with her sisters in Boston, young Fanny struggled with the convention of not writing too much about herself in her letters. Though fearing her adopted parents' disapproval, she longed to write to her parents of her delight in the artistic skills she was developing while under her sister Catherine's tutelage. With a plea that they not scold her, she begged their forgiveness for writing so much about the joy and excitement she experienced while mastering the arts.[16]

Beyond music and art, Fanny's other great loves were literature and poetry, and, again, she was influenced by Rev. Adams. He, having taught classical literature at the Bangor Theological Seminary before coming to Brunswick, was a voracious reader and read to his children from the works of the great poets, dramatists and novelists. Adams traveled frequently to Boston and New York to religious conferences and he invariably searched the book shops of the cities, bringing back the latest books of note, and also the classics. Shakespeare, Juvenal, Carlyle, R. H. Dana, and Coleridge, to name a few, were among his interests in the early 1840s. Fanny became a regular member of Brunswick's literary discussion groups, and was recognized as one who put much thought into her reactions to the discussed writings and theories. She was not afraid to offer her own opinions, and as one friend teasingly commented, Fanny's reasoning, "so poetical and ingenious," was "enough to puzzle even a Champollion," the scholar acclaimed for first deciphering Egyptian hieroglyphics. His observation that Fanny left people amazed, and "unwilling to allow *the truth* so different from previous convictions...," is some indication that some of Fanny's opinions were, at times, unconventional.[17]

The Brunswick family raised a daughter who could not only reason and think for herself, but could express herself in intelligent company. The rich intellectual atmosphere of her home led her to look and think beyond the perimeters of a "woman's sphere," that limited a woman's interests and concerns to home and family. Not many women of Fanny's time dared to display their intellectual abilities. Critics of education for women warned that intense mental activity for women was at best unfeminine, and at its worst could lead to physical illness or even insanity. In this societal climate, Fanny's willingness to offer opinions that did more than validate existing ideas, startled some and intrigued others.

Though quite comfortable and confident in her world of learned and talented adults, both as a child and as a woman, Fanny was not unshakable. Her aplomb could vanish, as when faced with her father's request to make a visit alone to Henry Wadsworth Longfellow in Boston. Confident enough to face the great man of American poetry if accompanied by a friend, she begged Rev. Adams not to send her on this visit alone. Audacious in some situations, she exercised caution in others. She approached her first riding lessons with a fearlessness that surprised her instructor, yet she showed an early apprehension toward sailing, though she discovered that the pleasures of it could overcome her fears. Fanny's caution in regard to sailing does not seem so surprising when considering the many examples of Brunswick seafarers who went to sea and never returned. Among Rev. Adams' many duties as minister was notifying and comforting Brunswick families when news came, all too frequently, of lost ships and sailors. On one occasion while visiting Brunswick, Fanny's birth-sister, Charlotte, teased Fanny for being the only member of a party that was "skeered" to ride a newly-built ship at its launching in Brunswick. Laughably, the ways broke midway into the launch, leaving the brig and its passengers "stuck in the mud." Perhaps Fanny's caution was, again, born from experience.[18]

As Fanny grew into womanhood, it has been said that her father became disturbed by what he saw as willfulness and stubbornness in her behavior. Most painful for him was Fanny's refusal to become a member of his Congregational community. Although Fanny attended her father's First Parish Church regularly, and played the organ for the choir, she refused to become a member of his church. Unable, in good conscience, to deny her own beliefs and convictions, Fanny rejected the dogma of Congregationalism and its adherence to biblical doctrines. The Reverend Adams, who led many into the Congregational fold and the promises of salvation it offered, must have felt great pain and frustration at being unable to touch the religious feelings of the adopted daughter he loved. But, as she demonstrated in later years, Fanny was more at home with the liberal theologies of transcendentalist Ralph Waldo Emerson, and the Unitarian minister, Starr King. As Catherine Clinton indicated in her book, *The Other Civil War*, choice of religion was one of the few decisions that society allowed a woman to make for herself. Obedient daughter Fanny strove to be, but she would accept no arbiter of her spiritual beliefs.[19]

The Reverend Adams also expressed frustration with what he perceived as flaws in Fanny's character—her tendency to be late for appointments and, as he saw it, remiss in attending promptly to social obligations, provoking her assiduous father to exasperated scolding. Adams, whose life of diligently attending, day and night, to the needs of the members of his congregation all through the years of his ministry, was baffled by his daughter's failure to emulate her father's perceptions of duty. But all in all, Fanny was her adoptive father's child. A bright little girl, brought up on religious debate, treated to literature steeped with philosophical dialogues, inspired to prize and glory in the arts, she became a reflective and dynamic young woman.

Fanny's father also provided a role model for his young daughter as one who stood by his convictions. Though sensitive to the opinions and attitudes of his flock, a number of whom had no appreciation for abolitionism in any form, in the early 1840s, Rev. Adams invited a black minister from Portland, one Rev. Freeman, into the pulpit of the First Parish Church. Three members of his congregation, all ship's captains who spent as much time in the South as in the North, walked out. Adams commented in his diary that Rev. Freeman "cast out three devils before he said a word." Young Fanny learned much from her father about having courage in one's convictions.[20]

Perhaps no member of the household, though, could be more critical of Fanny than Cousin Deborah, the sharp-tongued sister of Mrs. Adams. Deborah Folsom offered stern advice on what she perceived as Fanny's love of beautiful clothing. Her judgment has been used to describe Fanny Adams as a vain girl who put on airs inappropriate to her station in life as a minister's daughter. Yet Cousin Deborah loved to sew for Fanny and helped her shop for the beautiful materials and trims that she admired. Fanny did love beautiful colors and textures, as an artist will, and her taste was once described by her artist brother, George Adams, as "gorgeous." But Fanny described herself as having tastes quite different from anyone else, with no ambition to be dressed in the height of current fashion. Though Deborah was often critical and an unrelenting scold, there is little doubt that she loved Fanny and was often most generous and supportive. But she treated Fanny as her "silly child," unwilling to accept her passage into womanhood, and seeing Fanny's dreams and goals as unrealistic. Meddlesome and seldom tactful, Deborah was involved in any and all turmoil that occurred in the Adams family.[21]

Fanny must have relished the freedom of Portland, with the opportunity to order her own life and indulge herself in the arts. As she began to show her own talents in painting and music, she developed an ever increasing circle of talented and admiring friends. But as 1851 unfolded, Fanny's attentions to her painting, music and friends in Portland were interrupted by visits home to Brunswick. She had become increasingly aware of a tall, serious, gray-eyed student at Bowdoin, who had become the new director of her father's choir. And when Joshua Lawrence Chamberlain began to pay court to Fanny, before many months had passed, she found that they had much more in common than their mutual love of music.[22]

CHAPTER

2

Raising an Idealist

The young man determined to win Fanny Adams' hand had been named Lawrence Joshua Chamberlain at his birth in 1828. It is written in the family bible that he was named in honor of Commodore Lawrence, whose words of defiance in the face of defeat, "Don't give up the ship," won him fame in 1813. Yet the young scholar would enter Bowdoin College as Joshua Lawrence Chamberlain. Perhaps he merely saw his opportunity to reverse his names as he started his new life among strangers at Bowdoin College. But how significant was this wish to place his biblical name before that of the modern warrior? He would be known as Joshua Lawrence Chamberlain throughout his academic and professional life, though his family would always call him Lawrence.[1]

His early years might be seen as the quintessence of a son of Maine, his family's life dominated by timber and sail, and nourished by the soil. Born to a respected family in Brewer, a small town across the river from Bangor, Maine, one of the busiest lumber ports in America, he was the grandson of Col. Joshua Chamberlain, who had settled in the area in 1800 as a shipbuilder. Lawrence's father, Joshua Chamberlain, Jr., was a successful farmer and expert on timberlands, whose marriage to Sarah Dupee Brastow joined two of the area's pioneer families. Ships from all over the world made their way up the Penobscot River, carrying away the rich harvest of wood from Maine's forests. Sailors and woodsmen crowded Bangor's wooden sidewalks, riddled with holes from the spikes of the riverdrivers' boots. Only after loading timber at the city's busy wharves, would the ships pause briefly at a spring on the Brewer side of the river, to fill their barrels with sweet water before heading downriver to the open sea.[2]

How different those two towns on opposing sides of the river were, for though Bangor had outstripped Brewer in size and commerce, it was the latter community which founded the first church in the region. By the time Lawrence was born, Bangor had its own churches and even a theological seminary, but it also bore the brunt of the sailors' respite from months at sea and the woodsmen's emergence with the freshets of spring from their long winter in the wilderness. The jingle of coins in the pockets of these hardy men had attracted an array of bawdy and ale houses. Yet Bangor retained enough respectability for its houses of ill repute to discreetly advertise their trade, to those in the know, with signboards that declared "laundry."[3]

The daily passage of ships that sailed to and from exotic and faraway ports must take any boy's thoughts beyond the boundaries of his own world, which for Lawrence was bound up in the hard work of his family's farm and timberlands. Though it would not be the sea that would lure the Chamberlains' promising first-born son away, he would not remain to walk in his father's footsteps through field and forest. Lawrence entered Bowdoin to pursue the ministry, his longing to see those romantic foreign lands to be satisfied by becoming a missionary. But what influences of his home and childhood set him on this path?[4]

The family adhered to the stern Calvinist teachings of the conservative Congregationalist Church. Lawrence's father had been one of the community leaders who labored to see a new Congregational meetinghouse raised in 1828. Yet it was not until the 1840s that the children would hear the tenets by which Sarah and Joshua Chamberlain, Jr. raised their family echoed from the pulpit of that church by the river. In 1844, Lawrence's younger siblings, Horace, Sarah, John, and Thomas, were baptized at the church, and in 1845, at the age of 16, Lawrence became a member of the church after a customary testimony of faith. The family's rather lengthy hesitance to become active members of the church may have been in deference to the feelings of Lawrence's mother, Sarah Dupee Brastow Chamberlain. She was a woman of deep religious convictions, but her father, Billings Brastow, had left that Brewer Congregational Society with his family in 1822 over some unknown disagreement with its followers.[5]

Strict demands were made on the members of the Brewer church. Alcohol was a demon, though ale and cider, at least by the Chamberlains' reckoning, were exempt. Indulgence in drink or such seemingly innocent amusements as dancing or taking a buggy ride on the Sabbath were enough to bring excommunication on the offender's head. But what may have been the most narrowing restriction that the church placed on its members was its condemnation of reading any literature that was not religious in nature. This placed many works beyond the reach of young Lawrence, who reminisced in his memoirs of having been turned down flat when he asked his parents' permission to read James Fenimore Cooper's *The Deerslayer* in his youth.[6]

The Chamberlain household, however, cannot be viewed as a grim and sterile environment, devoted only to toil and devoid of warmth or joy. Consider Lawrence's life beyond hard work and the tenets of his church. Much of his unfinished memoirs are filled with fond remembrances of his childhood homes. One of his first memories was the scent of roses round the door of his birthplace, a small cottage that Joshua Chamberlain, Sr. had given to his son and new bride as a wedding present. Lawrence found it difficult to leave the large home his father had built for his growing family when it was time to part from these loved ones and follow his dreams. He relished the memories of working the earth on sunlit days, of riding headlong over the fields and taking a horse over the fences. The solitary pleasures of the woods and visits to the mysterious camps of nearby Maine Indians remained in his memories, while the treks that he made with his father through the forest wilderness of Maine and Canada were prized recollections.

Music was a great source of pleasure to Lawrence. Captivated with the sound of the bass viol, he mimed the finger positions and bowing on a dummy instrument of his own making, until he managed to acquire the real thing. His sister Sarah, called Sae by the family, would gradually acquire enough skill on the family piano to attempt duets with her enthusiastic brother. Mother Chamberlain, who devoutly instilled in her children a deep sense of duty to God and church, was a loving mother, whose eyes often sparkled with humor and shone for her young ones with the serenity of good family life. Father Chamberlain, though described as taciturn and stern, nonetheless proved to be a caring and supportive father. Lawrence's parents had great dreams and hopes for their talented son, and he, with much gratitude for all they provided and made possible for him, loved and honored his mother and father as long as they lived.[7]

Lawrence credited his father with teaching him that "obstacles irremovable can be surmounted." Father Chamberlain accepted no excuses from his young son when a job needed to be done, and his imperious command, "Do it, that's how!," became for Lawrence "an order of action for life."

Brewer Public Library

The Chamberlain home, Brewer, ca. 1840.

Something in this boy led him to place high demands upon himself, to create challenges beyond those made by his exacting father. The first goal he remembered setting for himself, was to learn to swim well enough to cross the Penobscot River to the Bangor side and return to his own shore. When this had been accomplished, the task was to make the crossing carrying a heavy stone under one arm. There were also the towering masts of the ships in the river to climb. Placing his cap on the top of the mainmast of every ship launched on the river during his youth became his special feat.[8]

Ambitious and daring by nature, Lawrence also possessed a strong sense of idealism, nurtured by the importance his family placed on moral and spiritual obligations. Like many youths, he agonized over his choice of career, for a man's profession in the 1800s was his identity and established his place in society. But it seems that he, torn between the demands of heart and head, suffered more anguish over his decision than many of his contemporaries. He felt keenly that his decision would determine nothing less than who he was, and who he would be, morally and spiritually.[9]

Lawrence's father wanted a military career for his son, as evidenced by the boy's attendance at Whiting's Military School in nearby Ellsworth, Maine. After all, Col. Joshua Chamberlain, Lawrence's grandfather, had led several companies of Maine militia, and had commanded a garrison at Eastport, Maine during the War of 1812. And Lawrence's father had been second in command of the militia that confronted the British during a border dispute between Maine and Canada in the early 1840s. Diplomacy settled the matter before blood was spilled, but the hostile posturing was known thereafter as the Aroostook War. The fates delivered no stirring exploits in the annals of history for either Col. Joshua or Joshua, Jr., yet their service is an indication of the Chamberlain family's willingness to pick up the musket in their country's defense.[10]

There were military contributions on his mother's side of the family as well. Lawrence's grandfather, Charles Dupuis, fought in the American Revolution, when a misspelling of his name on a muster list changed the family's surname thereafter to Dupee. But Sarah Chamberlain longed to see her son in the pulpit. It is tempting to speculate that this proud descendant of French Huguenots simply placed duty to God above duty to country. But there were many who thought of their new democracy as nothing less than the fulfillment of a divine plan, a consecrated beginning of a better future for the world. Guarding the nation's moral well-being was every bit as important as defending her shores. Considering this popular melding of piety and patriotism, or what some have come to call the "civil religion" of the United States, the dreams that Mother and Father Chamberlain held for their oldest son are not so disparate. They both envisioned their son as a leader of men in their new nation. The influences that played upon Lawrence as he made his decision were not only what he learned at his father and mother's knee, but the values and interests of his church and community, and of American society as well.[11]

Brewer's inhabitants gave testimony to their piety by being the first community in the region to build a meeting house, a full eleven years before their prosperous neighbors across the river in Bangor erected a church. Reform movements and schisms at the turn of the 18th century had challenged Calvinist doctrine. Yet the values of their Puritan ancestors still echoed in the theology and ethics of the Brewer

Congregationalists, who embraced the sanctity of hard work and self discipline. During Lawrence's childhood and adolescence, the Brewer church experienced, as did churches all across the nation, several "awakenings," or revivals. Thus, members were inspired not only to raise their own sense of piety, but to accept the duty of bringing more members into their fold.

The Brewer church was unique, given its location and size. From its earliest days as a congregation, the members looked well beyond their immediate vicinity, to a world in which much work needed to be done. This little church sent more than its share of contributions, in money and in manpower, to accomplish their ends in the frontiers of young America and in foreign lands. Between the years of 1850 and 1900, they could boast of having sent sixty missionaries into service, in the United States and abroad.

Some church members, well known to Lawrence, went from this river town to Oregon as missionaries to the Indians, while others went as far away as Turkey and the South Pacific. Lawrence would declare that "if he could also be a missionary and go to some really heathen Country, like Africa or the Pacific Islands where he could take part in civilizing a people and helping them live right in this world anyway," he would, much to his mother's delight, prepare for the ministry.[12]

Lawrence may well have decided to follow in the footsteps of a soldier for Christianity, Benjamin Galen Snow, a Brewer man who graduated from Bowdoin in 1846. Having returned to attend the Bangor Theological Seminary, Snow became an admired mentor to Lawrence. He advised his young friend on college and inspired him with the goal to become a missionary, for Snow, after graduation from the seminary in 1849, would be ordained at the Brewer church, and go to far-off Micronesia. Such an ambition would have appealed to Lawrence's idealistic nature, for he wished to "set his compass, and fix his resolve,—I will be worthy of what is best in me,—hold myself ready for what is noblest in doing or suffering, as the years of God unfold." Becoming a missionary may also have been a solution to Lawrence's primary objection to either of his parents' proposals. Displaying a streak of independence, Lawrence rebelled at the thought of a career in the army or the church, as offering "but little scope and freedom. They bound a man by rules and precedents and petty despotisms, and swamped his personality." As a missionary halfway around the world from the nearest church authorities, he would have to answer only to God and his own conscience.[13]

While the Protestant work ethic of Puritan descendants has been sung as the hymn of New England's Yankees, it is in harmony with the values of the age of Jacksonian Democracy, and its anthem of the self-made man. Lawrence's grandfather and father were hardworking and ambitious men. They taught their children that there were plentiful opportunities in the burgeoning new nation for any individual who was not afraid of hard work, and who grasped the opportunity to invest wisely and honestly. Undaunted by the financial and educational barriers to be overcome, Lawrence set a course for college in preparation for the ministry, for he had been taught to work for what he wanted.[14]

Joshua Chamberlain, Jr., having experienced prosperity, had invested heavily in farm and timberland, but the hard financial times of the 1840s had left the Chamberlain family in some difficulty. Lawrence needed to fulfill not only his own goals, but to meet his responsibilities to his family by working on the family's farm. He also worked in the brickyards and ropewalks of Brewer, and in early 1847 he taught school in the sparsely settled community of Milford. Just ten miles upriver from his Brewer home, this village was on the frontier of Maine's vast northern wilderness. One day, lessons were interrupted when local Indians killed the largest buck Lawrence had ever seen, just outside his classroom door. In this school, so little was expected from the children of the rough-hewn inhabitants of the settlement, that the school examiners of the region seldom bothered to visit. Lawrence invited them to assess the quality of education that he was giving his young charges, and he took great pride in their positive evaluation.

Some of the larger sons of the local woodsmen had been known to physically eject any unfortunate teacher who did not meet with their approval. They discovered, however, that this young academic was work hardened by wielded ax and scythe, and Lawrence proved that he could successfully win any such confrontation. While commanding their respect in the schoolroom, he won their hearts by starting a "singing school." Sending for his bass viol, these classes proved so immensely popular in this isolated community, that meetings were held three nights a week. While homesick for his family and friends at home in Brewer, Lawrence was also away from its strictures, and he took this opportunity to broaden his literary horizons. In a long and thoughtful letter to a favorite young cousin and childhood friend, Sarah Shephard, Lawrence quoted from Byron, a poet unlikely to have been on the church's approved reading list. He also confided to his cousin the anxiety he felt for the daunting task of preparing for college: "We are leaving the rosy paths of Childhood in all their innocence and joy, and are stepping with trembling feet and in hesitating steps on the verge of active life and new duties. He added that, "I sometimes wish myself a child always for then it is that sport is the most innocent and joy most unbeclouded."[15]

He considered accepting a position teaching in one of Bangor's schools on leaving Milford; instead he set himself upon a rigid course of study. He allowed himself one year to acquire Greek and increase his proficiency in Latin beyond what he had absorbed in the local academies and high school. Strength in both languages would be needed to qualify for entrance at Bowdoin College, a bastion for orthodox Congregationalism with strong ties to the Bangor Theological Seminary where Lawrence intended to complete his studies for the ministry.[16]

Seeking a quiet area for study, he furnished the spacious garret of the family home, and drew up a rigid schedule. Every hour of the day, from 5 a.m. to 10 p.m., he filled with the hard physical work of the farm or intense study. That summer, Father Chamberlain sometimes appeared in the open garret, enjoining his son to learn the art of the broad sword. Lawrence welcomed these strenuous respites from his taxing mental labors, but as his skill increased, he and his father's bouts of friendly swordplay threatened them both with a sort of head splitting well beyond the dangers of mastering Greek vocabulary. By mutual consent, the weapons were permanently retired. With the coming of winter Lawrence's hours of study were interrupted only by the splitting and carrying of his firewood up to his third floor study—work that he declared rivaled any scientifically designed physical culture, when the wood was yellow birch or rock maple.[17]

In the fall of 1846, Lawrence continued with his independent studies, as the freshman class at Bowdoin started classes. Advised by two local alumni who monitored his progress, he continued to strive for proficiency in the classical languages and joined his class late. His advisors felt, based on experience, that Lawrence's time would be better spent preparing for the rigorous entrance examination. Bowdoin sent its students home during the coldest months of the year, and as the scholars returned in February 1847 from their winter vacation, Lawrence, though "confused with mingled sensations of awe and awkwardness," nonetheless convinced the examining professors of the college that he deserved to be a latecomer to the freshman class.[18]

Early on his first morning, he joined the "yawning, motley crowds" whose day began in the chapel and with a first recitation before breakfast. He presented himself at Winthrop Hall, known to the students as "Sodom." His first step on the pathway to higher education resulted in his wandering into the wrong building and classroom, after "following along by force of suction, instinctively assuming for classmates the greenest looking fellows he could see...." Entering the room, he was confronted with "a dismal bank of jagged faces surrounded by blackened walls looking for all the world like so many galley-slaves at their benches...." No slave ship this, but students sentenced to Prof. Smyth's calculus class. On relating the story of his uninvited appearance in Smyth's classroom to his friend and mentor, Benjamin Galen Snow, Lawrence was congratulated on having taken the wisest course and leaving the room, "For if old Smyth had taken hold of you, there would not have been a grease spot left." Lawrence managed to find his own class in Latin with the gentler Prof. Upham in the building next door, but he would have his turn with Smyth for algebra. Courses in elocution, logic, and a heavy schedule of classes in Greek and Latin reading, grammar and composition awaited him.[19]

His health undermined by months of hard study and labor in preparation for Bowdoin, Lawrence knew that he must turn all his attention and strength to his class work. Snow expressed relief when Lawrence gave up his idea of trying to complete college in two years: "I am inclined to think that you will need the whole 4 yrs to rub off some of your greenness! As I and a good many others did." Part of being "green" at Bowdoin meant hazing from the upperclassmen. Lawrence credited his meek demeanor with saving him from some of their more rigorous pranks. His more defiant roommate, George Hayes from Rochester, New Hampshire, had been taken from Maine Hall one night, and with a rope tied around his middle, had been run up a pine tree, in a "highly insufficient state of dress." But neither Lawrence's mild appearance nor his late entrance to the freshman class spared him from the sophomores' notice. The newcomer was treated to a "smoke out," a visitation in which windows and door were closely secured before pipes and a plentiful supply of tobacco were produced. Smoke filled the room until "the lamp looked like a red moon in a foggy night." Lawrence, tipped off to the nature of this traditional greeting, outlasted his guests, scoring one up on the upperclassmen who had "twenty early missing and five left disabled on the field."[20]

Lawrence was invited to join one of Bowdoin's secret societies, the precursors of college fraternities. When he voiced his doubts about membership in these groups being consistent with Christian feeling, he received a rather impatient reply from his friend. Snow responded that if Lawrence felt he would be led into evil simply by associating with the less devout, perhaps it would be well to avoid such situations. But Snow tempered his response by reminding Lawrence that he could also influence them. Whether through Snow's encouragement or his own natural curiosity, he cautiously began to explore beyond the social and intellectual boundaries of his sheltered youth.[21]

While Lawrence became a member of Alpha Delta Phi, the same society that Snow had joined when at Bowdoin, he found kindred spirits in the Prayer Circle, an organization with special interest in the foreign missions. The circle required its members to "abstain from all intoxicating liquors," and "any immoral conduct, such as engaging in noisy and boisterous plays, scraping, or in any way disturbing good order,...." Members were expelled for "neglect of religious or relative duties or denial of any of the fundamental doctrines of the Bible...," quite a broad definition of immorality, as Ernst Helmreich, author of a religious history of Bowdoin, would note. By the end of the freshman term in late summer 1848, Lawrence had passed all freshman examinations, and traveled home for a much needed rest.[22]

Lawrence's second year at Bowdoin provided new challenges, academically and otherwise. Much of his attention focused on what he felt was his greatest weakness, mathematics. Refusing to accept defeat, he admitted that some of Prof. Smyth's problems kept him up all the night, before the "light would dawn." Also during this year Lawrence decided to wage war on an affliction that often prevented him from demonstrating his abilities. Though a bright and capable student, many of his classes involved recitation, and Lawrence, when faced with certain consonants, had a pronounced stutter. He later explained in his memoirs that "the initial letters p, b, and t well named in some of the grammars 'close mutes' had well nigh made one of him." Having long endeavored to keep his painful impediment a secret, it was only by what he considered eternal vigilance that he was able to avoid painful embarrassment. He grew adept at scouting pages for the offending letters and acquired some skill in having ready synonyms for words to be avoided. This defense had its limitations however, and he endured his teacher's wrath when, asked to recite the first line of Virgil's *Bucolics*, "Tityre tu patulae recubans sub tegminie fagi," he remained silent.[23]

Lawrence also realized that this disability was a major factor in his bashfulness in society. This combination of academic and social awkwardness had become all but intolerable. He determined not to avoid the letters that were his nemesis, but to command techniques that allowed him to conquer them. If he got a good breath behind him, a "pas de charge," he could touch on words quickly and lightly. Realizing the rhythm of the words, he could convince himself, without drawing the attention of the listener, that he was singing the words, rather than speaking them. Lest anyone should be critical of his claim that "anything that is worth saying is worth singing...," Lawrence pointed out in his memoirs that the old Spartans used to sing their laws, and that Spartan laws were no laughing matter![24]

Determination and practice smoothed his speech. In time he mastered these techniques so skillfully that at the end of his junior year, he won the college's prize for both oratory and composition. In later years, Lawrence believed that his skill at "scouting" the page in reconnaissance for the dreaded consonants of his youth, had given him habits of ready anticipation and quick reaction. He believed that the possession of such skills proved vitally useful against a far more lethal foe than an offending consonant.[25]

As his speech improved and his confidence grew, he realized his facility for and love of languages. He also gave credit to Daniel Raynes Goodwin, the professor of modern languages, for opening his eyes to the joy of learning, and giving him the ability to see not only the integral relationships of languages, but also the alliances that existed between other studies. At the end of his sophomore year, as one of Goodwin's highest ranking students, Lawrence was appointed assistant librarian by his mentor. It was a position that gave him ready access to the college's collection and encouraged his growing appreciation for the literature that the religious strictures of his childhood had denied him. Lawrence was also invited into his teacher's home, a highly valued opportunity to enjoy the many domestic pleasures sorely missing from a student's life.[26]

Lawrence allowed little time for any pursuits other than academic, and what time he did spend away from his books was often filled with religious meetings and the Prayer Circle. As Bowdoin students labored to finish the "spring" term that lasted well into the summer, the project dearest to his heart was a Sunday School he had started several miles out of town. With considerable pleasure in this, his first congregation, Lawrence would never forget the appreciative people, young and old, that over-flowed the small schoolhouse.

Despite his academic vigilance and cautious moral convictions, Lawrence was also proud of the acceptance he received from his classmates. Nicknamed "Jack" by his fellows, his determination to maintain his high principles did not exclude him from their circle. His obedience to his conscience, however, did not protect him from nearly being expelled from Bowdoin that year. Lawrence unwittingly joined a party of his classmates for a hayride that had been proposed for the innocent project of attaining a tree for the campus. But liberal indulgence in the contents of the flasks that soon appeared turned the errand into a riotous careening through the byways of Brunswick. This prompted a rash of complaints from townspeople who took a dim view of the drunken behavior of some of the participants. Lawrence's classmates were dismayed when "Jack," who had tried to dissuade them from these transgressions, was the one who was called on President Wood's carpet the next day. Threatened with expulsion if he did not inform on the offenders, Lawrence won many friends that day when he refused to do so. They rewarded his silence by promptly coming forward with testimony of Lawrence's innocence and admissions of their own guilt.[27]

By the end of his sophomore year in August 1849, exhausted by the strains of study, Lawrence traveled home for a three week vacation. His loved ones' plans for the celebration of his 21st birthday gave way to his family's anxious fight to save his life, when a fever threatened to make that birthday his last. Several doctors pronounced his case hopeless before Mother Chamberlain called in a homeopathic physician, who rejected the bleeding, purging and harsh medications then utilized by orthodox practioners. The cessation of such enfeebling treatments saved Lawrence's life. Left an invalid for months, he was unable to return to Bowdoin for his junior year. His classmates completed the year without him, and on his return to Bowdoin, he found himself a junior in the class of 1852.[28]

It is unlikely that Fanny Adams noticed his absence in the school year 1849-1850. If she had noted his presence at all in previous years, it would have been as a pale face in the South Gallery of her father's church. Then, too, Fanny was often absent from Brunswick during Lawrence's first years at Bowdoin. She spent a good deal of time staying with her Boston family and visiting the home of friends in Ipswich. There, she was so much in the company of a Mr. Ward, that friends believed that they were secretly engaged.[29]

Despite the admired poetry of Mr. Ward, in the fall of 1850 Fanny continued her vocal training with Professor Crouch, while painting in her Portland studio. Her adoptive father, Rev. Adams, lonely and depressed in the months after his wife's death, often left Brunswick to visit Fanny. He proudly attended her performances in Portland concerts, and in October of that year, accompanied her to Boston to hear the singing immortal, Jenny Lind. Immersed in her new life in Portland's art community, Fanny's trips home to Brunswick that fall were infrequent. But she did meet the quiet Bowdoin scholar, who, having abandoned the students' gallery at her father's church, began to sing baritone in a rich, pleasing voice with the choir.[30]

Lawrence had returned to Bowdoin that fall to begin his junior year, and though considered by many to be the college's most challenging term, it proved to be much less demanding for him than his first years at the college. Lawrence relished his study of German and Spanish. And his study of Hebrew with Professor Calvin Stowe offered a double pleasure, for Lawrence not only prized his academic association with Prof. Stowe, but was made welcome in his home. He enjoyed the warm hospitality of the professor's wife, Harriet Beecher Stowe.

It proved a fortuitous time to be in this remarkable lady's company. In late winter 1851, while sitting in a pew of Rev. Adams' church, Harriet Beecher Stowe had a vision. Despite her many family obligations, Mrs. Stowe began to write the tragic tale of American slavery that was inspired by that revelation. Lawrence and Fanny were among the young people who gathered to hear Mrs. Stowe read each chapter of her book as she wrote it, before the publication of *Uncle Tom's Cabin* made her name known around the world.[31]

Fanny also began to see Lawrence at the literary circle that met in Brunswick homes each week. Members discussed the latest literature and took turns writing and presenting papers. These were enlightening and revealing encounters, a far cry from the sterile exchange of polite pleasantries at college teas and neighborhood parties, for character and intellect were revealed. Fanny and Lawrence found much to admire in one another, but this would be no mere meeting of minds. Admiration became powerful attraction, and attraction turned to love during an intense and rather tumultous courtship.[32]

CHAPTER

3

"If You Could Love Me So"

Fanny Adams and Lawrence Chamberlain met for the first time as toddlers on their mothers' knees, when Sarah Ann Folsom Adams was visiting Rev. Adams' relatives in Bangor. Mother Chamberlain recalled that, although Fanny was several years older than her son, Lawrence was the same size as the Adams' petite adopted daughter. But it was in the choir of Rev. Adams' Brunswick church that Lawrence first felt the "mystery" of Fanny Adams' presence. That fall of 1850, he witnessed the slim figure of the minister's daughter seated at the church organ, and beneath her skilled hands, "soft strains breathe forth, or swell into loud, triumphant chords." She possessed a voice that made the songs she sang peculiarly hers. And the discovery that a pair of "soulful" brown eyes grew bright with a quick and active intellect, convinced Lawrence Chamberlain that he must make Fanny Adams his own.[1]

Casual observers no doubt wondered at the audacity of the Bowdoin junior who paid court to the talented Miss Adams. With all her accomplishments, and her ambitions and goals in art and music, Fanny Adams did not appear anxious to marry. In fact, Fanny, at 25, was somewhat flustered by the attentions of a 22 year old student who was hardly in a position to consider a serious relationship. Though he was subject to agonies of uncertainty about his chances of success, court her he did.[2]

In early 1851, Brunswick friends were unaware that he had declared himself to Fanny. After one evening with friends passed without them speaking to one another, Lawrence wrote to her in a state of despair:

I could not bear to come away from you tonight and not have you speak to me...not to the silly clown that I seem, but to the heart dark and dead within me. It cannot be dead for it would be still and there is no rest for it now. What am I living for and what am I doing. Will I not be driven mad. I turned away before you should see my tears, for I am sick of weak tears and I could not stay for it would trouble you. It is enough that I am full of such furious agonies, that I can only smile like a driveling idiot, to save myself from being a maniac. I am tempted and tormented by the old adversary, clutching at my heart and torturing it, murdering it and glorying over it with a devilish grimace. Why do I have a super natural impulse to read the minutest action and word, and contend with most powerful imaginings of my own fancy. I see with grief how you have to sacrifice to my unreasonable demands and I see how you try not to be too cheerful in company when I am looking at you. Try not to satisfy me, for I am all unreasonable, but I require of you all that I would give and can give you myself, and thank heavens, you do not know how much that is. I do not want you to try, for I do not have to try, for I feel always and everywhere the same to you. I am ready to show you how tenderly I care for you, but I know you would not like that, and you are right. Believing you do not understand me is the most charitable belief I can have, and I cling to the hope that at some time you will see but one single glimpse of me and know me. If I had not seen you that night, I would have spoken tenderly, and would not have suffered the demon to speak. If you could only have... but then it was I who let you go away as if you were nobody to me. I cling to you with the eager grasp of a sinking man, so earnestly hoping that you might only kiss me. Am I mad. What am I saying? Must I bear it long? It may be soon that the last dagger may be driven. How strange it will be to be at peace.[3]

No coy or cautious suitor, Fanny could have little doubt as to her admirer's tormented preoccupations. His apologetic acknowledgement of an unreasonable jealousy, his "demon," as he candidly admitted in this letter, is a theme that runs through a number of Lawrence's early letters. To Fanny, such thinly-veiled expressions of insecurity in one she found gifted and admirable were puzzling. While Lawrence felt thoroughly confident of his proficiency in forest and field, country and college classroom, he lacked experience in Fanny's world, especially when faced with some of her talented friends. Distressing manifestations of this vulnerability almost ended their relationship before it began. However bumpy their road of courtship, from the beginning Lawrence pressed Fanny for a commitment to match his own, though Fanny had just begun to explore her feelings of love for this man.[4]

In late spring of 1851, when Fanny went to visit friends in Bangor, Lawrence traveled home to Brewer. She later wrote that the time she spent with him and his family was "a dream I will never forget." Though her letter urged him to join her at the church conference she had traveled further downeast to attend, it was rather coolly addressed to "Dear Friend Lawrence." But a key to her tepid salutation can be found in her closing plea. "Lawrence dont you preserve this among the valuable and interesting documents in your portfolio, will you? but destroy it at once."

Lawrence was often greatly distressed that Fanny did not express her feelings as openly as he did. She protested, a number of times, that she did not often dare to bare her soul. For when Fanny wrote something that particularly pleased or touched him, he, in his bliss, sometimes read or showed her letters to his mother or to Fanny's Cousin Deborah Folsom. To Fanny's dismay, he persisted in this practice. The survival of this letter, despite her instructions, gives testimony that he kept it among his "valuable and interesting documents."[5]

They spent much time together in Brunswick when Lawrence joined Fanny in directing the First Parish choir, where he added the sympathetic voice of his cello to her own passionate music. Their choir gained such skill that the group performed throughout the area. But a little note, passed by hand to Lawrence, leaves little doubt of Fanny's feelings for him and her desire for more private moments: "I am disappointed at not seeing you last eve. Why not give Mary J. her lesson early and give rehearsal the

Pejepscot Historical Society

Rev. George E. and Helen Root Adams, 1851.

skip for I will be home alone. Father is away and Addie will be out. Will you come, that is if agreeable to yourself? Your singing book is here and you will need it for the next day." They would long remember the first time he dared to press Fanny's hand to his lips. And Lawrence eloquently recalled their first embrace, declaring Fanny's head upon his chest as "shedding its golden peace over all my tumult and instead of seeming to be any weight, bearing me up and upward...." As their feelings for each other deepened, they contrived to find times to be alone together.[6]

As Fanny was courted by the ardent Chamberlain, her adoptive father, Rev. George Adams, then fifty years old, courted Helen Root, a young woman just Fanny's age. He had met Miss Root during a nine week trip to Chicago for an annual meeting on Foreign Missions, and by October 1851 they were engaged.

The Reverend Adams had been a widower a respectable year and a half before their betrothal. Nevertheless, the great affection in which Sarah Folsom Adams had been held, and the secrecy and swiftness of his courtship of Miss Root, left little time for family or Brunswick friends to adjust to the idea of a new Mrs. Adams. On December 30 of that year, Fanny and her Boston family attended their wedding in Reading, Massachusetts.[7]

Though Fanny's demonstrations of caring for Lawrence did much to assuage the torments of his self-doubt, periods of separation still brought on reappearances of Lawrence's "demon." On the day of the wedding in Reading, not an easy day for Fanny, Lawrence restlessly went to the Adams' home in Brunswick. Cousin Deborah, sympathizing with Fanny's lonesome suitor, entertained him by showing him daguerreotypes. One of these images, of whom we know not, sent Lawrence into an emotional tailspin. In a fever of admittedly self-induced jealousy, he wrote:

> *I was perfectly and uncontrollably wretched.... It was not so much the thing, as the horrible train of mad thoughts it suggested.... Would to God that I might see you for one half hour, or that you had said the few words to me the other day, which would have lifted my soul out of such shadows forever— But alas! I thought that if there had been any thing to say you would have said it—and so all that I imagined and feared and shrank from was true—I will not, cannot trouble you now by telling you what I felt yesterday or what I feel now. It would not be kind in me; only I feel that I cannot help just telling you something now... you cannot know much about my mental constitution—my imagination and how strongly I am inclined to take it as a ground of belief.*[8]

Soon to leave Brunswick for home, Lawrence closed this letter with the wish for Fanny to "Be happy—even if to be happy is to forget me for a little.... May God be over you and in you and keep you till we meet again here or above." No better melodramatic exit could be wrought, though it was rather spoiled by a note Lawrence scribbled on the back of this letter: "You have the key to my box. All letters from *Bangor* be sure and open and send to me if they are important—I leave one of these chant books for you to play over the chants."[9]

Fanny was much shaken by what she later described as the "fearful, morbid states of feeling into which you so often fall." This was apparent when she shared her concerns with a Boston friend, Stephen Allen, during this time period. She knew that she must decide whether love and marriage with this impassioned and emotionally mercurial man were advisable. In response to her apparent doubts that such wretched unhappiness had any place in a love affair, Allen gave his opinions on the "character, habits, education and disposition of one she may share her life with:"

> *You say you love him—yet do not feel that sort of love for him of which you dreamed so wildly...your ideas of love are too highly colored with your early pictures of romance...the early ideals of love are colored by the ease or hardship or neglect with which a child is brought up, and the idol we set up, according to our nature, temperament and education, are of an impractical ethereal being, which no one ever found substantiated in the experience of married life... I wish that he was 5 or 6 years older than you and further advanced in his studies and profession. Having to wait 4 or 5 years is too long, but I wonder if it may be profitable. I guess that hints from you suggest that he is of a rather jealous, sanguine and ardent temperament, that makes large demands and might be hard to please or satisfy. If you cannot satisfy him now and inspire powerful confidence, you never will. If he cannot cast out of his mind all those notions of 'first love' with which he complains so bitterly, you should be cautious of giving him your hand. Jealousy is the mark of a small mind....*[10]

In Stephen Allen's letter, it is sometimes difficult to realize whose fears and foibles Allen addressed, Fanny's or Lawrence's, but Allen finally offered this advice to his anxious friend. He suggested that one aspect of love was an acceptance that it is not a perfect romantic paradise, but a caring search for mutual understanding and a willingness to labor for a meeting of minds as well as hearts.[11]

The Reverend Adams may well have had his own disappointments regarding romantic bliss. Just a few months after bringing his new bride home to Brunswick on the last day of 1851, there were hints of the turmoil that developed in the Adams' home. He recorded in his diary that he was concerned about Fanny, that Helen was dispirited and quite unwell, and later in the same month, he remarked, "trying times." It seems that Cousin Deborah had brought things to a boil, for it was her actions that Rev. Adams saw as symbolic of his family's lack of acceptance of the new Mrs. Adams. Cousin Deborah, half owner of the Adams' home, packed up some of the household linen to save for Fanny and her adoptive sister Anna. This gesture angered Rev. Adams, but Deborah compounded her error by presenting him with an inventory of the items in the home which she felt belonged to his adoptive daughters and to herself. While there were less than pleasant feelings in the Adams' household, there may also have been a falling out between Fanny and her adoptive father regarding her relationship with Lawrence Chamberlain, for Rev. Adams would bluntly state that he had no great confidence in the issue.[12]

Many who knew both Fanny and Lawrence may also have had reservations regarding their relationship. These two resolute individuals were perceived as set, immovably, on very different paths. Fanny had chosen a life in the arts, and if she had contemplated marriage at all, her previous suitors had all been of her own artistic inclinations. This young, would-be fiance had committed himself to the ministry, in a religion that Fanny could not embrace. Relatives of the Adams family stated that Fanny and Lawrence's relationship could not last, commenting that, "she is accomplished and amiable &c but then he can't think her suited to him." How could this pious, studious young man consider making a woman with Fanny's religious inclinations his wife? Yet that is exactly what Lawrence continued to do.[13]

Fanny's refusal to become a member of the Congregational Church was undoubtedly a serious consideration for Lawrence, as a prospective minister in that faith. But because she did not accept all the tenets of that church did not mean that she was without deep religious convictions. Her beliefs, apparently, proved to be ones that Lawrence found he could tolerate, and even admire. Long before Fanny was born, the Congregational and Presbyterian churches had experienced serious divisions. Liberal dissenters, many of whom would embrace Unitarianism, challenged the Calvinist dogma that declared man was born in sin and sinful by nature. These liberals favored the view of man as a creature of neutral predilections, who could by his own efforts draw nearer to God. Cloaked with the imagery of a sinless Adam, given a fresh start in the wilderness of the new world, these tenets were uniquely compatible with American sentiments and ideals. By the 1850s, Unitarians were perceived by the Congregational Church, and a number of other Protestant sects as well, as dangerous radicals who would destroy religion if their beliefs were allowed to spread unchecked.[14]

Fanny would have been witness to the continuing theological uproar and debate regarding the Unitarians' challenge to conservative religion. She may simply have been won over by the liberals' arguments for a gentler, humanistic theology, but we might also consider their position on that which was nearest to Fanny's heart. While the more conservative elements of Congregationalism looked with uneasy suspicion upon devoting one's time to the arts, the Unitarians embraced music, painting, poetry and literature. They believed that uplifting "moral taste" should be acquired and cultivated. The Unitarians professed that not only ministers of the church, but also artists, poets and authors, were agents for man's acquisition of spiritual awareness. Those who practiced and perfected the arts were seen as having nothing less than a moral obligation to provide a window on the beauties of the world as an aesthetic pathway to enlightenment.[15]

Religious conservatives may have found little fault with the high value Unitarians placed on observing the beauties of nature. They, too, presented "natural religion," the order and wonders of nature, as evidence of the divinity. Nor did the Unitarians seriously question the dogma of "revealed religion," that declared the Bible to be God's words. But many of the Transcendentalists did. And though many Unitarians considered themselves, philosophically, Transcendentalists, many Transcendentalists, including the father of that movement in America, Ralph Waldo Emerson, found even Unitarian theology too confining. Championing the ability of every person to discover and pursue their own theology and philosophy, Emerson renounced the Bible as a source of revelation, and with it, the religious dogma it had inspired.

While Brunswick had a Unitarian community of its own and Transcendentalist influence was felt throughout the country, Fanny's numerous trips to visit her Boston birth family may have provided the most influential introduction to liberal theology and philosophy. As the cultural leader of New England, Boston was a stronghold of Unitarianism and Transcendentalism, whose adherents were the elite, the "new lights" of the arts and literature. Whether Fanny's convictions and beliefs were influenced by visits to this hotbed of new theology and philosophy, or were formed in quiet contemplation at her home in Brunswick, is unknown. But by the time she met Lawrence, the arts and beauty were her religion, and she rejected the Bible as a source of divine revelation.[16]

Raised in orthodoxy, attending a college considered to be a conservative stronghold, Lawrence should, perhaps, have been shocked by Miss Adams' radical views. On the contrary, he was fascinated with Fanny's aesthetic crusade and impressed with her deep commitment to the arts. He already shared her love of music. But her belief in its spiritual power, as well as the power of poetry, painting and literature, to serve as an enlightening pathway to truth and God, was beyond his experience. This was a world away from the one in which he grew up, but it was one he would strive to know. And as Lawrence pondered over his own aspirations to serve God and his fellow man, is it any wonder that he viewed Fanny's confident celebration of the arts and their power for spiritual enlightment as nothing less than remarkable? Lawrence described Fanny's beliefs, as "worship of the holy, the true & the beautiful." In this, and in her desire to spiritually uplift others and transcend worldly and mundane concerns, he found goals much the same as his own. Though Fanny could not agree with Lawrence's determination to be a member of the Congregational clergy, she admired and blessed his desire to minister to his fellow man's spiritual needs. "Yours is a true life...a thing of intensity and depth," Fanny told Lawrence early in their relationship, and many times she described his beliefs and dreams as noble and beautiful. The differences in theology that existed between Fanny and Lawrence, which some saw as an insurmountable problem, would not keep them from respecting and loving one another.[17]

In mid-April 1852, Fanny traveled to New York to study music with Helen Root Adams' talented brother, George Frederick Root, founder of one of the first American institutions to train teachers of music. A distinguished musician and composer, Root's classical works are now forgotten, but he is remembered for his songs of the Civil War, *Battle Cry of Freedom* and *Just Before the Battle, Mother*. By mid-May, Lawrence, as he completed his senior year at Bowdoin, grew distraught at what he felt were short, dispassionate and infrequent letters from Fanny, and he was again assailed with doubt. His disappointment with one of her letters was such that Cousin Deborah had taken it and put it beyond his reach, and Lawrence declared, "I was needing much from you then, but your letter only made me feel how far away from me you were—it seemed, in something more than is measured by the mountains & waters that separate us now. There was no answer to my love." Pages filled with feverish apprehensions and petulant consternation culminated in a impassioned plea that she assure him of her love:

> *...if I may—only know that one thing it is no matter what else comes upon me—the world cannot touch me then. Oh. Fannie do not let any thing estrange you from me—Oh! do not But if it must be so do not hesitate to tell me. I know I have nothing to offer you—not one of those things to which you most incline—I know that I shall never be any thing, or do any thing in life—.... All that I had to hope for or to love in it was you...that is worth living for...if you could love me so.*[18]

The very next day, Lawrence received a letter from Fanny that was an answer to all his pleas. Fanny not only declared her love, but agreed to marry him. In a letter as joyous as his others were forlorn, Lawrence responded: "You do love me, as I love you—...What more do I ask—what can I not do—what can I not be, if that only be true." And from that day forward, though a lengthy engagement even by Victorian standards would intervene, he called her his wife.[19]

Much that has been written about Fanny, questioning the depth of her love for Lawrence or her ability to love at all, has been drawn from the anguished letters that he wrote during their courtship. Despite the barriers to their relationship, as well as Lawrence's candid admission of his unreasonable demands, any perceived hesitation on Fanny's part to enter into this relationship has been ascribed to character flaws ranging from selfishness to debilitating insecurities of her own. Sadly, few of Fanny's letters from their courtship survive. But it is not difficult to know, from Lawrence's letters of response, that Fanny, setting all apprehensions aside, answered his love with her own.[20]

CHAPTER

4

To a "Land of Strangers"

When Fanny promised to join her life with his, what a change occurred in Lawrence. Once assured of her love, he relinquished the role of tormented supplicant for that of protector and lover—all he envisioned as his responsibility and right as beloved husband to cherished wife. His affectionate support may have been exactly what Fanny needed most in the year 1852, as her relationship with her adoptive father, Rev. Adams, continued to disintegrate.[1]

Fanny continued her musical studies in New York, for though Lawrence would graduate from Bowdoin that summer, he was considering three more years of study at the Bangor Theological Seminary before she would become Mrs. Joshua L. Chamberlain. She had also agreed to reimburse Rev. Adams for the cost of her New York training. Determined to support herself as well, her training at Prof. Root's prestigious institution would be an invaluable asset.

If it was a sad relief to be away from the turmoil in her well-loved home of more than twenty years, being in distant New York did not save her from knowing of the continuing unhappiness at home. A letter from Cousin Deborah informed her that Rev. Adams had told other family members that there was prejudice against Helen in Brunswick. Deborah commented that he was mistaken, for Helen had always been well liked. She added, however, that Rev. Adams had expected people to fall down and worship her. The sharp-tongued Deborah added the suspect comment that "there is no danger for merit in time will always meet its full appreciation." But Deborah's appraisal of Rev. Adams' expectations, that others see Helen

Root's exceptional qualities, was valid. He wrote to Fanny that, once she came home, "we will all try to do better, & to be happy together. It is my opinion Fanny that you have great reason to be thankful in the prospect of having such a friend as Miss Root...."[2]

Helen Root Adams remains a shadowy figure in the conflict at the Adams' home. She left no evidence of her role or reaction to the unhappy uproar that followed her arrival in Brunswick. But she wrote many years later that she merited being "thought a fool because of my awkward way of doing things and my never making appear the good that I had intended." Whether tactlessness and indiscretion on Helen's part added fuel to domestic fires is only conjecture, but Rev. Adams' anxious entries in his diary indicate that Helen was often unwell and dispirited in her first months of marriage.[3]

Bowdoin College

Joshua Lawrence Chamberlain, 1852.

Though Fanny was disturbed by disquiet at home, her adoptive father's lack of enthusiasm for her engagement may also have caused her to reconsider her intention to return to Brunswick after her New York studies. In June 1852, Lawrence responded to her disclosure that if she returned, she would not stay in Brunswick, but would explore the abundant opportunities to teach in the South:

> *I see now the wisdom as well as the nobleness & independence of your present resolution & undertaking. I honor & respect you even more than I ever have. Be sure now my best & dearest one, that you are not alone in anything. Your Father has not much faith in our relation—I cannot call it engagement, it seems something more—he does not expect that much will ever come of it or that it will last very long. I do not need to be told that—I* <u>*see*</u> *it plainly enough. The lack of interest he evinces sufficiently shows that his opinion is the same as when he told me so frankly that he had no great confidence in the issue. Let it be so. I do not care for it in itself. The only trouble I have about it is that he does not seem to feel that I have much right to know of your affairs or to take much interest in you. As to this I simply say he has mistaken his man. I am not so easily managed. I suspect there is a plan getting up for you to go to Roxbury instead of coming here after you leave New York; &, if I am not mistaken, for the house to be vacated part of this summer as a step towards a quiet revolution in the household. I suspect that cousin D. will leave soon after Anna comes, or rather that such is the plan—and that the end will be that the former inmates of the house will be dispensed with. I have no thought that this will be the result of any unkind feelings; but of what will be deemed* <u>*expediency*</u>*,—that term covering up some sad things, & some things which it would not be well or easy to mention, I am certain that you are very dear to your Father, & that he would be*

very sorry if you could not be happy with him. But from what I know now, I have come to the conclusion that you are right, my prize-girl, in your ideas & your course.[4]

Having revealed his concern that Rev. Adams would insist that Fanny stay in Boston after leaving New York, Lawrence declared that Fanny ought to be in Brunswick a month or two before she went away, so far and for so long: "If anybody imagined you are not going to be here at Commencement, that person is cherishing a delusion & misjudging the nature of the elements he has to deal with." Lawrence, in his puzzlement over Rev. Adams' attitude and actions, commented to Fanny, "The truth is, I imagine, your Father thinks you do not like Mrs. A. very well & he is afraid you will prejudice Anna, if you are here this summer; & there is no knowing how strangely a man will act when he is just married."[5]

Anna Davis, Rev. Adams' other adopted daughter, was away from home visiting her birth father in the West during those first months after Helen's arrival in the Adams' home. But Anna was already voicing her own doubts about Helen's acceptance in Brunswick, well before her return home. She wrote to Fanny in March 1852: "How are things at home—now Fanny Is it pleasant. I have some fears that it will seem different to me. Helen gets along nicely dont she? How do people like to have her dress so much more than mother ever did? It must seem a little odd—"[6]

While Rev. Adams, understandably, hoped to keep Anna Davis from becoming embroiled in the unhappiness in the Adams' home, his suggestion that Fanny go to her Boston family that summer may also be indicative of his intention to try to keep Fanny and Lawrence apart. A letter from Lawrence to Fanny in New York in late spring of that year revealed that Rev. Adams' Bangor family and friends were apparently well informed about the unhappiness in the Adams home. Gossip had reached Mother Chamberlain's ear that the unsuitability of Fanny and Lawrence's relationship was being freely discussed. Along with this distressing news was Lawrence's confession to Fanny that a letter of hers to Cousin Deborah had been sent to him. He, in his desire for his family to know what Fanny was really like, showed it to Mother Chamberlain: "I *did* let Mother see your letter to Cousin D. & she told sis that it gave the lie to all that had ever been whispered to her by certain ladies about you—& that she knew you were good & just as your letter proved you to be—& that it was seldom one saw so beautiful a letter so full of good sense & full of good & valuable qualities—"

Lawrence undoubtedly meant to reassure Fanny of his and his family's support and confidence in her. But this airing of family unhappiness, coupled with the news that another of her letters had been passed around, could only have been disheartening for Fanny.[7]

Before Fanny left New York, harsh words came from Rev. Adams. In a letter that discussed the payment of her New York bills and Fanny's agreement to repay her father, he wrote:

Why need you say that you 'heard the other day that Helen said &c' Why did you not say if you mentioned any name, that Cousin Deba had sent you word that Helen said &c&c. What is the meaning of this? Did cousin Deba mention it merely from a disinterested desire to know whether all the money had

> *come safe to hand? Or for the purpose of giving you to understand that Helen was watching you &c? Had you any 'ugly' feeling toward H., which caused you to mention her name? Or, was your mention of her a mere accident? I shall make you answer these questions with rigid accuracy.*

Such unpleasantness over her New York bills, and the novelty of having to repay her father for expenses he had so cheerfully shouldered in the past, led Fanny to feel hurt and resentful over this debt to her father. And the postscript of his letter indicates that Lawrence was being drawn into the family squabbles, for Rev. Adams noted: "I perceive that Helen has been writing to you. I do not myself construe your letter as she does & Chamberlain also. I rather think you did not mean any reflection did you not? I w[oul]d not have had you say it for 5 tens. Helen cannot stand it long as things have gone lately."[8]

By the summer of 1852, Rev. Adams had apparently resigned himself to Fanny's betrothal and he urged Fanny to come home. But after she left New York in July, Fanny spent little time in Brunswick. She traveled several times to Bangor with Lawrence, ostensibly to visit friends, but undoubtedly to spend time with Lawrence and his family. Back in Brunswick, Rev. Adams confided to his diary that he was worn out over trouble with Cousin Deborah. The most disgruntled and outspoken of the lot, Deborah's correspondence, replete with quotes of what was being said at home, kept feelings running high.[9]

At the end of August, all parties were in Brunswick for Bowdoin's commencement. Despite all the agonies and ecstasies of courtship during his last two years at Bowdoin, Lawrence graduated a member of Phi Beta Kappa, with his honors including first rank in Greek; First Assistant Librarian, an acknowledgement of his high academic standing; First Honor in French; German, Junior Part at Exhibition; Prize for Declamation; Mathematics, Junior Examination; and an honorary appointment as First Assistant in Chemistry. Lawrence was also selected to deliver the First Class oration at commencement. It was this distinction that ultimately lessened the "pang of parting" that he experienced on leaving Bowdoin and Brunswick. Lawrence later reminisced that perhaps all would have gone well with his address, "The Last Gladiatorial Show at Rome,"

> *had it not been for the abnormal action of that mysterious 'tertium quid' called the nervous system. But the presence in the close-crowding and crowded galleries of certain friends whose love and pride were at utmost tension, gave occasion for the evil one to interpose some of his mockeries of human ambition. Some slight occurrence amongst the distinguished audience, for that was the occasion of the 50th anniversary of the organization of the College, and all the dignitaries of the nation were represented there, disturbed the anxious balance of the speaker's self-possession, and he stopped short. Our gladiator was hit; the adversary had broken down his guard. For a moment all around him swum and swayed into a mist. But he only reeled, half-turned, and paced the stage, grasping some evidently extemporaneous and strangely far-fetched phrases, then suddenly whirling to the front, with more blood in his face than would have flowed from Caesar's 'morituri salutamus,' he delivered his conclusion straight out from the shoulder like those who are determined to die early.*[10]

To put the success or failure of his oration into perspective, it is interesting to note that Rev. Adams commented in his diary only that "Chamberlain did well, tho' his memory failed in the latter part." But though Chamberlain later in life could jest at the faults in his performance at commencement, it rather undermined his new-found confidence in himself and his plans for the future. Lawrence was distressed enough at the time, he remembered, that "the experience revived the question whether it was best to go to West Point...." He was hardly oblivious to the fact that his upcoming attendance at the Bangor Theological Seminary would offer many more challenges in public oration. Had Lawrence been more impulsive by nature or less dedicated to his theological goals, he might well have opted for West Point, then under Superintendent Robert E. Lee, rather than the seminary. A decade later, Lawrence met many graduates of West Point, but he met them as a citizen soldier.[11]

Lawrence's classes at the Bangor Seminary started soon after Bowdoin's commencement, but before he left Brunswick, he placed an engagement ring on Fanny's hand. They did not know when they would see each other again, for Fanny was still determined to find a teaching position and strike out on her own. When Fanny's sister Charlotte learned that Cousin Deborah and Anna were both leaving Brunswick, and that her young sister intended to follow their example, she wrote of her sorrow that "there is no Brunswick now." Charlotte added, "who could have thought that one death could have changed everything."[12]

Bangor Public Library, Vickery Collection.

Dormitory at the Bangor Theological Seminary.

By mid-October 1852, both Deborah Folsom and Anna Davis had left the Adams' home. Cousin Deborah went to New Jersey to live with friends, while Anna Davis traveled to Mississippi to accept a teaching position. Though Anna seemed to manage, more than any other, to stay above the fray, she later commented that all of the letters she received from Rev. Adams contained reproofs for some misdemeanor. When Anna and Deborah's departure seemingly left Fanny to bear the brunt of her adoptive father's frustration and indignation, she arranged to escape these unhappy scenes. She wanted to go to her Boston family while she continued her search for employment, but a severe case of the chilblains that often plagued her in cold weather left her unable to walk, and she was confined to her adoptive father's house for six weeks. Worried over her ability to take care of herself if she accepted a position far from home, Rev. Adams spent many hours talking with Fanny, though he confessed in his diary that he spoke "perhaps not very wisely nor profitably."[13]

Fanny wrote to Lawrence of the heartache she felt as her estrangement from her adoptive father continued. For the second time in her life, she faced the possibility of permanent separation from her family. On the last day of October, 1852, Lawrence wrote to Fanny that, if she knew how he loved her, she would not say "she wished she had never been born." With sympathetic letters and little mementos, Lawrence did his best to cheer her. He sent a pair of soft and beautifully beaded Indian moccasins for her "poor little feet." And borrowing a photograph of himself that belonged to his sister Sae, Lawrence sent it to Fanny, insisting that, "If it didnt look so much like a simpleton I would let you keep it, I wont have another one taken till I get handsomer."[14]

The prospect of relief from her painful situation came with the arrival of a letter in early December. Recommended by Prof. Root, Fanny was offered a position in Milledgeville, Georgia's antebellum capital, to teach vocal music at Miss Lucia Bass' female academy. There, she would also assume the duties of organist at the Milledgeville Presbyterian Church, and instruct students privately in piano. At $800 a year, a generous salary for a woman in those days, her income would allow her to support herself and repay her debt to her father. Yet while Fanny felt she must withdraw from the painful situation in her Brunswick home, the thought of leaving Lawrence and all she knew and loved to take up a new life among strangers was all but overwhelming.

Before Fanny left Brunswick for Boston on December 22, she pleaded with Lawrence to meet with her one last time at her birth family's home before she began her long journey to Georgia. His letter of response arrived after she had gone, and it is hard to know when his letter caught up with her as she traveled south. Stating that he was too ill to travel, Lawrence declared, "I am scarcely able even if other things were free to go any where now. And then dear Fannie to see you only to part from you—it would certainly be too much for me." Though containing many endearments, it is an oddly detached letter, barren of his usual warmth and unusually suffused with the rhetoric of his conservative seminary environment. He suggested, "Do not let this world be all, Fannie—it is [of] little worth & unsatisfactory—and even, dearest, we must not make each other *supreme above* the higher worship of our Father above. He *may* see it to be necessary to remind us by a terrible lesson of his superior right to our affections—" If such a chilling farewell was the product of some new and sterner piety, it was not one that Lawrence would often endorse. It may be nearer the truth that, as a long separation became a stunning reality, Lawrence, heart-torn, required nothing less than a divine validation of the path he had chosen.[15]

Reverend Adams took comfort in the knowledge that Fanny would be spending her first days in Milledgeville with a distant relation, Mrs. Richard Orme, the former Abby Adams of Massachusetts. Sadly, Fanny may have left Brunswick aware only of her adoptive father's critical disapproval, but the real distress that Rev. Adams experienced is evident in his diary: "My poor Fanny left for Georgia at noon. Her prospects are good, if her health is sufficient, & if she has enough of energy & punctuality. But I fear. Poor child! God protect her! God have mercy upon her! Thus finally breaks up my family as it *was*!" Now alone with Rev. Adams in their Brunswick home, Helen shared with her husband her own sympathetic insights on Fanny's unhappiness, prompting the sad admission in his diary: "It seems as tho' my heart would break. I never knew anguish like this."[16]

Fanny arrived in Roxbury quite ill, but gathering her strength and courage, she made a tearful departure from her Boston family. The dark, threatening skies of the night she sailed for New York did little to ease Emily Adams' anxiety, as her daughter left for a "land of strangers." Nor would Fanny have a better passage from New York to Savannah. The steamer *Florida* was also plagued by winter storms, and seasickness confined Fanny to her berth for most of the trip. She wrote to her Boston family that, "I really believe I should have *died*, if I had suffered so, much longer, from starvation at least, even if seasickness had failed of dispatching me." Yet the misery of her trip did not prevent Fanny from taking account of her surroundings on landing in Savannah. What a different world she was entering, and she wrote to her sister Charlotte of her first encounter with slavery:

> *...a fine queenly, black woman with a very stylish turban disposed in a picturesque manner upon her head, came up towards the window of the car where I sat; her whole face beaming with joy, and then suddenly turning away again. I heard her muttering to herself 'O! if I did'nt think that was my dear, old Missis come from Savannah! and I thought maybe she'd be so pleased just to see her old Martha once more!*

Fanny pointed out to Charlotte, "Some people would have made it all tell on the score of the happiness of slaves with and their attachment to their masters."

She was astonished by the damp cold she found in Georgia, for not only had she expected more moderate temperatures that far south, but she noted that even the nicest houses were not built well for keeping out the chill. Her first days in Milledgeville were spent confined to her bed with a severe cold that left a lingering cough. Fanny gratefully realized the kindness of her hostess, for Abby Orme looked after her young relation with motherly care. And thoughts of home came to Fanny when she discovered a much-thumbed first edition of *Uncle Tom's Cabin* on a mantelpiece in the Orme home.[17]

Fanny felt some anxiety over whether she could meet her new employers' expectations, for Mrs. Orme had told her that the musical ideals in Milledgeville were very high. But before many weeks had passed, Fanny, with great relief, wrote to sister Charlotte, "their standard of music here does not terrify me in the least, and my confidence has been regularly increasing ever since I came here." Moreover, the kindness and attention of the community reassured Fanny that the warnings she had received, that teachers were looked down upon in the South, were unfounded.

Fanny found many differences between home and life in this Georgia community. The white populations of Georgia and Maine were both close to a half million in the 1850s, but the scarcity of public education gave Georgia an illiteracy rate eight times higher than Maine, while education for the state's black population was nonexistent. Nor would she find many kindred spirits who lived for the arts as she did. As it was, however, she would have no time for poetry or painting, for Fanny, as she took up her official duties, found that she had plenty to do. She also discovered that the very active social life of Milledgeville placed great demands upon her free time. It was an aspect of her new life that would tax her strength, and at times, her patience.[18]

Fanny's safe arrival in Milledgeville relieved some of Lawrence's anxiety, yet it is apparent that he felt uneasy at having her so far away and in conditions that he could not determine. One of his first letters to her in Georgia, while affectionate, seethed with barely disguised frustration. He criticized one of her letters that ap-

Georgia Department of Archives and History

The Orme House, Milledgeville, Georgia, c. 1900.

parently had left him feeling quite in the dark. Commenting that Fanny jumped from topic to topic, he also implied that she might not be telling him everything, or at least, not those things that she imagined would cause him to worry. Lawrence observed that among her many topics were her salary, her dreams of what she would do for their "little home," questions of whether he liked this or that, and a reference to a night dress that was "enough to drive a man mad." But he pointedly addressed Fanny's announcement that,

> *"Mrs. Orme has a son & two daughters." There your quick queer suggestive mind pounces on "the son" at once & as if I should have some mortal enmity with him as a matter of course, you array him in harmless "politeness" & invulnerable robes fairly out of my reach. There upon with an apology, and an absurd deification of me with an incense offering of kisses rather tempting to my saintship, you bound & sweep away in a perfect witchery of wildness to your subject again.*

Offering to make Fanny jealous by telling her of the sweetness of his Bangor cousin, Annie Chamberlain, Lawrence delivered the following tongue in cheek ultimatum to Mrs. Orme's son: "By the way you may tell your friend *Mr. Orme* that I am the best 'pistol shot' in this region. However he is at liberty to try to love you as well as I do if he can. We will then give the pistols the casting vote. I am ready any day—at 1000 miles!"[19]

Lawrence also expressed his disappointment at not having had more letters from Fanny, for he continued:

> *Well, now; after all I think this letter I have been criticising [sic] is a very nice letter—yes a sweet letter; even a—but I will not "cap the climax." You know what I think of it, especially when you were so very considerate as to allow me a month to anticipate it & whet up my appetite. I am happy to be able to announce to you that I am now strong enough to bear such things considerably oftener.... Fan you are too bad—thats a fact—not to write me any oftener, when I write you so often.*

Declaring that he would not write to her until she wrote to him again, he added, "Dont cry now. I only want to get you into better habits." But perhaps he was striking closer to his primary concern when he asked, "I would like to know what you do evenings—whether you sit & dream away 'rapt, inspired,' or whether the time is all taken up at the *toilette* as of old." While Lawrence's demand to know what Fanny did with her time when she was not teaching might be seen as a reoccurrence of his old jealousy, the conclusion to this letter suggests another concern. For Lawrence also stated his discomfort with the idea of Fanny working as a teacher, rather than practicing her arts in a more ideal and elevating setting. "I am rather afraid to trust you with yourself—I am afraid you will get *narrowed down* teaching, unless you *try try* to make improvement everyday. I dont feel very well about it." Lawrence's apprehensions regarding the stultifying effects of her teaching position would be expressed again and again in his letters. But given his enthusiasm to assume the role of husband for the one he already called "wife," perhaps Fanny's employment impugned his abilities as provider. Lawrence's offended sense of propriety is evident in his negative reaction to Fanny's later suggestions that she continue to teach after they were married. Middle and upper class wives simply did not work in mid-19th century America.[20]

Fanny's reply to this letter indicates that she, too, grew worried and unhappy when no word came from Lawrence. Though Lawrence may have carried through with his threat to remain silent until he received another letter from her, their letters took weeks to reach their destinations, and additional weeks sometimes passed before replies to questions or concerns were received. On this occasion, Fanny wrote anxiously:

> *My dear, dear Lawrence I have been looking for an answer to my last letter to you but it does not come; O what is the matter my own dear one? I am so grieved and anxious about you! so afraid lest you may be sick! and it is so long since you wrote me last; you told me then that you would send me another letter very soon, and it never, never was so long before. O! if I could only see your dear face, if it were only for a moment, what a comfort and relief it would be to me.*[21]

Though Fanny responded to Lawrence's distress at not receiving more letters, it may have done little to ease his mind:

> *...I wish I could tell you without being tedious, just how and why it is, that I cannot write to you oftener; you do not seem to realize about it; but one thing my Lawrence you may be assured of, and I know you will believe me when I tell you that you are in my thoughts and in my heart too, always, by night and by day. My eyes are troubling me so very badly, that a great part of the time, it is impossible for me to use them for writing, even if I am not obliged to be teaching every moment. I have now, let me think,—thirteen piano-scholars, and I am teaching almost forty girls, in Miss Bass' school, to sing. Then I am obliged to devote a great part of the little time remaining, to preparing Music to be performed at the Lyceum and on the Sabbath. I am the chief dependence in musical matters here, isn't it funny to think of dear?*[22]

After outlining the evenings of the week spent at rehearsals for the Lyceum and church choirs, Fanny explained that there were two nights of the week that she might call her own. But, she explained, "we always have company, and when I am called for, there is usually no reprieve, and I'm obliged to go down into the parlor, for one reason or another; the truth is, I cannot endure the thought of never seeming willing to do any thing for any body unless I am *paid* for it; and it would certainly have that appearance, if I refused to help the young ladies with their music, when they wished to entertain their friends with it." She reminded Lawrence of her many family members and friends who expected answers to their letters. Furthermore, she explained that it had taken her several days to finish this letter, for the morning after writing the first part, her eyes were so badly swollen that she could not open one of them at all.[23]

Lawrence, somewhat chastened, was less clamorous in his demands for letters. To make amends, he acknowledged that:

> *The respect I have for you, grows upon me continually; and I ought to tell you of the substantial comfort it affords me to think of you in the capacity of a friend, a companion, a helper. I feel very sure that we shall enjoy and improve very much from the similarity of our tastes and the employments to which they will lead us to devote at least some of our time. I allow myself to anticipate with something more than pleasure the time when I may have the privilege of unrestrained companionship & intercourse with that person who charms me not less by her rare qualities of mind, than by the thousand sweetnesses' of her disposition, and the enduring attractiveness of her person.*[24]

But he also advised Fanny to "...discriminate between what is essential & what is merely visionary—... where & how to take hold of things to the best advantage & to prevent one from doing every thing—.... what I said, or meant to say, was that your present employment will not *directly* help you so much...." Lawrence, though impressed with Fanny's ambition to fulfill her obligations successfully, chaffed at the all consuming nature of her position.[25]

In letters of love and loneliness that passed between Fanny and Lawrence in the years they were apart, they shared dreams and fears, hopes and heartaches. During their courtship of less than a year before their engagement and separation, they overcame many barriers to their relationship. While often imagining their future happiness, they continued to discuss their differences, old and new, persisting in their loving struggle against anything that would keep them apart.[26]

CHAPTER

5

"Be Sure & Burn This"

When Fanny and Lawrence parted in September 1852, earnest discussion regarding his entering the ministry was already well underway. Lawrence was aware, from the earliest days of their relationship, of Fanny's repudiation of Congregationalism, but he would also come to know that she held little enthusiasm for a clergyman's way of life. Raised in a parsonage, Fanny knew what that life meant, and her adoptive father's diaries contain striking revelations of the hard, demanding service he gave to his church. On hand for every trial and tragedy that befell his parishioners, at all hours of the day or night, not a week would pass without sharing another family's sorrow. The calls to the sick and suffering, to the death bed and the grave side, vastly outnumbered the happier duties of christenings and weddings. Though Rev. Adams was greatly admired and respected in Brunswick, such arduous self-sacrifice was considered to be his duty, and a minister's life was not his, or his family's, own. A minister's wife, more so than in any other profession at that time, worked in partnership with her husband, with duties and obligations of her own. If Lawrence accepted a pulpit after their marriage, he would not be doing so alone.[1]

If Fanny worried over his aspirations for the pulpit, she was appalled at his enthusiasm for becoming a missionary. While she may have had no wish to experience the isolation and trials of life in a distant, "uncivilized" land, there may have been reasons for her abhorrence. As a little girl, when Fanny first arrived at her adoptive family's home in Brunswick, the town gave a grand send-off to a local missionary on his way to the West Indies. The community was gripped with horror when word came back that he had been eaten by cannibals! And had Fanny managed to read Herman Melville's controversial novel of the South Seas, *Typee*, with its descriptions of the fate of young missionary wives among the heathen?

Fanny and Lawrence's first attempts to resolve the impasse ended in quarrels, but they reached an uneasy truce by the time she went to Georgia. The foreign missions would have to manage without him, while pulpits closer to home might not. But alternatives were still under discussion. Careers for which he was already qualified, with the advantage of cutting their three year wait for marriage short, were explored.[2]

While a number of Fanny's letters from Georgia have not survived, Lawrence's habit of quoting liberally from her letters as he responded to her questions is of great assistance. But establishing the sequence of their letters during this period presents a challenge. A number of them carry no date and letters that address serious issues are seemingly answered with ones of mischievous lightness. With the unreliability of the mails, while they waited for a reply to a question or suggestion, letters would arrive answering other queries made weeks before. An example of the confusion and seeming discordance of moods that often resulted can be found in a letter Lawrence wrote to Fanny in April of 1853, that addressed, "...your charge that I did not like your funny letter some time ago. Now Fan. I will not stand that; you keen little persecuting rogue, do you suppose I cant say a pleasant thing about you without being *critical*?"[3]

Lawrence's penchant for teasing also kept things lively. To the above letter he added, "Why, you mischief, I never thought for an instant that it was not a good letter, and as to *liking* it, I was as fond of it, really, I think, as I shall be of my first ****." It is no mystery what Lawrence's four stars represent, for he used this code regularly. The four letter word in this, and most cases, is "baby." It was not some sense of delicacy that led Lawrence to use this code, but rather his propensity for teasing Fanny. Babies, a subject guaranteed to get a spirited response from Fanny, were mentioned again and again, gleefully encoded as unmentionables by Lawrence. In another case of slow mail and delayed reactions, he asked Fanny why she did not laugh at the "'quit claim' deed for b**ies" he had sent her. As it was, "b**ies" would be yet another subject that demanded discussion.[4]

Lawrence adopted the role of paramour as well. With Fanny's promise of love and commitment came a noticeable lessening of restraint in his expression of lustier desires. "I want to kiss her. I want her to put up her lips to tempt me, so that I shall fall into her arms, as I used to try not to do...." Such expressions were designed to scandalize Fanny, for he seemed to like nothing better than to tease a blush to her cheek: "...Now, now I'm going to kiss her—there, only see her blush *now*—quite a sparkle in her eye—I guess she is a rogue; thats what I guess."

But, the one theme in his letters that eventually struck sparks with Fanny, was his great anticipation of a time when babies would come trooping gaily. In this letter from 1852, utilizing both stars and fill-in blanks, he wrote:

> *I dreamed last night that my F___ had a little 'gold-____' tossing him up in her arms & playing with him. I was very jealous, for she would not let me take him at all & I was so unreasonable as to imagine I had as much right to him as she. But there wasn't any quarrel. I wish I could tell you my*

> *feelings when I looked upon those two. I wish I could. Only I remember my starting when I thought that my F____. was not F____. ***********. yet.— After that I dreamed some thing else, which if it had been carried much farther, I am afraid would have made the two dreams come in rather an inverted order. now isn't that pretty well said. Dont scold me.*[5]

The stars in this instance spell "Chamberlain," and he would add in a side note, "*Be* sure & burn this. Mind, rogue." Another example of this maternity mischief declared, "I *will* plague you. What do you think of these?" His depiction of a pair of tiny shoes bore the caption, "She shan't—she shan't." Following months of such teasing, Lawrence soberly replied to a shot that Fanny finally fired across his bow. He wrote:

> *I believe it your opinion that marriage has no proper reference to children, being rather a more convenient or at any rate more congenial state or relation in which two persons by mutual agreement & attraction merge their individual lives & personal rights, & that children are the result of a tyrannical cruel abuse & prostitution of women. 2d That you rebel at all the Bible says about it & deem a man unreasonable who presumes to think of children as a natural offspring of marriage. Now I do confess that this did seem a little strange to me & what it presumed or implied most certainly had a tendency to cool a passionate love to a considerable extent. May I confess that it might make a person a little angry for a woman to try to ignore the fact that she was not above human passions & susceptibilities, & to imply that a husband should allow himself in no more personalities with his wife than he would with his sister. I must say that I think this would cool a passion about as effectually as if it were soaked in the Dead Sea. So much for what I am talking about,—now for what I think. If you had said nothing about the general principle, but merely that for some particular reasons you would shrink very much from the peril & pain of motherhood, & that you did not (although you loved me as a man & a husband) you did not dare to pass so great a hazard—at the same time admitting—that it was a matter requiring as much self denial on your part as on mine-that your love for me was to some extent a love in which difference of sex was quite an interesting & important feature & that you would be glad if the privileges & pleasures of the wife could be enjoyed without the perils of the Mother—why then Fan I would not have one word of objection to make—I would agree with you fully & confess the reasonab[l]eness of your fears & do all I could to find a sure safe guard. But then a warm blooded girl come & lie in a warm blooded man's bosom & think that he will not "touch" her ever! Why Fan, leave a girl to her own way about it, &, my word for it, she wouldn't lie very still a great while without extending her acquaintance I know that. I think on the whole for the best preservation of chastity a man & woman would do well not to sleep together. That's all. Well now, Fannie, we understand each other I think you are not so foolish as to suppose either you or I are destitute of a fair degree of humanity—you look upon it about as I want you to, dont you? If so Fan, we'll have no trouble about it again. If we are ever*

married (as Heaven grant we may be) we will not subject ourselves to any fears of this nature. I now here plainly give up all I have said about my love for a child (so prematurely foolish) & content myself with those touching dreams. I should like to have you answer me fully & frankly (as you may with perfect safety) & after that we will drop the subject. Let me only beg of you not to pretend that you have no passionate feelings. I do not like to contemplate you as a fossil remain.[6]

Fanny's hesitancy to accept motherhood with marriage might have stemmed from fear of the perils of childbirth, or perhaps she still cherished dreams of life as an artist or musician. But a more obvious reason lies in her offers to continue to work after they married. Fanny felt that, if Lawrence accepted her help, the three year deferment of their marriage would be unnecessary. This spirited exchange produced candid and positive discussion, and resulted in an agreement to limit their future family, at least in the first year of marriage. Employing euphemisms for contraception and sexual intimacy, it was agreed that Fanny should learn about "puddings and things," before the "two rooms"![7]

If Fanny was influenced by the early feminists of her time, there is no evidence that she numbered herself among these early crusaders. Yet she certainly was considering some of their positions on the duties of wife and mother. Many advocates of women's rights believed in "voluntary" motherhood, yet many did not endorse contraception, which they considered "unnatural." While many of the early feminists resented the myth that women did not have or should not enjoy any sexual feelings at all, they held to the principle that reproduction was the sole purpose of sexual activity. Temporary abstinence was the method of choice among these champions of women's rights. The more radical even created some enthusiasm for "companionate" marriages, in which the only intimacy was a meeting of minds.[8]

Fanny and Lawrence's exchange on intimacy and children in their marriage has led to speculation, not on her fear of childbirth, nor her advocacy of antebellum women's rights, but on her capacity to love or to be loving. It is apparent in Lawrence's letter that he was not scolding her for any lack of warmth or sexuality. Rather, he was insisting that she not forget her own feelings of passion and desire that he apparently knew could meet his own. Ironically, the above letter has also been used to argue that Fanny and Lawrence indulged in sexual intimacy before marriage. For this letter, so frank in its acknowledgement and endorsement of their mutual passion, ended with the following enigmatic words: "I will conclude by giving you one grand *scare*. You rem[em]ber the jar in the cellar-way. He would have been three weeks old to day."[9]

Ellen K. Rothman's book, *Hands and Hearts: A History of Courtship in America*, is an interesting consideration of the reputedly staid Victorians' expressions of love. Rothman cites the mysterious final words of Lawrence's letter to support the conjecture that Fanny Adams and Lawrence Chamberlain consummated their marriage before the wedding. Other writers, with less delicacy or discretion than Ms. Rothman, have averred that the "he" in the "jar" was the aborted or stillborn fetus that resulted from a premarital relationship. Rothman also refers to Fanny's note that encouraged Lawrence to visit her when her family was away. Rothman considers Lawrence's "Golden Baby" letter and the couple's proclivity for calling each other "husband" & "wife" well before their marriage. Lastly, she cites a letter Fanny wrote to Lawrence in 1854. "You know dear Lawrence that I may breathe to you, even as to my own heart, in all innocence and perfect trustfulness, those things which would ever sink me in the estimation and respect of any third person; for no other being can know what we are to each other." While this is likely another plea from Fanny to Lawrence that her words of love be kept private, oddly, Ms. Rothman does not cite another letter that could also be considered when making a case for Fanny's willingness for premarital intimacy. In the letter from the summer of 1852 in which Lawrence suggested kissing Fanny until she blushed, he also offered, "...then too when she invited me one night to sl_____ Wasn't I good, not to? But I shall remember that invitation till two rooms come—then we shall see."[10]

Much of Rothman's evidence can be explained by Lawrence's penchant for outrageous teasing and the couple's mutual delight in calling each other "husband," "wife," and even "mother of my sweet child," as Lawrence once addressed Fanny well before their marriage. But what of the "jar in the cellar-way. He would have been three weeks old to day."?

The Adams-Chamberlain collection at Radcliffe is large, and many letters are undated. Those letters that are dated, while organized chronologically, are also separated into files by the author of the correspondence when known. It would be easy to miss the letter that Lawrence wrote to Fanny immediately after the "jar" letter. Without date, salutation or signature, it begins, "I dont know when I have laughed so much as I have over the last note I wrote you—it *was* witty wasnt it—& over the concluding page of the note in this letter especially the final *idea.* I could not help roaring at the solemn ghostly stalking way it is managed."[11]

Was the "jar in the cellarway" no more than an attempt at the blackest of humor, with the grisly fate of the unwanted unborn as its theme? It seems unthinkable, but such incongruities often seem to widen the chasm between 19th and 20th century society. By that time, Lawrence had become quite a literary man, in a time when gothic horror was all the rage...a generation that read Poe and Mary Shelley. Even the works of Bowdoin's brightest literary star, Nathaniel Hawthorne, often dwelt on the darkest side of human nature.

Or perhaps the flood of reform literature of the day provided Lawrence's inspiration. Epics of fallen women, prostitutes, and innocents drawn into white slavery told tales of desperate mothers, haggard by the birth and care of too many children, at the mercy of back alley abortionists. Perhaps these tales, designed to scare nice young ladies as much as to address social evils of the time, provided Lawrence with a source for parody. While the significance of the "jar in the cellarway" might forever be elusive, it is apparent that Lawrence heartily enjoyed the joke, though he assured Fanny that he was serious about their future intimacy: "I am in earnest darling about the matter in the note—We can have mischief enough, without any *trouble.* I guess you will be as ready for it as I—" He could not resist adding:

> *I suppose you will be very angry if I confess to you what I have done. Can you believe it? I slept with a girl the other night. It came about queerly—I could not help it—such a sweet delicious maiden & then the opportunity— ...It was rather too much for human flesh & blood. And then her head laid on my shoulder so cunning & coy—can you blame me for*

> *kissing her so passionately when she was so soft & warm? It wasn't a dream.... You do not care, do you? You know you are above all such things—they are 'cruel' & 'unnatural'! If I am never to touch my wife, nobody can blame me for this. If you want to know who it was, why it was my own Fannie in the nice goldplate case I keep her in, so that nobody can see her except me.*[12]

While Fanny's appreciation for Lawrence's kisses and embraces gave him confidence that her desire answered his own in the months before their parting, there is evidence that she drew a line of propriety that Lawrence apparently tripped over. Teasing apologies for being "naughty," and his amusement when calling himself a "dangerous fellow" followed tiffs over his boldness. But shortly before Fanny left for the South, he expressed more solemn feelings for the promise of intimacies yet to be:

> *....how sweet how indiscribible [sic], how worth-waiting-for even in tears & tribulation will be some hours of one full soul communion—think of the glorious summer days; & of the wild, witching nights when your dear head will rest in my bosom as I hold to my heart all my earthly treasure. Dream if you can of the love that then first will speak & the thoughts that then first will fill our souls. O let us keep our hearts full of faith & purity & tenderness, blessing God for his great goodness & looking for that day of thanksgiving.*[13]

While a number of problems were discussed during their years of separation, the letters that best sustained Fanny and Lawrence were ones that expressed their longing for the day when they could be together in their own home. Dreaming of the future, they imagined "two rooms" where they would start their lives together. Though Lawrence could have had free tuition and board, he worked his way through the seminary by teaching German to a group of young ladies, and served as superintendent of schools in Brewer. He spent what little extra money he had on fine editions of their favorite books, that they would someday read together by their own fireside. Fanny would paint, and yes... Fanny could have a dog! But where and when this ideal could be achieved remained a topic of discussion.[14]

In early June 1853, they again discussed cutting short their three year ordeal. Lawrence voiced his fears regarding their original plan and their lengthy separation by stating, "I think that you & I dont know but both of us—will be so world weary that we can not enjoy any thing, if there is ever any thing to enjoy." Concerned about Fanny's health and her intention to work through the summer, he inquired, "what is of most importance to 'pay those debts' in 6 months, as it were 'out of spite,' or to regard yourself as having some higher obligations.... Now, Fannie, do not go to the last of your strength. Suffer yourself a little relaxation." Fanny admitted that she was unable to repay her debt to her father so quickly, for she would not receive part of her income until the end of her school term. And, she rejected the idea of going into debt for room and board. Fanny borrowed a character from Dickens' *David Copperfield* to ask Lawrence, "Won't you think your little *Dora*...evinced some little wisdom there, dear? isn't this principle the best one for her to adopt? tell her, you old comfort. O! I want to see him so tonight! I wish he might only fold me in his dear, *strong* arms if only for one minute! Be of good cheer my beloved one, there is brightness in store for us."[15]

Lawrence, no less anxious than Fanny to shorten the separation, entered upon a severe regimen of studies during his first year at the seminary, hoping to complete his work in two years, rather than three. After his ordination, he suggested, he and Fanny could go west, "after astonishing the natives awhile in this vicinity." But he also entertained the idea of abandoning his preparation for the ministry to teach, joining Fanny in the South or going out West. Yet the latter idea seemed to produce the greatest anxiety and uncertainty for Lawrence, for he was not only reluctant to give up the seminary, but he questioned his qualifications or desire to teach.

When Lawrence vacillated over his proposal to contact Prof. Calvin Stowe for assistance in finding a teaching position, he responded to Fanny's great disappointment in the following letter:

> *It is but just to you, my best one, that you should know what my plans are—though there are some things connected with them in which you could not sympathize with me—some things that trouble me which you would not be likely to appreciate—maybe some which you would not understand. I will only remind you of the difficulty of completely changing & giving up one's long cherished plans, even when there is not higher obligation or more sacred sanction than his own feeling. ...I do not wonder you write as you do & ask if it was 'all Talk' about Prof. Stowe. But, my dear, you do not trust me enough.... There is such a thing as 'striking' before the iron is hot.' ...You do not believe, I am sure, that I ever forget your wishes, or neglect any opportunity to do what you desire me to do.... Well, dear, I have not written to Prof. S.—it is rather humiliating to me, I can not easily bring myself to it. I thought it would be presumptuous & perhaps ridiculous if not suicidal, to make such an application within so few months from my first degree.... But I have thought that with somewhat more confidence I might make that movement after a year's deliberation & a year's distance from my Alma Mater's lap.... The 'Western project' (or Southern) is full before me. I do not see any hope for an other.... But you see if I could have so far mastered the Theological department as to be permitted to preach now & then a sermon, do you not see places would then be open to me on any condition to suit our convenience. I am afraid we shall yet see the day that you will be thankful that I could preach a sermon. Must I not then, dear, fit myself for a responsible, useful & honorable station? How do you suppose I should hold my head up at least among the little.*[16]

Lawrence agreed that they could live modestly, and perhaps Fanny could work for the first year of their marriage. Yet he felt uncomfortable with the idea that they rely at all on her income. He pointed out that Fanny might become ill, an apprehension he seemingly did not hold for himself. He also voiced determination to avoid any possibility of having to lean on his father for assistance, for he felt that his father had already done more than enough for him. But despite his reservations, and his obvious desire to defer such a move, Lawrence continued to entertain the possibility of pulling up stakes and teaching somewhere, for he continued:

So I mean to make the most of another year before I can hope to settle down upon any suitable place. Then I like to know pretty surely what I am about when I undertake to do any thing. I feel capable of something—with your dear help, of much. Ought I not to be careful & not make shipwreck of my life—I would indeed be willing to begin very small & trust to my own diligence & your blessed love, under Gods favor, to rise to the place to which I hope to attain.... I will be something for your sake. I am going to teach, dear, somewhere next fall or winter & get some money & then I will help you, dearest, if you will let me, to pay back some of those demands which you call 'debts.' I will not complain of their injustice. You will let me help you dear, if I can possibly manage to earn any money & carry out my other plans.[17]

To Lawrence's offer of financial assistance, Fanny replied, "No darling, *no indeed*, you shall not think of sending me any thing as you proposed; I would not have you for the world, I should think it very, very hard if with all my labor and strivings, I could not support *myself* here." But the letter also offered news on the first of many teaching positions in the South that she would draw to his attention. "Mrs Orme has an idea that you might get an appointment to a professor-ship in Athens College in Georgia; how would you like that, darling? O I want you to study all you can without working too hard, for I *must* see you honored and bowed down to for your intellectual acquirements and endowments."[18]

Though Fanny continued to propose alternatives to the ministry, she also gave Lawrence heartfelt assurances that he was capable of great things. Her letters of love and encouragement often helped him bear up under the heavy schedule of studies he set for himself. As he faced the prospect of delivering an oration at the seminary's graduation ceremonies for 1853, Fanny wrote, "I would advise you by all means to do as well as I know you can, at the Commencement exercises. if I can hear you next Summer dearest Lawrence, I wont complain at not being able to hear you now; and I feel that it would be a great advantage to you in more ways than one. Wont you try there dear? that is, if you can without doing an injury to your health." Lawrence, haunted by the memory of his last speech at Bowdoin, was filled with apprehension as the time drew near for another test of his skills of oration. He would credit Fanny's words of love and encouragement with bringing him through his "fiery ordeal." Lawrence wrote:

I thought of you on stage, and you will be glad to hear me say that I knew, I felt that you were thinking of me and that your blessing was on me; it gave me courage and hope—it was availing. I can not help thanking you again, now that in the award of prizes I am second to none. It was you Fannie, who gave me the strength—.... You will not think that I am unduly elated if I tell you that my success through all the examination was far beyond my best hopes.[19]

Many changes had taken place in Lawrence, for his letters of 1853, when compared with those of the courtship, were positively mellow. Yet in the letter above, he admitted to Fanny that during the pressure of his examinations, he had written a letter of "unimaginable wildness" that he did not send:

> *I went so far as to seal it and carry it down town, but judgement fortunately came to my aid. I felt that you are worthy of more consideration than that such a letter should be sent to you.... I was sorry that I had obliged you to write when it was inconvenient, but it is another proof of that real soul-kindness that is yours alone. I know that you will forgive me for all the demands I make upon you, and I know that you will tell me when I go too far.*[20]

Lawrence provided loving support for Fanny, too, for he filled his letters with reminders of their dreams for the future, and of his admiration: "...dear the thought just flew over my brain 'How proud I am of her';—for I was holding my pen suspended & I was gazing into vacancy. Yes, Fannie how proud I am of you, and how many hopes I have planted upon you & how tenderly I cherish them believing that one day they will grow up so sweet & beautiful & twine about us both, making us one." But Lawrence's plan to hasten that day, his attempt to do three years of work in two, suffered a blow in the summer of 1853, for he was exhausted. Realizing that he was unable to keep up the pace of work of his first year, his correspondence began to convey the growing intensity of his loneliness. In a letter partially composed in the third person, a characteristic of 19th century correspondence rather disconcerting for the modern reader, Lawrence opened a new line of negotiation when he told Fanny:

> *...darling he has just thought that may be she could come North in her summer vacation—how happy he would be if he could only have his dear Fanny where he could see her this beautiful bright summer. Can not you come, dearest? I suppose you will hardly stay there during the next two months. And then Mother wants to see her very much.... When I was telling her the other day of your present wearing & worrying labors she said she wished you would come & visit her instead.... I told her that I was afraid you were too proud & [thought] that it would not look well in the eyes of the critics.*[21]

By early July, Lawrence had received news from Fanny that she would not be coming to Maine, for after she finished preparing her students for their final exams, she would work through the summer in Georgia. This disheartening revelation apparently kicked off Lawrence's campaign to bring Fanny home, one way or another. On July 4, Lawrence wrote that he loved her more than ever, but that he was despondent, having been unwell for some time from an attack of pleurisy. He declared himself too ill to write and left the letter to be finished another day. Yet in a journal that Lawrence kept during that summer of 1853, he declared that he spent July 4 down river from Bangor in the town of Hampden. There, as a member of the Brewer Artillery, he marched in a long parade, after which the participants were treated to a sumptuous meal. When Lawrence finished his letter on July 5, he mentioned only that, "It rained here yesterday until afternoon. Towards evening I went down to my Uncles (only a few steps you know)—& stayed till 10 o'clock to see the fire works with Annie. It was a glorious evening & I could not be *alone* such an evening." With a description of a beautiful display of fireworks, enhanced by nature's own performance of lightening flickering in another part of the sky, he continued:

> *And then I had been having such a pleasant time with Annie that it made me think of you, dear, & want to see you very much. She treats me very dearly; but I do not suppose you would be a bit jealous if you were all the while on the spot. Cousins, you know, are very convenient friends, and no body can get up a story or a suspicion if you do love them some.... You were a very good girl to write me the 'note'; but I think my little Fannie took advantage of my permission to write only when she wanted to—consequently I have received only one letter from you for the space of twelve weeks, until this one came. I wont complain of her. I know she is busy; but then she has time to bestow upon Mrs. Orme's company &c; ....But not one word of fault to find with you, my dear,—if you are doing what you think you ought I am content. I want to help you all I can, even by keeping myself out of your way....*[22]

Congratulating her on not going into debt in order to pay her father, he suddenly interjected:

> *O Fan, a Bowd[oin]. graduate was asking me the other day about Bruns[wick]. matters, when among other things he said 'Well, Fanny Adams is married, I believe—I think I heard so.' You may be sure I felt rather sheepish—(yet I dont know why) and answered—'NO, sir, I-think-not', 'she is at the South.' Does not it look funny written down Fanny Adams is married? That name is rather familiar to me. It is too bad any man should want to spoil that pretty name, or that pretty maiden I used to know them both once. It would make me very sad to think that all those beautiful maidenly mysteries are at the mercy of a willful man. I should pity the poor girl. But no matter. I suppose she thinks she is happy.... you have a vacation, I presume, in the hot months. Where do you go? I had the offer of a free passage to Georgia in a new ship commanded by a cousin of mine, and I had even the courage to decline the very kind offer he made me. But it made me feel almost as if I had parted again from you to come so near seeing you. Please, darling, could not she just send a bit of a curl from her shiny hair, for her own dear one to love?*[23]

Thus an offhand remark about Fanny from a misinformed acquaintance had set off a dismal chain of imaginings, for the very suggestion of Fanny being married to someone other than himself worked upon Lawrence. Such unhappy musings, nurtured by a fertile imagination, offer evidence that Lawrence was still as capable of building dungeons of despair as he was castles in the air. With this incident to nourish his discontent, his letter veers from expressions of pique to those of melancholy. But the last few lines offer further evidence of his distress, for Lawrence asked Fanny to send more information on a teaching position in Georgia: "Oh, Fanny darling please tell me about Athen[s] Coll[ege] if you know any thing about it, but dont say to any one that I am anxious to know." Lawrence had apparently begun to pull out all the stops to try to bring Fanny back to Maine. Yet there is a subtle acknowledgement of the futility of such efforts, and an indication of his possible, though reluctant, capitulation.[24]

Lawrence's plans and ambitions conflicted with his desire to be with Fanny, but it seems that he was unable or unwilling to choose. Not only had the ministry been the goal for which he had dedicated years of intense work and study, but could he disappoint the mother who had dreamed of seeing her son in the pulpit? Yet if he continued his studies at the seminary, two more long years must pass before their marriage. Beyond the difficulties of supporting a wife while a student, seminarians were not allowed to marry.

Another issue is more difficult to assess, for it involves the depth of Lawrence's religious beliefs and his commitment to serve God through his church. Though he chose the ministry with some ambivalence, he had embraced what he felt was a calling from God to do His work by serving his fellow man. It was a calling he did not take lightly, but he had to decide, as does every seminarian, whether his service should be given as a minister of the church. He had once feared that the ministry would offer "but little scope and freedom, binding a man by rules and precedents and petty despotisms...." How assiduously he had been able to accept the theological teachings of his professors at the seminary held serious implications for his future as a Congregational minister. While Lawrence experienced no crisis of faith, a crisis of conscience may be nearer the truth.[25]

The Bangor Theological Seminary adhered to Congregationalism's Calvinist roots, a commitment ensured by its administrator, Rev. Dr. Enoch Pond. A dynamic and learned theologian, he had come to the institution as the former editor of a periodical titled *Spirit of the Pilgrims*, and the rest of the small faculty of the seminary had been chosen with equal care. When Lawrence asked if he could read part of his theology in German, his strongest language, permission was given grudgingly, for the faculty was wary of the radical writings that came out of Germany. His professor held him stiffly to the "old school," but Lawrence found that reading his work in both Latin and German presented "vital questions in widely variant lights."[26]

In the journal Lawrence kept during his first year at the seminary, he declared his intent to note those sermons and lectures that most impressed him. Only two works were recorded, and both could be considered challenges to the old Congregational dogma. One, delivered by a Unitarian minister, emphasized the limited number of theological differences that separated the Protestant religions. Lawrence, declaring it one of the best sermons he had ever heard, was taken with this minister's plea for fellowship among the churches, for while many other denominations were also striving to overlook their differences, they did so to combat what they saw as the Unitarian threat. The only other work mentioned in his journal was a lecture which controverted the Congregational dogma that held that, if we are all born in sin, children who died in infancy were sentenced to damnation. Lawrence subsequently conjectured that perhaps we were born without sin, a radical thought for a conservatively trained seminarian. The journal was soon abandoned, and however tempting it is to wonder whether Lawrence was unnerved by his own heretical inclinations, it is difficult to know how disturbing such considerations were for him. Nor is it easy to measure the strength of his commitment. But he admitted to Fanny in a letter that summer: "I will confess to you Fannie that I do shrink from a minister's life—as a life but I want to be able to do good as a minister though it should not be my profession." Lawrence had retreated thus far, while he would still enter the ministry, he would not remain in it long. By August 1853, Lawrence wrote to Calvin Stowe, and asked that he apprise him of possible teaching positions.[27]

Determined to fulfill her obligations, and prove to her adoptive father that she could succeed, Fanny remained in Milledgeville through the hot summer. She fell ill as autumn approached, much as Lawrence and her family had feared. During her first year in Georgia, she received little other than unpleasant news regarding her Brunswick home, for frequent letters came from Cousin Deborah. Fanny heard that, shortly after her departure, Helen had traveled to New York for medical treatment, while Rev. Adams remained alone in Brunswick. Deborah reported that Helen had been told that she was "*run* down from manifold cares & anxieties," to which Deborah commented, "rebellious children & family difficulties are at the root of all this evil in the estimation of some folks...." Deborah confessed that she was giving up her hope that, once they were all gone, Rev. Adams would "come to himself & see things in their true light.... The moulding [sic] he has been undergoing the past year has made him a very different character from what he was in your Mother's life time—When you [were] with him he [was] as kind & affectionate as possible...." Word had also reached Deborah that Rev. Adams was telling anyone who would listen among their family & old friends, that she was the "whole cause of all the difficulties..." and that she had caused the rupture between Fanny, Anna & himself. But Deborah encouraged Fanny to write as affectionately to her father, "as is consistently with the truth," for, she insisted, "I do not consider him responsible for the unpleasant occurrences since his second marriage—therefore dwell only on his over kindness, previous to that calamitous event."[28]

Though Deborah's letters demonstrated her caring for Fanny, her concern for her health, and her desire to know that Fanny was well situated, they could hardly have been comforting. One letter that diligently reported how many of Fanny's friends were getting married, also brought the grisly details of a mutual friend who had died a slow, painful death in childbirth, leaving several little children motherless. And Deborah's letters brought a good deal of unsolicited advice. Though she later commended Fanny for being so frugal, she warned her, "Do dress simply as becometh a minister's daughter & one who expects to become the wife of a minister.... Beads & furbelows, & finery depend upon it are very unbecoming one in your situation & your expectation—Your love for such things is a *weak* spot in your character & you ought to *fight* against it—" But, whatever Deborah's faults, Fanny confided in her, and, when Deborah heard from Fanny of Ashur Adams' rueful sorrow over the troubles that had come to his daughter, Deborah commented: "I do not think your Boston Father should regret giving you away—the gift has resulted infinitely to your advantage. I do not believe if you had remained at home [in Boston] you would have been *half* as much as you are—not meaning to say you are much any way, more than a silly child."[29]

If Rev. Adams had expectations that the trying times would cease with Deborah Folsom's departure, his hopes were disappointed. On leaving the home, Deborah, who held half ownership of the house, asked to be paid for her share, compelling Rev. Adams to seek assistance from his well-to-do sister. But beyond this financial inconvenience, he was embarrassed by what the community knew and thought of the upheaval in the household. He spoke with a number of family friends in Brunswick, hoping to make his views known.

While Rev. Adams would eventually accuse both Deborah and Fanny of prejudicing Anna against Helen, he reserved his harshest criticism for Cousin Deborah. He wrote to her that she had injured Helen's health, happiness, reputation and usefulness. Helen's frequent illnesses continued well after Deborah, Anna and Fanny's departure, and Rev. Adams often found himself alone as Helen sought treatment and tried to recover her health. In September 1853, he recorded in his diary: "I recal [sic] past years when my house was always full, people coming & going, the children around me often disturbing me with th[ei]r noise. Now, here I am *alone*, entirely *alone*! How different! How wholly unanticipated." During one of Helen's longer absences, he was dumbfounded to receive a note from Cousin Deborah. Hearing that Helen was not in Brunswick, she offered to return. It was an offer he did not accept.[30]

News conveyed by her family did little for Fanny's spirits, and undoubtedly reinforced her feelings that she could not return to Maine. Not only had the unpleasantness that surrounded her departure from Brunswick continued, but if she left her position in Georgia, she could not support herself, and she could not repay Rev. Adams. If she could not go home to Brunswick, she certainly could not go to Bangor, for she had no business there if she was not to marry for several years. Fanny's resignation to remain in Georgia and Lawrence's continued reluctance to leave the seminary resulted in a clash of conflicting responsibilities and disparate needs that seemed to defy resolution. The issues to be discussed and the decisions to be made would sometimes be difficult and painful ones for them both. With such obstacles, how could love, at a thousand miles apart, prevail?

CHAPTER

6

"Unless Somebody Cares & Loves Me All the Time"

In 1854, as Fanny began her second year in Georgia, it seems that both she and Lawrence were fast coming to the realization that being away from one another for another two years would be intolerable. Fanny was leading a rather spartan existence, her days and evenings filled with responsibilities, and her earnings swallowed up by her living expenses and her efforts to pay off her debt to her father as quickly as possible. But she was full of hope that some plan would be devised to allow them to be together before the year was out. Though Lawrence seemed willing to discuss alternatives to the ministry, he clung tenaciously to the seminary, and continued to try to find a way to bring Fanny back to Maine.

It was never intended that Fanny would live permanently with the Orme family when she went to Milledgeville. But Fanny's illness on her arrival in Georgia, and the affectionate friendship that sprang up between these distant cousins, caused her to remain with Abby Orme and her family longer than anticipated. In early 1854, Fanny moved into the home of Dr. Samuel Gore White, a prominent Milledgeville physician who had served as a naval surgeon during the Mexican War. A pillar of the Presbyterian Church, where Fanny played the organ and directed the choir, Dr. White and his wife Caroline invited Fanny into their home, where she would instruct the eldest of their two young daughters in piano.

Though Dr. White was known for his hospitality, when Fanny left the stately Orme home and the bustle of their large family, it is likely that she finally gained much longed-for time to herself. Fanny, who insisted she could not compose a letter to Lawrence unless she was alone, wrote frequently during this year, though the slowness of the mails, as well as lost and delayed letters, continued to plague their correspondence.[1]

Fanny was absorbed in her teaching in Milledgeville, but her letters to Cousin Deborah reveal that her thoughts often turned northward. When she confided in Deborah that she longed to come north, Deborah, who was boarding in Hoboken, N.J., responded with the wish that she could provide a home for her. But when Fanny told Deborah that Lawrence was pressing her to come and stay with his family in Brewer, Deborah advised her to work on in Georgia "till there is an unmistakable call...," and she added, "Never until you are married would I go there to abide." Whether Fanny agreed with Deborah or not, she still faced the necessity of earning her own income and completing the repayment of her debts.[2]

In late February 1854, Fanny wrote a long letter to Lawrence. The first few pages were dedicated to her continuing distress that her letters were shown to others:

> *There are many, many things that I would say to you, my dearest Lawrence...but I cannot write <u>freely</u> because I am afraid that what I may say will not be sacred to you alone. In truth I never write you without a secret, hardly acknowledged feeling that your mother and Cousin Deborah <u>at least</u> will perhaps know every word that I may say. It is not well for either of us that I should write so constrainedly is it dear Lawrence? it is so different with us from what I used so fondly to imagine it would be with my ideal love; I mean <u>in this respect</u> dear, and I would give the world to feel that every word between us was sacred to us alone; then I could tell you every thought and feeling in my letters, just as freely as I would whisper them into your ear, if I were resting in your bosom as of old.*[3]

Fanny responded to a theme in Lawrence's sentiments, that she keep herself "fresh & fair & cheerful," and also to his suggestion that the time that remained until his graduation was growing short: "...When you speak of a year and a half, does it dear? Ah! I am much afraid that if your poor little girl stays here toiling on for all that long, long time (as it seems to *her*) she will indeed have no youth left for you. I cannot bear to say this, lest it trouble you, dear one, but then it grieves me so that I cannot keep it from you." Fanny also assailed Lawrence for his opinion that a teacher's position could not supply sufficient income for their marriage. She reminded him that they had agreed to postpone starting a family:

> *You know I have told you before that I could help along by teaching at first at any rate. Now if you would secure a situation as teacher in a Theological sem. for instance, of course you would command* some *salary... and I should not be much expense to you for the first year at any rate. Why would it embarrass you to have me with you in such a situation tell me all about it you old comfort?*[4]

Addressing this issue, and Lawrence's continued assertions that his lack of qualifications for teaching still made starting off in the ministry the better choice, she declared:

Forgive me if I tell you that it seems to me that my dear Lawrence does not overcome difficulties quite so bravely as he might in this thing. Don't be too modest, learn to sacrifice a little of that over-fastidious pride that you and I have in so great a degree. You know that every great man that has ever succeeded in any thing in the world has had confidence in himself. Be brave then my dearest Lawrence, do not sink in discouragement, be all you are capable of being, and I will be strong to help you in all you undertake. You say you wish your 'little wife' was willing for you to take the course you think best, and could help you in it with all her heart; Well dear she is willing, and she feels that you know better about the matter than she does, for she does'nt pretend to any wisdom, but then she does not at all comprehend how it could possibly better the matter for you to 'begin in the ministry' even if you did not 'settle'. Would it not be very much harder to secure a different place then, than it can be now?[5]

You think, I know, that my tastes are very extravagant and 'gorgeous'. (as my brother George says of me) but trust me Lawrence, my happiness does not depend upon such things, although I do worship the beautiful in everything, I confess that. I wont say I could easily sacrifice all this, for the sake of being yours, because it would grieve you to have me use that word;.... But truly my Lawrence, that would be nothing to me in this case. It would be a joy to me to help you struggle through the darkness.[6]

I never felt so strongly before, my peculiar unfitness for being a minister's wife; it is not that her trials and troubles are so great, believe me it is not so selfish a feeling, but it is that my whole mind, character and temperament are entirely inappropriate for that position, and I never could be useful in it. It would grieve me to death to feel that I was necessarily a draw-back to your influence as a minister, and I know how important it would be to your success that I should be happy and free from such crushing anxiety.[7]

Before mailing this letter, Fanny received another from Lawrence. Dismayed at the fear he expressed of "sinking down into some unsatisfying position, *prematurely*, 'from which you might not soon emerge'...," she commented, "... as if you would not then be likely to rise or progress.... I am *certain* that I could help you to study and *grow*. I cannot bear to have you feel that you must forever remain at a stand, after you are once fairly married. Why I want to help you on in your 'excelsior striving!'" Noting that Lawrence's letters had become less frequent, Fanny also wrote, "I am so sorry you were sick my own one! but I hope you are better now. Do dear write me as often as you can, for I have some pride in not *seeming* neglected even, to others who notice how often your letters come, besides my own happiness in hearing from you."[8]

His response to Fanny's candid letter was a curious one. Lawrence, with distress, dedicated the whole first page of his reply to her remark that she might be perceived as neglected: "I dont know but I am over anxious about you; but tell me if you are not treated with some thing more than respect there—if they do not love you & know that you are such a darling, darling girl—" He also offered feeble reassurance regarding the privacy of their letters, stating that, "Why my child nobody sees or knows of your letters, only when I let Mother, on earnest solicitation, see just a bit.... What kind of a sensitive child are you? Who do you think would not love you more for seeing one of your dear letters?"

Indicating that she could still expect him to come south, Lawrence also explained, "Why no, my darling, it does not seem 'a short time' when I think of you. I was only looking back & it seemed a little while since I had come here—that is all dear & then I thought it was only so long till I should come to her at all events."[9]

Thus far Lawrence had responded to Fanny's concerns. But when it came to the ministry, his patience wore thin. He had previously extolled the practicality of the pulpit as a means of earning a respectable living anywhere. This time, with little effort to hide his frustration, he wrote with an outpouring of visionary assertions regarding the minister's role and his own sense of duty:

> *I will not attempt to reply to your arguments because it is of no use to reply. The only ground I should assume would be—not what was most favorable to my pride, or even to my thorough preparation & fitness for life—but the duties that lie between me & my God. I would not even speak of the sweet office of ministering to poor weary souls & of pointing them to the marvellous [sic] tenderness of that love that cared for them & would save them—I would say nothing of this—no one could feel it as I do sometimes—& how then all the riches & the fineries & the arts of this world fade away! No I will not try to tell you how things seem to me, but I pray God to forgive me if in my weakness I mistake.*[10]

Lawrence went on to proclaim his certainty that Fanny would do much for him, and he explained that it was not the lack of income he found embarrassing about a teaching position, but that it was a "bachelor" office, generally held by unmarried men. "...dear child she need not say 'she will not be much expense to me'—I do not fear that—only I want to do all for her I can." Teasingly he asked, "for *what* position she thinks 'her mind character & temperament' *are* 'appropriate?'" but he acknowledged, "I feel the precious power of your words about 'helping me'.... Tell me if you will come home—if you will come to my mother's a little while & learn something about *me*....love me a little longer...." Lawrence closed this letter of piety & persuasion with the cheeky request: "Be a good girl & make better *B*'s...," adding "Kiss me."[11]

By the end of March 1854, Cousin Deborah had heard from Fanny that she intended to go to Brewer that summer, but the above letter from Lawrence changed the climate. What had happened to Lawrence's promises to seek a teaching position, and of his ambivalence to the ministry? Also, Cousin Deborah kept reminding Fanny of the unkind remarks made by Bangor relatives at the time of her engagement. Of Rev. Adams' sister, Deborah commented, "I would hate to live within a hundred miles of Cousin Mary—"[12]

Fanny's reply to Lawrence's declaration of duty to the church has not survived, but his letter of response to it is revealing, and notably different in mood: "What a nice little wife she was to write me till her 'candle' 'expired' So I suppose she had to go to 'xxx' in the dark! Well, well, I am sorry *somebody* (not general, but particular) could n't have been *there first....* However I was half glad the candle did go out, for I see that a real scolding had begun—...." Claiming that Fanny made inferences too quickly, he declared, "How do you know I am n't 'doing any thing [at] all' &c You little torment, I wont tell you how I have done *every thing*. I can't. If you won't trust me I have not any thing left to try. I am expecting to hear from Prof Stowe soon, about the place at Galena...." Though he reassured her that he continued to seek a teaching position, Lawrence finally told Fanny that he was ill from the strain of trying to advance his studies too quickly. He admitted that he could not finish his work at the seminary in less than three years: "I am not well yet, my own darling, but if you were with me I would get well sooner—...I must keep cheerful or sink, & there is no one here who can love me as you do (though some would if they could)...."[13]

While Lawrence seemingly indicated that their marriage must wait, he nonetheless urged Fanny to prepare for marriage, and to come to Brewer. Reminding her of their agreement to postpone parenthood, he wrote: "Can not you come home again, Fannie, before I take you for my own little wife—why you know there are puddings to be made yet & all that—you need not think you are going to shirk all that sort of wife ship—if you dont know how to do 'things' you have no right to criticise[sic] them." He then gleefully related a family incident that no doubt led Fanny to despair of ever keeping some semblance of privacy. The joke revolves around the fact that pregnancy, if mentioned at all, was referred to as an illness or indisposition. When Fanny wrote of her concern that she might be ill when the heat of summer came again, Lawrence wrote:

> *You are looking for another illness then? Only think how funny it happened. Tom was in my room when the letter came & wanted to know what about Fanny! I told him she was afraid she would be sick again in the hot weather. So the little rogue went home & told Mother "Fanny's going to be sick" The next time I went home—there were one or two young ladies in the room—Mother spoke up "so Fanny is expecting to be sick is she?" (Such a comical way!) "not that I know of." (titter among the girls.) "at any rate it isn't my fault, if she is going to be sick it is 'on her own hook!'" There was a pretty general laugh here, in which Mother led.*

Lawrence went on: "Oh, did you know I had got a *little Fannie*—true—the very image of her sweet Mother;—and all without either aid or interference on your part. In other words I had that picture of you copied into a little miniature, baby picture—to carry in my vest pocket."[14]

Fanny never knew what to expect next. The following letter, written in late April 1854, seemed to indicate clearly that Lawrence was ready for something other than the ministry: "Father, funny man, told me the other evening that if he were in my place he would take Fannie & go to California & get up a College or start something. He said we had been long enough 'working for a dead horse'!! I am thinking of studying medicine this vacation. What do you think of it. Dr. Page offered me 'access to his library & to his patients' as well as general instruction."

Lawrence added that he was still pursuing teaching positions, though it was difficult since he must not let the faculty at the seminary know. Lawrence urged Fanny to return to Maine, stating that she had fully vindicated herself to those who doubted she would succeed in Georgia. At an unusual loss for words, he reminded her that she should "learn a few things more" and continued: "I want you to *get the hang* of things (I really dont know any other phrase to the point.) You will need to know how to manage affairs somewhat at all events."

Again asking Fanny to come to his parents' home, he suggested, "Whenever you think you are prepared to be married, it shall be done. Now isn't that satisfactory? Now I shall be half expecting to see you next Monday morning or so, to claim the reward." He added:

> *How true it is, I agree with you at last, that writing is a poor substitute for the magnetism of personal intercourse. I feel it now. If I could only see you & "touch" you—I dont think there would be much room for the "cooling down" you speak of, in the "effect of your letters." Though it is no such thing, as you say, that I do not feel the force of what you say. Fannie, you have been talking pretty plainly & pretty strongly lately, but then I dont blame you. I know how it must seem to you.*[15]

Fanny did not rush home to Maine. The knowledge that she was ill and discouraged during the month of May drew this response from Lawrence: "I want to tell you my poor precious little girl, how her 'chosen one' will cherish & sustain her—she thinks he will droop—*maybe not*, dear. He thinks he can bear up if only he can come to her & to his *own* blessed home." These reassurances prefaced reservations about a teaching position at Athens College in Georgia:

> *In the first place I am not equal to the place. I should appear inferior in any comparison. It is a department which presupposes & demands much polish & perfection in all branches of literature One is expected to have at least taken a second degree & to have been at all events some time out of college, & I should imagine it would be expected of him to have completed a Theological course. My studies you know have been it is true somewhat varied, but still mostly of the solid kind. In History—an important requisite—I am an ignoramus.*[16]

Lawrence also announced that a position would open up in the department of sacred rhetoric at the Bangor Seminary in the fall that would "suit me *at length* better than any other thing." He observed in a statement that would later prove to be ironic: "It is true I am not exactly fitted for a prof. of rhetoric That requires a man of rules—of *easy exactness*—of common place infallibility. Whereas *I* (begging your pardon) am a person of little respect for arbitrary rules & of a slight vein of originality in my style at any rate.—" And on the subject of one unidentified authority figure, he added, "I dont like Dr C very well, either. I have an impression that he is a stiff, overbearing, unreasonable man. I am not sure; I wont fawn, or cringe, or supplicate—scarcely *obey*!" Lawrence concluded that, at that time, he felt best suited for a department of languages.[17]

Fanny received word in late June 1854 that her birth mother, Emily Adams, had died suddenly of heart failure in Boston. While Fanny grieved at the loss of yet another mother, a letter arrived from Rev. Adams. "My Dear Child, My heart is full of love for you, of sorrow for your trials, & anxiety for your welfare." Relating the details of Emily Adams' death, he expressed his concern for Fanny. Questioning whether she had tried to repay her debt to him too quickly, he suggested that he would send her money if she found herself in need. Though he offered this support, there is much in the letter that hardly seems to belong in a letter of condolence. He wanted her to return his letters, an indication that he may have regretted his past words to Fanny, but he also wrote:

> *It grieves me that I should seem to have ever caused you needless sorrow. Some day, you may understand me better than now. You must suppose I should have suffered somewhat during the last year or two, seeing Helen so broken down in health & seeing her still the object of evil surmises & unkind feelings on the part of persons who would have felt differently, if* <u>*you*</u> *had not entertained the wrong notions which it seems from your letters that you have.*

He closed his letter with the news that they were expecting a visit from Anna Davis, and added, "[I] shall be very happy to see *you* whenever Providence may permit us to meet."[18]

The summer of 1854 was a melancholy one for Fanny, as she resigned herself to staying in Georgia. Letters from Cousin Deborah indicate that Fanny began to indulge herself as she had more time to pay her debts. Though Deborah criticized Fanny's love for beautiful materials and trims, her letters indicate that she was a willing partner in the composition of Fanny's shopping lists. Sending lengthy descriptions of the New York fashions, her only disparaging comments were on the limited value of buying bright colors that were stylish in the South, but would never do when Fanny came north. Deborah searched Canal St. and Broadway on her behalf, buying ribbons, laces, fabrics & patterns, to be shipped to Georgia along with new sheet music for Fanny's music scholars.[19]

Knowing of Fanny's unhappy resignation to stay on in Georgia, Lawrence wrote at the end of July:

> *My Own Darling, I have been rather anxious to hear from you this week, but I suppose I could hardly expect so soon to have another letter. So I am trying to think you are well, at least; for I fear I ought not to hope that you are very happy, my darling. I want to see you , dear, these beautiful summer days & nights—I get very lonely & I do not know how to bear it sometimes. I can not study even unless some body cares, & loves me all the time, & knows just what I am doing. By & by will there be an such body, darling; come & tell me.*[20]

Lawrence made an attempt at brightness: "Well, darling, I hope that we shall be very soon somewhere where you will never never have to go away at all again, but will have a right to go wherever I go; for I dont mean to join the free masons." But in a revealing flash of candor, he wrote:

It startles me to think how little a time it will be before I shall have to launch out into the world. I mean to be fit to do something. I know I do not write enough.... I mean to try a sermon this summer—one at least. We are not regularly licensed till next spring, but can by special permission go out for a day, & try our hand. For my part, I am more of a scholar than preacher & I shall have hard work ever to get up a sermon, I fear.[21]

Still plagued with doubts, Lawrence nontheless confirmed his intention to continue at the seminary. With a conscience-ridden defense of his attempts to find a teaching position, he renewed his plea for Fanny to return:

Do come home, dear, so that I can see you at any rate. Darling, do you ever smile? Tell me; for it seems to me all the time that you are so sad, that I hardly can have the heart to write a word that is not solemn.... Do not be disappointed, dear, at the result of my efforts (if you will indulge me in the word.) I did try and have tried so that it has made serious inroads on my proper interest & attention here. I feel all the time as if you were blaming me, & yet I am sure *I am not to blame for either want of energy or want of interest Still it has an effect on me, to have you think me remiss or negligent.*[22]

When Fanny, waivering, began to consider a visit in the North with her Boston family, a letter from Ashur Adams arrived with discouraging news. While Ashur assured Fanny that reports of typhoid in Boston were false, he informed her that New York City was quite another story. He encouraged her, if she came, to spend as little time there as possible. Though assuring Fanny that they would rejoice to see her, Ashur also related that Charlotte was in poor health. He explained, "We have it in contemplation to take a small family into the house, who will take Charlotte & me as boarders—We have not yet positively concluded to do it, but if we do, shall make arrangements for your accommodation, altho' matters may not be so pleasant for you as we could wish." Her Boston family's unsettled living arrangements may have convinced Fanny that she still could not go home.[23]

In September 1854, Lawrence returned to the seminary, and Fanny again changed her living arrangements in Milledgeville. She stayed with another of the Presbyterian Church's prominent families, in the large home of Dr. Augustus Williams. Ashur Adams directed letters to Lawrence in Bangor rather than to Georgia, when he wished to tell Fanny that Charlotte had become increasingly ill. Lawrence, advising Fanny to come home immediately, also mentioned that he intended to consult Rev. Adams about Fanny's return:

There are various other reasons which make us all think that it would be best for you to come home—& that with no intention of returning South again. I need not now tell you what they are, only that they seem to us conclusive.... As to the matter of your 'support' as you said in your last letter, I will write a word or two. You need not think of that at all in making up your mind. It will be made all right & satisfactory to you.... I do not know my dear Fannie, whether it would do for me to run the risk of going to Savannah now—indeed I should not like to go so far south at this season if

> *it were perfectly healthy. However if you hold me to my promise I suppose I must go...the only thing that troubles me about it is whether, if I should not go, you would have any escort at all....*[24]

With no indication that Lawrence's health was delicate, it is likely that his reluctance to set foot in Georgia was more a matter of facing Fanny on opposing ground. Willing to meet her in New York or Boston, he urged her to come immediately. Offering assurances that the Brewer Chamberlains hoped that she would visit them for four or five months, he added, "You would have only a few months left *to yourself*-only 8 or 9 months—if you... were to come north when I have mentioned. We get through here in July next year, and then____.... Fan, you have got to come. You may as well submit with a good grace."[25]

But Fanny did not come, and it is difficult to know how she viewed the alliance that had apparently formed between Lawrence and her two fathers to bring her home. Early in 1854, Rev. Adams met with Lawrence during a trip to Bangor. While the object of this meeting is unknown, by that fall Anna Davis returned to Brunswick for a short stay, and Rev. Adams even extended an invitation to Cousin Deborah to come back for a visit. Perhaps he wanted to make peace with Fanny, too. Lawrence also visited with Ashur Adams at his home in Roxbury in June 1854. Not only did Ashur fear that Fanny would ruin her health working in the South, but he also needed a companion for Charlotte. But while Charlotte was unquestionably ill with the disease that eventually took her life, it seems that Lawrence overplayed the seriousness of her condition.[26]

Little more than a week later, surprised at having no response from Fanny to his urgent summons, Lawrence described his frustration with the glacial pace of the mail service. In this letter, he all but abandoned the issue of a pressing need for Fanny to go to her Boston family:

> *I am getting so that I must see you. I can not do without you any longer. It is very needful that you should be a little nearer to me, dear Fannie; for I confess that writing to you now is no great pleasure or releif [sic] to me. I never get an answer. I have nothing which could be called correspondence with you. We can make no plan together; for it would be so long before I should get an answer to a proposition, that, by that time, a new set of actors would be on the stage & the opportunity would have passed by.... How very strange it seems to me. More than two years ago, I put the ring on my betrothed Fannies hand, & went out of her sight into the darkness & have not seen her since....*[27]

Comparing their love to a bridge over which had passed their messages of love and solitary sorrows, Lawrence inferred that she was not coming. "I think it would be better for you to come now, but if you like to be a missionary & feel that you must stay, why, I will try to get along without you six months." Scolding her that he knew nothing of what she was doing, he admitted that that was not wholly true, for Cousin Deborah had sent him one of Fanny's letters. He not only discovered that she was having trouble there over a cantata, but "...I understand that you are in need of 'a few pairs of _s_t_o_c_k_ings not too large'! Forgive Cousin D. for letting me into the feminine secret that you wear stockings. I am willing—nay, pleased that such is the *case* with those precious little ancles [sic] that support my idol.—"[28]

His spirits apparently lightened, Lawrence continued with news of his activities. He fretted at being "poorly fitted for a professional life of any sort—," and averred that he was trying to make the most of his time. He had again taken up the bass viol, and quipped, "when I can play better I shall call it *violoncello*—" He played German airs, especially Schubert, with Sae playing accompaniment on piano. He told Fanny that, "occasionally I take my gun & enjoy a hunt & a ramble some ten or fifteen miles & a successful returning." But the most intriguing, though seemingly innocent news was that he had taken up the study of Arabic and Syriac. As he would reveal many years later in his memoirs, he studied these languages with the specific hope of being a missionary in the Middle East. He concluded this letter with a response to one of Fanny's prior declarations:

> *You would not like to live in Bangor! On any condition? Well, I imagine you will have to be humored a little, till you get used to life—We shall "get along" (what a mulish idiom!) some how I am quite sure. I am going to sign my name to this I dont believe you know who writes to you half the time. J. Lawrence Chamberlain*

Though Lawrence displayed a teasing tolerance toward Fanny's outspoken rejection of Bangor as their home, he managed to have the last word. Beneath his signature was his notation that his letter was sent "To Rev. Mrs. C.F.C.," to Rev. Mrs. Caroline Frances Chamberlain.[29]

Still communicating through Lawrence, Ashur Adams wrote in October to ask Lawrence if Fanny would come to them for the winter. Though Lawrence had previously told Fanny that Charlotte's condition dictated her return home immediately, Ashur's letter expressed a contrary view. While stating his hope that Fanny and her sister would meet once more "before their final separation," he offered the opinion that she could live for months. Lawrence's next letter conveyed less urgency, but he still urged her to come north right away. And he offered to come to Milledgeville for her, "though I do not wish to. I will go to New York for you or any where else you may wish."[30]

Whatever Fanny gleaned from Lawrence's letters concerning her sister's health or his intentions, her next letter not only explained why she could not come north, but also conveyed the news that she had located a position for him in a school for young ladies in LaGrange, Georgia. She proposed that he "enlist" for a year, continue his studies in Georgia and return to the seminary for graduation in July. Fanny may have been more than a little surprised by the brisk, affirmative reply she found in Lawrence's next letter. Not only had Lawrence failed to acknowledge this proposal after first receiving it, but Fanny must have suspected that Lawrence had little or no intention of leaving the seminary.[31]

Written in the last days of October and early November, his letter spoke of dejection and loneliness. He wrote that he was more than ever "disposed to sink down into a silent gloom than to rouse myself to a cheerful energy—" He declared, "Fannie, my blessed Love, you are away from me. And now in a day or two I am to lose my darling cousin Annie, who has been my only comfort & solace here this long, long time that I have not seen you. She has been everything to me—so childlike, so sweet, so pure & noble hearted. She is going away, & I shall hardly ever see her again in this world I fear...." He explained that he had not been quite alone before, for when his heart was heavy he would "run down a few steps & be cheered by a radiant quiet smile, & come back happier." Having written thus far, Lawrence received another letter from Fanny, and when he continued his letter, he was seemingly ready to acquiesce to all that she asked of him. Employing the German word for fiancé, he wrote:

> *My darling, Fanny knew just when he would need a letter from his precious Brant didn't she? I shall call her "my darling comfort" as she used to call me. I was very lonely very, when she came & told her dear story into my ear to help & to encourage me. What a sweet little wife she is going to be, isn't she? Well, Fannie, I have thought almost two days of your 'little plan' and now reply viz; I am willing to enter into a correspondence with Mr. Bacon. I wish to know what he wants taught & when (as to vacations &c).... At all events I think favorably of your proposal, & if it is what I infer it to be from your letters, I shall hope it will be immediately arranged.*[32]

Proclaiming himself able to teach the girls a little Latin or German, conic sections and calculus, Lawrence related that his parents approved of the plan, but that he had not consulted anyone at the seminary. He also mentioned to Fanny, apparently for the first time, the faculty's disposition against student marriage: "probably they would be slow to consent, but that is no obstacle; only they might withhold a diploma of a completed course of study, and would not allow me to graduate if I were guilty of—marriage;—a crime I should probably commit, if exposed to violent temptation. However, do not think I shall be prevented from acting by any such obstacles." He also wrote, "By this same mail you will receive a deed duly made out & legally attested, a veritable deed of some property you were fearful, it seems to me, you might lose." Within days of the arrival of this letter, Fanny received the following "conveyance" from Lawrence.[33]

Warrantee deed.—For Sale by E. F. Duren, Bangor.

> *Know all Men by these Presents, that I Joshua Lawrence Chamberlain of Brewer county of Penobscot and State of Maine*
>
> *In consideration of the sum of the constant & sincere affections real & personal paid by Frances C. Adams formerly of Brunswick, county of Cumberland & State of Georgia, Lady. the receipt whereof I do hereby acknowledge, do hereby give, grant, bargain sell and convey unto the said Frances C. Adams and to her heirs and assigns forever, the following described premises, All that estate situated for the most part in the city of Bangor county & state first above mentioned, on the westerly side of Kenduskeag Stream, on Union Street, within the grounds of the Theological Institution and division numbered twenty-two, and bounded as follows; beginning at a block or elongated spheroidal mass marked in Paxton's plans of anatomy 'cranium' at the juncture of the sagittal and lambdoidal sutures thence south five feet ten inches & a half to the extremities of ten stakes*

marked as above 'phalanges digitorium pedis', & being sixteen inches in width at the widest part viz; at the articulation of the os humeri with the glenoid cavity of the scapula, but unequal in width owing to magnetic variations at the time when said premises were originally laid out. We above being well organized & under good improvement & inhabited by dispositions & qualities of great utility & rare attractions, & containing valuable privileges as yet unimproved; and being the same premises originally conveyed to me by Joshua Chamberlain Esq. of Brewer county of Penobscot & state of Maine & Sarah wife of said Joshua,...their certificates duly recorded in the clerks office in the town county & state aforesaid and to document on file in their possession. To have and to hold, the aforegranted and bargained Premises, with all the privileges and appurtenances thereof, to the said Frances C. Adams and to her heirs and assigns, to their use and behoof forever. And I do covenant with the said Frances and with her heirs and assigns, that I am lawfully seized in fee of the Premises; that they are free of all incumbrances [sic]; that I have good right to sell and convey the same to the said Frances and to her heirs and assigns forever,....

In Witness Whereof, the said Joshua Lawrence Chamberlain hereunto set his hand and seal this third day of November in the year of our Lord one thousand eight hundred and fifty-four. J. Lawrence Chamberlain

signed, Sealed and Deliver in presence of
Wellington Newall
Edward Buck

Penobscot, ss November 3 1854 personally appeared the above named
J. Lawrence Chamberlain

and acknowledged the above instrument to be his free act and deed.
Before me, Frank A. Wilson Justice of the Peace.[34]

To appreciate the significance of this tongue-in-cheek document, circumstances existing in Lawrence's life at that time should be considered, including the cousin whom he had declared he would so sorely miss. Hannah "Annie" Chamberlain, was the 22 year old daughter of Lawrence's uncle, Jefferson Chamberlain of Bangor, and a number of Lawrence's letters mention visits to Jefferson's home and being in company with Annie Chamberlain. It seems as if Lawrence sent thinly veiled attempts to arouse jealousy in Fanny regarding Annie, while dubiously stating that no one thought twice about cousins being seen together. Annie also attended Lawrence's German class for young ladies and the Chamberlain families were aware of their affectionate attachment for one another. But when Annie's father found a note that Lawrence had secretly sent to her, he was so alarmed by the nature of it, that he decided the relationship must end and that Annie should be sent away.[35]

Lawrence, embarrassed to be exposed in such an impropriety, repentant for having hurt a favored uncle, and indignant at his aunt's disparaging remarks about his character, struggled to compose a letter to Annie shortly after he had spoken to Jefferson Chamberlain. "I begin this letter to you scarcely knowing how I shall go on with it, for I am at a loss what to choose from the thousand things that are crowding upon me to say to you." Presuming that Annie's father had informed her that he would not be allowed to see her before she was sent away, he observed that, "I could not bear to have you go away while everything was enveloped in such a cloud of mystery, evidently so painful to all parties." Explaining that he requested an interview with his Uncle Jefferson, he reported that Annie's father stated that the intimacy between Lawrence and Annie had previously caused "remark & solicitude," but that discovery of Lawrence's note gave grounds for alarm and prompt action. Lawrence acknowledged that he was not surprised that his uncle found the contents of the note a "betrayal of trust" for on reading Lawrence's "extravagant & ardent expressions to you" he could be pardoned for thinking Lawrence was guilty of some wrong. Relating that he had stated to his uncle that he regarded Annie with "no ordinary nor temporary interest & affection," Lawrence explained to her father that "I felt that under my influence—I will not say instruction—you would grow in strength of mind & in beauty of spirit." Reflecting that he and Annie had an understanding that they would "act as not only under the eye of God, but so as to give cause for grief or regret to none," Lawrence assured Annie that her father did not charge him with deception or wrong intentions, but his uncle did insist that "*our* intimacy in its present shape both as to personal familiarity & written correspondence should not continue...." To his uncle's expressed concern of where the matter would stop if longer permitted, Lawrence replied, "we *do* know what would come of it in some sense—that is, what would *not* come of it" and he referred to his and Annie's "conscience & moral principle." With wishes that his uncle could understand their true relationship, which he felt was honorable, rather than a case of "silly blindness & indiscretion...," Lawrence admitted that the secrecy of their notes may have been a mistake, though "not wrong in any way I would blush to own." Declaring his hope that his own calmness and dignity of spirit would be soothing to Annie, Lawrence closed his letter by saying:

> *friend of my soul—there is a place for you in my heart which no other can fill, & I will sooner be blotted out of being than ever let you go. Annie let us be careful to keep our souls pure and without spot in the the eyes of Him...the judge of hearts & look for recognition to another world where we shall bring no pain to others, no reproach upon ourselves & sooner or later that day will come.*[36]

Annie's reply came just four days later from Lasell Female Seminary, in the Auburndale area of Newton, Massachusetts, where it had been arranged that she would teach Latin & composition:

> *Do not be grieved or angry when I say that I cannot answer such a stately letter, & one so evidently not intended for me.... I know that I asked you to tell me the conversation which passed between you and my father—but I did not mean you to arrange & deliver it to me as you have done—& so chill me & drive me away from you until I feel as if I never knew you—If the letter was intended for my father rather than myself (as it evidently was) then I can understand it better.... I have never known you so & I cannot think of you so If I love you at all it must be as I always have.*

Stating that she has suffered much for trying to be anything or love anything, Annie declared that her heart was broken, and she reminded Lawrence that she would have to bear it alone. "...I can bear it—but *you* never can bear on & *live* alone—I mean you never seem able to do so—you *must* have someone *near* you to love you & sympathize with you in all that comes to you—" Grieved to have hurt her father, Annie stated that she was unwilling to forward Lawrence's letter to him, for she felt her father would know it was unlike his others.[37]

No other examples of Lawrence's letters to Annie have been found, but she continued to write unhappy, rather desperate letters to Lawrence. The loss of his letters from this time period makes it difficult to interpret his intentions and feelings for Annie, but she suffered all the pain of lost love. An undated letter, likely written during Annie's vacation from Auburndale in the winter of 1854-55, is typical of her letters to Lawrence after their separation: "The day has almost gone—and you are not come—and I shall *go back* without seeing you dear, darling, go *back* I am afraid in more ways than one—for I cannot be anything there—You ought never to have been so good to me at home and to have helped me so much...." Wondering if she would ever see Lawrence again, Annie commented, "darling—I felt as if I were looking at you and listening to you for the very last time yesterday—.... The *last time must* come sometime—must it not darling—darling—and *soon* maybe— It will kill me I am sure." She declared that it might be best for her to again become more like the world, as she was becoming before Lawrence came. Annie added, "My own L_. if you come to Auburndale—(do as you think best—you *know* what I would say about it) come right up to my room & knock—I will be there if possible—all the afternoon. I want to see you *so* much but I will not urge you—you—darling know better than I about everything—"[38]

What had his relationship with Annie meant to Lawrence? Had her company simply eased the pain of a lonely and distressing period of his life or did he love her? Lawrence continued to write to her, and possibly met with her several times after she was sent away. Still, these questions are left unanswered. Perhaps the chance repetition of a phrase found in two letters, one from Annie to Lawrence, and one from Lawrence to Fanny, gives some insight into what caused him to encourage Annie's devotion. At the end of July 1854, he had written to Fanny, "I get very lonely & I do not know how to bear it sometimes. I can not study even unless some body cares, & loves me all the time, & knows just what I am doing." Annie, in her first distraught letter to Lawrence, used similar phrases: "...I can bear it—but *you* never can bear on & *live* alone—I mean you never seem able to do so—you *must* have someone *near* you to love you & sympathize with you in all that comes to you—"[39]

Annie's demeanor towards Lawrence sharply contrasts with Fanny's tendency to demur. Annie, who apparently saw Lawrence not only as the love of her life, but also as her mentor, deferred to Lawrence in all things. Fanny, on the other hand, consistently urged him to abandon his chosen profession, repeatedly refused to return to Maine, and rejected the idea of living in the area that was Lawrence's home.

Though Lawrence unfailingly spoke of his love for Fanny and affirmed their intention to marry in his letters, Annie's ready acquiescence to him might have made Fanny seem all the more recalcitrant. A further insight into Lawrence's relationship with Annie may be found in the declaration he made to her father: "I felt that under my influence—I will not say instruction-you would grow in strength of mind & in beauty of spirit." Beyond what Annie's adulation did for his self esteem, what satisfaction did he derive from "influencing," and perhaps we may even say "ministering" to his receptive young cousin? For Lawrence also stated that no one else would guide Annie's undeveloped qualities as he had, for, being like her himself, he might prevent her from struggling in darkness as he had or from being "forever fettered & dumb."[40]

At the end of 1854, encouraged by Lawrence's new enthusiasm for teaching in the South, Fanny confidently asked Deborah to purchase a piano in New York City and to have it shipped to Milledgeville. Her days were still filled with the duties of teaching, and she labored over her students' performance of the highly popular "Flower Queen," a cantata written by her former professor, George F. Root. It seems that Fanny would have been content to stay in the South, if Lawrence would be there, too. But his impulsive agreement to pursue a teaching position, made during the first painful and embarrassing revelation of his relationship with Annie, would be regretted. Beyond their society's perceptions of a wife's duty, did he believe that, on the strength of Fanny's love for him, he might still persuade her to be as Ruth, "for whithersoever thou shalt go, I will go; and where thou shalt dwell, I also shall dwell."[41]

CHAPTER

7

"Ready To Be Married"

Fewer letters survive from 1855 than from the other years of Fanny and Lawrence's separation, and one must wonder, as frustration and anxiety mounted, whether some of their letters were consigned to the nearest fire. But those that have been found are salient and illuminating. The teaching position in Georgia either was not offered to Lawrence or was not accepted. The discrepancies in their hopes and ambitions continued to obstruct the formation of any lasting plans, while letters stalled or lost in the mails between Maine and Georgia thwarted their communication. In this year of coming reunion, both Fanny and Lawrence would proclaim themselves much changed from the lovers who had parted in the last days of 1852.[1]

Anna Davis, after her visit to Rev. Adams in Brunswick, joined Cousin Deborah in Hoboken, New Jersey. She secured a teaching position in the area, traveled to New York City to study music, and assisted Deborah in choosing a piano for Fanny. Deborah engaged in sharp negotiations with the New York City purveyor, and managed to have a free piano stool and bundle of sheet music shipped with Fanny's piano to Georgia. Having arranged to ship a piano all the way to Milledgeville that February, it seems evident that Fanny planned to stay in Georgia until the spring or summer of 1855, if not longer.[2]

Fanny's Boston father, Ashur Adams, writing during the coldest days of February, expressed relief that Fanny had not come north to the sub-zero temperatures. "Altho' we long to see you, yet we are thankful that you did'nt attempt to come on last summer, as it would have been very hazardous.—& we are glad that you are not here now, as you could not have borne the cold.... 19 below zero—in and about Boston.—At Bangor it went down to 34 [below]!!!" Fanny's sister Charlotte was now confined to her room, advanced consumption making it impossible for her to leave her bed without assistance. But a cousin, Mary, had come to Boston to care for Charlotte. Though Ashur expressed no alarm, Charlotte would not live to see the pleasures of spring. Ashur described his loneliness since the death of Fanny's birth mother, Emily, and commented, "It seems that your views of life are different from what they once were—& I hope that you have found that the great business of life is to prepare for death—." This tenet Ashur and Emily Adams had offered to all their children, in the earnest desire that they live good lives.

From her letters, Ashur perceived change in his youngest daughter's "views of life." Before her three year exile to await her studious lover, Fanny had seen music, art, and poetry as the most important elements in her life. It seems her long, and as she saw it, compulsory stay in the South, and the demands of life as a music teacher, had changed her.[3]

The early months of 1855 were bleak for Lawrence. He received despondent letters from Annie, and although he was still received in his Uncle Jefferson's home, he was dismayed at their coldness. As Lawrence completed his last months at the seminary, a letter to Fanny at the end of March reveals his frustration regarding her stand on his entering the ministry. Confounded as to what his next step should be, he wryly acknowledged her protests:

> *You know there are only about four months left for my stay here, & I doubt not, I might,—If I would only try—know something of the next step. But being in ignorance of your feelings, I cannot have the heart to attempt any thing for fear you might feel that I was laying on you the necessity of dying, to avoid the miseries into which I might plunge you. So I am trifling away—not my time—but my energies—that is not directing them in any particular channel;... I think though after all I am gaining something but gray hairs. You little rogue of a girl away off there, how like a very mischief you do plague me. One comfort however I do have and that is that you never can plague me so by & by as you have these three years—now dont go off & cry & put up your little lip & look grieved—when I can see you & talk some reason into you, you will be just as sweet a child as ever need be. Being so far from the scene of things you can not understand their position & there fore can not be in very good condition to direct their disposition & movements. Let me see—the case is—You dont want to go where I do—you dont think I ought to ask you to—you do want me to go where you do—you dont know where that is—you dont think I have tried to find out—you do think I've been trying to kidnap you & carry you away against your knowledge or consent to slavery degradation & death. To carry out these base intentions & "effect my purpose" on you, I have been craftily staying at a Theol. Seminary making you think I was studying alchemy when I was "meaning to preach all the time" & while I was secretly thinking about my nefarious scheme of preaching, I have been pretending with an honest open look that I was pondering over the philosophers stone & waiting for some thing to turn*

up.—Well now, Fan, I know it is a serious affair with you & I treat it so but it does baffle me so, & prevent any effort on my part not to know how near to death my choice or action might happen to bring you. Will you be a good girl & tell me whether it would be "horrid" for you to be with me if I should chance to go for a few weeks some where to preach. I dont mean to plague you but I do wish you would write to me & good long letters.[4]

It is possible, in Fanny's anxious state, that yet another proposal that he preach for a while led Fanny to insinuate that his plans would be the death of her. But Fanny's distress likely had another cause; his study of Arabic languages at the seminary indicates that he had not forsaken the idea of being a missionary. It is also possible that Lawrence, in an attempt to reach a compromise, had upped the career ante from preacher to missionary, as a reminder that he had already been asked to sacrifice one of his original goals.[5]

If Lawrence was exasperated with Fanny in early 1855, he was also impatient with Annie. Her note to Lawrence in early April 1855 claimed that he had scorned her requests, and she demanded that he return a small portrait of herself which he had given away: "Please send it back and I will put it where it will trouble neither of us—My reasons for wishing you *alone* to have it are many and good to me—but *I* am only a silly child—and they would seem ridiculous to you as they did before—I shall expect the miniature on *tuesday*—not that *I* want it—I will never look at the hateful thing again—...."[6]

The beleaguered Lawrence received a letter from Fanny which struck a more conciliatory note, but did not entirely placate him. In his response, he wrote, "You did write, did n't you? I thought you would after a while. And you succeeded in writing 'a short letter' too. Well I have learned to be patient, & I suppose I shall need that grace most of all by & by." To Fanny's request that he send the address he was preparing for graduation, he teased, "...I dont think I shall let you have it. It is a great cumbersome mass of some 40 or 50 pages, & what can a child like you do with all that. Besides I want to write it over before I let you see it...it wont read so well though as it *sounds* when spoken." Fanny also questioned why he had not sent her any of his sermons; she received the surprising reply that none had been written. He explained that he had spoken extemporaneously when he practiced his skills at a Sunday school at Whiting Hill near Brewer.[7]

But, Lawrence found himself unable to maintain the rather cool and sardonic reserve he had employed in this letter when he considered a remark Fanny had made. He addressed a double entendre, intentional or otherwise, that Fanny's letter contained. With mock consternation he wrote, "About the 'insertion' I dont know what meaning you apply to it. I'm afraid you are getting to be a naughty girl arn't you? However I'll engage that you shall have just as much insertion as you want of any sort you may choose." Pleased with this sortie, Lawrence declared that he looked forward to Fanny's return. He informed her of his graduation date from the seminary, as well as the date of Bowdoin's commencement, where he would be awarded a Master of Arts degree for his theological studies. To Fanny's question of where he wanted to preach, he retorted, "You mischievously want to know what place in New England it is where I might go &c—now that is too bad tantalizing me about that when you wont let me go there...." But he added:

I feel that it will all come out right. I believe that God is over all things & that he will put me where he wants me & where I ought to be. You are a very dear girl & are pretty good to me—I am sorry though, my darling, that I ever should have given you the pain I have by what you call a "mistaken sense of duty[")] it grieves me to trouble you—I cannot think of it without pain But I feel that if my sweet wife could look into my heart or even into my eyes she could read there the tenderest love for her, resting on a broad & strong ground—my first & greatest duty to God. May he bless & keep you, my darling, shielding you from the terrible conflicts & scathing temptations that assail me, & prepare us both for all the way that is before us.[8]

The goal he had worked and argued so long for was within months of his grasp. Yet the pleasure he felt at achieving that goal was diminished by the hardships he had endured and had placed upon those he cared for most. Annie Chamberlain's pain was all too apparent, and though he knew Fanny loved him, continuing to test that love was placing a great strain on their relationship. Whatever bitterness, remorse or uncertainty he might feel, Lawrence was obliged to labor through the last requirements of the seminary. He had lost none of his drive to serve God by serving his fellow man, but all of his best laid plans seemed to be going sadly wrong.[9]

As Fanny planned her departure from Georgia in the weeks before Lawrence's graduation, he learned that despite the stress of the last months, he had been chosen to represent his seminary class by delivering a master's oration at Bowdoin. Faced with the preparation of two major addresses, Lawrence wrote to Fanny that he had also spent this last week of spring at the deathbed of Nathan Dole, the former minister of his Brewer church. Explaining that his friend's death and the attending obligations would limit his ability to answer what had been a long and apparently angry letter from Fanny, he wrote:

...my present letter must be chiefly confession. I will however premise by thanking you for the unusually long letter you wrote me last. You have not written so long a one for a great while. I believe the old Satin poets were of opinion that Love conquers all things; but I think that this time—something else has done what love could not do & you have written me a long letter. Still I know that after all such a terrible scolding you do love me, & as I love you too, I dont see any need of quarreling.—I confess I have written & seemed strange to you of late—just as I have to every body. I am strangely changing—I know it not that I love you, or any body, less than ever, but I dont know what it is about me that makes me so different. May be you wouldn't love me any, if you were to see me now; or, I mean when you do see me in a few weeks, you wont love me—I am so thin & pale.... I confess I have been indefinite & contradictory in my statements about my plans but I can only say now, you must not blame me for that—I can not bear it at all. Dont if you have any regard for my welfare, say any thing about my place of residence or labor at present.... Fannie dear, you must bear with me-you must. I tell you I can not endure one particle more of trial & burden. If I do not seem to you to be well do not reproach me with it.... I

am— have been—killing myself I know—but I could not help it. You must bear with me till you see me, & then you will forgive me all. I have not prepared even a subject for either of my orations & they come on in a month or more.[10]

Lawrence found no joy at his award of the master's oration at Bowdoin. On the contrary, he seemed distraught at having to prepare another address, a duty that would prevent him from accompanying her on her journey north. "It will be hard for me *not to* see you, but *I want you* & you must come. We will be married just as soon after commencement as you please. I will see that I am ready."[11]

By July 30, 1855, Fanny had traveled as far as Boston. Reverend Adams, on a trip to Andover, Massachusetts during which he visited Calvin and Harriet Beecher Stowe, exuberantly recorded in his diary, "*Saw our Fanny, a moment!*" Fanny arrived in Brunswick on August 1, in time for Bowdoin's commencement. Though details of Fanny and Lawrence's reunion are unknown, there is some indication of the strain of almost three years' separation. Their differences, as well as the acknowledged changes in themselves, could only have heightened the emotions of their reunion. Could Fanny understand all, as Lawrence had hoped, when she looked into his eyes?[12]

Few details about commencement week of 1855 are available, but one event is noteworthy, and would significantly affect Fanny and Lawrence's future. Lawrence's address at Bowdoin's graduation was a triumph. Years later in his memoirs, he remembered, "When he stepped upon that College stage, the flush on his face was far different from that with which he had left it three years before." His address, entitled "Law and Liberty," argued that "the superabounding life lavished in the universe was proof that the play of infinite freedom was to work out the will of infinite law. The whole Universe showed that Freedom was a part of Law." He reminisced that the "effect of this among those who heard it was an utter and overwhelming surprise to its author. The newspaper notices made him feel as if he had awakened in another world." Lawrence recalled that one notice, in the *New York Independent*, "opened a new current of thought in the mind of the young Master of arts. Life had another horizon. There might be a duty of choice as well as the power of it. There might be for him an illustration of his own doctrine of the freedom which subserves highest law." Bowdoin indicated interest in their young alumnus, and a proposed shuffling of positions suggested that there might be a place for Lawrence among the faculty. The acclaim he received at commencement opened his eyes to possibilities other than the ministry, and awarded a self-confidence that Fanny claimed he had been unable to realize. Some at Bowdoin suggested that he take over some duties of the professorship formerly held by the esteemed Prof. Calvin Stowe. There was also mention of a position in the department of rhetoric and oratory. Of the latter proposal, he declared it "the very irony of fate for one who had so struggled against what he had supposed disqualifying disabilities in this department."

Exhausted, Lawrence had much to think about as he returned home to Brewer after cpmmencement. Although flattered by Bowdoin's attentions, he awaited a concrete offer, for he had also received invitations from four different churches before his graduation from the seminary. And while Lawrence had promised Fanny that they would marry after Bowdoin's commencement, he now added the condition that he must first be settled in a stable and promising position. Fanny, determined not to return to Maine only to be dependent on others before she and Lawrence married, found herself in exactly that position upon her return.[13]

When Fanny first returned to Brunswick she stayed with her longtime friend, Alice Dunlap. Either Rev. Adams' house was filled with company during commencement, or relations between Fanny and Rev. Adams were still so strained that she felt herself an unwanted guest. Also, Helen's ill health continued, to the point that, after losing several housekeepers in early 1855, they took their meals at the Tontine, a Brunswick inn. But with summer came the realization that Helen, much to Rev. Adams' delight, was expecting their first child.[14]

On August 12, Fanny finally returned to her childhood home. A letter she wrote that day to Lawrence provides insight, not only to the emotional climate of Fanny's reunion with Rev. Adams, but to Lawrence and Fanny's reunion as well: "This is a wonderful day to me my dear Lawrence; I am all alone in the old house, amid the same old things that surrounded me long years ago, when life was all glorious and sparkling and full of the great poem of the future. Now how wonderfully changed am I, while the same dear old trees whisper the same kind things, only the heart they whisper to is changed." Of her reception there, Fanny wrote, "Father treats me very strangely; he says nothing unkind, but there is not the slightest vestage [sic] of his former manner of treating me. He asks me nothing of my plans or prospects, nothing of my success while I have been gone; has not one word to say excepting what belongs to the present circumstances about us. Helen is very polite and kind, but the thing seems forced rather." Fanny wrote that their old friend Samuel Gardner, had visited, and he thought there was a "perfect want of cordiality on Father's part." Fanny reported that Rev. Adams "has never once asked me anything concerning my being married, either *where* or *when*; so I feel decided fully to go to Boston for everything. I am upon the whole sorry that I did not go on to Boston at the time we intended, but perhaps my being here at the house may prevent some hard feeling in various quarters, so I'm willing to endure it all for a few days."[15]

Fanny also reported the rumors that Bowdoin's president, Leonard Woods, intended to offer Lawrence the upcoming vacant professorship in rhetoric and oratory: "Gardner said last night that Mr Woods spoke as if they expected you to come here, and I received the impression that the idea was for you to take the Professor-ship which Egbert Smyth was expected to leave,...what do you think of coming to Brunswick, if they offer special inducements here, as Gardner mentioned they thought of doing?" And she informed him that, "Every body here high & low, praises your Commencement performance." Fanny asked, "...do tell me frankly just what you think of doing from time to time. (I dont mean to trouble you about it) for I want to know what to do." In concern, she wrote, "How is your health now Lawrence? if you are sick, send for me *immediately*; you remember you promised me that." Though Fanny softened her questions with solicitude for Lawrence, she offered one observation: "I will not allude now to anything that occurred when you were here although there are many things that grieve me as much as they did then; indeed they make me very wretched at times." Fanny wrote this letter without mentioning that it was her 30th birthday.[16]

Lawrence, as he waited to hear from Bowdoin, began to cut his ties to Bangor and Brewer. It was with regret that he left behind well-loved people and places. The Whiting Hill Sunday School, where he had tried his wings as a preacher, sent him away with the gift of a Bible. Lawrence so valued it that he would carry it with him in the 1860s, through dark days and events that could then never be imagined. With a feeling of accomplishment, Lawrence left his position as supervisor of the Brewer Schools. He had persuaded the town to consolidate several of its schools into a new high school, with an improved curriculum to provide for students who wished to continue their education. He was adamant that academic opportunities be made available to all the children of Brewer, not just those whose parents could afford private schools. The citizens of Brewer voted for these changes, but the resultant increase in taxes caused controversy in the town.[17]

Fanny left Brunswick for Boston on August 19, and several days later Lawrence visited with her briefly at her family's Roxbury home. He brought disappointing news about the position at Bowdoin. The college had hoped to offer him the professorship of rhetoric and oratory then held by Egbert Smyth, son of longtime faculty member, William Smyth. But that vacancy hinged on Egbert's accepting the Collins Professorship of Natural and Revealed Religion, an appointment that was a position of influence. When Smyth declined, Bowdoin, just days away from the opening of the fall term, had little to offer Lawrence, for they were hesitant to offer the Collins Professorship to an untried man whose theology was a matter of speculation. Still anxious to engage young Chamberlain, their initial offer was a mere tutorship, with so small a salary that it was considered a bachelor's position, and a rather poor one at that.[18]

Lawrence, in a state of disappointment and indecision, turned to Rev. Adams for advice. A longtime overseer of the college and an intimate of the faculty and administration, he provided little information or encouragement. Confirming that Egbert Smyth had decided not to give up his position in rhetoric and oratory, Rev. Adams wrote: "I imagine you may have if you will,-the ordinary tutorship; [$]400;—part *of* the *themes* [$]150; preaching Saturday ev[eni]ng, *more or less*; preaching abroad— In a word, I judge without hav[in]g been very definitely informed, that you might,—if your health would allow you to do all the work,—pick up 6 to 8 hundred." Reverend Adams' qualifying statement, "if your health would allow...," was no casual warning, for the demands of a tutorship, with the additional obligations he had suggested, would be crushing. He acknowledged that, "This *may* be a good position to start from, (especially, if you should be able to gain some considerable acceptance as a preacher,) whether to a Pastorship or Professorship...." But, he added that Lawrence should not count on this position at Bowdoin leading to anything permanent.[19]

Though Bowdoin appointed him a provisional instructor in Logic and Natural Theology before the year ended, Lawrence started the fall semester of 1855 at the college as a humble tutor. Disappointed in his expectations and filled with anxiety over his future, Lawrence was also haunted by the unhappy events of the past year. That September, he wrote a bitter letter to Martha Chamberlain, Annie's younger sister. Declaring that he was not ignorant of her family's "pious detestation" of him and "want of common courtesy or kindness" towards him for some time, Lawrence reminded Martha that, unlike many of his classmates who had been "charity-students," he had worked his way through the seminary by his own efforts with considerable difficulty. He described himself as being among strangers, and though the members of the college respected his abilities and character, he felt alone and in a state of anxiety and gloom. Lawrence assured her, however, that he was not destroyed or afraid. He awaited the day that she and her family would speak of him "as you know I am."[20]

Miserable and anxious, Lawrence was not quite alone in Brunswick. His brother John Chamberlain was at Bowdoin that fall. Lawrence began boarding with Helen and Rev. Adams, and they seemingly got along famously. Though Rev. Adams discussed Cousin Deborah with Lawrence, and read some of Deborah's letters to him, it is not known whether he offered his opinions of his adoptive daughter and their upcoming marriage. Whether or not Rev. Adams influenced him, Lawrence wearily began again to communicate with Fanny by letter. The greater reliability and swiftness of the mails between Boston and Brunswick were a blessing, for the problem to be resolved proved to be painful. With his meager salary and the uncertainty of his appointment at the college, Lawrence suggested that they postpone their marriage until the start of Bowdoin's winter vacation in late November. With an invitation to spend several months with his family in Brewer, Lawrence was confident he could earn some much needed capital over the holiday. But Fanny, waiting in Boston for a September wedding, was dismayed at the proposed delay.[21]

Fanny was roundly scolded by Cousin Deborah that September for failing to inform her of her plans. "I do think you are entirely unpardonable for your remissness in writing to your friends.... I am in the dark, you have not taken the trouble to let me know any thing about your affairs." But during that month, Fanny herself hardly knew where or when her wedding would be. She began a Sept. 20 missive to Lawrence with, "I enclose *another* letter from Mrs Orme: think about it if you please, and write me what you think, immediately." It is hard to know whether Fanny expected Lawrence to seriously consider the position at Milledgeville's Ogelthorpe University. She also suggested that if Bowdoin knew of another college's interest in Lawrence, perhaps it would prompt them to offer more inducement for him to stay. But Fanny also informed Lawrence that Ogelthorpe promised the princely sum of at least $1,100 a year.[22]

Fanny related that she had received "a sweet letter from your sister Sarah...inviting me very cordially to go down to Bangor and see them...but I cannot until I hear again from you." Fanny also responded to what she described, paradoxically, as his "last dear, gentle, kind letter" challenging his denial that their circumstances were a "miserable affair," and taxing him for his conflicting statements regarding his readiness to be married: "you say... 'I am not ready to be married yet',— and then you tell me, that just as soon as I am reasonable ready, *you are all ready to be married, and will be*. As to this Lawrence, I will tell you that I never could be 'ready to be married' in the world, while things were hanging this way. I have not taken one single stitch in my sewing, for I have been almost beside my self with anxiety and suspense. I have seemed to be spending all my time either in writing to you or in crying."[23]

Fanny's feelings had passed beyond impatience to some degree of humiliation, for she wrote: "It has been dreadfully mortifying & embarrassing to be asked so continually by my friends, 'when are you going to be married?' 'why I thought you were to be married in Sept; what in the world did you hurry away from Georgia for then?'" Fanny also told Lawrence that a favored uncle from South Carolina, Harold Wyllys, who was visiting his family in the North after an absence of forty years, was delaying his return south in order to attend her wedding. Hoping to convince Lawrence of the merits of an October wedding, Fanny warmed to her subject as she warned:

> *It would have been a great deal better for me to have stayed South until Spring and then have come back to be married, for I cannot be exposed to the cold then; it is the most trying time in the whole year to one whose lungs are in the state that mine are. My dearest Lawrence does n't understand this, because he is strongest and well-est in the coldest weather,.... Be careful and tender of your Fannie, Lawrence, for you will love her some time not very far distant, with Consumption, I am afraid.*

While dreading the thought of trying to settle into lodgings in the cold of November, Fanny also explained that her Boston father, who "thinks everything of you," was in precarious health, and "it seems to be the only earthly pleasure left for him to see us married." She told Lawrence how one of her Boston sisters commented, "O poor man, I think he feels rather discouraged about it, we only hope he may live to see it!"[24]

Concluding this long recital of disappointment and demands, Fanny rather inexplicably wrote, "Thank you dear, for writing me such a blessed letter! You can never know how it cheered her heart." But Fanny had made her position clear; she did not want to postpone their wedding past the last days of autumn. Though she had received a kind letter from Rev. Adams, she did not want to return to her Brunswick home. And, while greatly disappointed that the wedding trip they had planned to make to Montreal and Quebec was out of the question, she loved the idea of going with Lawrence to his Brewer home. "How delightful it would be for us at your dear Father's— You made it seem so sweet in your dear, *bright* letter!" Though Lawrence said that he would work during their honeymoon, Fanny replied with, "Bless his heart! I imagined him coming home to dine with his little wife as he said at 12 1/2. I can see him coming now, and I'm looking out of the window to welcome him, as he comes towards the house."[25]

His reply to Fanny's letter is interesting. Lawrence's handwriting could never be considered of a copperplate standard, but it is usually readable. Though this letter begins clearly enough, by the time it reaches its conclusion, it is all but illegible. Several sections have been crossed out altogether, a great oddity for Lawrence's letters, and the look of it, let alone the tone of it, expresses agitation. Having received Fanny's letter just one day after it was posted, he answered it, first addressing yet another offer from Georgia:

> *I will reply 'immediately' to the letter I have just received. Really, Fannie, the proposition does not strike me favorably....the descent from my position now even...to a school is rather too great especially to a southern school.... Why Fannie I must be careful. I must not make a misstep at the*

very outset. It seems strange to me that you make not the slightest allowance for me, nor consider my part of the case very much. I cant bear to discuss these things with you. It is vexing me—this constant harassment & as you say 'uncertainty'....I am afraid I shall get out of patience with all this. Dont think I am not sympathizing with you; but I cant feel right till I see you here; I cant say any more about these things by letters. I am sick of it—completely....[26]

Reluctantly agreeing to use Fanny's "southern proposition" with Bowdoin, he doubted that it would influence them to keep him there. Regardless, Lawrence felt it best that he finish the term at Bowdoin before they married. Impatiently pointing out that it would be cold in Brunswick whether she were married or not, he wrote, "I think you would better come here immediately, if only for a little while if you choose; I *cant* manage this business at arm's length any longer. Do for pity's sake come where we can talk over these things & understand each other." He concluded his letter with, "Dont grieve. dont cry. I shall be offended if you do. There are better things to do, & you ought not to be wretched." Fanny agreed to come.[27]

Lawrence received a distressing letter from home as he awaited Fanny's return. His youngest brother, Tom, had been sick for some time and Mother Chamberlain wrote: "Again you might see me seated and seriously watching Tom's short and rapid breathing yes he is down again...he requires constant nursing At first I felt as if I could not endure it, but recollecting strength should be proportioned to my day I take courage, and hope he may soon recover—" The family was also anxious about Lawrence's brother Horace, who was returning from a trip to Europe, and short of money. Of Lawrence's troubles, his mother commented, "You know that to all your gloom and sorrow I am not indifferent, no, I sympathize with you most deeply, yet I rejoice that these feelings lead you to more entire trust in—and more intimate communion with your God—and determination to seek his guidance and direction—...if he has called you into his field be assured, he will find work for you just where twill be best for you and for his glory...therefore be cheerful a[n]d let not your heart be troubled." To his inquiries whether he and Fanny could come to Brewer during Bowdoin's winter vacation, Lawrence's mother stated: "I say what you already know, nothing could make me happier...." Mother Chamberlain sent love to Fanny, and in this letter, Lawrence's sister Sarah added, "I had a letter from Fannie and one from Annie last week I suppose Fannie's in Brunswick by now. It is more pleasant for you is n't it. I am glad she is there—"

The return of Lawrence's brother Horace, his closest sibling, may have had its bitter-sweet side, for the trip to Europe was a trip that he and Lawrence had dreamed of making together. But Lawrence did have the companionship of his younger brother, John, who had started at Bowdoin that fall. In the above letter to Lawrence, Mother Chamberlain included a page to "Johnny, my good boy Johnny," that sent her love and support to this son, too. Telling him how much she missed him, she implored him to "be careful of your health, mind Lawrence, be a scholar be a man be a christian obliging to your classmates do all the good you can to them..."[28]

Fanny returned to Brunswick and Rev. Adams' home on October 8. No more than a week had passed before he recorded in his diary: "I see I must change toward Fanny; I can't make her different; & can only treat her as kindly as possible;

& g[ues]s I must, or I sh[all] bitterly regret it, by & by." But Rev. Adams continued to reprove his daughter. Lawrence proved unmovable regarding the date of their wedding, and Fanny waited two months in this tense environment. And as Helen's due date approached, Rev. Adams suffered all the anxieties of a prospective father.

These were unhappy weeks for both Fanny and Lawrence. He was also, grimly, seeking absolution from his cousin Annie. At the end of October, Lawrence wrote to her, repeating a plea for her forgiveness. In a letter addressed to "My darling" in German, Annie leaves no doubt of her deep unhappiness. She questioned why Lawrence asked so often that she forgive him for, as she quoted from his letter, making her "sin or sorrow for knowing him." Annie responded: "You have made me love you—if that is sinning—there you have made me sin deeply...." But she protested that he had never taught her to call that a sin. Reminding him that he had Fanny to help him, Annie wrote that she would not have worried about him so much if she had known that Fanny was with him.[29]

At the end of October, Fanny received several directives from Cousin Deborah to find, pack up and ship the remainder of Deborah's belongings. One letter also brought disheartening news. Fanny had loaned Cousin Deborah her Georgia savings, and Deborah, who admitted to "spending it quite fast," warned Fanny that she would need at least a month's advance notice before she could possibly repay her. It is unknown if Cousin Deborah gave any of Fanny's money to Anna Davis, but several days later, Anna arrived in Brunswick from New Jersey with her intended husband, the impecunious Amos Atkinson. Anna and Amos's wedding on November 7, proved to be the last straw for Fanny. Reverend Adams commented on Fanny in his diary in the next week: "She & Mr C. have been very unhappy. I had better take Helen's advice & say nothing to Fanny; it does no good."[30]

After the Atkinsons returned to New Jersey, Fanny wrote a peevish letter to Cousin Deborah. Miffed at Rev. Adams' solicitous behavior towards Anna and her new husband, Fanny criticized her adoptive sister's failure to pay their father his usual fee for the wedding. She also wrote that Anna should have paid for other wedding expenses, such as the cake Rev. Adams provided. She implied that the gift of money that Rev. Adams gave to Anna before she came to Brunswick was likely used to get Amos Atkinson there for the wedding, for he could not afford it otherwise. By chance, because Cousin Deborah was suffering from a headache, she asked none other than the new Mrs. Anna Davis Atkinson to read Fanny's letter to her. Though Cousin Deborah apologized that Anna saw the letter, she wrote of her: "She has always thought that you *felt*, & *expressed* yourself very unkindly toward her & her feelings were very much injured...." And Anna wrote to Rev. Adams about it. In Deborah's revelation of this latest family tempest, which arrived a day or two before Fanny's own December wedding, Deborah also commented: "I should like to see Mr. C— & see you married but it cannot be—.... Time's effacing finger must pass over much before I could enjoy a visit in Brunswick."[31]

When the fall term of Bowdoin came to an end on November 20, Lawrence left Brunswick for Brewer. A letter from twelve students who had attended his Sabbath lectures reflects the college's offer to him to return as an instructor of rhetoric and oratory. But it also gives evidence that he had not yet decided to return for the spring term. Although the position of instructor was a desirable step up from tutor, it carried neither the salary nor the prestige of a professorship. And the word "provisional" that the college attached to the instructorship certainly emphasized the temporary nature of the appointment. In their letter, his students expressed regret that he was leaving. They thanked him for faithfully pointing out to them the "Path of Life," and also for his kind and brotherly interest in their temporal and eternal welfare. Had Lawrence discovered that the satisfactions and influence of a teacher could vival those of a teacher? Nonetheless, the limited income and instability of his position at Bowdoin left much to be desired.[32]

On November 25, 1855, Helen Adams gave birth to a son. The Reverend Adams, at 54 years of age, discovered all the anxieties and joys of having a new baby in the house. Delighted, though in awe of his new namesake, little Georgie, he worried over Helen, who suffered with milk fever in the days after delivery.[33]

Lawrence returned to Brunswick on December 2, but it is doubtful that he found many opportunities to spend time with Fanny. Much of her time was spent surrounded by the circle of friends who labored to finish her wedding trousseau. On the cold winter night of Dec. 7, Rev. Adams led Fanny and Lawrence through the marriage ceremony, one of the first to be performed in the First Parish's newly built meetinghouse. Reverend Adams' only comment on their wedding day seemingly fixed the responsibility for the couple's future failure or success squarely on Fanny's shoulders. He pessimistically recorded in his diary: *"I feel sadly about poor Fanny* fearing greatly she will not make herself happy."[34]

Whatever their fears or worries, Fanny and Lawrence found happiness. Spending their first night as husband and wife under Rev. Adams' roof before their journey to Brewer, the pain and perplexities of three lonely years began to fall away. They discovered that their love had survived many burdens and ordeals, and that, by resolving and overcoming their differences, they could build a happier life together.[35]

CHAPTER

8

"Light & Life"

Fanny and Lawrence spent their first night as man and wife in the little room that had been Fanny's chamber at Rev. Adams' home. Lawrence later reminisced about that night, "...my fairy honeysuckle girl came to the arms that once lifted her up among the leaves & roses, so sadly so tremblingly & yet so calmly came & laid her head in my bosom on that wedding night—that sweetest & purest & ever to be honored night."[1]

The day after their wedding, Fanny and Lawrence traveled to Brewer, and in the next weeks, Rev. Adams received several bright letters from his new son-in-law regarding their stay at his family's home. Lawrence also shared his feelings about his marriage to Fanny with an old Bowdoin friend, Samuel Gardner. In a charming letter that offered his best wishes, Gardner responded to Lawrence: "Allow me, especially to congratulate you. You are a married man. No one more heartily than myself, yields to you your full estimate of the dignity and solemnity of the condition." Gardner also offered fond reminiscences, for Gardner was Lawrence's confidante during the ups and downs of his courtship. Once quite smitten with Fanny himself, Gardner had gracefully yielded once convinced that Lawrence had secured Fanny's affections. Remembering their mutual admiration of Fanny, Gardner recalled in his letter:

> *You remember our worship of her sunset picture, and the pains we took with the window hangings to secure a mellow light. That sunset could hardly be more golden to your own heart, than it was to mine in those days. And the songs she used to sing, those so peculiarly hers,—they are still a memory by themselves, unapproachable.*

Remembering the melancholy days of the three year separation, Gardner wrote:

> *But now the consummation of all those hopes is realized. Society has suffered numerical loss for a time, by the interfusion of two heretofore distinct existences, but we may confidently hope that in actual possession it has made a great gain, by the mutual influence for good, of each factor composing the result of the union, and moreover, a train is laid, the natural tendency of which is to make good the numerical deficit.*[2]

As Gardner predicted, the newlyweds did make good on the "deficit" that they had caused in society, when their two separate lives had merged to one. With Lawrence's decision to continue at the college, he and Fanny returned to Brunswick at the end of January 1856, boarding in a room that Lawrence referred to as Mrs. Stanwood's closet. By early March, Fanny was unwell, likely suffering from morning sickness, for in evident resolution to their discussions of having children, she was already carrying their first child. Could Lawrence have been anything other than delighted that the baby he had so often talked and teased about was on the way? But he must also have felt keenly the new responsibilities that parenthood would bring.[3]

Lawrence began his duties as a provisional instructor in rhetoric and oratory at the college in early February. He was expected, as he soon discovered, to teach his courses as his predecessors had, leading his students through the examination and criticism of the writings of noted scholars. And such a number of mandatory themes were required, that the instructor would be hard-pressed to offer much constructive criticism. It was a regimen he remembered from his own experience that did little to improve students' skills. Whether it was the realization of the Bowdoin faculty's resistance to change, or his uncertainty regarding the college's intentions to retain him, Lawrence continued to look for a more promising situation. Nor had he forsaken the idea of trying his hand in the ministry, for even as his February classes began, Lawrence was also making inquiries about a pastorship.

The Congregational Church in Belfast, Maine, a coastal community a half day's journey south from his hometown, Brewer, needed a minister. But it was a pulpit, Lawrence discovered, that would be quite a challenge and would offer little of the financial security that he sought. A letter from Rev. Edward Cutter, who was leaving this pastorship because of ill health, was discouraging. The Congregational church in Belfast had an unsettled history, its congregation having separated from the town's Unitarian church a few decades before. They had a succession of pastors, none of whom stayed for very long, for the church did not guarantee an annual salary to its minister, but relied instead on voluntary subscriptions from members. In the past, some members had expressed approval or disapproval of their minister's performance by pledging or withdrawing their annual subscription. Though Rev. Cutter assured Lawrence that he experienced some success at the Belfast church despite the problems, it is likely that his letter discouraged Lawrence from seriously considering that church.[4]

In the last days of May 1856, little Georgie Adams was seriously ill, feverish and breathing rapidly. Much to his parents' relief, the baby recovered, despite the fact that he was dosed, according to his doctor's instructions, with ipecac every three hours for several days during his illness. Fanny visited the Adams' home during Georgie's illness, and soon fell quite ill herself, with what was identified as mouth and throat canker. Fanny recovered at the home of Mrs. Ross, where she and Lawrence boarded during the latter part of the spring term. When Captain Ross, a Brunswick ship's captain, returned home from the sea, the Chamberlains moved to rooms at an inn, the Tontine.

Fanny's correspondence with Cousin Deborah, who was living with Anna Davis and Amos Atkinson in Hoboken, was sparse in 1856. It is apparent from a letter that Deborah wrote in June of that year, that she was unaware of Fanny's pregnancy. Yet Deborah cynically asked, "...how many of those pictures have you painted that Mr. Chamberlain intended you should accomplish once you were married?" By the time Anna Davis Atkinson delivered a frail baby girl in August, Deborah knew of Fanny's impending motherhood. In the coming months, the hard feelings of the previous year forgotten, baby clothes started to arrive from Anna and Cousin Deborah.[5]

Though Lawrence had assurances from Bowdoin that he would be full professor of rhetoric and oratory for the fall term of 1856, the position was not official until the college's boards met in August. The additional income and security of his appointment must have provided considerable relief for this new husband and prospective father. But one among his proud family and friends did not approve of his commitment to Bowdoin. Cousin Annie's letters had abandoned the ardent expressions of her earlier missives, and by summer of that year, she had adopted the tame German salutation of "Mein Lieber Fetter," My Dear Cousin. In early July, Annie wrote that Lawrence should not stay in Brunswick. Suggesting that God might need him elsewhere, she commented, "*You* know whether you are doing all you can—" But Annie's pious challenge came at a time when financial stability and domestic tranquility were, perhaps, uppermost in his mind. After expressing her disapproval of his life in academia, Annie wrote that she was receiving affectionate letters from his former classmate at the Bangor Seminary, Peaselee Chamberlain of Vermont.[6]

In September, a family friend advised Fanny on the perils of childbirth, and expressed concern that Fanny had not yet engaged a nurse. This unidentified advisor wrote: "I am afraid you do not know the *danger* you will be in under these circumstances— A lady must have *constant* attendance, night and day, for a time— because the *least* neglect will endanger your life. Now with Mrs Dunning, you will be safe, so far as nursing can make you so, and comfortable *while you are sick*." At last offering some reassurance, the writer offered, "You know my experience in this matter will lead me to assure you that it is not as formidable an affair as you have always supposed. And I presume *you* are feeling differently about it now. I mean the suffering at *the* time." Fanny likely received little comfort or encouragement from this interesting example of 19th century euphemisms, demonstrating the reluctance, even among women, to discuss labor and childbirth.[7]

Less than a week before Fanny's "confinement," rooms were taken at a Potter St. home, known in town as both the Fales house, for its previous residents, and the Wilde house, for the current inhabitants. Reverend Adams, with Helen and Georgie away visiting the Root family at Reading, Mass., devoted his time to finding and securing these rooms, and assisting in the search for a nurse for Fanny. But two days before she went into labor, feelings were strained, for his diary records: "[I] feel unpleasantly ab[ou]t Fanny; I have reason to think she does not view things right yet." Had her father, again, pressed her to embrace his faith?

On Oct. 16, Rev. Adams heard that Dr. John Lincoln was with Fanny, and soon after, word came that she had given birth to a daughter and was resting comfortably. He visited the new family that evening and pronounced the baby "a beautiful child." Of his new daughter, Lawrence wrote many years later: "In the golden days of the Indian summer of that year, there came to his house an angel of God, who left his living smile,—for the loving earth part of the infinite heaven! There was a daughter of the house."[8] When word reached Brewer of the baby, Mother Chamberlain wrote:

> *For some mysterious reason, as we then supposed, for a few days past we had been thinking of you, wondering if all was well with you, so we were just taking our pens to enquire when Father came home from the City with the announcement Lawrence & Fannie have a daughter! You know I have always sympathized with L. whenever...any thing unusual happened to you—whether present or absent I always seem to feel it.*

Though relieved by their good news, Mother Chamberlain regretted that she had not sent a letter of advice to her daughter-in-law beforehand. She cautioned Fanny: "...you must not think the danger over—you must be extremely careful about taking cold or making much exertion, for two or three weeks, be content to keep to your bed mostly." She also offered, "I most sincerely congratulate you on having such a beautiful healthy and well behaved daughter—you have now, new duties, and responsibilities may your highest hopes, be more than reallized[sic] in her—may she be as obedient & good and prove as great a comfort to you as Lawrence has to me."

Mother Chamberlain was tickled by a letter that Fanny and Lawrence had whimsically written from the baby to her new grandparents. "I received a nice letter from her and now I must say a few things to her—I thank her for giving so particular a description of herself, her birth, &c.—and now if I could take her in my arms,...then I would rock her in the same chair in which my mother rocked her father some songs I would sing to her that so often lulled him in quiet slumbers." Mother Chamberlain instructed the baby to, "Say to father please roll me up in a nice little bundle an' put me in—Uncle *Johns valise then on board the cars direct to* grand-mother—...."[9]

Mother Chamberlain's letter, so expressive of love, concern, and delight at being a grandmother, contained a startling postscript. Lawrence's younger brother John was at Bowdoin preparing for the ministry, and Mother Chamberlain had gotten wind that John's enthusiasm for the pulpit was flagging. She minced no words, writing, "What is the matter with John why does he wish to go to W. *Point* dont let him think of it" This letter, perhaps more than any other, gives an intriguing view of Mother Chamberlain's nature. Strong and supportive in her love for her children, she nonetheless was affectionately described by her eldest son as having the quality of the "chasseur," a French military term for cavalry capable of rapid maneuver.[10]

Fanny and Lawrence spent the month after the baby's arrival at the Wilde house. On Nov. 25, as the college's winter vacation began, they traveled to Brewer to spend the next several months at Lawrence's family home. The Chamberlains were not only anxious to see their new little relative, but provided help and support for the new mother. Nor were Fanny and Lawrence free from worries about their expenses. Fanny expressed her concern to Cousin Deborah, and her answer contained a tactless question, even for Deborah: "*Does not Mr. Chamberlain still have access to his Father's inexhaustible purse*?" Before her departure, the indefatigable Rev. Adams presented Fanny with a Bible as a Christmas present, another indication that he was far from admitting defeat in his efforts to bring his daughter into his flock.[11]

Several days after the Chamberlains' departure, Rev. Adams noted in his diary that little Georgie showed signs of whooping cough, the beginning of a downward spiral for their 13-month old son. But, it is likely that he fell victim to the medical practices of the day as much as the disease. Several weeks passed without further notation of Georgie's illness, but by December 9, "oil & ipecac" were being administered every two hours. When there was no improvement, calomel, a commonly used remedy that contained a horrifying combination of mercury and chlorine, was ordered. In the anxious weeks of Georgie Adams' final illness, injections of morphine and doses of laudanum were administered, as three of Brunswick's most prestigious doctors were consulted. Sadly and surprisingly, their little son rallied, raising his parents' hopes before succumbing on December 27. On December 30, their fifth wedding anniversary, George and Helen Adams buried their firstborn child.[12]

Fanny, Lawrence, and their baby spent the last weeks of 1856 and early 1857 at the Chamberlains' home. Lawrence's family, delighted with their new little relative, soon had complete care of her. Fanny became seriously ill with a severe case of erysipelas, a streptococcus infection of the skin and tissues that is accompanied by a high fever and toxic reaction. Lawrence, to soothe his suffering wife, sat by her bedside and read poetry. The illness became so severe that Fanny's face was blackened by infection. By the time Lawrence had to return to Bowdoin, Fanny was recovering, though very weak. The day before his departure on Jan. 24, his grandfather, Col. Joshua Chamberlain, died, having outlived his wife, Anna Gould, by almost 24 years. Through their boyhood, Lawrence and Horace had regularly visited their grandfather's nearby home. With reluctance, Lawrence returned to his duties in Brunswick, unable to stay for his grandfather's funeral. Then too, he was leaving without his little family.[13]

Lawrence's first letter to Fanny from Brunswick was one of loneliness and reflection. He had spent his first night in their rooms at the Wilde's house, but would not do so again:

> *Our rooms are cold & cheerless. I think I shall live altogether at College It is not very pleasant to go cold & dark & desolate in to a room of the same character, & there is something oppressive in the intense silence. It is worse, of course, when other scenes have made those same rooms dear & sacred to me. I feel not merely a want, but a loss.... I miss some thing which was light & life to me.*

Lawrence also related visions of earlier days, for when invited to sing in church that first sabbath after his return, he sat "where I used to sit when I was first feeling the power & the mystery of *your presence*, to me. It is indeed still a mystery—... & more than ever a *power* that binds me to you dear Fanny forever." Lawrence managed a lighter tone as he reminded her that they must name their daughter. Having gone to see the newborn of a friend, Lawrence commented: "He is not so pretty as our little girl...I can see now what a *fine* look our baby has. *He* is *named!* Our baby will be "*it*" till you name her.... Do name her Fanny. I shall like any name which really suits your taste. I shall wear my lungs out, trying to make the deaf people here understand that she is not as yet named." Lawrence became somber again with the report of the death of a Brunswick toddler. "This led me into the most singular train of feeling.... When it grew too painful, I opened my eyes & recalled my self & recalled too dear Fanny one—*all*—to me—." Several times he assured Fanny that he would not "give way to my sad sense of loss," for "I rejoice that you are where you can be so comfortable. *You certainly could not be so here.* Great as the sacrifice is for me, & much as I must miss you & mourn for you, I will not be so selfish as to wish you here now."[14]

Lawrence had his brother John nearby, and his brother Horace, who had returned to complete his last year of study at Bowdoin. He also spent many evenings

Horace Beriah Chamberlain, c. 1857.

during Fanny's absence that winter at her old home, in George and Helen Adams' company. Pleased to report to Fanny that her adoptive father told him that, "he did 'like to have me around...,'" Lawrence also commented that he could see through their busy, cheerful demeanor to their grief over the death of their young son. Lawrence took an active role in the services at Rev. Adams' First Parish Church, delivering the prayer at sabbath services and leading prayer meetings during the week. But if Lawrence yearned for his own pulpit, the deep economic depression during 1857 meant that new ventures were unwise, now that his position at Bowdoin was secure.[15]

Fanny, too, expressed sad and lonely feelings that winter. In a letter written shortly after Lawrence had left, she admitted feeling discouraged that she did not regain her strength more quickly. She was yet unable to lift the baby, who, thriving and growing, had become quite an armful. She had "been downstairs twice only" and the baby had been afraid of her when her face was blackened by illness. Yet this letter to "Nonny," as Fanny called Lawrence at this time, was mostly bright, and filled with reports of the family and their baby's ability to charm them. Using the nickname that Lawrence devised from the German words for "lovely" and "child," Fanny reported that "little Minnikin heard her grandmother's voice and started up, first listening then laughing at the top of her voice, and calling ah-goo-oo-oo...." This behavior likely earned the baby yet another pet name, "little Gooley." In thoughtful musing that was nothing less than prophetic, Fanny wrote of their baby daughter: "I feel somehow as if she would live to be a great comfort to her dear Papa; her serene, angelic smile is just the thing you need darling." Grieved at his loneliness, Fanny wrote, "I miss your dear voice & step more than I can tell...."

Fanny expressed pleasure at getting to know Lawrence's sister, Sae, and thankfulness for the comfort his family's kindness provided, though she mentioned that no one, including herself, had any money. Father Chamberlain had to work especially hard to keep his two boys at Bowdoin that year. But the well-stocked larder and pantry of a farm kitchen helped the Chamberlains through hard times. Fanny and Lawrence could not have afforded the nursing and assistance that Fanny and the baby would have needed had they returned to Brunswick. Thus, in spite of yet another sad separation, they were grateful for the security that employment and a supportive family provided.[16]

Writing from his rooms at the college one stormy evening, Lawrence wrote: "Better can the untamed winds & driving storm whisper it to your heart to night.... So shall two angels have an errand & a charge to night, the one to bear a blessing to a pillow, & the other to a cradle." In the light of the next morning, Lawrence wrote, "I am almost ashamed to send you such desperate love letters as these. I will try to be more sensible hereafter—but the fact is Fan I *do* love you—I am beginning to find out that I *do*. So you will forgive me may be—you know a woman forgives *almost* any thing for the sake of love—*almost* any thing—*silliness* she will not forgive; so I mean to keep just on the hither verge of that region.—" Promising to send money whenever she needed it, it must have given Lawrence pleasure to suggest that, if his father came up short, he would pay John and Horace's tuition that term. But Lawrence also pondered how his family would ever manage in their small rooms at the Wilde house when Fanny and the baby returned to

Brunswick. Fanny encouraged him not to be disheartened. Anxious that Lawrence would consider his mother's advice and try to move into a house, Fanny expressed her belief that their present arrangement was best and the most economical. She suggested that, between Lawrence's endeavors in Brunswick over the winter and her proposed trip to Boston and its auction houses in the spring, they could add to the sparse furnishings of their little rooms and make them quite comfortable. This letter not only addressed Lawrence again as "Nonny," but Fanny signed as "Nappy," another pet name that defies explanation.[17]

Though frustrated by slow mail and lost letters, Fanny and Lawrence kept up a brisk correspondence in the winter in 1857. Lawrence described how he had fitted up his rooms at the college comfortably, with a "standing desk & a few little things which give quite a scholarly air to the room." With his habit of stopping by Rev. Adams' every day, Lawrence became aware of the plans to alter the house, alterations that would demolish Fanny and Cousin Deborah's old rooms. Assuring Fanny that he would remove her belongings, he expressed his distress:

> *It is sad to have all the old things going away—.... One thing however bears me up—that is they do not mark any happier days than I now have I am happier dear Fanny & growing happy every day—more than any house or outward memorial can witness for me. And yet, dear 'birdie,' I did love you in that house, most desperately.... Come & tell me if you think I love you any. And there are two to love? Why I wander in my brain, at the marvel. Oh how strange! Blessing on you both, my wife & my child.*[18]

Fanny answered the above letter with a love letter of her own:

> *It did delight my heart to find you so comfortable and happy last Friday when your dear letter came. How delightfully pleasant your College room must be; with the new carpet, beautiful desk and so forth! I wish I could come softly in Nonny, some evening while you were all alone in your room, dreaming, remembering, loving, blessing—and throw my arms around your neck before you could imagine your little 'honey-suckle' wife was there.*

While upset that Rev. Adams seemingly had no attachment to the old rooms of her childhood home, Fanny wrote: "This is one of those strange, wild, bewildering, rainy nights when one thinks of early child-days, and I am reminded of my youth's home now while I hear the rain pattering against the window-pane. My own dear old room 'at home'!.... where I have thought of you by night and by day, where I dreamed of you long before either of us had heard even the far-off echo of the other's name!"[19]

It is hard to imagine what could break the romantic spell that held the two lovers, but it would, indeed, be broken. Lawrence stayed at Rev. Adams' house while he and Helen were away, for Fanny had asked him to pack up some of the things in her old room before the renovations began. The impassioned letter he wrote on Feb. 8, 1857, was an unforeseen echo of the distraught, doubt-ridden letters of their courtship, and is key to the troubled thoughts that guided Lawrence's actions for the next several days: "...my heart misses you my own, my life, my bride, my *child-mother*—but I think of your sweet love—your early first love—for it was your first love, wasnt it, darling?" With expressions of terrible loneliness and longing, Lawrence continued with, "Come my sweet birdling, my blessed one my loved my cherished my tried & proved & faithful one.... Do you ever miss *me* so & love *me* so, Fanny? Tell me now when you have finished this letter, if you love me...." Among the things Fanny had asked Lawrence to remove from her old room was a portfolio filled with old letters. It seems likely that Lawrence had read some of Fanny's old correspondence with Paul Akers when he wrote the above letter. By the next day, he had read all of them, and he sent them to her in Brewer. He enclosed a letter to Fanny which drew a response from her that was eloquent in its distress:[20]

> *Lawrence! Lawrence! God help me my own Lawrence. Your letter has killed me. I would die for you if I could. If I did not know that you had misconstrued those letters of mine, and that there really was no reason for your feelings as expressed in your letter.... God only knows what would become of me. Lawrence I have been reading the letters I wrote Akers, which you send me, I see where you misunderstand them, and if you were here, you might "ask me any questions" you wished concerning them, and I would look into your eyes and answer, calling God to witness, answer everything in such a way as would calm your troubled heart and relieve every painful feeling. Lawrence God knows that I love you in such a way as it would satisfy even your heart to know.... There is nothing in those letters of mine which I have not told you of at various times Lawrence, and I thought you understood the thing perfectly. The letters I have meant to show you, but when I thought of it, was deterred by the fear of your looking at them in the distorted light in which you now see them.... God forgive me if I was wrong in this, and you will forgive this Lawrence, if you can. God knows this was the only crime. It was not that I would have kept any thing from you, only those fearful, morbid states of feeling into which you so often fall, are beyond endurance for me, they kill my very soul, and you will not blame me if I avoid what I see instinctively would induce them.... Lawrence I love you more than I ever could or ever can love any being, and when I think how I love you, this terrible blow which your letter gave me, sinks into insignificance. I knew the letters were in my portfolio, and I expected you would read them, but I hoped you would not misunderstand them;.... I will try to compose myself long enough to explain this thing to you. If you knew the person to whom I wrote those letters, you would see how peculiar the vein must be in which you would talk or write to him. I will show you the letters from him, which I answered in these, when I can find them. You know my wild enthusiasm for art, Lawrence, or you know what it might have been in those days when I was giving my mind especially to such things. Well, I was young & perhaps foolish when I first saw Akers in Portland, and I thought he felt a great sympathy with my love of art,...he used to tell me that he knew me and sympathized with me as no one else ever had, and I really began to think that there was a strange affinity between us, I felt a strong friendship for him, never thinking of loving him,*

only as one girl might love another.... Of course it was natural for me to believe him very noble, good & pure. If you had known him then..... After I had been dreaming everything that was noble and exalted about him, I began to find that it was after all, only what my enthusiasm had made him, not what he was; and that I had not found the friend I had needed all my life long....[21]

But perhaps it was Fanny's final words to Lawrence that would make this the last time that his jealousy came between them:

Dont grieve, dont grieve my precious, precious only loved-one. If you knew the wealth of my soul's love for you, you would not ask for more. Ah dear Lawrence your Fannie never doubts for one moment that you love her as you have loved no other, and yet dear she hears from time to time in one way or another, things that might trouble her as this thing has troubled you. When we see each-other again we will talk freely of every thing in the past, so that there can never again be any misunderstanding of any of these things.[22]

Fanny's reference to "things that *might* trouble her as this thing has troubled you" suggests that Fanny had heard something of Lawrence's relationship with Cousin Annie. Perhaps Sae, who got to know Fanny and spent a great deal of time with her during those winter weeks, spilled the beans. Or could it have been Annie herself? As Lawrence was leaving for Brunswick, Annie, back in Bangor, wrote to him of her distress that none in her family would accompany her so that she could call on Fanny in Brewer. But as soon as Lawrence left Brewer, she and her sister Martha went for a visit. Annie, who explained that she had fancied that Fanny was "not like other women," declared to Lawrence after their initial meetings that she was determined to get to know Fanny and love her as he did. Yet a note Annie wrote to her in the spring of 1857, holds little promise of warm feelings for Lawrence's wife: "My dear Cousin Fanny; These four words stare at me, from the corner where I have written them—with a very strange and unfamiliar air—as if I had been guilty of some misdemeanor or impertinence in doing so—yet what else could I have put in their place? Tell me—'Tis so long since I promised to send you some *names*.... I presume none of them would have pleased you enough to be chosen—you have looked too long—and expect something too beautiful to be pleased with these...."[23]

By the last of February, Fanny and Lawrence's correspondence was again affectionate, though Lawrence reported having a bad cold, and was feeling fretful and nervous, the results of sleeplessness and the effect of overwork. In his letter of Feb. 25, Lawrence wrote sheepishly, "I did not look at any thing else in your portfolio but those open letters. I do not ever look at your writings or letters addressed to you—unless you are present & permit me...." He offered that, "nothing of that kind will ever trouble me again." Yet he added, "The trouble is you were always inclined to take every thing for granted & so did not think it worth while to tell me what I *ought* perhaps to assume—that your love for me was—what it is. This accident has brought you to do what you might never have done. Its all over now

& better than before—though it was painful, the recovery is sweet & the health is better for it." Lawrence was as good as his word, for no other evidence of jealousy is found in their long life together. The "demon" was laid to rest, once and for all. But there were also the changes that marriage and parenthood brought to their relationship. Though Fanny's letters were affectionate and caring, much of her thoughts were of maternal and housekeeping concerns, perhaps an unforeseen development for this romantic new husband and father.[24]

A letter from Fanny the first of March offered Lawrence this advice. "*Cheer up* precious! there is brightness coming for us I know!.... I wont pretend to say that I dont miss you sadly dearest Lawrence, and that it does not rejoice my heart to think that I may so soon see you."

As Fanny regained her health and plans were made to return to Brunswick, her letters were filled with ideas about arrangements for boarding or housekeeping and how to furnish their rooms at the Wilde's. Several days before Fanny's return to Brunswick, Lawrence wrote: "...I was really made happy to find that you are really pretty well. So you have been to Bangor—have you—to look at *furniture* Gracious Fan what shall we do when we *get* all our furniture! How shall we employ our time? What theme can we have for hasty & frequent letters? I am actually afraid we shall be obliged to resort to some intellectual topics." Though declaring he was sick of chasing after furniture, he reported that he found a pier table and mirror that he liked very well, and he was ready to order a dining room chair, as a specimen of the style he felt would suit them, though he suspected Fanny preferred to look in Boston. Lawrence was still pressing Fanny to name their daughter, and at one point remarked that he would be satisfied with "any human name." Fanny had suggested naming her Leonie, Christine, Whilhelmina, Isidore, or Imogene. Lawrence, despairing that she would ever be able to choose, wrote, "...I shall name her *Grace Wyllys Chamberlain.*" And Grace it was, though her parents settled on Mother Chamberlain's maiden name, Dupee, for her middle name.[25]

Back in Brunswick on May 5, Fanny was at home no more than a week before she left for her family home in Boston. After the long confinement of pregnancy, birth and nursing, travel was encouraged, often ordered by the doctor, as a means of recuperation. Fanny had also experienced an additional seven months of inactivity due to her illness after Grace's birth. Such holidays were also a convenient, though unmentionable, way to ensure some separation between a woman's pregnancies. If that was a consideration in their plans, it had little effect. In the week after her return, and before her departure for Boston, Fanny and Lawrence's second child was conceived.[26]

Fanny composed a shopping list for Boston. In the furniture showrooms and auction houses, she searched for a lounge, two arm chairs, six dining chairs, two rocking chairs, a secretary, a carpet, curtains, an "open fire" and an extension table. John Chamberlain accompanied her to Boston, and she spent her first days there showing him around the city. She also shopped for silks for Sae, but on John's departure, Fanny wrote that she searched for furnishings "quite to the extent of my strength." In her first letter to "Nonny" from Boston, Fanny asked anxiously for "our little darling Daisy." After all the deliberation that finally resulted in their daughter being named Grace, laughably, the nickname Daisy or Daise lasted throughout her childhood. During her absence, the baby was cared for by several Brunswick women, for shortly after Fanny's departure, Daisy was unwell. Fanny, suspecting the problem, earnestly instructed, "*I dont want the baby to eat clear milk*, tis too strong for her stomack [sic]." The baby was then cared for by a Mrs. Berry, known for her experience with infants, and who might also have been a wet nurse for Daisy. [27]

Fanny asked Lawrence to send threads from their carpets and furniture to assist in choosing colors, and she asked him, if not scarlet, whether he liked green. Fanny's frequent questions to Lawrence on colors and styles, were, perhaps, unusual. While it was a "man's world" in the 1800s, the home was the woman's domain. But she was anxious that their home be pleasing to Lawrence. Fanny reported having little luck at the auctions, but was doing her best to buy a 200 year old chair, an impractical choice, but the first of Fanny's antique "finds." Suggesting that Lawrence send more money, to be replaced with money still due her from Milledgeville, Fanny asked if she might spend another week. Determined to find more furniture, she also wanted more time with her family in Roxbury. Her father, having again fallen on hard times, was considering abandoning the family home and going to board with Fanny's sister Catherine and her family. Fanny wished that they had a place for her father to come to, but she doubted that he could be happy away from his old business pursuits in Boston. She explained her family's feelings of embarrassment at their predicament and she shared her presentiment that she might be visiting her birth family's home for the last time.[28]

With an equal measure of loneliness and alarm at the money Fanny was spending, Lawrence answered Fanny on May 20, and explained why Fanny should come home. Her letter had fallen heavily on him, and he recounted being haunted by sad dreams, in which she did not care to be near him and had gone away to amuse herself. He wrote:

> *Dearest, how can I let you stay away from me another long, long dreary week? Will it ever be over, & will you care for me & love me & not leave me again? You will not think this wild & insane, will you, darling? Nor is it mere 'lover's talk—you know it is not that. I have no need of doing any thing for effect—if it were possible for me. Perhaps I am too much of a lover for a husband, as the world goes; but do forgive me dearest, & lay it to my love & sorrow for you.*

Though Lawrence insisted that he would not say she must come home & interrupt her visit, he suggested that she had accomplished all she could in Boston. Indicating that they were considering yet another move, he reminded her that there were just six short weeks left for them to enjoy being settled in their newly furnished rooms. As for sending her more money, he replied:

> *Darling, I dont know how I can possibly get any more money here—every thing is flat & every body in consternation Even the College is pretty hard up for funds.... Forgive me dearest, but I must remind you of our slender & precarious hold upon earthly things. I do not mean to be sick,*

dear; but at the best I can hardly keep up with our expenses.... I am ashamed to be obliged to say this, & to treat you so, You ought not to have married a poor boy like nonny. I do not know what makes me so sorrowful, Darling, but I cant help it. Little Daisy is not very well, but you need not be troubled. O my darling do remember your poor Nonny & love him & come to him soon.

By May 27, Fanny had returned. While the few pieces of furniture that she purchased were shipped from Boston, she carried home a rubber ring, a squeaking cat, and a toy rabbit for little Daisy. Their deliberation over the positioning of their furnishings at the Wilde house was perhaps curtailed by the fact that they would spend only the days of summer in that situation before moving to other quarters.[29]

In July, Lawrence attended Harvard's commencement and pronounced that it did not come up to Bowdoin's. He had the pleasure of seeing Horace graduate with honors at Bowdoin's commencement in August. It seemed uncertain whether John Chamberlain would return to college for the fall term of that year. In mid-August, he wrote to Lawrence: "Father thinks some of taking me back to Canada A notion which I do not object to in the least Even if it were proposed for me to stay out of college a year now I should not be at all dissatisfied. My private opinion is that I am too young and that were I in the class of 60 it would be much better for me" This was not the first time John exhibited restlessness regarding his studies at Bowdoin. Nonetheless, he arrived in the fall to continue his studies with his class of 1859, though he continued to look for a teaching position. Mother Chamberlain was yet determined to have a minister in the family. She had offered John advice when he first went to Bowdoin, to be like their former, late minister, Nathan Dole or like Brainerd Taylor. It would become a sad irony that Mother Chamberlain chose James Brainerd Taylor's life for John to emulate, for that promising young theologian achieved fame as a martyr to duty, who died young of consumption, the disease that would threaten John's life in the years to come.[30]

When Lawrence, Fanny, and the baby were at last together as a family in the summer of 1857 in Brunswick, Rev. Adams became quite attached to little Daisy, whose cheerful temperament charmed all who spent time with her. He and Helen enjoyed assembling and presenting a suit of "short clothes," that would be his "granddaughter's" first, after wearing the long dresses of infancy. Daisy, healthy during her first eleven months of life, was quite ill in the first weeks of September as Lawrence again took up his duties at the college. Helen Adams tried to assist Fanny in caring for Daisy, although she herself was pregnant with her second child. Helen's due date of Sept. 1 had come and gone, and the well-meaning Rev. Adams resorted to taking his wife for daily rides to encourage the onset of labor, with no result. Not until Nov. 2, a full two months beyond her supposed due date, did Helen deliver a baby daughter, Sarah Root Adams.[31]

In the first week of November, Fanny, Lawrence, and Daisy moved from the Wilde House to the Jewell's home on Lincoln St. in Brunswick, where John would board with them. On November 18, Rev. Adams reported in his diary that Fanny was not well. On the next day, Thanksgiving of 1857, Fanny delivered a son, three months premature, who lived but a few hours and was said by Rev. Adams to have been the "image of Fanny." Helen Adams wrote in her diary that she held the little boy and kept him warm during the hours that he lived. She and Rev. Adams had planned for Fanny, Lawrence, and Daisy to spend that day with them, but John Chamberlain was their only guest at a subdued Thanksgiving dinner.[32]

When news of their loss came to Brewer, Mother Chamberlain came to Brunswick. No service was held for the baby, and Lawrence and Fanny did not give him a name. On the morning of November 26, Rev. Adams accompanied Lawrence, as he had many other mourners over the years, to the cemetery in the pines near the college. Rev. Adams knew well such a personal loss. He had just arranged for the placement of a stone on his own Georgie's resting place, and his diary was again filled with sad reminiscences of his lost boy. Though Fanny fared well during the premature delivery and recovered her physical health quickly, on December 9, when the Chamberlains left Brunswick to travel to Brewer, Rev. and Helen Adams recorded that Fanny was miserable, and hardly able to start on this journey.[33]

The loss of an infant or child in that time occurred with tragic frequency, and there were few families who did not experience the pain of such a loss. Harriet Beecher Stowe put words to such grief in *Uncle Tom's Cabin,* when her character, Mrs. Bird, looks through the clothes of her own lost child to give to the fugitive Eliza's infant son. "And oh, mother that reads this, has there never been in your house a drawer, or a closet, the opening of which has been to you like the opening again of a little grave? Ah! happy mother that you are, if it has not been so."[34]

CHAPTER

9

"As Tho' in a Bad Dream"

After two years of marriage, a time that held much happiness, yet was not without sorrow, and sad loss, Lawrence and Fanny had settled into their roles of husband and wife, father and mother. Life was far different than either of them had imagined in early days, when they had dreamed of two little rooms, hours of conversation, reading to one another by their fireside, and days and nights of romance. And what of Fanny's music and painting? Though his children were one of the great delights of his life, Lawrence seemed rather baffled, though proud, of Fanny's necessary and willing transformation from artist and musician to homemaker and mother. Now committed to a career and family life in Brunswick, Fanny and Lawrence were successfully meeting the challenges of new responsibilities. But unforeseen trials awaited them.

The resumption of classes at Bowdoin brought Fanny, Lawrence and Daisy back to Brunswick in mid-January 1858 after a month's respite with the Brewer Chamberlains. It was a bleak homecoming for the family, for Fanny returned with a worrisome cold and Daisy was feverish as they came back to Lincoln Street. Perhaps those chambers evoked sad memories of a lost son for the family, for despite the fact that they had just moved into these rooms in late fall, by early spring, Fanny and Lawrence endured another of the domestic uprootings that marked their early marriage. And this third year of Fanny and Lawrence's marriage would also see Fanny's third pregnancy.[1]

Resuming his duties at the college, Lawrence again became active in the First Parish Church. In the last weeks of that winter, Lawrence often led evening prayer meetings during the week and he became a regular participant, offering the prayer

Pejepscot Historical Society

Frances Caroline Adams, c. 1858.

Bangor Public Library

Joshua L. Chamberlain, c. 1858.

or giving the reading during sabbath services. There was great religious interest in Brunswick at this time, and the many new converts who joined the church earned 1858 the label of a year of "revival."[2]

By the last of April, however, Lawrence was busy moving his family into the Berry house, a newly built home in the center of town that provided the Chamberlains with more room. New carpets were purchased and they supplemented their furnishings with pieces from the Brewer family home. Before sending Lawrence a secretary that he had used in his childhood home, Sae discreetly removed his letters, making separate bundles of those from Annie Chamberlain and those from Fanny. Having rented the whole house, Lawrence had room for more of his books, and Fanny, despite being six months pregnant, held a party for Bowdoin's junior class that summer. They both enjoyed the society of his students at Bowdoin, and Lawrence, when time allowed, had "many a good outing" with them "among the trout-brooks, or along the shores of the Bay..." His positive attitude toward the students at Bowdoin, with his favorable perception of their level of maturity and their potential for responsible behavior, was one of several opinions that placed him at odds with a number of the faculty members at Bowdoin.[3]

Lawrence, by this time, had experienced being both student and professor at Bowdoin. With the insights that each standing provided, he developed his own ideas of an effective role for a college professor, ones that did not always concur with that of the veteran professors. In his *History of Bowdoin College*, Louis Hatch described the conflicting attitudes at Bowdoin in the mid-1800s: "We have had two distinct theories of college life;...the great professors, Packard, Smyth, Newman, Cleaveland and Upham,...treated students as boys under parental discipline...in the grotesque aspect of policemen, patrolling the campus by night;

and in the more dubious role of detectives scenting out deviltry in Sodom and Gomorrah, as the ends of Winthrop Hall used to be called;...these grave professors were lending to mischief just that dash of danger which served to keep the love of it alive." The second approach to college discipline that Hatch described was the one practiced by then president of Bowdoin, Leonard Woods, of whom Hatch said: "The one ambition of his life was to touch what was best in the hearts of the young men entrusted to his care." While Woods "perfunctorily deplored... robbed henroosts, translated livestock, greased blackboards and tormented tutors," he did not deem them "specimens of total depravity, or cases of unpardonable sin." And when there were infractions of the rules, President Woods preferred to discover the culprits and have a heart to heart with them in his office, as opposed to chasing students around the campus. Years before, he had had Lawrence, or "Jack" as he was called then, on the carpet before him, in a futile effort to persuade him to provide the names of his rowdy classmates. But now, as professor, it seems that Lawrence's opinion of how students should be treated came much nearer to President Woods' with his exercises in the powers of persuasion, than that of many of the faculty, who considered their administrator far too lenient. Lawrence, like Woods, had a basic respect for his students. He recognized their need for guidance and encouragement, yet allowed for the possibility of enjoying their company.[4]

Lawrence also had his own ideas on teaching rhetoric and oratory. He recalled that during his own junior year, his professor in that subject, Henry Boody, had made a notation on one of his essays. He wrote that if Lawrence "could hold his imaginative powers well in hand, he will be heard from in due time." Puzzling over this mild criticism, yet determined to benefit from it, Lawrence found the solution, not by approaching Boody, but by pursuing his own course of study. The way his class in rhetoric and oratory was structured, as Prof. Boody also observed, there was no opportunity or time for interaction with individual students for more valuable criticism. Lawrence discovered Whateley's text on rhetoric, from which he realized his own tendency to "overload a subject with illustration." Practicing and perfecting the skills Whately's book offered on writing argumentative composition, at the end of his junior year, Lawrence took the college prizes in both composition and oratory. But he realized that, unfortunately, much of what he had learned in rhetoric and oratory had been acquired by his own exertions, rather than from the exercises and assignments in his class. With this experience still fresh in his mind, Lawrence approached the Bowdoin faculty with his ideas on changing the methods by which his students were instructed in rhetoric and oratory. He found them very resistant to change. They insisted that he hold to the practices and requirements of his predecessors, allowing Lawrence only those innovations he could introduce in addition to the usual curriculum. This arrangement meant that Lawrence took on even more than the taxing amount of work done by his predecessors. But he did it, for he was convinced that his methods would be effective and his students would benefit greatly from the valuable skills they would gain. And though Lawrence had managed to get permission to introduce Whateley's text to his students, he was left in some doubt as to whether the faculty would continue to grant him that concession.[5]

It was not only in matters of scholarship and discipline that Lawrence found himself at odds with his colleagues. When he first joined the faculty, he had much to learn about the political struggles and agendas at Bowdoin. The college was governed by two ruling bodies, the overseers and trustees. Many Bowdoin overseers not only wanted the college to remain a bastion of orthodox Congregationalism, but considered it a financial necessity. Maine Congregationalists were reluctant to support the institution if it did not clearly associate itself with their denomination. The overseers, therefore, gave as much consideration to a professorial candidate's theology, as to his educational credentials. In August 1856, the overseers failed to reelect their professor of modern languages for the sole reason that he was a Unitarian. The trustees, more liberal in their inclinations and wishing to register their disapproval, refused to approve any of the conservative candidates that the overseers recommended. Professor Upham, known for his diplomatic endeavors, suggested that if young Chamberlain could be persuaded to accept the chair of the department of modern languages, their problems would be over. In the summer of 1858, the first of many proposals was made to Lawrence that he relinquish the department of rhetoric and oratory for the professorship in modern languages. But this was not the only political struggle surrounding the latter position, for there were members of the faculty who questioned whether Bowdoin should teach modern languages at all, feeling that it drew the students' attention away from Latin. Such promotion of Latin in the curriculum by a number of the faculty, creates speculation as to how Lawrence's fellow professors felt about a popular optional course that Lawrence developed and taught in Anglo-Saxon and early English language and literature. Being a pawn in these matters could hardly have made the position in modern languages attractive to Lawrence, yet there was still another reason why he did not want it.[6]

In a letter to fellow educator and Bowdoin alumnus, Nehemiah Cleaveland, who was interested in his approach to rhetoric, Lawrence explained that the teaching of rhetoric should be more than methods and rules; it should be a nurturing of thought and the means for a man to know himself. Lawrence considered self-expression to be the very thing by which society measured ability. Convinced of the importance of this instruction, and the effectiveness of the new methods he was using, Lawrence told Cleaveland that, though he was beset to take the department of modern languages, "...so long as I feel the responsibility upon me of carrying out this system I have entered upon, I shall allow myself neither to be seduced nor driven from my place." Horace apparently shared his brother's sentiments, for on hearing of Bowdoin's offer, he encouraged Lawrence to continue with rhetoric and oratory. "I am aware of all these pleasant features in the Mod. Lang. Dpt. but still there's nothing so dignified, nothing so ennobling to a man after all, as straining through his mind the noblest thoughts & the finest dictions of his own native Language, & pointing them out to others." Among the "pleasant features" that Horace referred to was Bowdoin's practice of providing a salary to its professors of modern language while they went to Europe for a year or more to prepare for the position. Though Horace was well aware that Lawrence longed to travel, and even admitted that he would like to make that trip with him, he still suggested, "...I should stay in Rhet. & Orat. if I could without too much fuss-"[7]

Horace, now graduated from Bowdoin, missed the fellowship he had enjoyed with Lawrence while they were both in Brunswick. "You dont know how much I miss running in to see you once in a while to have a social talk—to congratulate, condole &c..." Horace, who planned to study law, was earnestly considering what to do with his own life and, in the spring and summer of 1858, he wrote a number of times to Lawrence for advice about going to Oregon. Hod, as he was called by his family, did not go west, but instead entered a Bangor law office. He married Mary Wheeler, a young lady who Lawrence had known well in earlier days.[8]

Hod also felt that younger brother John should attend the Bangor Seminary. He commented to Lawrence that John had "a good head—& perhaps the longest in the family," an interesting observation considering the academic prowess of both Lawrence and Horace. But John was restless, and he considered going south or to Europe to teach for a year before he returned to Bowdoin that fall of 1858. Sister Sae remained at home, attending local schools, although in this year she expressed dissatisfaction with the education she was getting. Sae's life, so typical of the young women of her time, had many obligations beyond her studies. In addition to her duties at the family home in Brewer, she was even sewing shirts for Lawrence and "drawers" for little Daisy. Tom, the youngest of the Chamberlain brood, was 17 years old in 1858, but there is no indication that he was preparing to follow his brothers to Bowdoin. In fact, he eventually took a job as clerk in a Bangor store. While his health was not the best, there are also hints that Tom, the baby, and the "pet" of the family, was a headstrong young man.[9]

Bowdoin College

John Calhoun Chamberlain, c. 1859.

On October 10, 1858, with Lawrence settled into another term at Bowdoin, Fanny delivered their third child, another son. He was a small baby, whose failure to gain weight satisfactorily caused considerable concern in the family. Yet he lived on tenaciously. The baby's birth prevented the customary trip to Brewer at the close of the fall term, and Lawrence, Fanny, the two babies and their nurse spent Thanksgiving at Rev. Adams'. A letter from Fanny's birth father in Boston that month asked anxiously after his daughter and the "newcomer." Expressing his wish to see his grandchildren, Ashur Adams, who described himself as a "minute man," liable to be called away at any minute, explained that his ill health made such a trip impossible. The first week of January, Mother Chamberlain traveled to Brunswick and offered to care for the children. Lawrence and Fanny took this opportunity to travel to see Ashur Adams. Fanny's family had had to give up their home in Roxbury, and shortly after moving into Boston, Fanny's sister Mary died. Fanny's brother, George Wyllys, had gone to work in New York, and would not live out the year. As Fanny and Lawrence were leaving, Rev. Adams sent ten dollars along with Fanny to give to her father.[10]

Lawrence remained in Boston only a few days before returning to Brunswick for the beginning of classes at the college on Jan. 20, 1859. Having left Fanny in Boston, Daisy was delighted to see him, but disappointed that Fanny had not come. Lawrence reported that he had presented the doll that they had chosen for Daisy in Boston as a special gift from Fanny, "& she sticks to it now that Mamma sent 'the baby' to her." Of their little son, Lawrence wrote, "The boy seems to be improving—... certainly no diminution of eyes, either in size or brightness." Fanny replied: "I was delighted to learn that our little boy is doing so well, and that you are all getting along so comfortable. I am enjoying my visit to my dear father & the rest very much; more especially as my father thinks it will be some time before he can come to see us in Brunswick. Dear, precious little Daisy! how I want to see her & ba*bee* too!" Asking for Mother Chamberlain, Fanny declared that she would not describe what she had been doing, for she would be home so soon. "I will merely ask you a few *business* questions now." Fanny's queries on the carpets, floorcloths, mirrors and bureaus that she hoped to find for the Wilde house, are the first indication that the Chamberlains would move again, but this time to their own home. Having boarded there when first married, the Wilde house had always interested them, for Henry Wadsworth Longfellow, as a young professor at Bowdoin many years before, had also lived in that house.[11]

News of Fanny's shopping expeditions, or perhaps reports of her other activities in Boston apparently convinced Lawrence it was time for her to come home. For Fanny had written that she had gone to hear both Transcendentalist Ralph Waldo Emerson and the well-known Unitarian minister, Starr King, speak in Boston. She also planned to attend the funeral of William H. Prescott, a revered Unitarian writer and historian. There is no indication that Lawrence tried to dissuade Fanny regarding her liberal ideas on theology. Yet such overt demonstrations of her proclivities were perhaps unnerving for him, given his position in a college so alert to their faculty's orthodoxy. Yet, Lawrence was re-examining some of his own feelings about tenets and practices of the Congregational Church. In his memoirs, years later, he recalled his distress at two-year-old Daisy's disappointment at being excluded when communion was given to the members of the First Parish Church. Watching communion being distributed, and being passed by, Daisy "nestled up to her mother and asked what this all meant. She was told that they were remembering God. 'Why then do they leave me out? Don't they know that I came from God a great deal littler while ago and I can remember him a great deal better than any of these big people can. They forget me, but he does not.'" Daisy was so grieved that they thought it best to take her home, "where we with her, remembered God."[12]

Lawrence's loneliness cannot be discounted. As he advised Fanny to get shoes for Daisy, books for herself and Daisy, and then come home, he also wrote: "...the house seems desolate with out you—my heart not otherwise...." Hard upon this letter, Lawrence sent another: "I see in spite of 'wanting to see us terribly', you are minded to stay as long as 'it will do for you' to, & I cant blame you much, poor girl; and yet we too want to see you terribly & there fore beg of you to come home as soon as you can." While he declared, "really painful as it is to me to limit in any way your few, brief seasons of relaxation & enjoyment...", he was at no loss for reasons why Fanny must come home. Mother Chamberlain was getting anxious about the family in Brewer, though she meant to carry out her promise to stay as long as Fanny wished to be away. And Lawrence also offered, "Little Daisy asks for you & I tell her Mama is gone. Then she says 'Want to see another Mamma, Papa.' What do you suppose the little constant-hearted thing means? Why to go & see your *picture*, which she takes & kisses & holds up for me to kiss...." Of Fanny's wish to find things for their new home, Lawrence stated: "...I should think you had stayed long enough for one place, even though it is *such* a place," and he added, "I am afraid my dear Fanny needs a little caution. She sees a good many things to buy in Boston & we could need them all if we would think so, & then remember we concluded that your other purchases in Boston were not *on the whole* very advantageous."[13]

After Fanny's return, Mother Chamberlain and Daisy traveled to Brewer. The family reported Daisy's delight in the sleigh ride home from the railway station with Father Chamberlain, and her shouts of "horsey" and "grandpa." Lawrence and Fanny had not officially named their infant son, but Sae wrote that Mother Chamberlain missed "little Willie," and hoped, if he did not gain at least a half pound a week they would send him to Brewer. Father Chamberlain encouraged this plan for the baby to come to Brewer, adding a startling endorsement for "Irish milk." He wrote, "We have got a high order of the perfect celt in our new house of the name of Rourke in full milk for young one..." He went on to assure Fanny and Lawrence that Rourke "is a name among the old soldiers of the revolution & tho Irish, are good blood & of pure milk & I believe in its being used." Over the years Father Chamberlain had a number of Irish families living on the farm, as tenants and workers in his fields and in his timber businesses. Though little Willie remained at home in Brunswick, Daisy stayed on in Brewer until summer. In May, Sae reported that Daisy was very happy, and apparently had charmed the saturnine Father Chamberlain as she had the whole family. She related that when Daisy called to "Gra'pa" it startled Sae to hear him answer, "What—, *dear*." Sae remarked, "You know he did not use to speak so to us."[14]

At the end of April 1859, having purchased the Wilde house by putting down half of the asking price, Fanny and Lawrence moved into their new home. A small New England cape, built in the 1820s by one of Brunswick's sea captains, Captain Ross, the Potter St. house had changed hands a number of times before the Chamberlains purchased it. While Lawrence was delighted with the "ample ground for as much garden as one man could well manage," a recital of the good and bad points of the house comes from Horace, who commented, "the location is bad, but then the *house* is plenty good enough for the present & the garden beautiful, & the distance handy to & from Coll[ege].... There is a good deal of room on the ground floor & fifty dollars laid out in door knobs &c would make a vast improvement." Sae wrote asking how Fannie liked her new house, but sympathized, "It is too bad she has no front *stairs*." There were no doorsteps or entry hall in the home to serve as a preliminary for the formal reception of callers.[15]

In those first months of proud ownership, Lawrence devoted a good deal of time to his new garden. Reverend Adams, an avid gardener himself, brought gooseberry and honeysuckle roots and tomato plants for the Wilde house garden. Lawrence went out regularly "at five o'clock in the morning, digging and scratching away at the genial and much-loved earth." One observer of the young professor's labors was Captain Joseph Badger, a Brunswick ship owner and president of the Pejepscot Bank. Impressed with Lawrence's "industrious habits," Badger "without solicitation...offered him all the money he wanted to pay for his house or anything else on his own personal note, and his own time." Lawrence accepted his kind offer.[16]

In May, as Fanny and Lawrence settled into their home, they made arrangements to bring Daisy home. Assuring them that Daisy had not forgotten them, Sae asked, "Cant you make your selves contented with one baby until some time in June?" Sae, who would accompany Daisy to Brunswick, described herself as very busy just at that time, but perhaps the Brewer Chamberlains were rather reluctant to part with little Daisy. Sae's letter is filled with Daisy's adventures, seeing robins' eggs with Sae, going to see the "proggins" down in the brook, and heading into the woods on Uncle Horace's back. When Sae brought Daisy back to Brunswick that summer, Mother Chamberlain wrote to Lawrence of her little granddaughter, "I have spared no pains with her—we love her as well as we do you, or any of our children—(*Thom not excepted*) I have learned something of her disposition, *a sweet child, much like yourself* when of her age...."

Mother Chamberlain also asked Lawrence to be attentive and kind to Sae, for Sae had taken on many of the duties of the family's Brewer home. Earlier that spring, Lawrence had suggested that Sae consider coming to Brunswick, where he would tutor her as a means of continuing her education. She did not accept his offer, expressing doubt that he should take on any more obligations. His responsibilities at school were, perhaps, weighing heavily on him at that time. Mother Chamberlain, in the conclusion of her letter, leaves room to wonder if Lawrence had again been the focus of the political machinations of his colleagues as the spring term ended, for she wrote, "Were you disappointed yester day? Your Father was afraid if he were there must have been danger—" Late that summer, the Bowdoin trustees expressed their concern over the "want of harmony" in the college faculty.[17]

A letter from Deborah Folsom to Fanny that summer suggests that Lawrence again considered leaving Bowdoin. She wrote, "When Lawrence gets President or Professorship out West then...I will come to your rescue." Knowing how busy Fanny was with home and family, Cousin Deborah wrote that she longed to return to Brunswick and see Lawrence and Fanny's children. But living with her brother's family on a farm in Cherry Grove, Illinois, Deborah explained that her own obligations would not allow her to come. In the first indication that things were not well for Fanny's adopted sister, Deborah went on to suggest that Fanny invite Anna Davis Atkinson to come and help out. Deborah related that Anna's husband, Amos Atkinson, planned to go to England, "to be absent an indefinite time" and that Anna was already planning to return to Brunswick. But help was secured when Sae brought Daisy home and stayed on to assist Fanny and Lawrence until August, when all of the Brewer Chamberlains, except for Horace, traveled to Brunswick for John's graduation. Horace, who had married Mary Wheeler that spring, was feeling his obligations as a new husband, and was busy with his work as a Bangor counselor and trial lawyer. Writing that Mary was not well and that he was hard pressed to meet the new expenses of housekeeping, Horace explained that he could take no holiday, but looked forward to a gathering of the whole family in Brewer after commencement.[18]

In the fall of 1859, Lawrence started a new term. Sae, on whose shoulders so many family responsibilities fell, took a much-needed holiday to Nova Scotia. But before leaving, Sae wrote to Lawrence and Fanny that she missed having the care of little Daisy. "I had become so accustomed to thinking of Daisy and 'keeping an eye' on her movements, that I am entirely lost without her. Isn't it surprising how one will get themselves bound up in a child." While Sae was gone, John Chamberlain, after helping Father Chamberlain take in his crop of grain, was afflicted with an illness that would prostrate him for the next three months. That same autumn, scarlet fever swept through Brunswick. Though Lawrence and his family escaped any serious illness, evidence of the fragility of life was ever before his eyes. He noted that there was so much death in the town that it seemed as if everyone was in mourning. Anxious for John and his parents in Brewer without Sae's assistance, Lawrence felt his own inability to be of much help to his parents, commenting: "It is rather a sad case to bring up children & have them all go away...." Bearing the knowledge that he was to be a father again in the spring, Lawrence struggled to pay the expenses of his growing family and new home, and he eventually asked his father for help. But despite his own financial tribulations, he advised brother John, who was regaining his health and his old restlessness, not to "be too much worried about money matters...", as he decided his future course. Lawrence urged his younger brother to at least try the seminary.[19]

At the end of October 1859, John Chamberlain was thought to be well on his way to recovery, but after an unexpected relapse, he remembered little of the month of November. Afterward, John reported to Lawrence that, "I cannot recall much but air castles...for the last month—Much was I disappointed on recovering from my pleasant delusion to find my Cuban plantation with its splendid castle had vanished and my $300,000 in the Banks [like] wise." However light he made of his illness, Mother Chamberlain had been desperately worried. With John finally on firmer ground, she told Lawrence, "I shall not urge you to come home, you see we are all alive—there never has been a time, I hope and trust, never will be again, when I shall so much feel the need of your aid as I have the past few weeks. I cherish the hope that we may once now find ourselves all in health—...." Trusting in God, Mother Chamberlain commented, "as thy day so shall thy strength be." Sadly for the Chamberlain family, Mother Chamberlain would need that strength, for the next year would bring more tragic illness to the Brewer home. And in Brunswick, though Fanny and Lawrence had met trials and difficulties during their first years of marriage, the coming months would be ones of unrelenting misfortune.[20]

Anna Davis Atkinson and her little daughter, Georgianna, called Georgie, had returned to Brunswick that fall of 1859, but Rev. Adams could give her little time. Helen Adams was in her eighth month of another pregnancy, and so ill at the beginning of October that, on their doctor's orders, Rev. Adams dosed her with laudanum and morphine. But Rev. Adams spent enough time with Anna to make the pronouncement that it was a "pretty hard case," for it soon became apparent that Anna had not only left her husband, but was expecting another child. When Helen Adams gave birth to their second daughter, Mary Leland Adams, on October 17, Anna and Georgie went to stay temporarily at Lawrence and Fanny's home. In the weeks after little Mary's birth, Rev. Adams became greatly concerned by the severe depression that Helen experienced. He also noted that baby Mary was much quieter than her sister Sarah had been. The injections that Helen received may well have caused little Mary to be what Brunswick people described as "slow."[21]

Unable to return to her adoptive father's, Anna moved into a room. By the beginning of December, she came down with a fever, and the home where she was boarding demanded that she leave. Though the doctor proclaimed that she had pleurisy, Anna had fallen sick at a time when many in Brunswick were alarmed about an outbreak of scarlet fever. On December 11, Lawrence helped Anna move to Mrs. Stanwood's. There the family's physician, Dr. John Lincoln, ordered a treatment in which blisters were raised on the skin, a profitless and painful procedure, widely accepted as a means of drawing out the source of illness. In these days, Rev. Adams was impatient with Anna, claiming that she would not be "molded or guided," while she complained to Dr. Lincoln that her father's talks were disturbing her. Reverend Adams felt that she should go to New York, where her husband Amos was, though he admitted that there was "no promise of comfort there." But he found a nurse for Anna, and when Helen Adams regained her health enough to visit, she described Anna as "emaciated & pale" and Helen was convinced she was dying.[22]

In the first weeks of 1860, Lawrence wrote to Mother Chamberlain that Fanny, now well along in her own pregnancy, had been "perfectly 'killed' with neuralgia—day & night—she has so much to do she cant afford to give entirely up by day—but at night—she has been almost driven distracted." As for himself, Lawrence reported that he was "never more plagued by pains & sleeplessness. Rheumatism or some such sort of thing seems to have got a fast hold of me, & has of late struck in to my head in such a way as to make me incapable of doing anything which requires attention or mental effort. I am hoping the powerful remedy I am using will give me some peace soon." Lawrence was also vexed with problems at the college, for he reported, "our usual amount of diplomacy this term—plotting & counter plotting. The game now is a professor of modern languages...& how it will turn out I cant predict. Your friend Prof. Upham still urges it upon me, & argues the point with his customary shrewdness; but I believe I shall stay where I am; unless some greater inducement than I have seen yet, is offered for the change."[23]

Although Dr. Lincoln held to his opinion that Anna was not very ill, on January 17, Rev. Adams recorded in his diary that he was "full of anxiety & dismal foreboding ab[out]t *Anna*. She declines seeing callers, refuses the Dr's medicines, eats nothing. H[elen thinks it] almost seems as if she were determined to die." Neither Helen, still feeble and depressed, nor Fanny, suffering from neuralgia, could do much for Anna when, on January 27, she went into labor prematurely, and delivered a stillborn son. On February 9, Dr. Lincoln admitted that the end was near for Anna, and Rev. Adams prayed with her. His distress that she had not embraced religion on her deathbed, is apparent in his diary entry: "All dark; tho' she did say "Lord h[a]v[e] mercy on me." He reluctantly left Anna that night, for word had come that Helen's condition demanded his presence at home. Returning early the next morning, Rev. Adams discovered that Anna had died just after midnight, and word was sent to her husband Amos of her death. After Anna's funeral service, Amos and little Georgie rode with Rev. Adams in a carriage to the cemetery, with Fanny and Lawrence among the mourners who walked behind. Helen was too ill to attend, and so disheartened that she wrote in her diary that day: "How near am I to the end?" During Anna's illness, Cousin Deborah had been unusually discreet, having little to say about Anna's situation other than offering to sell some of her stocks, should Amos "come up short in covering Anna's expenses." But when Deborah heard of Anna's death and Amos and Georgianna's departure from Brunswick, she wrote a candid letter to Rev. Adams regarding Anna's troubles. He reflected in his diary: "Letter from Deb[orah] telling what Anna has suffered from Atkinson, which makes us feel more sympathy for her & wish we had done more for her."[24]

Helen Adams, in the weeks and months after the birth of Mary Leland the previous October, suffered from a variety of symptoms and illnesses. On the day of Anna's death, Helen recorded in her diary: "Anna died about 1 o clock in the night. It is a sad sad event. my throat still very sore & baby's bowels bad—What *shall* I do? I feel as tho' in a bad dream—" Helen Adams, as so many other women of her time, had been fitted after childbirth with a pessary, in her case a ring of metal worn internally, designed to correct uterine irregularities, but also frequently used as a contraceptive device. While a prolapsed uterus does sometimes occur after a difficult delivery, this diagnosis seems to have been made with alarming frequency during the mid-1800s, often based on such varied and ill-defined symptoms as "ill turns, lassitude, back aches or general debility." Though Helen's doctor acknowledged only that she was suffering from bronchitis at this time, in the privacy of her own diary she reported that she was also in agony with pain in her back, hips and groin. Helen felt sure she was suffering from internal inflammation, but Dr. Lincoln disagreed. At last two consulting physicians discovered evidence of uterine inflammation and ulceration, and Helen was sent to New York for treatment and rest. Helen would be there nearly a month, still ill and suffering, before a city specialist finally agreed that the pessary should be removed.[25]

With the mild, dry April of 1860, came relief from the sad trials of the winter, and the promise of happier times. In a letter to Sae, who was teaching music at a school in Laurel Banks, New York, Lawrence wrote of his enjoyment at spending time with his children and the pleasure of escaping to the outdoors:

> *Such beautiful days & balmy air have tempted us out a great deal riding, walking &c the &c really of more extent & significance than the riding & walking; for that is applied to myself Daisy & Wyllys includes all the varieties of gardening, digging, hoeing, raking, scratching & all the rest. How I have wished you were here some of these fine mornings, like this, for instance, to ride or romp with us!*

In hopes of convincing Sae to stop and see them when she returned to Maine at the end of her school term, Lawrence offered: "You have always been here at my busy time just before commencement. You dont know how pleasant I can be! Fanny says I am very good when I am *asleep*—so I am too when I have nothing to do." He added: "By the way I should like to have you see & try to lift these two children of mine. They are solid, I assure you...." Lawrence also advised Sae that she was doing "a 'mighty' deal of work for a very small consideration. I would not on any account stay another term. I will give you more than that to teach Daisy her letters." In these days just prior to Fanny's fourth confinement, a visit from Sae that summer would have been a comforting prospect for Lawrence, though it is likely Sae would have had little time to "ride and romp."[26]

Pejepscot Historical Society

Sarah Brastow Chamberlain, c. 1860.

Sae would not return to teaching, and she would miss the many friends she had made among the students and faculty at the Laurel Banks Seminary. She had found the countryside around the school very beautiful, and she delighted in the nightly gatherings at the seminary where they took turns reading from Sir Walter Scott, Goldsmith, and Hawthorne's *The Marble Faun.* Sae brought the latter book to Lawrence's attention, and asked if he had read it. Perhaps she knew that Hawthorne had styled his fictional sculptor, Kenyon, after none other than Paul Akers, Fanny's artist friend from her Portland days.

As much as Sae had enjoyed her stay in New York, she worried how Mother and Father Chamberlain and her brothers were getting along without her. To Thomas, she wrote a letter of sisterly advice. "I hope you dont box, or jump much, or *dance* at all. Where there is dancing there is mischief for young men, & I wouldn't have you in it for anything in the world. Dont learn to smoke either." Whether Tom boxed, danced or smoked at this time is not known, but his later prowess as a rider indicates that he took the same pleasure that his brother Lawrence did in taking a horse at breakneck speed across the fields and jumping the high brush fences that bordered the pastures of the family farm.[27]

In May 1860, a new daughter was born to Fanny and Lawrence. Though Emily Stelle's birth brought joy, there were hardly enough hands to care for mother, new baby and two little children. Mother Chamberlain was ill in Brewer and Sae hastened home to care for her. Nor was it possible for Cousin Deborah to break free from her family obligations in the West. That summer, Lawrence was worn out, and a letter from Annie Chamberlain reveals that he was unwell and thought of going to Europe. Perhaps Lawrence was beginning to give in to the college's pressure and give serious consideration to taking the department of modern languages with its lengthy sabbatical to study abroad.[28]

Summer of that year brought a return to sorrow, for news came from Boston on June 16 that Ashur Adams was seriously ill. Fanny was also ill, having "tried to do too much" as Helen put it, and could not travel. Lawrence made the trip to Boston and found Ashur very low. The day after his return, a telegram arrived with the news that Ashur Adams, at age 82, had died. Fanny was distraught that she could not attend his funeral. Of her Boston family, only her sister Catherine, her three daughters and Fanny's brother Sam still lived. Sam, now married, prospered for a time as a bookkeeper for a railroad. Sadly, his prosperity did not last. Sam visited Fanny in Brunswick that fall of 1860, and though there would be times when years would pass with no news of Sam, he never forgot his little sister.[29]

Lawrence again refused the chair of modern languages, and began another year committed to rhetoric and oratory at Bowdoin. A few weeks into the fall term, he and Fanny again knew the pain of losing a child. Recalling that September of 1860, Lawrence later wrote that Emily Stelle "left but a summer smile and aching hearts, as she departed with the flowers." Mother Chamberlain, having regained her health, heard that the baby was not well and was on her way to Brunswick on the day little Emily died. Reverend Adams conducted the funeral service several days later, and though he tried to offer words of faith and consolation, he lamented in his diary that night, "I did not succeed very well." But there are indications that the shared sorrow might have helped to reconcile Fanny and her adoptive father.

During the weeks after Emily's death, Rev. Adams visited frequently, and they all spent Thanksgiving together. Joining the family circle that year were two students from South Carolina, but Rev. Adams, though intensely concerned about the troubles of the country, was likely too polite to introduce the subject of politics.[30]

As the Brunswick Chamberlains mourned, Father Chamberlain had stayed in Brewer, for Horace had not been well that fall, and his father looked after his chores. In a letter of sympathy, Lawrence's father assured him that Horace was decidedly better, though feeling "very tender" about Lawrence and Fanny's loss. But Horace would never regain his health. By the end of 1860, when he was again bedridden with what the family hoped was just a lingering, bad cold, the doctors shocked the family with news that they had detected a "cavity" in his lung. Horace had kept his good humor during his illness, Sae reported, relating one incident in which he had insisted on staying up all one afternoon, saying "it was so 'thundering gloomy, he wanted to *sit up and enjoy it!*'" But when he learned he had tuberculosis, Sae reported that "it perfectly prostrated him. He says he cant breathe since he heard it." Horace's wife, Mary Wheeler Chamberlain, was not well herself, and Horace was taken to his parents' home. Sae, who cared for her brother, as she had all the others in time of sickness, described Horace as patient and uncomplaining.[31]

What pain this news must have brought to Lawrence, in a year already dark with illness and death. The Chamberlain family clung to the hope that Horace might recover, and Lawrence sent letters to Brewer meant to cheer his suffering brother. That winter, Lawrence sent a description of a combination plow and sled he had built after a snow storm in Brunswick. With Daisy and Wyllys atop, "I have broke out all the paths around the house & clear out to the street. It works nicely & we have had a fine time. Dais has a splendid great black Spanish rooster in her arms for a muff—It's a kind of *pet*. Tell Hod I havent had such a grand time since the *dam* was carried away by a *tremendous freshet*." Lawrence could hardly bear to lose Horace. While all the brothers freely asked Lawrence for help and advice, it was to Horace that he turned when he needed brotherly counsel.[32]

Just five years married, Lawrence and Fanny had experienced enough sad loss and misfortune for a lifetime. Bitterness and disappointment can result from such unhappy burdens, but for Fanny and Lawrence, the trials of 1860 strengthened them and bound them together, preparing them to face the unimagined ordeals that lay ahead.

CHAPTER

10

"Mightier Things Than Personal Griefs"

The sorrowful events in Fanny and Lawrence Chamberlain's lives in 1860 could only have left them with melancholy memories. But no personal tragedies, nor even family happiness could insulate them from the menacing omens of the tempest about to break upon the country. The year 1861 opened with a dreadful sense of foreboding for many, and, while Lawrence witnessed the slow decline of his brother Horace, he feared that he might hear the death knell for his country as well.

It is difficult to determine Lawrence and Fanny's political feelings in the years before the war. Their correspondence with each other and with their families contained no political dialogue. But there are some observations that can be made regarding Father Chamberlain and Rev. Adams' political leanings. Their influence should be viewed with some caution, however, for in politics as in religion, the child does not always follow the father.

There is considerable evidence that Father Chamberlain was a devoted Democrat. While he named his first-born son after a naval hero of the War of 1812, he named two of his other sons for prominent Democratic politicians. Tom was named after Maine Democrat Thomas Davee, a remarkably successful mid-Maine businessman and politician, and a shining example of the self-made man. But it is the naming of his third son, John Calhoun Chamberlain, after the man best remembered as the fiery defender of states rights, secession and slavery from South Carolina, that many find startling. Biographer Willard Wallace cites a Chamberlain family tradition that Father Chamberlain was simply enamored of all things Southern after touring the region as a young man. But a look at the family's history, as well as that of the state, suggests ample ground for such a tribute. Many Maine people, feeling they had suffered from the national government's high tariffs and policies on trade and currency, saw John C. Calhoun, the mastermind behind nullification and its challenge to federal authority, as a champion.[1]

Father Chamberlain, as a young lad, knew first hand of his own shipbuilding father's near economic ruin when President Thomas Jefferson's embargo on trade, from 1807 to 1809, paralyzed the industries reliant on seafaring. Nor did ship masters fare much better under President Adams' Non-Intercourse Act, harassed as they were by both the British and the French. Many in Maine had also opposed the War of 1812, the conflict during which Lawrence's grandfather, Col. Chamberlain, suffered the destruction of two of his ships by the British at his Orrington shipyard. It was an economic loss from which it is said he never recovered, and an episode that would have left quite an impression on young Joshua, Jr. The Colonel held on in Orrington after the close of the war, with its promise of a resumption of trade. But the Tariff of 1816, designed to protect the United States' new industries, soon dashed the hopes of New England seafarers and shipbuilders, and those of the trade-reliant Southern states as well. In 1818, Col. Chamberlain abandoned his Orrington shipyard, and brought his family to Brewer to start over again, where farming and timber would supplement his shipbuilding. By the time Lawrence's father had grown to manhood and was seeking his own fortune, there was still considerable opposition in Maine to what was viewed as the national government's interference on issues of trade and currency, which were believed to have impacted negatively on Maine fortunes. In 1833, five years before John Chamberlain's birth, John C. Calhoun, in order to openly oppose national tariffs and defend South Carolina's nullification law, resigned as vice-president of the United States to again become senator for his state. As the champion of nullification, he was credited by many with forcing the confrontation that would result in compromise and a lowering of tariffs. In the year before John Calhoun Chamberlain's birth, many Americans also believed that the economic panic of 1837 was caused by President Jackson's policies on the nation's banks and currency. Senator Calhoun's previous denunciation of both Jackson and his policies had seemingly proved right, and Calhoun enjoyed such popularity in Maine that a movement in the state's Democratic party advocated his candidacy for president.[2]

While the demand for lower tariffs caused many Mainers to see their Southern countrymen as political allies, the defense of state's rights could hardly be divorced from that of slavery. While the views of Maine people varied from ambivalence, or allowance for a "necessary evil," to ardent abolitionism, there is no evidence of Father Chamberlain's position. But it is interesting to consider the Maine Democratic party in the years before the war, for it was, as in many states, a party in transition. As the Democratic focus became more pro-slavery, the party also courted many of the immigrants who flooded to the United States in the first half of the century. These changes disillusioned a number of Maine Democrats. With the demise of the Whig party in Maine, the formation of the Republican party was spawned by a puzzling fusion of die-hard Whigs, nativist Know Nothings, temperance supporters and abolitionists. This coalition occasioned the most improbable scenes, such as the appearance of the genteel abolitionist Harriet Beecher Stowe on the same stage with a ranting Know Nothing fanatic at one of the Republicans' first rallies in the state. In the 1850s, a number of Maine citizens were hard pressed to give wholehearted support to either party. But Father Chamberlain, apparently, continued to align himself with the Democratic party. By 1862, though there is no deposition of what policies he endorsed, he made it clear that he was against the war. The earliest and only evidence of Lawrence's antebellum political inclinations, and an indication that he had parted ways with his father, was his vote for Hannibal Hamlin for Maine governor in the election of 1856. Hamlin, the state's Democratic senator in Washington, resigned that office and renounced the party platform's endorsement of the Kansas-Nebraska Act and popular sovereignty. Hamlin embraced the Republican party, ran as their gubernatorial candidate in Maine, and won.[3]

Reverend Adams followed state and national politics avidly, and he recorded his votes and sympathies in his diaries. A Whig in the 1840s, he voted for the Republican John C. Fremont, the Free Soil candidate of 1856, and he continued to vote a Republican ticket through the 1860s, voting for Hannibal Hamlin and Israel Washburn for governor, as well as for the Lincoln/Hamlin ticket in the presidential election. Though there is no evidence that he preached against slavery, a subject on which his congregation of academics and seafarers was sharply divided, there are some indications of his sympathies. In 1841, Rev. Adams defied the conservative elements in his congregation when he allowed a black minister to speak from the pulpit of the First Parish Church. Several members of his congregation got up and left, and Rev. Adams commented in the privacy of his diary, that the aptly named Rev. Freeman had "cast out 3 devils before he had said a word." But perhaps the most telling demonstration of his feelings, considering the racial prohibitions of his time, was his uninhibited hospitality to a black man, as a guest at his family's dinner table.

When the Civil War broke out, Rev. Adams backed the Union cause, heart and soul. He initially expressed some anxiety that his stance would irritate some of his congregation. The war between the states was, as earlier wars had been, bad news for Maine seafarers, but it seemed beyond his power to abstain from overt demonstrations of his earnest support.[4]

Fanny and Lawrence returned from a holiday together in New York in mid-January of 1861, on a bitter night with a temperature of fourteen degrees below zero. Lawrence continued on to Brewer to see Horace. Shortly after his return to Brunswick and his college duties in February 1861, Lawrence wrote a letter to his brother Tom in Brewer that is a recital of his family worries: "I want you to look & see what brand of ale that is which Mother has." Lawrence explained, "I want to see if I cant put a little flesh on to Fanny's cheeks; she is as thin as a shadow—" And he sent advice to John, who was attending the Bangor Theological Seminary, but who still had thoughts of other ventures. Lawrence advised him to forget the school in the South where he had considered teaching, and suggested that it was probably broken up by secession. Lawrence sent a medicine for Horace to try, and, knowing his brother's fondness for the children, he reported on their winter activities: "We have been having great times with your sled this winter. I piled up a artificial hill against the barn, & made a long smooth track away out into the garden, & Daise & Wyllys have enjoyed themselves greatly.... Once in a while the sled would go off the track, & plump them headforemost into the snow, but Daise says that is *all the fun of it*." Lawrence also described his duties at Bowdoin: "I am just commencing double work in college again—so that I shall have a hard spring of it, but my health is good."[5]

Horace's illness weighed heavily on Lawrence's mind that March, and frustrated by his inability to help his brother, he invited Hod to come stay with him and Fanny in Brunswick. But it was a journey that Sae tactfully, but firmly, declared impossible. Though Sae clung to hopes that Horace would eventually recover, she realized that he was not well enough to make the trip, and out of concern for Fanny, she explained that Horace needed care day and night. "He seems so well to those who do not have the care of him, that it is almost incredible that he should require so much attention." Sae also acknowledged Lawrence's news, that he was again considering the professorship in modern languages. Mindful of the long European trip that appointment would bring, the thought of Lawrence going so far away for so long a time was her only objection to his accepting the position.[6]

The news of the Rebels firing on Ft. Sumter caused great excitement in Brunswick. That April, Lawrence also witnessed the commotion in Boston at the commencement of the war. Having heard that Fanny's family in Boston was in distress, Lawrence traveled there on her behalf. He wrote to her: "I got safely to this city of flags & bayonets...missing you very much. I find you have become quite a necessary article of travel for me." Distraught that he had not waited longer at the station in Brunswick with Fanny, he wrote, "I have felt troubled all day because I did not stay with you at the Depot until the last moment You have not thought of it I am sure; but I was ashamed to be seated *as I was* while you, poor little pale-face, were standing patiently waiting to get a last look at me." He added: "... you know that you have no reason to fear that I shall not always choose to be with you rather than any where else in this world." Lawrence told Fanny of her sister Catherine Lombard and her niece Mary Cate Le Cain:

> *I found Katie after a long search, having first to find Katie Le Cain. Poor little Katie has had a hard time of it. I went up in that 3d story room with her three little children to take care of—nearly all the time alone—sick—discouraged about Mr Le C. not getting business—standing between him & Mrs. Lombard & the girls, as also between these last & Mr. Lombard—chased up & dunned by Mr Le C's creditors & the officers when on her sick bed—so poor that after having sold every thing else she has at last pawned her wedding presents & her mothers pictures to pay her washing bills &c—you see how it has been with the poor little thing.*

Of Sam, the one success story in the family that had brightened Ashur Adams' final years, Lawrence also had sad news. Sam had lost his position with the railroad, and Lawrence's vague allusion to his ensuing failure in business has caused speculation that Sam had a drinking problem. Lawrence wrote, "Sam's oil business has slumped. It 'lubricated' his secret so that it slid off. Le Cain has gone to *soap making*, employing *Sam* as assistant." The family's Dickensian inability to get along in life must have been a sad worry to Fanny.[7]

After a return home, Lawrence again made his way to Brewer, in some anxiety. A letter from Sae at the end of April brought the disheartening news that Horace had experienced a hemorrhage that left him feeble and with little appetite. The family clung to the doctor's suggestion that the source of the hemorrhage was the throat, rather than the lungs. They knew the significance of the latter and what it meant for Horace's chances at recovery. Sae was also worried about Mother Chamberlain, and described her as, "quite well I *guess*, but she will certainly be deprived of her reason—if she doesn't stop worrying about Horace." Worn by family cares, and scenes of war in Bangor, Sae added, "What *terrible times*! The streets *full* of troops practicing and flags streaming."[8]

A month later, as spring approached, Sae sent a happier report to Brunswick. Hod had improved, and she wrote: "His strength seems more reliable than at any time since he was taken sick." Horace had walked out on visits and had even managed to mount a horse for a short time, though he found a buggy much easier. Sae wrote that Mother Chamberlain, too, was feeling much better, as the hopes of the family were temporarily raised. But family trials and the weight of his work at the college were taking their toll on Lawrence. Deborah Folsom wrote to Lawrence that spring, questioning him closely as to whether his "cares & duties" were "more than you have strength to endure?" Warning him to take care of himself, and instructing Fanny to "keep up good courage," Deborah wished that she could "lighten the cares that press so heavily upon you all." And she expressed her desire to see "those little immortals that are surrounding your table & filling the niches in your heart...." Cousin Deborah loved children, and it almost seems that she never quite forgave them for growing up. In this letter, Deborah commented to Lawrence about Fanny, now 36 years old: "How much I am pleased that Fanny comes out such a nice housekeeper & cook it is so much more than I ever expected, We see what can be done when we try—" Deborah overcame her reluctance, borne of past unhappy scenes, to return to Maine, and by July 1861, she was on her way back East.[9]

The first months of the war brought changes to Brunswick, as to every village and city in the country. While a company of Brunswick volunteers marched away with the 5th Maine in May 1861, the Bowdoin Guards formed at the college under the supervision of Charles A. Curtis, a young Maine man who trained at a Vermont military college. Curtis instructed his ununiformed but eager students in military drill. He noticed that Prof. Chamberlain took an interest in them, and "attended drills, listening to commands and observing the responsive movements."

In those first months, the boys also drilled without arms, so the arrival of 160 muskets from the government caused great excitement. Curtis issued one to each student with instructions on cleaning them, and sent the boys off with orders to return with a clean weapon the next day. Though Charles Curtis was well informed on the drill, he had a lot to learn about commanding exuberant young men. Curtis thought nothing of it when one of the boys arrived at his home later that day to inquire about how to make a cartridge. Having obliged this young man, another of his boy soldiers turned up and invited Curtis to go for a buggy ride, again without exciting the young instructor's suspicion. On his return to the college that evening, as Curtis described it, "...suddenly, from every window and every doorway of every dormitory blazed volleys of musketry filling the air with the rattle of irregular discharge." In the five hours since Curtis had left the campus, the boys had bought powder and percussion caps, and had made good use of their time. The "unceasing rattle of muskets" convinced Curtis that it would be a long siege. Approached by President Woods, Prof. Chamberlain, and several of the college tutors, Curtis gave the opinion that all they could do was wait it out. Woods was critical, while Chamberlain quietly acknowledged to Curtis: "The young scamps will have to carry their fun to the end, as the President will presently learn." As Curtis, Woods, and Chamberlain approached Appleton Hall, ablaze with gunfire, Curtis noted that an "irreverent sophomore" who recognized Chamberlain, yelled, "Oh, Professor!...First time under fire!—How do you like it?" Amused, Chamberlain turned to the president and said, "Doctor, I think Mr. Curtis is right, the boys will have to fire their last cartridge before they stop. We had better adjourn."

In spite of the general opinion that the war would be a short one, a second company, the Bowdoin Zouaves, was formed. Many of the boys from Bowdoin who went to war would come from these two companies of home guards. Several Bowdoin seniors enlisted in 1861, and one, George B. Kenniston of Boothbay, Maine, the orator of his class, was captured at First Bull Run. He spent what would have been his August graduation day in Libby Prison.[10]

In the first week of August, 1861, Lawrence accepted the chair of the department of modern languages, though the matters of salary and the length of his sabbatical remained to be worked out. There was no joy in the letter that announced it to his Brewer family. Indicating that he would rather postpone a Canadian excursion that Sae had been planning, he wrote that he wanted to come to Brewer soon:

> *We have not got through our bothering faculty meetings yet, so that I have had not time to day to consider the matter of the Quebec trip, & shall let it depend on your coming or not. In that case we shall try to "drop" down & see you at Brewer, & John & I will take a trip somewhere as we did last year.... It is likely then on the whole that you will see us, if you want & can stand the shock, some time the last of this week. I have got so worn out with work, that I must this time have freedom & rest, & I shall manage to have it some how.... Tell John to think up some good place for a camping & "duck shooting" time—I have this morning conditionally accepted the Professorship of Modern Languages, & am to leave for Europe, if I wish, by the last of October or first of November.*[11]

When the Chamberlains returned to Brunswick in early September, the women's circle of the church met at their home. The group devoted their work to the needs of the soldiers. Reverend Adams carried coffee and sandwiches to the depot for the soldiers who passed through, and Helen, having collected money in the town, sent mattresses and comforters to the 5th Maine's hospital. In the midst of this war activity, Cousin Deborah came to Brunswick in early October. Helen Adams, with some trepidation, made her way up to Fanny and Lawrence's to pay her respects, and reported of her visit, "made a call—with more comfort and pleasure than I feared."

Though the Chamberlains and Deborah did not dine at the Adams' home that Thanksgiving, whatever hard feelings or hurtful memories had survived thus far, if not forgotten, were overlooked. The Adams and Chamberlain families, including Cousin Deborah, soon adopted the habit of frequent cordial visits, and mutual support. The ladies were at each other's call when duties and obligations were pressing, and the latest from the gardens and the ovens of their kitchens was carried back and forth with pleasure. When Helen attended a party at the Chamberlains' in late October, Rev. Adams observed that it was the first time in two or three years that Helen had gone to a party. He commented that it was "exceedingly gratifying to have the old affairs put away."[12]

Fanny was glad of Cousin Deborah's company and assistance in early December when Lawrence and Daisy went to Brewer to be with Hod. It is not known whether Lawrence or his family suspected that Horace was dying. Horace, himself, did not accept that he had reached the end of his life until a few days before his death. Lawrence and Daisy spent the last three weeks of Horace's life with him, as Fanny, Wyllys and Cousin Deborah managed household chores in Brunswick. Anxious to assure Lawrence that they got along well in his absence, Fanny wrote in early December:

> *You will be glad to learn that we are getting along very comfortably in all respects; our coal fire has never gone out & is perfectly easy to regulate. We do all our cooking by it, keeping no other fire.... Never fear about Wyllys; the only trouble is, that he has too good a time,-too much attention. he has thick woolen under drawers, nice long, woolen stockings, longsleeved aprons and so on. I am only afraid he will get too tender staying with us almost all the time in the warm sitting room. Father comes in quite often to see us and he & Helen are very kind in remembering us in various ways....*

Employing Wyllys' name for the chickens, Fanny reported:

> *I feed the "Doo-doos" my self with your rubber-boots on. We have a nice number of eggs.... We have everything we want, and I hope I am truly thankful for all our blessings.... You must stay as long as you feel that you can with Horace; you need feel no care about us now, although we want to see you and dear little Daisy very much...If I had thought Daisy was going to stay so long as this, I would have sent more clothes, but I knew you would object to that,....*

Sending mother's love to Daisy, Fanny closed her letter to Lawrence as she had so many others: "Good bye a little while...." A week later, having news from Brewer, Fanny knew how distressed Lawrence was at Horace's condition, yet she did not know, as she wrote her Dec. 8 reply to Lawrence, that Horace had died the day before: "I was troubled to hear from you as so very sad and lonely, and I longed to be with you to cheer and comfort you, but it seemed hardly possible for me to leave Aunty and little Wyllys here entirely alone. I do not think it would be *safe* on many accounts; we have no girl yet you know." Fanny went on to say that Cousin Deborah did not hear well and she feared that she would never hear if the house were on fire. She was also alarmed that Deborah did not seem to notice "coal gas at night, for she never perceives it until I am almost suffocated with it."

Both photos courtesy of the Pejepscot Historical Society

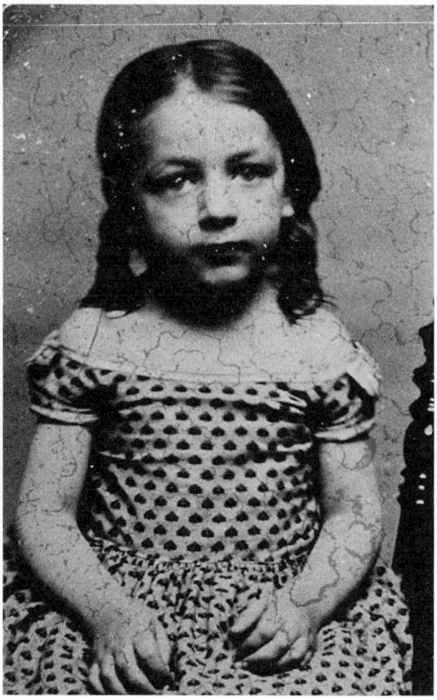

Grace Dupee "Daisy" Chamberlain, c. 1861.

Harold Wyllys Chamberlain, c. 1861. Wearing costume and curls customary for toddlers of the time.

Fanny asked about Daisy's cold, and also wrote: "I want to hear more about poor Horace; does he suffer much? is he able to see Daisy? I am glad you are able to be with him if it seems to comfort him." She ended her letter with, "Thank you dear a thousand times for your beautiful love letter, enclosed in your last! It was too bad that we could not be together last Saturday, the anniversary of our wedding!" She could not resist adding:

> *I want to answer the dear letter darling, dont think that I thought nothing of it, but I must tell you the answer when you get home, for I cannot trust it here, for fear of other eyes than those for whom it was meant. Dont leave this letter about, or show it, please dear Lawrence, I find myself checked when ever I write you, and compelled to write a mere, commonplace business letter, for I cannot bear that the sacred expressions of affection, should be bandied about, and left lying about the house like a tailor's bill.*

Fanny also included a plea for forgiveness at her "scolding" him. But she may well have regretted her admonitions when she discovered that the blow of Horace's death had already fallen upon Lawrence.[13]

At the end of December 1861, as they had the year before, Lawrence and Fanny traveled to New York. As if under some spell that allowed no relief from worry or misery, their trip ended unpleasantly. On finally arriving home, Lawrence related in a letter to Sae:

We got home the middle of last week, after great trouble, being out in the steamer in that great storm. The first twenty four hours however we lay in New York harbor but the next night we had a gale in the sound & the steamer trying to carry sail as well as steam had her yards carried away & we were tossed about considerably for two days & nights, the sea breaking clean over the ship, & washing the cabin wetting Fan's clothes &c &c Then we got to Portland two hours too late for the cars.

For Fanny, prone to sickness in heavy seas, the trip could only have been a nightmare. Lawrence pushed on from Portland to Brunswick the next day, but left Fanny with friends for several days to recover.[14]

As Lawrence settled into another spring term at the college, the town was alive with the news and commotion of war. On February 5, the bells of Brunswick rang out as the 14th Maine passed through on their way to Washington. They would ring again that month and the college would be illuminated as the town celebrated the news of the Union victory at Ft. Donelson. Several days later, a long cavalry train came through the town, and on Washington's birthday, Lawrence played the organ for those who gathered at the First Parish Church for a reading of Washington's Address. What was passing through Lawrence's mind as he witnessed the patriotic fever that gripped his town, as it had towns, big and small, all across the country? And when was it that a large map appeared in the Chamberlain home, on which Lawrence painstakingly tracked the movements of the armies?[15]

In the first months of 1862, Lawrence felt Horace's death deeply, as he revealed to his sister Sae:

...I feel very sad this winter, in thinking about Horace—in trying to realize that he is really gone from us. So it is not after all for him, as it is for the thought of the thing, for myself, & for us all, that I feel sad. That he should be cut down at the very opening of his career, & when he had so much reason to anticipate a prosperous course, seems almost against the order of nature. For him I have no doubt, the change is not a sad one. I do not think for a moment that it is not infinitely better for him, & that having once passed the great boundary he has no wish to be here again. And then I feel as if he experienced about all there was in life of comfort & happiness. I am sure, on the whole his circumstances through his short life were as pleasant as usually fall to the lot of any one. But I feel bereaved, as if a support & stay was suddenly taken away & one of the greatest sources of pleasure in this world was sealed up. I found a paper here containing a notice of his death, by the Bar. I could have wished that some appreciative friend had spoken for him, but perhaps it is all we could expect, & considering the way such things are usually done, we should be well content. I hope Father & Mother are well & cheerful. I am glad you are at home. I should insist very much on your coming here immediately, if it were not for the good you can do at home. It seems to me it will be lonely there without you. When you think they can get along without you, I want you to come at once.[16]

Sae Chamberlain went to Brunswick at the end of March, and her stay through the spring must have comforted her grieving brother. After Horace's death, Sae was the sibling to whom Lawrence wrote most often and to whom he confided his hopes or cares. It was in that spring of 1862 that Lawrence likely shared with his sister his thoughts of volunteering for the army. When attempting to gauge the family's reaction to this startling revelation, a quip in Lawrence's memoirs, that the "strife at home" proved good training for the battle he would have with the college over his decision, has led to much speculation. Which "home" he was referring to, Brunswick, Brewer or both, when he indicated that loved ones had protested his plan, is not known. Previous Chamberlain biographers have asserted that Fanny objected to Lawrence's military aspirations, based on the testimony of a 20th century family retainer's recollections of family conversations. Yet there is evidence that Fanny, however terrible the prospect may have been to her, understood and supported her husband's decision to go to war. Many years later, when introducing his wife to a group of Civil War veterans, Lawrence stated that, in spite of her being left at home to take care of two little children, Fanny had told him, "Your duty is with your country's flag in the hour of her deliverance." He also described Fanny as, "a broad-minded and richly endowed woman who loved her whole Country, in peace & in war, and honored brave men who did manly duty as they saw it in their own hearts." In conjunction with Lawrence's testimony for his wife's support, ample evidence is provided in their wartime correspondence and by Fanny's attempts to be near Lawrence as often as possible during the war.

A more likely explanation to Lawrence's reference to "strife at home" is provided by his father's disagreement with his son's sense of duty. Father Chamberlain expressed his feelings in a letter to Lawrence shortly after his departure for the front. And beyond his father's political stance, it is clear that, having just suffered Horace's death, it would be a great burden to the Brewer Chamberlains to have another son or brother in jeopardy.[17]

Evidence that Lawrence had made up his mind to enlist is found in a letter written several days after Lincoln's call for more volunteers in June 1862. Americus Fuller, a Bowdoin graduate who had run into Lawrence "in the cars," gossiped in a letter to a friend that Chamberlain thought of going in the military, feeling that he might be able to give valuable service. Fuller added: "By'way you are perhaps aware that he has been transferred to 'chair of modern languages—He is to go to Europe when he chooses have his expenses paid & his salary continued & 500 bonus not a bad offer. Says he intends to go as soon as war is over." While Lawrence had come to an agreement with Bowdoin concerning his salary and his leave of absence, his mind was not on Europe, but much closer to home with the Union army. On July 14, 1862, Lawrence took his fate in his hands, and wrote to the governor of Maine:

To his Excellency Governor Washburn:

In pursuance of the offer of reinforcements for the war, I ask if your Excellency desires and will accept my service.

Perhaps it is not quite necessary to inform your Excellency who I am. I believe you will be satisfied with my antecedents. I am a son of Joshua Chamberlain of Brewer. For several years past I have been Professor in Bowdoin College. I have always been interested in Military matters, and what I do not know in that line, <u>I know how to learn</u>.

Having been lately elected to a new Department here, I am expecting to have leave, at the approaching Commencement, to spend a year or more in Europe, in the service of the College. I am entirely unwilling, however, to accept this offer, if my Country needs my service or example here.

Your Excellency presides over the Educational, as well as the Military affairs of our State, and, I am well aware, appreciates the importance of sustaining our Institutions of Learning. You will therefore be able to decide where my influence is most needed.

But, I fear, this war, so costly of blood and treasure, will not cease until the men of the North are willing to leave good positions, and sacrifice their dearest personal interests, to rescue our Country from Desolation, and defend the National Existence against treachery at home, and jealousy abroad. This war must be ended, with a swift and strong hand; and every man ought to come forward and ask to be placed at his proper post.

Nearly a hundred of those who have been my pupils, are now officers in our army; but there are many more all over our State, who, I believe, would respond with enthusiasm, if summoned by me, and who would bring forward men enough to fill up a Regiment at once. I can not free myself from my obligation here, until the first week of August, but I do not want to be the last in the field, if it can be helped.

I am sensible that I am proposing personal sacrifices, which would not probably be demanded of me; but I believe this to be my duty, and I know I can be of service to my country in this hour of her peril.

I shall acquiesce in your decision, Governor, whether I can best serve you here or in the field. I believe you will find me qualified for the latter as for the former, and I trust I may have the honor to hear a word from you, and I remain,

Yours to command, J.L. Chamberlain[18]

He did not have long to wait for his answer. He readily responded to Governor Washburn's request that he come to Augusta on July 17. A conversation which he had with Gen. O. O. Howard, a Bowdoin and West Point alumnus, indicates that Chamberlain came back from Augusta with some confidence that he would be given a military appointment. He asked Gen. Howard, who had already given an arm to the Union cause at Seven Pines, for advice on how to prepare himself. Howard had come to Brunswick, as to a number of Maine towns, to urge men to volunteer. The Portland *Daily Advertiser* reported Chamberlain's introduction of the general at the Brunswick train depot on July 19:

The Professor said that his had been the lot to deal in words for some time past, but believed now was the time for deeds. He was willing to go to serve his country at once, if he could do more good elsewhere than by staying at home. It is no time to cry 'peace! peace!' but it is the duty of every well man to respond to his country's call now, when every man was needed. He spoke with a great deal of power & energy, and ended by saying that the gentleman was present, whom they were very anxious to hear, whose name had called so large a number together, he would give way for him.[19]

General Howard, who would head the Freedman's Bureau after the war, proceeded to speak for an hour to the people of Brunswick, and the following quotes are representative of the several themes he addressed. While giving praise to Gens. Banks and Pope, he described Gen. McClellan as a "cautious & able commander." Howard declared that, "If McClellan can have as many men as the enemy, he will take Richmond." Howard was also convinced that there were thousands of Maine men who were ready to volunteer, but were detained by the ladies of the state. He spent some time exhorting the women of Brunswick to make the sacrifice. To the married men who were worried about their families' well-being, Howard countered with, "What is the expense compared with the cause involved in the contest" and, "What are lives, compared with the great principles involved?" He also informed his audience that, "he was the only man in the State who dared to address an audience upon the negro question, and tell them what he thinks. He was one who had no political aspirations. He was in favor of using the negroes in the field or on the embankments—anywhere where they could save the health of our brave Northern soldiers. There is no reason in the world why they should not be used, except that some party might object. The negroes can take the place of other troops, who being relieved, can go to the assistance of Gen. McClellan."[20]

Two days after Howard's speech, on August 21, several newspapers in the state, to Lawrence's embarrassment, were announcing that Prof. Chamberlain of Bowdoin would be colonel of the new 20th Maine Volunteer Regiment. Not only had Lawrence not been appointed, but the formation of a 20th regiment was still in question, for Gen. McClellan had entreated the states to fill the rapidly dwindling numbers in their old regiments before creating new ones. It is likely that Gen. Howard had indiscreetly spoken to newsmen around the state. On the day that the first of the articles appeared, Lawrence wrote to Gov. Washburn:

> *I beg your Excellency will understand that these mortifying reports in regard to my appointment, did not come from me in any way that I can imagine. To Genl. Howard alone, in a private conversation, I stated that though it was scarcely probable that a new Regt. would be raised, yet in case it should be, I had received the impression that you thought favorable of my having it, and I asked the Genl what I had better do in the mean time. To others I had, of course, every motive to maintain a discrete silence, as to the result of my visit to Augusta.*
>
> *I hope your Excellency will not be as disturbed as I am, at these reports and contradictions which are so embarrassing and injurious to me.*
>
> *I do not know any way in which I am to blame for them, and I only hope that at some time I can overcome their mortifying effect by actual service in the field.*
>
> *I am persecuted with applications and propositions, but I urge all I see to enlist at once in the first Regt they can find.*[21]

One of those who lost no time in appealing to Lawrence was Tom Chamberlain, who was anxious to volunteer and saw his brother's appointment as his only chance. On the very day the erroneous announcements of Lawrence's colonelcy appeared in the papers, Tom wrote: "I see by the morning paper that you have been appointed Coln. of the 20th." He went on to explain that his friend, Capt. Farnham had offered him a lieutenant's position, "but you know how it is with mother." Tom added, however, that he felt Mother Chamberlain would have no objection if she knew Tom was going with Lawrence. Asking for an appointment as quarter-master or lieutenant, Tom admitted, "I don't care what so long as I go." Declaring that his health was better than brother John's and that warm weather agreed with him, Tom declared he could be ready to go at a week's notice.[22]

Another who saw Lawrence's announcement in the newspaper was Josiah Drummond, then attorney general of Maine, and a man who wielded considerable political power in the state. Rather inexplicably, Drummond wrote to the governor, "Have you apptd Chamberlain Colonel of 20th? His old classmates etc. here say, you have been deceived; that C. is nothing at all; that is the universal expression of those who know him." Drummond, who made a number of recommendations for other military appointments, likely had another candidate in mind for the colonelcy of Maine's new regiment. But the worst problem caused by this premature announcement of Lawrence's appointment was the storm of protest that arose at Bowdoin, for Lawrence had yet to tell the college of his plans. The faculty and administration, complacent at having at last gotten Chamberlain into modern languages, were taken by surprise when informed of his military intentions. As he described in later years in his memoirs:

> *With wise or unwise forethought the Professor had not consulted his colleagues about this movement. But the matter came out through the papers. Then there was a strife at home over this case which was a g[ood] rehearsal for the future field. The 'Faculty' objected. They remonstrated with the Governor, assuring him that the young Professor had no military stuff in him. They even sent a representative to the Capital to demonstrate that he was no fighter, but only a mild-mannered commonplace student. It was indeed a strange exhibition of affection. But this was not the ruling motive. The Professors were men of military experience in the religious contests for the control of the College. They had learned grand tactics. The young Professor held for them a strategic position. This chair was much sought for; and those competent to fill it were for the most part, not of the orthodox persuasion. In case this chair should become vacant, as the experiences and prospects of war rendered highly probable, the chances were that it would be filled by one of the adverse party. But they reckoned without both their hosts. The young colleague was not coward enough to let go his purpose under such injurious misrepresentations, and the Governor well knew the father and grandfather of his candidate, and had no thought of letting his own judgment be superseded.*[23]

Whether Bowdoin still felt they could persuade Chamberlain to stay, or whether they knew they could not keep him in Brunswick, on the first of August, the college voted to give Lawrence his sabbatical to go to Europe. Though Chamberlain still felt like a pawn in Bowdoin's political intrigues, Gov. Washburn considered the college's apparent reluctance to part with him little more than the desire to hold on to a good man. On Aug. 8, Gov. Washburn offered Lawrence a commission as lieutenant colonel of Maine's new 20th Regiment of Volunteers, at the same time announcing that Adelbert Ames, U.S.A. would be colonel. In his memoirs, Lawrence stated that he asked for a "subordinate position" so he could "learn and earn my way to the command." He replied to the Governor's offer immediately. "I should prefer the office you tender to any other. I shall accept. The College Laws require me to present the matter to the Faculty before the case is finally adjusted, but it can have only one issue, & an hour will settle it."[24]

The question of why Chamberlain felt he must go to war must be examined. As a 33-year-old married professor with two small children, he was an unlikely candidate for a soldier. But several paper fragments at Bowdoin, on which Chamberlain wrote, "Notes of my little speeches & doings which led to my going into the army in the war 1862" offer insight. Some thoughts from these notes were incorporated into his introduction of Gen. Howard, but he also wrote:

> *We have this war upon us & we want to stop it. It has cost us already too much precious blood. It has carried stagnation, starvation & grief in to too many villages of our fair land--brought death to too many noble hearts that we could ill afford to lose. But the only way to stop this war, is first to show that we are strongest we must prove to the South & to the world that we can afford to stop We cant afford to stop until we have taken the chief rebel cities & shown that we have the power as well as the right of the case I believe the war would have been ended by this time, if we had gone heartily into it at first, & had not given time for other issues to get at work, & complicate & mix up matters so that men of [worth?] do not know what they are fighting for. I feel that we are fighting for our country—for our flag—not as so many stars & stripes, but as the emblem of a great & good & powerful nation—fighting to settle the question whether we are a nation, or only a basket of chips. Whether we shall leave to our children the country we have inherited—or leave them without a country—without a name—without a citizenship among the great powers of the earth—...take the chief city of the rebels. They will have no respect for us unless we whip them. Europe will have none unless we whip them & I say it in all earnestness. There is no abiding peace till we conquer.... I spoke of Europe. We have learned a lesson there. I dont believe in that good will that has to be sweetened with sugar. I dont believe in that hollow breasted philanthropy that has to be stuffed with cotton. The Eng. govt. has no good will for us—north or south. We are two quarreling cats & she wants to decide our course for us.*[25]

Chamberlain's memoirs offer additional insights:

> *...Mightier things, than personal griefs then took possession of every heart. The flag of the Nation had been insulted. The honor and authority of the Union had been defied. The integrity and the existence of the People of the United States had been assailed in open and bitter war. The north was at last awake to the intent and the magnitude of the Rebellion. The Country was roused to the peril and duty of the hour. The summons rang almost strangely in the ears of one who once rejected West Point because it led to 'being a soldier in time of peace'. An irresistible impulse stirred him to have a hand in this business now that the moral forces of the people had summoned the physical to their defense.*

It is not hard to guess what kept Lawrence at home when war broke out in the spring of 1861. His family had been overwhelmed with cares before and during that first year of the war. Perhaps Lawrence thought, as many of his fellow citizens had, that the conflict would be quickly settled in the Unions' favor. It meant a great deal to Lawrence to be with Horace as much as possible in his last year. But perhaps his death, and Lawrence's brooding reaction to that promising life cut short, also influenced his decision to cast his lot with the Union. Discouraged by the political wrangling and conservatism at Bowdoin, Lawrence began to despair of ever realizing his dreams of doing something significant for mankind. Did he see his service to the Union as the worthy cause he had been looking for all his life?[25]

It is unnecessary to cite the hardships that this decision would bring to both Lawrence and Fanny, for men and women have endured such throughout the countless conflicts of history. Yet, because of their love and dependence on one another, it is easy to appreciate the pain they experienced. Lawrence faced the great dangers of battle, but caring anxiety about each other's well-being would flow both ways in the war years.

At some point, Fanny and Lawrence knew that life would never again be as it had been before the war. Perhaps they knew this even before Lawrence became a soldier, for Fanny learned that her uncle, Harold Wyllys, a favorite for whom they had eventually named their son, was in a South Carolina jail. He had openly opposed secession in his adopted state, and was imprisoned in 1860 on a charge of "incendiary papers." And Fanny had many friends in Milledgeville, a number of whom were wearing Confederate gray. If Fanny, at any time, tried to dissuade her husband from going to war, once that decision was made she proved to be a loving and supportive wife.[26]

Pejepscot Historical Society

Frances Adams Chamberlain, c. 1861.

CHAPTER

11

"Where Duty Called Me"

On September 2, 1862, less than one month after Lawrence accepted his commission as Lt. Colonel, he and the 20th Maine left the state for Washington, D.C. The bustle in the Chamberlain home during those weeks when Lawrence made the transition from professor to warrior was considerable, as his family prepared for his needs. He traveled to Portland on August 18 for his first taste of army life at Camp Mason. Two days later he was back at home, hoarse and sick with a cold. With him came the 20th's pride, their new regimental color, for Fanny and Helen Adams to stitch on the gold fringe.[1]

When the 20th's colonel, Adelbert Ames, arrived at Camp Mason at the end of August, he quickly informed his new volunteers that they had a long way to go before they could consider themselves soldiers. The son of a Rockland, Maine ship-master, Ames had not followed in his father's footsteps, but he had grown up with a rough and ready model of what it took to command men. From the West Point class of 1861, and already a battle-scarred veteran, the 26 years old Ames was a stimulating mentor for Chamberlain.[2]

A few days before departure, several Brunswick men, deciding that Lt. Col. Chamberlain should know how the people of Brunswick felt about his going to war, made a collection in the town. The results were so substantial that the most admired horse in the area, a dapple gray known as the Staples horse, was purchased and equipped with handsome trappings. On Sept. 1, 1862, the 20th Maine formed a hollow square for the presentation. Though Lawrence's powers of oratory were well known, he was at his best when speaking extemporaneously. Particularly moved by his town's extravagant gift, he declared:

United States Military Academy

Mass. Commandery, USMHI.

Adelbert Ames
(Left) as a West Point cadet; (right) as colonel of the 20th Maine Infantry.

> *A soldier never should be taken by surprise, and it would be doubly inexcusable in me, were I to deem anything surprising in the way of generosity on the part of those whose sentiments and deeds of kindness I have known so long.... I know at least how to value kindness and a compliment like this. I accept it, as a bond to be faithful to my oath of service, and to your expectation of me. I accept it, if I may so speak, not to regard it as fairly my own, until I have earned a title to it by conduct equal to your generosity.*

He bid his townsmen farewell, drawing their attention to the soldiers of the 20th Maine, and "commending the brave men who surround you, to your remembrance and care; and all of us to the keeping of a merciful God on high."[3]

Two who witnessed the presentation were Fanny and Rev. Adams, who had come to bid Lawrence goodbye—a bleak farewell, for with orders for the regiment's departure early the next morning, Lawrence, Fanny and Rev. Adams spent the night of Sept. 1 in a tent at Camp Mason. Rain and wind swept the encampment as they awaited the three a.m. reveille that would see the 20th off on a six a.m. train. The next morning, Adams followed the regiment through the rain-soaked streets of the silent city, while a place was found for Fanny in the coach of a Bowdoin graduate, Lt. Charles Howard of New York. No bands with patriotic music or cheering crowds intruded upon the Chamberlains' sad thoughts of parting. A Portland newspaper reported on September 3 that "The Maine 20th regiment, Col. Ames, left this city yesterday morning at 6:00 o'clock, so quickly and quietly that our citizens were hardly aware that they had moved."[4]

Tom Chamberlain, who enlisted as a private and was elected sergeant of Co. I, was forced to stay behind, his health eroded by an army diet of coarse food and coffee. On regaining his strength, he carried Father Chamberlain's note of anxious and austere last minute advice to Lawrence:

> *Lawrence You are in for it So distinguish yourself as soon as possible and be out of it tis long & sanguinary if we lead, short and bloody if they lead. It has got to be settled in 3 mo[nths] for them or 3 years for us—Shape yourself accordingly And come home with honor as I know you will if that luckey [sic] star of yours will serve you in this war We hope to be spared as tis not our war Take care of Tom, as well as you can by way of easy work until he gets seasoned to the Trenches. Good luck to you.*[5]

Maine Historical Society

Joshua Chamberlain, Jr.

In a postscript he emphasized his youngest son's abilities: "Tom is the sharpest on a post of observation there is none like him for that—so over military stores or any other post—correct vigilant—no drone nor dunce He must be detailed out of the ranks to a higher post if he dont receive an appointment." It is likely that Father Chamberlain's instructions increased Lawrence's feelings of responsibility for his brother, coupled, as they were, with his mother's begrudging approval of Tom's going into the army only if he would be in Lawrence's regiment. Perhaps it eased his worries when Tom was chosen sergeant. This position, as "file closer," whose appointed place was behind the two lines of battle, afforded him some protection. Tom understood the benefits of that position, for he wrote to reassure Sae: "If you shoot a sergeant, you have to fire through two men first. A sergeant never fires his gun until the men in front are killed & then not unless you want to show off." But Tom's presence in his regiment was a worrisome responsibility that the family placed on Lawrence's shoulders.[6]

A number of Fanny and Lawrence's letters are unavailable to scholarship, including several letters that he wrote home after the 20th's departure. But it is not hard to realize that his letters held thoughts of home, as well as descriptions of the confusion and tribulations that every green regiment faced in their first weeks. Just two weeks after leaving Maine, the men saw their first scenes of war. On September 17, the 20th was held in reserve as the bloody battle unfolded at Antietam. Lawrence wrote to Fanny that night from a bivouac near Sharpsburg, Maryland: "We passed through one battlefield on our way & became accustomed to the sight of dead bodies piled up & laying in every conceivable position." Expecting the battle to resume the next day, Lawrence told Fanny, "...tomorrow we expect to be in the thickest of it all day & as for me I do not at all expect to escape injury. I hope I should not fall; but if it should be God's will I believe I can say amen. I think of you all whom I love so much & I know how you would wish me to bear myself in the field. I go, as twice today I went serious and anxious but not afraid. God be with you & me."[7]

Several days later in a letter to Fanny, Lawrence told her that, contrary to his expectations, the 20th Maine had remained in reserve at Antietam, but that the 7th Maine, three members of whom had been his students at Bowdoin, had been all but annihilated. "Hyde got out of the battle alive—but 2 Bowdoin boys in his Regt. fell. H. P. Brown; & Haskell who may survive." Lawrence's letter continued with a graphic description of his and the 20th's first trial under fire, a lively, though far less lethal affair. In pursuit of the Rebel army as it returned to Virginia, the 3rd Brigade, 1st Division, Fifth Corps attempted to cross thc Potomac at Shepherdstown Ford. Though there were indications that the Union troops who had crossed before them upriver had met a substantial enemy force, the 20th followed orders to make the slow and difficult crossing, impeded by the swiftness of the water. With his own regiment across, Chamberlain was sent back by his brigade commander, Col. T. B. W. Stockton, to steady the rest of the column that had been checked by the severe Rebel fire that began to sweep the ford. Mounted, and taking up a position in the middle of the river, Chamberlain steadied the men, urging them over. Meanwhile the 20th had no more than gained the other side and scrambled to the top of a bluff, when orders were received for them to cross back immediately. On September 21, Lawrence wrote:

> *Since I wrote you last, we have gone through a good deal. I wrote you a few lines a day or two ago which I have had no opportunity to send, so I enclose. Just after writing those we were called up to defend a new position on the left, where the terrible storming of the bridge over the Antietam took place. We did not find ourselves much exposed however. But the next morning we started in pursuit, & on the second reached the ford at dam no 4 the only place left the enemy to recross. Here our batteries pounded their rear, & our Division was ordered to cross. Of all the unearthly dins I ever heard that was the worst. The banks on both sides were high the rebels were in line of battle to meet us across & 25 or 30 pieces of artillery on our side shelling them over our heads as we forded leg deep. The Col. [,] Mr. Brown & I on horseback. The rebel sharpshooter were hard at work. I was ordered to stand in the middle of the river & urge on the men who halted for fear of the fire. The balls splashed all around me during the whole time & just as I reached the shore two struck just over my head in a tree. Sometimes our own shells would explode right over our head, & scare the men dreadfully. No sooner had we got over, & in line than we were ordered to recross. The General sent Col. Ames with six companies to defend the ford by lying behind the bank of the canal, & me with four companies to support the batteries on the heights. We had four wounded, not seriously.*[8]

The 20th had made a respectable job of recrossing the river under Rebel fire that one soldier described as coming down on them like hailstones; and while Capt. Ellis Spear questioned whether it was their "steadiness of nerve, or the difficulty of running in three feet of water," he, too, acknowledged that there had been no disorder. The 20th's major, Charles Gilmore, had loaned his black horse to Chamberlain at Shepherdstown, for it was not difficult to realize that the handsome gray that the fond citizens of Brunswick had presented to Chamberlain was apt to draw unwelcome attention from the enemy. Lawrence commented to Fanny: "My horse I keep a little in the rear. I should have been killed if I had ridden him in that crossing of the Potomac." As it was, the horse he was riding was struck by a bullet near the bit of the bridle, while the rider came through Shepherdstown unscathed. But the regiment had not entirely witndrawn from danger. Lawrence continued:

> *...at dusk we were sent out as pickets & we have been lying here all night—the whole Regt.—crouching along the banks of the river. The rebels firing every time they saw a head, & we doing the same for them. The river is narrow. At about mid night I rode softy along examining our pickets, & whenever the horse stumbled—whiz—would come a bullet in the dark. All this moming, & at least as often as every three words I have written, a bullet or a shell has hissed over my head either from our own sharpshooters or the rebels—5 in that last line. I am lying in a hollow where I am not much exposed, & really not at all disturbed. Glancing down at this moment I see a rebel ball that had struck right by my side, but I suppose, before I came. I hope to be relieved soon, & get somewhere where I can live like a civilized being. Our eating, drinking & sleeping arrangements are not remarkable for comfort. I can see plenty of dead & wounded men lying around, from where I sit. As soon as it can be done we are going to rescue some wounded who are calling to us from the rebel shore. Our Regt. has not done much yet, but we feel as if we could. I am very well, & happy as one need be, not at all sorry I came, I assure you. I think I did right & whatever comes of it, I have no fears. Some of our Regt. have just crossed the river at the risk of their lives to bring away the wounded we can see, some have died since we were looking at them. The poor fellows some 8 or 10 we have got are badly hurt in all sorts of ways. They belong to our brigade & were shot in our crossing yesterday. Two were dead when they got over. I took some letters about them to find out who they were. affectionate letters from wives, & answers written but never sent. I sent the letters to the Col. of the 118th Penn. Regt which they belonged to.*[9]

In the weeks that followed, the 20th Maine was frequently on the move, and Lawrence learned the limitations of the mail. On Oct. 10, he wrote to Fanny: "It is very evident that you do not get all my letters & perhaps I dont get yours. Now it occurs to me that it would be a good idea to *number* the letters...." This was his sixth letter to Fanny since leaving home, while he had received only one of hers. Telling how he "could *talk* hours together, but writing does not answer at all," he tried to describe life at camp:

> *Does your innocent little head imagine that I could get a photograph(!) taken here? My stars! I fear you have not a high idea of my position. If we can get any thing to eat: or any thing to sleep on except the ground: or under, save the sky; if we can find a bit of paper, or get a little thimble ful [sic] of ink of a sutler; if we can see a house that is not riddled with shot &*

shell, or left tenantless through terror, or if we could get a glimpse of a woman who does not exceed the requirements of sweepers in College, we think we are in Paradise. Why you have not the least idea of the desolation that has swept through this part of the country. You are a very dear little wife to suggest that Mrs Col. Merrill & Mrs. Col. Sewall are coming this way. Well the difference is this Their Regiments are stationed in permanent fortifications, or camps, & are quite in the rear as I understand, while we are in the very front, & as shifting as a night hawk's flight. I should wonder to see a woman in our camp. Really I think the exposure & hardship would kill her in a week.... My rubber blanket is not quite big enough to accommodate even so sweet & welcome a guest on the hillside, or in the drenching valleys that constitute my changing homes. I have my care & vexations too: but let me say no danger & no hardship ever makes me wish to get back to the College life again. I cant breathe when I think of those last two years. Why I would spend my whole life in campaigning it, rather than endure that again. One thing though I wont endure it again! My experience here & the habit of command, will make me less complaisant—will break upon the notion that certain persons are the natural authorities over me.[10]

Though a check to their hopes that Fanny could join him, the letter provided her with blessed proof that he was alive and well. His descriptions of the living conditions were a cause for anxiety, but this letter must also have reinforced the alarming realization that their lives would never again be the same. Lawrence wrote again on October 26 from the 20th's camp near Antietam Ford:

My dear Fanny;

It is some time since I have written you, & a great while since I have heard anything from you. I dare say you have written me often, but there is great irregularity about the mails. It is rather discouraging to me to look over a bushel or two of letters & find one for every body but me.... The Col. & I are crammed in this little tent. Last night after dark we became enterprising. We rushed out, ripped up a seam in our tent, built a fire place of stones & mud, topped out the chimney with a flour barrel & stuffed newspaper into the immanagable gaps, thinking to have a comfortable air inside. Since that time we have not been able to see out of our eyes for smoke, & a dull north-easter coming on, we have to stay inside & be smoked, or outside & be soaked. Thus far I have preferred the smoke. You notice by my blots & mistakes that I am occasionally smitten with total blindness. Multitudes of callers are chatting as long as they can stand the smoke, & I am keeping up two or three characters while writing... However that does not prevent my thinking of you & the darlings whenever my thoughts are not absorbed in military affairs, & dreaming of you every night.... I dont dare however to dwell too long on those dear names; it makes me rather disposed to pay you a short visit, which I dont expect to be able to do very soon. One of our Captains has the pleasure of having his wife at Boonsboro six or eight miles from here, but with my duties I could get away ten miles once in a month. If by any chance we get into winter quarters, I shall let you come some where *near. You are coming to Washington at any rate this winter—you & Daise. I want you to do everything you wish, & go every where you like. I dare say my $100. a month for you, has not reached you yet. As soon as you do get it, I want you to use it.... Every third day I am detailed as Field officer of the Day for the Brigade & I have charge of all the outposts & advanced guards for miles around. That gives me a fine chance to ride over the country. I wish you could be beside me on some gentle palfrey plunging into some rich shaded vally [sic], craggy defile, or along some lovely stream.... I have enjoyed these rides very much. Often I am 12 or 15 hours a day in the saddle. We are having rather a peaceful time now—though I did jump up a minute ago, to see what our batteries on the hill were banging at across the Potomac. We have got over being startled by sudden orders to be "ready to spring to arms at a moment's notice." I study,—I tell you—every military work I can find. And it is no small labor to master the evolutions of a Battalion & Brigade. I am bound to understand every thing. And I want you to send my "Jomini, Art of war" in a package. The Col. & I are going to read it. He to instruct me, as he is kindly doing in every thing now.*[11]

Sending love to "all those friends who think of me kindly & treat you so kindly....," Lawrence added:

I feel that it is a sacrifice for me to be here in one sense of the word; but I do not wish myself back by any means. I feel that I am where duty called me. The "glory" Prof. Smyth so honestly pictured for me I do not much dread. If I do return "shattered" & "good-for nothing," I think there are those who will hold me in some degree of favor better than that which he predicted. Most likely I shall be hit some where at sometime, but all "my times are in His hands" & I can not die without His appointing.... I know that prayers are going up for me from dear hearts & loving lips. I long to see you, to rush in & have a good frolic with the children, & a sweet sit-down with you in the study—take tea with you & Aunty—then dash off again into my work. I tell you Fanny the estimate of men & things is very different here from the popular one at home. Our Maine Regts. & our prominent officers, have quite a different name from the one they are given in the papers.... We employ no reporters—have no partizans [sic] at home—the papers do not load us with praise we do not deserve but in the Army & by the Regular officers we are already said to be a marked Regt. We have been applied for by three Generals out of our brigade, & I believe that no other new Regt. will ever have the discipline we have now. We all work....[12]

He did not exaggerate the intensity of the training. Many members of the regiment, both enlisted men and officers, said that Col. Ames was a hard man. Tom Chamberlain wrote home to John: "He is about as savage a man as you ever saw," and that the men hated him "beyond all description." While Ames attributed the regiment's achievements to the "hardhearted men at its head," and he and his lieutenant colonel got along well, Chamberlain gained the respect of the men without antagonizing them.[13]

Interminable drill was only one misery in the camp near Antietam. The men of the 20th were sturdy, but country boys proved susceptible to measles, bronchitis, pneumonia and dysentery. While the regiment was encamped on low, malarial ground near Antietam Creek, 300 of its members fell ill. Despairing comrades tried to nurse them on hardtack and salt pork. But both Lawrence and Tom Chamberlain thrived in these rough and risky conditions. Lawrence claimed that he never felt better in his life, and Tom, whose slight build and poor health worried those at home, eventually bragged in a letter that he weighed 150 lbs., "which is 30 Lbs more than I ever weighed before."[14]

Except for the sadness at leaving behind many comrades who would march no more, the regiment had little regret at leaving that scene of pestilence. On Nov. 3, Lawrence wrote to Fanny from Snicker's Gap. Expecting a fight, he declared it "an undignified name for a battle field...," while he confidently asserted that the 20th was ready. The 979 men who had left Portland two months before were whittled down to 550. Of those who remained, he wrote:

> *...what there are left are of the right sort. We marched suddenly from Antietam at night, the loveliest night you ever saw & thro one of the richest countries two days more of marching brought us here. You can find the place on that map I used to look so longingly at. If not buy a map, or send for one...so that you can keep the run of me, if I do run. We are now under Hooker who has command of the 1st Army. Hooker's Porter's & Franklin's corps are joined to make the finest army of the war, & the appearances are that we shall not be slighted in the coming battle. We shall certainly beat the Rebels this time, though I expect a hard fight. They are admirably handled & fight with desperation.*[15]

While Lawrence was exuberant at the army's movement, he had received two letters from Fanny, and several more from the family, containing requests to describe life with the army. Offering the testimony of his friend, the 20th's adjutant, John Marshall Brown of Portland, he wrote:

> *You have not much idea of how I look & fare. You may imagine that I am in a suffering condition, but I am not one of that sort. Mr. Brown says I am the most careless & improvident fellow he ever saw—take no care of myself at all—sleep on the ground when I have the whol [sic] Regt. at my command to make a house for me. But I hate to see a man always on the spring to get the best of every thing for himself. I prefer to take things as they come, & I am as well & comfortable as any body, & no one is the worse for it.*[16]

John Marshall Brown,
1/Lt. & Adjutant, 20th Maine Infantry.

Lawrence described settling down on the night of a bitter cold north-wester:

> *I take my saddle for a pillow—rubber talma for a bed—shawl for a covering & a big chestnut tree for a canopy & let it blow. A dashing rain & furious gale in the night make me put on a skull-cap (given me by the Major) & pull the talma over me—head & all—curl up so as to bring myself into a bunch—& enjoy it hugely. I would confess to any body but you, that I was cold— feet especially. However I enjoy it I say, & get up, (I don't say wake up) bright as a squirrel & hearty as a bear.*

He described his diet as sometimes coarse, with "salt pork or hard bread, with, maybe coffee with out milk & alas! without sugar," and sometimes "some luxury such as *you* seldom get. Say a supper of fig paste, jellies of all sorts, cans of preserves & fruits, &c—bought of some sutler at double price."

If Lawrence's selfless disregard and precarious lifestyle caused Fanny some anxiety, perhaps the following description of himself brought a smile:

> *Picture to yourself a stout looking fellow—face covered with beard—with a pair of cavalry pants on—sky blue—big enough for Goliath, & coarse as a sheep's back—said fellow having worn & torn & ridden his original suit quite out of the question—enveloped in a huge cavalry over coat (when it is cold) of the same color & texture as the pants; & when warm, the identical flannel blouse worn at Portland—cap with an immense rent in it, caused by a Picket raid when we were after Stuart's cavalry, a shawl & rubber talma strapped on behind the saddle & the over coat (perhaps), or the dressing case, before—2 pistols in holsters. Sword about three feet long at side—a piece of blue beef & some hard bread in saddlebags. This figure seated on a magnificent horse gives that peculiar point & quality of incongruity which constitutes the ludicrous. The Col. says the Regt is recognized every where by that same figure. Rebel prisoners praise the horse & the sword, but evidently take no fancy to the man.*[17]

More seriously, he added, "Do not be worried about me. I am in the right place, & no harm can come to me unless it is wisely & kindly ordered so. I try to be equal to my duty & ready for any thing that may come." As he finished his letter, he gave scant, almost impatient attention to Fanny's questions about preparing the house for winter.. His bright mood returned as he signed his letter, "With much reason to love you, & being as I contend, a reasonable man, you may draw the inferences. L!"[18]

He pointed out, when he wrote to Fanny the next day, that he almost burned the above letter, hoping to write a better one. But when the mail carrier came, "I put the poor thing in rather than miss sending any thing by that mail." Still near Snicker's Gap, the 20th now camped in a "fresh, sweet valley." Though on better ground, this region was still unpleasant. He wrote:

> *...it is difficult to get anything here, because the Rebels who live here will neither sell nor give. One amiable lady of whom we meekly requested some milk, said she would like to kill the whole of us. It is quite possible however that she indirectly contributed to our good living, for I am afraid*

our naughty boys helped themselves to a few pigs & turkeys & other delicate articles of diet, which must be had even if they could not be bought or accepted as presents.[19]

Such hostility is not likely to sweeten anyone's disposition, but there is a startling contrast of mood in these two letters, from exuberance to pessimism in the space of a day. Two months into his transition from civilian to soldier, and with time to consider Fanny's questions about the house and garden, Lawrence was likely beginning to realize the demands of being a military officer, while still a husband and father. A growing list of household tasks, all beyond his power to affect, likely weighed heavily upon him. He gave extensive instructions for his much-loved garden, and suggested moving the stoves and installing double windows. Fanny had also reiterated her wish to be near him. He offered "I do not expect you to spend the winter in Brunswick, though Aunty & the children will I suppose...." He suggested that she, after stopping to visit friends in Boston and New York along the way, could make her way to Washington or Baltimore. But all depended on the army's movements in the next months, a thing hard to predict, and his hope for any decisive action before the end of the year seemed to be dwindling:

I suppose our present campaign will be closed by Christmas at least, but I dont know where we shall go into winter quarters. Maybe near Washington, we hope Richmond, but possibly near here. We shall keep on fighting, I imagine, through the present administration. I see no signs of peace. Good fighting on both sides, but while we will not be beaten, still something seems to strike all the vigor out of our arms just at the point of victory. We have confidence in our officers, & are well prepared for the campaign, & hope for more decided results.[20]

Although all of the family wrote to Lawrence, he commented to Fanny: "Your letters are the only ones I receive. They do not come so often as I could wish, but I read them over often enough to make up. I like to hear all the little particulars you mention." Then, his spirits plunged, for he exclaimed: "Bless the dear children. I dont dare think of them too much. It makes me rather sad, & then I do not forget that I am here in the face of death every day. You must not let them dwell too much on me, & keep me too vividly in their affections. If I return they will soon relearn to love me, & if not, so much is spared them." As Lawrence continued the painful musing of an absent father, yearnings for a winter frolic with the children prompted him to scold Fanny about their winter clothing: "Provide all they need. *Dont* have them so lacking as they were last winter." He could well imagine, with not being there to initiate the outdoor romps that took him and the children out in all sorts of weather, that they might spend the winter cloistered near the warm parlor stove. Lastly, Lawrence addressed expressions of sadness and anxiety from Fanny, who was learning of the loneliness, anxieties, and new responsibilities of having a husband gone for a soldier:

I want you to be cheerful & occupy your mind with pleasant things, so as not to have time to grow melancholy. You must n't think of me much. I am in earnest. Invite the Juniors over to spend the evening with some of the

> *young ladies, as we used to, & keep up your character for hospitality, & your spirits at the same time. I shall write you as often as I can get an opportunity,—& you need not worry if you hear of a battle, until you know that I was in it: If I am injured, you will hear at once. I expect to get some sort of a scratch when we "go in", but the chances are it will not be serious if anything. Give my regards to my friends, & tell them I am beginning to understand my business, & shall probably be enabled to look them in the face again if I get home.*[21]

This letter, as well as conjecture over a possible debilitating fear of abandonment as a result of Fanny's early childhood adoption, has been offered as evidence that she was subject to bouts of reoccurring depression and instability. It is far more reasonable to view Fanny's expressions of concern and loneliness for her husband, gone just two months, as typical of anyone with a loved one gone to war.[22]

Fanny's response on Thanksgiving Day, 1862, minced no words regarding her ability to put thoughts of him aside: "We are all here together at Father's the children playing in great glee around us—making such a noise that we can hardly tell what we are thinking about. I, for one am hardly at a loss on that point however, for you have not been out of mind for one minute today, naturally enough. We have wanted you with us *terribly....*" She continued: "it has been very pleasant here, a beautiful dinner, the children all well and perfectly happy, tonight a charming table of fancy-cakes, bright red apples, nuts, candies and so forth, which made four pairs of bright eyes shine especially when the little hands that go with them had full liberty to help themselves." While assuring Lawrence that the children were happy, she made no such claim for herself: "...it is about time to go to our lonely home, you cannot imagine *how* lonely to *me*, this Thanksgiving night, when you ought to be at your own home, with all those who long to see you so." Perhaps taking assurance from the same salutation as in days gone by, she concluded: "Good bye for a little while With all love Fannie." During these difficult first weeks, Lawrence and Fanny, each dealing with stress and loneliness in their own way, had to learn ways to express love and support for each other as they adjusted to the new roles and duties that the war years demanded.[23]

Far away in camp, Lawrence brooded over the army's inability to strike a decisive blow against the Rebels. Lincoln, again impatient with McClellan, removed him from command, and appointed Gen. Ambrose Burnside in his place. Under Burnside's command, the Army of the Potomac began a promising movement to the southeast. But by December 2, Lawrence wrote to Fanny from Falmouth, Virginia, with an interesting description of the preparation of what, years later, he would call Lee's "death trap:"

> *We have been a week & are waiting nobody knows for what. All sorts of rumors arise of course, but our business is to obey orders & something will be done with it, I have no doubt. Saturday I rode over to the front, on the banks of the Rappahannock, only a few rods from the Rebels opposite in Fredericksburg. I rode along for some miles, & of course I had no difficulty seeing Rebels. They were busy as bees throwing up fortifications & planting cannon. They kept as much out of sight as possible in order not to show*

> *their force & movements. I did not feel fully comfortable, I own, in full view & reach of every one of those ugly looking cannon they are training to slaughter us by & by....*[24]

Assigned to picket duty in the last days of November, additional encounters with hostile Virginia civilians caused Lawrence to wonder at the wisdom of Union policy, for he continued:

> *The country is nearly all devastated in this part of the state & starvation pretty sure for some I cannot but believe.... Our generals are kind enough to place guards around every house that is inhabited & Rebel property is carefully protected from pillage. Our quartermasters it is true take whatever we must have & give receipts for it which are presented to the Govt, & pay obtained on them I suppose. I do not think the Rebels are treated very severely however. If this were really war we should not leave rabid secessionists within our lines to observe & give information while we protect them from loss or harm. I do not mean to question the propriety of the present policy. But regardless in a merely military point of view, the war would seem to be much more effectively carried forward if we should leave no Treachery in the midst of us or behind us—We should take horses, forage, cattle, &c send women & children & all nonresistants over the lines all active rebels to the rear that is to confinement within our line, & for every ship burned at sea fire a rebel courthouse, or even private houses worth $20,000 to $50,000. I tell you we should not have to fight the same ground over again, as we have here so many times. In that way we should weaken & crowd the enemy & at the same time strengthen & advance ourselves. Of course the country would be laid waste absolutely, but it would be war. We have not got over the old idea of suppressing a mob. Whatever cruelty there might seem to be in the course I indicated would be countervailed if the great saving of life & treasure in a speedier ending of the war. Now we take no advantages, use little or no strategy, but gain what we do by main force, by bearing on. Perhaps I speak strongly.... You may think I am very savage in what I have said, but it is to lessen animosity. I looked over at the Rebels in Fredericksburg, without the least blood-thirstiness though if the order had come to "charge" on them, I could have gone in with all the vigor & earnestness in the world.*[25]

Lawrence related his attempt to discover news of Fanny's uncle, Harold Wyllys, by questioning a prisoner from South Carolina. The Rebel officer knew nothing, and Lawrence offered the dubious reassurance: "I don't believe he was foolish enough to get hung after all his knowledge of the world." He also wrote his gratitude for a package of clothing Fanny had sent, and described how varied the weather was in camp:

> *The first day of December was a lovely day. I thought of you in my rude tent & grew rather lonely, till some duty took me away. You may imagine how warm it is, or perhaps how tough I am, when I say I took a full bath in 'Potomac creek' the first day of winter, without the least inconvenience. To be sure ice*

formed to quite a thickness the night before, but the days are delightful when it does not rain. Sometimes it snows—a wet driving snow—then I beg to assure you it is not particularly agreeable weather to experience.[26]

By December 6, the 20th Maine arrived at Stoneman's Switch on the railroad between Aquia Creek and Fredericksburg. There, they experienced a night so bitter that two men froze to death in their tents. These temperatures moderated, but not until December 13 did the Union attack of Fredericksburg begin, giving the 20th Maine their first real trial by fire.[27]

Fanny learned on December 11 that the bloody confrontation, expected for weeks, was underway. When the Army of the Potomac began to lay bridges to cross the Rappahannock, Rev. Adams, who avidly followed the news of the war, came to the little house on Potter Street to tell Fanny. By December 16, he glumly recorded, "disheartening news that Burnside w[a]s obliged to recross the river." How long it was before Fanny learned that Lawrence had survived the battle is not known. But he did not come through unscathed. Though he suffered only a slight wound on his right ear and neck, he also carried sights and sounds of that first battle that would be never forgotten,...forever remembered. The tortured days and nights that the 20th Maine spent on the field at Fredericksburg would, years later, inspire some of the eeriest and most moving of Chamberlain's writings of the war.[28]

James Frasca Collection

Fanny Chamberlain.

Several days passed before anyone in the North, other than high officials in Washington, knew of the disaster that the Army of the Potomac had experienced at Fredericksburg, where brigade after brigade was "handed in piecemeal, on toasting-forks" as Chamberlain bitterly described it. No soldier in that army needed to be told they had been dealt a bloody defeat. They had every reason to believe that the fighting was over for 1862, but unusually dry weather in December encouraged Burnside to attempt another strike against the Confederates. The failure of Burnside's infamous "Mud March" finally consigned the army to the harsh discomforts of unusually cold Virginia weather and the tedium of a winter camp plagued by shortages and disease.[29]

At the end of January, Chamberlain applied for a leave of absence to return to Maine ostensibly to oversee the appointment of new officers to fill vacancies in the 20th Maine. By February 6, he was on his way to Brunswick, and on the 10th, he was home. After months of hardship at the front, he would relish the quiet comforts of home and the solicitude of a loving family. How strange it seemed that life at home had gone on, unaltered, during all he had experienced in those five months. To his friends, he would say little of his experiences, or of the army's grim determination to pursue elusive victory. But he wanted Fanny to know something of his new life, and as he traveled to Augusta on the regiment's business, Fanny prepared to accompany him when he returned to Virginia.[30]

Lawrence went directly from Augusta back to the army, stopping in Brunswick on February 17 just long enough to meet Fanny, who traveled with him to Washington. It is unlikely that Fanny continued on with Lawrence to the 20th's encampment until a pass was arranged and some accommodations were made at camp for her visit. But as she waited for permission to join him, she was already getting her first views of the army in wartime Washington. Lines of wagons and artillery, cavalry and infantry troops passed through at all hours of the day and night. Soldiers crowded the sidewalks and hotels of the capital. The many hospitals in the city brought sad sights of sick and wounded who arrived in streams of ambulances, as well as their distraught families and friends who had come to search for them.[31]

In the weeks that Fanny spent at the 20th Maine's camp, she experienced many aspects of camp life, from the captivating serenades of the regimental bands to the all too frequent processions that accompanied lost comrades to their final resting places. With Lawrence, she rode on horseback through the countryside, and shared one night when a storm assaulted their flimsy shelter with snow, hail, thunder, and lightning so fierce that one wag commented that the Rebels had flanked them again, for they had "got overhead."[32]

Fanny returned to Washington near the end of March, hoping to obtain another pass and return to the regiment, but when she applied on April 9, the situation had changed drastically. In the last weeks of March, the men of the 20th had received tainted vaccine against smallpox, which, far from protecting them, brought the most dreaded disease of the war into the regiment. Fanny's request for a pass was forwarded with the statement: "The brave, wife of Lieut Col. Chamberlain of the 20th Reg. Me Vol is very anxious to visit her husband at the Camp near Stoneman's station and he as earnestly desires to see her." The first man died on April 11 and succeeding days brought more deaths. By April 17, 84 of the Maine men were laid low, 32 of them gravely ill. By April 21, a fence was put up around the regiment. And on April 23, the regiment was moved away from the brigade.[33]

As the 20th Maine moved into quarantine, rumors abounded that the Army of the Potomac, now under the command of Gen. Joseph Hooker, would soon move. Fanny waited for news of Lawrence in Washington, where any hint of army action brought great excitement. Though his soldiers were calling it "Camp Small Pox," Lawrence discreetly headed his letter of April 24, "New Camp," and though he seethed with frustration, he managed a relatively upbeat opening:

> *It has rained pouring ever since we started to move camp, so that the most we could do was to get our things into a tolerable compact heap, & keep them from a thorough wetting. I had some important letters to write this evening, & have been scrambling about to prepare for it— looking up the dry side of a board for a table— ransacking after a piece of candle & pen, ink & paper— humming a little air meantime to counteract the gloomy influence of storm & confusion, when I found that I had been singing in the air of "Sleeping I dream Love," this very foolish & boyish song, "First to my Dear one, First to my Love. Because I am always thinking first of you. You were too sad, Darling, when you wrote, but my mind was dwelling on you, even more than usual, all that very time. I do not think you can have any particular occasion to feel apprehensive either for yourself or for me. I trust that before this time you are in a happier mood.*
>
> *The most that troubles me now is that I may not be able to take part in the next fight. Here we are in an isolated camp, with direful looking placards posted at every entrance 'Small Pox', the Surgeons giving opinion that we cannot move for a fortnight at least. If in the mean time there is a battle, & I am left here in a pest-house, I shall be desperate with mortification. I have tried to make conditional arrangements to get placed on some General's staff but things are so uncertain in regard to the Army & our Regt. that even this could not be done at present.*[34]

To make matters worse, word had come of the death of Lawrence's Brunswick patron, Capt. Joseph Badger, the banker who provided financing for the Chamberlains' home. Chamberlain was named an executor of his estate, and the immediacy of this obligation, with its lucrative compensation, only heightened Lawrence's frustration. He informed Fanny:

> *Meantime I have had printed notice of an appointment for the proving & allowing of Capt. Badger's Will on the first Tuesday in May, & if I have any thing to do with it as an Executor, it is necessary for me to be present, at that time & place. Nothing would induce me to be absent from my Regt when they went into a battle, and even if they did not engage, I should make every effort to...obtain permission to render some service personally on the field. Now if I were at all sure there would be a movement within a fortnight, & I could be permitted to take an honorable part in a battle, I would throw up all idea of serving as Executor in this case. But you see every*

thing is uncertain—the probability is that I could attend to this matter & return before the Regt., at any rate, moves. At the same time it seems half disgraceful to ask for leave of absence just when it is possible there may be a battle impending. You see my perplexity. If the settling of this estate were a matter of ordinary importance I might easily forego all thought of it. But it seems hardly right for me to neglect a business of so much interest to me personally; for I suppose Capt. B. intended by appointing me to do me a favor in the pecuniary advantage it would be to execute this trust. If I should give it up now, & then find that I must stay here in this hospital camp a longer time than I should require to transact the business it would be a great vexation. I feel quite puzzled,—cornered expresses it.[35]

When he completed this letter on April 27, his obligations were clear. Ames had managed to join Meade's staff as a volunteer aide. Chamberlain now commanded the regiment:

Well here we are at length—left—the Col. [Ames] gone, & I put in charge of the Regt. we saw our Division & Brigade move off, & we felt lonesome, I assure you. However by not granting me permission to go forward, I suppose the Regt will be ordered to move very soon. I wish you could be here now. I could endure it. I suppose I shall have to give up the Badger Will case which I am sorry to do. You do not know how I want to see you, dearest, this disappointment in not being able to go on with the army, nor obtaining leave to go & attend to the will business, keeping me in a sick camp I do not at all enjoy. I have not the slightest idea when or where I shall go next. You had better go on without me where ever you wish.[36]

Fanny, realizing that she could not go to Lawrence, nor could he come to her, left Washington. Beset by the worry of Lawrence's exposure to small pox, as well as his determination to get himself into the impending battle, she traveled only as far as New York City. On her arrival at the St. Germaine Hotel, Fanny notified Cousin Deborah, who had charge of the children in Brunswick with the assistance of a Mrs. Harris as housekeeper. Fanny also wrote Lawrence of her whereabouts, but it would be many weeks before he received her letter. Nor would all her letters to Deborah reach their destination.[37]

At the end of May, Fanny still waited in New York for word from Lawrence. Sae, at home in Brewer, expressed shock that Fanny was away from home for so long, and commented in a letter to brother Tom, "Did you ever *hear* of such a thing." Yet perhaps the ever-dutiful Sae longed, at times, to be a part of the exciting events beyond her world. For she responded curtly to Tom's question of whether she, too, had been away: "All sorts of work are to be done in the spring, you know," and she reminded him that John, now the only son at home, worked all the time in the garden. Sae also told Tom of the hero's welcome Bangor had given the two-year men of the 2nd Maine on their return from the front. As for the marching soldiers, "...nobody could get a chance to speak to their friends Some women ran right in among them and kept along in the procession, talking & crying. I didn't blame them a mite—. I dont know but I should have done just so—"[38]

Thomas D. Chamberlain as a captain.

When Fanny's next letter failed to reach Brunswick, Cousin Deborah wrote to Fanny's sister Catherine in Boston, voicing her concern. On June 1, Katie, as she was called, responded to a letter she had received from Lawrence by sending along much of Cousin Deborah's news: "My letter I have received enclosed in yours to Fannie, shall keep hers until I am fortunate enough to hear from or see her, which has not been my fortune as yet—" Katie cited passages about Daisy and Wyllys from Deborah's letter that would warm their father's heart: "...the children are busy as bees, making their gardens & digging the sand. They are getting to be quite helpful. Daisy's daily task is to feed the chickens which is a great pleasure to her. Yesterday she aspired to washing dishes and succeeded admirably. They are very good children easily governed." But Katie also included a quotation from Deborah's letter that was less pleasing: "Wyllys asks *where Mama's house is now*, & Daisy would like to see her but they are very happy." Katie had another reason to be annoyed at her sister's failure to write or appear, for Lawrence had invited Katie's daughter Julia to accompany Fanny when she returned to the 20th's camp. "Julie was delighted with her invitation to visit the Army but as Fannie has not been heard from, conclude the matter settled, that she will be to [sic] late to return to you this season." Fanny and Lawrence had expressed concern for Julia over the past months. They feared that in her anxiety to find a husband, as Lawrence described it, "...Julia, sweet girl that she is, will...throw herself away on some chance acquaintance for the sake of securing that apparently 'only hope' which they speak of so much."

Katie also speculated, though incorrectly, on Fannie's whereabouts:

I think she has gone to see Sam[ue]l, who has recently buried his wife, and who is now living at David's Island. He has a situation at the United States General Hospital there—I am sorry she neglects writing you of all others. It is too bad unless there is a good excuse. Cousin Deborah says, "that her last letter to her was 29th April St. Germaine Hotel, NY. She intimated in this letter that she should soon be in Boston and I supposed she was long ago—" But no. She may come this week. I hope she will and relieve all anxiety.[39]

Catherine's letter was hardly a missive to cheer a weary soldier or reassure an anxious husband. Unaware that one of Fanny's letters had never arrived, Cousin Deborah, receiving a letter from New York in early June, wrote, "Oh Fanny if I am not vexed with you awfully vexed with you, to think you should let your indolence so far overcome your sense of propriety as to be all this time at the St Germaine & not write to any living being to let them know where you are." Declaring that the children could have been dead and buried without Fanny's knowledge, she conceded that Daisy and Wyllys were, in fact, "wild as hawks" running after the chickens in the yard. Deborah described herself as quite lame, and reported that several women were helping with work around the house. Though writing that she had not paid any bills that were due during Fanny's absence, Deborah answered one of Fanny's concerns: "Do not feel any apprehension that we do not have enough to eat & that which is good, we fare sumptuously every day...." She also wrote that Catherine and family, unbeknownst to Fanny, had moved from their old address in Boston. Lost and late letters continued to cause anxiety and confusion for all.[40]

On June 13, the 20th Maine marched to join the Army of the Potomac in its northerly pursuit of Lee's army. While halted near Manassas Junction on June 15, Lawrence wrote a quick reply to a letter from Cousin Deborah: "Have been on the double quick for two days. We are expecting an attack every moment. Clouds of dust following our rear promise a little sport by morning. We are only a few miles from the old Bull Run Battle field, & probably shall have Bull Run 3. I have 500 men & we are in good spirits, though hard-marched. Look out for news from these parts." Replying to Deborah's inquiry if he would consider selling his house, Lawrence wrote, "My house I will sell (if you & the children can find shelter for your heads) for $2,500 dollars. It cost me that in money." Oblivious to the fact that Deborah now knew where Fanny was, Lawrence told her: "Fanny is not here & I have no idea where she is."[41]

Fanny, unaware that none of her recent letters had reached Lawrence, believed he knew that she waited for news of him in her New York hotel. With no word since she left Washington, she was determined to know something of her husband before she traveled toward home. In the first days of July, city papers poured forth news that the Army of the Potomac had met the Army of Northern Virginia at Gettysburg. At home in Brewer, Mother and Father Chamberlain, with sister Sae, could only guess where any of their three boys were. John Chamberlain, having finally succumbed to his brothers' invitations to visit them at the front, had left Brewer on June 1. Sae, also invited, had, as John later observed, "debated a long time the propriety of accepting" and "wisely gave it up." After a series of misadventures, John reached his brothers at the end of June in time to look after Lawrence, prostrated with sunstroke, but insistent on traveling with his column. John would get to see more of army life than he ever wanted.[42]

Recovering sufficiently to lead the 20th Maine in their historic stands at Little and Big Round Tops, Chamberlain, managing to find paper, pen, and ink, scribbled a note to Fanny, one day after the Union victory at Gettysburg. Directing his letter to Brunswick, he wrote:

> *Dear Fanny,*
>
> *We are fighting gloriously. Our loss is terrible, but we are beating the Rebels as they were never beaten before. The 20th has immortalized itself. We had the post of honor in the severe fight of the 2d, on the extreme left where the enemy made a fierce attempt to turn the flank. My Regt was the extreme left & was attacked by a whole Brigade. We not only held our ground but charged on the Rebels & drove them out of all sight & sound, killing & wounding over 100 & taking 200 prisoners, including 6 officers one the inspector Gen. of the Brigade. I received the thanks of my superior officers on the field. After our charge I was asked if my men could carry a high hill, which was a strong hold of the enemy—being covered with trees & large rocks. I had lost at that time almost half the effective men I took in, but I went in with charged bayonets & line of battle & swept every thing before us, taking many prisoners. Col. Vincent is mortally wounded—the greatest loss that could have befallen the Brigade. Six officers in the 20th wounded—130 killed & wounded. I am receiving all sorts of praise, but bear it meekly. Our army is in fine spirits. Many Generals on our side are killed. Ames & Brown of the 11th Corps have covered themselves with glory. You shall hear from [me] soon again, if I am spared. I shall tell of little incidents, such as my taking officers prisoners, & receiving sword & pistols &c. We captured one whole Rebel Regt. Hoping you are all well. Yours. L.*[43]

Fanny waited through the alarming reports of the battle at Gettysburg and its aftermath. When a week passed, she dared to believe that no news of Lawrence meant that he had survived unhurt. But any attempt to leave New York became impossible. On July 11, violence against the draft became rioting that paralyzed the city. During the chaos, Fanny finally received news from Lawrence when Cousin Deborah included one of his letters in her own. Relieved to have word at last, yet dismayed that her letters were reaching neither Brunswick nor Lawrence in the field, Fanny's reply to Deborah on July 16 displayed an uneasy state of mind, jumping from subject to subject, as she was wont to do when upset or excited:

> *I was rejoiced to receive the letter from you just now. What about your lameness? You never told me of it at all. You cannot have received the letter I wrote you before the last one, for you have not answered it, and you make no allusion whatever to any thing in it. I was perfectly*

rejoiced to have the letter, (short as it was) from Lawrence. I knew he must be safe, as I told in my letter, but I wanted to see his own hand writing. As for candy for the precious little children, I bought them some the first week I was in the city; I do not forget them I assure you. You are mistaken my dear Cousin D. in thinking it was my fault not hearing from you and Lawrence. I have written Lawrence three letters that I can distinctly remember, to which I have received no answer. They will perhaps reach him some time, if the Rebels have not taken them. As to your drawing the money from the bank, I expected you to do it. it was put there to use, and I hope we shall be having some more soon. I hope you are having and have been having, everything you want. The children shall be dressed up when I come. Poor Daisy's shaker must be looking forlorn. Did you get a letter from me beginning "I have just been to see Mary Larabee" and so forth? if not, then the one before the last you did not receive. It was a great risk sending the money in the letter, but thanks to Providence it came safely. I should not risk it again, however. The proprietor here says it was not safe. Do you know at all what terrible scenes we have been through with in New York since last Sunday? and the end is not yet they say. Fifth Ave. Hotel last night had 400 soldiers inside as a guard besides cannon in the door-way and cavalry in the park opposite. Murders & robberies are committed any where & every where in the Streets even at noonday. Houses are burned all over the city. Negroes are caught in the Street and literally drawn and quartered and hung upon lamp posts and trees. Every gentleman that goes out of our Hotel takes his loaded revolver with him. One of them came in the other night with his face beaten black, his costly watch stolen, and pocket book with $180 in it. There is no police-man to be seen; they are murdered by the whole sale. The fiendish mob has had entire possession of the city. It began in resistance to the Draft. I have not been out of the house since Monday [July 13], and it was not safe, but I had been at Mrs Darling's to dinner Sunday and had spent the night there (by invitation) and wanted to get home. They are expecting an attack upon the Fifth Ave. Hotel tonight. A foreigner in the house tells me he has been in revolutions in France, and this is much worse than he ever saw there. Soldiers with bayonets and citizens with revolvers perambulate the Streets, but they are powerless in the hands of the terrible mob. Horace Greeley just escaped with his life. And they were going to hang Mr Hitchcock of the Fifth Ave. for being an Abolitionist, if he had not secretly fled for Europe.[44]

At the St. Germaine Hotel on the corners of 22nd St., Broadway and 5th Ave. in New York City's 18th ward, Fanny had every right to be frightened. The mobs waged their worst fights with the police and soldiers within a few blocks of her hotel, where the gunfire and the volleys of the troops were clearly audible. Under siege for days, the police station of the 18th ward was burned. Yet Fanny's thoughts again flew to worries of home and Lawrence at the front:

I hope your lameness is not going to be serious dear Aunty. what in the world caused it? I think I shall start for home in several days now, but if I hear that there is to be another battle very soon, I shall stay awhile. I expect to stop in New Haven long enough to see about our sewing machine, but I think I cannot stop in Boston now, as Commencement is so near. Your letter was written July 11th and now it is the 16th. How was it so long in coming? It is now only about 2 weeks to Commencement only think of it. I am afraid to have the Children go across the Railroad track alone Aunty dont let them do it. With great relief at having heard from you, and rejoicing that the children are well, I am your's affec. Fannie[45]

On July 17, Lawrence at last received one of Fanny's letters. From a camp near Berlin, Maryland, he wrote:

My dear Fanny

I was much surprised to have a letter from you dated New-York. I have been writing you at Brunswick. I wrote you on my knee in the battle of Gettysburg, after our terrible fight, in which the 20th held the post of honor on the extreme left of the whole army where the fiercest attack was made. I will tell you some time of the magnificent conduct of the Regt. I was attacked by a whole Rebel Brigade & after two hours fighting during which we exhausted our ammunition & snatched the full cartridge boxes from the dead & dying friend & foe, & when that was gone & we were pressed two to one, & had lost one hundred & forty from the field, we charged & utterly routed the whole Brigade—killed & wounded 150, & took 308 prisoners & 300 stand of arms.

Afterwards I was ordered to carry a height with my remaining 200—& did it—at the point of the bayonet—an achievement which Gen Sykes said was one of the most important of the day, & for which I recd the personal thanks of all my commanders. When we were relieved & I rode off from the field at the head of my little scarred & battle-stained band the Brigade Commander took me by the hand, & said "Col C. your gallantry was magnificent, & your coolness & skill saved us." I left 32 noble fellows dead—gathered them all & laid them side by side in the grave, one hundred wounded, some are dying some recovering—one of my finest Lieuts. was killed— Kendall & Capt Billings very seriously wounded 5 other officers wounded not seriously. Poor Vincent fell early in the fight & died a day or two after. I grieve for him much. The Pres. made him a General before he died, but he was unconscious. I am going to write Mrs. V. & I wish you would.[46]

Lawrence spared Fanny a description of his near lethal confrontation with one Lt. Wicker of the 15th Alabama, who fired his pistol at Chamberlain's head before surrendering his sword. He merely quipped, "Fanny I took several officers in the fight prisoners—& one of them insisted on presenting me a free pistol—as reward of merit I suppose. Sword &c plenty." Of the harrowing sights of the battlefield on July 5, he only said: "What fighting that was. 1000 dead horses lay on field torn by shell, & half as many men, in one small field." But he returned to his expressions of pride at what he & the 20th had accomplished: "These prisoners of mine were fierce fellows from Texas & Alabama—they said they had never before been stopped." Turning to Fanny's dilemma in a riot-torn city, Lawrence exclaimed: "But New York! I am sorry you are there. It is not safe to try to get away is it? I wish you were at home. You should have been there before."[47]

While the last pages of this letter are missing, his last words, "I have been very danger-..." undoubtedly informed Fanny of his serious illness before Gettysburg and his precarious health ever since. Though ill and new to command, Chamberlain had proven to himself and his men that he had the courage and cool head to command. Writing to Fanny, as he did, on his knee the day after the battle, Lawrence wanted her to know how his life had been irrevocably changed. The weeks before the battle had cut off all communication between them. Yet Lawrence came to understand that Fanny, through days of anxiety and perplexity, had waited for him, ready to go to him should he be sick or wounded, or to be with him should he be spared. The fates of war would often separate them, yet new bonds formed between them that the difficult years ahead would nearly sunder, but never break.[48]

CHAPTER

12

"There Can Be No Home without Country...No Life without Honor"

There was little opportunity for the 20th Maine to rest or refit. The remaining days of July were spent with the Army of the Potomac pushing down the east side of the Blue Ridge, in hopes of intercepting and striking at Lee's army. Lawrence, in temporary command of the 3rd Brigade since mid-July, wrote to Fanny on the 24th from Manassas Gap near Front Royal:

My Dear Girl,

You must be astonished to see where successive letters are dated: especially if you happen to have (as I once suggested) a tolerably minute map of the theatre of war. Here, for once, in this famed 'Gap' of the Blue Mountains. Your noble '5th corps' is up here with the 3d to take this important pass from the Rebels. Well, my dearest, they have done it; so don't worry. We have just returned from the final pursuit, one of the very hardest we ever had in the way of natural obstacles, craggy ascents, deep ravines—mountain torrents, treacherous morasses—wild vines & woody thickets—all these in the burning sun & at the 'double quick'. I tell it wears men out to encounter all these for twelve or twenty four hours. Last night the 3d corps had a fight—a pretty severe one in carrying a crest—murderously shelled by the Rebels. at sunset we went up to relieve them & this morning Griffin's Division was ordered to clear them off a very steep & densely wooded hill at the outer throat of the pass. The pleasant duty of taking the front was assigned to the 3d Brigade, the left the most exposed to a flank attack was given to the 20th. up we went like tigers— 'your friend & servt. about twenty five yards ahead of his gallant boys— with a good solid company on the flank as skirmishers to prevent surprise—up a mountain side of the roughest sort. The Rebs. left. we got only two specimens. We had to bury half a dozen of them afterwards but the stronghold was free from them, & so we have just marched back a little & gone into camp—tired to death completely wet through as a result of toil & heat.

What a lovely spot this is where I am camped on a...mountain side overlooking all the beautiful valleys—on one side the valley of the Shenandoah lying like a sweet meadow as seen from here—in the distance an immense Rebel column moving rapidly down toward some lower pass of the mountains, but too many or too far away for us to attack—on our side twenty thousand men to fight encamped in their little white tents, or winding down the hill sides opposite. What a magnificent scene. Would that you might lie here under my one little piece of shelter tent—in a cosy [sic] cleft of rocks—the glorious stars & stripes our loved color—the 20ths—more battle rent than ever, but the fringe still on, clinging like true love, because fastened by the true and loving hands—marking my head Quarters gaily streaming out in the mountain breeze. How happy I should be with my darling here for a little while just to enjoy this with me. You know I am not well yet that will account for my slight unsoundness of mind in a remark I just made to Col. Rice about a sweet smiling valley between the soft blue hills— 'It is a vale of love, between the breasts of the Mountain'. Shall I be forgiven? and yet I half believe I should have said it to you, if you had been here—a soldier is bold you know. I am writing you though I shall not have a chance to send the letter for several days. night—moonlight—we move very early so I try to send this to Washington. Good night darling I shall lie looking at the moonlight on the mountains—& in that 'vale' & dream myself there. A kiss & thousand thoughts of you till the early bugle call.[1]

Considering the hard marches, rough living, and his precarious health, Chamberlain was in high spirits when he wrote this. Within days, however, his strength was gone. On the night of July 25, in command of the division's pickets, he rode with Capt. Spear of the 20th to the front, hoping to get the pickets out before a threatening storm broke. But drenching rain overtook them as they posted their men, aided only by flashes of lightning as they moved through dark unknown fields and woods. By July 27, he asked for a 20-day leave. "I am convinced that I can no longer continue these duties without the most serious consequences." The examining surgeon pronounced him to be suffering from nervous exhaustion and leave was recommended. By July 30, Lawrence was on his way to Washington, D.C. for treatment, the very day Fanny arrived home in Brunswick, unaware of his illness.

Lawrence left Washington on August 3 with a fifteen-day leave, arriving home on August 6. That evening, a service of thanksgiving in Rev. Adams' church celebrated the Union victories of Gettysburg and Vicksburg. In an informal address that Rev. Adams pronounced "capital," Lawrence spoke to the congregation. The members of the First Parish Church closed their meeting with the singing of "America."[2]

Rest and good care at home, where the cooler air was a tonic after the stifling heat of Virginia, revived Lawrence. By August 12, to his parents' delight, he traveled to Brewer with Fanny and Daisy for a day or two. After returning home on the 17th, his Brunswick doctor insisted that he could not return to the field for another week. But news of Col. Rice's promotion to brigadier general arrived, as well as Chamberlain's appointment by Gen. Griffin to replace Rice as commander of the 3rd Brigade. Some senior officers were absent and Rice, who longed to go home to his wife, asked Chamberlain to return to duty. By August 25, he was back at the 20th's encampment at Beverly Ford.[3]

Several days after Chamberlain's return to the army, a ghastly duty was performed that troubled the soldiers of his brigade as no battlefield horrors had done. The 1st Division of the 5th Corps formed three sides of a hollow square to witness the execution of five Union deserters. In this week of brutal realities, an affectionate letter from Fanny provided a reminder of the world away from such scenes. Lawrence replied:

> *Dearest*
>
> *The bugle has just sounded before my door on this hill. '3d Brigade, Extinguish lights!' Your sleepy head is tired—but the dear letter just received must have a word of answering love before any lights are extinguished in these quarters. I am happy to think of you as at home again—now my little dear ones are all nestled together— 'all'—I paused over that word—the tears filled my eyes—a dull, heavy pain flowed over my heart. I could not have spoken then. But it is all well & bright with her, whose sweet face still shines in my heart. Come & let me kiss your dear lips precious wife—sad mother—let our hearts worship together God's love & wisdom & mercy. Yes all is well—well with us, darling—well if we can only meet at last, as I pray God we may, never to part. I overheard you & dear Daisy making your prayer for me, & I thought how many a night when I was out on some perilous duty, or in some fierce storm & hardship, that gentle prayer has gone up for me. Then too on other nights not outwardly so dangerous, I dare say I have been in peril of forgetting God & his goodness, & that prayer has been heard for me. You were in "two moods." So I am, always, when I write you Especially last night when I wrote you. You would not miss it at all if you were to tell me of the "dreamy love." If you are tempted to write of "facts"—write about that fact. I do not have much of the beautiful & spiritual said or done to me here. Oh, ho! you want to be liked. Well, that will do—a girl that is loved so much that she longs to be liked! But there's sense & logic in that too. And did you ever think of that word like—it carries an idea of things reciprocally befitting—of a certain agree-*

ableness—of similarity—likeness in fact. Yes, Miss Fanny I like you if I may pay myself that compliment after the analytical definition. If I might be so bold, I do like you for I am like you. Sufficiently unlike for all practicable purposes (& some impracticable ones!) & all the more "like" for being not the same. I suppose you think you are a pretty likely girl intrinsically & absolutely & it was doubtless my opinion to the same effect which set me to liking you.[4]

I told you about the "two eyes" didnt I. Dont you get my letters? Oh yes it hadnt time to reach you by the 27th. Well you will see how they struck me. I had no business staring in a girl's face, but I could not help just stepping out to take a nearer view of that one somehow. But where is the picture—the card picture of you? and can you send me a "proof" of mine? Love & liking.[5]

Secure in the support of a loving wife and family, Chamberlain enjoyed the confidence of his commanding officers, many of whom recommended in the fall of 1863 that he be appointed a brigadier general of volunteers. But it was many months, and under dire circumstances, before he achieved that rank. Chamberlain shouldered the responsibility of a brigade commander with relish. Successfully meeting the challenges of military command appealed to his ideals of manhood and duty. But it is no small puzzle how this man of peaceful pursuits so readily adapted to the role of soldier. Previously a champion of spiritual and academic enlightenment, who had now forsaken both callings, where on the bloody fields of war did he find that ideal that sanctioned, even blessed his defections from pulpit and schoolroom, home and loved ones? Did he believe that any cause was worth the carnage and suffering of the war?[6]

The answer to these questions may be found in the thousands of words that Chamberlain wrote after the war, for himself, his comrades and their families, and his countrymen. In an address made shortly after the war, Chamberlain gave perhaps his most intimate feelings on the conflagration. It may explain why he embraced this calling with a passionate satisfaction, so enhanced by a sense of self-sacrifice for a cause he called worthy. He declared, "There can be no home without a country & no life without honor," for he held that failure of the Union cause would not only be the death of the country, but of our experiment in democracy, letting a "darkness fall upon the anxious eyes of humanity." For those who believed, as he did, that the principles on which the United States was founded provided the best hope for the future of mankind, their defense took on aspects of a holy mission. Yet it was the faces of those dearest to him that rose before him in the terrible moments of battle. He asked his fellow veterans:

Tell me if in the fierce carnival of death, in the mad uproar of charge and countercharge did not then a fair pale face amid the hideous phantoms of smoke and flame lure you on more than the tempting batteries you were sweeping to win? And when summoned to storm the crest rolling down an avalanche of fire, which it were madness for mortal to dare, tell me were there not visions that beckoned more brightly than your advancing banners?

He asserted, "Is it not thus also that love may conquer death?" For him, the soldier's strength, what kept them fighting during the blackest days of war, was the knowledge that they fought, not only for the future of their loved ones, but for the common good of all people. Is it any wonder that years later, he referred to the men who gave their lives at Little Round Top, as the "sons of God!"[7]

Still encamped at Beverly Ford, a letter to Fanny on September 12, 1863, begins brightly enough, but drops into sadder reverie. It is an odd, yet revealing expression of his reverence for a symbol of the sacrifices being laid on the altar of home and country:

> *Are the cheeks pale or rosey[sic] this hot noon tide? I hope the Darling of my home is happy. How I think of you sitting here evenings under the shelter of the "fly," in front of my tent, looking out upon the waterfall foamy & misty, & farther upon the broad spreading river reflecting the trees upon the banks & winning my gaze & almost my feet like the "Green River" of my school boy days. I dreamed last night that many ladies were coming to camp, & I was all excitement to have you come. But I suppose we shall have something else upon our hands before a great while. This war, I suppose you can see, is rapidly coming to a close issue, & the heavy fighting is nearly over. We may see one or two battles more like Gettysburg, though many doubt even that. I did not tell you about Mrs Vincents present from the Col's. staff. It was an oval breast pin, nearly two inches long—the stone was onyx—an emblem of mourning I believe. Inlaid—cut in—was an exquisite oval wreath of forget-me-nots in diamonds—The border (outside edge of setting) was of little pearls, close-lying, & each riveted with a gold pin, the head of which projected slightly & seemed to add beauty even to the pearly beads. On the reverse was written— (inscribed somehow is a better word) in ornamental characters (the name at least was) His Staff in remembrance of Gen. Strong Vincent The back was hinged—making a locket inside of which might be placed any gentle memento such as a lock of hair—How sad—sad—sad—& yet could any thing be more exquisite in taste & significance? To me it was a poem—unutterable sad—yet darkly beautiful. I have sat, or lain, dreamily gazing with an inner sense, on that wonderful memento hours together. We rough soldiers have at least some remnants of feeling & taste—dont you think so—or else such a gem as that never could have been conceived of.*[8]

Here he launched into the saga of a different kind of loss—evidence that he returned to the army before his strength was regained. With fond exclamations and mischievous teasing, he continued:

> *It is hot noon, my precious one, but I love you even at noon! Before dinner too;—Ah rogue you scold me about losing the sweet pickles, but the logic was poor...would you have me "lug" that big heavy thing all the way to the Rappahannock—weak as I was? Moreover if you were late in getting to Boston & had to drive like John to reach the New York Depot, would you have dragged that great pack into a coach already crammed full of men.... Fan, you pretty butterfly, how you do spell. 'advise', you ask for;—bussiness*

inadvertent no doubt, and then—dont think I would care how an angel spelled a loving word to me—'dreamyly'—you darling, sweet girl, it is dreamily. How are your pretty roly-poly horns, or 'rats'—or whatever you call the puffs of hair I plague you about. Good day![9]

On October 1, Chamberlain was assigned to serve on a court martial board, some indication that his health was failing. But he rejoined his brigade for a grueling series of marches and countermarches that brought the army to Rappahannock Station on November 7. Weak with malaria and overworked, his condition reached a crisis when he slept unsheltered on the ground during a snowstorm. On Nov. 15, Chamberlain signed a request for sick leave, his signature all but unrecognizable. By the time he was sent to a Washington hospital in a railway cattle car, he was unconscious.[10]

Constantly changing camps had delayed all mail to and from the brigade. Not until November 21 did Fanny receive a letter from 3rd Brigade's headquarters telling her of Lawrence's illness:

Madam—I am muched pained to be obliged to inform you that your husband, our Colonel, is quite ill. He was taken sick Friday evening; he had seemed during the day indisposed and late in the afternoon was so much worse that a Surgeon was summoned. He is attacked with malarial fever. He is not in serious danger, but the fever is slow in spending its force and leaves one very low. He will probably start for Washington tomorrow, and thinks of entering the Officers' Hospital in Georgetown, D.C. "Seminary Hospital," where all letters will reach him. It is possible that the Surgeons there may think it best for him to proceed North. The Colonel insists that his illness has been brought on by his own carelessness. For the past two weeks we have been greatly exposed and your husband has, I am sure, endured greater privations than any private soldier. Allow me to tender you my warmest sympathy, and to express the hope of the colonel's speedy recovery.[11]

With no help at home and unable to leave the children in the aging Deborah's care, Fanny must have been relieved when Sae "volunteered for service," traveling to Washington to care for her brother. Several days after his arrival at the Georgetown Seminary Hospital, Sarah Sampson, a remarkable woman from Maine who nursed the state's soldiers and supervised getting supplies to the men during the war, wrote to Fanny that Lawrence showed no signs of improvement. But by the time Rev. Adams and his family gathered at Fanny's on Thanksgiving, they had reassuring news that Lawrence, though still confined to bed, was slowly gaining.[12]

With the deficiencies of the mail service, it is hard to know when a letter that Cousin Deborah wrote on October 25 found Lawrence. Deborah wrote that it had been many weeks since they had heard from him, while she praised Fanny for writing to Lawrence every week, though she despaired of her letters reaching him. But this was the only compliment Deborah gave Fanny. Though she had great affection for the family, Cousin Deborah was still capable of being as critical and tactless as ever. Describing their misery since they had lost their "girl of all work," she offered a recitation of Fanny's faults: She did not get up until 9:00 a.m. Nor did she remember to feed the chickens until 4:00 p.m. And when visitors came, Fanny kept them waiting until she dressed, "which you remember is not done in a minute. I talk and scold and advise, but to no purpose." Deborah also reported that "Rev. Whittlesey is disposed in his widowhood to be quite social, he has taken tea with us twice once by invitation once by proposition. He comes with a covetous eye, your commission in the army & your house here would satisfy him.—" Reverend Eliphalet Whittlesey had become professor of rhetoric and oratory after Lawrence, but was then a captain in the army. He was, in fact, anxious to buy the Chamberlains' house. Deborah, aware of Lawrence's former jealous proclivities, should have been more judicious in expressing her observations. Yet Deborah redeemed herself with descriptions of the children as miracles of health. Her portrayal of the homey scene of Fanny washing dishes as Daisy read Mother Goose and Wyllys played with his blocks presented a charming scenario. She also wrote: "They seem to realise [sic] more & more every day that they have a Papa somewhere in the world & when he comes, skin horses and pony rides will be every day amusements."[13]

Not until December 18 could Lawrence endure the trip to Brunswick, arriving home feeble and exhausted. With his family for Christmas and New Years for the first time since 1861, he regained his strength, and by the middle of January 1864, he attended Brunswick gatherings. Assigned to light duty on a court-martial board in Washington, D.C., by February 1, he was in the nation's capital, where Fanny joined him several weeks later. By mid-March, as Gen. Ulysses S. Grant was appointed general-in-chief of the armies, Lawrence grew apprehensive that the spring campaign might start early.[14]

As winter ended, Lawrence and Fanny made a trip to Gettysburg. The dead of the 20th Maine had been reinterred in the new National Cemetery. But for Lawrence, they would always be there on Little Round Top, where their comrades had placed them, "side by side, with the touch of the elbow still." He walked with Fanny over the rocky hill, of which he would declare, "every feature of this ground is emblazoned on my very sight."[15]

During their stay at 402 13th Street in Washington, Lawrence and Fanny took advantage of the theater and other amenities in Washington, which Fanny enjoyed very much. But by mid-April, Lawrence was unhappy anywhere but with his command. He wrote to Cousin Deborah: "My health is pretty good will be better when I get to the field which I have been trying to do for a month. This Court Martial is very tedious to me." Disappointingly, he was sent to another court martial in Trenton, N. J. where he continued to request orders for field duty, while a reappearance of the symptoms of malaria added to his misery. As Lawrence and Fanny were returning to Washington, they received news from Brunswick that so unnerved Fanny, she started immediately for home. The housekeeper she hired to help Cousin Deborah with the children was not working out. Torn between Lawrence and home, Fanny sent word to Cousin Deborah from New York:

> *I have only a moment to tell you where and how I am.... I came here last night from Trenton where I left Lawrence at the Depot, waiting to take the Philadelphia train for Washington. He was quite sick again in Trenton; That miserable malaria showing itself again which no one ever gets fairly*

rid of. He was very anxious for me to go back to Washington again with him, but I thought it was not best, unless he became very sick. He wants me to wait here until I hear from him from Washington. If he does not insist upon my going back, or if he is better, I shall start from here in several days, shall not be able to stop in Boston, as Caty asked me too [sic].... I am very anxious to get home and see you all, and it worries me to think you cannot depend upon Hannah, as I had hoped you could. I wish I could hear from you again here, but suppose I cannot. In case L. sends for me positively to go back, I shall wait to hear from you again I think. I wish I could know that you were all well and comfortable...I cannot date this, for I know neither the day of the week or day of the month.[16]

On May 7, Lawrence sent a telegram to Fanny in New York: "Come to Washington on the first train immediately without fail Answer immediately." It is uncertain if Fanny was still in New York to receive it. When Lawrence had arrived in Washington, news of the Battle of the Wilderness gripped the capital. Desperate to get back to his command, Chamberlain discovered that the request he had sent from Trenton for return to field duty was never received. On May 9, he again asked to return to the field, and the next day he was finally relieved from court martial duty. As he left for the front, the capital was in a state of celebration. Oblivious to the bloody outcome of the battle, the public was much taken with Gen. Grant's statement after the Wilderness: "I propose to fight it out on this line, if it takes all summer." This generated such optimism that the war in the East would soon be over, that many congressmen stayed on beyond their session to be in on the end. Lincoln, dismayed at the premature festivities that spring of 1864, told a friend, "I shall be happy if we are over with the fight in Virginia within a year."[17]

Chamberlain returned to a changed army. Grant had reorganized the Army of the Potomac into three large corps, and on June 6, 1864, Gen. Gouverneur Warren, the 5th Corps commander, appointed Chamberlain to the command of the "new" 1st Brigade of Gen. Griffin's 1st Division. It consisted of "veterans of 5 battered regiments of the old First Corps, & a new regiment, the 187th Pennsylvania...." Chamberlain assessed his weary veterans and the green regiment that made up his new command:

...six regiments as good as ever took arms. Veterans, in fact, the five old regiments, having passed thro untold hardships and slaughter at Gettysburg, and in truth, some of them looked upon as somewhat shorne [sic] of their honor there as well as of their numbers, by reason of not holding on after all was lost,—or perhaps for holding on until one of them lost their colors. At any rate, I found them somewhat disheartened when I took them, after Cold Harbor, and I set at work to restore spirit.[18]

The men needed all the confidence that a good commander could give them. Late at night on June 17, Chamberlain, aware that an attack would be made on the well-defended Confederate works of Petersburg in the morning, walked among his sleeping soldiers. He experienced an "unreasonable yearning over them, thinking of what was before, and wishing I could do what no mortal could do for them." He was oppressed by a premonition that the next day's battle would be his last, a feeling he shared only with his friend and division commander, Gen. Charles Griffin. The next day, as he prepared his brigade for an attack on Rives' Salient, this nagging certainty prompted him to give particular instructions to senior colonels most likely to succeed him.[19]

Chamberlain's men advanced on a deadly field of fire with shouldered muskets and bayonets fixed. Within minutes, the brigade flag was down. Taking the flag from the dying man's hands, Chamberlain led the advance. Finding himself on the border of a bog, he turned, raising the banner with the red Maltese Cross high over his head, signaling with his saber to the left. "...So signaling, I felt a sharp hot flush that seemed to cut my back-bone. A twelve-pound shell or case-shot had exploded right behind me as I was faced, and the pieces came thrumming by my ears. My thought was that I had been shot in the back,—in the middle of the back, below the belt. This was all I could think of for a moment, and the shame of it was worse than death. To be shot in the back "in the face of the enemy!" Though the blow was strong, Chamberlain had not fallen. Bracing himself with the staff of the flag and his sword tip, brought to the ground, he was determined that he would not fall: "I remember and always shall, the looks on the faces of my men as they came up to me in line,—dear brave fellows...as they broke files gave way to the left 'to pass obstacle.'" As his second line passed, he felt blood gushing in his sword hand:

> *I looked down,—then, for the first time. I saw the blood spurting out of my right hip-side, and saw that it had already filled my long cavalry boots to overflowing, also my baggy reinforced trousers, and was running out at both pocket welts. Not shot in the back, then! I do not think I was ever so happy in my life. My first thought was of my Mother, my Huguenot-blooded mother; how glad she would be that her boy was not shot in the back!*[20]

Chamberlain lay on the field under heavy fire for more than an hour before taken to the division hospital. The surgeons ran a ramrod through his body, the wound far too wide for a surgeon's probe, before they discovered the ball just behind his left hip joint. As evening approached, he knew by the surgeons' behavior, not their words, that his wound must be mortal. On a leaf taken from a field order book, he penciled this note of farewell and love to Fanny:

> *My darling wife I am lying mortally wounded the doctors think, but my mind & heart are at peace Jesus Christ is my all-sufficient savior. I go to him. God bless & keep & comfort you, precious one, you have been a precious wife to me. To know & love you makes life & death beautiful. Cherish the darlings & give my love to all the dear ones Do not grieve too much for me. We shall all soon meet Live for the children Give my dearest love to Father & mother Sallie & John Oh how happy to feel yourself forgiven God bless you ever-more precious precious one Ever yours Lawrence*[21]

That night, Generals Griffin and Bartlett brought word that Grant had promoted Chamberlain to Brevet Brigadier General. Lapsing into unconsciousness, he had no memory of the visit Gen. Warren made to him that night. With his next conscious thought came "a flood of tearing agony. I never dreamed what pain could be and not kill a man outright." Chamberlain soon saw Dr. Abner Shaw, surgeon of the 20th Maine, brought to him by his brother Tom. Dr. Shaw and Dr. Morris Townsend of the 44th New York refused to give up on their old commander. Townsend eventually suggested that they stop what seemed nothing more than futile torture, but Shaw's last effort to stop the bleeding saved his life. Through the night, Tom and a comrade, from the 20th Maine, "True-hearted [Ellis] Spear," watched over him. Chamberlain remembered:

> *After Midnight, I became aware of some one fumbling about my beard, trying to find my mouth. T[he] great iron spoon made its way along the uncertain track made by his trembling hand. I opened my eyes and there knelt Spear, his red beard in the gleam of a lurid camp-fire making him look like a picture of one of the old masters. He had been turning the spoon bowl as he thought in the right place, but had missed it by an inch, and the beverage he was offering had taken the course nearest to the earth, which was down my neck and bosom outside. "Now, plese [sic] give me some" I plaintively murmured, taking a little cheer, if I can be believed, in making a joke of it. The tears were running down his cheecks [sic]...but he smiled....*

Chamberlain remembered of that night: "At times the agonizing pains would get the better of my patience. But the suffering of those lying around me, particularly of the poor forlorn southerner close to me, were some counterpoise. 'A fellow-feeling makes us wondrous kind.'"[22]

Mass. Commandery, USMHI

Maj. Gen. Charles Griffin.

Maine State Archives

Maj. Ellis Spear.

In the morning, Gen. Meade sent a stretcher party to carry Chamberlain six miles to City Point, and friends gathered to see the "forlorn hope move out." Placed on the hospital steamer *Connecticut*, the surgeon in charge was noticeably drunk, but happy accident brought one of Chamberlain's old students from Bowdoin, Dr. Tom Moses, to his side to do what he could for his old professor. Arriving at the Naval Hospital at Annapolis, Maryland, Chamberlain lay on the wharf for some time before being placed, as lone occupant, in a tent. Lying alone for hours, eventually a woman's voice asked, "Who are you?" He felt, "'What are you,' would have been justified," for he was still "booted & spurred, blood-soaked & smeared, hair and beard matted with blood and earth" just as he was when taken off the field. Mary Clark of Boston, who nursed him at Annapolis, would be counted as a friend for the rest of his life.[23]

When the dreadful news reached Fanny, she, accompanied by two friends, made the agonizing journey to her husband's side. Sae, not knowing what else to do, wrote to Lawrence on behalf of the family on June 23:

> *I hardly know whether it is proper to address a letter to you now, but feel as though I must. We received a dispatch from Annapolis yesterday that you had arrived there and that your wound seemed more favorable. Mr. Tenny sent us a dispatch the day before from Brunswick an hour or two before it came out in the Bulletin at first we were entirely over come and could hardly endure the suspense. Mother and I, both are entirely sick to-day. The telegram yesterday relieved us a good deal, and we are hoping to hear some thing more to-day.... We so long to be with you. Fanny I suppose is there. She has written us two bountiful letters which we should have answered but she forgot to mention her address, it is a great comfort to us to think she is with you or near...It is strange that as well as we knew that we have liable to hear this news for two years, it seemed as great a shock to us as though you had never been exposed We could almost annihilate distance and fly to you. Mother says every hour, how "this or that would be for poor Lawrence" Of course the surgical care is better than could possibly be at home. We long to hear the particulars. Whether it was a gun shot wound (we suppose it was) and whether Thomas was with you at the time. We concluded as the dispatch came from a stranger that he did not go with you to Annapolis. No doubt he has written us, but it takes so long for a letter to come and we are so impatient.*[24]

Sae's letters to her brothers at the front were always filled with gossip of family and friends. Even this letter shared the latest family news:

> *There is a Hospital now in Bangor, you know at Gymnasium Hall, opposite City Hall, and Mother went over to see the soldiers. There are a good many transive ones there from the 20th, but none the day Mother was in. While she was there some one asked a fellow if he knew the Chamberlains. A voice replied from the opposite corner. 'I guess I do know Col. C— didn't he pick me up himself when I had fainted and the Reg. had left me far behind, and carry me to a place of safety. I shall always remember that I guess, as long as I live.' He belonged to the 5th Maine. It was very pleasant to mother.*

Sae added: "If Fanny is with you—do let her write if only ten words every day or two, at present. You dont know what a stay it is to us. Mother is too anxious and sick to send any thing but her warmest love." It was with joy that they soon received a note in his own hand.[25]

The slow mail was maddening for those who waited for news, and often, rumor and erroneous reports muddied the waters. Lieutenant Holman Melcher of the 20th Maine probably gave the family a shock with his undated letter of condolence: "intelligence has reached us of the death of Gen'l Chamberlain—*very* painful—for as a commander I had learned to love him—...."[26]

Lawrence lay "under the eyes of the dear, suffering wife who had taken up her dwelling in the adjoining tent." She witnessed his pain, so agonizing that it caused nurse Mary Clark to "wonder why God allowed it." She saw the convulsions and fevers as she watched beside his hospital bed, wondering if the child she carried would have a father. But during August, he slowly improved, and by the end of the month, he could sit up most of the day and spoke of returning to his troops.[27]

Recent research by urologist Dr. George Files, who made a careful study of Chamberlain's military, medical and pension records, and subsequent treatment, allows some assessment of Chamberlain's wound. It is impossible to know, incontrovertibly, the path of and subsequent internal damage done by the ball that passed diagonally through Chamberlain's pelvis. Setting aside the issue of physical idiosyncrasies, as well as the lack of documentation of Chamberlain's exact height and weight at the time he was wounded, Chamberlain's position, the precise twist of his body as he turned to exhort his men at Rives' Salient, would need to be known in order to make a definitive statement on the bullet's path.[28]

Chamberlain, by his own description, experienced bleeding at both hips, at the entrance wound on the right, but also on the left, though the ball lay below the skin. It is suspected that a fragment of bullet or bone exited through the skin at the left hip. The ball, during its diagonal passage upward, encountered the urethra, so near the juncture of the penis and scrotum that it might have opened the wound that, due to prolonged use of a catheter, developed into a fistula, an abnormal tract or opening, in this case leading from the damaged urethra out to the surface of the skin. Chamberlain not only experienced leakage of urine from the fistula, but also through the original track of the bullet, urine coursing out through the entrance wound on his right hip. During his hospital stay, he endured severe infection of the wound and urosepsis, an infection in the urinary system, both of which would have caused chills and high fever. In those days before aseptic treatment and antibiotics, it is impressive that he survived. His surgeons likely warned him of the wound's seriousness, but it would be many months before he realized, let alone accepted, the full extent of the condition inflicted upon him by that Petersburg bullet.[29]

Able to begin his journey home to Brunswick on September 20, in the following weeks he tried to answer Mother Chamberlain's concerns regarding his determination to return to the army:

> *...I confess, Not a selfish ambition: for I assure you not all the honors & titles that can be given or won, would tempt me to hazard the happiness and welfare of my dear ones at home, nor would they be any equivalent whatever for these terrible wounds as must cast a shadow over the remain-*

der of my days, even though I should apparently recover. But what it is, I cant tell you. I havn't a particle of fanaticism in me. But I plead guilty to a sort of fatalism. I believe in a destiny—one, I mean, divinely appointed, & to which we are carried forward by a perfect trust in God. I do this, & I believe in it. I have laid plans in my day, & good ones I thought. But they never succeeded. something else, better, did, and I could see it as plain as day, that God had done it, & for my good. So I am right, be sure of that, happen what may. Not for any merit of mine, but for divine & living mercy all is bright with me, in this world & beyond. So dear Mother, with a more appreciative love and a growing gratitude towards my Parents, as I recount their faithful care & unfathomed kindness & the trust that I may never do dishonor to their name, I am your obedient & loving son, Lawrence[30]

While Mother Chamberlain could count on her oldest son being safe for the next month, she still had a boy at the front. Word that Tom was brevetted a major for gallant and distinguished service while fighting with the 20th Maine at Peeble's Farm, Virginia, possibly arrived during Lawrence's visit back to Brewer that October. Yet the family could not escape all brushes with tragedy. Reports of the death of Lawrence's cousin, Billings Brastow, a captain serving in the 9th Maine with the Army of the James, had reached Brewer in late summer. False hopes were raised that the report might be erroneous when a letter from him, long in transit, arrived at his family's Brewer home. But Bill had, in fact, been killed on September 29, leading his men at Laurel Hill Church, Virginia. His three year enlistment had ended several weeks before, but with action expected, he had volunteered to stay on. The news of Bill's death was particularly hard on Tom, for he and Bill Brastow were childhood friends, and often talked about the possibility of one of them dying in battle. Tom told Sae that he had always known that one of them would die. Now Tom had to live with the inscrutable and painful weight of being the survivor.[31]

On October 29, little more than a month after his release from the hospital and before he could mount a horse or walk 100 yards, Chamberlain left Brunswick to return to the field. After a successful but exhausting raid against the Weldon Railroad, Lawrence responded to a letter from Sae urging him to have some care what he wrote to Fanny, waiting and worrying at home as she neared the end of her pregnancy. He wrote "Thank you for your valuable criticisms &... hints. A woman knows so much more than a man, after all. I wrote Fan another letter almost exactly the same & yet totally different in the turn & bearing of it. You would be much amused to see how the same words could be made to do such different duty." Yet Lawrence must have felt that Sae was made of sterner stuff, for he described what Rebel guerrillas were doing to 5th Corps stragglers. While he made no mention of his health after that strenuous week, a letter from Tom assured Sae that Lawrence had stood the march against the Weldon Railroad very well. Perhaps they conspired to keep up the spirits of the folks at home, for only in a letter to John did Lawrence confess the realities of his physical condition:

...I am managing to do full duty without much injury, & not a great deal of suffering. Still I was not fit to return to field duty, & it is very hard to take such chances as we had on the Weldon raid;.... I ride some, too much,

probably & to tell the truth, I dont feel right yet; though the "Herald" proclaims my "perfect recovery," & all that. I shall have to take to the knife again & am making up my mind where to go to have it done....[32]

Whatever reassurances Lawrence and Tom wrote to the family in Brewer, Mother Chamberlain feared that Lawrence was in no condition to bear the hardships of the front. On the first day of 1865, Sarah Chamberlain wrote to her son in the field:

A'rent you too forgetful of your own safety? We rested quite easily, in the last movement assuring our selves you would not attempt, even an engagement without a long march and were surprised to learn that you endured oft the cold & exposure of that dreadful march & came out alive! do dear child take care of your self surely you have done & suffered & won laurels enough in this war to satisfy the most ambitious not that I would say you were eager for the praise of man alone but moved by nobler motives I trust. And not wishing to dictate—yet daring to hope you may soon retire from those scenes of strife in which you have bourn your part so faithfully.... I hope, you will soon go to the hospital & avoid the coming battles which must be terrific....[33]

Bangor Public Library, Vickery Collection

Capt. Billings Brastow, 9th Maine Infantry.

Chamberlain left the front several weeks later, sent away by his corps commander, Gen. Warren. Traveling to Philadelphia and then to Boston for treatment, he also faced the nagging fear that he would never enjoy a complete recovery. He arrived home in Brunswick on January 20, four days after the birth of a new baby daughter.[34]

During the weeks he recuperated from his surgery, deep winter in Maine brought sub-zero temperatures, blizzards and sleet. Housebound and inactive during those severe winter days, yet knowing well how much sooner spring would come to Virginia, Chamberlain grew impatient. Lawrence wrote to his father on February 12:

Though still confined mostly to my room, I am fast recovering and by proper caution think I shall be able to get away by the first of next week. I am anxious to be back with my command: if I am to hold my position there I want to be at my post. The campaign will soon open, & it will open strong. I have been considering the past week whether to accept the office of Collector of Customs in the District of Bath, [Maine] which has been offered me. I believe it is considered a very good position, second only to the similar one in Portland held by Governor Washburn. I do not at present encourage the idea, preferring, if possible, to continue my duties in the Field, where my services were never more needed, or more valuable than now.

I shall probably resign my professorship here this summer, and be ready to throw my self on the current of affairs, & either remain in the military service (as is most congenial to my temperament) or strike into some other enterprise of a more bold & stirring character than College chair affords. I take no steps at present, waiting to see how my wounds are to turn.[35]

Tom was also back in Maine, run down by the bronchitis he had suffered with since the previous December, as well as symptoms of diphtheria. Discovering a wide gulf between soldiering and civilian life, Tom was so uneasy at home that his parents were worried. Lawrence observed:

I enjoyed your letter much, but was sorry to hear both from you & from Mother, that Thomas was so restless & roving while at home. However, I think you need have no fears of his indulging any incorrect habits whatever. He annoys me chiefly by being too sensitive, & allowing a few cowardly fellows [to] disturb his peace of mind. It is more creditable and more safe to have such men enemies than friends, & in my opinion it will be a good thing for him to have to stand his hand among men just as they come.

Reporting that Fanny and the new baby were well, Lawrence welcomed the suggestion that Mother Chamberlain visit them. He explained that he could not visit Brewer this time, for "I am so much over my time of leave from the army."[36]

Mother and Father Chamberlain were dismayed to learn of the customs position that Lawrence stood ready to refuse. To his father on February 20, he tried to explain:

I appreciate fully the view you & Mother take of the Collectorship offered me. It is natural and proper advice, & such as I certainly expected. But my own consideration of the subject has not, as yet, brought me to favor the proposal any more than at first. I owe the Country three years service. It is a time when every man should stand by his guns. And I am not scared or hurt enough yet to be willing to face to the rear, when other men are marching to the front. It is true my incomplete recovery from my wounds would make a more quiet life desirable, & when I think of my young & dependent family the whole strength of that motive to make the most of my life comes over me. But there is no promise of life in peace, & no decree of death in war. And I am so confident of the sincerity of my motives that I can trust my own life & the welfare of my family in the hands of Providence. And then as far as mere human probabilities go, my position & prospects in the Army were never better. I am now among the senior officers of my rank. And after all I have gone through, I am not willing to back out just at the decisive moment, & leave the rewards & honors of my toil & suffering to others. I had a great deal rather see another man in that Custom House, than see another next commander of the 1st Division. Nor will my claims be any less for an honorable post in civil life after still longer & better

> *service in the Field, nor for having declined advantageous offers for myself personally, rather than to abandon our cause in the hour of its need. At all events I must return to the army, and if I find I cannot stand it I shall not be foolish about it but shall take proper care of myself. I shall leave tomorrow. Have not yet been out of the house, but think I can bear the journey.*[37]

Chamberlain "stole the march" on his doctors, and started a painful journey back to the army. He became so ill on the way that he could not continue. In a letter to Brewer, he declared: "I was detained in Philadelphia by the state of my wounds; but that misfortune proved a good fortune; for besides the warm courtesies & compliments I received from every body there, I found the services of Dr. Pancoast—the most skilful [sic] surgeon in the United States—not only relieved my existing disabilities, but put me in the way of a more rapid recovery.[38]

At the end of February, back with the 1st Brigade at Hatcher's Run, Lawrence assured Sae:

> *You can not imagine how favorable this kind of life is to my health. One would not think me fit to walk a half mile if I was home; but here I ride as fast & far as the best, and ask no favors. I have no doubt that my recovery will be greatly promoted by my return to the field, and I do not in the least regret my choice. I shall not feel obliged to lead any more charges unless it becomes necessary and hope to escape any further injuries. I have no insane desire to deprive my little family of my protection & support I assure you. On the contrary I look forward with delight to a speedy return to the happiness and affection of my little home No man's ever was dearer or more blest. And to no man could it be a greater sacrifice to leave them far away and face the dangers which in threatening me threaten them ten-fold. Still let me say the course I take is not only that which honor & manliness prompt, but the one which will prove best for them & for all who belong to me or to whom I belong. Please understand that my wounds are now doing finely, and I am encouraged to hope I may not have to leave the field again till we finish campaigning.*[39]

Chamberlain had, despite all odds, managed to return to the Army of the Potomac in time for its last campaign. At the Battle of Quaker Road, while leading a charge, he was again thought to be mortally wounded. A ball, passing through his horse's neck to strike a leather case of field orders and a brass bound mirror in his breast pocket, left him slumped, unconscious, over his horse's bloody neck. Someone who caught a glimpse of him afterward sent a dispatch to the New York *Times* reporting that Gen. Chamberlain had been killed. Yet Chamberlain went on that day to rally his men again and again. As General Griffin would reportedly comment, it was a magnificent sight to see Chamberlain in battle. Gen. Warren saw to it that he received a brevet commission as major general, "for conspicuous gallantry in action at the Quaker Road." For a man who had assured his family, "I shall not feel obliged to lead any more charges, unless it becomes necessary...," he had done quite a day's work.[40]

On the cold, rainy night of March 29, he began a letter to Fanny, but was unable to complete it for many days. As news of the last battles traveled north, she could only wait and worry. The months of anxiety took their toll on her, at home

Janet and Bedford Hayes Collection

Bvt. Maj. Gen. Joshua Chamberlain.

caring for the baby, Willie and Daisy. Faithful Cousin Deborah was worn out, too, and took respite away from Brunswick, while friends and sister Catherine came to help. Every day, little Willie was sent to the post office to see if there was a letter from "Poppa."[41]

At the White Oak Road, at the Battle of Five Forks, and finally, at Appomattox, Chamberlain took a distinguished role in the Army of the Potomac's final campaign. His last impetuous advance afforded him a sight he would never forget. On the slopes of the Appomattox Valley lay the Army of Northern Virginia, and he would remember: "We seemed the possession of a dream. We are lost in a vision of human tragedy."[42]

The news reached Bangor and Brewer before daylight on April 10. Booming cannon and the clamor of bells proclaimed the momentous event. The next morning, one Bangor citizen recorded a thrilling sight across the river: "...some one in Brewer made a large kite, twelve feet long, and on the cord, some twenty feet below the kite, made fast a flag, and sent up the whole, two thousand feet into the air. Looking at it from this side, the cord did not show...and it appeared as though the beautiful flag, doubly dear and precious now, was supported by unseen hands in the Heavens."

Early that morning, there was shouting in the streets of Brunswick and the church bells began to ring. No word of explanation was necessary, for everyone in town knew that the anxiously awaited news of Lee's surrender had come at last.[43]

CHAPTER

13

"Providence Will Both Open & Guide My Way"

Late on the night of April 9, Chamberlain was called to headquarters and informed that he would command the troops to receive the formal surrender of the arms and colors of Lee's army. Though Grant's terms of surrender were thought to be generous, on one point he had stood firm. Though the Confederates had entreated to be allowed to stack arms and depart, Grant insisted that the surrendering army should lay down "all tokens of Confederate authority and organized hostility to the United States, in the immediate presence of some representative portion of the Union Army." Chamberlain asked to be given command of his old 3rd Brigade, with whom he had fought at Gettysburg. He claimed no personal reason for this request other than the conviction that, on this historic occasion, these veterans deserved such recognition.[1]

Quickly the end of strife turned hostility to friendly overture, and curiosity brought many into the "opposing camp." What little food the Northern soldiers had left was shared by Yankee and Confederate alike. After a night of slumber strangely free from picket fire, many Federals awoke the next morning with an inquisitive Rebel standing over them. With no food available now on either side, the men began to trade in that ageless custom, the quest for "souvenirs" of the war. Order among the soldiers was so disrupted that the men were ordered to their respective camps.[2]

At sunrise on April 12, four years to the day from the firing on Fort Sumter that had begun the war, one of the Confederacy's great armies ceased to exist. Chamberlain's pride, old and new, the soldiers of the 3rd and 1st Brigades of the 1st Division, were formed along both sides of the main thoroughfare near Appomattox Courthouse. Waiting with a small group of officers to meet the head of the Confederate column, Chamberlain determined that this occasion would be marked by some "token of recognition." Though he knew it would be criticized and condemned by some, it was a gesture that would lighten the spirits and spark a heart-felt gratitude in many others. Instructions were given that when the head of each division came opposite their formation, the bugle would signal each Union regiment in succession from "order arms" to the old "carry"—the marching salute. General John B. Gordon, downcast as he led in the first of the Confederate corps, would never forget Chamberlain's gesture. Quick to catch the meaning of the shifting of arms, Gordon ordered his own troops to return the salute.[3]

National Archives

Gen. John B. Gordon.

In a letter written to the family in Brewer the day after the surrender, Lawrence, still defending his decision to return to the army, explained what it meant to be a part of those last days of battle and the incredible scenes that followed:

> *I am glad I was not tempted to leave the army this spring. I would not for a fortune have missed the experiences of the last two weeks. It seems like two years, so many, & such important events have taken place, within that time. Father said in his last letter to me that 'the glory of battles was over'. But if he had seen some of these we have had of late, in which we captured the enemy by [the] thousand & carried their positions by a dash, and at last at Appomattox Court House received the surrender of Genl Lee & his whole army he would think differently.*[4]

Lest the family should recognize the momentous nature of the events, but still question the necessity of Lawrence's participation, he continued:

> *For my personal part I have had the advance every day there was any fighting—have been in five battles—two of them being entirely under my own direction and brilliantly successful—twice wounded myself—my horse shot—in the front line when the flag of truce came through from Lee—had the last shot & the last man killed, in this campaign... The bare fact seems like boasting, but I assure you I do not feel any of that spirit. I only rejoice that I was here & bore my part in the crowning triumphs of the war. It was a scene worthy of a pilgrimage, yesterday, when the old 'Third Brigade' of the 1st Div. was drawn up to receive the surrender of the Rebel arms. My Brigade you know consists of 9 Regts! The remnant of the old 5th Corps, veterans of thirty battles. They number about six thousand men all told— ...With my*

staff & the old flag—the red Maltese Cross on a white field with blue border—I took post on the right at 5 a.m., & received first Maj. Genl Gordon with his Corps— Stonewall Jackson's—then Longstreets Corps with Hoods Andersons & Picketts old Divisions—men we had faced a score of times & almost recognized by face—Picket[t]s splendid Div. only stacked 53 muskets & not a single stand of colors—we had so completely used them up at 5 forks. Last came Hill's Corps—by Divisions—Hill himself being killed. We received them with honors due to troops—at a shoulder—in silence— They came to a shoulder on passing my flag & preserved perfect order. When the head of their column reached our left, they halted faced towards our line & close to it—say 4 or 5 yards—stacked their arms & piled their colors. Poor fellows. I pitied them from the bottom of my heart. There [sic] arms had been well handled & the flags bravely borne. 15000 stand of arms & 72 flags were stacked before my line. I saw & conversed with nearly all the Rebel Generals, & shall have some thing to tell you of by & by.

The conversations that Chamberlain held with the Rebel officers were gracious and heartening exchanges, but for one. Lawrence saved the tale of Gen. Wise, who chose to continue the war with words, for another time.[5]

Chamberlain's 3rd Brigade, still suffering from lack of food and shelter, left Appomattox on April 15, heading east in a driving rain. Promised rations at the end of their march never materialized, and well after dark, the brigade settled in for a wet and hungry night. Resuming the march the next day, skies and spirits brightened on reaching Farmville, where the soldiers received the long-awaited rations and mail from home. Lawrence answered a letter from Fanny, to whom he did not have to defend his unyielding loyalties. He wrote on April 19, adding to a letter he had started weeks before on the night of the battle at Quaker Road:

My darling wife, a good-morning kiss for you with big brown eyes & peach-bloom cheeks, and vol—no ...vel vet lips! That, I had written just three weeks ago, seeming like three months or years if you please—so much & such momentous things have since transpired. That night I had fought a battle— the first of the campaign, and the fiercest—and more than four hundred of my men lay dead or wounded on the field—I too suffering from two wounds either of which was a miracle of an escape. Now I say the same thing to my dearest love, & if I could see her would have many many things to say. What tremendous scenes I have participated in within these three weeks. I told you I think that I fired the first & the last gun of this campaign—that I was present at that conference of officers—ever to be memorable—preliminary to the surrender of Lee's army. I had not then passed through the last & most intensely interesting scene. I happened to be designated to receive the formal surrender of the arms of that great Army of Northern Virginia... You can imagine what it was, when these veterans of a score of battles were drawn up to receive the surrender of the army they had faced so many times... I shall have something to tell you of this, as of other matters never to be forgotten.

The exhilarating promises of peace had begun to dawn on Lawrence, as they had on all the soldiers of the 5th Corps at Farmville. With the inner man finally restored, the sun shining, and those overdue missives from loved ones in hand, soldiers could begin to believe that the tragedies of the war were over. But that very afternoon the 5th Corps received the terrible news of Lincoln's assassination. Lawrence exclaimed:

> *But, Fannie, in the midst of all this triumph—in this hour of exaltation, in this day of power & joy & hope, when our starry flag floats amid the stars of Heaven, suddenly it falls to half-mast—'darkness sweeps athwart the sky', & the President of the United States, with his heart full of conciliation & charity & forgiveness is struck down by the assassin's hand. Words will not tell the feeling with which this Army received this news. I wish you could have been present to day at my funeral service for the President—the field—the drooping flags—the dirges of the bands—the faces of the men, the words of the chaplain from his text—'Give me here the head of John the Baptist in a charger'! You should have been here. You of all, I missed. The chaplain is an Irishman, & the Celtic soul took fire to day you may be sure. I ordered this service on my own responsibility, as it is the day of the Presidents funeral, & all duties of a military character were suspended. It will take a life time to tell you all I have to tell. These are terrible times, but I believe in God, & he will bring good at last. We march at 7 in the morning, to make a camp & rest for a little, when I shall write you more fully God bless you, sweet love; I thank you for your letters. I learn that some of the papers commend me. For your sake I am glad.... Sae speaks of your 'most sweet & beautiful of letters'. Thank you darling. What is our baby's name? With a goodnight kiss & a long one. Your own.*[6]

The terrible news from Washington, of Lincoln's death and the attack upon Secretary of State Seward, struck a cold fear into the minds of the commanders of the Army of the Potomac. Was it possible that what the Rebels could not accomplish militarily, they would gain by treachery? Nor could the officers predict the reaction of their soldiers to the tragic news. Fearing that sorrow would turn to rage and revenge, the men were confined to their encampment. But the soldiers of the Army of the Potomac, as they had on other black days in this war, patiently accepted the blow.[7]

After Appomattox, Gen. Griffin appointed Chamberlain commander of the 5th Corps' 1st Division, and on April 20, when the corps was assigned to take up a position along the Southside Railroad, the 1st Division marched seventeen miles from Wilson's Station to Sutherland Station near Five Forks. Chamberlain was responsible for a large area on either side of the tracks, and the civilian population that lived there. Residents who had lived in the pathway of two warring armies, were now at the mercy of marauding bands of hungry slaves and the stragglers of both sides. The area was without courts or officers of the law, and though the 5th Corps did not try to settle questions of property, a court was set up to deal with issues of conduct. Great difficulties were caused by the government's policy at this time that strictly forbade the army to furnish food to citizens unless they took the oath of allegiance to the United States. Chamberlain later commented that "conditions compelled us sometimes to take responsibility not strictly authorized," for he felt it a matter of common humanity to set to work to feed the people in his jurisdiction as quickly as possible. He directed mills and stores to be reopened and the wagons, tools and animals that had been confiscated from the Confederate army were distributed in order to put people back to work.[8]

As a provost marshal, one of Tom Chamberlain's duties was to administer the oath to those who came to the camp asking for assistance. The result of one such application, made by a beautiful young lady from the nearby town of Dinwiddie, was an encounter of the sort that inspired many a romance novel after the war. Her charming but recalcitrant refusal to take the oath so robbed Tom of his usual official demeanor, that he "did not consider himself wholly fit for duty." When Tom asked to bring her case before a higher authority, Lawrence, commenting that he was not yet on the superannuated list, agreed to meet the "Belle of Dinwiddie." A spirited conference led to the young lady's agreement to take the oath, but Lawrence noted that from that day forward, "there was a daily unaccountable diminution among the finer delicacies of our private headquarters' mess-stores," and that "on moonlight evenings," their provost marshal was often reported "present but not accounted for."[9]

Before the 1st Division left this area, Chamberlain, who admitted he had dealt sharply with the lawbreakers in the area, had apparently exercised his autocratic powers with fairness toward the stricken residents under his authority. The citizens of Dinwiddie County planned a dinner in his honor, testimony to the services he had rendered. Knowing that this gesture would overtax their slim resources, Chamberlain declined their invitation, but made sure that they knew of his regard and mutual respect. The 5th Corps marched toward Richmond in the first days of May, passing many desolate battlefields. They passed their position on the White Oak Road that had been forsaken to do battle at Five Forks, and the scene of their struggle on the Quaker Road. They marched past the site where Chamberlain had been shot down at Petersburg, where Ft. Mahone and Ft. Sedgwick, later known as Ft. Hell and Ft. Damnation, dealt out further death and destruction after his wounding. With great interest, the 5th Corps entered hard-won Petersburg. General Warren commanded the force left to occupy the town, and Gen. Griffin persuaded him to see the Corps pass in review. The men of the 5th Corps let Warren know how they felt about their former commander with ringing cheers.[10]

The next days were spent marching to what Chamberlain called, "the famed city which the newspapers had ordered us 'on to' since 1861." As the 5th and 2nd Corps entered Richmond on May 6, there was silence in the ranks as the men caught a glimpse of Libby and Belle Isle prisons. Chamberlain recalled his advice to his men—to prefer death to prison, "by which desperate tactics they sometimes saved their lives, cutting their way out of capture like madmen." The 5th Corps, ragged but proud, marched on through the famed city, now marred with burned out ruins and rubble, and passed Gens. Halleck and Meade in review. Their last sight of the city was the imposing, now empty fortifications that had guarded the Confederate capitol.[11]

The 5th Corps marched to Washington at such a pace that it seemed as if they were still in pursuit of Lee. But a schedule and route for each day, covering many miles over bad roads, was ordered by some distant authority who did not have to make the march. Finally, on the morning of May 12, they went into camp on Arlington Heights. For once, time and plentiful supplies allowed a camp such as they had never been able to construct in the field. On May 20, Sherman's Army of the West began to arrive in Washington, and the stage was being set for a Grand Review of the armies, scheduled for May 23.[12]

It was probably not until Lawrence and Tom arrived in Washington that a letter from Brewer reached them bearing somber news. John Chamberlain had suffered a severe hemorrhage from the lungs and the specter of tuberculosis hung over the family again. After resting at home for more than a week, John seemed well, and he had lost none of his determination to pursue employment in New York City. John's interests had turned away from the ministry in favor of a government position. Sae brooded over John's ambitions, fearing that "he will wear himself all down as Horace did and disease will fasten upon him." Mother Chamberlain implored Lawrence to help John secure a position, suggesting that "it may save his life."[13]

Reverend Adams arrived in Washington on May 17 to witness the last review of the Army of the Potomac. At home in Brunswick with the new baby, Fanny missed the last triumphant procession. Though Chamberlain found time to see to Rev. Adams' accommodations, dined with him, and took him on visits to two of the hospitals where soldiers of his division were being treated, Rev. Adams saw that the life of a division commander was a busy one: "...men coming for passes, all sorts of papers, all sorts of complaints, dissatisfactions, crooks, quirks." He also realized that Lawrence was not well. One 5th Corps surgeon had commented to Adams that he "never saw a man who w[oul]d continue work[in]g so when really unfit to move."

It did not take long for Rev. Adams to become privy to the headquarters' grapevine, and his diary records a sampling of camp gossip. Of Sheridan, who was to go to Texas to restore order, and be a visible challenge to the French and Austrian incursion in Mexico, it was reported that he wanted the 5th Corps to go with him, having declared that they could "outmarch & out fight anything he had ever seen." But Gen. Griffin was afraid of losing command of the 5th Corps, having angered Meade with his outspoken criticism. On the night of May 20, Chamberlain visited Sheridan to intercede for Griffin, returning with Sheridan's word that Griffin had nothing to worry about.[14]

May 22 was an evening of camaraderie for the officers of the 5th Corps and the presentation of a tribute from the 1st Division to Gen. Griffin. Four large hospital tents were brought together for the occasion. Chamberlain, entrusted to design a jewel-encrusted miniature of the 5th Corps battle flag, was chosen to present it and speak for them all. Chamberlain offered heartfelt words of respect and affection for their corps commander. Griffin expressed regard for Chamberlain in his response: "You yourself, General, a youthful subordinate when I first took command of this division, now through so many deep experiences risen to be its tested, trusted, and beloved commander,—you are an example of what experiences of loyalty and fortitude, of change and constancy, have marked the career of this honored division." Rev. Adams was called upon to say a few words, and he remarked that he was too great a coward and too old to enlist, but he had sent his boys from Bowdoin College, and not content with that, had sent his son-in-law, Gen. Chamberlain. With the applause that greeted this comment, Adams agreed that he could not have done better. Expressing his wish that he could be permitted to wear the badge of the 5th Corps, no less than four were pinned upon his coat.[15]

At 4:00 a.m. the next morning, the 5th Corps crossed the long bridge, moving through Washington toward the Capitol. They moved down Pennsylvania Avenue to such a tumult of sound and color that Chamberlain described their passing as "like the children of Israel walled by the friendly Red Sea." The officers and men of the 1st Division had chosen to eschew new uniforms, as well as the trappings of sashes and epaulettes... a decision, Chamberlain admitted, that might be "a scornful pride more sinful than that of vanity...," for their very plainness made them conspicuous. Reverend Adams watched the entire six hours of the review, and declared that none had shown to better advantage than Chamberlain and his command. Chamberlain was invited to watch the rest of the review from the president's stand, and the faces of the men of his own division soon brought him recollections of lost comrades. Greatly moved, he would declare, "More were passing here than the personages on the stand could see.... It was as the morning of the resurrection!...." When they had passed, Chamberlain commented: "So has passed the First Division,—and with it, part of my soul."[16]

Several nights later, this army of veterans invented its own spontaneous ceremony of farewell. After dark on May 25, the soldiers of the 2nd Corps used a recent issue of candles to "illuminate" their encampment. The idea quickly spread until tens of thousands of candles glowed in the night. Spontaneous parades were formed, and Chamberlain's Division as it marched to headquarters was described as "an immense column... a line of living fire." The cheering men demanded a short speech of Chamberlain, and the radiance of their procession ended only when the candles expired.[17]

The next day, Rev. Adams prepared to leave, and he recorded in his diary that Lawrence, "begs me to remain with him, is very lonely & homesick, now that active service is over." But Rev. Adams, whose health had been fragile the past year, had endured camp life as long as he could.

Perhaps it was during the long march to Washington that Chamberlain began to notice the anomalies in his life with the army. It was no longer necessary to note the lay of the land, or consider what was over the next crest or beyond the next bend in the road. The enemy was not there, and the way became commonplace and the march weary. The weeks since his arrival in Washington were filled with floods of paperwork. Was this the life of a peacetime commander? His division would soon be gone. The Army of the Potomac would soon be gone. If the border between Mexico and the United States remained peaceful, those who remained in the army would likely be sent to the South as occupation forces, and he had already had a taste of that. Yet how could he let go of all this? He had declared since his first weeks in the army that he could never return to the life of a professor.[18]

On June 6, Lawrence wrote to Sae with assurances that he had plenty of options, yet his letter indicates a discontented and unsettled state of mind. Nor did what Lawrence saw as a scarcity of letters from Brewer or Brunswick sweeten his mood:

> *It is a long time since I have written. I doubt however, if I have had the pleasure of a letter direct from you since my last. You doubtless know very well that we are now reducing the army as fast as possible. What will happen next we do not know. I suppose the rest will be ordered into the interior of the Rebel states some where. My own affairs are in an exceedingly uncertain state. But I am by no means disturbed about them. I have plenty of 'strings to my bow', or in better words, Providence will both open & guide my way. You see I was right in sticking to the Army to the last. I have now been recommended by all my superior officers for the rank of full Major General, besides the Brevet recommended at Five Forks. Whether I shall get the full appointment, I dont know. Any body else would if he had half the record or the recommendation I have. But the political gentlemen of Maine have not particularly interested themselves in me. It is only those who know me & have seen me, in the field who take much notice of me. I can afford to be let alone however. It makes me perfectly independent. I am not much beholden to the State of Maine. I am far better known in New York & Pennsylvania than in my own state. Do not think I say this complainingly. I am not obliged to complain. My position is all I could ask—all I coveted, the command of 12,000 men whose record as soldiers never was surpassed. Of course, I shall soon be reassigned, where I dont know. If I dont like it I shall resign. My wounds trouble me still. I tried to ride into Washington to night in my wagon & had to give it up. The saddle does not trouble me so much. I am in good spirits though, and ready to do any thing I am called on for.*[19]

Asking for his mother and father, he commented, "They need not have a particle of anxiety about any of us now." While Lawrence and Tom could now claim to be without an enemy in the world, John had gained a well paid position as a tobacco inspector in New York City when Lawrence signed the necessary $3,000 surety bond. Lawrence added, "Don't let Mother get low. I could not bear to lose Father or Mother any more than if I were a boy of 10." Referring to Brunswick, Lawrence petulantly commented, "As for my own home I shall have to refer you to your own latest intelligence. I am not favored in that particular."[20]

At home with Daisy and Wyllys, and devoted to the care of her new baby, Fanny found that her world was now limited to Brunswick. Throughout the war Fanny had demonstrated her willingness to go to Lawrence. Now, during this climax to the hostilities, this hour of triumph that, nonetheless, brought change and uncertainty, Fanny could not be with him. With his Brewer family's outspoken protests regarding his last return to the army, Lawrence was perhaps more reliant on Fanny's support than ever before. Distressed and lonely at not having her near, he extended invitations to a number of others in early 1865. Mary Clark, his nurse at Annapolis, was asked to visit camp before the last campaign. Although pleased by the invitation to become one of Lawrence's "staff," she could not accept the offer. Old friends of the family, the Abbots, were offered the same hospitality, but could not go. How Lawrence appreciated Rev. Adams' presence during the glorious but difficult days of the Grand Review and the dissolution of the Army of the Potomac.[21]

When an order officially disbanding the Army of the Potomac was issued at the end of June 1865, Chamberlain was appointed commander of the 1st Brigade, 3rd Division in the newly formed Provisional Corps. He filled days of inactivity by writing out his field notes of the last campaign while the events were fresh in his mind. But during this interlude, without the challenges and distractions of pressing duties, the debilitating nature of his wounds seemed to force itself on his attention. On June 26, Chamberlain wrote to a well-wisher:

> *The old Army of the Potomac is gone. Very few of the familiar faces are seen among us now. In a few days we expect to be broken up by explicit orders, and distributed & assigned in widely different places. I have no idea of my own fate. To my great astonishment I learn that Genl. Meade has sent my name to the President with a few others—all by far my seniors & superiors—for the full appointment of Major General. I appreciate the compliment at this time when the effort is to get rid of officers. But my feeling now is that I shall return very soon to private life. Soldiering in time of peace is almost as much against my grain as being a peace man in time of war. My wounds too, I find, now that I am called on no longer to bear up against them, are very troublesome, and I need to be vetted at home a while... It is now my expectation to go north in the course of a month.*[22]

On July 6th, Chamberlain requested:

> *...that I be relieved from service in the field, & ordered to some duty in the state of Maine, or in Washington City, or wherever my services can be of most benefit, until I no longer require surgical treatment for my wounds. I have been in the field for nearly three years, having had only four days leave of absence in that time, except when sent away for medical treatment.... The state of my wounds is such as to require care and attention. I shall be obliged to undergo a severe surgical operation as soon as the heat of summer is past. I do not apply for a leave of absence, because I believe I am able to render full service, if placed in a favorable position, until the operation referred to can be performed; and I am unwilling to be off duty without absolute necessity.*[23]

By the middle of July, when Washington diplomacy had succeeded in diminishing the threat of an armed confrontation with the French and Austrians in Mexico, the Provisional Corps was disbanded. The 20th Maine received word that they would be returning to Maine to be mustered out, and Tom Chamberlain, now a lieutenant colonel, went with them. Tom's disappointment at the turn of events that sent him back to civilian life is evident, for he declared: "...if there was a Foreign *War*, I would enlist tomorrow morning as a private if I couldn't get anything better." John Chamberlain wrote Lawrence from New

York, putting the best face upon events, and suggested that perhaps Lawrence could get one of the foreign appointments he had been mentioned for before he returned to the army for the last campaign:

> *I am glad to learn the Provisional Corps is to be mustered out as inactive life must be tedious to you old veterans. You need about three years rest. I think a foreign appointment the thing for you now. If that will not be a rest it will be a change and gratification to your old desires for a continental tour almost equivalent to it. And how suitable that the same agent for which you sacrificed those plans which had been culminating for a life time should now become the direct means of consummating them. Such reciprocations sometimes come around in the order of providence, so that the specific things which in heroic self sacrifice we turn our backs upon we are startled in the end to find before our eyes and within our grasp. Really I know this is the thing for you unless your wounds are too troublesome and serious. And now is the time for you to accept it—You could grace an imperial Court—and no republican but a military man can do it. Am I right?*

Seemingly free from the debilitating symptoms of consumption, John related that he was in good health and good spirits, and he commented on his position as a tobacco inspector: "I am doing pretty well, some weeks very well. Perhaps my position does not sound very dignified but it is responsible & lucrative—I relish making money. I feel no regrets..." But John was anxious about Lawrence, and asked to hear from him.[25]

When his brigade command disappeared, if there was still any hesitation on Chamberlain's part to cut his ties with the army, one last incident may have influenced his decision to return to civilian life. As he revealed years later to one of his dearest friends, Gen. Alexander Webb, Chamberlain did, in fact, receive the commission for which he had been so highly recommended, as full Major General. But for reasons then unknown to him, he was asked in a private letter from the Secretary of War to return it. He would later learn that "there was another Major General to be appointed from Maine and so its 'quota' would be full." Francis Fessenden, son of Lincoln's Secretary of the Treasury, William P. Fessenden of Maine, received the commission, and though an honorable man and soldier, his service record paled beside Chamberlain's.[26]

Lawrence returned to Brunswick at the end of July, and though a newspaper article described him as "quietly ensconced here in his pleasant home," tranquil moments with Fanny and the children were few and far between. Lawrence returned just before commencement week festivities at Bowdoin, and the homecoming scheduled for Bowdoin's sons returning from the war increased the usual large number of visitors to a flood. The news that Gen. Grant might extend his visit in Portland to accept invitations from Chamberlain and Gen. Howard to attend commencement only increased the deluge of guests, and the Chamberlain home had an influx of visitors.[27]

Chamberlain had left his home town a professor admired for his scholarship and patriotism. On his return, he was embraced as the town and college's own war hero. A local paper wrote:

Gen. Chamberlain...attended by the benedictions of the literary and patriotic—the representative of Bowdoin in the war—her proud testimony to the honor of learning and patriotism as one and inseparable. The General is in excellent physical condition but is suffering somewhat from those hideous wounds at the Petersburg assault, where he blazoned his name before the country in the full romance of enthusiastic courage, fearless and peerless as the knights of the tournament. Few men could have rallied from such fearful wounds—transverse axes he humorously terms them. Another surgical operation will be demanded before those wounds will turn to honorable scars. The General looks brown and hardy despite rebel bullets, grayer than four years ago, but hardier, and grafted into fame. And none have better won their laurels! [28]

Lawrence transformed his library during his first few days at home with the relics of his wartime experiences. The 5th Corps' flag from Appomattox graced the wall, along with several captured Rebel flags. He also displayed the division flag that he had taken from his fallen flag bearer and was carrying when shot at Petersburg. Over the mantelpiece was hung the dented scabbard and sword that he wore at Gettysburg, and a number of documents, orders and dispatches covered his study table. But his most prized possession from the war did not arrive until August 2. Charlemagne had survived shot and shell to return home with his fond master.[29]

His homecoming became more hectic when Gen. Grant accepted the invitation to come to Bowdoin's commencement. The college intended to confer an LL.D. on Gen. Grant, and a local newspaper quipped that it was about time that Gen. Grant received his "literary brevet." The article also suggested that Bowdoin would counterbalance the "great mistake" they had made when they conferred the same degree on then senator and former Secretary of War, Jefferson Davis when he visited Maine in 1858. On Gen. Grant's arrival in Brunswick on Aug. 2, he and Mrs. Grant went to the Chamberlains' home before attending the veterans' welcome at the First Par-

Pejepscot Historical Society

The Chamberlain house on Potter Street, 1866.

ish Church that evening. The patriotic Rev. Adams was aglow, describing in his diary Grant's entrance, and that Chamberlain had escorted Mrs. Grant into the church, where the crush of people caused one Brunswick resident to recall that it was the "greatest jam I ever saw in this place." Chamberlain responded briefly to an enthusiastic call to speak. His comments elicited the only public words Grant uttered during his visit. Chamberlain declared, "I have tried to get Gen. Grant to speak, but he says 'No,' and when he says that word he means it. Lee knows it means something." Amid the cheers, Grant, affirming his unwillingness to speak, quipped, "I continue to fight it out on that line."[30]

More peaceful days came after the excitement of commencement, and Lawrence turned to contemplation of what the future might hold. He had already decided to write a history of the 5th Corps, but there was the immediate reality of having a family to support. Despite his intention to never return to college life, by the middle of August, Lawrence again held the chair of rhetoric and oratory at Bowdoin. Moreover, this month that should have brought the joys of a family reunited, seemingly could produce only sorrow. On August 17, seven-month old Gertrude Loraine, Fanny and Lawrence's fifth and last child, was seriously ill and died in the night. Reverend Adams officiated at the funeral of "poor Fanny's baby." One week later, Lawrence received notification that he had been mustered out of the army. This premature action came as a blow, for, beyond it being the official severing of his ties with the army, he had expected to be retained in the service until the surgery he needed had been performed. At the end of this difficult month, six year old Wyllys was ill, and Daisy was sent to stay with the Brewer Chamberlains. As September began, young Willie improved, and some respite from heartache came with the cool days of autumn.[31]

October brought guests to lift Lawrence's spirits. General Griffin and his wife came to Brunswick to visit for several days. Esteemed as commander and friend, Chamberlain described Griffin as "alert and independent, sincere to the core, at his ease, ready for anything,—for a dash at the enemy with battery front, or his best friend with a bit of satire when his keen sense of the incongruous or pretentious is struck...." What reminiscences must have passed between these two comrades during this visit, before Griffin, who would be assigned to Texas, went back to the life of a soldier, and Chamberlain, to academia. In the last weeks of 1865, along with his duties at the college, he also threw himself into preparation for the 5th Corps history. Having prepared circulars to go to all the corps' regimental commanders, he began the laborious effort of collecting field and staff rosters. This period also brought the first of hundreds of invitations that Chamberlain would receive over the years to speak about the war. Each speech would be carefully prepared, labored over with the precision of the historian, the soul of the dramatist, and the love of a father that made Chamberlain, for the rest of his life, a champion for the Union soldier.[32]

However deeply Lawrence immersed himself in his old duties and new endeavors, a milestone in his and Fanny's life did not go unnoticed. Lawrence conceived a design for a bracelet to be made by Tiffany's of New York—his tenth wedding anniversary present to Fanny. Two oval bands of gold would hold twenty-four tiny hourglass-shaped tablets, symbolizing "the weary hours away from home" during the war. Each tablet was engraved with the name of a battle or engagement in which Lawrence participated. In the center of the bracelet on a field of white was a red enameled Maltese Cross surrounded with small diamonds, a diamond star in the center, reminiscent of that in the 5th Corps badge that Chamberlain designed for Gen. Griffin. The back of the bracelet held a replica of a general's shoulder strap, dark blue enamel with two stars, each set with a tiny diamond. The cost to have it made, $250.00, was extravagant, but sentiments were presented with this loving creation. One recalls the brooch that had been given to Col. Strong Vincent's widow after Gettysburg, that had so moved Chamberlain with its beauty and significance. But unlike Vincent, Lawrence had managed to come home, and present Fanny with this symbol of his service and their mutual sacrifices.[33]

Late in December 1865, when a number of influential Maine politicians became aware of Chamberlain's physical condition and urgent need for treatment, they petitioned the government to restore him to his rank in the army. Prompt action facilitated the approval of this request, and Chamberlain underwent surgery before the year was out. He again returned to Brunswick to recuperate during the cold days of Maine's winter, but this time he also had to face a bitter truth. The newspapers' prediction that his "wounds will turn to honorable scars" was not coming true. No doctor possessed the skills that could repair his wound. The Rebel bullet at Petersburg had damaged his body beyond its capability to heal. Urine still seeped from his damaged urethra out through the fistula that could not be closed. The path of the bullet did not heal, and it remained an open conduit for infections that continued to rack his body. Prey to reoccurring infections of the bladder, an acute attack would result in infection traveling through the seminal tubes to produce inflammation of the testicles. At its worst, infection throughout the abdomen caused abscesses that could only be relieved by surgery. Though the bullet may have missed the blood vessels and nerves involved with sexual potency, the pain and inflammation, as well as the psychological trauma of his condition, may have denied him any possibility of sexual intimacy.[34]

During the first months of 1866, he had to come to terms with his physical condition, knowing that there was little or no hope for improvement. The strength of Lawrence and Fanny's love for one another had stood the test of many hardships, but the months and years just after the war would prove the hardest of all.

CHAPTER

14

"We Have Looked Our Sorrows Fairly in the Face"

Chamberlain continued to receive offers in early 1866 to lecture and deliver addresses about the war and on behalf of the soldiers and their families. He also continued to reflect, not only on his personal experiences and trials, but on those of all who participated in the war, North and South. While Chamberlain followed national politics with great interest, nearer to home, Maine politicians showed great interest in him. By the first of the year, he knew that many in the Maine Republican party saw him as their next candidate for governor. In the first weeks of the new year, Lawrence was preparing a speech to deliver in February before a gathering of veterans in Philadelphia that would establish a new organization, the Military Order of the Loyal Legion of the United States [MOLLUS]. Recuperating from his latest surgery during Bowdoin's winter break, he also began to write his history of the 5th Corps. As they often would in the future, the family vacated the house in order to give Lawrence the quiet he needed to write. Fanny made a short visit to friends and family in New York City, the first of several trips to the city that winter.[1]

On New Year's Day, fearing that her son was trying to do too much, and dismayed that he was at home on his own, Mother Chamberlain wrote: "Are you still alone! I suppose you are pressed with business & considerably tensed beside—perhaps perplexed beside but I hope not—here I sit longing to write something to you, that will help sustain you under your cares & responsibilities how can I, one in your position I can only ask for you that wisdom wisdom which is so freely given You must feel your need of it—" Mother Chamberlain and Lawrence had been talking politics, and between her consideration of the foment over Reconstruction, and the influence of Lawrence's previous observations, his mother offered:

> *I think this a very perplexing time politically—since the war I have been quite a <u>politician</u>—even studying all the political speeches that fall in my way—I declare I find myself with Congress rather than Johnson for better have left the Slaves in bondage than set them at liberty & withhold protection from them now they must suffer unless they are protected from the rage or violence of their former masters and put in the right way of taking care of themselves—May be I dont understand all about it—but you do & I trust you are right.—*

Of Lawrence's possible candidacy for governor, she added: "While twould be most gratifying to me to see you in the chair of state I would not have you yield your conscientious convictions of right to gain any position earth can give. Be sure you are right—in sympathy with *Heaven*, I know all is well I have no fears on your account you have always been on the right side, & trust are now—" Several days later, Sae, an ambassador conveying the family's concern for Lawrence, came to Brunswick to visit until Fanny's return the next week.[2]

Brewer Public Library

Sarah Brastow Chamberlain.
In the dress she wore to her son's first inauguration.

Additional insights to Chamberlain's thoughts and political inclinations can also be found in the MOLLUS speech over which he labored. In this address entitled "Loyalty," Chamberlain entreated his listeners to not only cherish their memories of loyal and costly devotion," but to "pledge hearts anew to the faith of freedom under the law; to perpetuate the ascendancy of immortal ideas over temporal interests and passions; to celebrate the enfranchisement of the People...." He optimistically asserted that, "...we know now what we are, and what we belong to, and what character is under this name of Country...What all this was for will be made manifest; what we shall be will appear."[3]

What the character of the country would be after the war, however, was a matter of passionate debate in early 1866. Though Republicans had a three to one majority in Congress, the party was far from united on the nature of Reconstruction. Radical Republicans, who had assumed that Lincoln's vice president and successor, Unionist Democrat Andrew Johnson, concurred that the Rebels must be punished, were, by the time Congress met in December 1865, enraged. By that time, Johnson had ordered that all land that had been confiscated from former Confederates must be returned to its former owners. He also issued pardons to thousands of Confederates who had been excluded in the amnesty proclamation, issuing an average of 100 pardons a day in September 1865 alone. Moderate Republicans urged that Johnson's tactics be given a chance, but worrisome reports from the South eventually convinced most Republicans that more must be done to protect the freedman from violence and discrimination. When Johnson vetoed the bill that extended the life of the Freedmen's Bureau, and would have affirmed freedmen ownership of confiscated Confederate lands, Republican moderates were dismayed. Refusing to address the fact that the Constitution contained no provisions for civil war or reconstruction, Johnson declared that the legislation contained in the Freedmen's Bill was unconstitutional. Adding fuel to the fire, he declared that the military courts maintaining order in the South had no jurisdiction in time of peace. He also made the alarming assertion that Congress, in the absence of Southern representatives, could pass no legislation. News of Johnson's veto came only a few days before Chamberlain delivered his speech in Philadelphia, and Chamberlain had little time to incorporate his reaction into his address. But he did observe that there are "two aspects and spheres of politics: one is that of practical detail, the minor tactics of particular policies, the machinery of methods and measures,—questions upon which opinions may naturally differ, parties arise, sharp discussions and perhaps serious dissensions ensue; the other is that of the great whole, the vital principles, the moral convictions and purposes, the guiding ideals of a people's life and movement." Regarding the constitutionality of Congress' attempts to pass Reconstruction legislation, Chamberlain asserted that the laws and constitution were not meant to remain fixed and unchangeable, but were "creations of its advancing life, —afterthoughts, not prototypes."[4]

On one issue the Republicans seemed united—the reentry of Southern representatives to Congress. Congress held the right to accept or reject any representative. When the roll was called in late 1865 for the 39th Congress, by prearrangement, the names of Southern representatives who had presented themselves were not called. A passage of Chamberlain's speech reveals his feelings regarding the participants in the rebellion and their rights. He suggested that with the surrender at Appomattox "an over-ruling spirit as arbiter of human destinies hushed all thought of hate and petty vengeance...," but he also declared that, during the years of attempted compromise before the war, "Loyalty to freedom was held in abeyance by Loyalty to the Union...," and that, "The slaveholding spirit was not contented with toleration; it demanded mastery of the Country. And it got it. What a century of concession could not do, secession did,—with marvelous demonstration, its own weapons turned to its destruction." Declaring that the principle of local self government was no less dear to the people of the North than to the people of the South, Chamberlain asserted, "But when this is made a war-cry only to warrant the right of slaveholding, alien to our convictions and contrary to our declarations as a people, and thus set above the life-law of the whole Country, then there is a disturbance of equilibrium which is fatal to all in its results." Chamberlain believed that there were "those who erred through ignorance or imperfect vision of the deep issues pending, or illgrounded though honest conviction of duty or in the spirit of a splendid but ill directed chivalry...." But he declared that the "Leaders of men are deeply charged," as he drew attention to "those who precipitated upon our Country that direful war...." Believing that "the innocent have suffered more than the guilty," he stated that ultimate judgment of all must be left to a higher tribunal.[5]

With optimism and a profession of belief in man's better nature, he concluded that he perceived "a common faith," shared by people of the North and South, that was a ground for hope:

> *Now that the stumbling-block of slavery is removed, I can see how these vital principle[s] at the centre of our life will at no very far-off day, bring us into a closer union than ever before,—closer, perhaps, than ever could have been without that terrible ultimate appeal. When the bitterness of the evils attendant upon war has been assuaged, and the immediate consequences of the overturn of industrial and social systems have been adjusted, as in the interchanges of a renewed common life must come to pass, the whole Country will be drawn together under the law of its larger life, its deepest convictions, its highest aims.*

Chamberlain assured his audience that he did not ignore the difference between the "country's defenders and its assailants. But it is to hold in view, and believe in making real, the very object we strove for,—the American Union;—a free people by the strength of righteous law; one people with the brotherhood of man its living bond. If we do not reach that end, then our victory is vain."[6]

Chamberlain also addressed the "great and difficult duty...laid upon us all to help the poor, surprised race among us, whose enfranchisement was the signal incident of the war, to make themselves truly free." Nor did he discount the difficult challenges that the South faced, for he noted: "Still greater and more difficult is the task for the States now restored to their place in the Union, having on them a double burden; of dealing with this multitude among them suddenly let loose from slavery; and settling in a new order, civil, social and industrial relations which have been shaken to their very foundations." He saw the enfranchisement of the freedmen, not as a task the North would impose upon the South, but as "A work that can effectually be done through the best minds of the South, although lately swept into the ranks of the Rebellion." Chamberlain did not think such tasks beyond his countrymen's capability. With his insistence that our nation "cherish reverence, honor, truth, justice and brotherly love," he charged his listeners to consider the even broader work of sharing our "dear-bought blessing with other peoples far off and waiting for the light... to the greater hope that this world's advancing edge shall touch the better one." He set out the challenges, as he saw them, that the country must meet, and the ideals he discerned as the fruits of Union victory. At such a cost in national suffering and sacrifice, he could accept nothing less.[7]

Fanny had accompanied Lawrence to Philadelphia to hear him give his address. She remained in New York while Lawrence returned to Maine to do a week long lecture tour. Sae commented, "She will get nicely rested in New York. I am glad for her—& wish I was there too." The children, though they had remained in Brunswick to attend school, were staying outside the home, and even the family pet, Coladnus, boarded with another family. After he arrived home, Lawrence wrote that he had a terrible cold and was "lonesome as a cat," but he instructed Fanny: "I want you to have a good time, & not deny yourself anything you desire." Before she received Lawrence's letter, Fanny wrote that, though a stubborn cold and cough restricted her activities, she was visiting friends, had gone to the theater to see Booth in *Richelieu*, and had attended a Sabbath service at the Old Trinity Church, famous for its surpliced male choir of 50 and its high church Episcopal pageantry. As in earlier days, Fanny exclaimed, "I can not see or hear anything beautiful without you, it all comes to that. How do you do now my darling? are you rather lonely or do you have such uninterrupted time for writing, that you enjoy it?"[8]

On receiving his letter, and learning that he missed her, she continued, "I have just received your 2d letter dear, am sorry, I mean *glad* that you are lonely!" Twelve days later she wrote to him from New York, concerned that she had not heard from him after his travels. "My dear Lawrence I have been hoping to have a letter from you since your return from your lecturing tour. Your [sic] received my letter I suppose, on your return. I am anxious to know how your cold is, and many other things about you." Although Fanny had not seen him, Tom Chamberlain, still plagued by respiratory problems, was also working in New York in early 1866, as clerk to brother John. Fanny reported that she had seen John, and though the symptoms of his tuberculosis had apparently not reoccurred since he had been working in New York, she expressed her concern for him. "John... came very kindly with a carriage the other night and took me to the opera. He seems so very sober, as if something weighed heavily upon his mind." Fanny also asked Lawrence if he knew anything of the rumors John had related to her, that Lawrence was to be offered a colonelcy in the regular army, and that he had also had an offer to teach at West Point. She added:

> *I have no idea when you will go back to Philadelphia, why dont you let me know more about things dear? Where is Aunty? Where are you and how are the children. I think I will be going towards home soon, but I want to hear from you. What are you doing dear? are you writing for your book? and how was it with your lecture in Brunswick—was it the one Gettysburg? I look at your picture when ever I am in my own room, and am lonely for you. After all, every thing that is beautiful must be enjoyed with one you*

love, or it is nothing to you. Dear, dear Lawrence write me one of the old letters. My eyes are paining me so badly that I must not write more now. With love to those two dear little ones and hoping to hear from you soon...I am as in the old times gone bye Your Fannie.[9]

Lawrence was indeed writing, for he had accepted an invitation to open a fund-raising fair for the widows and orphans of Maine's soldiers and sailors. The irrepressible Sarah Sampson, now that her wartime duty as a nurse was over, shouldered the responsibility of seeing that justice was done to those who lost loved ones in the war. Thrilled that Chamberlain had accepted her invitation, she wrote, "May the Angels of little children 'Who always behold the face of the Father' you know[,] hover over you every moment you are writing your lecture for those who will receive the benefit." The speech he wrote for the widows and orphans' fair at the end of April 1866, provides insights to his more intimate feelings on the tragedies and sacrifices so many bore during and after the war. But his work on this speech also produced brooding thoughts of how his own life had changed forever.

While his letters had expressed weariness, a letter to Fanny written on March 23 gave way to despair: "...I have a bad cold, & have had a rather hard time of late, & many services & duties in prospect which prevent my resting much. The address at the opening of the Orphans' Fair in Portland falls to me, among other things. Have as good a time as you can while you are away. There is not much left in me to love. I feel that too well. The last six months experience has finished me. L." It was a sad response to the love letter Fanny had requested.[10]

Uncertainty ruled their lives in the first half of 1866. Though they were now married for ten years, it is reminiscent of the time before their marriage. With the possibility of Lawrence being a political candidate, the questions of where they would live and what Lawrence's career would be remained unanswered. At the end of March, they even experienced the old confusion that lost letters could cause, when a letter in which Lawrence rescinded his offer to meet Fanny in Boston or New York apparently went astray. Unaware that Fanny was still expecting him to join her, Lawrence wrote on April 7: "To tell you the whole truth we are getting rather lonesome without you. I am not going to revoke my permission for you to stay as long as you want to, but you will be very welcome when you do return. I feel a little babyish perhaps now, because I am quite near being sick with a cold & influenza. I have had a suspicion of diphtheria but do not fear it now." He reassured her that, "The children are well and stout as two little 'bulls of Bashan'. We are having very pleasant times, only you are wanting to our complete happiness." But, he added, "I am full of cares and labors, & not being well for some few days past, have grown rather thin and pale....," In an unenthusiastic comment on his political future, he said, "I am summoned to Augusta today by a dispatch—to see some of the gentlemen interested in having me nominated I suppose—I hate these things."[11]

Another cause of uncertainty came with the realization that the family had outgrown their little house on Potter Street. Lawrence told Fanny in his letter that he had made an offer on Prof. Upham's house, asking "How would you like to live in that house? Would you rather have ours put upon the 'White' lot & the roof raised? I prefer this place to Prof. Upham's.—"[12]

Fanny replied with questions of her own. It is likely that she agreed with the advice that John Chamberlain sent along:

> *I rather hope Prof. Upham will not take your offer for his house, for I dont think you want it, and you bought one house which you didn't really want, you know. I see no reason you should change unless for the better. John says he thinks it very foolish for you to buy another house, or go to any other expense now, when everything is so undecided with you. You will not probably stay in Brunswick long, and if you should do any thing with the old house it would only be a great expense to you, and no particular advantage when you wished to sell. Is it not so?*

In the Spring of 1867, the Chamberlain's would move their house to a more desirable location on Maine Street, an apparent resolution to maintain a home in Brunswick.[13]

On April 25, Chamberlain opened the fair in Portland that would raise funds for Maine's war widows and orphans. His speech contained eloquent praise for the soldier and sailor, and saluted the men and women of the Christian and Sanitary Commissions, and the Relief Associations, who sent help, and went with willing hands to the front. But he opened his address with uncharacteristic bitterness. He declared that those who had gathered there that night, proved by their very presence that they were:

> *...not of those who can see no good in the soldier of the Union who took upon his breast the blow struck at the Nation's and look only to our antagonists for examples of heroism—those over magnanimous Christians, who are so anxious to love their enemies that they are willing to hate their friends. I wish not to obtrude my sentiments upon you but I am sure I speak yours in saying that no man shall go before me in appreciation of a generous foe; nor in recognition of personal valor or virtue wherever I meet it—in friendly rivalries of peace or in deadly front of battle. I can gladly share my biscuit or my blanket with a brave enemy whom after the feverish struggle, midnight finds a weary, cold and hungry prisoner in my hands.... But I have no patience with the prejudice or the perversity that will not accord justice to the men who have fought and fallen in behalf of us all,-but must go round by way of Fort Pillow, Andersonville and Belle Isle to find a chivalry worthy of praise.*[14]

Chamberlain next offered his thoughts on the many who had made such terrible sacrifices during the war, reserving his highest praise for those who would be the recipients of their efforts that night. He explained:

> *I do not think it any superhuman merit to stand in the ranks of battle and to receive wounds there. It is easier to have physical courage than moral. It may be harder to send your friend into danger than to go yourself; and to languish in prison is doubtless a severer task than to encounter the fortunes of the field. A wound may be a proof of peril, but it is wrong to demand such proof, and folly to be proud of it.... The torture of a mangled body is indeed a bitter experience and a stern discipline, but it is not the worst.*[15]

Not even to those who died for their country did Chamberlain assign a martyr's crown of greatest sacrifice. He reserved that for those who "send forth the joy and stay of life and to wait in dread the heavy blow." He declared:

> *... the worn and wasted and wounded may recover a measure of their strength, or blessed by your cherishing care live neither useless nor unhappy....A lost limb is not like a lost brother, an empty sleeve is not like an empty home, a scarred breast is not like a broken heart. No, the world may smile again and repair its losses, but who shall give back again a father? What husband can replace the chosen of your youth? Who shall restore a son? Where will you find a lover like the high hearted boy you shall see no more?*[16]

Chamberlain gave one more tribute that night. Acknowledging all whose earnest and affectionate encouragement had helped sustain the soldiers in the field, he delivered a declaration of what his own wife's love and encouragement had meant to him during the trials of the war:

> *Lord Bacon was not a true philosopher when he said that wife and children are "impediments to great enterprises." For History tells us too well that in the times that try men's souls the Women and the children are leaders of the men. And the stronger love of life which a man might feel in such relations would not lead him to dishonor himself or them. But rather a sense of pride of duty, of manliness would impel him to be worthy of those who bore his name, that they might at least receive it without stain.... Did they not bear you up with their inspiring messages, my comrade? In the trying hour, when sore worn, and hard-pressed, when desperate valor could win nothing but death, when the heart grew sick with hope deferred, and manly fortitude could endure no longer, were you not roused by the helping, heroic words, "I ask you not to come home, but would to God I could be by your side!" Tell me if in the fierce carnival of death, in the mad uproar of charge and counter-charge did not then a fair pale face amid the hideous phantoms of smoke and flame, lure you on more than the tempting batteries you were sweeping to win? And when summoned to storm the crest rolling down an avalanche of fire, which it were madness for mortal to dare, tell me were there not visions that beckoned more brightly than your advancing banners? If a sweet calm voice did not thrill you with more than bugle or cannon call—"Forward my hero!" though all that made life dear were cast upon the word? And did not then your soul rise mightier than the storm? Could patriotism grow weak, could manhood falter then? Could doubt, or dread, or danger or difficulty unnerve your resolution? Is it not thus also that love may conquer death?*[17]

Sadly, Fanny was not there to hear these words. Still convinced that Lawrence was coming to meet her, she had stayed on in New York. When she found that this was not the case, she wrote a cool note on the 1st of May:

> *So you have given up coming to Boston, as you were going to do when you wrote me. You said that after your address in Portland, you were going to make the trip "to Boston and so forth." I didnt know whether the "and so forth" referred to the little town of New York.... I was surprised when Aunty said that you had been expecting me for a fortnight, for I thought that you were surely coming to Boston at any rate. How did you succeed with your address in Portland?... John brought me some papers from Bangor, with articles upon the gubernatorial question and yourself. John thinks it is a sure thing for you.*[18]

Fanny explained that she was "bothered to death about a dress-maker" who had not completed when promised the clothes that she was having made, and she declared that she would come home as soon as they were finished. Nor had she had any luck finding a woman in New York who she hoped would have news of her brother, Sam. Questioning whether Lawrence could possibly have received all her letters, and in some doubt at what guided him and what he really wanted, she asked, "Do you have any time for writing your book now?" In closing, she wrote, "I am glad you are all so well and happy. Give my love to the dear children. I am quite disappointed that you could not come on to Boston 'and so forth.'"[19]

What had Fanny imagined life would be like with the blessed end to the bloodshed and strife in the country? The cause her husband had given himself to for three years had been won. Had she dreamed of peaceful hours and the sweet communion of uninterrupted days with the husband that had miraculously survived the slaughter to come home? What could separate them now? Was there yet some duty that must be performed? It is hard to imagine that Lawrence had returned to his Bowdoin professorship with anything other than reluctance, but his pursuit of material for a history of the 5th Corps provided some satisfaction. He also savored his opportunities to lecture, though the preparation of his addresses was an ordeal. But after the end of the war, as he confronted the terrible cost that the conflict had inflicted on all Americans, and on his family and himself, a powerful conviction took hold that some good must come after the horrendous price that had been paid. Political machinations should not be allowed to threaten the soldiers' victory, purchased with patriot blood. Lawrence did not relish the life of a politician, but if that was where his duty lay...and Prof. Smyth's terrible prediction, that Lawrence would return from war "shattered" & "good-for-nothing," must not be. Sanity and salvation lay in the proof that he still had important contributions to make and a valuable purpose in life. After the war, though Chamberlain had always been idealistic and dedicated to public service, there is evidence that he was a driven man. But could Fanny, after supporting Lawrence through three years of the national nightmare, understand her husband's need, when his military campaign was over, to take up a political one?[20]

On June 21, 1866, the Maine Republican Party, now calling itself the Union Party, adopted a platform of equal civil and political rights for all men. A sharp contest developed between Chamberlain's supporters and those of Samuel Springer, a wealthy Portland businessman. The opposition demanded to know whether Chamberlain supported the president or Congress, and pointed out his lack of political experience. Satisfying the convention that he aligned himself with Congress, Chamberlain was offered the nomination, which he accepted several days later with his endorsement of their platform. The party had also pledged itself to the ratification of the revised 14th Amendment that Congress had passed in the second week of June. The amendment redefined American citizenship, reduced representation in states that withheld black suffrage and prohibited former government officials who had supported the rebellion from holding office. Congress had also passed a revised version of the Freedmen's Bill over Johnson's veto. Many moderate Republicans, despairing of Johnson's intention to control volatile conditions in the South, were adopting a more radical stance. One Republican instrument in the state of Maine made this quote from Chamberlain their campaign's rallying cry:[21]

> *All must unite in demanding security for the future. We must have guaranties good and sufficient, against any future attempt to destroy this Government whether in the exercise of a pretended right by open war or by more artful and insidious assaults against the principles on which this nation was founded. These are points we cannot yield without danger and dishonor; and when the Southern states shall have complied with those conditions in good faith, they will be in a condition to ask association and fellowship with the loyal commonwealth of the country which they deserted with such violence and scorn. Until that time, in my judgment, it is wise to hold them in strict probation.*[22]

In the days before the election, Fanny and Lawrence held several parties or "levees" in conjunction with Bowdoin's commencement week, just as they had before the war. At the end of August, Lawrence, Fanny, Cousin Deborah, Rev. Adams, Helen and all the children managed to spend a day on nearby Orr's Island, enjoying the peace of the seashore and roasting corn. Several days later, Chamberlain received a letter from his former commander, Gen. Warren, who had been asked by Gen. Grant to submit a list of candidates for field officers in the regular army. Warren informed Chamberlain that, though he doubted he would accept a commission, he had nonetheless put Chamberlain's name at the top of the list. How Chamberlain would spend 1867, for Maine's governors were elected for one year terms, was decided on September 10 with a decisive victory. Elected as Maine's next governor, Chamberlain would never serve as one of his country's "regulars." Perhaps his election as first commander of the Maine chapter of MOLLUS by his boys in blue in the fall of 1866, helped assuage any last regrets.[23]

Change seemed to be the watchword for the Chamberlain and Adams families that fall. Three days after Lawrence's election, John Chamberlain, with the confidence of continuing good health, married Delia Jarvis of Castine, Maine. The newlyweds came to Brunswick on their honeymoon to celebrate Lawrence's victory at the polls. At the end of October, the winds of a violent storm felled the spire of Rev. Adams' church, sending it crashing end over end into the street. Reverend Adams declared it just as well, for the steeple was beyond repair. So, too, was the relationship between the First Parish Church and its minister of almost 37 years. The church was, again, far behind in paying his salary. He had just turned 65, and suffered with chronic digestive problems, among other things, from what he felt was overwork and fatigue. At a temperance meeting that winter, he spoke on the propriety of using liquor for the relief of pain, for he dosed himself with whiskey when the abdominal pain that accompanied his bouts of indigestion became intense. He and Helen dined with the Chamberlains on their 11th wedding anniversary, and he ate only bread and milk from a feast of roast duck and plum pudding that Fanny had prepared. Deborah Folsom, "Cousin Deborah" to Fanny and Lawrence and "Aunty" to the Chamberlain children, was seriously ill in November 1866, and she died in the middle of the month. For all her meddlesome and critical ways over the years, she had been a faithful stay in the Chamberlains' life. That fall, even Sae faced a decision that would significantly change her life. She was contemplating marriage, though apparently with no girlish dreams of romance, for she wrote to Lawrence:

> *Which would you choose for me a man all intellect and not a very warm heart who perhaps would take care of himself and let me do the same but who would no doubt be eminent in his profession— or one all heart with no thought aside from my comfort and happiness, but inferior in intellect both equally high-minded, honorable men. That is just the way the case stands with me. I abhor marriage, and would never enter into any such relations if I could always be situated as I am now but when one is older it is better to have a family—It is impossible for me to tell how much I shrink from assuming such duties.*[24]

The trustees of Pennsylvania College bestowed an honorary Doctors of Laws on Chamberlain in late 1866. Bowdoin did not confer such an honor on their man until 1869, but, in their own way, they did recognize Chamberlain. Before he began his duties as state governor, which at that time did not demand his full-time residency in Augusta, the college turned to him when long-time president, Leonard Woods, retired, and asked him to be interim president of Bowdoin. Chamberlain's exasperation with their offer of less than full salary was explicit in his reply. Having resigned his professorship because of heavy public commitments, he explained that the duties of Bowdoin's presidency, even temporarily, would mean he would have to give up lecturing and would also have to hire a private secretary. These obligations he would consider only if given the full salary. Bowdoin agreed.[25]

When Chamberlain was inaugurated in January 1867, his address was a coalescence of the Republicans' agenda and his own concerns and goals. Mindful of the great losses the people of Maine had endured, he reassured them: "We have looked our sorrows fairly in the face and found that we could bear them." A Republican victory the past fall had preserved their three to one margin in the national Congress. But Chamberlain warned that the instigators of the war were again at work, promoting a Southern solidarity against the reasonable demands made upon them for their states' reentry into the Union. He supported the ratification of the 14th Amendment, considering it a testimony to "our conciliatory disposition." But he considered it imperfect, for "hazarding one of the very fruits of our victory by placing it in the power of the South to introduce into the Constitution a disability founded on race and color...." Observing that the just results of the war might not be speedily apparent, Chamberlain insisted that, "Loyalty...can wait but will not yield." He reminded the people of Maine that, of its estimated 72,945 soldiers who fought in the recent war, over 20,000 were killed or seriously disabled. Nor did he feel that a final account could be taken, for he added, "... how many more who manfully resist as yet the sharp encroachments of disease will be forced to yield to them at last, and how many will live lives of pain & bitterness, with the strength of their youth broken forever, no one can say." Instead of erecting monuments to Maine's soldiers, Chamberlain urged assistance for the disabled and the widows and orphans of the dead. He drew the legislators' attention to the recently instituted home for soldiers' orphans that was imperfectly provided for. Maine's schools and colleges had a new champion, and Chamberlain put forth ideas for attracting industry, utilizing the state's tremendous natural resources, and developing transportation, all to help stop the flow of Maine's young and ambitious out of state. Ironically, Chamberlain also requested, as had several of his predecessors, that the legislature either outlaw the death penalty or mandate the governor's responsibilities in the enforcement of execution. Their failure to do so would result in a storm of controversy during Chamberlain's gubernatorial years.[26]

In the midst of Lawrence's labors as new governor, painful news came from New York. In a letter addressed, "My dear General," Tom wrote that John had again experienced lung hemorrhages and was bedridden. Delia, John's wife of less than 4 months, was having a difficult time caring for him, and Tom asked that Sae come to New York. He wrote proudly that now he, too, was a tobacco inspector, earning $2,000.00 a year, with a chance of earning a $1,000.00 more. Several days later, Tom wrote that John was better, but that over-exertion or excitement could bring on a hemorrhage. John and Delia were in good spirits, but Tom warned that neither had been told by the doctors how sick John was, and Tom felt Lawrence should come to New York to speak with the physicians. While the doctors said that John might live for years, they thought it would not be for many, and only a move to Florida might bring about a complete recovery. By January 16, with renewed hemorrhaging, John's condition deteriorated to the point that his doctors gave him a 1 in 100 chance of recovery. Sae, who had rushed to New York, wrote to Lawrence: "He does not know his condition, though I think fears it is so from what he says to me. He said if he were '*dangerous*' he should want you." Tom added, "Poor John does not yet know that in all probability he will never go to his office again & still he inquires after his business all the time. We shall of course tell him the worst if he does not change for the better within 48 hours—You had better come right on—if it is possible anyway—for he could not die without seeing you—"

Lawrence did travel to John's Brooklyn home, but when it was time to depart, he was unable or unwilling to admit that he might be taking his final leave of his younger brother. Sae told Lawrence, "John asked me after you left, what made you go away so, as though you were only going over to New York? [John] said he had been thinking about it, and he supposed it was so that he should not feel that you thought he was very sick." When Lawrence returned to Maine, Fanny traveled to Augusta to be with him. John rallied enough to leave New York in the spring and travel south. Sae, though she knew Tom would be terribly lonely, was so exhausted that she could think of nothing but going home.[27]

As winter turned to spring, Congress passed measures that divided the ten unreconstructed Southern states into five military districts. But President Johnson held considerable power over the enforcement of these measures. His propensity to remove officials who did not conform to his agenda soon brought the military into the conflict between him and Congress. Closer to home, in April 1867, two men, Clifton Harris and Luther Verill, a black man and a white man, were arraigned in Androscoggin County, Maine on murder charges. Their fate would become a source of great debate in the state, and lead to considerable political turmoil for Chamberlain. Having only served six months as governor, the convention process began again, and in June 1867 he was again chosen as the Republicans' gubernatorial candidate. That summer, he was relieved of one of his duties, when Prof. Samuel Harris of the Bangor Theological Seminary was elected president of Bowdoin.

Sae made her choice and married Charles O. Farrington of Brewer. She chose the man with the big heart over the one with scholarly achievement, for though Sae's Charlie was a successful Brewer businessman, he was no intellectual. The end was near for John Chamberlain, who had come back to Maine with his wife, Delia, that summer, and Sae's first weeks as a wife were spent nursing her brother. A Chamberlain relative would comment that, in the weeks leading up to John's death, Sae "exemplified the true nature of sister's love, in all her toils for him, whom she strove to rescue from an early grave—" Lawrence returned home to Brunswick after John's funeral, having lost another brother just entering the prime of his life. It is believed that John Chamberlain most likely contracted the disease that took his life while he served with the Christian Commission in the squalor and suffering of the hospitals during the Gettysburg campaign. Thus, it was an irony of fate that slowly took the life of the Chamberlain brother who had been safe behind the lines, while preserving the lives of his two brothers in the maelstrom of Little Round Top.[28]

In September 1867, Chamberlain was reelected by a smaller margin than the previous year. The Democratic party had made gains across the country in the off-year state elections. Republicans around the nation feared that there had been a conservative shift in public opinion, indicating a growing opposition to black suffrage. But Maine was already one of the six states in the North that allowed Negroes to vote. Though Maine Republicans had not included one word for or against temperance legislation in their platform, they considered the drop in support for Republican candidates a reaction to the Republican-dominated state legislature's passage of stringent new laws prohibiting the sale of alcohol.

One popular issue in their platform that year was an affirmation of Gen. Sheridan and the other military commanders of the military districts in the South. Sheridan, in command of the 5th Military District with headquarters in New Orleans, was relieved from duty by President Johnson after removing several Southern officials who allegedly were obstructing government policies. Johnson took this action against the advice of Gen. Grant, who was serving as interim secretary of war after Johnson had dismissed Stanton, spitefully flaunting his power over Congress' Tenure of Office Act. Grant's considerable popularity would only be enhanced by his compliance with Congress' later order that

Stanton be reinstated, and the public relished the open confrontations between Johnson and Grant that ensued. Sheridan spent the months after his dismissal touring in the Northeast, and kicked off the campaign that would see Grant as the Republican party's next candidate for president. He was feted in Maine during his visit at the end of October. General Griffin was to have replaced Sheridan in New Orleans, but in the middle of September 1867, Charles Griffin died of yellow fever in Galveston,Texas. Many months later, Chamberlain re-

Maine Historic Preservation Commission

Governor Chamberlain's office. The ornately carved chair is now displayed in the study of the Chamberlain House Museum in Brunswick, Maine.

ceived the sword that he had given to Griffin when his own was lost, as well as the cap that Griffin wore during the war, a familiar sight to every 5th Corps soldier. With these remembrances of his friend were the division flag and bugle that was used at Appomattox.[29]

Chamberlain's first year as governor was successful, and his party and constituents were well satisfied with his performance. But Chamberlain biographers, citing the writings of his 20th century secretary, have claimed that Chamberlain spoke of Fanny's hatred for his service as both soldier and Maine's chief executive. This has created speculation that she did not support him during his governship, though she was eulogized elsewhere as having dutifully attended receptions and provided "generous hospitality." Since Fanny did not move to Augusta, it has been deduced that she "refused" to go to Maine's capital with Lawrence, but this interpretation of events is ill conceived. The governor's duties, in those years, did not demand a year-round presence in Augusta, nor was a residence provided for the governor. There is no reason to assume that the Chamberlains did not rise to the new challenges that Lawrence's life in the political world imposed, but the archives are curiously devoid of correspondence for the year 1867. While it seems that Lawrence and Fanny made a success of public life in their first year as Maine's governor and first lady, we can only speculate upon the stresses in their personal life as husband and wife. In following years, the correspondence of a family friend implies that Chamberlain was, physically and mentally, coming near the end of his tether. And one surviving letter, from Lawrence to Fanny in the fall of 1868, reveals that by that time, Fanny may have considered divorce. Whatever tension the Chamberlains might have experienced in Lawrence's first year as governor would have increased immeasurably during his second term. In that year, he would find out what it was to have political enemies. The virulence of the attacks made upon her husband offer ample justification, if Fanny did, in fact, "hate" Lawrence's life in politics.[30]

CHAPTER

15

"In the Midst of All the Uproar"

In the last year of the war, before Lawrence returned to the army for the last campaign of 1865, he addressed a letter of condolence to the family of Rev. John S. C. Abbott of New Haven, Connecticut. Formerly from Brunswick, the Abbotts were long-time friends of Rev. Adams' family with whom Lawrence became well acquainted. Abbott's soldier son, Waldo, had died of disease in Florida in the summer of 1864. In his letter of sympathy, Lawrence sent a photograph of himself and an invitation for Rev. Abbott and his 31-year-old daughter, Jane, called Jenny by the family, to come and visit when he returned to the field. Abbott, a prolific writer of histories and biographies and a popular speaker, was involved in a lecture tour, and he and Jenny were unable to accept the invitation, but Lawrence was enthusiastically received by the Abbotts when he stopped to see them in Connecticut in the summer of 1865. Reverend Abbott pressed Lawrence after the war to allow him to write a biography of him for his series, "Heroic Men." But Lawrence begged off, exclaiming to a friend, "I couldn't have the face to do that."[1]

Jenny Abbott, who suffered from a back condition that sometimes left her bed-ridden and confined to a wheelchair, continued to correspond with Lawrence and a warm friendship developed between them. By 1866, one of her letters indicates that Lawrence had dealt with expressions of love from Jenny. In early 1866, she wrote in response to an apparent admonishment from him, "I will never say 'love one all you can'! I had no thought of the 'fallacies and pitfalls' which 'lurk' under the cover of the word! Perhaps I ought to have said feel all the 'friendship' or 'esteem' you can, but love has to me so many phases I used the word in a more general sense than you understood it. I never weigh my words to you." It is apparent, however, that Lawrence came to rely on Jenny as a friend and confidante, and in the late 1860s and early 1870s, her letters were brimming with sympathetic observations and advice on his troubles, personal and professional. In 1868, Lawrence, again laid low by the pain and inflammation of his wound, consulted a surgeon, and was told that little could be done. Anxious for him to see a physician she had great confidence in, Jenny wrote:

> *...As soon as it is safe you shall have a cordial welcome here where we will nurse you back to health. When I see how much vigor there is still remaining to you, when I recall all that you have triumphed over I cannot feel that there is not still a great possibility of restoration to comfortable health. But it cannot come by unaided nature. If Dr. Bacon speaks encouragingly you may safely trust him. Only think for a little what it would be to have that dreadful wound put in a healthy condition! Since there is no vital part injured help must be possible—Please, please, listen to me! You have borne for four years this cross—I for fourteen have borne a similar one and I know time does not make it easier. It is worth a great sacrifice to do all one can to avert it. If your surgeon could give you no more encouragement than he did oh pray try Dr. Bacon who may help you—We will pray and God will hear. If His answer is a denial to all our hopes we will accept it humbly and lovingly—but we will not sit quietly by, doing nothing when so loudly warned, and then say the 'Lord's will be done' not having tried to do it or even to know it! It can never be right to be ill if we can be well—or even better— It is false courage which makes us endure if we can conquer—You who are so brave, so strong, so noble my heart rejoices in the thought of you, and my life takes new hope because of you, I may trust you to be entreated by these words of mine. I think God suggested this in answer to my prayers—Do not be vexed with me, and think I am overstepping friendship's bounds—How can I not beseech you when I see what may be your loss if you let this time pass. Dont learn to dread my letters because of my nagging—I do dislike to be a tease and still more impertinent....*[2]

Though suffering from his wounds, there was no retreat from his obligations as governor, nor any abatement of his commitments. Chamberlain began the year with his inaugural address, in which there was a perceptible shift from the previous year's postwar issues, to the state's internal needs and problems. Equitable taxation and a slow economy were on Maine people's minds. A method for fair distribution of the debt created by wartime enlistment bounties attracted considerable interest. Chamberlain again requested legislation regarding the state's law on capital punishment. A number of Maine's governors had simply neglected to issue warrants for execution to carry out death sentences handed down by the state's courts. In this way, Maine experienced a period of *de facto* abolition of execution without addressing the controversy or passing legislation. Several of Chamberlain's predecessors were unhappy with this arrangement, but had failed to convince the state legislature that it must be changed. Chamberlain stated:

> *Nothing can be more plain than that the law contemplates the death penalty as the extreme of punishment. It declares even the method, and requires the judge to pronounce the awful sentence, but leaves a weak place in providing for its execution by which a Governor, if so disposed, can shirk a painful duty. It begins a tragedy and ends a farce. I am not prepared to say whether public sentiment demands a change in the law, but I deem it proper to inform you that I shall consider it my duty to dispose of cases under sentence of death which come before me for action, and shall either see that the law is duly executed, or shall interpose the Executive prerogative of commuting the sentence to imprisonment for life.*[3]

Chamberlain also made his opinion on pardons clear, stating that they should be based upon either, "new evidence since conviction, mitigating circumstances unknown to the Court, indisputable proof of thorough reformation, or some peculiar hardship in the case which the law could not take into account." Declaring that the dignity of law should not be mocked with sentences of the court set lightly aside, Chamberlain asserted that the "burden of proof" is upon the petitioner for pardon, "to show why it should be granted and not upon the Executive to show why it should not."[4]

Chamberlain gave only passing mention to recent temperance legislation, but it would become another great controversy in Chamberlain's second term. Early in his first term, he accepted the invitation to chair Maine's annual temperance convention like his predecessors before him. But in 1868 he declined with the explanation that, since the organization was meeting to "affect certain legislation now pending, upon which my official action may be required, it appears to me that the proprieties of the case do not leave me free to participate...." The more radical men of the state's temperance movement, far from accepting this explanation of his position, were highly offended.[5]

Once relieved of Bowdoin's presidency, Chamberlain again began to accept the many invitations he had to speak. One such occasion is typical of the hundreds Chamberlain would attend in his lifetime. In mid-February, Fanny and Lawrence traveled to Bangor, where he delivered "The Surrender of Lee" to a large, appreciative audience. The Bangor *Whig and Courier* reported:

> *Governor Chamberlain, in response to the invitation of prominent gentlemen of this city, and the lecture committee of the Union St. Course lectures, delivered his account of the surrender of Gen. Lee, to a large and delighted audience at Norumbega Hall, on Saturday evening. Despite fast falling snow, the people began early to flock to the hall, and continued to pour in till every seat was occupied. The Governor was introduced by his Honor, Mayor Wakefield, in a few pertinent remarks, and was received with a round of applause; The Cornet Band, which was in attendance, playing 'Hail to the Chief.' The lecture was a scholarly and eloquent production, replete*

with thrilling incident and glowing description. In the language of a contemporary, "It was the scholar narrating the deeds of the soldier, with all the grace and eloquence of the one, and the modesty and gallant bearing of the other." The lecture was listened to with breathless attention, interrupted at times by bursts of applause. All present were gratified at the opportunity thus furnished them of hearing the particulars of the final & closing scenes of the war, not only from one who was on the spot, and had peculiar advantage for giving a correct and minute account of the affair, but from one of our own noble sons so honorably and closely connected with it....

After the lecture, the audience was invited to the home of a local official and "a large number of our citizens availed themselves of the opportunity of paying their respects to the Governor & his lady..."[6]

In February 1868, the House of Representatives started impeachment proceedings against President Johnson. Grant had stepped aside in January when Congress reinstated Stanton as secretary of war, but Johnson removed Stanton again on Feb. 21. This time, Stanton not only refused to be dismissed, but barricaded himself in his office. With the Senate serving the function of jury and the chief justice presiding as judge, the trial began on March 4. Every Republican state convention endorsed conviction. But there were a few Republican senators who, despite how they felt about Johnson, doubted that he had committed any legally impeachable offense. Nor were they comfortable with the precedent this case would set. If Congress could impeach any president they could muster a two thirds majority against simply because they disagreed with him, the presidency would be seriously handicapped, and the balance of power in the country destroyed. William Pitt Fessenden of Maine was one of the Republican senators that held these views. In the days just before the vote was taken, when it was known that Fessenden had not been swayed by the outcry for Johnson's conviction, he began to receive vitriolic and threatening mail. Chamberlain supported Sen. Fessenden's position, and shared, in some part, the storm of criticism that was heaped upon the senator when Johnson was acquitted in May.[7]

Johnson had little time to enjoy his acquittal, for 1868 was a presidential election year. Ulysses Grant was, as expected, the Republican Party's candidate. Both cavalry commander Gen. Alfred Pleasonton and Gen. Daniel Sickles, who was a Republican at that time, stumped for their old commander, appearing that summer at the Maine convention that again chose Chamberlain as their gubernatorial candidate. The party, convinced that the state legislature's concessions to the temperance forces cost them many votes in the previous year's election, had seen to it that the legislation was repealed. Angered by this setback, and still smarting from the governor's failure to appear at their convention, temperance radicals in the state focused their discontent on Chamberlain. At a Maine Methodists' convention on temperance, a resolution was proposed criticizing Chamberlain, but Rev. Adams, while putting in an appearance, helped defeat the measure with a few well chosen words.[8]

Reverend Adams considered retirement in early 1868, feeling that he must leave Brunswick before he broke down completely. But by late summer, he considered taking the pulpit of a newly organized congregation in Orange, New Jersey, in hopes that a change would be beneficial to his health and sagging spirits. He also pondered whether a new man at the First Parish Church might instruct the members on the need to support their minister. That summer, Sae and Charlie became the new parents of a baby boy, named John Chamberlain Farrington. Prior to the gubernatorial election, a hasty note from Lawrence to Fanny indicates a hectic and unsettled lifestyle, full of obligations and travel. Asking that she bring recent newspapers and any important mail, Lawrence wrote, "I hope you got home safely & found all well. I have plenty of work on hand. Go to Waterville this afternoon & return Thursday morning. We are going to Mr Sanborn's Friday and would like to have you come up Thursday P.M.. I am sorry I have not my black suit for Waterville & the sleeve button I was going to borrow."[9]

Chamberlain had not endeared himself to the Republicans party stalwarts by his opposition to Johnson's impeachment, nor to Maine's temperance radicals. But the Sept. 14 election was a triumph, with Chamberlain winning handily over his Democratic opponent. In November, Gen. Grant swept to victory in the presidential election. Many years later, an acquaintance would recall a conversation he had with Chamberlain regarding Grant, in which he claimed Chamberlain remarked, "He never ought to have accepted the Presidency in the first place. He should have been as wise as was Sherman who refused it again and again." He also reportedly said of Grant: "He falls too easily into the hands of shrewd, designing men." Perhaps Chamberlain first perceived this failing in Grant during those days of the last campaign, when Sheridan alone seemed to win Grant's favor and confidence. And with his 5th Corps history laid aside, had Chamberlain seen the pamphlets that Gen. Henry Tremain, one of Sheridan's cavalrymen in the last days of the war, had circulated in Washington? Tremain considered the battle at Quaker Road, "a severe contest," but he would state that, "it was comparatively resultless. The enemy withdrew at its conclusion, believing us too strong for further aggression." Tremain also quoted Sheridan as stating that Gen. Warren at Five Forks, had "wished for the sun to go down before the dispositions for the attack could be completed."[10]

But, Chamberlain had plenty to hold his attention closer to home. Maine law mandated a one year waiting period between a sentence of death and execution. In October 1868, that period had expired for convicted murderer Clifton Harris. It cannot have been a surprise to the people of the state when Chamberlain made known his intention to carry through on the court's sentence. He had stated in his second inaugural address that it was his duty to do so, unless he saw grounds for commuting the sentence to life imprisonment or a pardon. The controversy that arose over Harris' death sentence is curious. Clifton Harris, a young black man, was born on a Southern plantation, the son of former slaves. He had confessed to and been convicted of the 1867 murder of two Auburn, Maine women. The victims were robbed, sexually assaulted, murdered and dismembered. His admission of guilt, and the barbaric nature of the crime, should have made him an unlikely candidate for public sympathy. But Harris, after his own arrest, had implicated another man, Luther Verrill, a white man who pleaded innocent. Tried separately, Harris was found guilty and sentenced to be hung. Verrill, maintaining his innocence, asked for another trial based on new evidence, and was eventually released by the courts.

Clifton Harris, 1867.

There was much interest in Maine and around the country regarding reform of capital punishment, but many of Harris' champions came from the ranks of ardent abolitionists. A state senator, John L. Stevens, declared to Maine's senate of Harris: "His ancestry was torn from a barbaric land by agents of Anglo-Saxon cupidity. His father was whipped and robbed; his mother had vile indignities heaped upon her.... Shall this uninstructed, friendless, defenseless creature who since his advent among us has no one to care for him but GOD—shall he die on the gallows of our rearing?" When the editor of Portland's *Daily Argus* questioned why Chamberlain had pardoned another convicted murderer, other Maine newspapers joined in the fray. While some supported the governor, others implied that he was willing to sign the warrant for Harris' execution because he was a black man. Chamberlain was furious.[11]

At a distance of 120 years, it is difficult to analyze the political goals of those who arrayed themselves against Chamberlain in this year. If the temperance radicals were not partisans of the capital punishment reformers, they likely enjoyed his discomfort. Oddly enough, Chamberlain may also have proved to be too popular a politician, for there were those, even in his own party, who wanted to diminish his power at the polls. But on the day that Chamberlain signed the first warrant for Clifton Harris' execution, he had more than political foes on his mind, for he also wrote a letter to Fanny. It is a startling revelation of the impasse they had reached in their marriage. On November 20, Lawrence wrote Fanny:

Dear Fanny,

In the midst of all the uproar of obloquy now hurled at me by the friends of Harris & the rampant temperance men I find my self assailed by only one thing which distresses me. On arriving here last night sick & worn-out, I had hoped that even if I could have no other care and nursing I could at least have that of sleep. Things have now however come to that pass that I must trouble you by referring again to the suggestion I made to you some time since in regard to your making a confidant of unworthy persons. I have had abundant & concurrent testimony from many—all as much your friends as mine—that you were complaining to every one who came in to the house of my conduct & treatment of you. I have passed that over for a long time not thinking it worth while to notice it. When I found that you were still disposed to do this, & in the last instance in a direction that would do you more harm than me, I ventured to give you the warning I did some time since. You received it with apparent kindness & I was satisfied. I then referred to it again just before I came away & you spoke in a way that made me nearly happy. Now last night after I had gone to bed, Mr Johnson came in with a very distressed manner & begged me not to be angry with him but he saw such grief & ruin impending that he must tell me. Miss Courlaender it seems is freely telling people that "you told her (& Mrs. Dunning also as well as every body else) that I abused you beyond endurance—pulling your hair, striking, beating & otherwise personally maltreating you, & that you were gathering up every thing you could find against me to sue for a divorce." Mr Johnson says this is doing immense harm, whether the fact is so or not, & the bitter enemies who now assail me on public grounds, will soon get hold of this & will ruin me. He is in great distress & begs me to do some thing—what he does n't know. You must be aware that if it were not you who were so clearly implicated in this business, I should make quick work of these calumniators. I fear nothing for myself. But you must see that whatever come[s] upon me; comes upon you too with even more effect & for your sake I must again offer the suggestion that you act with wisdom and discretion. If it is true (as Mr Johnson seems to think there is a chance of its being) that you are preparing for an action against me, you need not give your self all this trouble. I should think we had skill enough to adjust the terms of a separation without the wretchedness to all our family which these low people to whom it would seem that you confide your grievances & plans, will certainly bring about. You never take my advice, I am aware. But if you do not stop this at once it will end in hell. I am sorry to say this to you, when I have so entirely confided in you—& have been so reassured of late in this confidence, as my interest in your matters & in your friends must convince you. Of course this has given me a troubled night & I am taking up the duties of the day wholly unfitted for them. The thing comes to this, if you are contemplating any such thing as Mr Johnson says—there is a better way to do it. If you are not, you must see the gulf of misery to which this confidence with unworthy people tends. You have this advantage of me, that, I never spoke unkindly of you to any person. I shall not now do so to you. But it is a very great trial to me—more than all things else put together—wounds, pains, toils, wrongs & hatred of eager enemies.[12]

Lawrence's letter to Fanny is open to interpretation, but ultimately it seems to be neither a confirmation nor a denial that he had been an abusive husband. Maine law on divorce, from 1849 to 1883, was liberal, comparable to the modern "no fault" divorce. Maine's Supreme Court could grant a decree of divorce if it were deemed, "reasonable & proper, conducive to domestic harmony." Fanny would have had no reason to invent grievances in order to bring her suit. But divorce decrees were granted by either the state's Supreme Court or the state legislature. As Lawrence pointed out, it would have been a great public embarrassment for them both, and for the Chamberlain and Adams families.[13]

Fanny apparently agreed to Lawrence's suggestion of a separation, and though Maine's law had provisions for legal separation, it seems that they settled the details of their arrangement privately. In mid-December, when Lawrence returned to Brunswick, he stayed with a neighbor, while Fanny apparently remained in their Maine St. home. In the months to come, Fanny often traveled to New York with one of the children. Lawrence, with another term as governor to serve, was often away from home on state business or lecturing. The couple communicated with each other through their letters to the children, and it seems that when Fanny and Lawrence were in Brunswick at the same time, the house was filled with company.[14]

The controversy of Clifton Harris continued, for the warrant which Chamberlain issued for Harris' execution in late November 1868 had not been carried out. The sheriff designated by law to be the executioner had disappeared, and a Bangor newspaper suggested that this was merely a delaying tactic on Chamberlain's part. There was speculation that, given this extra time, the legislature would change the "barbarous law" that permitted Harris' execution. But when they did act, both the house and senate voted to preserve the law that mandated capital punishment in the state, a stance that probably strengthened Chamberlain's resolve to carry out the sentence. Maine's attorney general, William Frye, not only joined the voices that spoke out against Harris' execution, he did so officially, including his objections in his official report for the year 1868. Previously, though there was no question that the 14th Amendment would be passed by the Maine House, William Frye plied the legislature with a lengthy speech in its favor. For Frye, though no doubt sincere in his support for Freedmen's rights, had political ambitions. Though Frye stated, "I have no hesitation in giving my opinion that the Governor is right; that a strict observance of the oaths he has taken required of him this action....," he followed this legal defense of Chamberlain's actions by saying, "While I fully sustain the position of the Governor, I do not think that justice requires the execution of Harris." Pointing out that Harris had "turned State's evidence," Frye also asked why, in another recent decision, a well educated white man who had murdered his wife had escaped the death penalty, while "Harris, born on a Southern plantation, educated only as to his brutal instincts, compelled into ignorance and degradation, and a subserviency to a white man by force of law itself, almost in his legal infancy influenced by a white companion, commits a murder and is executed. The proposition does not commend itself to my sense of justice."[15]

Janet and Bedford Hayes Collection

Governor Joshua Chamberlain, c. 1868.

No less than a quarter of Chamberlain's third inaugural address was dedicated to answering his capital punishment critics, especially William Frye. Chamberlain explained that in cases where there were mitigating circumstances, he had commuted death sentences to life imprisonment, but he declared that the "peculiar atrocity" in Harris' case admitted no leniency. With barely concealed disdain, Chamberlain stated:

> *I should have contented myself with this simple statement of my action without comment; but as it has pleased the Attorney General in his official report to protest again this execution, although candidly admitting that it is the Governor's duty to execute this law; and as his careful official statement must be taken as the best expression of dissent which can be made, I may be warranted in giving you the reasons why I am not influenced by that kind of argument.*[16]

Chamberlain turned the tables. He questioned why, when the case was still in the hands of the court and the attorney general, they did not avail themselves of the opportunity to reward Harris for his attempt to implicate an accomplice by "withdrawing any portion of the indictment in token of services rendered." Nor, Chamberlain pointed out, had the jury or judge recommend mercy to the executive. He suggested that Harris' state's evidence against Luther Verrill, who was released for lack of evidence, had "either implicated a guilty party or an innocent one." He declared that if Verrill was innocent, Harris tried to add a "third murder to the former two," and if guilty, Harris' later withdrawal of his accusation against Verrill, "virtually shielded the guilty from justice, in either case but adding another to his horrible list of crimes, and crowning the whole with perjury." Chamberlain added, "I fail to see the extenuating force of any such State's evidence as this."[17]

Addressing the extenuating facts of Harris' early life that Frye and others cited, Chamberlain retorted that, "they were a ground of gratitude that no man nursed of woman was left to do these horrors—and of congratulation that this precocity of guilt was nipped in its 'legal infancy,' before its blossom and full fruits had come." Chamberlain observed: "'Previous good character' is a plea in mitigation—but to plead a 'previous bad character' is a novelty of jurisprudence." Of the convicted wife-murderer, Knight, he offered the opinion that he also should have been hung, but that Knight "still protests his innocence while Harris boasts of his guilt." He also pointed out that since his predecessors had failed to issue a warrant of execution for Knight, he had already served twelve years at hard labor, and he questioned the justice of taking Knight from what had unofficially been a commuted sentence of life imprisonment. As to whether Harris was really the guilty party, Chamberlain stated that he had nothing to do with any other suspect, for the attorney general had discharged Luther Verrill from custody, "presumably, because he could not convict him." Adding that neither his own personal opinions nor the present state of public opinion in the state affected his duty to execute the law, Chamberlain reminded his listeners that the state legislature, well aware of his intention to carry out court sentences, had rejected a bill to abolish capital punishment in the state.[18]

Chamberlain ultimately offered his opinion that the death penalty should be retained, and remarked, "It is urged to be merciful. But to whom? I ask. To the violator of all sanctities—the assassin of all defenselessness—the pitiless spoiler of the peace and order of society? or to the innocent, the good, the peaceful and well-doing, who rely upon the protection of the State which they serve and adorn?" In a statement that reveals how deeply he felt the personal criticism he had received during this vitriolic debate, he observed that the, "virtues of Harris the ravisher of his murdered and dying victims, are compared with the crime of the stubborn executive in not withholding the just penalty of the laws."[19]

On January 8, 1869, Chamberlain again signed a warrant for Harris' execution. At the end of that month, he wrote to his mother that he had not been well, and, still under great pressure, was seeking wisdom from above on great issues. "Many are bitter on me about capital punishment but it does not disturb me in the least." He had received an abusive, threatening letter from a man who had apparently known the family when Lawrence was "a little good boy." Asking if his mother knew who this man was, he denied that he was scared by threats of vengeance. "He is mistaken his man. I do not think I have a particle of fear in me of any thing that walks or flies. I go on in the strength of conscious rectitude & you cant scare me." His usually plain spoken father rose to the occasion when he let Lawrence know how he felt about the "Cavil of Clowns" that tried to prevent his son from doing his duty, and his contempt for "over reformed attorney generals odious."[20]

In mid-February, Lawrence traveled to Philadelphia to deliver a speech at the Academy of Music, taking twelve-year-old Daisy with him. Fanny and Lawrence's little girl was becoming a young lady, and an amusing and delightful companion. Abandoning her childhood nickname for her given name of Grace, she addressed her brother at home, "Darling Bill," and with irreverent affection described her now silver-haired father's performance: "The snowy cap the Sacred Mountain still looms above all Father perfect in every way. Good voice—and the same presence. Our path is strewn with Generals and Admirals and old friends galore God's in His Heaven All's well with the world Yours Grace." Lawrence added: "...The academy of music was packed to its utmost 24 hours before the time not a seat to be had. I think I got on pretty well. The lights plagued me somewhat But Grace says my voice was good. Everybody in the house heard every word of mine not of the others, I am told I am tired & head swimming perhaps too rich food. L." When Grace was but a babe in arms, Fanny had the presentiment that their daughter would be a great comfort to her father, and her prediction had come true. While daughters were often cast in the role of companion to their fathers in the 1800s, Grace's cheerful nature and enthusiasm for her father's activities promoted a special relationship between father and daughter. Grace's relationship with Wyllys was also one of deep affection. Sae related how Wyllys, who was also called Will or Bill, while visiting them, had kept half of everything nice he received during his stay to bring home to Grace.[21]

When Chamberlain returned from Philadelphia, he went to an Augusta physician, who examined him for an application he made at the end of 1868. His condition was described as, "Bladder very painful & irritable—whole of lower part of abdomen tender & sensitive—Large urinal fistula at base of penis in front of scrotum, which is exceedingly troublesome—suffers constant pain in both hips from wound—also struck in left breast by bullet which bruised integuments severely from which much lameness in that region—" The physician offered: "I think his general health much affected from his wounds, especially the first named & that it will materially abridge his life." Chamberlain was awarded a pension of $30.00 a month.[22]

It is likely that a lecture Chamberlain gave in Massachusetts kept him out of the state on March 12 when Clifton Harris was executed. The executioner botched the job, and Harris, who is said to have faced his death bravely, died a slow death by strangulation. As recently as 1974, the degree of Harris' guilt has been questioned with an unsubstantiated story that Harris claimed, once again, on the eve of his execution, that Verrill instigated the crime. Harris had withdrawn his accusation against Verrill because, he claimed, "They told me I would be pardoned if I got Verrill clear, but now I can't say anything but my first story is true."[23]

Chamberlain had clearly fought for a change in the law that left the action of the governor, rather than the judge and jury, with the final judgment on convicted and condemned criminals. But while the legislature refused to change the law on capital punishment, and judges continued to hand down death sentences, that responsibility was forced on Maine governors. Though Chamberlain supported suffrage for the Freedmen in his first inaugural address, because Harris, the only man executed during his governship, was a black man, his attitudes on race were called into question.

An examination of Chamberlain's attitudes toward race and equality yields little hard evidence. A biographical piece, "Chamberlain, a Sketch," written in 1906, has been attributed to Chamberlain, and it states that he did not believe in immediate suffrage for Freedmen. This and other significant errors in the "Sketch," provide evidence that, while he supplied material for the work, it is unlikely that he authored it. But there is no question that Chamberlain wrote a speech entitled, "The Old Flag," that he delivered in 1878, in which he reviewed what he believed were the causes of the war and principles won. Though it provides insight to Chamberlain's attitudes toward the races, the speech was written ten years after the Harris controversy, when the country was dealing with the failures of Reconstruction. Chamberlain criticized those who would use armed force to defend Negro rights in the South, and commented that we would, "keep the plighted troth to the black man, the red man, the yellow man and the white man," but he added:

> *...some say we cannot have peace here because the negroes do not have good treatment in the South, and because the Rebels are back in Congress. The negroes are abused in the South, it is true, but so are the Chinese in California, so are the 40,000 poor girls in London, so are the Indians. We must do the best we can for the negroes. While I am sorry that they cannot vote without interruption, I want to ask if that is the thing for which all that toil and sacrifice was given, for which the best blood in all the land made those mountains and rivers and fields immortal, that the negroes might have no one to stop them in going to the polls.—For my part, if I am to die for it—I think it was for something else, something a long way before that. I think it was country, the whole country, dear because of the precious foundations in which it was laid; sacred, because of the divine commission laid*

upon it to hold the van in the great but slowmarching enfranchisement of man. The free country—first the men who made it so, and then the men who are cast upon it. Yes, I say it. The men who have made a country what it is or given it character and built their very lives into its history are to have the foremost hand if we would keep the country true to its mission, true to its ideal. The voting business in the South will regulate itself.[24]

It seems that Chamberlain believed that other states, given time, would adopt his own state's position. Maine had allowed black men the vote in the years before the Civil War, and in the town of Brunswick a number of well-respected black residents went to the polls with no question of their right to do so. But perhaps he saw a distinct difference between the Freedman of the North and newly-freed slaves. In his book, *The Passing of the Armies,* he wrote that his encounters with the former slaves under his jurisdiction in Virginia immediately after Lee's surrender did not make a favorable impression. Acknowledging that stragglers of both armies roamed the area, Chamberlain commented:

We found the negroes especially unruly. All restraints which had hitherto held them in check were set loose by the sudden collapse of the rebel armies. The floodgates were opened to the rush of animal instinct. The only notion of freedom apparently entertained by these bewildered people was to do as they pleased. That was what they had reason to suppose white men did. To act according to each one's nature was liberty, contrasted with slavery. Numbers gave them a kind of frenzy. Without accustomed support, without food, or opportunity to work, they not unnaturally banded together; and without any serious organization, and probably without much deliberate plotting of evil, they still spread terror over the country. They swarmed through houses and homes demanding food, seizing all goods they could lay their hands on, abusing the weak, terrifying women, and threatening to burn and destroy. This was an evil that had to be met promptly, and we construed our orders to protect the country liberally. So the First Brigade...was sent out charged with the duty of protecting the homes of the people and the peace of the community, more especially against the depredations of the lawless negro bands, of whom there were about a thousand within my jurisdiction.

It is difficult to know if Chamberlain's impressions of the newly freed slaves influenced his judgment on how readily they could integrate into Southern society. It is of some interest, but perhaps of questionable significance that he did not use racial epithets that were common during the 19th century. While Tom and John Chamberlain both used the word "nigger" in reference to contrabands and black servants during the war, no example exists of Lawrence doing so.[25]

Chamberlain's attitudes toward the nation's newest citizens can also be examined by considering a project which he, as governor, endorsed with enthusiasm. Convinced that vast tracts of land suitable for agriculture were going undeveloped, he seized on a project that encouraged Scandinavians to immigrate to Maine. "My conviction is strengthened that it would be greatly to our advantage to induce colonies of these hardy, frugal and industrious people to settle in this State." In a nation teeming with recent immigrants, it is interesting to consider why Chamberlain found this particular project so attractive.[26]

The history of immigration in the state, and in particular, the area where Chamberlain grew up, sheds light on the issue. The city of Bangor and nearby town of Brewer experienced tremendous growth and prosperity in the 1800s, and attracted many Irish who fled from famine and disease. The Irish who first came to the area were those who could afford to leave their mother country with some assets, and by starting businesses or offering skilled labor, they were assimilated into the communities. But as the suffering continued in Ireland and the number of those desperate to escape starvation increased, many who came to America were not only destitute when they arrived, but were also suspected of bringing with them the diseases that scourged the old country. The shoreline of Bangor became lined with their shanties, and disease and crime flourished in the growing ghettos.

Chamberlain grew up a witness to the raw life of this impoverished class, and when he traveled from the Bangor Theological Seminary to his home in Brewer, he passed by and through the worst neighborhoods of the city. Along with the problems this influx of destitute Irish brought to the area, they were also held in disfavor for their Catholicism by the Protestants, and it is said that a number of the Bangor seminarians labored to save bodies and souls in the Irish slums. Battles took place between the laborers of Bangor and the new immigrants, who were perceived as a threat to their jobs. But the propertied inhabitants of the area, while disparaging their religion and sordid living conditions, welcomed this new pool of workers to their mills, woodlots and farms. The Chamberlains, over the years, had many Irish workers in their home and working on their properties. Little is known of the family's attitudes toward them, other than Father Chamberlain's preference for the Irish who arrived early in the 19th century, as opposed to the desperate latecomers. And John Chamberlain, during his labors with the Christian Commission, pondered at great length over the Sisters of Charity he had encountered in the hospitals. John had read the sensational novels that achieved notoriety in these years, books that accused the Catholic clergy of the worst sort of depredations and fantastic immorality.[27]

While it is interesting to consider the early influences in Chamberlain's life that made him a champion of the project that brought hardy Swedish Protestants to Maine, these are hardly conclusive. Perhaps it is sufficient to say that Chamberlain held a strong belief that those who had worked hardest and contributed the most to the country were the most deserving of success in America. Lawrence and Fanny, by anyone's standards had attained success, yet the price paid seemingly robbed them of their marriage and the comfort of their loving dependence on one another. In the next year, their lives would be largely spent apart, yet marks of the respect they still held for one another remained.

CHAPTER

16

"Where Worries Cannot Reach You"

The spring of 1869 found Lawrence pressed with state business, while Fanny visited New York. Tom Chamberlain had stayed in the city, though the tobacco business dropped off that winter. In April, he wrote to Sae in Brewer, asking about her five month old son. "In the first place I want to know how old the boy is, and whether he talks any or not. I take considerable interest in babies some how lately—" Tom also asked for John's widow: "I want to know how old Delia is—Can you tell me?" By June, Tom was apparently in financial distress. Fearful that he might lose his job, he asked Lawrence for help in obtaining another position. Lawrence responded from Augusta that it was impossible for him to come to New York:

> *I am as much distracted with the pressure as you are with your dropping off of business. I declare I would not have an office, if I were you, which requires so much 'fixing-up'. I would be more independent somehow. I am under bother enough as I am, but I dont have to beg any body to favor me & I hate to have you do it. I will do every thing I can to have your matters go well, & had hoped to go to N.Y. before this but we were obliged to hold session of the council which took me this way instead. I dont see now how I can take time to go there before July. You must make the best of the situation, & with the backers you have I think you can carry it.... I am*

sorry to disappoint you but cant help it. If things get too blue, you must let me know because I can manage to come in a case of life & death.

Tom scrawled on Lawrence's letter, which he may have sent to Fanny: "I wrote L. today not to think of coming for me, as I was O.K. and not to trouble himself one bit for me as I could get along without him by paying 100$ to a man I know. TDC"[1]

Chamberlain was also urged that summer to reconsider his refusal to be a candidate for a fourth term. In his inaugural address that January, he had made it clear that he was serving his last year. But the Republican Party could not secure a viable candidate by the time of their June convention. Chamberlain acquiesced, and received two thirds of the delegate's votes, while radical temperance members supported their own candidate. Fanny, in New York with Wyllys, was haunting the auction houses for antiques and works of art. The disruption of their lives from frequent travel and poor communication is apparent. She wrote home:

My dearest little Daisy I thank you for your last little letter, it was very welcome. The check came safely tell Papa, but it was so long before I got it, that of course the things I told Papa about, were snatched up and we lost them. Miss Alice Cary (tell him) got the beautiful china set, and the Italian picture, the beautiful Magdalen, went immediately. I am very sorry you have a cough dear. Be sure and do not sit in draughts, or sleep in damp bed clothes or put on anything that is not thoroughly aired. It is a very bad time of the year for getting rid of a cough. How did you get the cold? You and Wyllys ought to be especially careful about coughs, as both your Papa's and Mama's families are so subject to them.... I want to see my little Daisy very much indeed and so does good, old Wyllys. He is writing you now, I believe, at Uncle Tom's office. I will enclose an old letter I wrote you long ago, because it may amuse you, although most of it means nothing now. Papa's change of plans made it of no use. How funny it was that Papa did not know where to send to me, or felt in any doubt about my plans with regard to going to Boston or Brunswick! He wrote me and Wyllys too, for me to meet him in Boston at a certain time; I answered, telling him what day I would be in Boston, asking where I should meet him there and sent for the check in full season for it to reach here, and for me to do with it what I had written him about. Then came the telegram...proposing that I should stay in New York until he came and saying that I could not find him in Boston. Of course I did not think of going after that, as I knew that any great change in going to house keeping or any excitement with regard to it, would ruin his oration for the Fourth, which is a very important thing. By all means it is better not to open the house until after he gets back from New York, and by all means I had better stay here till then. I hope Papa is coming on well with his writing, I know he will do well, but I appreciate the labor and care it is to him. This morning's paper brings news of his nomination again.[2]

Lawrence presented his oration to a new organization, the Society of the Army of the Potomac, in New York City on July 4 of that year. The address provides another window to Chamberlain's thoughts, four years after the end of the war. It is eloquent in its expression of the gulf that widened in the years after the war between the veterans of the field and a number of those at home, who "charged upon us that our campaigns were feeble, our battles indecisive, and even our victories barren." He declared that "the hour is not yet, nor even near, when the history of this Army can be adequately or impartially told," noting bitterly that, "Men are so constituted that what they but imperfectly understand they still make up their most violent judgment upon; and works in which they had no hand seem easily achieved and of little worth; and it is not impossible—such is the 'rarity of human charity under the sun'—that envy and enmity even should be the tribute paid to superiority of merit which cannot be denied." But, declaring his ambition to adopt a defensive stance, rather than an aggressive one, Chamberlain defended the Army of the Potomac. He described the region in which they operated as a "constant series of natural fortifications, thinly settled & with few & bad roads" in which one could "neither apply the maxims nor imitate the example of the great European masters of the art of war." The chief fault found with the Army of the Potomac was that they "did not 'move.'" To this, Chamberlain responded that the nation's capital was "practically in enemy territory" and that the adversaries could hardly "afford to exchange queens." He wished to remind the critics that, with their responsibility for the defense of Washington "our friends behind us had quite as much to do in determining our campaigns as did the enemy before us." He pointed out that even Grant found it was not "quite so easy to keep up the prestige of his western victories, when he came to confront Lee and the Army of Northern Virginia. Offering that the army had been "organized from the debris of defeat," Chamberlain praised the men of this army for their patience, discipline and intelligence. He acknowledged "McClellan, the magic name; Burnside, the magnanimous; Hooker, the chivalrous; Meade, the victorious—" But here Chamberlain took a bold stance; for he commented on the men of the Army of the Potomac:

> *Nor do they forget tonight those officers, once the favorites of fortune, whom misunderstanding, impatience, or jealousy has stricken from our rolls. Pardon me, comrades, if I venture here to express the hope, knowing all the pains and penalties of so doing, that tardy justice (if that can be called justice which is tardy) may be done to officers whose character and service in behalf of the republic, deserve something better than its hasty and lasting rebuke.*[3]

Frustrated in his ambition to write the history of the 5th Corps, it is likely that Chamberlain offered these words in defense of Gen. Warren. Former commander of the 5th Corps, Warren had been removed from command after Five Forks by Gen. Sheridan, and thus died a broken man. Chamberlain defended Warren despite the fact that Sheridan, as first president of the Society of the Army of the Potomac, was one of his listeners. Chamberlain went on to declare: "God be praised that in the justice of his ways, this same much-suffering old army—scoffed at for not moving, but never that I have heard for not dying enough—should be the chosen one to push the rebellion to its last field...." He added, "In triumph, too, obedient still, which is more difficult; masters of their enemies—masters of themselves, which is more noble. No sacked city cries out against them from its ashes...." However much Chamberlain longed for and loved his old comrades, their bonds forged in the sharing of this amazing trial, he observed: "...though sometimes the heart will yearn for the stirring duties and high companionship of the field, yet when I think of all the noble spirits 'passed in battle and in storm'...I thank God that no bugle at tomorrow's dawn shall wake us to a reveille of blood." Chamberlain's oration would draw prolonged cheers from his audience.[4]

Back home, the gubernatorial election battle was in full swing. Radical temperance supporters, having failed to make their man the Republican candidate, formed a third party. But Chamberlain won handily over both the Democratic and temperance candidates. When he returned from New York, shocking news came from Brewer that the Chamberlain family's house had been badly damaged by fire. Fanny, using Wyllys' childhood name for his Grandmother Chamberlain, expressed shock at hearing that "Garky's house" burned. Mother and Father Chamberlain boarded out as plans were made to restore their home. Mother Chamberlain was ill that summer, and Sae, also caring for her seriously ill baby, did the best she could to help. Mother Chamberlain wrote to Lawrence shortly after little John Chamberlain Farrington died that fall:

Pejepscot Historical Society

Sarah "Sae" Chamberlain Farrington, c. 1870.

> *I am sorry to give you so much anxiety on my account—certainly I should wish to be a stay & comfort to you & help you to bear the burdens which must press so heavily upon you instead of your taking one of mine (which I think at present I am able to bear) While I was sick with out friend or comforter—Saties babe at the same time so very sick, but poor Sae did n't forget me—sent her girl to me did all twas possible for her to do to alleviate my condition—*[5]

Mother Chamberlain was impatient to see their home repaired, and felt that her illness had slowed the project, so that they must board out all winter. She exclaimed: "...I am as brave—as self[-]sacrificing (I won't say as great a sufferer) as any that fought on the famous field at Gettysburg! I won't complain... if I live to see the old home stead properly fitted up—I shall try to forget the past—but twill never seem home to me again—" Mother Chamberlain wrote that Tom had said that if she could keep herself alive until the next October, he would take entire care of her, for he was going to be married, and had declared "we will all be happy." She commented: "Poor boy they hope his anticipations may be realized but fear not."

Though she related that it was difficult for her to get along alone and that she must be near one her children, she insisted: "Please don't be anxious about us—we are well situated here for the present—better than making interruptions in your family—think of us as happy." Mother Chamberlain expressed longing to see her grandchildren, and stated of Grace, "She is a good house keeper now, and must make home happy-" Concerned for Lawrence, she asked, "Why will you work so hard? ...I pray you take proper time for sleep you are wearing yourself so fast I fear you can't hold out long so you know how suddenly persons are called away—"[6]

In the fall of 1869, Fanny and Grace were in New York. Lawrence, in Boston signing bonds for the State of Maine, wrote to his daughter, "Glad to hear that you & Mamma are enjoying yourselves so well. Let me know all your intentions." Lawrence had been lecturing every night, and he noted: "It is doubtful now if I can go home Thanks giving day... But you & Momma can come & make me a call when you go 'home along,' if you go before I do. By next mail I will send you a list of my engagements so you will know just where I am every day. I do not find it very hard to lecture every evening, though few people could stand it. My powerful constitution keeps me up." Lawrence closed his letter: "I would write Mamma instead of you if the little scamp would answer me. Mrs. Darling *wants to come* & keep house for us. What does Mamma say. Let me know your plans."[7]

On December 7, Sae gave birth to a baby girl. Named Mary Alice, she would be called Alice. Lawrence wrote to Father Chamberlain: "I have to thank you for your letter so promptly conveying to me the agreeable intelligence of Sarah's happy deliverance from her perils, and the birth of another daughter of our House." Still another holiday would pass with the family scattered, for Lawrence said that Wyllys alone would be traveling on Christmas eve to visit the Brewer Chamberlains. On New Year's eve, Lawrence, as he wrote his inaugural address for his last term, wrote to Fanny from Augusta:

We are winding up the year, and I write to wish you a Happy New Year. I have been digging away at my Message, here & at home, as the rush on me was more or less. I have had a severe rheumatism, so that I had to invade your little boudoir bed room so as to have a softer bed. I got a mortal cold by it though I had the furnace going a whole day beforehand. However I am well enough now except being tired. My Message will be long & dull, but there is plenty of hard work in it. I was expecting you almost every evening the last week when I was in Brunswick. You will stop there to get your things I suppose.... I shall go home again tomorrow to put the last touch on the message. Half expect to see you there. I came to Augusta Tuesday for good; though if you are in Brunswick I shall go there again Saturday. Let me know if you get this. Draw on me, or leave the bill at Stevens House if you find necessary. Wyllys happy as a king.

Sending New Year's greetings to "Daise," he signed his letter, "very aff[ectionatel]y & anxious to see you again. Your old boy"[8]

Chamberlain's inaugural speech in January 1870 addressed a number of problems that carried over from the past year and needed resolution during this, his last term as governor. Scrutiny of the records, regarding the monies still owed by towns and cities to the state for soldiers' bounties, had uncovered many irregularities and sparked controversies. But Chamberlain insisted that it was no time for timidity in dealing with "vexed questions." Declaring the need for "the insight and foresight of the best minds of the state for all the high ends for which society is established and to which man aspires," he declared that, "We cannot expect much that is good from laws enacted under clamor or to meet some crisis, nor from statesmen who are chiefly concerned in contriving to keep their place and power." Chamberlain eulogized William Pitt Fessenden, who, having incurred the wrath of many of his own party by voting against the impeachment of President Johnson, died before it became his fate to feel their disapproval when he sought reelection:

The man who will calmly resolve and give judgment with understanding, unmoved by the voice of those who seeing not so clearly, feel more violently—the man who aims for the ultimate right, rather than for the near advantage—the man who in the tremendous hour of responsibility when great issues hang upon his action, hearing above the tumult of taunting foes and supplicating friends, the deeper voices of reason and conscience, fixes his single eye on duty, and stakes his all upon the blow—that man it is hard to find, and hard indeed to lose.[9]

On temperance, another controversy that fractured Maine Republican solidarity, he remarked that it was a difficult issue, for it was a "question of social ethics, or public morals, on which even good men might be divided...." Obviously stung by the campaign the radical temperance men had led against him, he declared that "various elements of disaffection availed themselves of the confusion" in the temperance movement, and Chamberlain commented, "...let me here deprecate the practice so recklessly resorted to in the last campaign, of aspersing the motives of official conduct, and of misrepresenting private character for political and sinister ends." In this, Maine's 50th year as a state, Chamberlain also expressed his grave concerns for the state's lack of capital and industry, and his desire that Maine use its resources wisely. Nor did he see the state's prosperity as a simple estimate of the "operations of capitalists and the balance of trade. They will also look upon the great masses, and see if they can live upon their daily labor...." In this, his last address, a certain weariness, or admittance of discouragement seems to intrude. He finished his address with the words, "The ways of Providence seem slow to our brief, impetuous lives; but they are swift in the centuries of God."[10]

By 1870, many of the idealistic hopes for a reformation of American society after the war were proving illusionary. George Fredrickson pointed out in his treatise on Northern intellectuals and the war, *The Inner Civil War*, that, "Instead of purging the nation once and for all of self-seeking, materialism and corruption, the war opened the floodgates for the greatest tide of personal and political selfishness the nation had ever seen." September 1869 saw the first links of corruption with the Grant administration, when it became known that Grant's brother-in-law had been involved in the schemes to corner the gold market that led to panic on the gold exchange. In Congress, the battle over the future of Reconstruction waged on. Moderate Republicans feared that military enforcement of freedmen's rights in the Southern states set a dangerous precedent in centralized government. The Fifteenth Amendment, giving freedmen the vote, had finally passed in February 1870, but they and white Republicans were left to face the violence of the Klan or like groups. Though several enforcement acts were passed, it was not until April 1871, when Klan violence exploded, that steps were taken to protect voters' rights. Years later, an observation that Chamberlain made on President Lincoln's hopes for the years after the war offers insight to his own political disillusionment:

> *In after years we were almost glad he was removed from a scene of strife yet more trying to him. Fortunate perhaps in the time and manner of his going. In his great love for the whole Country, he would have desired a policy of re-construction more accordant with his thought and character. But this field he could no longer control as chief of the war power of the people, and his wishes would have incurred the opposition, and perhaps enmity of a majority of the party into whose hands the task of restoration almost wholly fell. This unwisdom of power, this division of friends, this new 'domestic insurrection' would have grieved his spirit and shadowed his later years He might have gone down to death overruled, disregarded, disrated. His last acts were thought to show too much mercy, too easy return for discomfited rebels, too rash a restoration to civil and political rights. Had he lived, the reconstruction policy would doubtless have been quite different from that executed, and the long agony of the recovering South been mitigated or averted. But for him the task would have been more trying than that when he had extraordinary powers in the military sphere. Welcome then, for him, if not so well for the dismembered Country his swift release at the high tide of his fame.*[11]

In 1870, Rev. George Adams faced a difficult, disheartening decision, after a year of vacillating on whether to accept a new church in Orange, New Jersey. In February, he asked the First Parish Church's standing committee to support his going to Orange for a season. Yet Rev. Adams still seemed a bit reluctant to leave "his dear home." On his return from New Jersey to Brunswick, he commented how "very pleasant the old ch[urch] seemed." But by the end of that summer, he tendered his resignation.

Not a word did Rev. Adams write in his diary of the break in Fanny and Lawrence's relationship, though he surely knew of their troubles. Miss Courlaender, whom Lawrence identified as the "unworthy confidante" who was spreading rumors of the Chamberlains' impending divorce, was a close friend of the Adams' whom they saw frequently.[12]

A letter from Lawrence to "Daise" on Apr. 27, 1870, provides other views of the difficulties that arose with Lawrence and Fanny's transient life styles. It also provides an amusing peek at Chamberlain's work habits and personal filing system. Fearing that Grace would try to clear up his rooms while he was away, he wrote that he had left some important papers scattered about, and asked her not to disturb "anything on desk floor mantelpiece pocket wastebasket or where ever else I keep my things." He also expressed doubts that they could keep house that summer if Fanny did not find a housekeeper, or at least someone to do the scrubbing. Lawrence worried that it would spoil the bright plans for summer if Fanny failed to find someone. One of the "bright plans" for that summer probably entailed the 26 foot sloop, *Wildflower* that he purchased late that spring.[13]

Chamberlain made it clear that summer that he was not a gubernatorial candidate. The Maine Republican party, as a compromise, nominated a moderate temperance man, Sidney Perham, a move that alienated liberal party members and friends of Chamberlain. The Maine Democratic party was also splintering, with the young men of the party, including a number of veterans, insisting on change. At their convention that June, a number of speakers demanded that Chamberlain be approached to be the Democratic candidate, as the best man available for governor or senator and, as one delegate pointed out, as the man who could win. The old line Democratic party members were horrified and demanded that the convention be postponed until just before the fall election. It was eventually brought to the party's attention by "General Chamberlain's friends" that he would not accept a nomination from the Democrats, and that an offer from the opposition "would embarrass him." He was, in fact, being spoken of for one of Maine's U.S. Senators. The Democrats finally nominated a former colonel of the 2nd Maine, Charles Roberts as their candidate for governor. In great confusion, with a temperance man running for the Republicans and a veteran running for the Democrats, the gubernatorial race was on.[14]

If Chamberlain's thoughts were on the U.S. Senate in June, by July they were roving even farther afield than Washington, D.C. Americans took great interest in the conflicts that united the German states under the banner of Prussia. Though the victors' rule was acknowledged to be despotic, many saw the unification as the first step toward German democracy.

Americans also admired Prussia's military expertise, and their requirement that every citizen do military service appealed to the American sense of equality. Many also considered the Prussian educational system as second to none in the world. But a more subtle attraction was the esteem that many American Protestants held for Germany as the home of the Reformation. In the summer of 1870, when war broke out between Prussia and France over disputed territories, many Americans sympathized with Prussia, not only because of their admiration for Germany, but because of a decided antipathy to France. Louis Napoleon's attempt to intervene in the American Civil War on behalf of the Confederacy, was fresh in the minds of many Northerners. Nor did the South have any affection for the French ruler because of his ultimate failure to intercede for them. Also, the French incursion into Mexico was perceived as nothing less than an assault on the Monroe Doctrine. And Napoleon III was widely suspected of having had designs on U.S. territories that lay vulnerable while the country was torn by civil war. The only real support that France enjoyed in the United States came from American Catholics. On July 20, in the first days of the Franco-Prussian War, Chamberlain composed a letter offering his services to the Prussian king.

To His Majesty, William, King of Prussia

Sire,

The undersigned respectfully presents to your Majesty the tender of his services in the war now opening in Europe. He has the honor to refer to the fact that he has served through all grades from field officer to that of General Division. His last two promotions were made on the field of battle under circumstances which warrant him in referring to them as testimony of his capacity. The office he now holds of Governor of the State of Maine he proposes to resign in case your Majesty shall be pleased to accept his service. While no great principle of international right is involved in the present impending war, the honor of manhood is a point on which a soldier may well be sensitive. In this feeling & sympathizing with your Majesty's political & personal attitude, well acquainted with your language & admiring your people I tender the best service of my sword.

Written in Chamberlain's hand, on the letterhead of the State of Maine's executive department, this letter was marked "copy/translation." If Chamberlain actually sent his offer to the Prussian king, no response has ever been found. Did a longing to return to the military, where duty was clear and his ability unchallenged, prompt him to consider such a thing? Could unhappiness at home or in his role as governor have reached a point where he would walk out on either or both?[15]

Correspondence between Lawrence and Jenny Abbott apparently suffered another interruption in 1870. In what may have been another attempt by Jenny to take their relationship beyond friendship, she had offended Chamberlain's sense of propriety. In a letter written as they resumed their correspondence, Jenny addressed a number of Lawrence's concerns:

You dear Goosie to think anything could be as hard or as bad for me as the sense of separation! Your letter has braced and strengthened me so that my heart leaps under its burdens I grieve that my naughtiness has made you reserved, or robbed you of the slight comfort that could have come to you from me—I will try to 'be good,' dear, if you will forgive me—I have been so hungry for a word of kindness that some times where no ingenuity could screw any such out of a letter, I have [made] an outcry which ought, perhaps to have been suppressed. But to share or even to know your troubles is only good and precious—Is it not one of the most blessed privileges of friendship? So now, again, I grasp your hand and hold it close, praying God that the sufferings of the past months may be spared me in the future—Whatever sorrow comes to either of us let us stand loyally true to our friendship....[16]

Jenny expressed her delight over Lawrence's yacht, and "to know that you are off among the islands where worries cannot reach you with their usual power—" He expressed dissatisfaction with discomforts at home caused; it is likely, by the continuing absence of the homemaker, and Jenny responded:

Do try to throw off the troubles that belong to this life only—After all, dear, housekeeping discomforts have too much power over us sometimes...I wish you would give up the attempt to keep house; take board in a large enough boarding house to escape criticism, in Portland perhaps, send the children to school and spare your dear soul struggles in a hopeless cause. I am sanguine you would be less uncomfortable. Sell off your house and try to make a home in a few rooms—...I believe expense of soul and money would be saved—And this brings me to Daisy— I have thought over the plan you proposed when here and have asked the girls about it—They all want me to take her and seem to think I could make her happy—...If you have made no other arrangements and if you still wish to have me take her I will do this; let her be at home as my own little sister, and attend school in town.... This would secure her from lonliness [sic] and I need not assure you that [I would do] everything in my power for the happiness and good of your child.... And dear, if you will forgive me for saying so I think perhaps it would be better to have the dear little girl's wardrobe prepared here as much of her peace and happiness will depend upon having it like other children's. I will cheerfully take the charge of this and feel richly rewarded if I can do what pleases you.[17]

If not for her plans to accompany a friend on a trip, she wrote:

I would ask you to take me to your home without regard to anything that might trouble you in the housekeeping—it would not hurt me if I could see your dear face untroubled. I would try to make it easier for you too—without meddling—I am afraid you will always be too careful to let me have this glimpse into your daily life, your study, your stable (for I always think of Charlemagne among your household) which I desire—But you shant be teased. If the time comes I will go if possible; if it does not you must not be troubled or over-sensitive about it.[18]

Though Chamberlain was under consideration for Maine senator, it seems that he did not actively lobby for it. Asked if he would go after it, he replied, "I hate to but if I do I dont like the idea of seeming to ask the people for something and being denied. However we shall see." The elections in September

1870 were a triumph for the Democratic party. Though the Republican, Perham, won the governor's seat by a slim lead, and the party still controlled the legislature, the Democrats made great gains. Louis Hatch, in his *History of Maine*, written in 1919, claimed that the September gubernatorial and legislative elections of 1870 were a veritable referendum on Chamberlain's candidacy for senator, for supporters of Chamberlain's opponent for the senate seat, Lot Morrill, were elected. According to Hatch, when Morrill men won dominance in the legislature that would chose Maine's next senator in January 1871, Chamberlain had already lost. But Chamberlain's supporters either did not know or would not accept that their man was beaten. Apparently Morrill's supporters were not entirely convinced either, for they saw to it that partisan newspapers launched an attack against Chamberlain in the last weeks of 1870. One attack, however, Chamberlain did not let pass. A letter written by a correspondent for the Boston *Journal*, a young man that Chamberlain had at one time refused to hire as his private secretary, directly accused Chamberlain, among others, of criminal and impeachable offenses. Chamberlain commented in a letter to his lawyer, "I intend to make these parties understand that this sort of political campaigning 'wont do'...."[19]

By the end of August, Rev. Adams, Helen, and the children, bid farewell to Brunswick. The people of the First Parish Church presented a table laden with silver to their minister of over 40 years. Fanny's childhood home was sold in September and another family celebrated Thanksgiving in the Brunswick house that year. An invitation that came from Father Chamberlain to come to Brewer had come too late. Lawrence who had seen Tom in New York, commented that, although Tom had enough business on hand, he was still worried about being turned out of office. Lawrence commented: "For one I dont care much if he is, for I doubt if his associations...are profitable." Lawrence also had contacted a portrait artist, Mr. Willard of Worcester, and engaged him to paint portraits of Mother and Father Chamberlain. With the family home restored, Lawrence suggested that Willard utilize the good light in the garret room, where had he labored over his Greek in preparation for Bowdoin many years before. Lawrence asked about Sae's baby, who had been seriously ill in the fall. Little Alice recovered, and would live to be a great favorite of her uncle's in his later years.[20]

A hint of mending hearts and renewed communication are contained in his last words to his father in this November letter: "The children & all of us are hearty & well. I send our best greeting."

A letter from Jenny Abbott to Lawrence at Christmas indicates that he, Fanny, and the children spent the holiday together in Brunswick. Jenny's letter is remarkable for its change in attitude and tone from the previous summer, when she clearly encouraged Chamberlain to try living on his own, sending the children away to school. In this subdued letter, Jenny seemingly acknowledged that Lawrence's family was intact. And her Christmas salutation was a far cry from "You dear Goosie" of the summer, for Jenny began this letter, "My Friend." She wrote that she was sending gifts by express to Brunswick that "included all your circle." Along with presents for the children, Jenny, "at the risk of intrusion," was sending a trifle to Mrs. Chamberlain, "that each one may share the package as each one has my good wishes." In this letter, Jenny also mentioned for the first time a "Dear Mr. Johnson." She questioned Mr. Johnson's piety, commenting that the "lovely letter" that had accompanied his gift to her, "showed he was yet outside the circle of full recognition." But Jenny would be writing more and more frequently of Mr. Johnson in the months to come.[21]

In January 1871, the Maine legislature chose a senator to send to Washington. The result was 195 for Morrill, 34 for Chamberlain. In the years to come, Chamberlain's name would again be mentioned as a senatorial candidate, but his political career was over. On January 21, Father Chamberlain invited his son to come home for a grand social event in his honor. With a father's pride, he declared that Lawrence's was "a perfect triumph in rising above party to the heights of purity & public virtue."

Father Chamberlain also wrote that Tom, too, was a hard one to put down. In late 1870, he had married John's widow, Delia, and Father Chamberlain wrote that she had taken her property and set up a business with it. After paying them a visit, Lawrence declared that they were "happy as gulls on a rock."[22]

In the spring of 1871, Grace was away at school in nearby Gorham, Maine and, unexpectedly, had not come home for a weekend. Fanny and Lawrence responded, each in their own way, to her absence. "Papa" wrote:

> *I did not know what had become of my darling, but I see that she is there still. Perhaps I have a morbid tendency to feel forlorn—my life lies rather far from most that I see around me. So I count on my bright glimpses of companionship, & cling pretty closely to those who respond to me with kindred thought & feeling. That makes you more than a daughter to me.*

From a poem entitled *Gertrude of Wyoming* he quoted, "*For thou hast been to me all tenderness And friend to more than human friendship just.*" He added, "I say no more about love for fear it will spoil you!" He commended her for her energy and resolution in her studies "which are soon to interest you." Of home, he commented: "Your hope that we are well & happy is realized, we are. I am going to the Yacht to day to paint her &c Probably I shall keep her. Certainly shall unless I am sure of a better one." With fondness for the good times they had enjoyed on the "Wildflower," he suggested that, though they might change boats, they would use the same name. "Perhaps next winter I will build one, & name her *Wildflower*, a schooner (two masts)." He continued enthusiastically:

> *I will not keep you from school for Yachting, but do just as you wish. Indeed you can remain there & I can telegraph you when we want to take a trip & you can return there as to a home, maybe that would be best. At any rate we will have a happy summer. It is now likely that I shall live in Brunswick. If I do, I am going to 'take to pieces' the House again!! I shall raise the whole main house & put a new a spacious suit[e] of rooms in the lower floor, letting this present lower floor become the second story! Mamma will send several things soon.*

And from "Mama:"

My dear little Daisy, for you are just as much my little Daisy as when you were not so big; I was very glad to receive your nice little letter which Wyllys brought to the tea-table to me last night. I was disappointed that you did not come home Sat[urday] and I dont see but that you took just as much time from your school by going out to Hollis Fri[day], did you not? I am glad you are so ambitious with regard to your school, and I should be afraid you were studying too hard...if I did not know that you were not of that kind. You never did study hard you know.

I have no doubt you are doing nicely, and it makes me happy to think so.[23]

Of home, she wrote, "Papa and I sat down alone together at the tea-table last night for the first time for years. It seemed like old times when you were a baby...." Later that spring, Fanny wrote Grace how pleased she was that her studies were going so nicely: "I knew you would like philosophy." Asking that Grace write often, she added, "and tell me of every thing that concerns you." The house on Maine St. under her supervision again, Fanny stated that while "Papa is off again on his yacht," she was going to put the house in order. Free from all obligations, Lawrence enjoyed that summer. Time on his boat was time spent away from the problems of the world. Though Fanny loved the sea, she was never much of a sailor, and Lawrence's "crew" often consisted of Grace and family friends. One of these companions, to whom Lawrence had mentioned he was getting old, responded, "When you get flying around in your yellow coat & pants on the deck of the 'Wild-flower' I expect you will be as gay as ever."[24]

Lawrence enjoyed tidying up the grounds, and getting his "little farm" back in shape. But could a summer of sailing and gardening provide a remedy for the trials of the past eight years? What the war had done to mind and body had not been relieved by four tumultuous years as governor. But Fanny and Lawrence began slowly, cautiously, to put their relationship together again. The coming years would bring new and difficult trials, but they would, once again, be there for one another.[25]

CHAPTER

17

"Old Bowdoin"

By early 1871, Chamberlain knew that Bowdoin wanted him as their next president. Dr. Samuel Harris, the college's president since 1866, came to Bowdoin as a respected professor. But he soon discovered that he had no liking for the president's role as disciplinarian, and admitted that the upperclassmen's practice of hazing "gave him the 'jim-jams.'" Nor did he claim any particular talent for fundraising, and Bowdoin's finances reached a low ebb during his term of office. When Yale offered him a professorship in 1871, Harris accepted. Chamberlain had been offered the presidency of Maine's agricultural college at Orono, but his sights were set on his alma mater. His unanimous election by the trustees to succeed Dr. Harris broke precedent, for only ordained ministers had ever held the presidency at Bowdoin. Though he had graduated from the Bangor Theological Seminary and received an MA from Bowdoin, never having accepted a pulpit, he had not been ordained. He assumed the duties of president in September 1871, and at the outset of shouldering the college's many problems, he wrote optimistically to his mother in his annual letter to her on his birthday:

> *I have been full of business all day & it is almost twelve at night; but I will not miss my letter for the birthdays are never forgotten by me. I have to thank you for many things: not the least of them is the right care & training which have given me a strong constitution & cheerful mind. I tried every thing working pleasantly in regard to my opening a larger field for the college to work in. It looks as if I could do some good here, and I can stand a great deal of hard work.*[1]

Chamberlain would need all his strength. Having been a student, professor, acting president and trustee of the college, he could hardly have entered into his new duties blindly. Though almost all the formidable old professors of his student days were gone, he still faced a conservative board of overseers. Changes were necessary at Bowdoin. They had to compete with three other colleges in Maine, as well as the prestigious colleges in New England. While Bowdoin could rest on its laurels as a college for classical education, if it did not compete with institutions that offered broader, more liberal studies, many believed that the school's days were numbered. As a condition of his acceptance of the presidency, Chamberlain was armed with the overseers and trustees' permission to expand on the introduction of science courses that President Harris had initiated. Something also had to be done to improve Bowdoin's financial standing. Cognizant of their fiscal troubles, Chamberlain accepted a salary of $2,600 a year, while, as one student pointed out, a cook at Boston's Parker House earned $4,000.[2]

Chamberlain's speech for his inauguration at Bowdoin's next commencement is a clear and powerful presentation of the future he foresaw for the college. It drew praise as the "best inaugural the College has ever heard in terms of a new president's willingness to express a vision in very concrete terms." Chamberlain saw his duties as defined by their acknowledgment that the college needed "some hold on the public confidence, some share in the living sympathies, through which a college can find its life and its work." He perceived "the dear old college" as "proud even in its isolation," but warned that "Men meant all too much when they said 'Old Bowdoin.'" Chamberlain charged that officers of finance had "satisfied themselves with the laudable duty of preventing the funds from being spent instead of studying how they might be enlarged," while "the times had shot past the college." The boards realized that young, talented professors invariably were drawn away to more promising positions. Yet, they had hesitated, lest "the remedy might be worse than the disease!.... The college had touched bottom, not so much by the fault of men, as by the fate of things. But how to rise again? and how to begin? Young men passed by the college, because they demanded a kind of education she could not give." Chamberlain offered the answers in military terms: "...advance boldly to the key point of the position, and begin in right earnest to entrench," though he admitted that they were taking this step "before we had force enough to hold it at all hazards, and even before our supplies had come up." Yet they decided to "*move on*, even though it were upon a scale of expenditure that would exhaust our whole capital in a dozen years, and then either die gloriously or be worth saving, than to dwindle along until men began to doubt whether we were worth a decent burial, and left us to rot above ground." This plan necessitated adding a new course of studies to the old, and Chamberlain outspokenly observed:

It was the cloister spirit, after all that made most mischief with the old college. Its tendency was away from life; the natural affections rebuked; the social instincts chilled; the body despised and so dishonored; woman banished and hence degraded, so that even to admit her to a place in the higher education is thought to degrade a college. The inmates separate, secluded, grown abnormal and provincial, came out into the world strangers to it, and in its own simple phrase, fools. Now that is not exactly what the college wants to make of men.[3]

Yet Chamberlain defended classical studies that teach of heroism, aspiration and devotion with "a glory all its own," as an antidote to the age of materialism. "Better to me is this than the self satisfied, self felicitating spirit of him who in these days of abundant fruition, easily wins and wastefully uses, that makes haste to be rich and is slow to do good, that increases possessions and dwarfs the possessor." But he suggested that the lessons of Greece and Rome might be known by reading them in translation. And he dared to suggest that French and German, languages rich in philosophic thought and investigation, should replace Greek and Latin.[4]

Chamberlain realized that churches and their affiliated institutions viewed liberal education in the 1800s with apprehension; many saw the "age of science" as an "age of skepticism." While admitting that "our men of science may be quite right in their science and altogether wrong in their philosophy," he averred that "after all they are following in God's ways and whether they see him now or not, the lines will surely lead to him at the end." He declared that, "No society, no study, no science, no philosophy is sound and complete which does not recognize the highest in man—his relations with the supreme." Demanding that the banner to be set on their towers should declare, "To Christ and the Church," he insisted that it not be the "church of sect and dogma, not the church with a stake in its creed...but the church of brotherly love,...the church Universal!" Suggesting that the college embrace all, he appealed to fellow alumni to let old feuds be forgotten:

Let love and loyalty rally us here! Joined hands make warm hearts and warm hearts make liberal hands! Let the people understand this college. It is not a rich man's college, but one where we would that all, rich and poor alike, might be trained for man's highest estate! It is not a sectarian but a Christian college. It is not a place to make orthodox ministers...but it is a place to make even masters of themselves and ministers of all good.[5]

Woman too should have part in this high calling. Because in this sphere of things her "rights," her capacities, her offices, her destiny, are equal to those of man. She is the Heaven-appointed teacher of man, his guide, his better soul.... Let the college rise but let her also stoop a little to reach as many uplifted hands as possible.... This is my hope and ideal for the college—that it may be indeed a lofty seeker after truth, but more than all a lifter up of men. I fear not the age, with all its hot haste. Let it come and stir all minds and all hands. Let it be a new Elizabethan age—dazzling discoveries, broadening science, swift-flowing invention, arts multiplying, civilization advancing, new fields of thought and labor, new prizes of courage, new rewards of toil.... Let labor be wedded to thought...God grant that we may do our part![6]

Bowdoin had admitted that things must change. Many alumni demanded it as a prerequisite to their financial assistance. But as Chamberlain formulated the changes to take place, he had little idea how much would be tolerated, and how much support he would receive.

In late summer 1871, Jenny Abbott visited Lawrence and Fanny in Brunswick, though the trip from Massachusetts to Maine was arduous for her. Disappointed in her hopes of finding Lawrence well rested after his summer of sailing and gardening, she continued to express her concerns to her cousin, Dr. Butler of Hartford. Though Butler explained that he could draw no conclusions about Chamberlain without an examination, he admitted that the symptoms Jenny described sounded grave, and could not be long endured without resulting in "brain trouble." Acknowledging Jenny's instructions that her friend's identity be protected, Dr. Butler suggested that a confidential interview could be arranged. In the months to come, Jenny continued to press Lawrence to seek help.[7]

Beyond his duties at the college, Lawrence also began the enormous task of having his house raised, and he labored over plans for the new first story that would be built under the original old cape. The Chamberlains had many obligations to entertain, and were convinced that they needed a larger home, yet they both prized the house as a former home of Henry Wadsworth Longfellow. In the spring of 1867, they moved the cape from its original site on Potter St. to join the beautiful homes on Brunswick's Maine Street. At this point the red Maltese crosses appeared on one of the house's chimneys, testimony to Lawrence's pride in the old 5th Corps. They added a new first floor that provided spacious rooms for entertaining guests, while preserving the Longfellow rooms on the second floor, keeping them for the family's private rooms and guest rooms.[8]

Pejepscot Historical Society

The Chamberlain house, c. 1880. Chamberlain stands at the front door.

Pejepscot Historical Society

The Chamberlain Drawing Room.

Pejepscot Historical Society

The Chamberlain Library.

This radical alteration to their home became a labor of love for both Fanny and Lawrence. When it was completed, guests at the Chamberlain home first entered a dramatic entrance hall with its large, black oak gothic archway and circular staircase that Lawrence had designed. The deep red walls and dark, varnished floor were an impressive setting for the oil portrait of Mother Chamberlain that hung at the base of the staircase. Guests proceeded through a small arched doorway to enter a reception room just off Lawrence's private study. Or if visitors came to see Lawrence in his official capacity as college president, they were shown into his library. With its deep red, flocked wallpaper, it housed Lawrence's rapidly expanding collection of books, and his prized possessions from the war. It was to the comforting warmth of the fireplace of this room that he turned to when the pain of his wounds banished sleep. Just beyond the library was his office, the setting for official Bowdoin business or a heart to heart with students from the college. For their parties, or student levees as they were called, or when the students were invited to the weekly evenings of tea and music, Fanny and Lawrence designed an elegant parlor. The walls were a vibrant sky blue, as was the satin upholstery of the Victorian settee and chairs. Here was Fanny's piano, with Lawrence's bass viol leaning against it. The back wall of this room gently curves, enhancing the acoustics of the room for the music they both loved so well. The fireplace, set into a bay window, was Fanny's idea, and she designed the crystal chandelier that sparkled in the mirrors and glass set above the mantel. The parlor's nine foot ceiling has a decorative painted border and a plaster center medallion, surrounded by diminutive American flags and vignettes. Guests who stayed for dinner were led to the gray-green dining room with its frieze of forest green stylized leaves and fleur-de-lis crowning the walls, accented with the same shade of garnet that banded the family's formal French tableware.[9]

Chamberlain's demanding schedule was interrupted in the Fall of 1871, when President Grant's special train stopped in Brunswick en route to Bangor for the dedication of the newly completed European and North American Railroad. Bowdoin's entire student body welcomed Grant, and gave a grand send-off to their college president, who boarded the train to join his former commander for the journey. Celebrating the completion of the rail line that was meant to link New England and the Canadian Maritimes, Bangor went all out for the first American president to visit the city while in office. Upon arrival, his party was escorted by two hundred firemen carrying torches, and bands and soldiers marched through the gaily decorated streets. Some of Bangor's belles, each representing a state, received a presidential kiss from Grant, and the governor-general of Canada, Count Linyard, said that "the girls were so beautiful that one felt like embracing the whole Republic."[10]

Grant, who would face reelection in 1872, was still immensely popular, but he had accumulated a fair number of critics, including members of his own party. Though personally honest, cases of spoilsmanship and corruption in the expanded government bureaucracy were laid at his door, giving rise to the uncomplimentary term, "Grantism," for all that seemed wrong in American politics. In January 1872, dissatisfied Republicans, realizing that Grant would be nominated again as the party's candidate, called for a meeting of "liberal" Republicans with the intention of forming a third party. Their platform called for civil service reform and demanded an end to bayonet rule in the South. This stance was taken to win the support, not only of those Republicans that had no faith in the Radicals' brand of reconstruction, but of "a better class of Democrats" as well. The Liberal Republicans, though attracting a considerable number of adherents, were not unified in their goals, and by way of compromise chose a surprising candidate, Horace Greeley of New York. Though influential and nationally known, Greeley was an unpredictable loose-cannon of a man, and the press had a field day lampooning his past crusades. In April 1872, a New York paper listed Chamberlain as a possible vice presidential candidate, though there is no evidence that he encouraged such consideration.[11]

Resisting any temptation to re-enter politics, Chamberlain continued to establish Bowdoin's new scientific department, and his efforts regarding another program of his own design began to bear fruit as well. In January 1872, the War Department granted his request for an officer, and Chamberlain chose Maj. Joseph P. Sanger as Bowdoin's new instructor in the military sciences. He also asked for breech loading rifles from the federal government and requested four Napoleons from the state for artillery practice. Hatch's *History of Bowdoin* implies that Maj. Sanger was universally liked by the students, outfitted in West Point-style gray tunics for drill. But the biography of a student from that era indicates otherwise: "The students were ready to like their distinguished, newly-elected President until he appointed Major Joseph Sanger of New York as Professor of Military science. Major Sanger introduced Military drill as a required subject, not a popular move even though Pres. Chamberlain was in back of it." That January, Chamberlain also made gymnastic exercise mandatory for all Bowdoin students, under the instruction of Dudley Sargent. This unlikely candidate for a college instructor, who acquired his skills as a circus performer, finished high school and began his college education while instructing at the college. Whatever the Bowdoin students thought of Maj. Sanger, Dudley Sargent and his gymnastics program were a rousing success. The students found ways to make this preference perfectly clear, for as a Bowdoin man commented in later years, the "late 'sixties and early 'seventies were years which brought to this famous institution the most nerve-trying students that ever sought intellectual development in the quiet town of Brunswick."[12]

That spring, Lawrence and Fannie were raising their own young man of science. Wyllys, now thirteen, announced his ambition to expand his menagerie, which consisted of a rat and four mice, and to establish an extensive collection of local flora and fauna. Collecting deserted birds' nests, and only one egg from inhabited nests, he also expressed enthusiasm for reptile skins, and all specimens of flying or crawling creatures on land and in the sea.

Grace, now fifteen, spent less time sailing with her father this year, for she had places to go and friends of her own. Shy and self-effacing with strangers, Grace's wit and liveliness charmed those who came to know her. That summer of 1872, she often visited and traveled with friends. Having missed a voyage with her father, she wrote: "How do you do, and what kind of a voyage did you have? It was ugly in me not to go with my good Boy, but leave him to go back without any girl!" The friends she had stayed with in Portland had invited company to "meet Miss Chamberlain," Grace said that her hostess had remarked, "she does not wonder I am such a *splendid girl* having such a father & mother!" Grace commented, "So you see I am behaving well!"[13]

Jenny Abbott continued to worry about Chamberlain this year, and wrote to him, "...tell me whether you received my dear Dr. Butler's letters and mine? I am anxious to a most painful degree...the human heart will grieve throughout all its nature at such words as 'grave peril,' applied to a friend." Jenny declared that she knew Chamberlain's case was "beyond the cure" of the yacht and she felt he needed medicine. Offering her own ideas on rest and respite, she wrote: "If you were here and liked it, you should lie on my lounge, which is drawn up to the window...and feel this soft breeze play among your hair...there are roses,—pink, red and white—on the table; the air is full of fragrance, and your temples are throbbing—Let this eau de Cologne cool them. There! isn't that better? Now a little more for the hot palms that have their feverish pulses."[14]

For all Jenny's concerns, Lawrence enjoyed his summer. Between sailing excursions, he and Fanny traveled together, for Fanny also relaxed during Bowdoin's summer vacation. Father Chamberlain relieved financial constrictions in July with a loan, when Lawrence explained that he would be caught short until September, "when my 'ship gets in.'" Whether referring to his income from the college or, literally, the income he received from part ownership in the ship, *Bombay*, Lawrence commented, "...on the whole my affairs are very satisfactory." Responding to his father's concern for Tom, who returned with his wife Delia to Maine in this year, Lawrence wrote: "I would be glad to assist Tom, if I can. Would like to have them come & make me a visit. Plenty of room now for a grand family gathering. I wish you would all come & stay a week, this summer. We could have a good time." To Grace, still away with friends, Lawrence wrote between sailing excursions, "I 'happen home' over night & find your dear little letters." He told her that "Momma," who was visiting friends, had sprained her ankle. "She is not seriously hurt, but she bears real pain like a hero." On the proofs of pictures she had had taken, he was candid, if not tactful. "Your picture with Annie Cole is fine. Take some of them. But the others are bad. The full face execrable—the profile better but the thick under lip is much in excess even of nature. I had just such a beauty myself till I was twenty one." With belated diplomacy, he added, "Your mouth is sweet perfect, but this lip must not be open (in a side view) to catch the light & become exaggerated."[15]

During the fall term at Bowdoin in 1872, a Portland newspaper reported that, "Half a dozen young women, graduates of Brunswick High school, have applied for admission to a select course of study and their request will no doubt be granted." Though certain courses were made accessible to women, one request from a Miss C. F. Low for admission to Bowdoin's medical school caught the institution by surprise. Miss Low explained that she was a student at a women's college, "but wish to graduate on equal terms with my brother students...." Offering sympathy for her request, Chamberlain firmly denied her admission: "I perceive the reasonableness of your proposition, and regret that not having contemplated such applications we can not make such arrangements as would be fit & proper in [this] case. I am sure that with the high character & earnest purpose you evince, women will soon find those equal terms which they so justly desire...." In fact, Bowdoin's governing boards would not vote in favor of coeducation until 1970, almost 100 years later.[16]

President Grant was easily reelected, but trouble was on the horizon. Though Chamberlain found it difficult to raise funds for Bowdoin, he had some success in his first year, doubling the enrollment of the college. But the next year ushered in a deep, decade-long economic depression in the country, threatening all that he hoped to accomplish at the college. Before this storm broke, however, Lawrence, Fanny, Grace and Wyllys celebrated Christmas 1872 together with much to be grateful for. Included in their household was Miss Carrie Pennell, who came to the family as a domestic servant, but whose kind ways and intelligence would elevate her to the position of Chamberlain's secretary and a valued family friend. Also living in the Chamberlain's home as caretaker was Andrew Tozier, the former color sergeant of the 20th Maine and his family. The day before Christmas, Ellen Bacon, an old family friend from Portland, wrote an affectionate, teasing letter that has caused confusion for Chamberlain scholars. Knowing that Lawrence had expressed the whim to have a jew's harp, Ellen wrote to him, "My dear little Joshua...In obedience to a summons from Santa Claus," Ellen hunted among the Christmas favors heaped up in the city for the "bonnie, bonnie bairn's" wish for a jew's harp to come true." Though fearing that "Mama Fanny Sister Daisy or the kind Miss Carrie who are always so eager to indulge in all his fancies" may have already given him one, she sent hers, hoping it would be "pleasant as a token that his old friend remembers the nice little boy at Brunswick."[17]

Chamberlain spent the first days of 1873 personally appealing to a number of Maine's most wealthy citizens to help meet Bowdoin's urgent need for money. Chamberlain refused to consider raising Bowdoin's tuition, for, as he pointed out to one potential benefactor, "that will keep poor boys out." That spring he was discouraged by his lack of success in raising funds. With no reference to the hard financial times that the state was experiencing, he simply offered, "I am a poor beggar." But by commencement day, 1873, Chamberlain had begun to realize that all was not right with the college. Some former contributors were withdrawing financial support. A subversive minority proved to be protesting the decisions that were made for new courses of study, a situation that Chamberlain considered nothing less than disloyal. One who openly opposed him was his friend and former professor, Daniel Goodwin. In a speech before the alumni that year he declared that it was a "breach of trust to use money which had been given to a classical and mathematical institution for the new departments...." One Bowdoin historian concluded that Chamberlain, during his years as college president, was "obliged to meet not only hesitating support but both open and secret opposition." By the summer of 1873, on the day before commencement, Chamberlain addressed a convention of the board of trustees and overseers and tendered his resignation:

> *When I assumed the duties to which you honored me by your election, I was aware that they involved difficulties and trials from which older and abler men than I had retired in despair. I have exerted myself beyond any previous experience to be equal in this place and meet your wishes. I hoped to succeed, but I have not met my own expectations. A spirit seems to possess the college with which I cannot harmonize, and under which I cannot advantageously work. I owe the world some better service, and it is my duty to seek it.*[18]

The boards did not accept his resignation. Instead, they expressed appreciation for his efforts, stating: "That while engaged in this grand experiment to meet the public demand for a more liberal course of college instruction, the President and Faculty are entitled to the moral support of the guardians and friends of the College until such time as the Boards authorize the discontinuance of the experiment." It was a small victory, but it helped Chamberlain perform his duties as Bowdoin's president at the graduation ceremony with a measure of confidence.

Though some chaffed against the changes at Bowdoin, they had little cause for dissatisfaction with the ceremony of commencement, conducted in the manner of Bowdoin's earliest days. "Pres. Chamberlain addressed the graduates in Latin and asked them to rise. 'Candidati pro gradu baccalaureati, assurgite—' Then the President's question, 'Placetne?' 'Placet,' responded the President of the Board of Overseers. 'In cujus testimonium baece membranas litteris scriptas accipite.'" "In witness thereof, receive these diplomas."[19]

After the July commencement, Lawrence could again indulge in peaceful sailing off the coast of Maine, but he had found another refuge from his cares. During the difficult months of early 1873, when *Wildflower* was hauled up until the snow and ice of winter had passed, he had had a greenhouse erected. By May he told his father: "I am sure you would all enjoy my splendid Green House...where there are over fifty different kind of flowers in full bloom. It is the wonder of the town." Thus began the lovely flower garden that Lawrence added to his "little farm." He added: "For myself I am almost ashamed to say I weigh 180 pounds. It looks as if I had a pretty easy time but that is not the case exactly."[20]

Late that summer, Fanny, accompanied by Wyllys, visited an oceanside resort, seeking the solace of the sea. Wyllys, still interested in collecting specimens of wildlife, wrote to his father, "The seals, loons, ducks, sandpeeps, and mosquitoes are so thick here, I think I must have my gun.... We are having a splendid time here and I have been in swimming 3 or 4 times. The breakers keep roaring all the time and Ma especially loves to hear them...I wish you could come and stay with us here, for I think it is a splendid place for a rest." Lawrence also received a belated birthday acknowledgement from Jenny, who had married her Mr. Johnson that summer. Relating her happiness, she also confessed: "My friend, I could not keep my promise and burn your letters. It was simply impossible. Letters can never be rewritten. These are mine and they are, most of them, rarely beautiful. I have told my dear husband about them and he has promised, if he outlives me, to burn them as reverently as I would. They rest where they have lain these many years in a box I had made for them." Asking if he would continue to write to her, Jenny assured him that it would grieve her husband "if I were to lose your friendship and my gladness in it by our marriage."[21]

Chamberlain, when he assumed the presidency at Bowdoin, not only carried the school into a period of change in its curriculum, but took a different approach to his duties as disciplinarian at the college:

> *In establishing my relations with the students I made them see and understand that I should deal with them as gentlemen, that I should hold a man's word of honor as better than foreign testimony, that I should allow neither spy nor suspicion to hold any place between me and them, and that I*

should not abandon my confidence in them until they were false to themselves. But where a man dealt untruthfully, I regarded him as rotten at heart and good for nothing.

Chamberlain was as good as his word. In dealing with infractions of the college's rules, particularly hazing, any prevarication on the part of those found guilty was dealt with severely. He expressed satisfaction with student response to his policies in his first years. Yet it was during his presidency that Bowdoin experienced the worst student rebellion in its history. In November 1873, the first shot fired in what became known as the "drill rebellion," was a student petition. Delivered to the board of trustees, it called for abolishment of the military department. Annoyed by an order at the beginning of the term that made the purchase of a uniform compulsory, 126 upperclassmen signed the petition. It cited, among others things, "loss of a large proportion of time otherwise devoted to study," and "abundant facilities for more popular and profitable exercises" as reasons for their opposition to military science. A committee appointed by the board met with student representatives, but when the board took no action, the seeds of discontent were sown.[22]

If Chamberlain was consulted, it is unlikely that he would have countenanced the board's neglect to respond to the students' petition. But in the winter of 1873-74, Chamberlain may have been satisfied to leave such matters in other hands. Wyllys came down with rheumatic fever at the end of 1873, so ill with this frightening disease that he would not fully recover until the next summer. Fanny, troubled with periodic pain and swelling in her eyes for as long as she could remember, was finally compelled to consider surgery to halt the deterioration of her vision. When confident of Wyllys' recovery, Fanny submitted to an eye operation performed by a Dr. Green. Judging from the gradual loss of her eyesight over the next twenty years, little was accomplished by the treatment she received that summer.[23]

When the college board of trustees met in January 1874, they again failed to deal with the students' petition. Though some members gave the students reason to believe that they, too, opposed military drill at Bowdoin, officially the students were told only that they had committed an impropriety by addressing their petition to the board instead of the faculty. When drill resumed in the spring of 1874, the students, bitter at having been ignored, took matters into their own hands.

Graffiti about military drill and Major Sanger appeared on the chapel walls and one of the school's Napoleons was dismounted. The junior class persisted in boisterous demonstrations after breaking ranks from drill, and the faculty voted to dismiss the entire class. After an investigation, disciplinary action was taken against six students. However, the junior class, in response, vowed never to drill again, soon followed by the sophomore class and eventually the freshmen. At the next scheduled drill, the sophomore and freshman classes massed in front of the chapel. Only two men obeyed the order to fall in. The faculty appointed a number of professors to meet with the recalcitrant students, but they remained firm. The juniors failed to report to the next drill, and the men were called before the faculty. Each man, as he refused to obey the college rules, was sent home. The faculty authorized Chamberlain to send a printed letter to the parents of the suspended students. The letter notified them that students who failed to send a renewal of their matriculation pledge, a promise to obey college rules, within ten days would be expelled. Chamberlain added that all who submitted would be given an honorable dismissal to another college at commencement if their objections to the drill were not removed. This was a generous offer, for expulsion from Bowdoin barred a student from being accepted at any other institution. In the end, all but three students renewed their pledge and returned to the college.[24]

It is difficult to judge the causes behind what was a good deal more than just a confrontation between Chamberlain and the students. While the introduction of military science had created opposition, student resistance was strengthened by the personal sympathies of members of the boards and faculty. And Chamberlain's belief, that outside influences encouraged disorder, seems less fantastic given the field day the press had with Bowdoin's dilemma. Reactions from newspapers broke down along partisan lines; Chamberlain's critics proposed that he was trying to turn the college into a military school. One paper, the most notorious "copperhead" instrument in the state during the war, claimed that college alumni were disgusted by the sight of cannon on campus. It offered that "the President and Professors wished to hide their inferiority to their predecessors by substituting show for brains." Another suggested that the students expel the faculty. Rumors abounded that Dartmouth College had offered to admit all the suspended students, gossip that the president of Dartmouth quickly refuted. Scathing letters to the editor poured in to the newspapers. One anonymous letter declared that, "elderly men are too apt, in their own passionate fondness for military exercises to forget how painful and repulsive the art of war is to the bashful and ingenuous youth whose proverbial fondness for retirement and study should not be rudely disturbed by duties so unsuited to their tender years." Although many conceded a need to maintain order, there was little support for continuation of military drill. Perhaps Bowdoin historian Charles Calhoun's observations on the mood in the country, a weariness with war and soldiers and Reconstruction, help also explain the dynamics of the drill rebellion.[25]

At the spring term's end, Chamberlain suggested that students be given an option between military drill or gymnastics. An impartial committee made the same recommendation, but also instructed the president, faculty and boards that the "President of the college must deal both with Faculty and Students face to face with unswerving directness of statement.... The Faculty must avoid cabals, refrain from depreciating one another, either carelessly or maliciously, in the hearing of enemies or intermeddlers, and guard most carefully against sowing among the undergraduates the sense of distrust or want of confidence in the President of the college or in any of its departments." They instructed the boards that they "also have duties, among which are to remember that variety of opinions temperately expressed is a good and not an evil.... It is in the stress of weather that the good seaman sticks to his ship. Let the Boards also remember while it is their right to investigate, to demand explanations, to criticize, and finally to decide, yet the basis of all is just confidence in the branch of the College Government whose views of collegiate requirements are the result of daily experience and observation."[26]

During the months that Chamberlain dealt with the havoc created by the rebellion, Bowdoin's financial problems continued. A letter from one college supporter who attempted to assist Chamberlain in fund raising, gives insight into the difficulties encountered. Beyond the controversies of the curriculum, some also disapproved of Bowdoin taking a non-sectarian stance. Others felt that they had not gone far enough in separating themselves from conservative Congregationalism. One party, who threatening to withhold a promised donation stated that Bowdoin was still in the hands of the old fogies, and that Chamberlain and Bowdoin were "too sectarian" for his taste. But the worst blow came in the summer of 1874, when the college boards began to withdraw their support for Bowdoin's expanded curriculum in the sciences. It had been hoped that the new scientific program would help finance classical studies, but when it was realized that science was not even paying its own bills, the boards withdrew any further funds for expansion. Though Bowdoin had not officially abandoned its new department, newspapers reported it as such, and it was the beginning of the end for the new science program. Some students, fearful that the courses they needed would be withdrawn before they completed their college work, felt compelled to go elsewhere.[27]

Lawrence wrote to his mother that summer: "More thanks than I can speak for the kind words. It seems as if I have not heard anything like them for a long time.... Have had to work 14 hours a day for three weeks. I am not very easily cast down & dont mean to be now...Just refused an honorable position...I am going to carry this point here for I can do good. Am in the right place now." Having moved in with mother and father Chamberlain, Sae and Charlie Farrington had another baby boy in the summer of 1874, named Charlie. The first week of September, Lawrence attended the Maine militia's encampment in Bangor, and Fanny visited the family in Brewer. After the experiences of the spring, did it do Chamberlain any good to be among those who were not offended by the sight of a cannon? He wrote to Daisy:

> *We have had a [working] day of it, & are now all safe & sound in camp. The men are singing stirring old army songs & seem happy. We had a beautiful parade at Sunset; the bands played an hour afterwards. Many people were here. Beautiful ladies were plenty. I succeeded in keeping my heart free. This morning I took a run over home. Went all over the house before I found any body. Momma first in Sadie's kitchen washing handkerchiefs. Then one by one all the rest. Well & happy.*[28]

While "Poppa" teasingly signed his note, "your aff. affiance Joshua, Jr.," Seventeen-year-old Grace was apparently entertaining thoughts about the man who would one day become her fiance and husband. She had met Horace Allen, son of Fanny's friend and confidante of long ago, Stephen Allen, in Boston. Openly interested in Grace, he wrote her several letters, and was disappointed to receive no response. A mutual friend explained that "Daisy" made it a "principle not to write to young men." But by September, Grace made an exception to her rule.[29]

The year 1874 had not been easy. Illness, as well as intrigues and calamities at the college created tremendous stress. Life was full of pressures and duties, but the family was together, their beautiful home a source of great pride and pleasure. This year also held the promise of another change. As Grace blossomed into womanhood, her doting father would have to learn to share his little girl and cherished companion with another.

CHAPTER

18

"All Doing Good Work in Our Way"

In 1875, while the boards of Bowdoin committed themselves to raising a $100,000 endowment, Chamberlain labored on with his own fund-raising efforts. He traveled across the country meeting with college alumni, and even sent a letter of solicitation to the former commander of the 20th Maine, Adelbert Ames. Married into the family of the wealthy and powerful Gen. Benjamin Butler, Ames was then the beleaguered carpetbagger governor of Mississippi. While he refused Chamberlain's request with a plea of having recently made several unsuccessful speculations, Ames wrote of his frustration and fears to his old comrade:

> *I often of late think of my old army associates in connection with a possible war. The old rebel here is ripe for any thing. Exactly why they should love our country—the Union—which they sought to destroy and which took from them their slaves is not so apparent. I fail to remember having heard a Union loving sentiment from any of them. Just at this time they are devoting thyselves to misrepresenting those of different politics. The Whole question south is that of the personal liberty and security of the negro. He has them not in the democratic states. Thousands are coming here from Alabama and Georgia and had they the means the last one would come. You can have no idea of the true state of the case here.... We do hope the north will stand true to the rights of the colored men. Let the democracy prevail and the negro will rue the day he was made free.*[1]

The Democrats' big wins all over the country in the fall of 1874 gave them control of the U.S. House, causing many Republicans to examine their Southern policies with trepidation and concern for the 1876 presidential election. Continuing economic woes in the country distracted Northerners from the plight of freedmen. Disgust with violence directed against black and white Republicans in the South was turning to disinterest as military intervention on behalf of carpetbag rule was fast falling out of favor. Ames would be one of the first victims of the Republican party's changing policies in 1875, for when he requested troops to quell violent attempts to suppress Republicanism in the state, he was denied. The result was that the Republican majority of 30,000 in Mississippi would become a 30,000 majority for the Democrats. The Northern public was listening to influential spokesmen for the South and the Democratic party, such as Gen. John B. Gordon. Just six years after meeting Chamberlain at the surrender of the Army of Northern Virginia at Appomattox, he was in Washington, seated as a senator from Georgia. Along with declarations of support for a unified country and peace, Gordon insisted that removal of remaining Federal troops and home rule in the South would put an end to the violence in the region. Gordon, who denied any knowledge of the Ku Klux Klan in his state to an investigating congressional committee several years before, was, in fact, an organizer and leader of that organization in Georgia. But he proved to be an effective spokesmen for an end to Reconstruction. In a much publicized speech before the Senate in 1875, Gordon condemned "hate and vindictiveness," declaring that "wherever in the Southern states people of intelligence, integrity, and honesty have control of public affairs, property and life and rights, political and personal, are as secure as in...any state of this Union." Beside the turmoil over reconstruction, additional accusations of corruption in the Grant administration added to Republican woes this year, with two of the president's cabinet members having resigned when it was discovered they had accepted bribes for their political influence.[2]

Chamberlain's attention, however, was focused much closer to home in the summer of 1875, as he continued to answer the critics of Bowdoin's attempt to offer scientific and liberal education. To those who insisted that the college should have waited until funds were raised before launching these endeavors, Chamberlain described it as "a slow way and some of us would drop off into our graves before any land of promise was reached.... No man would put his money into Bowdoin because it looked like a sinking ship." Chamberlain admitted, "Where things could not otherwise be secured we gave our own personal obligations and paid our own private funds." In another effort to save expenditures for Bowdoin, Chamberlain volunteered to teach courses in mental and moral philosophy, and did so from 1874 until 1879. In spite of the continuing controversy, Bowdoin enjoyed one of its most celebrated commencements in 1875. Henry Wadsworth Longfellow returned with the class of 1825 for the 50th anniversary of their graduation. He delivered his famous poem, "Morituri Salutamus,"... "We Who Are About to Die Salute You." The Chamberlains were honored with the poet's visit to their home, and when he entered the upstairs rooms where he had lived as a young, newlywed professor at Bowdoin and found them virtually unchanged, Longfellow wept. In happier days, before he lost his young first wife to puerperal fever, he had, he said, composed many poems by the fitful light of the fireplace in the old parlor.[3]

In August 1875, Sae gave birth to another son, named Lawrence Joshua Farrington. It might have been several weeks before Lawrence learned of his new namesake, for he and Fanny were enjoying the last days of summer. Rev. Adams sent Fanny a letter of introduction for her visit to his old friends in Portsmouth, N.H., while Lawrence continued sailing in the Isle of Shoals. In the five years since leaving Maine, Rev. Adams had, at times, found his duties at his new church in Orange, New Jersey, almost beyond his strength. During these years, he faithfully kept his diary; though Lawrence's name was mentioned in relation to business, no word of Fanny, nor Grace or Wyllys, was written during his five years in New Jersey. During that summer of 1875, Rev. Adams was so ill that his old parishioners pleaded that he be brought back to Brunswick for his funeral. But Adams lived on until Christmas Day. He was buried from the First Parish Church on December 30, 1875, the 46th anniversary of his installation at that church, his and Helen's 24th wedding anniversary, and the anniversary of the burial of their baby son, Georgie, nineteen years before. In the years after Rev. Adams' death, Lawrence designed and had constructed the magnificent stained glass window at the east end of the First Parish Church as a memorial to his father-in-law.[4]

First Parish Church

The Rev. George E. Adams.

In the last days of 1875, the Chamberlains sought a tutor for Grace and Wyllys. Able to do strenuous chores about the grounds of their home, Wyllys had made a good recovery from his bout of rheumatic fever. But his parents still worried over his health, and, fearing that Fanny's condition might be genetic, cautioned Wyllys about taking good care of his eyes as he prepared himself in Latin and Greek for his entry to Bowdoin. Failing to procure a desirable tutor, Wyllys went in early 1876 to Bangor for instruction, staying in his father's old garret room at the Chamberlains' home. Tom Chamberlain operated a business in Bangor, selling stationery, newspapers and periodicals, while he, and presumably Delia, lived with Mother and Father Chamberlain.[5]

In March 1876, Grace was attending the Gannett Institute in Boston and visited frequently with family friends, including Horace Allen's family. A letter she wrote to Horace in early April indicates that little "Daisy," now 19 years old, was beginning to have a mind of her own. Grace related a confrontation she had with the school regarding which church would be her regular house of worship. She was quite angry when the school refused to give her permission to attend the church of the Rev. E. E. Hale, a prominent Boston Unitarian. Her request caused quite a storm, and when her father announced he was coming for a visit shortly afterwards, Grace told Horace, "We *shall* have a tear if he comes!" While Chamberlain had declared his liberal stance of nonsectarian education at Bowdoin, it apparently did not carry over to home and family. Grace's defection from Congregationalism appalled her father, who likely blamed Horace, a Unitarian, for this calamity. The situation was awkward. Not only were the Allens old friends, but Horace's father, Stephen Allen, was supporting Chamberlain's consideration for an appointment as U. S. minister to Great Britain.[6]

Grace knew that she had deeply upset her father, and a letter that he wrote to her indicates that they had quarreled. It is not hard to imagine that Grace had presented some variation of the age old protestation of daughter to father...that she was no longer a little girl, and fathers, their perceptions colored by their special love for their daughters, do not always know best. Though Lawrence attempted to reassure Grace that he loved her and admired her for the fine woman she had become, he was still very angry:

> *I have been waiting long for your letter & now I have come home from faculty meeting 11:30 p.m. & find it. Thank you & bless you for it. (Private & confidential) I don't love you too much because you are my daughter—that is a mere physical law of time & earth—a mechanical management.* I *love you because you are a splendid soul & belong to eternity. I should love you any way daughter—sister—woman more especially the latter Dont consider this a Paternal epistle in which fathers say what is proper for father to say to daughters. I go back to first principles. Father & daughter is an arrangement of temporal & earthly law for the present sphere. If you were not a woman to command my love, you would not have it—daughter or no daughter. You do command it—& I want to tell you that it is something worth having. I am glad of all the things you tell me of. You do not tell me of every thing You have good reasons. I dont care what they are if they are not the miserable ones of 'afraid to tell my father!' Let me tell you nobody will ever love you more or more deeply or widely than your present addressor!!*[7]

Suspicious of Horace's influence over Grace, if not furious that he might encourage her to alter her religious beliefs or values, he continued: "I love you as a father *properly* & *regularly* I love you besides as a true, solid, genuine splendid *woman*, whom if God had given to *me* I would have looked on as God's representation on earth—(as *a woman should be to a man*) & I would have been something more than I am." Despite all he had been and was, it seems that Chamberlain still harbored some deep-seated resentment at having relinquished his own religious commitments for the sake of love. In a fit of pique, he continued:

> *If you don't like this burn it up & me too. I am in a hurry, & have been sick ever since my return. I wrote you a long letter & burned it! It did me just as much good & you no hurt! God bless you, for a sweet true woman, my joy & hope. If you want anything of me as a daughter let me know—Tear up & burn if you dont like. Written in 10 minutes after—3 days of small hell-torments.*[8]

We do not know Fanny's reaction to this turmoil, but it likely brought sad memories of her confrontations with her adoptive father over much the same issue.

Stephen Allen's efforts on Chamberlain's behalf proved unfruitful. It seems puzzling that President Grant, at the head of an administration noted for its spoilsmanship, hesitated to bestow an office on a highly qualified comrade in arms. But these appointments were not necessarily Grant's to give. In a system that rewarded political and financial support, the appointments were often the "spoils" of the Congressmen, and all that Grant's Secretary of State, Hamilton Fish, could tell Stephen Allen regarding the ministry in England was that the appointment would be decided by the president's cabinet. General Nathaniel Banks, now a Massachusetts representative, wrote of Allen's recommendation of Chamberlain, "A better appointment could not be made." But Banks seemed to discourage any thoughts of success. Allen commented to Chamberlain, "I am fully persuaded that unless he [Grant] turns...to the advice of such as you, his administration, as well as he himself will go down to posterity as a perfect failure;—more than that under the circumstances, a disgrace." Fearing that the Republicans were headed for a major defeat at the polls, Allen advised Chamberlain to remain as neutral as possible in the upcoming fight for the Republican presidential nomination. He assured him that there was plenty of time to decide what course to take after the candidate was chosen. He also advised Chamberlain to avoid a movement that would seek him as an independent candidate for governor of Maine. Allen stated: "I am fully persuaded that you can & will be the instrument of saving your state—," but he advised Chamberlain to, "Be patient."[9]

Senator James G. Blaine may well have been on Allen's mind. One Maine historian described Blaine as the "best loved and the most hated man in Maine history." In 1860, Blaine had become chairman of the state's Republican committee, and for the next 20 years, he dominated state politics. With few exceptions, he chose the candidates, dictated the platforms and assigned hundreds of appointments to his constituents. Elected to the U. S. House of Representatives in 1862, he became speaker of the house in 1870. He went on to the Senate in 1876, appointed to fill Sen. Lot Morrill's seat when he became secretary of the treasury. In this year, as Grant's supporters sought a third term for their man, Blaine believed that he would be the Republicans' presidential nominee. But allegations of bribery for influence tainted his candidacy, and Civil War general and Ohio Governor Rutherford B. Hayes won. Once the nomination was decided, Blaine supported the usurper, Hayes, perhaps more dutifully than gracefully. For Blaine was a man who had experienced great success by backing the party, no matter who the candidate or what the platform might be, and he did not condone any dissension in the ranks. This value system did not allow for men who did not toe the party line or who could not be controlled. Considering Chamberlain's independence as governor, Blaine was unlikely to have supported his appointment for such a sought after position as the British ministry.[10]

Though hope of a diplomatic mission had faded, in June 1876 Chamberlain wrote a letter of resignation to the boards at Bowdoin:

> *Indeed all that has actually been accomplished during the last five years does not yet fully appear, and some labor has perhaps been wasted. But I am happy to leave the College in so good a condition, as will be apparent if any one is disposed to consider it. Our funds are nearly doubled: our Buildings greatly improved; our means of instruction and the number of our students largely increased; and we have every prospect of an unusually large entering class, and of continued additions to our funds.*[11]
>
> *Having been connected with the College in offices of instruction or of government ever since taking my second degree in 1855, I was well aware of the difficulties I should encounter, even had not the task been laid on me of establishing a new department of study without adequate means—without, indeed, any means at all. Some difficulties I have met with were unexpected and, I think, unnecessary, and some doubtless the result of my own too sanguine & self-reliant spirit. However that may be I am willing to leave to time the justification not only of what I have done, but of what I have attempted and not been able to carry through.*

If Chamberlain submitted this letter, his resignation was not accepted. His ambitions and plans for the school continued, and while Chamberlain sought the peace of the summer sea, a six week, coed school of science, incorporating chemistry, botany, and mineralogy commenced at Bowdoin.[12]

What a sad year 1876 was for the Chamberlains. In April, Sae and Charlie's eight month old baby, Lawrence Joshua, died. In July, Tom Chamberlain's health was so broken that he could not work. That same month, the Farringtons lost two year old Charlie. Father Chamberlain's brother, Elbridge, who had been in the Midwest for over 40 years, felt his brother's sorrow, and wrote:

> *Your deeply affecting letter of the 1st inst came duly to hand and as I read its contents, I think I caught a full view of the dark shadows of the vally [sic] in which you sadly mourn. Tears filled my eyes as I read your vivid description of that dear, cold form, with its upturned, beautiful face, whose spirit had fled away—I thought of you, a man of 76 years, inured to all the rough experience that that time of years implies, bowed down with grief—*[13]

Joshua L. Chamberlain, President of Bowdoin College.

After the election of 1876, there was uncertainty as to who won—the Republican, Rutherford B. Hayes, or the Democrat, Samuel J. Tilden. Accusations flew that violence, intimidation and fraud had cost the Republicans an estimated 250,000 votes, and the disputed returns from South Carolina, Louisiana and Florida would decide the question. As officials from both parties poured into the Southern states, rumors of bribery by both Democrats and Republicans abounded. Talk of upholding state and presidential candidates' election by force fueled fear of another civil war, and a congressional committee devised a plan to handle this unprecedented situation. Cautiously accepted by both parties, a commission of five representatives, five senators and five Supreme Court justices served as arbitrators of the disputed returns. As it became apparent that Hayes would be victorious, several leading Southern Democrats, including John B. Gordon, met with Hayes' representatives. They asked for assurances that, once president, Hayes would complete the removal of military forces from the region, and give support to the Democratic gubernatorial claimants in the Southern states. Though the Democrats held few cards, those assurances were obtained by the time Hayes was declared president by the commission on March 2, 1877.[14]

Hayes' campaign had promised everything to everyone. While the Republican stand on governmental reform seemed relatively clear, at least part of the funds needed to run the campaign were collected, as they always had been, by a 2% assessment on the salaries of civil servants. Hayes promised his support to "honest & capable local government in the South," while he encouraged his supporters in the North to "wave the bloody shirt" against Southern outrages and the inherent dangers of their domination in Congress. Such sentiments helped Hayes win Northern votes. But four days after his inauguration, he ordered government troops out of South Carolina and the Southern state capitals, where Republican governments collapsed and were succeeded by Democratic rivals. While a number of old guard Republicans condemned Hayes' betrayal of the Freedmen, the country as a whole shed no tears for the end of Reconstruction. Many felt that, given the apparent failure of enforcing equal rights with military force, Hayes had little choice. Even Frederick Douglas supported the action, stating: "What [is] called the President's policy, might rather be considered the President's necessity."[15]

That summer of 1877, when Maine Republicans held their annual convention, Chamberlain moved that a moderate statement of support for President Hayes be included in the state's party platform. Others insisted on a condemnation. Blaine successfully urged that both measures be tabled, though he had no love for Hayes. Blaine opposed Hayes' efforts to separate civil servants from political activism. And he resented Hayes' refusal to grant his request that a cabinet appointment be given to William T. Frye. Frye, Chamberlain's old nemesis of the Harris execution controversy, had served as Maine's representative in the U.S. House since 1870. Blaine was also appalled by Hayes' appointment of Carl Schurz as secretary of the interior. Schurz, a Civil War general, and senator from Missouri, was one of the founders of the Liberal Republican Party and a serious advocate of political reform. Blaine ultimately labeled Schurz' lack of party "allegiance" as distinctly un-American. But many New England intellectuals gave their support to President Hayes in this first year of his presidency, as did many veterans.[16]

On the eve of the state election in 1877, Chamberlain spoke to Massachusetts Republicans at Boston's Faneuil Hall, urging them to support their administration and the party's candidates. Chamberlain, though he acknowledged to his listeners that they may not "think the President wise in everything," declared that "we must all think him honest." Chamberlain added, "I do not see why all reasonable men, not embittered by prejudice, nor blinded by self-seeking, why all right-minded men, of whatever party should not rejoice in the accession of such a man to carry out such salutary ideas. For my part I believe he is thoroughly right and wise." Regarding government reform and Hayes' stand against "prostituting the civil service," Chamberlain commented, "You may call this poor strategy, but it is thorough going sincerity. You may call it foolish, but I call it heroic." There were those back in Maine that year who urged Chamberlain to lead a movement of Republicans who felt that, "too long have they obeyed the crack of the master's (James G. Blaine) whip...." Chamberlain was urged to call another state convention that would adopt a platform that included support of Rutherford B. Hayes.[17]

If national politics weighed heavily on Chamberlain's mind during the summer of 1877, when he returned for the fall term as Bowdoin's president, he was also fighting for the survival of science at the college. The boards' inconsistencies regarding support, financial and otherwise, for the sciences and for the professors who taught them had taken a heavy toll on the enrollment of students in these departments. But while fighting this battle, there were the usual mundane matters to deal with. Bowdoin sophomores continued to violate the rules against hazing incoming freshmen, and were dealt with accordingly. Chamberlain was even asked, by the father of one Bowdoin scholar, to find the culprit who had stolen his son's best pair of pants.[18]

At Thanksgiving that year, Lawrence expressed regret that they could not spend the day with the family in Brewer. His description of his family's activities indicates that relative peace again reigned in the Brunswick home. He told Mother Chamberlain that though "There is no great virtue in Thanksgiving day unless we can gather in the old home.... We are all well, & all *doing good work in our way*." Wyllys was at Bowdoin as a freshman that fall facing conditional status in several subjects. Lawrence wrote that Wyllys,

> *...is taking a noble stand in college. Daisy is maturing a fine character in body and mind. All their prospects are good. Fanny is young & bright & happy, I think. I am working along well satisfied with results. I never cease to think of you & all your loving care of me, & my respect and affection for you & father increase the longer I live, & the more I know.*

The Chamberlains extended an invitation that year to any Bowdoin students who were in town over Thanksgiving to spend an informal evening at their home.[19]

In mid-winter, Wyllys wrote to "Ma," who was visiting the Brewer Chamberlains with Grace, that he had made up all his conditions, though he was unsure about "Cosine," as the students referred to the professor of mathematics. He was also enjoying his part in a comedy "gotten up" by a theatrical club at the college. Wyllys also asked, "When do you intend to come home? If it were not that Pa & I were so tremendous busy all the time and had our minds taken up with study, at least six days of the week, I don't know how we would get along without you and Daise. It has been lonesome here today especially." In early 1878, Grace was still trying to work things out with her father, for she wrote to Horace: "Papa goes away tomorrow to lecture.... He will probably say something to me of your letter tonight as he has not mentioned it yet. Don't worry about me being tried, Dear—I shall get along—" For Chamberlain, the tiring efforts to set Bowdoin in a better financial situation finally were succeeding, as the country began to emerge from the economic depression that had gripped it for nearly a decade. He wrote wearily to a friend, "The College has received many favors of late, & is in a fair way to be well funded before long. The toil & trial to me has been far beyond any thing I ever experienced 'in the field' but I believe I shall be justified in the end."[20]

Early in 1878 Chamberlain spoke again in Boston, this time delivering the lecture, "The Old Flag." Having many times given his lectures on the war in Massachusetts, he asked his audience's pardon "if I bring you nothing exciting or sensational tonight, but ask you rather to walk with me an hour in [the] mind." Realizing that his audience understood too well the horrible costs of the war, he suggested, "... it seems we well might spend an hour thinking—thinking whether there was anything at stake worth all that struggle, whether anything has been won to recompense the sacrifice, whether there was any righteous cause there, so that these deaths & losses may enter into an immortal life—anything to look forward to, into which we also, the living, may build our lives."[21]

Observing that the conflicts which had torn the country had meant resorting to the sword, Chamberlain asked:

> *...can we say it was settled by the sword? That will depend on who was right. The sword does not make right; it will make peace, but it is a wrong peace; out comes the sword again, you may be sure of that, sure as there is evil on the earth.... And more than that, unless the right is seen to be and well understood, then the battle may have to be fought over and over again until the right is seen and acknowledged.*

Chamberlain identified the main issue as whether the states or all the people of the United States would have supremacy over questions of general welfare, and added, "The question of slavery was a successful expedient, and on it the South became united." He observed, "The battle was fought, fought so well and thoroughly, and ended so completely, that I do not think it needs to be fought over again, either on the field of honor or behind the entrenchment of parliamentary rules. Not fought over, but thought over." He expressed confidence that when the army of the rebellion laid down their arms, they also surrendered the doctrine of absolute states' rights. Chamberlain further asserted that the officers and men who surrendered with Lee understood this, and were ready to "receive, support and maintain the integrity & rightful supremacy of the United States of America." He insisted, "I know that they thus understood it. They are men of honor, and they meant it, and their word of honor is good."[22]

Chamberlain also offered that something else had been yielded at Appomattox, though it was not included in the terms of surrender—slavery. "Slavery & freedom cannot live together. Had slavery been kept out of the fight, the Union would have gone down. But the enemies of the country were so misguided as to rest their cause upon it, and that was the destruction of it and of them." Chamberlain claimed that, though they had not entered the war to strike at slavery, God had ordained that it be so. Referring to an unnamed senator [quite likely James G. Blaine], who had condemned President Hayes' refusal to continue to "redress private wrongs of the negro in the South," Chamberlain stated that armed interventions, "even if they executed substantial justice in a particular case, would in the long run be dangerous to liberty, and to justice also. The Senator, I am told, aspires to the Presidency himself, and if he is sincere, if he means to say that if he were President he would take his army and settle private injuries and local rights in every State in this union, after the fashion of monarchies, I, for one, should not be so willing to trust him with that office as I am Rutherford B. Hayes." Nor did he want such power in the hands of Congress, for he observed, the president was simply obeying the Constitution, and the Southern states received exactly the rights of all others. So important was the issue at hand that he warned, "Look to it, men of New England, or you may bitterly rue the day. Some other issue may arise and we be the ones who want our rights respected."[23]

The country had recently experienced the destruction of Gen. Custer's troops at the Little Big Horn, Gen. Howard's attack upon Chief Joseph and the Nez Perce, and anti-Chinese rioting on the west coast. Chamberlain reminded his audience of the many issues with which the current administration must deal:

> *...we will keep our plighted troth to the black man, the red man, the yellow man & the white man...some say we cannot have peace here because the negroes do not have good treatment in the South, and because the Rebels are back in Congress. The negroes are abused in the South, it is true, but so are the Chinese in California, so are the 40,000 poor girls in London, so are the Indians. We must do the best we can for the negroes. While I am sorry that they cannot vote without interruption, I want to ask if that is the thing for which all that toil and sacrifice was given, for which the best blood in all the land made those mountains and rivers and fields immortal, that the negroes might have no one to stop them in going to the polls. For my part—if I am to die for it—I think it was something else—something a long way before that. I think it was country, the whole country, dear because of the precious foundations in which it was laid; sacred, because of the divine commission laid upon it to hold the van in the great but slow-marching enfranchisement of man. The free country—first the men that made it so, and then the men who are cast upon it. Yes, I say it. The men who have made a country what it is or given it character and built their very lives into its history are to have the foremost hand if we would keep the country true to its mission, true to its ideal. The voting business in the South will regulate itself.*[24]

Again responding to the unnamed Senator, Chamberlain stated: "As for the presence of rebel Generals in Congress, you yourselves took back the states which they represent, and besides they have sworn to support the Constitution and the laws of the United States." For those who continued to "wave the bloody shirt," he commented, "they are willing to stir up the dregs of anguish in the nature's soul and rouse the beast in man.... Let us not assist at such a spectacle. If the kings of death and terror have finished their awful banquet I will not wait to see the court fool's mockery. The great tragedy that has wrung our hearts, let it close without a farce."[25]

Exclaiming, "To oblivion with hate and malice, to immortal memory the righteous cause...," Chamberlain warned, "There never was a peace but straight away there are new enemies to encounter, new interests to guard and keep. In this warfare there is no rest and no discharge." He entreated:

> *Oh, my young countrymen, into whose hands we commit these sacred trusts, remember well, and do not forget, but face to the front. That flag shall be the beckoning signal for human eyes in many a good fight yet. Men will love it and die for it and glorify it on many a field to come. Great things are coming on—I know not what. Be ready. God is before us as well as behind. Nations are borne onward to their destiny. In the shock of empires, the world moves, and from the smoke and flame comes forth redeemed, regenerated man.*[26]

Later this year, after violence permeated the fall elections in the South that ended in a strong Democratic victory, Rutherford B. Hayes continued to express hope that the "better element" in the South had simply been disorganized, and it was just a matter of time before improvement would be evident.[27]

Despite his outspoken defense of President Hayes and his administration, there would be no foreign mission for Chamberlain. But in the spring of 1878, he was offered an appointment to represent the United States as commissioner of education at that year's Paris Exposition, an offer he nearly refused. But in March, in a letter to Fanny, who had traveled to New York City with Grace, Lawrence wrote, "I may go to Paris after all—am now corresponding with the Secretary of State about it." Worried over the expense of such a trip and hoping to curtail Fanny's shopping in New York, he added:

> *If so I shall be sorry you have bought so many things, & expended so much money; for I should try to take you & Grace if I could possible get money enough. It would cost $3000 for all of us—to go as I expect to if I go at all June 6th...& stay till Oct. 1st—4 mos. But as you think best only it seems to me poor policy to pile more things into the house to shut up & leave liable to be burned up before we return. You shall go, if you will be good!, & I want Grace to go. Wyllys cant.*[28]

But Wyllys would, in fact, go abroad with the family that year, as Lawrence's dream of seeing Europe at last came true. Aboard the steamer, *England*, Lawrence wrote to Father and Mother Chamberlain just before their departure in June: "I reserved a day or two to run down & make you a little visit, but matters came in so nearly on me the last week I had to work day & night without interruption except for three or four hours sleep just before day light. We all are off for France, & are well & happy." Referring to the Chamberlain ancestor, William, Count Tankerville of Normandy, who came to England with William the Conqueror, he commented: "It will be a great thing for the children to have this opportunity of seeing Europe with us, & we shall try to write you from *Tankerville Castle* & many other interesting places." Relating that they planned to be away five months, their first stop would be in London. He planned to take a house in Paris, and "*keep house* with a French housekeeper. We can learn how they do it."

It is easy to see that the father shared the son's enthusiasm as Lawrence wrote that, "Wyllys is happy as a sea bird. The ship is magnificent—Five thousand tons—& our cabin was the first choice." Lawrence bid his mother and father farewell: "We all send our dutiful & affectionate regards, with much love to dear Sadie, & wish the best things for you & the best prayer from you for the welfare of all until our next happy meeting." Several weeks after the Chamberlains' departure, Sae gave birth to yet another son, who would be named Dana.[29]

Letters from Grace to "dearest" and "precious" Horace mark the Chamberlains' passage through Europe. In August 1878, Grace wrote that she was less than impressed with Paris or the French, exclaiming, "What w[oul]d I give for one good New England Sabbath...." But her absence from Horace may well have inspired such sentiments. At the end of her letter, Grace used the closing that Fanny had so often written to Lawrence when they were apart: "Good bye...for a little while...." Enjoying the natural beauties of Europe, as well as the art treasures of the old world, the Chamberlains visited Venice, Verona and Milan, the Alps, Switzerland and Germany.[30]

When the Chamberlains returned from Europe at the end of 1878, the Bowdoin students met his train. With a band in the lead, they led his carriage to the Chamberlain home. When he gave a speech of thanks, "the air was rent with cheers for President Chamberlain and B-o-w-d-o-i-n." Perhaps the joys of his "grand tour" and the rousing reception from the students took some of the sting out of an otherwise great disappointment for Chamberlain. In 1878, the scientific department at the college was crumbling. As one history of Bowdoin explained, many students had begun to avoid the degree for fear that the new department would be abandoned before they could complete their studies. This history also acknowledged that Bowdoin had been competing, on one hand, with the free tuition and lower requirements at the state's agricultural college, and on the other, with the Massachusetts Institute of Technology with its superior facilities. Hatch commented, "...General Chamberlain succumbed to the odds against him, but in yielding he refused to accept blame for what he had done and tried to do." By 1880, only the engineering department remained at Bowdoin. And it, too, would vanish, when the professor who was its leading light accepted an invitation to MIT, taking some of his best students with him.[31]

During the Chamberlains' time in Europe, Maine had experienced a difficult state election. The Republican governor, Selden Connor, a Civil War veteran whose wounds rivaled Chamberlain's in their severity, failed to win a sufficient majority for reelection. Thus, the next governor of Maine was chosen by the state legislature. With heavy support from Maine's disgruntled farmers and others who suffered during the depression, a Greenback party had made major strides in the state. When Greenbackers and Democrats formed a "fusion party," Republicans could do nothing other than throw their weight to either the Greenback or Democratic candidates, choosing to support Democrat Alonzo Garcelon. This political scenario was repeated in the election the next year. Chamberlain, who had served for a number of years as commander of Maine's militia, would be faced with the threat of insurrection in his own state that he would describe privately, to Fanny, as rivaling the challenge he had faced at Little Round Top.[32]

CHAPTER

19

"Counted Out"

The Greenbackism that threw Maine politics into three party turmoil had reached the state as the movement was waning in other parts of the country. But events on the national political scene were far from peaceful. The 1878 fall elections in the South were dominated by rampant violence and intimidation. The Democrats added control of the U.S. Senate to their majority in the House. In the 1879-1880 sessions, eighteen Confederate generals sat in Congress with ninety percent of the Southern congressmen having served in the Confederate Army. In March 1879, the Democrats made the first of a number of attempts to repeal voting enforcement laws by attaching riders to appropriation bills, while no Southern jury would hand down a conviction on electoral crimes. The Republicans had painted themselves into a political corner. Enfranchisement of black voters in the Southern states, whether they actually could vote or not, had allowed those states additional congressmen. The Republican Congress of 1872 had also removed disqualifications for holding office from all but a handful of ex-Confederates. All these actions were efforts to defuse the threat of a Liberal Republican and Southern Democrat coalition electing a president that would end Reconstruction. Everything had been bet on the Republican party winning enough votes, North and South, to maintain a majority in Congress. In 1878, that wager had clearly been lost.[1]

Republicans, including James G. Blaine, presidential hopeful for the 1880 election, responded by again "unfurling the bloody shirt." Their campaign would be an attack on their Democratic counterparts, not as political opponents, but as traitorous rebels who now had the upper hand in the country. Republicans counted on war veterans to spread the alarm. On Decoration Day in May 1879, Chamberlain spoke before a large group of Maine veterans, again addressing what they had fought for and what many of their comrades had died for. While GAR policy forbid the discussion of political issues during meetings, Chamberlain's speech is crowded with his ideas and concerns on the political state of the country. Underlying his words was his disillusionment with some of the members of his own party and his distress with the intrigues of party machines. Also evident was his strong, presiding faith that the basic structure of government that they had fought to preserve would survive this and other storms.[2]

To his fellow veterans, Chamberlain offered, "New thoughts, stronger justifications, wider ranges of vision as the great future opens on us, show us the true measure of the sacrifices that have been offered up, the true meaning of the conflicts in which we were called to bear a share, the high reach of those toils and sufferings which sometimes have seemed unavailing, and give us glimpses of the immortal structure into which our poor work was builded." Chamberlain drew their attention to others who had died for their beliefs. He told of three simple tablets at a cathedral in Berne, Switzerland, that "touched me more than anything I saw there of human art, or even nature's work." Dedicated to the men of the Swiss Guard who, to the last man, had defended Louis XVI of France against the mobs of the French Revolution, Chamberlain commended these soldiers as men who had died "for duty, for their honor's sake—for their sacred oath..." Chamberlain declared, "...a living power from them passes into the souls of all who see and kindles in every manly heart a new devotion to truth and valor." He reminded his audience of the Spartans who fell at Thermopylae. "Stranger, go tell the Lacedemonians that we lie here in obedience to their laws!" Though Chamberlain averred that earthly laws were not supreme, he asserted, "Were it not for laws, freedom would have no guarantee, Liberty would be license and soon there would be no liberty." He added, "We thus see that men are held in honor who fight not merely for personal and civil rights but to illustrate and defend certain great principles dear to the spirit of man, and needful in the long campaign of history in the great deliverance from evil." While acknowledging the sense of honor and loyalty that inspired the Union soldier, Chamberlain suggested, "It was a peculiarity of our war that we were fighting for an idea." He observed that, with Southern secession, they had been threatened with no particular loss of material interests, nor had Northern homes been invaded. The Union soldier was not trying to throw off a yoke of oppression, nor had he struggled for personal or civil rights. He stated:

> *We were fighting on a purely political question, gentlemen. A question of politics, comrades, and by the rules of our order politics must not be discussed. But I am going to speak of politics a little and I promise you that I will not violate in the slightest degree the letter or the spirit of our constitution. The politics we must not discuss is the party, partisan or personal politics, for in these times it has come even to mean the tricks by which the machinery of free institutions is made to subserve petty ambitions or corrupt schemes, and the people are made to think this is for their interest and their cause! But politics in the true sense means the art of living together....*

How do we undertake to achieve this in this country—what is the nature of that organic life by which we are the people of the United States of America? That is the political question which so far from being banished from our fraternity should be the theme of our thought, of our study, of our discourse or discussion....[3]

Emphasizing his belief in the necessity of maintaining the delicate balance between local and national government, Chamberlain asserted:

The distributions of sovereign power in this country and the institutions of government are altogether peculiar.... Our peculiarity is that we have a National life and being, and we have also local governments not subordinated to the general government...except in times the most extraordinary, when a State is unable to exercise its powers, the general government under the constitution has no right to interfere. Now there is nothing like this elsewhere, and we look upon this system as a happy and almost an inspired thought of our fathers.... We need both these forces. Either alone would be destructive—one tending to imperialism and cramping despotism of the weaker just as we see England doing to Ireland—the other disintegrating, breaking asunder and bristling with antagonisms full of petty jealousies as we see in the South American States to-day.... How to hold both forces in equipoise...that is our study and our task. There must always be two parties in this country, whatever temporary issues may now and then break them and commingle them. There will be one party emphasizing the central ideas of the government, and one to emphasize distributing ideas. Both are needed....[4]

Chamberlain borrowed from Lincoln's immortal definition of our democracy, to assert that, "the war was an act of defense *by* the people *for* the people, against the hostile acts of State organizations pretending to be supreme in this country, pretending that it was in the power of any of them to say that henceforth there should be no more a people of the United States. This is what it was exactly, and we accepted the issue and settled it!" He further suggested:

There will be bad men and good, in Congress and out, bad measures and good, bad theories and good. It is the part of statesmanship, and manhood to deal with existing evils, to take things as they are, and make them what they ought to be. And this should be done under the constitution and through the laws and by all the machinery of government, connected expressly to avoid the appeal to brute passion and brute force. That's what constitutions and laws, and courts, and congresses, and ballot boxes are for. Let us not be afraid to discuss questions fairly, and to vote upon them squarely.[5]

In an appeal to end sectional hatred and bitterness, he gave an analogy of an old man in Virginia who erected a monument to his sons after the war. On one side it said, "To the sacred memory of my eldest son, who fell fighting for the Stars and Stripes." On the other side it read, "To the sacred memory of my youngest son, who fell fighting for the lost cause." On the third face of the stone, he had inscribed, "God knows who was right." Chamberlain asked, "Which of the boys was right? God indeed knows and He alone. Into men's motives, which constitute one essential element in the character of actions, men cannot see." With pity for those who died in a wrong cause, Chamberlain insisted that God would remember all the blood noble souls had offered "in the name of right." To continue the work of the patriots and martyrs of the past, he declared that they needed the spirit of the Spartan obedience to the laws and the faithfulness of the Swiss to their sacred word of honor.

Chamberlain again declared the need to keep their word to "all men—the black man, the yellow man, the red man and the white man." He warned his comrades that "many a good fight yet will call for manly hearts and hands."[6]

One Republican newspaper reported Chamberlain's oration as the best ever given on such an occasion; another saw his speech as a thinly-veiled condemnation of those Republicans who attacked the character of Southern Democrats rather than their political opposition. How far these men were willing to inspire animosity toward their opponents is illustrated by the vindictiveness they turned upon Chamberlain after the speech. In an article entitled "A Dead Senator," a mean-spirited declaration to Chamberlain that he would never sit in the U.S. Senate, the article commented, "Probably the most remarkable Decoration Day speech ever delivered in Maine was that of Gen. Chamberlain...report of his remarks leads one to believe that he had changed his residence from Maine to South Carolina, and that the orator of the day was a Confederate Brigadier." Fastening upon Chamberlain's story of the father with a Union and a Confederate son, the writer said:

> *Well, there is no mistaking that sentiment. Gen. Chamberlain plainly says he went into the South, ravaged homes, burned the country and killed people, and yet he is not sure whether or not he was doing right. A man who skulked at home, or who fled to a foreign country, is preferable to one who will engage in all the horrors of battle, and then returning, say, "God only knows which was right".... Even a man who did so noble service for that cause as Gen. Chamberlain, will not be allowed to question the motive of his comrades, unchallenged.... It is impossible to conceive the object Gen. C. could have in taking the course he has taken—this year above all others.... If we do not mistake the sentiments of the soldiers and citizens of Maine, this will prove to be Gen. Chamberlain's last 'political' utterance before the loyal element of this State.*

Chamberlain's critics were right; he never would confront them in the U.S. Congress. But he was on a collision course with the party leaders in his own state, and before the year 1879 was out, an amazing battle for the Maine Statehouse would begin.[7]

Chamberlain realized several dreams in his personal life in the summer of 1879. He purchased a 10-ton, clipper bowed, 2 masted schooner which he named *Pinafore*, for Gilbert and Sullivan's widely popular comic operetta, "H.M.S. Pinafore." In late summer, Chamberlain also purchased five acres of land at Simpson's Point on Middle Bay, four miles from the Chamberlain's Brunswick home. Once the scene of a prosperous shipbuilding industry, as well as the site of "new wharf," the berth for all of the area's passenger and cargo ships before the coming of the railroad, the land and buildings at the point had been abandoned with the decline of Maine's shipbuilding industry. With plans to completely refurbish the big house, home to gangs of shipbuilders who had worked in the surrounding yards through the first half of the century, Chamberlain credited the building's salvation from vandalism to its reputation of being "haunted." Debris of those earlier years—the work-shops, saw-pits, steam-boxes, piles of sawdust and great timbers were strewn over the property. But Chamberlain saw beyond that, to a beautiful summer home for the family. They would call it Domhegan, hearkening back to an Indian chief who is said to have occupied the land before white men came.[8]

The desire to sail *Pinafore*, and work on his land at Simpson's Point undoubtedly played some role in Chamberlain's decision to tender his resignation as major general of Maine's militia that year. But he was urged to retain his appointment, and many of Maine's citizens were glad he did. Maine's state election in the fall of 1879 had again failed to elect a governor, though the Republicans held the majority in the legislature that would chose the next executive. In an atmosphere of great mistrust between the parties, a number of the state's voting returns were challenged. With his council, the seated governor, Democrat Alonzo Garcelon, who had himself been chosen by a coalition of Greenbackers and Democrats the year before, rejected or "counted out" a number of returns as suspect. The Republicans maintained that they were eliminated for nothing more than minor technicalities. Significantly, the number of returns that Garcelon and his council disallowed were sufficient to create a "Fusionist" majority of Democrats and Greenbackers in the Maine legislature. Such a turnaround in the legislature that would chose not only Maine's next governor, but also its next U.S. senator, caused an uproar. Republican leaders called "indignation meetings" all over the state, and had little difficulty convincing citizens that they had been denied their rights. Senator Blaine called on Chamberlain to "get up an indignation meeting in Brunswick," but Chamberlain refused, replying that such demonstrations had surely already impressed Gov. Garcelon of the state of public feeling. Chamberlain declared, "What we need to do is not to add to popular excitement which is likely to result in disorder and violence, but to aid in keeping the peace by inducing our friends to speak and act as sober and law-abiding citizens." He also informed Blaine that he had written to Garcelon urging him, before his term as governor expired, to submit pertinent questions to the state's supreme court. Maine's constitution provided that its supreme court could give its opinion upon points of law. Confident that Blaine endorsed this course, Chamberlain expressed his fear that "our friends may take some step which would put them in the wrong.... I hope you will do all you can to stop the incendiary talk which proposes violent measures.... I cannot believe that you sympathize with this...."[9]

Governor Garcelon was indeed impressed by the anger expressed around the state. In fear that the legislative chambers were in danger of being taken by storm, he assembled a force of a hundred armed supporters, men of no civil or military authority, to defend the State House. Garcelon's order to ship arms and ammunition from a Bangor arsenal to Augusta in late December did little to quiet the ugly mood growing within the state. On January 5, 1880, just before his term expired, he summoned Chamberlain, as commander of Maine's militia, to Augusta, ordering him to protect state properties until the next governor could be qualified. Chamberlain assumed command on January 6, facing a situation of no governor, no state government, legal or acting, no legislature—instead, two rival bodies attempting to pass legislation, and phalanxes of worked-up partisans, ready to fight for their rights. Chamberlain first dismissed Garcelon's armed band, who had barricaded themselves in the State House, and replaced them with members of Augusta's police force and county sheriffs. He hoped that civil authority could keep the peace without having to call out the military. However, Chamberlain had militia units at the ready with arrangements to bring them to the capital by train. On January 7, he wrote to Fanny: "Every thing is confusion here yet, although I succeeded yesterday in getting a good many awkward things straigh[t]ened out. But what vexes me is that some of our own people (Republicans) do not like to have me straigh[t]en things they want to have as big a mess as possible. They actually blame me for disarming the State House." He wrote to her again on January 9:

There is such confusion here—no Governor & no legislature—that to prevent positive anarchy & mob-law I have been obliged to assume the defense & protection of the Institutions of the State as you will see by my Proclamation to the people which you perceive bears a very quiet & unassuming mien. I do not dare to leave here a moment. There would most assuredly be a coup d'etat, ending in violence & bloodshed. I am determined that Maine shall not become a South American *state. I wish you were here to see & hear. But there is not a great crowd of ladies here I assure you.... No one knows what will come next, & I cant tell when I can get home. For the last two days & nights I have scarcely slept. It is a critical time & things are greatly mixed. But I know my duty thoroughly. Thanks to a good Providence my health is quite good. Hoping that you are all well & happy & not worried about me....*[10]

Chamberlain's duty, as he saw it and stated it to the press, was not to interpret the law nor recognize any political claims, but to maintain order until the question of a legal government was acted upon by the Maine Supreme Court. While many saw this as reasonable, some wanted to get Chamberlain out of the way. At some point Chamberlain realized that, while Blaine outwardly appeared to want a peaceful solution, Republican threats of force against the Greenback-Democratic fusion emanated from Blaine's Augusta mansion. Describing the forces arrayed against him, Chamberlain later called it a "three-cornered fight. There were three policies and three camps at the capital: one, the fighting wing of the Republicans, with headquarters, or at any rate, point of departure, at the house of Mr. Blaine; another, the fighting wing of the Fusionists,...and the third, the modest combination of the General and the Mayor, in one of the small offices in the State House." A letter written on January 10 by Blaine's protege, Maine's U.S. Representative, Thomas Reed, to a Portland newspaper editor provides an interesting view of the atmosphere at the Blaine mansion:

I have much grieved this week over your absence from the seat of war. I have been living at the house of J.G.B. and have been in the thick of it with [Capt. Charles] Boutelle [Republican newspaper editor, future U.S. Congressman] on my right hand and [U. S. Rep. William P.] Frye on my left. I have heard all the fundamental principles of law pronounced 'pusillanimous' and have seen the loudest bluster end in congenial smoke. But at last we have peace broad, white winged beneficent and headed by a Major General.... Need I say that the resplendent figure shining like one of the sons of the morning which has brought to us this tranquil joy is the figure of Joshua Lawrence Chamberlain to whom Lee surrendered.... He walks the State House stairs master of the situation and Lord of the Ascendant.... While we contemplate with rapt eyesight the Solidity of our massive position we are haunted by one of those vague distrusts which underlies all human happiness. Can a State be preserved by a Major General whose staff is only partially organized!.... But it is a great sight entirely. A Major General doorkeeping the State House and issuing passes to members of the Legislature!.... The Constitution of our dear old State is a delightful instrument but unfortunately only made for 'middlin' rascals. When the framers contemplated the broad horizon of possible disaster and shame they never dreamed of a knave like Pillsbury [Democratic leader] or fools like Garcelon and his council and we find ourselves heinously unprovided.... These fellows that I see certainly don't govern it and as certainly wont let anybody else.[11]

Chamberlain was careful to keep the public informed of his intentions, and took the precaution of having all his conversations recorded by a stenographer. Even so, partisan newspapers maligned and misrepresented him, and he was under attack from all quarters. Newspaper headlines declared him to be a "Traitor to his Trust," the "Serpent of Brunswick," and, ironically, the "Tool of Blaine." But what surprised and hurt Chamberlain most were the headlines of a leading Republican newspaper, which labeled him the "Republican Renegade," the "Fusionist Sympathizer," and also called him the "Most Dangerous Man in Maine."

His resolve was also assailed by a committee selected from his old army friends, "sent to him with the distinct proposal that he should permit an attack on the legislative chambers where the discordant elements congregated, for the purpose of 'pitching out' the falsely certificated members elect." His refusal to condone such action stopped the movement, but intensified the animosity against him. Though tremendous pressure was placed on Chamberlain, the number who actually participated in the aggressive posturing that permeated Maine's capital at this time was very small. Many anxious citizens of the state, and by this time, throughout the country, had little or no sympathy with the perpetrators of this astonishing confrontation. Many letters of support reached Chamberlain in his besieged office at Augusta, including one from a former soldier of the 20th Maine:

Dear General

Seeing the unsettled state of affairs at the Capital & thinking perhaps you may require more men than you have at your call, I would say that at a verry [sic] short notice we can raise a Company here for you (mostly Veterans) that can be relied upon & that would stand by you as we of the old 20th did at Round Top. I lost one leg in that Charge & if you require it am ready & willing to risk the other in either your defense or that of our rights. hoping to see this affair settled right I remain as ever Awaiting my old Commanders orders.

Respectfully F. B. Ward Co. F 20. Me[12]

No fewer than three men, elected by various combinations of those who considered themselves duly elected to the Maine legislature, presented themselves before Chamberlain, demanding to be recognized as Maine's governor. He refused them all. On the day that Chamberlain published his reply to one such demand, he was called into a committee room by an effusive politician, who flattered him with, "that document will go down in history famous as the speeches of Cicero in the Roman Senate." Chamberlain bowed and left the room, but the door had no more than closed before his "admirer" declared, "What we want to do is to get rid of that Major General." Another gubernatorial claimant, Joseph S. Smith, announced his governorship, and declared he was removing Chamberlain from command. Declining to "vacate the office," an attempt was made to arrest Chamberlain for disobeying orders, but as he would later dryly comment, "It was not successful."

The terrible days of Maine's "Count Out" were not without elements of a farce. Superintendent of public buildings and ardent Fusionist, Bradford F. Lancaster, alarmed as a group of Republicans attempted to meet at the State House, grabbed the keys from the doorkeeper and ran off. When another set of keys was obtained, Lancaster reappeared, this time making off with the gas lighter for the chamber. But, the situation became less laughable when Chamberlain notified James Blaine and his Republican cohorts that he had gotten word of a plot that was well underway to assassinate Blaine and destroy his house. Though Blaine had been urging Chamberlain to call out the troops for some time, once the Senator and his supporters grew "alarmed at the effect of their call to violence," their pleas became strident. Blaine wrote to Chamberlain, "I may be obtruding but pardon me—Mobs are not regular forces—nor are they governed by the same laws—The presence of one company of organized militia would speak peace to the mob that may be gathering while I write—Do not I beg you let any scruples detain you from calling out the militia—It is the one sure way to preserve order, uphold Law & avoid bloodshed."

Chamberlain again refused, insisting that he could keep order without it, and maintaining that such a show of force would only incite the opposing force and precipitate a bloody conflict. Chamberlain himself received threats of bodily harm. When a well-wisher rushed into his office in the State House to warn him that a mob of some two dozen men had come to kill him, Chamberlain buttoned on his coat and went out to meet them. Mounting the steps in a short corridor off the State House rotunda where Maine's Civil War battle flags were enshrined, Chamberlain declared:

> *Men, you wish to kill me, I hear. Killing is no new thing to me. I have offered myself to be killed many times, when I no more deserved it than I do now. Some of you, I think, have been with me in those days. You understand what you want, do you? I am here to preserve the peace and honor of this State, until the rightful government is seated,—whichever it may be, it is not for me to say. But it is for me to see that the laws of this State are put into effect, without fraud, without force, but with calm thought and sincere purpose. I am here for that, and I shall do it. If anybody wants to kill me for it, here I am. Let him kill!*

Chamberlain dramatically threw open his coat. But there was, as he suspected, an old veteran in the crowd who responded, "By God, old General, the first man that dares to lay a hand on you, I'll kill him on the spot!" The crowd melted away.[13]

On the 15th of January, Lawrence wrote to Fanny:

> *Yesterday was another Round Top; although few knew of it. The bitter attack on me in the Bangor Commercial calling me a traitor, & calling on the people to send me speedily to a traitor's doom, created a great excitement. There were threats all the morning of overpowering the police & throwing me out of the window, & the ugly looking crowd seemed like men who could be brought to do it. (or to try it) Excited men were calling on me—some threatening fire blood & some begging me to call out the militia at once. But I stood it firmly through, feeling sure of my arrangements & of my command of the situation. In the afternoon the tune changed. The plan was to arrest me for treason,...I should be kept in prison while they inaugurated a reign of terror & blood. They foamed & fumed away at that all the evening.... At about 11 p.m. one of the citizens came & told me I was to be kidnapped—overpowered & carried away & detained out of peoples knowledge so that the rebels could carry on their work. I had the strange sense again of sleeping inside a picket guard. In the night Gen'l Hyde of Bath came up with 30 men & Col. Heath of Waterville with 50 men; sent for by Republicans I suppose & greatly annoying to me & embarrassing too. I wish Blaine & others would have more confidence in my military ability. There are too many men here afraid of their precious little pink skins. I shall have to protect them of course; but my main object is to keep the peace & to give opportunity for the laws to be fairly executed. Do not worry about my safety.*

Chamberlain was, however, worried about Fanny. He suggested that, if she were afraid, she should call on the Brunswick selectmen to have the police watch the house. He reassured her, "...I dont believe any body will think of troubling you," but he wrote, "Somebody else beside Annie ought to be in the house with you."[14]

The Maine Supreme Court, when the question was put before them, decided, unanimously, in favor of the Republican claims. Fusionists, stunned, then angry, threatened violence, and the capital city still teemed with an ugly crowd. But Chamberlain, three of his staff members, including his friend, the old adjutant from the 20th Maine, John Marshall Brown, and the stalwart constables of Augusta would see peace regained on the streets and in the halls of the State House. On Jan. 17, 1880, Republican Daniel Davis declared himself Maine's duly elected governor, and Chamberlain's duties were over. An investigation was instituted to probe the causes and wrongdoings of Maine's infamous "Count Out." Chamberlain was not called as a witness, and Blaine eventually claimed credit for resolution of the conflict and bringing the hostilities to a peaceful conclusion. Many years later Chamberlain related that two of the most influential members of the Democratic-Greenback fusion had approached him during the crisis. They promised that, if he would

Civil War Library & Museum, MOLLUS, Phila., PA.

John Marshall Brown, Maine National Guard, c. 1872.

recognize their government, they would elect him as the next senator from Maine. They remarked that, "Blaine and his drive are the bitterest enemies you have in the State." A confidential message had also come from Blaine at nearly the same time: "Mr. Blaine says he will give way, and leave the way clear for you to go to the Senate if you will recognize the Republican organization of the two Houses." To this Chamberlain responded, "...they mistake me. I am not here for self. I will recognize the right,—rightfully declared, and take the consequences."

The consequences were that Chamberlain never again held political office. Nor would anyone who openly acknowledged friendship with Chamberlain be able to secure office or obtain a government contract. But there were many across the state of Maine and across the country who admired what Chamberlain had done. Perhaps Grace's future husband, Horace Allen, best captured the admiration many felt for him and the stand he had taken. Asking if "Daisy" had seen Massachusetts papers praising her father for bringing Maine out of trouble, he commented, "What the press *says* of your father, all decent people in Mass[achusetts], irrespective of party, *think* of him. Well you may be proud of a father, to whom the whole militia of Maine send word, 'We take orders, from you alone'." The Philadelphia *Times* declared that "Chamberlain of Maine is a 'bigger man than Blaine,' and that it will be a glad day for the State when she turns from the Blaines and the Hamlins to a 'scholar and statesman like Chamberlain.' He is the first Republican in the State that has dared to raise his voice in opposition to Blaine. This single fact would be sufficient, did he not already enjoy the distinction, to ensure him the lasting honor and respect of every good citizen of the Pine Tree State."[15]

There was little respite from controversy for Chamberlain in 1880. That spring, he traveled to New York to testify at the hearing to investigate Gen. Gouverneur Warren's dismissal from command of the 5th Corps at the battle of Five Forks. Warren had requested such a hearing for years, and had been denied. Finally in 1879, President Hayes granted his request. Warren still faced a daunting situation. Chamberlain commented, "The traditions of the whole War Department were for sustaining military authority. We would not expect a Court to bring in a verdict of censure of General Sheridan or anything that would amount to that." Nor would it be easy to find officers who were willing to testify. Who among those who had remained in the regular army could or would testify against Grant and Sheridan, the ex-president and the Lt. General, soon to be commander of the Army? And Griffin, who could have told much, was dead. Lawrence wrote to Fanny on May 11:

> *Genl Sheridan has been in the witness stand the two days I have been here & will be tomorrow probably, so that my evidence will not be given before Thursday & I shall very likely be kept under cross examination at least another day. The cross-examinations are very searching & as my evidence will be important I expect quite an ordeal. I dislike very much to be away so long a time, but this is something I cant be absent from. We are bound to have the true history of this thing out now.*[16]

Lawrence reported a "warm greeting from Sheridan and Hancock, and a great many others including *Genl Sickles* (your friend)." Not only would Warren's fellow officers be called on to testify, but also, as Lawrence told, "some of the Rebel officers will be here soon." Warren had communicated with many officers over the years. A number of them had decided opinions and had kept voluminous notes on the campaigns, but were not prepared to reveal them. Nor would all the Confederate officers who testified feel that they could be entirely candid. General Thomas Munford, who commanded Fitzhugh Lee's Cavalry at Five Forks, wished to avoid the storm his description of Gen. George Pickett's lapse in command that day would cause. Munford ordered that his papers be kept secret until 20 years after his death. Yet the Confederate officers brought a valuable perspective to the proceedings. Munford took exception to the idea that Warren was removed from command because he had not been "in the fight." It was his own dismounted cavalry that Gens. Warren and Crawford had encountered, and as Munford pointed out, the official reports of Union casualties stated that Crawford's Division suffered one half of the total loss that day.[17]

Chamberlain was closely questioned about his own actions and the movements of his troops, as well as his observations of and encounters with Gens. Warren and Sheridan. He responded with considerable care, making it clear when he was estimating times or distances, or when he simply did not know. Of events that did fall under his direct attention, he offered forceful testimony. Though he "edited" some of Sheridan's colorful oaths from that day, Chamberlain repeated, word for word, Sheridan's directive to his forces as he pushed them on into the darkness at Five Forks: "I want the South Side Rail Road. I want the men to understand that I have got a record to make before the sun sets that will make *Hell tremble*." Chamberlain testified again that fall of 1880, this time questioned about the actions of Warren and 5th Corps officers before the battle. Contrary to Sheridan's assertions that Gen. Warren and the 5th Corps did not exert themselves to get into position for battle, Chamberlain testified that Warren constantly superintended arrangements for the movement, and his men had been eager to get upon the ground and begin the fight. Only the state of the rain-ravaged roads caused delay. The Warren court of inquiry sat for three years, and did not deliver its verdict until 3 months after Warren died. The court exonerated Warren of most, but not all of Sheridan's accusations. Warren left instructions that he not be buried in his uniform, nor did he want any patriotic emblems at his funeral.[18]

In the summer of 1880, when the Republicans met to choose their presidential nominee, James Blaine suffered another setback to his ambitions. Hayes, as he had promised, would not serve for more than one term, but the Republican party was at no loss for presidential hopefuls. While one of the strongest factions of the party supported Blaine, another urged a third term for Grant. So severe were the disagreements between these two elements that after a deadlock of 35 ballots, a dark horse, James Garfield, emerged with the nomination. While a disappointment for Blaine, it was not considered a defeat, for Garfield was one of Blaine's cronies. Blaine's opponents had only managed to grab the second spot on the ticket when Chester Arthur was chosen as Garfield's running mate.[19]

Disagreements and controversies at Bowdoin in 1880 perhaps seemed tame or even petty in comparison with the other struggles Chamberlain participated in that year. A feud between two professors of chemistry at the college, Robinson and Carmichael, raged on with battles over who would use which laboratories. Though things were looking up for Bowdoin financially, the boards of the college voted to abolish science, but retain engineering. By the next year, however, when Prof. Vose asked for more salary, engineering died, too, for the boards rejected Vose's request and he accepted an invitation from MIT. The majority of the faculty voted to abolish military drill in 1880, but the boards continued to support Chamberlain. He observed that some of the very schools who initially criticized Bowdoin's offering of military sciences were now starting such courses of study themselves.[20]

Of all the blows he received that year, however, none hit harder than the death of his father on August 10. His father had taught him to meet challenges head on, and instilled in him a tenaciousness that refused to be overwhelmed by adversity. The work-hardened, leathery exterior of Joshua Chamberlain, Jr. had belied the tender feelings of a loving father and the boundless pride that he felt for his son. Father Chamberlain was laid to rest with his sons, Horace and John, in the family plot in Brewer.[21]

In September, James Garfield won the presidential election over the Democratic candidate, Gen. Winfield S. Hancock. That December, Garfield appointed James G. Blaine as his secretary of state. The fight for power between Republican factions in 1880 left little more than the wreckage of a party. In Maine that fall and winter, some tried to urge the members of the next state legislature to consider making Chamberlain Maine's next senator. It must have been some consolation to Chamberlain when the legislature chose Republican Eugene Hale, a man who had worked for a peaceful solution to the "Count Out." In the fall and winter months of 1880, Chamberlain traveled extensively, invited to speak in towns and cities all over New England, their citizens anxious to hear his lecture on Appomattox and to meet the man who had stood up to James G. Blaine. Mary Clark, who had nursed him at Annapolis after his Petersburg wound, regretfully refused an invitation from the Chamberlains to come to Brunswick. But she urged Lawrence to visit when he came through her area, and encouraged him to make her "little country home, your headquarters."[22]

No great public upheavals or controversies intruded upon the Chamberlain family in the year 1881, yet it would be a year of profound changes in all their lives. Grace married her beloved Horace in April of that year, and left an unfillable gap in the Brunswick family circle. Lawrence wrote to his "dear Daisy" that February, hoping that she could accompany him when he traveled to Washington, but Grace was occupied with the preparations for her wedding. Her father wrote, "If you want a $75 dress you may get it I want you to have all you want. You have been a good girl to me, & good to your Mother & deserve every recognition." Lawrence commented that he half envied the quiet time that he imagined Grace was having while staying with friends, reporting that in Brunswick, "It is not so here, for me. House full, mails full, hands full." He expressed relief that Carrie Pennell, his secretary, was there, for it seems that Carrie was indispensable. Going far beyond her clerical duties, she pitched in cheerfully whenever and wherever needed. A friend of Fanny's wrote to her before the wedding, sympathizing with the family's reluctance to part with Grace, commenting, "...tell Horace, for me, that he has won a prize. I am glad he is such a kind and good man."

On April 28, Grace married Horace Gwynne Allen. The ceremony took place in Brunswick at Rev. Adams' church, the church of her childhood, the First Parish Congregational. In May, as Grace settled into her new Boston home, she sent for their wedding presents. In response to a letter from her father, she wrote, "Friends share our 'mingled feelings' you say, 'Ay[e] there's the *rub*' my blessed ones. But I have much to be thankful for in my new life. Horace does every thing and is every thing he can be for me—" There are indications in July 1881 that Grace may have become pregnant shortly after her marriage, for she did not remain in Boston while Horace worked at his law office during the heat of summer. Horace's doting comments in letters to Grace of, "how much depends on your general health," as well as his wish that she will "return to your hubbins with a good appetite," suggest an early stage of pregnancy. So does a quip from Horace regarding an encounter he had with one of the "baldheaded fraternity...who sat near me in the cars" & "never even bawled." If, indeed, Grace and Horace conceived a child in 1881, the result was a sad one, for Fanny and Lawrence would not become grandparents for many years.[23]

In summer 1881, President James Garfield was shot in the back as he walked through a train station, arm in arm with James G. Blaine. A disappointed office-seeker, a member of one faction that bitterly resented Blaine's influence over the new president, was the assassin. Garfield lingered until the end of September, his death making way for a new president, opposing faction member, Chester Arthur. James Blaine, with little to show for his nine months of intrigue since the Republican convention's nomination of Garfield, resigned as secretary of state in anticipation of his dismissal.[24]

That fall, as Chamberlain entered his 11th year as Bowdoin's president, he had decided that the time had come for a change. There is no indication that Chamberlain suffered any serious ill health in his years at the college, but by the end of 1881, his labors, and likely the trials of the past few years were catching up with him. Just before Christmas, while Fanny stayed with Horace and Grace in Boston, Lawrence made his first trip to Florida, apparently to consider a proposal he had received to accept the management of a large business in that state.

He wrote to Grace from New York, where he had given a lecture before departing for his destination near Jacksonville. "Every body was good to me in Brooklyn & N.Y.," but he admitted, "I found out how used up I was when I tried to make a speech.... Am on board Steamer San Antonio ready to sail for Fernandina."[25]

For more than 25 years, Lawrence, now 52 years old, had served as a champion for causes that he perceived to be for the "common good," in roles as diverse as dedicated educator to that of soldier defending the Union. These years had taken a toll on Lawrence and on Fanny. Beyond the threat that years of such labors and stress posed to their health, a simple desire for a change could certainly be understood. But could a lifetime of service be exchanged for the worldly comforts and temptations of the "gilded age?" Or was Lawrence simply beginning another crusade?

CHAPTER

20

"To Transform the Wilderness into a Garden"

In the 1880s, as American entrepreneurs sought new fields to conquer, Florida was a state whose time had come. Many were willing to overlook the hazard of tropical disease in order to take advantage of the abundance of land, so plentiful that it inspired plans for developing, not just new communities, but new cities. The potential of the state's citrus groves was also being realized, while the unspoiled beauties of Florida held great promise for attracting Northern tourists. Beyond the lure of lucrative investments, some Northerners who were discouraged by political conditions in the South, hoped that the economic recovery of the region might cure many ills. They theorized that with opportunities for both races, the resulting stability might lead to progress in social equality that was not being achieved at the polls.[1]

Chamberlain was first drawn to Florida by an offer from the Florida West Coast Improvement Company, an enterprise based in Ocala, a growing little metropolis in north central Florida. Among other things, the company would build the Silver Springs, Ocala and Gulf Railroad, with a charter to run from Silver Springs, a budding tourist mecca and steamboat terminus near Ocala, to the tiny village of Homosassa on the Gulf Coast. One of the leading directors of the railroad would be a key figure in many enterprises with which Chamberlain would be involved over the next decade. John F. Dunn, though known as Col. Dunn, had served as a private in the 4th and 7th Florida Infantry. Captured and finally released from Camp Douglas prison in June 1865, Dunn came to Ocala after the war. There he rose from law clerk, to lawyer, to the founder and president of the town's first bank, the Bank of Ocala.

Dunn was also banker, stockholder and land agent for the Homosassa Land Company, which had invested in substantial acreage that would sky-rocket in value with the completion of the rail line. Other businessmen who had an interest in the SSO&G Railroad included Solomon and Simon Benjamin, kin of the Confederate cabinet officer Judah Benjamin, and Summerfield M. G. Gary of Ocala. "Colonel" Gary, once a member of Florida's Secession Convention, was a former captain in the 9th Florida Infantry, before serving as aide-de-camp to his brother Gen. Martin W. Gary, CSA. While Summerfield Gary was paroled at Appomattox, Gen. Gary had cut his way out and eventually escorted Jefferson Davis to South Carolina, where, it is said, the last Confederate cabinet meeting was held in the Gary brothers' childhood home. While it has not been discovered how Chamberlain became involved with this group of Ocala businessmen, it is not difficult to ascertain why they were interested in him. Such grand plans demanded capital that could only be gotten, at that time, from Northern investors. What was needed was a respected and trustworthy figurehead for their enterprise. But what was it about this particular business venture that appealed to Chamberlain?[2]

After landing at Fernandina on Florida's east coast, Chamberlain traveled to Ocala by train through the wild and unspoiled beauty of the state's interior. Offering a landscape intriguingly alien from that of New England, Florida still teemed with wildlife, from deer and bear to the more exotic panther and alligator. On reaching Ocala, the last stop on the rail line, he traveled another 60 miles to Homosassa by horse and buggy, through virgin lands of unique beauty. The village was set at the mouth of the crystal clear Homosassa River, a fisherman's paradise, its banks lined with giant cypress and its waters teeming with waterfowl. Writing to his sister Sae from Washington as he returned north, Lawrence wrote of what he had seen and the dreams it inspired:

> *I made quite a visit to Florida, & saw much there to invite energetic & resolute young men. There are great opportunities to get health & wealth, & also to do good, & help other people. I was most warmly received by all sorts of people, & had many invitations to take positions of responsibility which naturally suit my temperament & aspirations. I always wanted to be at the head of some enterprise to transform the wilderness into a garden—both materially & spiritually—to be a missionary of civilization & of christianity at once. Here is a great chance to do it, & in my own country, which is peculiarly dear to me. It would be a delight to me now to give my energies to bringing forward the true results of all our struggle & sacrifice for the Country, & to secure the blessings of so great a victory for the right.*

As yet I have made no plans, for I owe a duty yet to the College, & must see that all fulfilled before I think of new fields. Health surely could be found & kept in that wonderful climate where the sea sands & corals have made a land of strange contrasts of soil, & the days & nights are glorious above, & the airs sweeping from the Atlantic & the Gulf keep a constant & delicious evenness of temperature. I mean to take Fanny there next winter, & I think it would cure her of all her ills. It may be I shall have more to say & do about Florida by & by.[3]

Chamberlain's idealistic observations on what was, after all, land speculation may be startling, and he may not exemplify the entrepreneurial spirit of the "Golden Age." But Florida developers of this era did consider themselves pioneers as well as businessman, and the "founding" of towns and cities was a reality. Enterprises such as the development of Homosassa involved a great deal more than just the selling of land. In order to attract both settlers and visitors, the development of businesses and industries, and the transportation that would foster them, was a vital ingredient. And the region's development of new citrus groves must have appealed to Chamberlain. For a man who never lost a sense of delight in making things grow, here one could literally "transform the wilderness into a garden."

The resurgence of his "missionary spirit" is a little harder to grasp. Perhaps he believed, as a number of Northern intellectuals did, that once raised above the pressures of subsistence living, man's "better nature" could be cultivated. In Chamberlain's approach to business, as in his politics and his religion, to strive for the common good was his highest ideal.[4]

On leaving Florida, Chamberlain had traveled to Petersburg. Seventeen years had passed since his wounding in front of Rives' Salient, and he told Sae:

...I visited the battle fields of Petersburg & spent 4 hours trying to identify the spot where I fell on the 18 of June 64 in leading a charge upon the Rebel works. All is changed there now. What was a solid piece of woods through which I led my troops is now all cleared field, & the hill side so smooth then is now grown up with little clumps of trees—marking some spots made more rich perhaps by the bloody struggles made on them. At last, guided by the rail road cut & the well remembered direction of the church spires of the city, I found the spot—or a space of 20 or 30 feet within which I must have fallen. It is now a plowed field—too rich, I suppose, since that 18 of June to be left barren by the owner—& there are in it the remnants of a last years cornfield. Standing & musing there remembering how I thought of Mother in that calm ebbing away of life amidst the horrible carnage, I looked down & saw a bullet, & while stooping to pick it up, another & another appeared in sight & I took up six within as many feet of each other and of the spot where I fell. You may imagine what the havoc must have been that day. And for 17 years relic hunters have been carrying away lead & iron from that field—amounting, I was told, to cart-loads. I could easily no doubt have found many more had I searched, or kicked away the earth a little. But these I have, & that other that made so straight a way through me, will do.[5]

Yet Lawrence's thoughts reached beyond the effect of his Petersburg wound:

You can not imagine, I believe, what thoughts came over me, as I thought of all those who stood there on that day—for & against—& what it was all for, & what would come of it—& if those who on the one side & the other thought there was something at stake worthy of dearest sacrifice. Such thoughts never would end had one time to ponder, & it is well perhaps that the common cares & the inexorable duties of life call us away from too long thoughts.[6]

His amiable encounters in Florida with former participants in the rebellion perhaps reinforced his unwavering faith that there were men of the South who should participate in the restoration of their region, and the rebirth of the country. Writing from Washington, where he stopped during his journey home, the sights of the nation's capitol intruded upon his thoughts:

Another study is this capitol. Here are gathered the representatives of all sections & parties & creeds & countries, within little space. It is like a spectacle—a scene in an amphitheater. Here is the little world around which the whole great country moves. Self-seeking marks too many faces, & all the strifes of peaceful times, less noble often than those of war,—are seen here in their little play, or great one, as the case may be. All is not evil here, however, I went to a church thronging with earnest people this morning, & heard words of deep impressiveness, & witnessed a wonderful scene of infant baptism which also set me to thinking long of how we are responsible for each other.[7]

Returning to Maine, Chamberlain faced the continuing uproar over a case of hazing at the college in the fall of 1881 that had resulted in the injury of a student. When a freshman was hit in the eye with a piece of coal, allegedly thrown by one of a group of sophomores, the father of the aggrieved student sued seven Bowdoin students for $10,000. One trial ended in a hung jury and another verdict was set aside on a technicality. Meanwhile, the press had a field day, often exaggerating the wanton behavior of the Bowdoin student body. These attacks on the college by partisan newspapers prompted Chamberlain to wonder if his political liabilities were detrimental for the college. By spring 1882, though he would continue as president at Bowdoin, Chamberlain decided to accept the presidency of the Florida West Coast Improvement Company.[8]

In 1882, as Bowdoin commemorated its Memorial Hall, built in honor of the college's war dead, the faculty voted again to abolish the military sciences. Chamberlain finally capitulated, releasing the officer and aid supplied by the War Department to Maine's agricultural college at Orono. In the fall term of that year, he returned to what he described to Fanny as "a world of work...." Nor was this year free from instances of student hazing, for in the coming winter, he dealt with the fiasco one Bowdoin historian dubbed the "War of Smith's Moustache." Sophomores had traditionally prohibited moustaches on freshmen, and when a freshman named Smith began to grow a moustache, upperclassmen decided to take action. Masked students entered his room and clipped off his moustache with a pair of scissors. Considering this act just the tip of the iceberg, the faculty was well into a serious confrontation with the sophomores by the time Chamberlain, who had been away when the incident occurred, returned. Faced with a list of demands from the professors, Chamberlain needed little encouragement to act on what he, in disgust, called the "mutilation of Smith." Eleven sophomores would leave Bowdoin, never to return.[9]

In early 1883, Chamberlain was worn out, and so ill that he consulted a graduate of Bowdoin's medical school, well-known Boston surgeon Joseph H. Warren. Dr. Warren told Chamberlain in early March, "You must absolutely stop your work, for a time at least; You must have surgical treatment for your wounds. Both these things should have been done before. The condition is now critical. You have worked too hard, & been neglected too long." Suggesting that he consider a change in climate and recommending Florida, Warren declared: "I shall not be responsible unless you obey these orders." On April 19, after visiting Warren in Boston, Lawrence wrote to Fanny that he would go ahead with the surgery that very day. The use of ether worried the family , near as much as the operation that was to relieve the abscesses that pulled Chamberlain down and attempt reconstructive surgery to close the penal-scrotal fistula. Grace wrote to Fanny immediately after the operation, first of all, that "Pa" was coming out of the ether "nicely," and then that Dr. Warren believed the operation was successful. Wielding the unquestioned authority of the 19th century physician, Dr. Warren allowed no one to see Lawrence for at least a week.[10]

With many months of recovery ahead of him, perhaps the best medicine of all was when, with Dr. Warren's permission, he could return to Brunswick and Domhegan. Since its purchase in 1879, Lawrence had transformed his land at Simpson's point, clearing away the years of rubble left by the ship builders' trade and restoring the pleasing contours of the land. The old house had been expanded and renovated, "all in a simple manner after old-time fashion." Hitching a light plow to Charlemagne, Lawrence traced a path along the steep bank of Morningside Cove. It led to a sheltered spot of shade and wild flowers that would bear two names, the "Squirrel Path," for its inhabitants, and "Lovers' Retreat," for its privacy. Lawrence would quip of the latter name that "retreat" might be a "misnomer under such conditions." The other side of the point along Sunset Cove was a haven for songbirds, and as Chamberlain described it, an ideal site for a hammock or a walk. The bay itself was home to seals and a variety of waterfowl, while eagles and osprey circled above. Lawrence delighted in the many views from the porches of Domhegan, particularly when sunsets turned the rocky islands in the bay flaming red and yellow, and even the humble clam flats caught and reflected the tints of the setting sun.[11]

The family kept the problems of the world at bay, withholding all "business" mail, and delivering only the letters of well-wishers. Shortly after his surgery, a letter came from John Bigelow, the former Captain of the 9th Massachusetts Battery, whose soldiers had carried Chamberlain from the field at Petersburg: "From time to time, when I have had the pleasure of meeting you, you have spoken so lightly about your Petersburg wound, that I was led to believe it was not causing you much trouble. A few weeks ago, however, I was undeceived...." Remembering that Chamberlain had tried to send away the stretcher party that went through hot fire to carry him to safety, Bigelow defended his soldiers' decision to ignore a general's orders. Praising Chamberlain's contributions to his state and to the college, Bigelow observed that it gave abundant evidence that "it is better to follow...the order of a well Captain than those of a wounded General." At the end of June, a letter from the 20th Maine's Ellis Spear, expressing his delight at the reports of Chamberlain's favorable health, indicates that there was still optimism regarding the results of Dr. Warren's operation. But by the end of July, the New York *Times* picked up a news story from an Augusta, Maine newspaper that stated Chamberlain's condition was little improved, and that he would never entirely recover from his wounds. It is hard to know how high Chamberlain's hopes were raised by the reputed skills of Dr. Warren and the initial reports that his operation was a success. Three months after his surgery, he could do no more than sit up and attempt a few "strolls." Once again, he had to recover from the effects of surgery, and bear the knowledge that he must continue to live with the torments of his Petersburg wound.[12]

Bowdoin was apparently taken by surprise when Chamberlain resigned in the summer of 1883. The boards imposed on him to continue as a lecturer on economics and law, while they began what would be a two year search for a new president. Chamberlain, though failing in a number of his goals, had had a considerable impact on the school. Though the science department was no more, science had, nonetheless, come to Bowdoin, and a number of courses continued to be offered at the college. The departments of modern languages, rhetoric and literature were strengthened, and courses in American and world history had been introduced. During his presidency, students were given an option between Greek and Latin, and were offered more choices in advanced mathematics. As the search for a new president proved fruitless, some suggested that Chamberlain, as he regained his health, be urged to return. However, not all expressed gratitude for Chamberlain's accomplishments. Some alumni blamed him for the decline in enrollment after the demise of the science department, and some claimed that he had offended the "ultra-Congregationalists" during his presidency. At a Bowdoin alumni banquet, his old political opponent, U. S. Senator William P. Frye declared in a speech that "he did not like the Unitarian drift that the college had been taking for the past twenty years...."[13]

After his resignation from Bowdoin, Chamberlain received several attractive offers for the presidencies of other colleges, which he refused. Early in 1884, the private thoughts he shared with a friend, an ambitious young professor, perhaps best reveal his frame of mind after his release from the duties and worries of the college. He wrote, "I want to set a caution against your young ambition, that however pleasant and useful the life of a College Professor may be, that of a president, in I may say any of our common or best New England colleges even, is about the most thankless wearing wasteful life that can be undertaken." Though Chamberlain admitted that he was not ready to commit himself to any undertaking, he said that he had rejected the proffered college presidencies, and commented, "...no more of that sort of thing for me if I can help it."[14]

Wyllys graduated from Bowdoin the summer of 1883, and entered Boston University that fall to study law. Fanny and Lawrence found themselves on their own at home in Brunswick. Early in 1884, Lawrence told Grace that Fanny was pretty well, except for her eyes, and a Boston physician was consulted for advice on how to halt the deterioration of her vision. Though Fanny could still write and sew, she was steadily losing ground. Lawrence spent the first part of 1884 lecturing in Massachusetts and visiting with Grace. While he also sold Florida lands during his travels, he may well have felt some concern about his Southern ventures. It had become obvious in the previous year that the Florida legislature had issued too many charters to railroads, and as overlapping claims caused legal uncertainties, selling Florida properties and bonds became more difficult. This year also brought a brief, but sharp financial panic across the country, and in Florida, a freeze killed many of the orange groves. In March, Lawrence again sought a diplomatic appointment, this time to the Russian mission in St. Petersburg. President Arthur, in the last year of his presidency, did not offer an appointment.[15]

Bowdoin College

Harold Wyllys Chamberlain, 1881.

In this presidential election year, there was a heated battle for the Republican nomination, with Blaine and President Arthur both seeking the number one spot on the ticket. Liberal Republicans were dismayed at the prospect of having to chose between these front runners, and meetings were held to pursue alternatives. Carl Schurz, still leader of the reform movement, now dubbed the "Mugwumps," called on Chamberlain to attend one of his New York conferences in February 1884. Explaining that commitments to lecture would prevent his attendance, Chamberlain responded: "I regret it much, for I fully sympathize with the feeling that it is absolutely necessary for the success of the Republican party that their nominations should command the respect of sincere and thoughtful members of that party, who are not self-seekers but are looking to the real interests of the Country." While a number of Schurz's followers made known their willingness to break with the Republican party altogether if it did not provide an acceptable candidate, it is not known whether Chamberlain approved of so drastic a step. He cautiously offered:

> *If I could be present at the meeting I should doubtless find occasion to express....my opinion as points came up for discussion, but without knowing what questions may arise or what measures may be proposed, I can not say anything here of any value. I only desire to have all influences brought to bear to hold the Republican party up to its high ideals and make its practical measures correspond with its proposed principles.*

Chamberlain likely found much to admire in this tireless crusader against the spoils system. Of the many prominent guests who called on him in Brunswick, in later years Chamberlain was proud to tell that Carl Schurz had visited his home.[16]

After finally winning the Republican party's presidential nomination, James G. Blaine faced the man who had taken the state of New York away from the Republicans when he won its governorship, Grover Cleveland. In one of the dirtiest campaigns in American history, a lack of strong issues led to an exchange of personal attacks. This was the campaign that produced, "Ma, Ma, where's my Pa? Going to the White House! Ha, Ha, Ha!," after it was revealed that Cleveland had fathered an illegitimate son. The Democrats, meanwhile, found fertile ground by reopening the issue of Blaine's questionable financial dealings. While Blaine had consistently claimed himself innocent of any reproachable or illegal transactions, he was a very well-to-do man with no visible means of support. Though it is difficult to judge how much this mudslinging influenced American voters, two events at the end of Blaine's campaign are credited with losing him the election. Anticipating a close election, both parties realized the importance of carrying New York. But Blaine, after courting the Irish Catholic vote in this crucial state, grew worried that he might have alienated the Protestant voters. During the last days of the campaign, a meeting was arranged for Blaine and a large number of Protestant clergymen. The result was an address by one Rev. Samuel Burchard, who attacked the Democrats as the party of "Rum, Romanism and Rebellion." The Democratic papers lost no time in publishing this inflammatory remark, and their reports that Blaine, that same day, dined sumptuously at Delmonico's with a number of New York millionaires increased the damage. The election of 1884 was decided in New York, its 36 electoral votes going to Grover Cleveland.[17]

John Dunn traveled north from Ocala in the fall of 1884 to visit the Chamberlains in Brunswick. Having decided to throw his energies into his Southern ventures, Chamberlain commented that Dunn had liked what he saw of Domhegan, and believed he knew a man that would purchase or lease the property. By the following summer, Domhegan would be in other hands. Though Chamberlain did not sell, he arranged for a member of the Simpson family that had originally owned the property to manage it as a summer hotel. Chamberlain became president of the newly organized Homosassa Co., with John Dunn its leading director. The company purchased 12,000 acres of land, much of which was already controlled by Dunn. It included the plantation and orange groves of Florida's controversial former senator, David Yulee, on Tiger Tail Island and at the mouth of the Homosassa River. Wanting a more active role, Chamberlain offered to oversee the development of the company's land into a community that offered the business opportunities of a budding railroad terminal, seaport and resort, and residential properties laid out with consideration given to maintaining Homosassa's natural beauty.[18]

In 1885, two major roadblocks stood in the way of Homosassa's development. Until the SSO & G Railroad was completed, other transportation must be found for passengers and material. In order to entertain potential property buyers and investors, comfortable accommodations must be built in Homosassa. Chamberlain committed to go to Homosassa in July 1885 to take steps to rectify these problems, but those responsible for raising the funds for these projects failed to acquire the needed capital. Postponing his trip south until the fall, Chamberlain spent that summer in the North, helping find investors.[19]

In August, before Chamberlain left for Florida, he joined the nation in mourning for Gen. U.S. Grant. Whatever he may have thought of Grant's susceptibility to wily politicians, Chamberlain was deeply moved by the passing of the commander who had ultimately driven the Union armies to success. Traveling to New York for the funeral in early August, Lawrence shared with Fanny the scenes, and his thoughts during Grant's elaborate funeral and interment:

> *The great scene is over. Grant is laid in his tomb. You may imagine—few others can—how strange that seems to me. That emblem of strength & stubborn resolution yielding to human weakness & passing helplessly away to dust. I wish you could have seen the faces of Sherman & Sheridan & Hancock as they stood over that bier before the body was laid away. What thoughts—what memories—what monitions passed through those minds! The pageant and the tribute of honor were grand—Worthy of a great nation. I wish now very much that I had brought Wyllys with me. This is the last of the great scenes.*[20]

Embarrassed, yet grateful for the position he was given in the procession to Grant's final resting place, Lawrence stated:

> *By Genl Hancock's kind attention I was treated with marked distinction—too much in fact. I had a carriage directly in the group of Cabinet ministers & the most distinguished men of the country. It chanced that I was far ahead of the Governors of states & the officers of the Army. I would not have chosen that position because it was too much. But Genl Hancock's staff officer did not seem to understand that I was only a private citizen.*[21]
>
> *It strangely happened that Governor Connor of Maine was left out without notice & without provision by carriage for a place in the procession. I stopped my carriage when I saw him & took him & the commander in chief of the Grand Army into my carriage & my place—far ahead of that to which they would have fallen if they had had a carriage! By this means they had a chance to see the whole ceremony & at the burial service they were with me not ten feet from the central scene the casket before the tomb-door, while the last services were paid—the last prayer offered....*[22]
>
> *...the tattoo! The evening roll call—you remember—the end of day—the signal of silence & darkness. They who stood about—most of them—could not feel all that said to me. I looked in vain for a face that seemed to express what I was feeling. But not till I saw the faces of Sherman & Sheridan & Hancock did I meet that response, & that deepened all my own feeling. The great men of the nation were there. But nothing seemed great to me—but what was gone; except the multitudes that crowded miles on miles, & the tokens of mourning that overshadowed the city. Grant himself seemed greater now than ever. And he is.*[23]
>
> *Do not think me foolish & egotistic. It is not that spirit that prompts me to speak of myself; but you know I have had great & deep experiences—& some of my life had gone into the history of the days that are past.*

Though they have seen much death, the soldier is uniquely moved at the death of an old comrade in arms. Grant's funeral would be the last of Gen. Hancock's public duties, before he, too, was lost to the world.[24]

Chamberlain traveled to Homosassa in September 1885 with instructions from the company's directors to build a moderate sized hotel. But when the plans were submitted to local builders, the bids were much higher than expected. The company had had little or no success arranging regular transportation to Homosassa, and the contractors cited its isolated location as the major reason the cost was so high. Denied the possibility of starting the hotel, Chamberlain pressed on with the building of offices and a store, while choosing the site for a warehouse that would offer optimum accessibility at all tides. Chamberlain was hard pressed to get the materials shipped from the nearest point of civilization, Cedar Keys. And when the company's secretary was called away, Chamberlain found himself encumbered with an impossible variety of responsibilities that kept him constantly on the move. In October, he wrote to Fanny:

> *...I am glad enough to have the sight of your hand writing again. It has been a very hot day & I have had a very hard days work & to no small degree an annoying one. You would be surprised at the amount of business I have had on hand & have accomplished today. I am very tired and should no doubt write you a much better letter if I waited until morning but I am so rejoiced to have a word from you I can not help writing you something. The night is glorious, the moon high in the heavens—fleecy cloudlets feathering the blue. All is still except the fine chirrup of the cicadae, & a plaintive negro song floating from a distance on the soft air.*[25]
>
> *Still it is dull & lonely here. I do not mean that I miss people, or long for society, for I do not. But nature herself though soft & sweet lacks richness & body, so-to-speak, & fails to fill my spirit to perfect satisfaction. How I should delight to have you here though! & I am sure we should find worthy & profitable themes for converse, & even nature would please me better by having more body in it then!*[26]

Relating that no work got done unless he was on the spot, he also told: "The worst now is the great expenses that have been run up for the company in my absence—unnecessary it seems to me, & using up our money in a way that embarrasses me in pushing forward my works." Lawrence also reported that he was gamely trying to transform the plan for one of their work buildings into something that could serve for a hotel. The alternative was to let another season go by without attracting investors or selling land.[27]

On a brighter note, Lawrence described how promising the oranges in their own grove looked and he reassured Fanny: "I have been at Homosassa & all over our lands & waters. I walked scores of miles, & never once tho't of snakes! Nor have I seen one in *all* my three weeks of travel & tramping." But he also related a condition that would have been far from consoling for Fanny:

> *It is a trying season of the year & people are dying suddenly & strangely. Several of my Florida friends here have been taken suddenly sick to day. I feel entirely well. But I have taken some risks, being obliged to expose my*

self much to all weathers, & especially to work too hard. Once or twice I have had a 'queer' feeling in my head. But a small pill of quinine—or what is better a lime or a lemon—has immediately put me right.

Looking forward to coming for Fanny in November, Lawrence related that she might stay at either his log cabin near Ocala or in Homosassa: "... it will be something like camp life for a time. But you will like it I think. The oranges will be ripe by that time." He concluded, "Our enterprises here are full of promise, & really are worthy of my best powers. I feel that we are making history, & good history."[28]

Though Lawrence may have convinced Fanny that Florida was a land of promise, a letter from Sae to her brother in January 1886 expressed amazement at Lawrence's situation. It leaves little doubt that she questioned his judgment:

Your letter was duly received, addressed to Mother; and we were very glad to hear from you, were beginning to worry some. It conveys the impression that you are undergoing hardship and privation down there—To what end? simply—of business enterprise? If so, it seems to me you might do better with yourself. I do not know any thing about it except what I gather from the circulars. There are men not worth so much to the world who can do such things—[29]

Sae not only expressed disapproval of Lawrence's ventures, but her letter also contained disturbing news of Tom. Having worked in pension offices since 1879, Tom was being turned out of his position and was again returning to Brewer. Sae exclaimed, "What in the world will he do? There is absolutely no business here. Is there any thing there? I doubt very much if he has money enough to take the

Brewer Historical Society

Thomas D. Chamberlain, c. 1880.

journey! *Probably,* he will never see the day when he will have such an opportunity to lay by money; as during the past 5 or 7 years. *If* he hasn't done it, the outlook for the future both for him and us, is very discouraging." Of Tom's wife, Sae wrote:

> *Delia called on Mother for money during the fall, not getting any from him, & being obliged to pay her board—where upon I wrote him some plain if not wholesome advice, which he received with the utmost courtesy admitted his deficiencies, and pledged himself to do better. Soon after he sent Charley's old bill of $40.00 with a cheque for the same. I feel sure if Tom had any money he would have sent Delia enough for necessary expenses— If he has no money he is in a very dangerous way, in short on the highway to ruin.*[30]
>
> *I have more fears about Tom than I wish to express here— I havn't seen him & know nothing about him— Thats the trouble— If he could live in a Christian manner with his wife, and attend to some rational business— But I dont know, sometimes I think circumstances make no kind of difference; a man will over come those, if the right spirit is in him, and all the effort in the world and I might say, as I believe: God himself can not save him—if that is lacking—*

Sae went on to reveal an experience that had shaken her deeply, and goes a long way in explaining her willingness to lay censure far and wide. Referring to her husband Charlie's brother George, who spent his entire wages "in dissipation," Sae said that, after having a pleasant visit with Grace and her family in Boston, she and Charlie had returned home "just in time to provide a place of *shelter* for George to *die* in—" Sae's hopes that George would "make his peace with God" were disappointed, and she said, "That whole experience with him has wrought upon me—I honestly think, more than all my other experience in life—"[31]

That winter, Lawrence and Fanny anticipated a respite from the cold of the Maine winter. Instead, Florida experienced a freeze so severe that it brought all work to a halt. Yet Lawrence managed to finish the building that would provide hospitality to the company's guests. He had even secured an experienced manager for it, Capt. A. E. Willard, who readied it for its opening in February 1886. But even this small victory was undoubtedly spoiled by a warning from a friend that Willard was as "deceitful & cold blooded a rascall [sic] as is to be found any where—" Willard, who was married to John Dunn's sister, remained the manager of the establishment that became known as the Homosassa Inn. Chamberlain's later pronouncement that the hotel's comfort and table were second to none in Florida, indicates that he continued to find Capt. Willard's efforts acceptable. Another of his accomplishments in early 1886, however, gave Lawrence unmitigated pleasure. Failing to secure dependable transportation between Cedar Keys and Homosassa, he purchased the steamer, *Mistletoe*, to carry the Homosassa Company's passengers and freight.

Chamberlain had not only found a boat that could handle the Gulf passage in all weather, but one that had a shallow enough draft to be brought to the wharf of Homosassa's store and the Inn at ordinary tides. Proudly he reported, "I loaded her completely full of freight and with twelve passengers, and after encountering an extremely low tide at the outer bar which caused us to wait for the flood, brought her directly to the wharf at our Inn."[32]

Lawrence had little time to enjoy his successes, for by March 1886, he was seriously ill with malaria. In July, he attempted to make his way north with Fanny, while Wyllys, who had come to visit his parents, stayed on in Florida to look after his father's interests. When Lawrence took sick en route, he and Fanny were detained for two weeks in Chattanooga before they could continue their journey. A letter from Wyllys to Grace indicates that Fanny and Lawrence never made it farther than New York that July, for there, Lawrence was again taken ill with the pain and fevers of malaria. In addition, the Chamberlains learned that Grace, who had come south to visit her parents, had returned to Boston with the same taxing illness. In August, Wyllys wrote cheerfully to Grace from Ocala: "I have had no fever of any account as yet and am reading law out on the place for a while— The banjo occupies most of my leisure time and I am learning some songs and accompanyments [sic] with which I occasionally entertain (?) my friends the Martins." He confided to Grace that he had "got up quite a flirtation" with one of the Martin girls, but complained that he was now having to share her attentions with another. Having heard that Grace had not yet recovered, Wyllys offered, "I'm sorry it milled you down so and hope you will be yourself again when you answer." He suggested a dubious remedy. "Better take quinine & iron & strychnine—the druggist can give you the proportions."[33]

In the fall of 1886, Lawrence attempted to return to work. Still president of the Homosassa Company and vice president of the Florida West Coast Improvement Co., he limited his endeavors to working in their New York offices. But in December, after Fanny traveled to Boston to visit Grace and Horace, Lawrence was again taken seriously ill. After a lengthy silence, Grace received a long letter, written on December 13, from her father: "You & dear Mamma must not think I would willingly let all these long days pass without a word from me. But I really have not been able to write until now your dear beautiful letter makes it impossible not to do so." Describing Fanny's departure from New York, Lawrence wrote, "I was not well for several days before our poor tired 'little one' went from me to you. When she went I stood on the bridge in the gallery of the Grand Central Depot and watched the train bearing away,—at first so slowly but so strongly & sure,—my dear one committed to its trust, till it had passed out of sight, and only the circling wreaths of steam told of its track. Then that vanished."[34]

He wrote that the hotel room, that had been their "little home for so many weeks & months," seemed desolate as he left it, sending his bags on to the home of the Uphams, the friends with whom he would be staying. "I afterwards brought myself—depressed in body & in mind. There was a dinner party there that evening, and all remarked my *peculiarly* 'poor looks.'" The next day was stormy, the snow gusts whirling in the air, & circling around in eddies & making the fences & posts & yards look like a field of graves." He commented, "I would have given any thing to be able to stay quietly in my room & think & rest. I wanted to write dear Mamma a letter, & did begin one. But I had to come out, & be entertained, & spend the day in a false position, & had but little rest." Over the next few days,

Lawrence tried to go to his Wall St. office, but on December 7, his wedding anniversary, he became so ill that when he rose to leave, he sank back into his chair. "The kind friends those not Wall Street 'sharks'—I assure you, nor 'Bulls & Bears' to me—" saw that he was accompanied to the Uphams. By the time he arrived, his body was racked with "spasmodic, congestive chills... seemingly from hip to hip...," his hands and feet cold as ice. The Uphams flew into action, sending for several physicians and enveloping him in flannel and hot water bottles. Though his agony was eventually eased, the pain continued to spread, moving into the region of his heart. "...I did not know what was coming but thought it best to give instructions about many things.... I was not in the least frightened, nor afraid, but I was thinking much of dear Mamma, & you & poor Wyllys, I knew not where." The first physician to arrive relieved Lawrence's mind concerning his heart, but he was particularly glad at the arrival of his own physician, Dr. Jackson. The attack was diagnosed as, "long over worked & over worn nerve & vital force," as well as malaria. Refusing to let Mrs. Upham write to Boston, Lawrence determined that it would be better to wait until he could write himself. He explained, "...as it was, no good could come of making you anxious & agonized."[35]

The promise of a new and healthful life in Florida had proved to be a cruel illusion. With his health impaired and Fanny exhausted, a return to Florida was out of the question. Lawrence realized that he must relinquish responsibility for the work he started in Florida to others. There is reason to believe that Lawrence had invested heavily in the companies he labored so hard for in Homosassa. Wanting to maintain a key role in company proceedings, Fanny and Lawrence had to contemplate yet another drastic change in their lives. Far from the pines of Bowdoin and the exotic palms of Florida, they made their home in the country's center of finance, New York City.

CHAPTER

21

"A Blessing Somewhere Yet to be Given & Received"

In early 1887, the Chamberlains were still weary and unwell, but Fanny managed to make a visit to Grace, who was still ailing in Boston. Her husband Horace sent a cheerful, mischievous report to Lawrence in New York. "Mrs C has improved wonderfully since she arrived. She *almost* gets up to breakfast and retires at a reasonable hour, has a good appetite & seems to enjoy dancing (with the cat) very much. But for the ugliness of her son in law, of which she complains bitterly at times, she would be happy." Grace had bemoaned the fact that she could not be more help to her father, and Lawrence wrote to her: "You must not think I could possibly feel that you were indifferent to me, or any otherwise than the best & dearest & most dutiful daughter. I am now more concerned for you than for myself, & I trust you will plan to take a long & good rest.... I think that is what I need too. The Doctor of course thinks my trouble is simply '*malaria.*' I know better. It is overwork...." But he reassured her, "I am about well... You know I recover so quickly....," and he commented that a trip to Florida would actually do him good. Telling her that he often visited with his and Fanny's New York friends, he admitted:

But I do miss 'Mamma' very much. New York without her is desolation to me. I dont want to go any where or see any thing without her. But I do have many invitations from choice people. The lady cousins of Lady Randolph Churchill are those who invite me often... & many other of my 'millionaire' friends. Dont worry about me. I am glad for Mamma.[1]

After an absence of nearly a year, during which he had depended on others to look after his interests, Chamberlain returned to Florida. The trip did little to benefit his health or relieve business anxieties, for as he prepared to return north in late March, he expressed his desire to go home to Maine in the summer for a rest. Weary of hotel living and frequent travel, he explained, "I have no abode," describing the places he stayed as "Arab bivouacs." By the spring, some mortgaged lands of the Homosassa Company were sold to a New Jersey corporation. Businessmen who would ultimately reap the financial benefits from Homosassa's development came on the scene. Chamberlain, though his involvement in the Homosassa Company would continue for some time, was not among them.[2]

Though Fanny and Lawrence had some peaceful moments in the summer of 1887, by the end of August, Lawrence was again in New York, stating that he was "in the midst of great cares & responsibilities, & am not feeling quite well." His annual letter to his mother on his birthday, expressed some discouragement. "Perhaps I have not made all that was possible of my life, but I trust that God has still use for me, and has spared me through so many perils and so many years, for a blessing somewhere yet to be given & received." He added, "...I am happy and ready for any thing to which I may be called."[3]

That October, Lawrence sent a ring to Grace as her 31st birthday present:

I have an impression that you fancy the sapphire. I therefore had one placed between diamonds. For the sapphire though deep & rich, needs like some other precious gems I know of, to be set in the midst of lights to show its own beauty best. Things that are sufficient to themselves inspire our admiration: but those that need others, win & hold our love. Accept this little token of my grateful appreciation of your goodness to your mother & to me when we needed much light & love.[4]

Fanny was in Brunswick in early January 1888, and wrote to Grace as she prepared to return to Lawrence in New York. Now almost 60 years old, Fanny mentioned her apprehension when trying to get around in wintry Brunswick. "It is as much as one's life & limbs are worth to try to walk down to the post office, for the streets and side walks are the slippery*est* [sic] of ice." Fanny had regained contact with her Boston brother, Sam Adams, who had again fallen on hard times. In answer to an inquiry from Grace as to whether her mother and father really wanted "Uncle Sam" to have their latest New York address, Fanny wrote:

...<u>it never will do to refuse to give the poor fellow Papa's address</u>, after having been on such good terms with him as we were in N. York. He would surely find your father out, in one way or another, and it would hurt Sam's feelings dreadfully to have him think we were keeping aloof from him when we were living in the same city. I think upon the whole he would mortify us

less by coming to our up town place, than by frequenting your father's down town offices. I could face the music better than Papa could, & ought to take the brunt of it, because he is my brother & not Papa's. I do not think his applications would be so hard to refuse as many others. He is not a selfish man, but has too little self respect, I am very sorry to say. He is a much truer man than Tom, although not making so good an outside appearance. I think he understands that your father has much to stagger under, & would not willingly add to his burdens as some would.... I dont know what I should do if he were to meet the Uphams or Kendalls or some other of our friends there, but even that would be better than to have him meet the business friends of Papa's.... It almost killed me to have him come to the hotel where we were in N. York, appearing as he did sometimes, but I would not deceive or lie about him, & I marched right up to the cannons mouth, for it actually seemed like that.

Explaining to Grace that Sam had always been kind to them, Fanny instructed her to send her brother their address.[5]

In early April 1888, Chamberlain again journeyed to Florida, most likely on behalf of yet another Florida venture for which he would serve as president, the Ocala Company. Backed by northern investors, including James Gilfallin, former Treasurer of the United States, the company purchased the Ocala House. It was Marion County's answer to the extravagant new resort hotels springing up in Florida to court northern tourism. The first year of the company's operation was marked by an ill omen, when the yellow fever swept Florida. With medical science yet unaware that the disease was spread by mosquitoes, the frightened citizens of Ocala refused to allow any passengers off the trains in their city. The Ocala Company, as did the Homosassa Company and the Florida West Coast Improvement Co., had an office in New York City, and though Chamberlain still made occasional trips to Florida, his work was primarily in New York. Preparing to return north for another stretch of work, Lawrence wrote to Grace, once again expressing his loneliness: "I write Momma often, but have not heard from her directly for a long time." Fanny's vision continued to fail, and the pain in her eyes and their sensitivity to light might alone have caused her silence. But for Fanny, too, this must have been a difficult and lonely way of life. Each year, as her sight faded, Fanny became more and more unwilling to travel away from Brunswick. And when she did, the transient lifestyle and weeks in hotel rooms, watching Lawrence work himself, again and again, into exhaustion and illness, were undoubtedly unhappy experiences.[6]

On a more cheerful note, Lawrence reported having found Wyllys, who had stayed on in Ocala, "bright & hopeful." Opening a law office, Wyllys tried to establish himself as an attorney, while keeping an eye on his father's property and orange groves near Ocala. A long drought threatened the new orange trees that were set out that year, but Wyllys optimistically reported that he thought a good percentage of them would survive. Having escaped the fevers that struck his father and sister, Wyllys nonetheless expressed his desire to escape the Florida summer with a trip north. With Lawrence's encouragement, Tom Chamberlain had also gone to Florida and entered into a partnership in a store in Homosassa with Captain Willard, the manager of the Homosassa Inn. While Willard provided the capital, Tom supplied the labor and would share in the profits.[7]

In July 1888, Lawrence returned to Gettysburg on the 25th anniversary of the battle, where 25,000 "pilgrims," as he called them, came to the field. Lawrence found himself unexpectedly elected president of the Society of the Army of the Potomac. Elated, he wrote to Grace from New York on July 13:

> *It was a remarkable honor, on such a field & such an occasion, for one who was only a colonel on that field to be chosen President.... I shall have to do something to prove myself worthy of it. But a fellow couldn't get such a recognition unless there was something about him to draw men's minds, or hearts. I was not a candidate, & it was a surprise to me, for there were candidates who 'ranked' me out of sight.*

Occupied with business, Lawrence commented that he was pretty well, but much in need of a yacht trip. Soon to be traveling to Maine on business, he wished Fanny would consent to leave home and travel with him. "I hope to have our little 'Mamma' with me. Shall call & try. But she may refuse me, as she did Horace."[8]

In the fall of 1888, Lawrence wrote of a plan he had hit upon to give Fanny and himself more comfortable living arrangements in New York. In the little time he had away from his office, he had been preparing some rooms that he had taken in a house, for a "little 'home' in this city where I hope soon to see 'little Mamma'—" He added:

> *I am not going to have the responsibility of housekeeping; but have an arrangement by which I can have my own rooms & 'come & go' as I please, & be sure of the home whenever I want to come to it & feel safe about it when I want to leave it. We are going to bring some of our home things here for our rooms & keep up a reminiscence of the dear old rooms in Brunswick. We have a good place, near Central Park & near the Hudson River.*[9]

Though Lawrence decided not to travel to Grace's for Thanksgiving, he was called away from his work that month. Mother Chamberlain, in her 85th year, died on November 5 and was laid to rest in Brewer's Oak Hill Cemetery beside Father Chamberlain, Horace and John. Here, too, were the Farringtons' baby sons, John, Lawrence and little Charlie, though Sae and Charlie had the comfort of their daughter Alice, now 19 years old, and their son, Dana, age eleven.[10]

Lawrence persuaded Fanny to come to the city in the fall of 1888, but by early 1889, she was back in Brunswick. Displaying an obsessive attention to business, Lawrence wrote Grace from New York: "I have wanted to write you a good letter in response to your dear little note; but no such quiet time has come to me yet. I have had to be out every evening to keep myself in good relations with the *gentlemen* I am associated with, so you must take this sort of a letter for the one I would (& will) write." Neither the veterans nor the alumni of his alma mater had their usual power to draw him away, for he continued, "I am trying to see my way to come to Boston & give the lecture the 'boys' want me to... but it is very hard for me to break out & give *one* lecture when my mind is so absorbed in other business. I have promised to come to the Bowdoin dinner.... It is a great draft on me to do either." Yet he reminisced, "They say I made a real Chauncy Depew speech at the Bowdoin dinner here, & I enjoyed it, but may not be able to do it again." Although he had to go to Florida at the end of February, he wanted Fanny to come to New

York as soon as she could, to enjoy "the season." But of all the details Lawrence shared with Grace about his whirl of business and socializing, it was his last statement to her that gives some impression of how anxious he was to make some mark in the financial world. "I have an invitation to take a *very important* place in a great Railroad system in the north. *I may do it.* It is a great opportunity, if I can master the 'technique' of it, so as to fill the position with credit. People here say I can make myself famous in a new sphere, if I take this.... Full of *train, & brain-work*, but with a little heart kept for my dear ones...."[11]

This same month, Chamberlain wrote to those preparing Bowdoin's catalogue of alumni that he should now be listed as president of a railroad company. He also began to withdraw from some of his Florida interests. Wyllys expressed regret at this, for it meant that his father would not come there very often, but he also said, "...still I want you to do what is best for you and will give play to your varied experience and talents." Through the rest of the year, business letters indicate that Chamberlain was involved with a project that would extend the New York and Albany Railroad. Working with Henry Hill Boody, his rhetoric professor from his student days at Bowdoin, now a New York banker and railroad developer, Chamberlain likely crossed swords with some of the most notorious financiers and speculators in the country.[12]

In 1889, the Silver Springs, Ocala and Gulf Railroad finally reached Homosassa. Yet this long anticipated event had come too late, for in this year, the Homosassa Company sought another mortgage. But the most painful news that came to Lawrence from Homosassa was of Tom Chamberlain. Captain Willard reported difficulties that began when he asked Tom to bring the books of their store up to date. When Willard found errors in the accounts, Tom, without a word to Willard, left town. Willard also wrote that Tom refused to pay room and board, insisting that Lawrence had said that his board would be free. According to Willard, Tom had stated that if Lawrence did not make good on that promise, he "would hold you responsible if otherwise, & if you did not pay it, that he would sue you for the am[oun]t (such were his exact words)." Tom's return to Bangor in the fall brought yet another letter to Chamberlain from one of his brother's business associates, who said that he, too, had had a falling out with Tom, due to his "taking life too easy." By the end of the year, Tom applied for a pension, citing reoccurring bronchitis as the cause of his disability.[13]

That autumn, Lawrence spoke at Gettysburg for the dedication of the memorial statue for Gen. John Reynolds. In response to a glowing introduction, Chamberlain told his listeners:

> *Your courtesy is great, but it makes the object of it in this instance seem small in comparison. This memorable field is honored to-day by dignitaries of highest rank—Presidents and Governors and corps commanders, orators and artists, judges and doctors of laws. But what am I? On this field only the Colonel of a little regiment over yonder on the far slope of Little Round Top, lost from the world's sight amidst rocks and trees and the whirl of overwhelming foes, knowing—we and others,—what reach of sequence depended on it. Only a colonel among others....*

Here, Chamberlain was interrupted by Gen. Daniel Sickles, who yelled, "Ah, but without such colonels as you, what would have become of us?" Chamberlain went on to express his admiration of Reynolds, "noble man and true...revered and beloved through the whole army....," and praised the regiments that had stood with him, from Stone's and Biddle's Brigades. Chamberlain also reminded the Pennsylvanians that Hall's Second Maine Battery and the 16th Maine had stood shoulder to shoulder with their own men that day. He declared, "The associations of this day are more—far more—than a memory. They are living power. Far more than a new bond of union, they are part of what shall be."[14]

Three weeks later, Chamberlain again returned to Gettysburg to speak at the dedication of the 20th Maine monuments. Twenty-six years had now passed since the Battle of Gettysburg, and though Chamberlain had returned to Little Round Top a number of times, each visit brought a flood of memories and inspired him to seek the meaning of that terrible strife. Though few would consider Chamberlain an underachiever, the intervening years had held a number of disappointments for him. Denied advance in politics or entry to diplomatic service, he had returned to academia, but was unable to reach the goals he held for Bowdoin. As his numerous forays into the financial world had yet to bring success, his military record during the Civil War became for Chamberlain the one well-recognized and unblemished achievement in his life...one that no one could take from him. Or could they?[15]

In this year that saw the formation of the United Confederate Veterans, Gen. John B. Gordon would lead his comrades in gray into a decade that would see the veterans of the North and South meet upon the battlefields with a new-found spirit of brotherhood. Paradoxically, this era also ushered in a rising tide of bickering and bitterness among the soldiers who had stood shoulder to shoulder. Clouding efforts to preserve accurate history, differences of memory or perspective became petty quarrels. Meanwhile, recognition for the achievements of 26 years before came under attack, as reputations were jealously sought and guarded. It was into this atmosphere that Chamberlain came back to Little Round Top in 1889. On the afternoon of Oct. 3, the regimental reunion was held. In this more private of the two ceremonies that were held that day, he addressed many of the men who had stood with him on July 2, 1863, as well as their families and friends. "A quarter of a century ago on this rugged crest you were doing what you deemed your duty. To-day you come with modest mien, with care more for truth than for praise, to retrace and record the simple facts—the outward form—of your movements and action." Chamberlain assured his comrades, "But far more than this entered into your thought and motive, and far greater was the result of the action taken than any statistical description of it could import. You were making history. The world has recorded for you more than you have written. The centuries to come will share and recognize the victory won here, with growing gratitude." Aware of a number of the controversies that had developed over details of the battle, Chamberlain entered the fray, addressing those issues that, apparently, had most distressed him.[16]

He first observed that the positioning of the 20th Maine monument on a great boulder, while it was "so conspicuous an object during the terrible struggle—the centre and pivot of the whirlpool that waged around," it was, he insisted, quite to the left of the centre of our regimental line when the final charge was ordered." To his officers who claimed sole credit for bringing information during the chaos of

Maine Historic Preservation Commission

Little Round Top, October 2, 1889. Chamberlain is number "2".

battle, Chamberlain observed: "I take note also of the surprise of several officers to hear that it was some other than a single one of them who came to me in the course of the fight with information of the enemy's extended movements to envelop our left. Now, as might well be believed of such gentlemen and soldiers, they are all right; no one of them is wrong." To those who claimed that another conceived of and initiated the bayonet charge, Chamberlain answered:

> *The enemy...were gathering in the low shrubbery for a new assault. Our ammunition was gone. It was manifest that we could not stand before the wave that was ready to roll upon us. Knowing all this I resolved upon the desperate chances of a counter-charge with the bayonet. I at once sent to the left wing to give them notice and time for the required change of front. Just then the brave and thoughtful young Lieutenant commanding the color company, came up to me and said, 'I think I could press forward with my company, if you will permit me, and cover the ground where our dead and wounded are.' 'You shall have the chance,' was my answer, 'I am about to order a charge. We are to make a great right wheel.' What he did, you who know him, know. What you did, the world knows.*[17]

Chamberlain flatly denied that some men in the 20th Maine did not advance with their comrades. "I am sorry to have heard it intimated that any hesitated when that order was given. That was not so. No man hesitated. There might be an appearance of it to those who did not understand the whole situation." He explained that it took some time for the bent back left wing to come up into the line of their general front, but by the time that had been accomplished, Chamberlain told his listeners, "the centre and salient, you may be sure was already in motion. Nobody hesitated to obey the order. In fact, to tell the truth, the order was never given, or but imperfectly.... There was only time or need for the words, 'Bayonet! Forward to the right!' The quick witted and tense-nerved men caught the words out of my lips, and almost the action out of my hands." But, here Chamberlain made clear how offensive he had found the challenges offered regarding whether or not he had conceived the charge and taken steps to initiate it. He declared, "And while every one here, officer and soldier, did more than his duty, and acted with utmost intelligence and spirit, you must permit me to add the remark that I commanded my regiment that day."[18]

Putting controversy aside, Chamberlain told the soldiers of the 20th Maine:

> *The lesson impressed on me as I stand here and my heart and mind traverse your faces, and the years that are gone, is that in a great momentous struggle like this commemorated here, it is character that tells...a firm seasoned substance of soul. I mean such qualities or acquirements as intelligence, thoughtfulness, conscientiousness, right-mindedness, patience, fortitude, long-suffering and unconquerable resolve. I could see all this on your faces when you were coming into position here for the desperate encounter; man by man, file by file, on the right into line.*[19]

To the veterans' families and guests, he offered, "I do not know whether any friends who now stand here on this calm and sunny day, comprehend how the weight of such a responsibility presses on the spirit. We were young then. We do not count ourselves old yet; and these things were done more than twenty-six years ago. We believe we could do them now; but we wonder how we could have done them then." Chamberlain attributed it to their character, formed "by the mother's knee and by the father's side, which stood you in such stead in the day of trial." Chamberlain told:

> *I stood on that summit not long ago with Longstreet and officers of our own army, not so much disposed as he by the events of that day's fighting, to praise the Fifth Corps, and they one and all acknowledged that this was by nature and in fact the supreme position.... All honor to those who seeing it, seized it in thought; who gained it, who held it, who glorified it. All honor to Warren, first and last and now forever, of the Fifth Corps; to Vincent, to Rice, to Hazlitt, to Weed, to Ayres,—chief commanders here. Peace be to their spirits where they have gone. Honor and sacred remembrance to those who fell here, and those who fought here with us and for us, and who fell elsewhere, or have died since, heart-broken at the harshness or injustice of a political government. Honor to you, who have wrought and endured so much and so well. After life's fitful fever, may you, also, sleep well. And so, farewell.*[20]

What perceived political wrongs might have wrung such a statement from Chamberlain is a matter of conjecture. This was Benjamin Harrison's first year in office after he defeated Cleveland in the 1888 presidential election. The Republican party had courted the veterans' vote by portraying Cleveland's veto of a pension bill as nothing more than an insult to the boys in blue. Chamberlain had taken an unpopular stand against this bill that would have cost the country as much as $50 million a year. Much was also made of Cleveland's order that the Civil War battle flags, both Union and Confederate, that were mouldering away at the War Department, be returned to their respective states. While there was sincere opposition to the return of the Confederate flags, Cleveland's political enemies took every opportunity to discredit him as a lackey of the Southern Democrats. These issues, as well as a heavily financed campaign by the nation's industrialists to convince voters that Democrats would destroy the country's economy if allowed to tamper with protective tariffs, won the Republicans the presidency and both houses of Congress. James G. Blaine was credited with Harrison's election. Harrison reciprocated, though reluctantly, by making Blaine his Secretary of State.[21]

On the night of October 3, Chamberlain addressed a large audience in the Gettysburg courthouse. He addressed familiar themes—the causes of the war, why they fought, North and South, and why the struggle must continue if the righteous results of that war were to be realized. But Chamberlain also brought to this occasion something more, something religious, and mystical. He shared his vision of the United States as a sacred trust to its people, and described what he believed had ultimately brought victory to the Union armies:

> *There is a mysterious law of our nature that, in this sense of membership and participation, the spirit rises to a magnitude commensurate with that of which it is part. The greatness of the whole passes into the consciousness of each; the power of the whole seems to become the power of each, and the character of the whole is impressed upon each. The inspiration of a noble cause involving human interests wide and far, enables men*

to do things they did not dream themselves capable of before, and which they were not capable of alone. The consciousness of belonging, vitally, to something beyond individuality; of being part of a personality that reaches we know not where, in space and in time, greatens the heart to the limits of the soul's ideal, and builds out the supreme of character. It was something like this, I think, which marked our motive; which made us strong to fight the bitter fight to the victorious end, and made us unrevengeful and magnanimous in that victory.[22]

Chamberlain ended the speech with the words for which he is best remembered:

In great deeds something abides. On great fields something stays. Forms change and pass; bodies disappear; but spirits linger, to consecrate ground for the vision-place of souls. And reverent men and women from afar, and generations that know us not and that we know not of, heart-drawn to see where and by whom great things were suffered and done for them, shall come to this deathless field, to ponder and dream; and lo! the shadow of a mighty presence shall wrap them in its bosom, and the power of the vision pass into their souls. This is the great reward of service. To live, far out and on, in the life of others; this is the mystery of the Christ,—to give life's best for such high sake that it shall be found again unto life eternal.[23]

While there were those in the 20th Maine who questioned or begrudged the fame of some of its members, there were those who would deny the whole regiment its due. Several years earlier, Jacob Hoke's book, *The Great Invasion of 1863: General Lee in Pennsylvania*, was published. Mentioning only the 20th's desperate plight on Little Round Top, he proclaimed that the Pennsylvania Reserves of the 5th Corps, 3rd Division saved the day. By the time the soldiers gathered for the 30th anniversary of the battle, Col. Joseph Fisher of the Pennsylvania Reserves, undeterred by others' unwillingness to substantiate his earlier claims, took full credit for himself and his men for the seizure and occupation of Big Round Top on the night of July 2, 1863 in his account published in *Pennsylvania at Gettysburg*.[24]

By the last of 1889, powerful agents worked against Chamberlain and the developers of the New York and Albany Railroad. Efforts to raise capital were futile if the company could not first secure contracts with adjoining carriers, but there were forces at work to see that the New York and Albany did not get them. Chamberlain's remaining businesses in Florida were failing, but things were going very well for some of his associates. John Dunn, now elected to the Florida senate, prospered in banking, and E. W. Agnew, owner of Ocala's largest store, established a second bank in the city. Captain Willard hoped to end the year profitably, with a commission earned on the sale of 40,000 acres to northern investors. But by the next year, Florida's big railroad tycoons outflanked the SSO&G Railroad with their own lines, threatening to put it out of business and turn the little communities along its line into ghost towns. Only as the line breathed its last was Chamberlain allowed into the inner circle of administration of the SSO&G Railroad. But fate smiled on John Dunn. In the fall of 1889, Dunn learned of valuable phosphate finds in his region of Florida. He set out to buy all the property he could get his hands on before the owners knew its worth. Land that sold for $1 an acre would bring as much as $250 an acre should phosphates be found on the property. Though he came near bankruptcy, Dunn bought 13,000 acres of land, and the ensuing flood of speculators and prospectors turned the town he founded, Dunnellon, into a boom town.[25]

By January 1890, Chamberlain was again ill in New York. Though the news of the phosphate finds in Florida revived the sagging SSO&G Railroad, it did not save the Homosassa Company. In March, Chamberlain and the other officers ordered all the company's assets sold to pay the company's debts of around $80,000. A stockholders report reveals that all profits for the previous year went to the Central Trust Co. of N.Y. Those who gained control of the Homosassa Company's properties built a resort on Tigertail Island, with a stable for 70 saddle horses and a clubhouse called "Rendezvous." A hideaway for the wealthy with a list of stockholders that read like "Who's Who in America," those who came to enjoy the pleasures of Homosassa's fishing and hunting included John Jacob Astor, Grover Cleveland, Henry Ford and Thomas Edison.[26]

Wyllys remained in Ocala, practicing law, though he met with little financial success. While he had business and won his cases, he had difficulty collecting his fees. Wyllys chalked it up, in part, to what Fanny called "Chamberlain luck." There is no evidence that Tom Chamberlain ever returned to Florida, or answered the questions and demands of Captain Willard. The petition that Tom had made to the government to receive a pension for full disability was followed up by a declaration that he had experienced several hemorrhages from his right lung. In the spring of 1890, a medical examiner reported that both lungs were diseased and evidence of heart trouble was found. As Mother Chamberlain's estate was settled, Tom took the opportunity to repay Lawrence and Sae the money he had borrowed from them. By summer, Chamberlain was again hard at work in New York. In June, he got as far as Boston on his way home to Bowdoin's commencement when urgent telegrams drew him back to the city and business. But sometime that summer, he managed to supervise the building of a Gothic-style piazza to be added to the back of the Brunswick house. It would become his favorite place of repose when he managed to be at home.[27]

By 1891, Wyllys' "luck" ran out altogether when he became so ill that he had to leave Florida. Early that year, he traveled north, and after partially recovering his health in Boston, he went to stay with his father in New York. Lawrence, again afflicted with an infection of his wound, wrote to Fanny, who had apparently questioned what goal was worth all the misery:

> *I have your beautiful letter that quickens all my great love for you so that I am impatient of any conditions that seem to keep you away from me. All I am doing is with the fixed and undismayed purpose of being able to realize our ideal home & its sweet society. I have patiently and not unwisely planned & toiled to secure the command of the things necessary for this freedom. I have been delayed & baffled as to some of these plans. But I am still active and full of courage, & I cannot but believe some of the things I have in hand will be brought to results before very long. You well know my present plan for living included you near me & your place was set apart & prepared. But our dear Wyllys seemed to be providentially brought back to me—*[28]

Acknowledging that their small quarters were really only big enough for two, Lawrence nonetheless encouraged Fanny and Grace to come. But perhaps Fanny also complained of their frequent separation, his dependence on and relationships with others, and her own loneliness. The reflective, self-absorbed mood of the invalid is evident in his reply:

> *Meantime do not feel bitterly that others have of me what you cannot. I do not think that is ever so. It is doubtless an advantage to any who have souls or minds to appreciate, to catch even the overflow of my thoughts and fancies But all that is best—all that is most mine is kept for you & is most yours. Nor do I indeed see...many, nor much of the few I most enjoy. Those in the house are good, and faithful & reverential and careful of me & for me. The patience I have longed for has wrought a strange peace & calm in my spirit. And now in the days of my convalescence, which is slow, in that the old wounds were the occasion & location of my illness, I am impelled & inspired to write & I do so to the extent of my strength, not allowing anything to tempt me from it. I have a little brochure in hand on the astral soul or 'In two worlds.' You will like it.*[29]

Wyllys also shared his thoughts with Fanny, writing, "I owe you an apology for not answering your good letter before; but have been engaged in a sort of struggle for subsistence and trying to decide what to do. I am still in the stage of being neither sick nor well...." Relating his great enthusiasm for scientific and mechanical studies, Wyllys was working on several patentable ideas. Still hoping to collect monies owed to him in Florida, Wyllys planned, on recovering his health, to test his inventions and secure a position as a patent attorney. He also reported, "It has been such a tough old time for us both here, that perhaps it was better that you were not in it, after all." Optimistic about his health and his goals, Wyllys offered:

> *I have good reasons for hoping that in not over a year, I will be in a position to give you and poor old Father a good lift, after all, and see you both able to follow up the advantages you have. So keep young, and we will have some fun, yet...*
>
> *Two of Father's companies are coming to the front, three of them in fact, and I hope he will see that he gets something for himself out of them. But I am coming to realize better than ever what you have seen so long, that our man cant be best at everything, and Father can not ever be relied upon to look out for himself, but always for that other fellow. I think my out-look is providentially timed, so as to be a relief before things get any worse. Father has sunk so much of his money, and gotten his property most of it all tied up besides. I don't say this to worry you, but think it best for you to know some thing of how things stand—Just as soon as these companies are beginning to prosper, they begin to retract and cut down Fathers share It makes me very mad. Father stands it very well on the whole, and his reputation is still bright in every way.*[30]

At this time, Chamberlain was president of the Mutual Town and Bond Company of New York, as well as the Ocala and Silver Springs Company, whose plans to develop a Silver Springs resort ended in failure. He was also involved with the Kinetic Power Company, developers of the "Car Lillie." Chamberlain traveled to Chicago in the fall of 1891, meeting with the Pullmans to get estimates for construction. He was also engaged in business with Gen. John B. Gordon, who in this year was returning to the U.S. Senate after serving as Georgia's governor. It is ironic that these two champions of sectional reconciliation joined forces in business. If ever there was a man who energetically pursued financial success only to have it totally elude him, as it had Chamberlain, it was John B. Gordon.[31]

The end of 1891 found Lawrence in New York, Fanny in Brunswick, and Wyllys, still ailing, in Brewer with Sae and Tom. Wyllys's hopes of being on his feet physically and financially had been disappointed, and while he tried to earn money by working as a patent attorney, his father contributed to his support. Wyllys wrote to "Dear little Ma" in early December: "I am busy, and reaching out for work to do—Think I can get into a store for the holiday season at any rate..." Hoping for more work on patent applications, he said he could board with Sae and have a desk in Uncle Tom's office. "He also is very kind to me. Knows how it is himself to be out of health and out of work at the same time. He had a time of it here for a year, but all is going well with him now. We think and speak of you often. Aunt Sae is a true woman if ever there was one—" Wyllys assured his mother, "My health and courage are both gradually coming up." But he was concerned about Fanny. "I hope you wont stay in cold rooms to work, as it is really unsafe. You ought either to have a furnace or stove going, or to move out as Winter is getting in."[32]

Lawrence echoed Wyllys's concern for her in a letter to Grace in mid-winter. Hoping to bring Fanny away from Brunswick, he wrote, "She may not think she can get ready; but I do not like to have her there, & shall make every effort to take her with me.... Your assistance may be needed to induce your Mother to come away. If you can write her to be ready to come with me, I may be able to get her." He had also asked her to go to Florida with him at the end of February, and commented, "... I shall be glad to have her away from the lonely house in Brunswick." But as Fanny lost her vision, she became more and more unwilling to leave her home. By the end of 1892, she was blind in her right eye and had constant pain in both. Wyllys, though still hoping to practice law, moved to Brunswick, and contented himself with studying electricity and working on his experiments as he saw to the upkeep of the home. Despite Fanny's affliction, Wyllys told his father in the late fall that Fanny was getting rooms ready in the house and searching for suitable tenants, while Wyllys arranged to sell wood from a family wood lot.[33]

Chamberlain applied for an increase of his disability pension from $30 to $50 a month, due to his frequent need for medical and surgical attention and attendants during recuperation. Applications for this increase were handled by Tom Chamberlain, now a partner in a pension agents' office in Bangor. An official from the Pension Bureau instructed the examining physician that only if the gunshot wound through both hips and the "alleged" resulting infections of the bladder and testicles with general debility caused him to be in a completely and permanently helpless condition would his claim be approved. But Chamberlain was, again, overtaken by illness, and too ill to attend the Pension Bureau examination.[34]

The Chamberlains' life at this time presents a grim picture, but they were not alone. As the rich grew richer and the poor grew poorer, the protests of farm and labor organizations in the country grew louder. In 1892, at the failure of Benjamin Harrison's administration and the Republicans in Congress to lower tariffs or curb industrialist greed, the country stood on the brink of a major depression. Though Harrison and Blaine were friends before Harrison's presidency, these two potential rivals for the 1892 presidential election had been circling each other like two fighters since 1888.

The Republican party that Blaine knew and loved to manipulate had changed. The politicians of Blaine's day seized political power as an end in itself. But the new leaders of the party, in a wedding of big business and politics, wanted control of the country's financial policies. Nor was Blaine the man he had once been. In the early 1890s, three of his adult children died suddenly. Whether it was due to the deterioration of his own health or serious depression, Blaine gave all appearances of a broken man. But in June 1892, he gamely resigned as secretary of state to free himself for his party's presidential nomination, only to have the Republican convention choose Benjamin Harrison to run against the Democrats' comeback candidate, Grover Cleveland. The Democrats not only took the presidency in the fall of 1892, but swept Congress, placing the entire government in Democratic hands for the first time in 36 years.

Cleveland's victory may have been hollow, for just one month after he reentered office the country fell into a severe financial crisis. Credit disappeared, debtors had to liquidate their assets and many companies went bankrupt.[35]

Several months after the election, at age 63, James Blaine died, it is believed, of Bright's disease. One of his biographers, however, claimed that it was simply a matter of having nothing left to live for. Unfortunately, history is denied any real investigation of the decades of Blaine's political intrigues, for by his instructions, a private secretary burned all of his papers and correspondence. But enough evidence exists to show that Blaine had subtly and effectively disarmed Chamberlain and his political supporters on both the state and national level during the many years that he wielded power in the Republican party. Blaine could not tolerate, nor perhaps even understand, a man that did not tend the party machine. He undoubtedly perceived Chamberlain as a loose cannon and a dangerous political rival. And in a country that elected six of its presidents from the ranks of its Civil War veterans, had Blaine probably cursed his own lack of military service as the one missing ingredient that had denied him that office?

John Dunn of Ocala also died in early 1893 at age 49. Though his Silver Springs, Ocala and Gulf Railroad was not swallowed up until after the turn of the century, the beginning of the end was evident one month before Dunn's death, as the line entered into an agreement with Florida's west coast railroad giant, Henry Plant.[36]

The Chamberlain family was in financial straits and precarious health, yet they lived on, loving and supporting one another. And though financial success and security still proved elusive, Lawrence's reputation, as Wyllys declared, was "still bright in every way."[37]

CHAPTER
22

"An Inextinguishable Instinct to Go Forward"

In late December 1892, Chamberlain suffered another serious infection of his old wound. He made a difficult journey to New York City for treatment, and was bedridden there during the first weeks of 1893. His doctor's report to the Bureau of Pensions described a severe infection, resulting in an abscess that left him debilitated and disabled. Friend Fitz John Porter also offered his affidavit regarding the seriousness of Chamberlain's condition. As he regained his strength though still bedridden, he began to write. Periods of invalidism, though devastating for his work and finances, provided Chamberlain with time to chronicle his war years. During these winter weeks, he wrote a paper on the action at the White Oak Road that would later be incorporated into his book, *Passing of the Armies.* Chamberlain sent a draft of this, and a request for copies of letters and dispatches, to his old friend, Gen. Alexander Webb, who had been Gen. Meade's chief of staff in the last campaign, and was now president of the College of the City of New York. Chamberlain's work struck a chord with Webb, reawakening feelings and memories of those last hard days with the Army of the Potomac. In agreement with Chamberlain regarding the controversial days before the battle of Five Forks, Webb responded:

> *My Dear Chamberlain*
>
> *The little 'white Oak Road' should be relabeled*
>
> *Sheridan Used Up By Josh!*
>
> *It is a powerful little book and it is so full of repressed contempt for the mean plotting and sacrificing of men for a single purpose. I saw it all & Meade <u>felt</u> it night & day It is all coming back to me—I can sit by the camp fire & see & feel & hear it over again—....*[1]

Chamberlain also accepted the presidency of the Institute for Artist-Artisans in New York City, founded in recognition of the talents of America's artists and artisans. Dedicated to making art education more available and affordable, the school provided courses not only in painting, sculpture, architecture, and illustration, but also in the "domestic arts," stained glass, ceramics, carving, metal working, interior decoration and textiles. Still unable to leave his bed, Chamberlain corresponded with potential patrons, including Andrew Carnegie.

His months as an invalid also gave him time to reflect on the decade he had spent immersed in business pursuits and the elusiveness of financial success. These years had taken a terrible toll, and he had little to show for it. Limiting his undertakings to the art institute, he made a startling and premature statement of abdication in early May 1893. Though the friend to whom this letter was written is not identified, it was likely to "Andy" Webb, who called Chamberlain the "best & most loyal of all my friends...true as steel."

> *Dearest friend—of friends!*
>
> *Your kind & strengthening letter came this happy 'Lords day'—& gave me heart comfort and courage. I have 'burned my ships behind me' in turning away the offers elsewhere, of late, & clinging to New York & the sense of duty here—with it comes a sort of reaction from the strain I feel very weak now, & in the hands of God. I had to be brought to this patient trust & faith— It has always been my pride to be so active, & trust too much (I fear) to my human strength— Still I suppose it was right then, when nothing but "example" & "proof of deeds" would satisfy citizens—now it is done—the responsibility has passed from me to them—It is their Cause, Country, Civilization, City, their Young, their Commerce—*[2]

At the end of May, however, a speech to his old comrades in Boston on Memorial Day held no sentiments of "passing the torch" to others. It was a declaration of continuing determination and hope:

> *Comrades—I greet you with the password of youth; for this fellowship is for all time and for all place. You still hold your front, compact and calm. The blasts of death cut through us as of yore. Our ranks are thinning faster with the years. But the same firm look is on your faces as when you heard the old familiar order, 'Close up!' thrilling through the smoke and roar. We are closing up; pressing to the head of the column; rear rank passing to the front; the heart strong with the presence of all it has loved and lost, an ever-power. So we close up today; elbow to elbow; heart to heart; soul to soul. We stand together, held by one mighty thought, forever ours, that many or few, here or otherwhere, we are something greater than ourselves, and that which seems to perish is part of things that cannot die.*[3]

Acknowledging the power of Spring to awaken an "eternal expectancy of the blessing yet to come," Chamberlain asked:

> *Do you remember those spring mornings when day after day drawn up for battle yet unseen, knowing that before the night darkened above us a darker wing would surely settle down upon us; among all things uncertain*

this one thing certain, waiting in the shadow for its chosen—which one? or how many? Yet when those soft airs of morning touched the cheek, what flush of strength, what throb of blood, what thrill of soul, what deep, far gaze of forward-looking eyes, told of great purpose, great endeavor; the infinite hope, the mortal self-surrender![4]

What means this eternal "Forward" sounding the heart's depths with its call? The far off good allures; the answering impulse becomes an imperative command. There is an inextinguishable instinct to go forward, till the ideal of the mind be fulfilled of fact, till the deed make good the dream.

Asserting that man's affinity for declarations of reason and justice are in accord with nature and the universe itself, Chamberlain asked:

All the heroic toils and sacrifices and martyrdoms of the ages, are they but wild caprices of frantic thirst for a phantom freedom? Is the passionate human struggle only a treadmill toil, beating over and again the same weary round upon ground which ever slips away under the feet? No! with all its eddies and back tides there is an onward current in human experience. With all its changing bodies there is a living spirit of history. The great hope has its haven.

Chamberlain noted the world's achievements, in the spread of constitutional and representative government and the many institutions dedicated to humanitarian aid. He cited the end of slavery and praised the laws that secured all men's civil rights, a hope easier clung to in these last few years before a Supreme Court decision made segregation constitutional.[5]

Free from personal bitterness or disappointment, he told his comrades:

And for ourselves let us keep our forward record clear in all well-doing, in the ranks and roll of honor. Such services as we have been permitted to render cannot be measured by pay; nor such sacrifices and sufferings by pensions. Let it be ever a debt of honor, with no other requital than the proud consciousness that we have given of our best and uttermost to the noblest nation that is carrying forward the great deliverance from evil fulfilling those high behests which are the prayer of history.[6]

A number of veterans were awarded the Medal of Honor years after the war. Alexander Webb, who received his in 1891, was determined that his friend would be similarly honored. In a letter written in May 1893, Chamberlain thanked Webb for his efforts: "The requirement of witnesses I do not regard as unreasonable. The curious transformation of the rear rank to the front now that it is profoundly peaceful and safe there, is quite noticeable all along the line, and makes a fellow of my temperament reluctant to put in any claim for recognition...." Adding that he wished the government had required proof years ago, he acknowledged that he was unfortunate, for many who had witnessed his actions "fell victims of their 'environment'" and were killed. He offered the names of Major Joseph F. Land and Gen. Ellis Spear, both former captains with the 20th Maine at Little Round Top, as witnesses. His service at White Oak Road and Appomattox Court House, Chamberlain observed, was recognized by his superiors at the time, "but circumstances,—my own peculiar habit of reticence (in those days) and the absorbing interest which followed the event of Lee's surrender, being among them,—prevented me from thinking much about myself,—or others of me; and so my story ended with the war." It was thus, he explained, along with his lack of political patronage, that he was denied a full major generalship. Having just been asked to recommend Gen. O. O. Howard for the medal, Chamberlain quipped, "I seem to be in danger of being made conspicuous by being left out." Fitz John Porter also recommended Chamberlain for the Medal of Honor, claiming that he was one of the deserving heroes of the Fifth Corps who had received no recognition of his brave deeds. Porter expressed urgency in his recommendation, for having seen Chamberlain so ill from his Petersburg wound, he stated, erroneously, that Chamberlain was not long for this world.[7]

In the fall of 1893, Sae wrote to Fanny in Brunswick. Disappointed that Lawrence and Fanny had not come for Thanksgiving, she still expressed happiness that her brother had recovered his health and was again speaking around New England. The family anxiously awaited the birth of Horace and Grace's first child, and Sae hoped that Grace's health would improve after her confinement. Writing that she prayed for Grace and Fanny, too, every day, Sae advised, "Fannie—we need...wisdom & patience—every day of our lives—to stay us up—" Fanny would need patience and courage. While Grace successfully delivered a healthy daughter, Eleanor, Lawrence was taken seriously ill in mid-December during one of his many trips to New York that year. Stricken with a particularly acute infection of his wound, he wrote to Fanny at the end of January, 1894:

> *You have not, I hope been allowed to know how very hard a time I have had with sufferings and disabilities since Christmas. I have told Wyllys to write you such particulars as he thought proper, and he has no doubt, and rightly, softened the story down so as not to distress you. But now I am getting up, and shall recover rapidly—having no poison in my blood from miserable drugs. I dont know how the attack was prompted—probably by a seizure with grippe, which caught me by the throat, & then went to the 'weak spot.' But now I want you here. You certainly have stayed long enough in Brunswick; & I am much concerned to have you exposed to the inconveniences and uncongenial surroundings that beset you there. You can be made comfortable and happy here, where we shall welcome you with love and I can give you as much good as you can me. So please be ready to come right away. Make a very short stay with Daisy now, & plan for a longer one when we leave here very early in the season.*

Having had a letter from Boston, Lawrence told Fanny that Grace and her one month old baby, Eleanor, had been out into the sunshine, and were wonderfully well. "She wrote me the brightest letter I have ever read." But he also wrote that their old friend, Horace's father Stephen Allen, had died suddenly. Regarding the funeral, Lawrence commented, "I am glad you are not there for that. It would be too much for you."[8]

The country remained in the grip of economic depression and widespread unemployment in 1894. Chamberlain's railroad days were officially over, and he asked that "president of railroad" be replaced by "president of an arts institute" in Bowdoin's alumni catalog. He commented, "I resigned the Railroad office & it was not worth mentioning at all, except to *locate me* temporary."

Chamberlain initiated an eight-week summer course for the art institute at Domhegan, where he could enjoy his seaside home. By fall, he was traveling again and wrote to Fanny from Boston, on his way home to Brunswick: "Have stood the journey pretty well.... I suppose I shall have to go right down to Domhegan to see about the yacht." He reported that Grace and Eleanor were well and Wyllys, who was living in Boston, was hard at work on his inventions. Fanny's failing eyesight had robbed her of the joy of reading, for Lawrence wrote, "I shall bring some good books to read to you. We will have a happy winter I think." He expressed his hope to write and, in fact became editor of a collection to be entitled *Universities and Their Sons*. The first volume would be published in 1898, while the last came out in 1923.

That winter, Chamberlain tried to sell what Florida land he still owned. His orange groves were neglected and drought was affecting the crop. A real estate agent reported that he had put a "darkey" off the property and placed another man in charge, but with the lack of rain, his trees produced only five crates of fruit that year.[9]

Chamberlain continued to be popular on the New England lecture circuit, and in demand as an orator before the region's veterans' organizations. In September 1895, he addressed the men of the 20th Maine on the 33rd anniversary of their muster date. At the conclusion, he turned to Fanny, who was in the audience. He told his comrades that she could not go to the war, for he had left her at home to take care of two little children. But she had told him, "Your duty is with your country's flag in the hour of her deliverance." Introducing her, he said, "here she is and her heart is with you." At the veterans' applause, Fanny rose to take a bow. In early 1896, he was invited to speak in Philadelphia, where men from the old Corn Exchange Regiment, the 118th Pa., planned to greet their old commander. As a mark of their respect, he was asked to write the introduction to their regimental history, published in 1888.

Chamberlain continued to write about the war and frequently corresponded with other veterans, sharing reminiscences and information. In the spring of 1896, he corresponded with former Brig. Gen. Frances A. Walker, economic theorist and, at this time, president of M. I. T. Walker sent some of his writings to Chamberlain to review. They shared an interest in political economics, but it is likely that this material was for Walker's biography of Gen. Winfield Scott Hancock that was published the next year.[10]

In the summer of 1896, Chamberlain made one of his last attempts at high finance. He and several partners sought investors both here and abroad to purchase an extensive landholding in Minnesota. The short-lived flurry of correspondence over this project suggests that it was not completed, although the country was beginning a financial recovery. Blamed for the depression of the 1890s, the Democratic party was also associated with the increasing labor foment across the country, and drew their foes' accusations of having a penchant for "anarchy." In the 1896 presidential election, promises of renewed economic prosperity influenced the voter, and the Republicans' candidate, William McKinley, rolled over his Democratic opponent, William Jennings Bryan. The Republican platform had also announced its support for a peaceful solution to freeing Cuba from Spanish rule.[11]

That summer of 1896, Fanny and Lawrence visited Horace and Grace at the birth of their second daughter, Beatrice. Lawrence, declaring that he was more tired than he could remember since his hardest yachting days, left Fanny in Boston to help Grace, as he and Wyllys returned to Brunswick and Domhegan. Lawrence wrote teasingly to Fanny on his arrival home, asking how his "brave girlie" was today after her "hard pursuit of pleasure." He hoped the "dear little ones" were a joy and would help Fanny recover her youth. Mrs. Drew was housekeeping again for the Chamberlains. Lillian Edmunds, a distant relation of Fanny's, had also joined the household, first as a secretary for Lawrence, but eventually as a companion for Fanny in her last years. In this age when black-face comedians and sentimental "plantation" songs were the rage, Lawrence wrote that Wyllys had read to them the night before, and done an "inimitably funny impersonation of a darkey making a speech on the times."[12]

Lawrence later wrote to Fanny from Domhegan: "I trust all is well with you & 'ours'. It has been so cold here all this month that I have been half-reconciled to your being away. Especially when I see how needful you are to our dear Gracie and how your own youth is renewed by the companionship of the sweet little ones." Telling her that she was greatly missed by friends at Bowdoin's commencement, he reported that "dear little Hatch of Portsmouth...your pet student who liked to come to our house—not so long ago...," was now prime minister of the Republic of Hawaii. Another old friend of Fanny's, Kate Furbish of Brunswick, had also asked after her. Furbish, who attended Deborah Folsom's school in the 1840s, had, after years of study and exploration, gained national renown as an artist and botanist. A warm admirer of Fanny's, Lawrence invited her to visit them at Domhegan when Fanny returned.

Lawrence closed his letter with sad news from Brewer. "Poor Tom is seriously ill. Sae is with him all the time, & she thinks he cannot recover." Tom did not live through the summer, dying in mid-August at age 55 of a "Disease of Chest." A Bangor obituary cited typhoid fever and heart failure as the cause. Sae, as she had their two brothers before him, nursed Tom to the end. Whatever troubles Tom and his wife had had in their marriage, Delia Chamberlain was left forlorn at her husband's passing. Tom was buried in her family plot in Castine, Maine, where she would, many years later, be interred beside him. His gravestone, surmounted by a Maltese cross, is inscribed, "a faithful and distinguished Soldier of his country."[13]

Interest in establishing and recording the details of battles of the war increased in the 1890s. In the fall of 1896, Chamberlain was a member of a commission gathering material for the book *Maine at Gettysburg*. While his official reports and some of his material were used, Chamberlain did not write his own account. Instead he was asked to review and consolidate the accounts contributed by members of the 20th, including Ellis Spear and the regiment's historian, Howard Prince. With admirable patience, Chamberlain did not mention the fact that Prince was not on Little Round Top with the regiment. But he did say that, while his account was "admirable in its historic truth and...masterly style," he felt it was affected by "ex parte" or one-sided data. While writing his account, Prince had not consulted Chamberlain, and failed to avail himself of the large amount of material Chamberlain could have made available to him. In a letter to Spear, Chamberlain expressed concern over the influence of the former commander of the 15th Alabama, William C. Oates, on both Prince and Spear's accounts. Oates had not only published an article in 1878, but Spear and Prince, disappointed when Oates did not attend a reunion at the battlefield in 1882 as expected, had traveled to Washington to visit him. Oates, then a U.S. Senator, had thoroughly impressed the two Maine men. Letters passed between Chamberlain and Spear, not only to discuss details of the battle, but also Spear's writing style. Ultimately Chamberlain pronounced that trying to reconcile these accounts was the "hardest work I ever did in the literary line." He overcame what he felt were discrepancies or inaccuracies in Prince's account by footnoting certain passages and attributing the information to a specific source, such as "Statement of Colonel Oates."[14]

Chamberlain up to this time had not seen Oates' account of the second day, "Gettysburg—The Battle on the Right," that had been published by the Southern Historical Society in 1878. This work by the "One-armed Hero of Henry County," as Oates had become known, was an angry response to a paper by Gen. James Longstreet. Published in a previous issue of the society's journal, Longstreet suggested that the blame for the loss of that battle must be shared. Not until the autumn of 1896 did a copy of this article fall into Chamberlain's hands, inspiring him to write to Oates in order to compare notes on the battle. Meanwhile, Chamberlain wrote candidly to Spear in late November 1896:

> *As to Gettysburg itself; quite a number of things have been put in distorted perspective lately. The influence of Colonel Oates' statements has extended to color the accounts of the whole engagement.... I think you have been somewhat affected by this late account. No doubt all that*

Officers of the Army and Navy Who Served in the Civil War

Ellis Spear, c. 1894.

State of Alabama Dept. of Archives and History

William C. Oates, C.S.A.

Oates says of his own command is perfectly correct. But to reduce our whole fight to an encounter with his regiment is to falsify history. There is no room for question that our right was engaged with the enemy some time before Oates came on us. The time, topography, &c of the movements make this almost self-evident. The history of the 83rd Pa. is explicit on this point. My own recollection is clear. An account I wrote soon after the battle without motive for distortion, puts this truthfully. The status of the prisoners we took corroborates the testimony. Some of the 4th Ala. and of the 4th and 5th Texas were taken.[15]

Nor had things settled down among the members of the 20th Maine. Apparently the claim that the 20th Maine's Lt. Holman Melcher had conceived of and led the bayonet charge persisted, for Chamberlain also commented to Spear:

The Melcher incident is also magnified. He is now presented to the public as having suggested the charge. There is no truth in this. I had communicated with you before he came and asked me if he could not advance his company and gather in some prisoners in his front. I told him to take his place with his company; that I was about to order a general charge. He went on the run, and did, I have no doubt, gallant service; but he did no more than many others did,—you for instance, on whom so much responsibility devolved in bringing up the left wing and making it a concave instead of a convex line in the sweeping charge. There is a tendency now-a-days to make "history" subserve other uses than legitimate ones. "Incidental" history, even if true in detail can be made to produce what used to be called in our logic, "suggestio falso."[16]

In a postscript to Spear, Chamberlain mentioned another interpretation of the day's action that might be traced to Oates' influence. In his 1878 article, Oates made no mention of the 20th Maine's bayonet charge, only that he ordered his men to retreat, though they made no attempt to retire in order. According to Oates, when the 15th Alabama "ran like a herd of wild cattle," they ran right through a line of dismounted cavalrymen, taking several of them prisoner as they ran. They escaped what Oates believed, due to reports brought by his officers, was an impending encirclement by the enemy. Though Oates would forever insist that they met this body of Union troops, there is no evidence of any cavalry, dismounted or otherwise, at the Round Tops on the afternoon of July 2, 1863. Nor did infantry approach the 15th Alabama rear. The only possible explanation is that Oates or his officers mistook the 20th Maine's Company "B" and its small contingent of sharpshooters for this phantom regiment. The role of then Sergeant Walter Morrill, who commanded Company "B" far out off the 20th's left flank during the Confederate assault was also being debated, and Chamberlain commented:

Now it seems it was Morrill that won the battle. He did good and praiseworthy work. But one might ask why he did not make some demonstration while Oates was advancing on us, and not wait until we had fought him as long as we could stand and then turned on him and got him running. The 'whole truth' is sometimes quite different in its bearings from what is called truth. But to make a part truth displace the whole is not in accordance with old-fashioned ethics.[17]

A fragment of a draft of the first letter Chamberlain addressed to Oates in February 1897 reveals that he questioned if and why the 15th and 47th Alabama had ascended Big Round Top before their advance on Little Round Top. Chamberlain wrote:

I am having some controversy with some of the "Gettysburg Commission" of this State in regard to points of our respective movements on the Round Tops on the afternoon and evening of July 2nd, 1863. They think it impossible that you should intend to say you came over the summit of the Great Round Top to attack our extreme left. They think you and most of the Confederate commanders called Little Round Top the "mountain"; and their specific argument in your case is that the line of direction indicated by the position of our extreme left, and also the very great difficulty of surmounting the rugged sides of Great Round Top, make it almost certain that it was one of the lower spurs of the Round Top, and not its utmost summit which you crossed in your advance and near approach to our left.[18]

Chamberlain also addressed the 20th Maine action before the 15th Alabama attacked:

My right was struck some little time before your regiment enveloped my left; the 47th Ala. had reached my front before this. I think also, that the attack of the Texas regiments, I think, extended over so far as to reach my right even before the 47th struck. If I am correct, all the accounts I have...harmonize. You could not, of course, have struck my line as soon as the regiments which had more favorable ground to pass over, and your attack coming some little time later gave me the impression that it was by what I then called "apparently a new line" that the really heavy blow fell upon me which made me reel and recover so many times.[19]

Chamberlain received two letters of response from Oates, a correspondence that Chamberlain felt left their view of the battle in accord, except for Oates' claim of their encounter with dismounted cavalry during their withdrawal. Meanwhile, Chamberlain continued to investigate new sources and gather material. In that same year he received diary entries from Albert E. Fernald, former lieutenant of the 20th, who confirmed that the author of *Reminiscences of the War*, Theodore Gerrish, was not with the regiment on July 2, 1863, though in his chronicle of the 20th Maine, Gerrish had described the Battle of Gettysburg in detail.[20]

Fanny, Lawrence and Wyllys spent Christmas 1896 in Brunswick, and a letter from Lawrence to Grace in late December told of looking forward to Grace and her family's visit. Thanking her for her Christmas remembrances, Lawrence wrote that the old house did not need more things to remind him who was still "its light & joy, for the hearth stones of Christmas glow with many a bright, sweet face, traced in

William C. Oates, U.S.A., 1898.

the glowing embers & reflected in mystic lights & shadows on the walls...babies of babies rose, rank above rank & made an amphitheater of more than clouds of witnesses...these being part & partici-pants of their loving dreams." Fanny's nick-name of long ago, when she was a new mother, was revived, for Lawrence said how much "Nappy" enjoyed her Christmas present from Grace.[21]

By 1897, Lawrence severed his last ties with New York City and the world of finance. In the spring, Fanny was in Boston, Lawrence in Brunswick. He told that, after making an address in Springfield, Massachusetts he would "go to New York...to take away what furniture is to be brought here. There is no use in leaving it there any longer." Writing that both he and Wyllys were rather "run down," he had not felt like writing a Memorial Day address, though he had to do it. While Wyllys wished they were at Domhegan, Lawrence commented on his old Brunswick home, "I would rather be here now,—as I have less care here than any where."[22]

By early 1898, much had transpired between Spain and the United States over the rebellion in Cuba. While American business interests hovered in the back-ground, the birth of yellow journalism and its stories of Spanish atrocities fed the country's war fever. Many Americans sympathized with the Cubans' and Philippinos' quest for independence from Spanish rule. But far fewer felt confident in the na-tives' ability to rule themselves. Beyond these perspectives, the country was in an expansionist mood. In February 1898, the battleship *Maine* exploded in Havana harbor, killing 260 American sailors. An investigation of the explosion uncovered no evidence of Spanish involvement, and Spain had already agreed to American demands for Cuban independence. But in April 1898, President William McKinley sent a declaration of war against Spain to Congress.[23]

Chamberlain offered his services to the governor of Maine, stating, "I have had some experience of affairs and I am not aware that my powers are impaired." To the Secretary of War, he wrote, "I hereby tender to the Government in the exigencies of the impending war, my services in any military capacity for which I might be deemed qualified." To William P. Frye, now president pro tem of the U.S. Senate, Chamberlain sent a detailed plan for raising and training troops in New England. Though Frye was no friend to him over the years, Chamberlain asked for his advocacy in an appointment. He wrote:

> *My motive is by no means that of personal preferment; but wholly for the interests of the public service of the Country in her hour of need. Still, I cannot but think that my day is not yet over for the service of my Country. You gentlemen in Congress and in the offices of the Government, are in your right places; I desire to be in mine. And it is not unbecoming in me to express the conviction that by temperament, education, and a peculiar experience of public service, I am capable of taking a part like that suggested. The condition of my wound is very much better than for years; and while I would not think it advisable for me to go into Cuba at this season of the year, I should be ready, by the time the stress came, and the troops were ready, to take the field wherever called.*[24]

On April 30, the Secretary of War responded to Chamberlain: "I have your patriotic letter of the 22nd instant offering your services in the impending war, which has been placed on file for consideration at the proper time should an opportunity occur making this possible." This 19th century equivalent to a form letter, was undoubtedly perceived by Chamberlain as a painful snub. But it should be mentioned that there were many with military pretensions wanting a commission at the outbreak of the Spanish-American War. Soldiers, old and new, battled for a regiment, and as a friend of Chamberlain's commented, "The rush of all sorts of applications seems to swamp the service. There is utter confusion in Washington at the War Dept—" He told Chamberlain facetiously, "There are a million colonels in N.Y—I may be *one*" But there were those among Chamberlain's old comrades who would command again. Adelbert Ames reentered the service, and one of a number of ex-Confederates who served as officers in the Spanish-American War was William C. Oates. Though appointed a brigadier general in May 1898, he reported having a devil of a time procuring what he felt was a desirable command.[25]

An even more startling ambition of the now 69-year-old Chamberlain than a return to camp and battlefield is revealed in a letter from a supporter who urged his appointment as governor of the Philippines. This post was eventually claimed by William Howard Taft. In retrospect, it is well that Chamberlain did not receive the appointment. The seizure of the Philippines became a nightmarish struggle between American civilian and military authorities, and a horror of personal ambitions and intrigues that ultimately ended in unnecessary warfare for both Americans and Philippinos. By August 1898, the United States emerged victorious in its war with Spain, and in possession of Cuba, Puerto Rico and the Philippines. American opinion was mixed as to what the United States should do with these acquisitions. The Republican party, in this election year, remained relatively mum on the subject until after the voters went to the polls that fall to elect their congressmen. The details of the treaty with Spain and the intention of the American government to retain Spain's former possessions were, conveniently, not revealed until after the election.[26]

If the rejection of his services pained Chamberlain, his family could only have been thankful that he was not called to war or a diplomatic mission. In late 1898, Grace was expecting her third child, and Fanny faced total blindness. With as much cheer as he could muster, Lawrence wrote to Grace in December 1898:

> *You are greatly in our hearts and minds in all these days. I am glad to hear from time to time that you are enduring your trials so bravely and well, and I pray God to give you all strength and grace. We were preparing to see our dear little one here before this time; but as I thought it best to take our dear little Mother for consultation and treatment for her eyes, we took a journey off in a quiet way, where I could myself see the Doctors and find out what they could do for her. The truth is none of them seem able really to do much good; but their counsel is valuable as to general conditions. We did not want to worry you by leading you to fear anything critical or newly dangerous for our dear one. But now that we believe she is really going to be materially helped & perhaps partially restored, I can mention it to you as you will be cheered to know of the prospect for her improvement, & possibly recovery of comfortable seeing.*[27]

In this letter to Grace, just before the birth of the Allen's third daughter, Rosamond, Lawrence offered:

> *Now I wish to give you our affectionate remembrance and constant, tenderest love. As the days advance you will have added strength of spirit & soul for every issue or experience. You have part in the Lord's creation, and it is a divine office, and the divine love will sustain you. We will hold ourselves ready to answer all your wishes, and to share in your experiences as it may be given us to do.*[28]

Though Lawrence tried to impart some words of encouragement to Grace regarding Fanny's vision, it is clear that he held little hope that she would be helped by the doctors. But Fanny, now desperate to try any available treatment, stayed with Lillian Edmunds in Boston under a doctor's care. Lawrence wrote to Sae at the end of April 1899:

> *I thank you for your beautiful letter. Do not worry about me. I am wonderfully upheld, and am pretty well. As well as I ought to be considering that I do not spare my strength much. Fanny is blind; but <u>will</u> stay in charge of this magnetic Doctor who dares not tell her that he cannot help her—if it needs telling I do not see how Fanny keeps up. She exhausts all her energies, physical & spiritual in frantic un-reconciliation (and who can*

blame her?) to this affliction. Lillian is wearing herself out. We fear she will be a confirmed invalid out of it. I cant get them home, & Lillian writes me that it would do no good & make me not only unhappy, but wretched to go up there. Still I am going—as I ought to—soon.[29]

Lawrence also told Sae that he had spent much time writing over the winter, and finished the first draft of his book on the last campaign of the Army of the Potomac and the Army of Northern Virginia. Lawrence thought Sae would especially like his chapters on the "passing of the armies." He also wrote a paper that he called "The Charge at Fort Hell," a graphic and highly personal description of June 18, 1864 at Petersburg that has never been published. During this winter, Chamberlain corresponded with Gen. John B. Gordon, who since 1893 had been engaged around the country delivering a well-received lecture, "The Last Days of the Confederacy." Gordon and Chamberlain discussed joining forces, and lecturing together on the last campaign and Appomattox. Although Gordon's manager wanted to publish Chamberlain's lecture on the surrender, he discouraged the idea of joint lecture tours.[30]

In the spring of 1899, Lawrence received a letter from the son of the late William Pitt Fessenden, who had served as Lincoln's Secretary of the Treasury. Having found a letter that Gen. James Rice wrote to his father shortly after Gettysburg, Francis Fessenden sent it to Chamberlain, remarking, "The enclosed letter from Genl. Rice pays such a handsome tribute to your bravery and skill, that I think you ought to have it." Rice's letter to Fessenden, written September 8, 1863, recommended then Col. Chamberlain for promotion, stating, "...My personal knowledge of this gallant officer's skill and bravery upon the battle-field, his ability in drill and discipline, and his fidelity to duty in camp, added to a just admiration for his scholarship, and respect for his Christian character." Of the 20th Maine, he noted: "The conduct of this Regiment at the Battle of Gettysburg has rendered, for all time, the prowess of the arms of your State, imperishable; conduct which, as an eye-witness, I do not hesitate to say, has its inspiration and great success from the moral power and personal heroism of Col. Chamberlain." Moved by this tribute from his long-dead friend, Chamberlain wrote back to Francis Fessenden: "I thank you for the kind letter enclosing that of Genl Rice, as brave and true a man as ever went 'booted & spurred' from the field to report to the God of battles. His letter does me more good now than it did then. And, yours as much as his." It was to Frances Fessenden that Chamberlain lost his chance to become a full major general in 1865, when "there was another Major General to be appointed from Maine and so its 'quota' would be full."[31]

The disagreements and hard feelings that developed among some of the 20th Maine veterans contest whether there really was, as one veteran stated that spring, "glory enough earned on Little Round Top for every participant." Chamberlain had recommended Color Sergeant Andrew J. Tozier of the 20th Maine for the Medal of Honor the previous year, writing that, "At a crisis of the engagement when our whole center was for a moment broken and the enemy seemed about to overpower us, I saw, as a thick cloud of smoke lifted, Sergeant Tozier standing alone at his advanced post,—the two center companies having lost nearly half their numbers, and the color guard entirely cut away,—the color staff rested on the ground and supported in the hollow of his shoulder, while with a musket and cartridge box he had picked up at his feet, he was defending his color; presenting a figure which seemed to have paralyzed the enemy in front of him, who might otherwise have captured the color." Regarding this testimony, Chamberlain received a letter in the spring of 1899 from a former member of the color company who took exception to Chamberlain's description of Tozier's solitary stand, for he and another surviving member of the 20th's color company, he insisted, had never left the colors. "...why special mention is made of him [Tozier] defending the colors alone when he was not and the guard represented as absent when the colors was in such peril I cannot understand. Neither of us was wounded if 'cut away' it must have been by smoke or fright." William Livermore, who unlike some of his comrades had never entered into the fray over details of the battle, was obviously distressed, but he nonetheless concluded his letter by saying he hoped that "providence would allow" him to meet and greet his former commander when Chamberlain spoke in his home town that Memorial Day.[32]

By the end of 1899, Chamberlain was in desperate financial straits. Sending instructions to his brother-in-law, Charley Farrington, to sell some of his Brewer property, Chamberlain's customary patience with Wyllys's years of inventing and unsuccessful attempts to sell his ideas was also wearing a bit thin, for he suggested to Charlie that he wished Wyllys would curtail a visit to Brewer and get back to his "proper work." In late fall of 1899, Chamberlain, at the death of the Collector of Customs for the port of Portland, Maine, asked for an appointment to that position which had been held by a number of former governors of Maine, and was generally awarded on that basis. The ensuing struggle over the appointment would be a humiliating, yet ironically heartening experience for Chamberlain in this, his 71st year. Fanny eventually came home to Brunswick and blindness, but she was never the same. Though this affliction, that had stolen upon her so slowly over years, may alone have changed her and darkened her spirit, there is evidence that other illnesses came to steal away her strength and personality in her last years. As aging parents, Lawrence and Fanny became increasing dependent on the love and support of Grace and Wyllys, while their grandchildren, Eleanor, Beatrice and Rosamund Allen continued to be a source of great joy.[33]

CHAPTER

23

"No Responsibilities, No Duties"

The family gathered at the Chamberlain home in Brunswick on Thanksgiving Day, 1899, with Grace, Horace, the three grandchildren, and Wyllys joining Lawrence and Fanny, to fill "the circle, long broken," as Lawrence later commented to Sae. Dining with them was Lillian Edmunds, who Lawrence said did not have as much time to tend to his matters, for she now had the responsibilities of family housekeeper. Also at the large table was Miss Hodgdon, a new special attendant for Fanny, and a Mrs. Curtis, whom Lawrence described as their "old smiling-faced rear-guard."[1]

Earlier that year, Fanny had celebrated her 74th birthday. But she had already encountered a number of the limitations and vexations that are the infirmities of old age. Her blindness meant a staggering loss of independence and mobility, and it was accompanied by the pain of becoming an object of well-meant, but debilitating pity. From the time when complete blindness overtook her, Fanny's health began to deteriorate. Other undefined illnesses robbed her of her strength and equilibrium. Fanny's role in the family changed drastically, from having been a source of strength and support, to becoming a needy recipient of family care. Fanny's world narrowed, more and more, to the Brunswick home and Domhegan. It was, at times, a lonely existence, as the rest of the family carried on with their busy lives.[2]

Though financial security was a pressing necessity, Chamberlain also needed an outlet for his undiminished enthusiasm for public service. He openly made known his desire for the post of Collector of the Port of Portland, Maine. In the last weeks of 1899, the people in his state and Chamberlain's friends around the country petitioned the government for his appointment. Though many letters simply presented Chamberlain's qualifications and details of a life of dedicated service, one candidly addressed the extremity of his need. Old army comrade Ellis Spear wrote to a Maine representative in Congress:

> *There is one view of Genl. Chamberlain's case I would like to present, not at his suggestion. He is seventy years of age, and is poor. He keeps up the best appearance he can, and is sensitive and proud, and is the last man to plead, or even admit poverty. What public position he has held you know. In the Army I know that he stood high. He was on the best of terms with Griffin and Warren, his superior officers, and was relied on by them, and, as you may remember, was promoted on the field by Genl. Grant, who also mentions him particularly in his memoirs, in the highest terms. Chamberlain is also 'solid' with the old soldiers, in Maine and elsewhere, and they would feel gratified if he were favored. This seems probably the last chance to do something for Chamberlain, and it is exactly what he needs. It will save his last days from the distress of penury, most galling to a man of his standing and sensitive feeling. If he does not get this, I dont know what he will do. He gets but $25- per month pension and his wife is now totally blind. I was with him when he was wounded, and I know how severely it was. The common belief was that he would not recover from it. His is the most conspicuous and singular case in the State—of distinguished service in the war, old and poor.*[3]

Chamberlain traveled to Washington, D.C. in late November to press his case, but the position of collector, a lucrative political plum, was promised to another, and Chamberlain was begrudgingly offered an appointment as Surveyor of the Port, a secondary position with little or no responsibility and few duties. Dr. Abner Shaw, the 20th Maine's surgeon who had saved Chamberlain's life at Petersburg, was still his physician and friend, and knew that his old comrade was mortified by the offer of this secondary position. But Shaw entreated him to accept the post of surveyor, suggesting that it was "too good a thing to throw away." He observed that the post carried a good salary, was easier, and there was "no political work expected such as attaches to the Collectorship." Shaw added, "Your best friends advise this, and hope it will be done before it is too late." Chamberlain accepted the office, but wrote to a friend that his humiliation was eased only by the wide support of many friends:

> *Your kind heart suggests a delicate way of congratulations to confer me in my defeat for a place which I thought it fitting to aspire to, and very many others of the highest character and standing thought me competent for and entitled to. It is this testimony which is the real reward for any service I may have rendered, this recognition rich in character and volume, which cannot be bought nor held cheaply, nor be given to the exchangers to be traded on or off.*[4]

Guy Gannett Publishing Co.

Joshua L. Chamberlain, Surveyor of the Port of Portland, Maine.

Chamberlain commented, "The surveyorship is a good little office, no doubt; and I ought perhaps to be thankful to get it....," but he added that it had "no responsibilities, no duties, no power, no prominence...and requiring no ability. Whether this description of the place should inflate my vanity when I am told that I am 'entitled to it,' is a question for the meek, who are said to be about to 'inherit the earth.' To me it suggests a free bed in a hospital. It has a good salary, I confess...that is something of a silencer." While it was President McKinley who appointed Chamberlain as Surveyor of the Port, all involved recognized that responsibility for the decision lay with Maine's congressional delegation in Washington, an indication that the spoil's system had lost little of its power. Chamberlain, far from holding any grudge against McKinley, declared that the president was a fair-minded man who had, privately, given him recognition.

Chamberlain was also pressing another's case in Washington. General Webb sought the full military retirement that could be granted by Congress to Civil War veterans, and Chamberlain told his friend, "Somehow, I can do more for you than I can for my self." Expressing his pleasure at being able to help, Chamberlain stated, "You must feel free to command me. I am no half friend. With all that can be felt by one man for another *man*...."[5]

Chamberlain took office as Surveyor of the Port in the spring of 1900. Despite his light duties overseeing the harbor's facilities for shipping, in the years that he held this post, he worked, if his health allowed, every weekday, all day in his office at the Portland Custom House. But by fall, he was again prostrated by illness and infection of his Petersburg wound. Having applied for a two-month leave of absence, he planned a trip to the Mediterranean to recover his health. In his application for a passport, Chamberlain described himself: "age, 72 years; Height, 5'9"; Weight, 170 pounds; Complexion, fair—(somewhat browned); Hair, grey, (nearly white); shoulders, broad; Forehead, high; Face, square; Eyes, grey-blue; Nose, medium size, somewhat Roman; chin, square; mouth, medium size;...scars, right thigh & left hip."[6]

Vickery Collection, Bangor Public Library

Custom House, Portland, Maine.

Before Chamberlain left for Europe, he heard from an old friend, known from her nursing days at the field hospitals. Sarah Sampson, who was refused a pension for her own service during the war, worked in Washington at the Bureau of Pensions. Her supervisors considered her an incorrigible because she wrote personal notes of appreciation to veterans who applied for assistance. She told Chamberlain:

Since I first knew you, you have given me more encouragement and assistance in my life work than any other person living, or who ever did live—.... So many glorious men have gone who were interested in my work and so few are left that sometimes I feel lonesome— When I am gone and before I go, I want you to know that I appreciate all your

Maine State Archives

Mrs. Sarah Sampson.

kindnesses to me in so many ways—ways that you have forgotten but I never shall— Don't think from this that I am expecting to go soon—I am not, and again I thank the 'Master' as Howard says that I am able to be at my desk each day and beside my official work do something to make an old veteran or oftener now, a veteran's widow glad.[7]

Lawrence wrote to Fanny before the departure of his ship, *Columbia*, from New York:

If I did not feel that it would be better for you & for me that I should take this trip abroad, I should be very sad at leaving you now, even for so short a time. But it will interest you to keep "the run of me" in your mind and heart as the "little people" trace from day to day my course on the waters and over the lands. My thoughts will be with you always, and I shall feel charged and commissioned and empowered to see things for you, and bring you whatever of them can be taken into the soul. You can send me word when they write me.... I pray God to have you in his holy and healing care—you remember we are "engaged" again,—not to sink down under any evils in our absence, but to keep whole and well, for other days to come. What is it that Dante says,—not this exactly but nearly,—"And other songs in other Keys, God Willing". Soon again.[8]

Fanny, at home with Wyllys and her attendants in Brunswick, did indeed "keep 'the run'" of Lawrence's progress, and with relief, received news from Grace in mid-November that the *Columbia* had arrived at Gibraltar. Grace reassured her mother, "All danger of shipwreck is now passed for the outward voyage anyway." But later news was less reassuring. He wrote to a friend of his journey:

I had rather over estimated my strength in what I undertook to do and see in Rome. I had got on well enough in other places—Naples, Genoa, Pisa and Florence—but in Rome I ran into the worst weather conditions ever experienced there, constant cold rains and deadly chilling airs especially at evening and getting myself overtired with my daily walks and task of seeing so many places, old and new, and there being in Rome no houses and hotels a means of warming above the corpse degree, I very naturally and necessarily went down to that degree myself and came near not getting out of it. But when they told me I could not live two days if I stayed in Rome, and though [I] could not "sit up" but an hour at a time and could not take even a cup of hot milk—my only food—the old war spirit got command of me and I took a train for Naples where I learned a ship was to start

> *for New York in five days. I was resolved to get what ever was left of me on that ship, body or soul, together or separate. But then I came into the care of my friends, who would not let me take that very hazardous experiment. They took me in one of the great, grim, old East African liners by way of the Suez Canal to Egypt where the conditions for recovery from just the kind of attack I had were the best possible. I have been here nearly a month and have wonderfully recovered my normal condition and am fast regaining my strength. I had to ask for 30 days extension of my leave of absence.... I have taken passage for the 7th of February from Alexandria on the steamship Columbia of the Hamburg-American line. My doctors here protest against my leaving so soon, declaring it is a great risk for me, but I think I know my strength better than they do, especially of will.*[9]

In spite of his precarious health, he visited Heliopolis, "built by Ramses II, where Joseph got his wife, & Moses his education, & Plato & Pythagoras & so many other of the old scholars & philosophers found it worth their while to stay *years*. No vestige of the famous city is left now but great heaps of ruins. I could see the bricks down among the rubbish, which were some of those (I have no doubt) made by the 'children of Israel'...." Britain's Lord Cromer, who knew of Chamberlain's military reputation from a visit he had paid to the Army of the Potomac many years before, provided him with valuable introductions, including one to the powerful, medal-bedecked Egyptian leader, Forduse. This "descendant of Mohammed," took quite an interest in the Medal of Honor Chamberlain was wearing, and he saw to it that the old soldier was given every attention while visiting in his country.[10]

By the middle of March, Chamberlain was back in Maine, working at the Customs House and traveling home to Brunswick on the weekends. Sae's relief at his return was explicit, as she told Lawrence: "We were rejoiced to get your letter from home once more in your own hand writing—It is great for you to go on such a journey at your time of life & return safe & sound-we are thankful—It will divert you from many a harrassing [sic] experience I hope & think." Lawrence would always fondly remember his journey. Statues of Hermes, Cupid and Psyche, as well as scarabs and other Egyptian relics were now among the treasured possessions that he kept in his Brunswick study. His stay in Egypt left him in good health, and he seemed relaxed and refreshed in a letter to Grace after his return. He told her that Wyllys "was quite fine with his beautiful old-gold jacket & his 'tarbush' (or 'fez')" that were his father's presents to him from Egypt. Reporting that he had also brought back gifts for Grace and the "dear little ones," he suggested that he might visit Boston for a weekend, "though dear little Mother will miss me if I do not go to see her." Well satisfied with arrangements made in Brunswick for housekeeping and Fanny's care, Lawrence commented, "All is so bright & sweet at home it rests me to go there now. Lillian is a blessing to all."[11]

In the summer of 1901, a young admirer wrote to Chamberlain about his war record, closing his letter with, "Hoping that in the decline of life you have health and comfort, and that after you answer the last roll-call here your chivalrous soul will find repose in the Valhalla of the brave...." Chamberlain responded graciously, but took exception to one of the young man's sentiments, "I accept with gratitude your good wishes for what you naturally consider my 'declining years.' I do not feel as if my years were declining,—except as to their numerical remainder. In all that makes their value I look upon them as mounting. 'The best is yet to be.'" Putting his disappointment regarding his minor post of surveyor behind him, Chamberlain sought other spheres of influence. Though still frequently asked to speak on Appomattox and other war reminiscences, he began more frequently to speak on current issues. In the 1901-1902 issue of *Who's Who in America*, Chamberlain was described as "writer & lecturer on public questions." Though he defended the United State's right to retain the Philippines after the Spanish-American War, he was outspoken in his criticism of the military's role in subjugating its people, stating that, "military temptations precipitated hostilities & war unnecessarily," and that the Philippino leader, Aguinaldo, "should have been our friend." Convinced that the diversity of the people, as well as their inexperience with self-rule made them poor candidates for independence, he still insisted that they were not "spoils of war, but wards of providence." He maintained that the U.S. had a serious responsibility to "teach" them the skills necessary for self-government.[12]

In the fall of 1901, when an assassin again struck down an American president, Chamberlain was moved to make a number of startling assertions. William McKinley and his running mate, Theodore Roosevelt, had sailed to a Republican victory in 1900. Though criticized for an imperialistic foreign policy and accused of apathy toward the growing stranglehold of big business and trusts on the American economy, the voter's association of the Republican party with general prosperity saw McKinley easily reelected. Many felt that the United States was entering the 20th century as a new and beneficent world power, and seemed oblivious to omens of the internal problems that were shaking European societies. In these last years, before revelations of the sordidness and suffering beneath the country's prosperity brought earnest demands for social and economic reforms, the assassination of McKinley shocked the nation. The foreign birth of the self-proclaimed anarchist who had shot the president twice at close range ignited fears that the violent mood precipitating the deaths of a number of European leaders was being brought to America by her recent immigrants.[13]

Chamberlain addressed several audiences shortly after McKinley was shot and lay dying. He was incensed that government officials quoted in the press offered little more than the observation that it was the act of a madman. "I protest against this impotent helplessness... the practice must be stopped." In spite of the assassin's Polish birth, Chamberlain suspected him of being associated with an Italian-American group who had made known their intention to murder a number of world leaders. He called these self-appointed executioners of the ruling class "... aliens in blood, in birth, in spirits, in principles, in faith, in habits of life and thought...associations organized, instructed, encouraged, sworn together for the overthrow of government and the foundations of society everywhere...coming here to wreak a misdirected and impotent vengeance upon the country which offers an asylum for all the oppressed of the suffering earth." Chamberlain angrily asked, "Shall we tolerate such nurseries for disorder?"[14]

Proposing that new laws must be considered and new vigilance must be practiced by municipal and police officials, Chamberlain marveled that the country had legislated the exclusion of the "simple-minded, patient and faithful Chinese," only to "admit freely the off-scouring of other races and lands full of all uncleanness...." He added, "We are too reckless in our political harangues and publications.... We permit the sensational newspapers without rebuke to run a tirade of false and libelous assertions and scurrilous abuse against our judges of the highest courts, the ministers of the country's honor and dignity, and the chosen President himself. Witness one of them of late calling our beloved and now almost martyred President this 'red-handed violator of the people's rights, the pampered aristocrat gloating over the miseries of the down-trodden.'" Speaking before Bangor's MOLLUS, Chamberlain declared, "Companions, these things must be stopped; or they will come to a pass where we shall be tempted to forget we are older than we were forty years ago!.... I do not know but we shall have to define treason more sharply.... Some limit must be given to our boasted and much abused maxims of 'free speech' and 'free press.' It is a difficult matter to reach such things without over-reaching. Freedom of criticism is a salutary agent in discussing public measures and personal candidacies." He admitted that there was sometimes a need to bring a people to spontaneous action, but he denied unchecked speech and writing to those who proclaim the nation's leaders "deserving of destruction and death...." Chamberlain's conclusion was a far cry from his usual, optimistic declarations for the future:

> *Is Christ dead? Is Lincoln dead?.... This punishment will teach our nation what deadly vipers we have taken into our bosom with their dangerous anarchistic teachings, which stand in opposition to the home, the church and the state. We have given them the freedom of the press and speech. And now we are stung by them.... Oh God, let this lesson be enough. Spare us from any more such costly teaching!.... It is time that we forbid further public meetings of this kind and forever bar them from this fair land as the heathens were from the house of Israel. What has transpired will cause our nation to realize the degradation into which we have fallen. Men and women are rebelling against the established institutions of God. Why we have the vice in our very midst. Even in our own city we find enough seed for anarchism in the growing disrespect for law and church. O may this nation confess the sins and repent. May the grace of God still protect our government and nation. "His will be done. Not ours."*[15]

Chamberlain was terribly shaken by the assassination. And for a man who had already seen his country through some very hard times, his distress at what he obviously perceived as a grave threat to the United States, is extraordinary. In this speech, Chamberlain expressed his appreciation for the wisdom and courage the president had shown in guiding the country. For in spite of the many detractors of his administration, Chamberlain believed that McKinley, the last of the Civil War veterans in that office, had the good of the country at heart.

History remembers him as a president who did nothing to address big business out of control and the problems of a growing and suffering underclass. Yet it is interesting to consider a forceful speech that he made at the Pan American Exposition on the day before he was shot. McKinley's statements held the promise of challenging Congress to address the stranglehold of the trusts on the American economy. He spoke of working to resolve issues too important to allow partisanship to interfere. McKinley died on September 14, and those Republicans who desired to preserve the status quo, who had seen the vice presidency as a place to put that loose cannon of the party, Theodore Roosevelt, safely out of the way, were dismayed.[16]

Whatever political tumult gripped the country that year, domestic tranquility could be found at home in Brunswick. Lawrence wrote to Grace in December 1901, telling of his and Fanny's celebration of their 46th anniversary:

> *We had a lovely anniversary of our wedding. I took home a beautiful Arabic seat-cushion & a Persian shoulder-rest for your mother's dining room chair where she spends much time; & two beautiful aprons to guard her fine dresses at meals; and I gave her one of the lovely napkin rings you know something about, so as to keep her napkin entirely distinct to her own feeling, from all others. We had a very fine wedding day dinner & another on Sunday. Nappy took two pieces of mince pie & a good glass of sauterne.*[17]

Lawrence wrote that Fanny wished Grace and her family would come for Christmas. "She sets her heart on it, & everything is so pleasant now in the house I should much like to have you there too." But in that month, Lawrence was again overtaken by ill health. At the end of December, he wrote to Wyllys, who was in Boston in search of a position, "I am pretty slow in my getting about.... At office half a day at a time, using great care." Worried over his son's continued lack of success at finding some niche in life, he commented, "I suppose you find it hard to get into just what you want. But I would keep trying & w[oul]d take what I could get in any line to begin with. I dont want people here to think you made a failure." Wyllys owned rental property in Brewer, which Charley Farrington managed for him. But Charley deferred to Lawrence when decisions needed to be made regarding the upkeep and improvement of Wyllys's holdings. It seems likely that a concerned father had turned over some of his own property to his son in order to provide him with some income and financial security for the future.[18]

Lawrence continued to work in Portland and travel home to Brunswick on weekends, but his busy schedule of speeches and his membership in veterans' and civic organizations sometimes kept him away. A letter written in May 1902 to Fanny from the New Falmouth Hotel in Portland is evidence of his busy lifestyle:

> *It was hard for me to come away again last Monday in such a pressure for the train as not to be able to go up and see you. I felt the loss to my self all day & the next. Ever since my return I have been on the "jump" & the "stretch." Monday evening at Judge Putnam's for the "Fraternity" Club; and last evening at the Anniversary of the "Thacher Post" Grand Army "Banquet"—where I had to make quite an elaborate speech.... I trust you are bearing up as beautifully as you have begun doing. So many people now are praising you & sending loving greeting for your brave & cheery way of bearing this great affliction, you must feel the influence of it carrying through the air, or ether, or whatever other finer element our souls are floating in. I am making plans to give*

you as pleasant a summer as you can have. This is only a little love-greeting between whiles—I shall soon be home again.[19]

Despite Lawrence's good intentions, the summer of 1902 proved difficult for them. Fanny's courage disintegrated, and her spirits plummeted. The narrowness and loneliness of her life may have brought on the changes that Lawrence claimed to see in Fanny. But the illness that weakened her physically may have robbed her of the strong and supportive character that she displayed through their many years of marriage. It is sadly ironic that Fanny, who had such an aversion to having others read her personal correspondence, had to have her letters read to her. And, she had to dictate her thoughts for some one else to write when she wanted to communicate with absent loved ones. Lawrence, who was none too well himself in Portland, wrote a distraught letter to Fanny in July:

You do not know how much I am thinking of you, and wishing to help you, and be of some good to you. You were so gentle and patient and receptive and appreciative, and in all ways so sweet, when I left you, a strong tenderness continues to hold me to you ever since. I see that you need me, and I wish, of all things, to meet that need. It is the deepest wish of my heart to be able to bless you—to bring, to be a blessing, & not merely to pray for me to come, in vain words & vague thought. But when I try to do it, and think & study & plan how best to do it, I do not seem to succeed. Somehow I am turned off—baffled, almost driven to the very contrary of what I so earnestly meant. Your affliction seems to have made you hard, rather than tender,—& I feel as if I were smitten in the most sensitive place in my heart. This I know is a part of your affliction—a symptom of your disease. It is hardest of all to see these physical deprivations affecting the mind and spirit—by nature so bright, so dear, so sweet. This must not be. We cannot let this tendency go on. It will become a new distress— a terrible condition. We must strive to restore that sweetness and clarity I might say in the true sense of the word, that charity,—which makes you in your real self so lovable. You need love—most of anything; & that is exactly what you can have if you will receive it—as indeed you sometimes do even now. But I sometimes see you scorning a service or attention brought to you in love and for love's sake, & you are missing & losing much by this, which you need & deserve, & could have, if you would receive it. You have good & true friends who should be near you in such days as these. I wish you to have them, & to make these dark days full of an inner light. Do not be too critical & exacting, & do not scorn what is brought in love. It makes you so unhappy—that is the worst of it all, & that makes me so more & more as I see your need.[20]

Other stresses and strains that summer upset the family. Grace, so supportive and attentive to both her parents, was sick for weeks in Boston with bronchitis and had to cope with the necessity of surgery for her little daughter Beatrice to relieve a condition of the adenoids. Though Wyllys had come home to Brunswick to fill the breach, Lawrence wrote to Fanny later in July, with this plea:

Dearie: I have had a beautiful letter from our Gracie. She is considerably troubled about my condition and yours, and I have written her as reassuring a letter as I could. It is true, dear; I am much reduced from my usual condition, & note a serious diminution of my recuperative force. But this contemplated yacht trip will probably help me up. Dr. Shaw says I must have a respite, & ought to be off three weeks. That I cannot manage. But if I could feel happy about you—I mean that the best is being done that is possible, and that you are looking more at the blessing-side of things than at the hard & dark side, a very great burden would be taken off my spirit. And it is this, more than any thing, that makes my heart so heavy. Now you have all your own, old sweetness and brightness, if you could let it appear. And this seems to me your best comfort & compensation. Surely we must not let you fall off into darkness of spirit. It will work fourfold trouble for your physical condition. Think how many are loving you & caring for you, & wishing to come nearer you so as to be of real good. Wyllys is nobly resolved to stay by you now,—much as he needs a change,—while I find it absolutely necessary to be off the "dead line" a while. Now, dearest, cherish all you can the things which are "not seen"—& are of the "eternal." They are in us—not out of us—& they are yours.[21]

In late August, President Theodore Roosevelt visited Maine. He received an enthusiastic welcome in bunting and flag-bedecked Portland. A news account proclaimed him a "good fellow," and commented that there was some foundation for the funny political cartoons that caricatured TR as a pair of glasses and a set of teeth. Chamberlain was one of a large party of local dignitaries who greeted the president at the train station. There were still enough boys in blue, many of them members of the veterans' organizations that wielded considerable political power, that it comes as no surprise that Roosevelt recognized the old commander in his speech that day. Throughout his oration, he spoke to and of Joshua Chamberlain:

I was greeted here not only by your Mayor, not only by other men standing high, but by your general, to whom it was given at the supreme moment of the war to win the supreme reward of a soldier of honor to a man; and may we keep ourselves from envying him because to him fell the supreme good fortune of winning the medal of honor for mighty deeds done in the mightiest battle that the 19th century saw, Gettysburg.[22]

Addressing the contributions of all Civil War soldiers, Roosevelt exclaimed, "Now, general, and you, and you who wore the button, when you came down to the root of things in war time, you had to depend upon the qualities of manhood which had made good soldiers from the days when the children of Israel marched out of Egypt...." Speaking of the self-sacrifice and tenacity of the men of the Army of the Potomac, and their service, Roosevelt offered, "The army of the Potomac could never have seen Appomattox, if it had not been for the spirit that drove you from the office and the factory and the farm to take up the burden of war. And when you went to war, you staid there till you saw it through." Again addressing Chamberlain, he stated:

Some such service, general, as you rendered at Appomattox. But normally...what we want is not genius but the faculty of showing that we know how to apply the copy book moralities that we wrote down when we were small, and as long as we think of them only as fit for the copy book there is not much use in them. It is when we come to apply them that they count. We need in our public life, as in our private life the virtues that everyone could practice, if he would. We need the will to practice them. There are two kinds of greatness that can be achieved; there is the greatness that comes to the man who can do what no one else can do; that is a mighty rare kind, and of course, it can only be achieved by the man of special and unusual qualities; then there is the other kind, the kind that comes to the man who does the things that every one could do, but that every one does not do, who goes ahead and does them himself....[23]

Lest anyone doubt his ability to know the value of men who do their duty, Roosevelt amiably pointed out, "Now, general, I was a very little time in my war, you were a long time in yours, and I did not see much fighting, but I saw a lot of human nature." Chamberlain remained Roosevelt's companion throughout the hours he was feted in Portland, and when he left the president's car as it prepared to leave Union Station, he was carrying a single rose. Plucked from one of the bouquets received by the exuberant commander-in-chief that day, he had received it from Roosevelt as a keepsake of the occasion.[24]

Lawrence's advice to Fanny earlier that summer did little to encourage or pacify her, and in the fall of 1902, Fanny waged a full-scale revolt. The initial provocation probably occurred when Lawrence and Wyllys went off on the yacht in mid-September, derailing a plan for Fanny to spend the weekend with them at Domhegan. In the weeks that followed, Fanny came down with a heavy cold that caused Lawrence to consider postponing a scheduled trip to Washington. "If you are very sick I will give up the Washington trip & will come home to be with you.... You are to be put *first* in all my plans and doings, as you are in my affections. Let some one write me tonight for morning mail." But apparently all deemed Fanny's health sufficient that Lawrence might make his trip. When he returned, he found himself in a perplexing situation. Fanny had dismissed the woman who took care of her, packed up and taken herself to Portland to the home of friends. Lawrence wrote to Grace in some desperation, "I have got home from Washington (through a great storm) an hour ago, & find your mother at Charlotte Thomases [sic] waiting for me to take charge of her. She has dismissed Blanche...," and, he added, Fanny refused to consider Blanche's return. Asking when Grace could come, Lawrence worried over what friend or relative might be able to help. Explaining that after being away for eight days, he had an office full of work and a speech, already announced, that he must deliver, and exclaimed, "...I certainly cannot take care of her..."[25]

Whether the family's busy summer or some other grievance inspired Fanny's unannounced trip to Portland, this assertion of her personal wishes certainly got everyone's attention. Fanny, back in Brunswick in November, had communicated some of her desires and needs, and a letter from Lawrence to Fanny addresses several issues. Using one of their grandchildren's names for their grandmother, Lawrence wrote, "Dear 'Gorgan,' But what a name! I shall have to stay here and work up my paper for wednesday evening, & look after stripping & laying up the yacht—no small task! So I cant come home Saturday or Sunday. But will try to come towards the middle of next week & stay a day with you. It must be lonely for you. Our little pleasant-voiced Edith—table girl—wants to come over & be with you.... I will just bring her over for an over-Sunday visit sometime soon & let you try how she will do." A soothing voice, in what was a world of voices for Fanny, was easily found.

But, one thing Fanny craved, stimulating companionship, was hard to provide. In early 1903, having found no satisfactory solution, Lawrence was exasperated. He wrote in February:

> *I fear I may have seemed to you almost harsh in my extreme anxiety to have you work out of the gloomy mood which seems so darkly to envelope you, when I urged you too emphatically-I know well such things cannot be brought about by argument nor emphasis of suggestion. Evidently we must do something. I am studying this all the time. It happens that the things I think of are not such as suit your feeling. Very naturally you perceive the disadvantageous thing in any proposition intended for your help quicker and more forcibly than the helpful or agreeable things. In your condition, perhaps, this is inevitable; you are so shut up & shut in, that the relief of surrounding circumstances cannot come in to lighten a vexation, as it can with us who see the whole compass of things around us. If you could have a little reading & conversation 'club' or circle to take up some distinct and continuous line and work up an interest, it would be a good thing! But I am aware you do not see, or have at hand those who you would like to form such a circle. So with a music circle, I suppose. Your ideals & cravings are so high, your needs seem beyond ordinary reach. I cannot see what I can do more than to give you pleasant change by bringing you to Portland as often as possible. That I am planning to do whenever I myself am able to carry it through. Many demands on my time & strength leave me scarcely an hour to keep my own mind properly fitted for the work I have to do.... I think you do wonderfully well under your deprivations & positive ills. The natural course of time will bring some of these, anyway.*[27]

In late winter 1903, Lawrence's life of working during the week and commuting on weekends, as well as frequent speech-making around the state, caught up with him. After having been laid up in Brunswick, he wrote to Fanny on his return to Portland in the first days of spring, "You will be wishing to hear how I am this evening. I have gone through the day pretty well, I think. The soreness of the chest from the hard cough & the internal oppressiveness are the main things to trouble me. I found much work awaiting but am 'taking it easy,' and shall, no doubt, be better in the morning." Lawrence's convalescence had, perhaps, provided Fanny with the best medicine, that of being needed, for Fanny rose to the occasion. Lawrence commented, "You were so good and thoughtful in your care of me that I escaped a serious sickness." Dangerous illness struck another household member that year, for a quarantine was placed on the family home in the summer of 1903. There are indications that it was Wyllys who suffered a debilitating illness.[28]

After an absence, Lillian Edmunds returned as housekeeper for the Chamberlains and companion for Fanny. In late June, Lawrence, who had recently seen Grace in Boston, wrote to his daughter from Brunswick, "I have had no time to tell you of the delight I felt at our little heart-talks, & the good you have done me. But I trust we shall have this opportunity before very long." After years of living in hotels in Portland, Lawrence rented a small house in the city. Although he earned a generous salary, the expense of maintaining two households and the staff needed for Fanny's care was putting a strain on the Chamberlains' finances. Regarding an attempt by Grace and Horace to help out, Lawrence continued:

> *I found the checque here, which I took with me to return, for I cannot think of keeping that. You cannot pay...any to see me—in any other way, at least, than the task and trial it is to you to have to share my cares and anxieties. It is cheerful here to day. Lillian is at home & your Mother is lovely to her, & to us all. I think she feels much helped by Lillian coming. Now I look for better conditions...we shall go to the shore,—although your mother at present, rebels against it. I have had a great pressure on me for a month, & until July. Then I must take a rest.*[29]

With a home in Portland where he could make Fanny's visits more comfortable, in early August Fanny and Lillian made an excursion. Lawrence reported to Grace:

> *Lillian brought your mother in to the city last week & got her a beautiful black dress, fashionable & becoming, for an every day dress—also a beautiful white silk waist, and a very fine & (somewhat expensive) peplum—all much to your mothers delight. They came in & dined with me and spent the afternoon. Then I went to the store and selected another dress black with a delicate white figure in it,—not very expensive but very becoming to her, matching her grey hair, &c. So she is well supplied.*[30]

Lawrence's efforts to get Fanny away from Brunswick had also included a trip to visit Grace in Boston. He continued:

> *But of course the dear little woman following her old & indulged habit, got hold of a very rich black silk skirt, elaborately barred & flounced &c, & insisted that she wanted that, too. I did not think she needed this, as she has a beautiful new silk she had made at your house, I think, & the opportunities for her to wear this lately desired one are now very rare & unlikely to occur. So I dissuaded her from buying this expensive silk skirt at present. She has waived the matter for a while.*[31]

With no sight, but with hands to touch, the delightful smoothness of silks and the patterns and rows of trims still held some magic for Fanny, who had always enjoyed design and rich fabrics. Fanny expressed no interest in the mundane undergarments Lillian said she needed, so they purchased necessary items, with Lillian "*giving*" them to her, "to silence objections." Later that month, Fanny traveled to Brewer to visit with Sae and Charlie, as Lawrence and Wyllys, both out of health, sought time on the yacht. Lawrence relinquished manning the sails to others, saying that an "outing where I do not have to work hard will do me good."[32]

Chamberlain accepted additional responsibilities at this time with his election by the state's Civil War veterans as commander of the Maine GAR. Though gratified by the recognition from his comrades, with this position came many obligations, including visiting and speaking at many posts in the state and around New England. Lawrence told Fanny that he had so many requests to speak in 1903, that it would take him all summer to make the rounds. He observed, "I would rather fall back on the profound sentiment of 'unwritten history that was never recorded.'" But never doing things by half, Chamberlain made a number of speeches that year. An account of his visit to the little town of Oakland, Maine, reported:

> *The mere announcement of the official visit of the department commander is usually enough to bring out nearly all of the old boys, but when the hero of a hard fought field, he of the never ceasing painful wound, the man who...was promoted by the general commanding...the old boys of the blue perk up a bit, make believe they are young again and swarm to see the famous man.... Sections may have their grand old men but never were, are not and never will be, grander than Maine's hero soldier, ex-governor, and greatest orator, Gen. Joshua L. Chamberlain. The comrades...began practicing on the old time manner of cheering about as soon as they got out of bed this morning and they rehearsed so well that when the dust settled this evening, the welkin and everything akin to what is well had rung to the limit. Those who recall the Joshua L. Chamberlain of his prime, remember a handsome man. Those who looked upon the famous war officer tonight saw that early beauty enhanced by the silver of age, the warm handshake, the kindly smile and the cordial greeting, the grand old warrior and the honest Christian man. His commanding figure brought the war back again, and it seemed to many that yet the great guns were pounding away at the heart of the nation. Then the story of what had been, what might have been and what is. From out of the gleam of the old warrior's eye, came the enlightenment. It was all over and the men who passed it over stood there in reverence before one of the greatest commanders of the Civil War. Young and old did homage to the great soldier for there was a crush at the public reception in Memorial hall.*[33]

The speech that Chamberlain gave before the New York MOLLUS the next month was, perhaps, before a more sophisticated and refined audience. But it is likely that the obligatory banquet featured oysters, a delicacy that was placed so often before Chamberlain, that it is possible he couldn't bear the sight of them. But whatever town or city he was in, Chamberlain never failed to respond to such enthusiasm, and perhaps this warmth and respect kept the old soldier going. Beyond his enthusiastic welcome from the veterans, he had a number of other tributes paid to him that year. His cousin Annie Chamberlain Keene, widowed in the 1870s, was now Mrs. Annie Chamberlain Smiley, as well as something of a poet. She added her own efforts to the "immortalization" of Lawrence. Her poem, entitled "Private Witherell's Story," proclaimed:

List to the story that I shall tell,
As told by private Witherell,
Who fought in the stalwart Twentieth Maine,
With dauntless Colonel Chamberlain
'Our Colonel', he said, "left his college hall,
To answer 'Here!" to his Country's call;
And we who followed with quickened breath,
Would have marched with him to the gates of death...

In his *Reminiscences of the Civil War*, published in October 1903, Gen. Gordon, when speaking of Appomattox, wrote of his friend, "One of the knightliest soldiers of the Federal army, General Joshua L. Chamberlain of Maine...." And among the roads built to bring the aging soldiers and their guests to the far-flung sites of strife forty years before, there was now a road at Little Round Top, named Chamberlain Avenue.[34]

The battles and veterans of the Civil War were hardly forgotten in the new century, and Chamberlain enjoyed a place of relative fame and enduring admiration. But there were still skirmishes to be waged between the facts and fictions of the war, as history grappled with growing mythologies. There were wrongs, real and imagined, to be made right before the old soldiers joined that growing number of those who had gone before. Lawrence and Fanny would also have to deal with the infirmities of old age, though they were armed, each in their own way, with a still pressing sense of duty, and a reluctance to part from loved-ones and life. Lawrence, for all his encounters with the life-threatening infections of his wound, had many years before him, but Fanny was coming to the last of her days.

CHAPTER

24

"We Have Been So Long Spared to Each Other"

In the summer of 1903, Chamberlain experienced a period of such acute illness, that many, including Chamberlain himself, had doubts that he would recover. General John B. Gordon, though his own health was precarious, came to Maine to see his old friend. Gordon was reported to have leaned over Chamberlain, saying, "Dear old fellow, can't bear to lose you." Another friend who consoled Chamberlain during his painful illness was Myra Porter, a Maine woman who worked for a New York orphanage. Having sent her regards to "Mrs. C" in mid-July, commenting, "how hard her lot!", Myra wrote to Chamberlain on the 21st of the month: "...I am so sorry to hear that you are suffering and hasten to send my most earnest and heart-felt sympathy. Yes, you *can* bear pain like a hero, as you have borne it for years— suffering in silence; but I know full well how hard it must be even for your brave spirit." Myra was involved with the Orphan Train Society, an organization that sent thousands of orphaned and abandoned city children to new homes in the Midwest. The daughter of a veteran of the 19th Maine from Old Town, just up the river from Brewer, it is possible that the Chamberlain and Porter families knew each other. But it is likely that Fanny and Lawrence came to know Myra from her work with destitute children in New York City. Myra subsisted on a small salary, prompting Chamberlain to send small sums of money in his regular correspondence with her, letters in which he would come to confide some personal problems and concerns.[1]

John Brown Gordon, 1896.

As Chamberlain recuperated in August 1903, the commission that superintended what is now a national park at Gettysburg, contacted him regarding the placement of a memorial to the 15th Alabama on the battlefield. This began an exchange of letters that provided plenty of stimulating, if not pleasant, diversion for the ailing Chamberlain. General William Oates had proposed that a stone be placed at the Alabamians' farthest point of advance on Little Round Top, despite the commission's policy that monuments be placed at the point where regiments began their first advance. General John Nicholson, chairman of the battlefield committee, sent Chamberlain a copy of the letter that Oates had written to the Secretary of War, which described the area to which he claimed the 15th had advanced before they were stopped. Nicholson commented, "Some of the statements are so much at variance with the records that we thought we would ask your opinion on the subject." Chamberlain responded, "I should feel no objection to the erection of a monument to the honor of a regiment that had pushed its way so far around the flank of the Union line and made so gallant an attack; but I should expect it to be placed on ground where it actually stood at some time during the battle,—at the extreme point of its advance, if desired,—so that it might not only represent the valor of a regiment but the truth of history."[2]

Chamberlain was troubled by statements that Oates made, which differed from established records and from Oates' previous statements. Nor did these agree with that which Chamberlain had received several years before in personal letters from Oates. That correspondence, Chamberlain commented, had left him "much gratified to find so close an agreement between our impressions and recollections as to our contest there." A confusion of lefts and rights in Oates' statement to the Secretary of War led Chamberlain to believe that Oates was now asserting that the 15th had driven the 20th Maine's right from their position, when in fact, Oates apparently meant the left wing of the 20th. But there was no confusion in Chamberlain's disavowal of Oates' claim that the 15th Alabama also fought the 83rd Pennsylvania and the 44th New York. Chamberlain insisted that the 15th Alabama "never saw the front or flank of the 83rd nor 44th regiments in this engagement. It could have seen only their rear, and that for a brief season in their extreme advance upon us." He also averred that the two regiments that Oates described as threatening his rear were, in fact, a skirmish line comprised of the 20th Maine's Company "B" and the sharpshooters who had joined them behind the stone wall. Chamberlain concluded his letter to Nicholson: "I cannot venture to advise as to the erection of the monument proposed by Colonel Oates. That would involve the entire policy of the U.S. authorities in charge of the battlefield. But as to the location of this monument, I should regret to see it placed near the monument to Vincent, who fell near the right of our brigade line, on ground never seen by the 15th Alabama during the battle. Placing their monument there, as I understand Colonel Oates to desire, would indicate that the 15th. Alabama had run entirely over the 20th. Maine and annihilated it. The facts are, quite curiously, nearly the converse of this." In the next weeks, Chamberlain heard only that the commission wanted permission to send his letter to the Secretary of War, but his involvement in the controversy was far from over.[3]

Chamberlain visited Pennsylvania in the fall of 1903, meeting with a number of veterans he had commanded at Petersburg on June 18, 1864. This inspired him to travel to the battlefield and to Appomattox later in the year. He found the town of Petersburg busy and prosperous. And when it became known that he was the commander who had brought order and safety to their region in the chaotic days immediately after the surrender of Lee's army, he was greeted with enthusiastic hospitality, including a cordial meeting with the A.P. Hill Camp of Confederate Veterans. Here, he met a veteran from the ranks who had been at Rives' Salient on June 18. They shared their experiences, and though Chamberlain's own wound had left many amazed at his survival, he related that this old Confederate soldier "was as badly cut up with wounds as any man I ever saw alive."[4]

With a local guide, Chamberlain discovered that the field at Petersburg was relatively untouched and overgrown with brush and trees, though part of the Rebel earthworks had been cut away for fields of sweet potatoes and peanuts. Chamberlain saw only one monument on the field, which was dedicated to the 1st Maine Heavy Artillery. Fighting as infantry at Petersburg on the same day that Chamberlain was cut down, the 1st Maine lost 600 men in a disastrously ill-conceived charge. Chamberlain later commented of their monument: "The sight of it was a fitting overture for the tragic reminiscences of the day before me." During his passage over the battlefield, he encountered small hillocks and depressions, the unmarked graves of those who had died there. He could not help but compare the fate of this battlefield with that of Gettysburg:

> *...there the constructive work of man uppermost, here, the covering work of nature, that made a magnificent mausoleum, a splendid spectacle; this, the bald fact, held fast, cased in amber; there, highest art in headstone, monument & statue; here, grim trees, wild grasses, clinging mosses; there luxurious avenues laid out with artistic effect, for easy access, or convenience of visitors, even though confusing the old battlelines; here, only the very lines themselves...there, the remaining gathered in a noble cemetery consecrated with immortal eloquence, cherished in eternal honor; here, sleeping in their blood, canopied by swaying branches growing out of it; the lost resting-place marked by the chance staying of some wild rose, named only by the birds singing love-notes above them. There, all remembered; here all but forgotten!*

Refusing to choose which was most grand or impressive, Chamberlain declared that it depended on the man and his mood: "I have memories of both, but hold largely of the forgotten." Finding the spot where he was wounded, Chamberlain cut a small cane from a thriving sassafras bush, musing that his own blood had nurtured its growth.[5]

He found Appomattox, by contrast, vastly changed since 1865. Except for the jail, all the buildings were gone, including the old courthouse and the McLean house. Even the road on which his division had entered the town had been obliterated. Only bronze tablets, erected by the government to identify the positions of Union troops around the field, gave evidence of what happened there 38 years before.[6]

On his return from the South, Chamberlain recorded his thoughts and impressions of the old battlefields, and he wrote an address that he delivered around the state in the first weeks of 1904. One who heard it given to the Maine MOLLUS in Bangor wrote, "Gen. Chamberlain at times seemed to be on the old battlefield again and the next moment would return to the company and make a bright sally for which he is well known." A formal version of the oration was presented to and published by the Maine MOLLUS, in which Chamberlain wrote of Petersburg: "For here when last seen by me before, on the one side and the other, mighty masses and serried ranks of brave, true men stood, and struck, and went willingly to death for what they, strangely contrariwise, deemed the right...." He declared:

> *It was the travail of the people. This is not too strong a figure. For was not this undergone? Sorrow, suffering, sacrifice, surrender, devotion, death,—that something for the world's good should be born into being? Know you not that the tears of this were drawn up into the heavens to descend on these fields in the ever new-creating rains to consecrate this mingled blood to the building of 'the house not made with hands,' here upon the earth? But for such thought, how desolating would this vision be!*

Haunted by his visit to the scene of so much death and destruction at Petersburg, he also wrote: "... the shadow of that whole, dark campaign of 1864 came over me,—which up to that June day had cost our army seventy thousand men. Then I was nearing the crest of manhood, where life looks back and forward, the middle-point of our allotted years,—but it seemed that experience was at the climax."[7]

But Chamberlain also wished to set the record straight on his role at Appomattox. There were those who refuted his role at the formal surrender of the Army of Northern Virginia on April 12, 1862. Chamberlain quipped that finding the bronze tablet at the site, that stated that the "First Division, Fifth Corps" had received the surrender near that spot, had "restored my confidence in my personal identity." He added, "I think I need not take advantage of the kind rule which permits the accused to testify in his own behalf. If necessary, I might call attention to the testimony of General Robert E. Lee and General John B. Gordon, as given in their autobiographies."[8]

Chamberlain received sad news in the first month of 1904. On January 9, just one week after Gen. Longstreet's death, Gen. John B. Gordon died at his home in Florida at age 71. When he received the news of Gordon's death at the Custom House in Portland, "he stepped into a stairway, sat down and wept bitterly." Chamberlain was tired and overworked in the final days of winter that year, and Fanny boarded at a nursing home. Staying at the Mary Brown Home in Portland from mid-May until the latter part of June, Fanny wanted to return to Brunswick in time for commencement week at Bowdoin. Lawrence wrote:

> *I have just left your mother. She now insists on going home to Commencement to see her friends; & she wants you there very much. Florence will be there, & I suppose, Miss Donovan...she is as good as any body we could get. Your mother wants one more intellectual, but when I offer to get one, she says, 'she cant be entertaining her all the time'—so I dont see but we must keep Miss Donovan if we can.*[9]

In late summer, Grace visited Brunswick. Hearing that Fanny was much improved, Lawrence wrote to Grace from Portland: "I am getting myself together again,—but rather slowly, but able to be in my office all office hours." Having abandoned his rented house in Portland, he had been staying on the *Pinafore*, docked in Portland. He hoped to sail up the coast to Domhegan and spend the next Sunday in Brunswick. Still using the grandchildren's nickname for Fanny, Lawrence wrote: "I will not be out of speaking-distance from dear Gorgan any time, & will be within an hour's reach of her. When we are at anchor for over a day in any place, Wyllys or I will go to Gorgan." Thanking Grace for her visit, Lawrence added, "I trust some good may come to you by your generous visit to Gorgan—you do not know how much good your visit—& our heart-talks have done me. Nothing has made me so nearly peaceful and happy for years." The constant traveling and worrying over conditions in Brunswick were catching up with Chamberlain. He feared that his own health, frequently undermined by infections of his Petersburg wound, would give out altogether under the strain of his responsibilities. Another indication of his

Pejepscot Historical Society

***The Schooner* Pinafore.**

discouragement is found in a letter from Myra Porter to Chamberlain in the fall of 1904. Myra not only voiced her personal admiration for him, but seemingly exhorted him to embrace the tenets of Spiritualism. She remonstrated:

> *Say not you have lost something. Shall it not rather be that this which you call 'lost' is but transmuted into vitalizing, potent, uplifting energy on another plane? You are more than you are! I get glimpses and I am charmed. I feel that you have never fully understood what sweet power this high nature of yours has to hold me in its keeping. But not for this do I most rejoice at its recognition. With all your honors, so well deserved, and attainments so befitting, you have never truest satisfaction, but it is for you. Infinite love waits to crown your life. And here and now. Nothing earthly can ever satisfy a nature with an element of eternity in it. I feel sure I have the key.*

Myra acknowledged that Chamberlain planned to see her when he next visited New York, in all likelihood to discuss an opportunity for her to return to Maine. Fanny and Lawrence had taken an interest in an orphanage, the Good Will Farm in Hinckley, Maine, and by summer of the next year, Myra would be one of their agents, raising funds for the institution.[10]

During Christmas 1904, Lawrence wrote to Grace from Brunswick:

> *The box of lovely, generous things came this morning, and I have 'stayed over' to take your mother out with her splendid Hood this mild winter day (if I can get her to get ready before night.)...and my picture! well you know I never let any body select a picture for me; but if 'Mr. Allen', as the card said, selected this one...I will just get him to do all my selecting pictures hereafter. It is an exquisite piece of color & form,—'impressionist['] & dreamy as it is. It suits my present prevailing moods quite perfectly. I hardly know where I need it most, but think I will take it to Portland, and let the contents of the other box...serve my realistic needs here at home!.... I am now urging all forces & elements to get your mother ready to 'drive out' with the new hood. We are all well as we can be.*[11]

Having returned to work in February 1905, after suffering another severe relapse, Lawrence wrote to Grace, telling her that he did not think she needed to come. He reported that Wyllys had made a great "coup de jamb," or literally, "victory of the leg," for despite Fanny's protests, Wyllys managed to get her shoes away long enough to have much-needed new soles put on. Lawrence commented, "...we think we see good effects Still the patient was a little querulous yesterday because she could not drive out." That same month, he received a letter from Ozark, Arkansas, that told the tale of a Confederate soldier's attempt to shoot Chamberlain at Little Round Top. He told that a private of the 20th Maine jumped in front of Chamberlain at the very moment the writer had pulled the trigger, and was killed by the bullet meant for his colonel. Expressing his highest regard for Chamberlain, this assailant of yesteryear wished to correspond. This was not the only letter that Chamberlain received from an old adversary that winter, for in late April a letter arrived from William C. Oates. The controversy over the placement of the proposed 15th Alabama monument was far from over, and the commission at Gettysburg suggested to Oates that he take the matter up with Chamberlain.

Oates had replied to the commission: "...I have no hope of an agreement with General Chamberlain. I have heard and read enough of his statements to know that he and I are not likely to agree on the place or point to which I advanced." Oates, whose book, *The War Between the Union and the Confederacy and its Lost Opportunities*, had just been published, had added in his postscript:

> *I am not vain or boastful enough, if I ever was in my old age to perpetrate a falsehood forty two years after the occurrence by erecting a monument to the memory of my dead comrades on ground they never reached in their assault. If you see my book I concede the gallantry of Chamberlain and the 20th Maine & acknowledge my repulse. He was duly honored & promoted. It seems to me that so gallant a gentleman would not deny an honest claim made by his defeated competitor.*[12]

Chairman Nicholson forwarded a copy of Oates' letter to Chamberlain, who replied to Nicholson on March 16, 1905:

> *I have your notice of the book of Colonel Oates, as also a copy of his letter concerning the monument he proposes to mark the point of his extreme advance on Little Round Top. I am wholly at a loss to know what Col. Oates wants me to do. He seems to have satisfied himself that I am incorrigible on the point he wishes to establish and that he never can agree with me. As he looks to you to vindicate his rights in the matter of what he thinks our conflicting claims, I infer that you submit the case to me hoping that if possible I may make some modification of something I have said or done.*[13]

Chamberlain asserted: "I have never set up any 'claims' at all about the action of Round Top. I have simply stated the facts; first in my official report written on the march away from Gettysburg, and since in a more extended account on the same lines in a lecture...." While wondering whether the contents of his lecture had been inaccurately reported to Oates, he stated:

> *I cannot change the facts, nor any statement of my own about them. I remember saying in a letter to you some time ago referring to the statement of Colonel Oates then made that his regiment advanced until confronted by the 83rd Pennsylvania and the 44th New York, that this regiment never reached that ground, nor encountered a shot from these Union Regiments. My own regiment held by its extreme right, but all the rest of it was pressed back entirely from its ground two or three times, but finally regained its original position. I am more than willing that the monument of the 15th. Alabama should be placed inside my lines, for some of these men were doubtless there, and I should feel honored by the companionship of the monument of so gallant a regiment on that historic crest, as I was honored by its presence forty years ago.*[14]

Referring to their prior correspondence, he expressed surprise at Oates' sentiment that they could never agree. Chamberlain remembered that, to his own gratification, their statements and recollections had been so remarkably similar. As for the article that Oates published in 1878, Chamberlain stated that he had taken exception only to his statement regarding an encounter with Union cavalry. He added: ...I greatly regret that he should now find occasion to accuse me of withholding from him any measure of just recognition of his skilful [sic] and bold attack, and the splendid gallantry of the 15th. Alabama, for which I have ever felt a peculiar regard." Chamberlain concluded, "The matter of monuments is in your charge, not mine. All I could wish is that they be placed in accordance with historical truth."[15]

Nicholson stirred this brew of controversy by sending, without prior leave, Chamberlain's letter to Oates. In mid-April, Oates wrote directly to Chamberlain:

> *Col. Nicholson has sent to me your letter to him of the 16th ult. which I have carefully perused, and take pleasure in writing directly to you on the points involved. General neither of us are as young as we were when we confronted each other on Little Round Top nearly 42 years ago. Now in the natural course the memory of neither is as good as then. You speak in that letter of having corresponded with me and that you had received two letters from me. I will not dispute your word for you are an honorable gentleman, but I have no recollection of ever writing a letter to you except at the present moment, nor do I remember ever to have received one from you. I have heard and read much about you—among other things, the very complimentary notice of your soldierly and gentlemanly conduct at Lee's surrender, in Gordon's book of Reminiscences[sic], but never had the honor of meeting you after the close of the war.*[16]

Reiterating his desire to place a monument at Gettysburg in memory of the fallen of the 15th Alabama, including his brother, Oates told that he had traveled to Gettysburg the previous summer to meet with the commissioners. Only part of the commission accompanied him to Little Round Top, and afterwards they informed him that the point to which his regiment advanced was a matter of dispute. Regarding Chamberlain's letter to the commission on that matter, Oates wrote:

> *In that letter you, unintentionally, I presume, misrepresented what you understood me to have claimed to wit: that I drove back your right and advanced up the slope a good distance. That letter of yours was what did the work and caused my application to be turned down. That was what made me conclude that you were incorrigible, and especially when I read a letter from Col. Nicholson written me, I think, last November, in which, as I recollect, he stated that you were opposed to my erecting the monument inside your lines.*[17]

Having established that he did not claim to have driven back the 20th's right, but their left, Oates continued to press his case. Referring to Chamberlain Avenue as "the driveway," he explained that he wished to place his monument "something like 75 or 100 yards at an elligible [sic] point near the driveway." With hopes that Chamberlain would write the commission that he had no objections, Oates assured him: "...there will be no inscription upon the shaft derogatory to your command and if mentioned it will be complimentary, for well do I know that no regiment in the Union Army fought any better or more bravely than yours at that spot." But Oates had one more bone to pick with Chamberlain:

One other remark. You stated that in a former letter of mine that I said I was confronted by Union cavalry. In that General, you are mistaken. I said that when my men were retreating that they encountered a thin line of dismounted cavalry men through which we run and took two or three of them out as prisoners. About that I am not mistaken. They belonged to Kilpatrick's cavalry and we encountered them near the foot of Big Round Top.... No one man can see all that occurs in a fight even between two regiments. My statement that we encountered the left oblique fire of the 83rd Pa. and 44th N.Y., was true, but this was before my turning movement began around your left.

In a postscript, Oates stated, "If you & I were on the ground together I do not believe that there would be any very material difference between us about what occurred & the ground on which it did occur." If these two old soldiers had been able to walk the ground together, that may well have been true, but they would never meet.[18]

A month passed before Chamberlain responded to Oates' letter, and he explained that, having been prostrated by an attack of his old wounds, he had been prevented from answering promptly. Angry, and perhaps puzzled by Oates' denial of any previous correspondence, he began:

In this letter I find your impressions place me at a disadvantage in your estimation on two very different grounds; first, in that our former correspondence by way of letters made so little impression on you that you are led to deny having such correspondence; and secondly in that you ascribe to my influence with the Government authorities their refusal to permit the erection of a monument to the 15th. Alabama on the ground where they fought.[19]

Oates had indeed corresponded with Chamberlain; one of his letters, an eleven page missive, still exists. After checking his records, "to see if I could have possibly been mistaken on topics of so much importance as to involve my word of honor," Chamberlain continued:

I find that I did receive, in answer to a letter of mine, two letters purporting to be from you, and so regarded by me, and that I based important statements in public addresses on what was given in them very perfectly confirming my own recollection and reports on the minor points of the conflict on Little Round Top. Looking also at my correspondence with Colonel Nicholson, Chairman of the Gettysburg Commission, I find that in the private correspondence instituted by him on this subject, I made no objection whatever to the erection of a monument by you on the ground attained by the 15th. Alabama or any portion of it during the battle, expressing only the wish that this ground be accurately ascertained....[20]

Acknowledging that Col. Nicholson had sent copies of his personal correspondence to Oates, Chamberlain asked Oates to note:

...the expression of my complete and cordial willingness to have the monument of the 15th Alabama placed within my lines on the slope of Little Round Top, on ground actually reached by portions of that regiment in the sharp

passages of the fight. As to exact location, I cannot say from mere description what was the extreme point to which my left was driven by you, but certainly it was not doubled back upon my right, nor was the right driven materially from its connection with the 83rd. Pennsylvania; I should say it was to a perpendicular within the line of my right front, that is, a quarter circle.[21]

Chamberlain concluded:

It is really my desire to have your monument set up, only let us make sure of our ground for the sake of historical fact. I really do not know what more you could desire as to my present attitude in the matter now at issue. I should be glad to meet you again, after your honorable and conspicuous career of which the trials and tests of Gettysburg were so brilliant a part.

The stalemate between Oates and the Gettysburg Commission over the monument site continued, and a memorial for the 15th Alabama was never erected at Gettysburg.[22]

In early summer of that year, Grace had again been to Maine, and Lawrence wrote to her from his office at the Customs House, of his plan to sail the *Pinafore* to Brunswick: "I can see that her sails are on; but dont know yet what condition her *paint* is in." He resigned himself to taking the train home, but as soon as the paint on the yacht was dry, he would bring it to the shore off Domhegan. He insisted to Grace, "I shall get into my usual condition in a few days." But he worried over Grace, advising her, "Now, take care not to overtask yourself, nor let any there, nor *any body*, overburden you."[23]

In the summer of 1905, Domhegan was operated, as it had been for several years, as a summer hotel. Excursions on the *Pinafore*, under Chamberlain's or his employee, Captain Henry's command, were a favorite past-time of the guests. A log was kept by one of Domhegan's visitors that summer that described a voyage from Portland to Simpson's Point with Chamberlain aboard. Having raised sail at Portland, they were soon "off at a good clip up the harbor." But the uncertainties of traveling by sail soon became apparent:

Pejepscot Historical Society

Domhegan House at Simpson's Point.

All went well until we reached Great Chebeague Island when the wind died out and we were becalmed at the northern end of the island where we had to cast anchor for the night. We had expected to reach Domheagan [sic] by night where we were to meet the other members of the party and I began to fear that we would be hungry, but after the anchor was cast, the General went below deck and in a few minutes he called us to partake of a very refreshing supper of imported sardines, toasted pilot bread and butter, hot tea and milk, Damson plums, banannas [sic] stuffed olives, pickles, raspberries, and cake. We ate heartily and leaving the table in care of Capt. Henry, who filled the office of Cook as well as captain, we went on deck with pillows, wraps, mandolin and Guitar.

We were treated to a very beautiful sunset and through the twilight, into the starry evening we sat on deck amongst the pillows, playing and singing. At last we went reluctantly to our 'bunks' below and were soon rocked to sleep by the gentle motion of the yacht. We were awaked at 5:30 a.m. by Gen'l Chamberlain and after a row to the shore for some wild flowers we set full sail for Domheagan [sic]....[24]

Several photos of Chamberlain were included in Phinehas Stephens' log of his excursion on the *Pinafore*. The first presents him in an uncharacteristic pose, his usual dignity and immaculate attire giving way to that of a relaxed holiday-maker, lounging against the piling of a Portland dock. The other shows Chamberlain near the ship's wheel, having donned a sailor's cap and assuming the pose of captain. They are pictures of a happy man.[25]

Myra Porter, who returned to Maine and was working in Portland, wrote often to Chamberlain in the summer of 1905. Her letter of July 8 indicates that he was once more struggling with his family's expenses. Chamberlain was again living in a Portland hotel during the week, but was about to change his living arrangements. Myra commented, "I shall miss the little calls in your 'supper room' now that you are moved out." Planning an extended visit with her family in Bangor, Myra exclaimed, "And when I leave Portland how I shall miss you! I am not foolish over it, but no friend has ever come into my life just as

Bowdoin College

Chamberlain at the* Pinafore's *berth, Portland dock, August 2, 1905.

Chamberlain at the wheel of the* Pinafore, *August 2, 1905.

you have come. Oh, I am so glad that this life does not end all—there are deeper joys—and they will never end. Let us be ready to 'enter in.'" Myra added, "I hope to hear that 'things' are better in your house (Mrs. C's suffering and the care I mean)."[26]

Having sailed aboard the *Pinafore*, Myra addressed another letter to "Gennie," the name Chamberlain's grandchildren had given him, she wrote afterward, "I hope you all had the loveliest trip imaginable and I wish to thank you all for the dear, sweet little outing I had with you. How precious the memory of our sail will ever be! I hope you will get off for many such trips this summer." Hoping to see Chamberlain once more before she left for Bangor, she flirtatiously offered, "I want you to see my new dress too for you have never seen me with anything frilly on." Several days later, she invited him to dine with her:

> *I'd love to have you if you think best. You will know better than I. Most of the gossips are away I think. Come whatever time will be most restful for you.... I am so glad you are coming, and we will have the sweetest...little hour together—only I want it to be longer than that for I shall not see you again soon, and I wish to talk to you heart-to-heart of some thoughts I have.*[27]

Further indication of the nature of the "thoughts" Myra was having, is in her conclusion: "I am so delightfully indolent today that I did not even attend church—had breakfast sent to my room and have been around in my negligé writing, and napping." Chamberlain, in his choice of a confidante and friend, may have again acquired an ardent female admirer. He did have dinner with her that week, but disappointed Myra's hopes for his return later that same evening. Her salutation switched abruptly from "My dear Gennie" to "My General Chamberlain." She wrote, "You did not come back to me last evening." She asked, "Didn't we have a restful little hour together?" Gathering steam, she added, "You must come again and soon. I will dress for you alone, in my sweet new gown. I'd rather dress for you than anyone else, and was so sorry last evening I could not do so." Asking him to bring along the oration he wanted her to read, she commented: "...you know how I always love everything you write—(not everything you say)." In 1908, Myra married Ralph Edwards, a railroad engineer from Brooklyn, New York. He was 27; she was 41.[28]

On August 4, 1905, three days before her 80th birthday, Fanny, while attempting to cross a room, slipped on the hardwood floor, and fell heavily, breaking her hip. The pain of this injury strained her already failing health. Lawrence wrote to Fanny on her birthday:

> *...although your condition is far from being what I could wish and constantly pray for, I cannot help sending you a word of loving greeting with thanks that we have been so long spared to each other, a life...so rich in blessings. You have had a useful and honorable,—& I trust on the whole,—a happy life. Your husband & children 'rise up & call you blessed'—as the old scriptures represent the crowning grace of a good woman. Every body is send[ing] me letters of sympathy & love for you—more than I can answer for some time—But I am returning greetings for you to them all. The dear little girls have been working at some little tokens of affection for your birth day, & you will have them by this time. I shall soon come to see you & try to cheer you. With all love & prayer for blessings to come to you.*[29]

That same month, Chamberlain began writing old friends, asking their advice and support for legislation that would provide an Army pension for the volunteer field officers of the Civil War. How many of his problems would have been solved if he could have afforded to retire, in this, his 77th year. Adelbert Ames expressed his opinion that the number of beneficiaries would weigh heavily in the possibilities of such legislation being considered by Congress. Chamberlain and Gen. Webb discussed who among the general officers should be considered, and Chamberlain outspokenly suggested:

> *Would it not over-burden the proposed list and defeat the measure, to put in all who attained or received the rank of a general officer? Should it not be of such as commanded troops in the field,—and not officers of bureaus &c? Would you put Colonels into the 'bill' unless they actually commanded brigades in the field? and would you include all those who secured brevets of brigadier general, including almost everybody who had a friend at court after the war had ended? It would appear to me that the list should be somewhat discriminating and a roll of honor. Otherwise, I really do not want any part in it. There have been enough of such things. A brevet, which used to cost all the blood that would run out of our bodies, is not worth now a real old brass button: and the medals of honor are no sure token of distinguished service or merit, after the raid on them from the rear.*[30]

Of the volunteer officers, Chamberlain commented, "If they are not worthy of this or if this would degrade the army either in its history or in its present rare tests and superior estate, then I would accept the situation and be content to be buried in an honorable grave. That is better than to go into an unseemly struggle to obtain recognition and be denied it, and go down under the shame of it." Writing from his fifth story hotel room in Portland, looking out over a night sea, Chamberlain told his old friend: "I will try to give a more politic answer when I come to my desk and to a 'realizing sense' of actual life and the probabilities..."[31]

Fanny died the night of October 18, 1905. It is not known whether her death was expected, and if, on this mid-week night, Lawrence was called home to be with her. Fanny and Lawrence had been looking forward to the celebration of what would have been their 50th wedding anniversary that December. Described as a rare and gifted woman, an obituary stated that she had borne her blindness and suffering from a combination of diseases with admirable patience. Her funeral service was held in the First Parish Church, and the Rev. Dr. E. B. Mason provided a touching tribute. Calling upon memories and images in the church itself in earlier days, Rev. Dr. Mason described:

> *The door opens and a father mother and little girl softly enter the sacred place. Little Fanny Adams has come from her home in Boston, to live with her cousin George, who loves children, and longs to have one in his house. The little girl grew up, listened to her adopted father, your honored pastor, Dr. Adams, preaching Sabbath after Sabbath, and became a part of Brunswick life.*[32]

Mason continued:

> *Years have passed away, this impressive church, which always deeply affected her, has risen on the site of the old meeting house, and each sabbath morning, there is seated at the organ, a young woman who loves music, and knows how to lead the congregation in its public and solemn worship. Soft strains breathe forth or swell into loud triumphant chords, while the people sit and reverently wait for the uttered words of prayer praise and religious instruction. Once more Fanny Adams is taking her part in the church life, and for years continues to render this important service. Among the members of the choir and for a time leader of the choir, is a young man between whom and the organist grows a beautiful friendship, which ripens into a warm deep love, and which we know now was to last for half a century.*[33]

He presented a third vision:

> *It is a wedding. The bride and groom walk slowly up the aisle, and stand before this altar while the solemn words are spoken, which make them husband and wife. The picture is easily filled out. All its details come back. We see the throng of friends, and hear the thrilling organ notes, and the full melodious voice of the minister, as he recites the impressive and touching marriage service. Fanny Adams again goes out of the church, and this time as the bride of the young man who helped her in the choir.*[34]

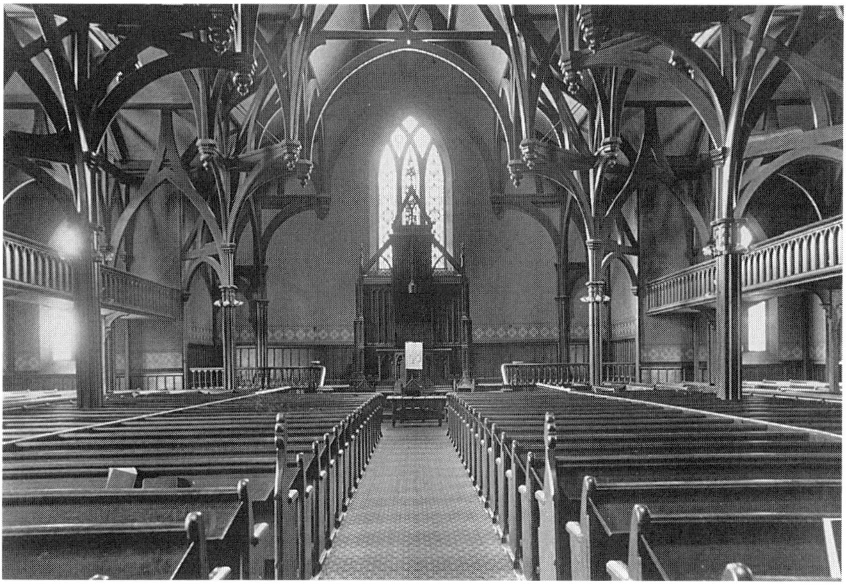

Interior of the First Parish Church, Brunswick, Maine.

Then, forty years later:

> *...we are in the Congregational church, on almost any Sunday evening, when the door slowly opens and three persons carefully enter; a father, a mother and a son. They move cautiously down the aisle, at almost a creeping pace, and we soon see that the mother is totally blind. A devoted son and husband support her at every step, and seat themselves at her side. She sits motionless during the service, and at its close smiles brightly on friends who stop with a word of greeting before being led back to the other side of the street, and the home made as comfortable as love can make it, but always in darkness.*[35]

Reverend Dr. Mason suggested, "Those who fill in the events between the four scenes described can rehearse the story of a strong useful and beautiful life." He said that he had not addressed the many incidents in Fanny's life outside of that building:

> *...her experiences in the war, the days in Augusta as governor's wife, with receptions and social obligations; nor the college life when her husband was president of Bowdoin College, and students gathered in their home, or came to her with their troubles and questions for sympathy and direction; not the home life which is too sacred for strangers to meddle with; nor her regretted inability to unite with the church, because of a scrupulous conscience which could not assent to propositions beyond comprehension.*[36]

He concluded:

That little Fanny Adams, who appeared one Sunday morning in this church seventy or more years ago, who later played your organ, was married before your altar, and worshipped here on Sunday evening with her husband and son, has gone on into the bright and glorious life and light which is immortality and joy and peace. Old and tried friends have brought in for the last time her mortal body, and will lay it in the grave, but her spirit, with its music, and brilliant gifts, and memories of the past, and treasures gathered in this world, has gone to God who gave it, and will abide with Him forever.

Fanny was laid to rest in Pine Grove Cemetery. The stone that marks her resting place bears the word, "Unveiled."[37]

CHAPTER

25

"We Pass Now Quickly From Each Other's Sight"

In the months after Fanny's death, Lawrence gathered together those things most dear to her and most exemplary of her life. He wished to create a memorial to her in the family home. She had cherished the bracelet that he had designed and given to her on their 10th anniversary, and Lawrence kept it in a small jeweled casket. Treasuring her paintings of Hamlet and Mary Magdalene, Lawrence wrote to Helen Adams. He asked for paintings that Fanny had given to her adoptive father many years before: one of angels, and a Madonna, as well as several landscapes. Though Lawrence explained in his letter that he cared about these paintings as others could not, Helen, then widowed almost 30 years, refused to part with them, claiming her own sentimental attachment. She commented on his efforts to gather Fanny's most prized possessions: "I know the 'treasury' you are putting together will indeed be a choice one, for Fanny could never resist the possible acquisition of beautiful things." Another letter from an old family friend expressed more empathy for both Lawrence and Fanny. In his letter of condolence, James McKeen echoed the sentiments of others regarding Fanny's merciful release from suffering. He also reminisced about the last time he had seen her, for "... she talked with her old time vigor of art and literature, and seemed for the moment to quite forget her blindness and helplessness." Little would change in the Chamberlain home in the coming years, and a visitor to the house several years after Fanny's death remarked, "On every side and in every room of this old mansion can be seen the evidence of her skill and artistic taste."[1]

Lawrence's life would, of course, change when Fanny was gone. There were fewer trips to Brunswick, and he visited Boston more frequently, cherishing his time spent with Grace and her family. Always, the news that "Gennie" was coming was a cause for celebration to his granddaughters. The youngest of the three, Rosamond, today still remembers her grandfather's kind ways and great gentleness, describing him as "just the opposite of pompous." She recalls that her mother, Grace, enjoyed pampering him, and made his favorite popovers for breakfast. But she also remembers her grandfather's "fuzzy" mustache, commenting, "I'd hate to kiss him, I'll tell you that."[2]

In late October 1905, Chamberlain made a belated reply to a letter from Gen. Thomas Munford, who had commanded Fitz Hugh Lee's cavalry at Five Forks. He began his letter, "The death of my wife, who was a broad-minded, and richly endowed woman who loved her whole Country, in peace and in war, and honored brave men who did manly duty as they saw it in their own hearts, has come upon me since the receipt of your letter, and my delay in acknowledging it is thus to be pardoned." Munford had asked for his writings on the Battle of Five Forks and, Chamberlain, wishing he could have spoken with Munford earlier, asked the Southern commander to criticize his work and add suggestions. Munford was fighting his own battle for the truth regarding the Battle of Five Forks, which he referred to as the "Waterloo of the Army of Northern Virginia and of the Confederate Government."

Today, the notorious shad bake that caused the absence of Gen. George Pickett and Gen. Fitz Hugh Lee from the front that day is accepted as fact. But Munford was discouraged from publishing his account of the battle, advised that it would only bring him into acrimonious controversy. Munford declared that in his account, "There was not a word said that could not be *substantiated*," for "these are facts which have been *established*, but as the *trial* of Warren was suppressed, the real story has never been compiled in its true colors—" General Munford accepted his comrades' judgment and left instructions that his paper, "Narrative of the Battle of Five Forks, April 1, 1865," be published twenty years after his death.[3]

Chamberlain's thoughts did not dwell solely on the details of long ago battlefields. Powerful memories softened life's painful losses. In the months after Fanny's death, he finished writing "The Last Review of the Army of the Potomac, May 23, 1865," a narrative both vivid and intimate. Here, Chamberlain declared that all his old comrades-in-arms had passed in review that day. "They belonged to me, and I to them by bonds birth cannot create nor death sever. More were passing here than the personages on the stand could see. But to me so seeing, what a review,—how great, how far; how near! It was as the morning of the resurrection." In his stirring descriptions, Tom Chamberlain was not forgotten, but remembered as "my brave young brother." And Fanny took her place in his moving recollections of the women whose tender care eased the suffering of the wounded. "You in my soul I see, faithful watcher by my cotside long days and nights together through the delirium of mortal anguish,—steadfast, calm and sweet as eternal love. We pass now quickly from each other's sight; but I know full well that where beyond these passing scenes you shall be, there will be heaven!"[4]

Chamberlain delivered this address on the Grand Review, which became a significant part of his book, *The Passing of the Armies*, for the first time in May 1906 at the dedication of a Civil War memorial at York, Maine. Though such monuments adorn the center of thousands of towns and cities across the country, the residents of this small Maine coastal town still ponder over the granite warrior in their midst. His slouch hat and vandyke beard strikingly bring to mind a Confederate soldier. Thus, York residents suspect that, through an error in shipping, the town square of some small Southern town is dominated by a statue of Billy Yank.[5]

In early 1906, Chamberlain renewed his efforts to have a private bill presented before the Senate that would grant him army retirement. He was 78 years of age, in poor health, and holding an appointment that could be swept away with a change in the administration. He was encouraged by the success of several volunteer officers, who were granted retirement based on their outstanding service records. But Chamberlain's timing could not have been worse. Veterans' organizations had an "Omnibus bill" placed before the Senate that would qualify all brevet generals for army retirement. This would have included Chamberlain, but he firmly believed that Congress would never approve the costly addition of so many to the army's retired list. But beyond its slim chances for success, a major sticking point for Chamberlain was the bill's inclusion of all brevetted generals, regardless of when or how they received their brevets. Of the 1,940 Union generals commissioned during the Civil War, 1,207 reached brevet rank after March 1, 1865. This last-minute flood of brevets had, in Chamberlain's opinion, robbed its bestowal of significance as an award for extraordinary service. He told his friend, Gen. Henry Merriam, a retired regular who championed Chamberlain's case in Washington, that when asked to support the "Omnibus Bill," he was torn by conflicting feelings:

> *Brevets were scattered so promiscuously after the war that they are no indication of service in the field or anywhere else. It seems to me hardly just to base the application of this measure upon the brevet rank rather than on the actual service rendered. I cannot truthfully say I approve this bill. And yet it seems a little ungracious for me to withhold assistance to old comrades deserving consideration, on account of the inclusion of some who do not stand on the same ground.*[6]

Though generally unperturbed by demands from many supporters of the bill who continued to press him for endorsement, Chamberlain was worried that two of his friends, Gen. Charles Grosvenor and Gen. Ellis Spear would be offended if he did not endorse the measure and continued to pursue his private bill. "I hate to set myself up above as distinct from my old comrades in arms. The rest of them I do not mind." Eventually he and Gen. Webb, who was influenced by Chamberlain's views to withdraw his support of the bill, made a noncommittal statement, an endorsement of the general principal of retirement for volunteer officers. To those who campaigned for the bill's passage, this was not good enough. Chamberlain and Merriam were convinced that they should wait to submit his private bill until the controversy over the "Omnibus Bill" subsided. But in March 1906, illness drove Chamberlain from Portland to convalesce in Brunswick. Feeling that he could wait no longer, he wrote to Merriam that, "...a sudden 'set-back' threatening a bad time of the old sort with my wounds, lets me see the necessity of my seeking immediate response in the best way I can." Chamberlain admitted, "...I am in a depressed and dispirited mood...and cannot make myself rally as I wish."[7]

The "Omnibus Bill" ended up being sent to its demise in committee, as Chamberlain had warned it would be. Because he did not give his endorsement for their bill, lobbyists for the national veterans' organizations withheld their crucial support when Chamberlain's private bill was considered. Chamberlain also lacked another essential for the success of his bill, the political support of Maine politicians. William P. Frye, a member of Congress since 1871, had served as Maine's senator for twenty-five years, and was president pro tem of the Senate for ten. While he submitted a bill for Chamberlain in May 1906, and another during the next term, no action was taken.

When the bills were quietly buried in committee, Chamberlain knew his hopes for retirement were over. He not only faced the necessity of continuing to work. Having felt that the passage of private retirement bills for others was the government's recognition for their outstanding service, the failure of his own bill was a cruel disappointment.[8]

The desire to offer testimony for Chamberlain's bills in the Senate may well have inspired a short biography published in 1906. "Joshua Lawrence Chamberlain A Sketch," was published by the Chamberlain Society, a genealogical association of which Chamberlain was president for a number of years. No author is acknowledged, and an introduction stating that "several persons...procured the material or assisted in the preparation of this sketch," controverts speculation that Chamberlain wrote the piece. But there is additional evidence that someone other than Chamberlain wrote the manuscript. Comparison of the sketch with Chamberlain's unpublished memoirs reveals that they contain very similar subject matter and include many of the same incidents and anecdotes. In some cases, even the same wording and expressions are used. But while Chamberlain supplied a good deal of information for this project, and probably saw its potential for setting the record straight regarding his political career, it is unlikely that he wrote the biography in its final form. Throughout the sketch, a number of words and phrases that the unknown author took directly from Chamberlain's writings are set apart and placed within quotation marks, leaving the great bulk of the text in another's hands. And it seems unlikely, for instance, that Chamberlain would have described his own writings and addresses as showing "a tendency to reaches of thought somewhat abstruse." The sketch also contains a puzzling and clumsy interpretation of Chamberlain's political views on the vote for freedmen:

> *He was in some disfavor with his party because he did not approve the policy of conferring the privilege of the 'suffrage' on the lately liberated slaves. He thought so delicate and difficult a task as the 'reconstruction' of the South, after its terrible disasters and the overturn of its industrial, civil and social system, could be effected only by and through the best minds of the South, and by no means by hasty and sweeping measures tending to give political preponderance to the most inferior.*[9]

It is true that Chamberlain disapproved of the disbarment of the ablest minds of the South from political leadership because of their Confederate affiliations. But he supported the amendments that gave suffrage to freedmen. The above interpretation of his views not only implies elitism, but in its choice of words, yokes them with an implication of racism that Chamberlain did not embrace. It has also been suggested that Chamberlain, at the very least, had editorial privileges over the sketch before publication. This, too, seems unlikely, for simple errors remained uncorrected. For instance, the sketch asserts that Chamberlain was absent from the army in late 1863 due to injuries, when in fact, he was ill with "malarial fever." Scrupulous in his attention to detail, this is not a mistake that he would have let pass had he edited the work. Written by well-meaning admirers, who meant the sketch to be a tribute, there is also indication that Chamberlain was less than comfortable with the Chamberlain Society's pamphlet. Though he sent a copy to an old family friend shortly after its publication, he asked that she not let it fall into any other hands.[10]

Despite the many infections of his wound that threatened his life, Chamberlain outlived many of his old comrades. Sarah Sampson, nurse and friend to Maine soldiers and veterans, widows and orphans, died in 1907. And his old friend, John Marshall Brown of Portland, partially paralyzed by a stroke, suffered another attack in the fall, and died during a surgical attempt to save his life. Chamberlain coauthored a MOLLUS tribute, in which he remembered young Brown, the recent graduate from Bowdoin who he had helped select as adjutant in the new 20th Maine in the fall of 1862. Brown, who eventually served as lieutenant colonel of the 32nd Maine, had been severely wounded at Petersburg, the day after Chamberlain was shot, which ended his military service. But the war was not the last adversity they had shared, for during the tumultuous days of the disputed election in Augusta in 1880, one of the very few people Chamberlain called to the capitol to assist him was John Marshall Brown.[11]

As the 50th anniversary of the Civil War approached, public interest in accounts of the battles increased. In early 1908, Chamberlain contributed material to a Washington writer who intended, with Gen. Munford's encouragement, to write an article on Five Forks. While his collaborative details were appreciated, the opinionated author commented: "...this article has nothing to do with the 'Yankees' in any way whatever. It has to do with the errors of our own side which made Sheridan a present of a glorious victory when by all the laws of war and patriotism and soldiery he ought to have been given a most astounding thrashing."

Later in the year, Chamberlain was privy to other skeletons in the Confederate closet. A copy of a letter purported to have been written by Col. John Mosby of Partisan Ranger fame, was sent to him. It stated that after the Battle of Five Forks, Lee gave his aide, Colonel Venable, an order for Pickett's arrest. Later passing Pickett during the retreat from Petersburg, Lee was reported to have "called out with vexation, 'Is that man still with this army!'" This letter also claimed that when Gen. Pickett visited Gen. Lee in 1870, he received a very cold reception from his old commander.[12]

The approach of spring meant getting *Pinafore* ready to sail and opening up Domhegan for the season. Spring also meant weekends of sailing the Maine coast and spending time at the shore. After visiting Grace in late summer 1908, Chamberlain sounded very chipper when he wrote upon his return to Maine in mid-September: "Thanks to all your sweet care in so many ways, after my charming visit to your two lovely homes I am very well this morning, and full of abiding thoughts and strength therefrom." He quipped that they would keep in touch: "I shall keep the 'wireless' 'attuned' to a certain confidential communion till that meeting is materially realized." But he was denied the pleasure of another trip to Boston. By the middle of October, he was so ill that Grace came to him in Brunswick. This time, it was not the old wound that laid Chamberlain low. As he explained in a letter to sister Sae:

> *I am afraid you may be troubled at hearing possibly that I have been ill. It was a sharp little turn, of a new kind for me,—inflammation of the tonsils. The effect of it and the excessive pain I suffered, have disabled me for some little time but I am getting over it all. Grace is here for a few days—and most glorious days they are. Did you ever see anything like them? The leaves & the earth are full of glory. I wish we could enjoy them together.*[13]

In February 1909, once again healthy, Chamberlain traveled with Grace to Philadelphia for a ceremony to mark the one hundredth anniversary of Abraham Lincoln's birth. In his address, he spoke of Lincoln's great strength:

> *Great crises in human affairs call out the great in men. They call for greatness. This greatness is of quality rather than quantity. It is not intensified selfhood, nor multiplied possessions. It implies extraordinary powers to cope with difficult situations; but it implies still more, high purpose—the intent to turn these powers to the service of man. Its essence is of magnanimity. Some have indeed thought it great to seize the occasion in troubled times to aggrandize themselves. And something slavish in the lower instincts of human nature seems to grant their claim. Kings and conquerors have been named 'great' because of the magnificence of the servitude they have been able to command, or the vastness of their conquests, or even of the ruin they have wrought. But true greatness is not in nor of the single self; it is of that larger personality, that shared and sharing life with others, in which, each giving of his best for their betterment, we are greater than ourselves; and self-surrender for the sake of that great belonging, is the true nobility.*[14]

He asked what combination of qualities marked the man who could face such adversity, who "could mount above this storm, make his voice heard amidst these jarring elements. It was a divine providence which brought forth the man, to execute the divine decree, in a crisis of human history. It was a strange presentment and personality,—this deliverer, this servant and master, this follower and leader of the law...." Chamberlain concluded, "More and more the consecrating oath of that great purpose: 'With Malice towards none; with charity for all; following the right as God gives us to see the right,' will be the watchword of the world."

It is said that Chamberlain's friends considered his oration on Lincoln his masterpiece. Speaking of the terrible challenges that Lincoln had to meet, and the strength and courage with which he met them, it is obvious that Chamberlain found Lincoln to be a hero, not only of his own time, but for all time.[15]

During the winter of 1908-09, Gen. "Andy" Webb fought his own battle with ill health, writing to Chamberlain, "How are you my dear young friend—I am *better* but it has been a hard winter for me—I hope to be myself again this summer—" Several weeks later, Webb wrote, "I am anxious about your health—You do not write any longer the treasured short notes to your old friend. Well! I will keep it up and will pester you—two or three times each month just to blow off a little of that affectionate regard for you 'Old Boy'." Chamberlain also heard from a mutual friend, Maine veteran Selden Connor, who wrote that Webb had stated, "...Connor, you and Chamberlain are my 'beaux ideals' and I have always an affectionate respect for both of you." Connor added to Webb's tribute by stating that it was "especially gratifying to me since it links me with you in his regard."[16]

Alexander S. Webb.

In the spring of 1909, Lawrence planned a trip to the Virginia battlefields with Wyllys, Grace and the children. It would include a visit to Gettysburg on the 47th anniversary of the battle. Savoring a mild morning, Chamberlain wrote to Grace from Brunswick, "...I wish to write you this little note while the airs make me wish you to be here, or to receive a 'wireless' message from me." Wyllys was still in Brunswick, as was Lillian Edmunds, who kept the old home ready for the family's visits. Lawrence told Grace, "We were all at home yesterday, and had a lovely dinner on the veranda and then an hour's walk among our pines, and a bright evening...the fireside in the library—wanting you all the time." The Chamberlains did make a tour of the battlefields that summer. While little is known of their trip, at least part of the journey was made by automobile, with Grace behind the wheel.[17]

In mid-September, Chamberlain reported his health as being in "limbo." Though not seriously ill, he was far from well. Dr. Abner Shaw, former surgeon of the 20th Maine, who still treated his old friend, advised him to give up a trip to Boston and postpone a proposed stay at Domhegan with Grace. A month later, when Commander Robert Peary arrived in Portland after his expedition to the North Pole, Chamberlain was still too unwell to be one of the welcoming party. He sent word: "I should have been the first to greet you on your return home from so arduous a task and honored, as you deserve, had I not been entirely disabled by the recurring consequences of my old war wounds." Chamberlain had not abandoned his policy of believing in his students' veracity, as he wrote to this member of Bowdoin's class of 1877: "Be assured I am of those whose faith in your deed as your word admits no doubt or diminution. The first honors are yours and we are all proud of you."[18]

In December 1909, Chamberlain wrote to Sen. William Frye about the feasibility of submitting another bill for his army retirement, but he received little encouragement. Though Frye was willing to present another bill, he stated that ongoing efforts of the veterans' organizations for a general retirement of volunteer officers left no room for consideration of individual cases. Frye added that Congress was also heeding President Taft's instructions for strict economy. Chamberlain would, therefore, work on, going to his office at the Custom House whenever he had the physical strength to do so. Knowing he would be kept in Portland for the foreseeable future, Chamberlain had the family home in Brunswick closed up for the winter. He purchased a house on Ocean Avenue overlooking the city's Back Bay. He took a trolley to work each day, and he was a familiar figure to the residents of Portland. With a soldier's posture and bearing, even in his advanced years, people remembered him in the dark suit and black tie he habitually wore, a striking contrast to his white hair and full mustache, while a blue shirt and white starched collar emphasized blue eyes that still had plenty of snap. Carrying a stout, hand carved Japanese cane, on cold days he wore a long black overcoat against the winds that sweep through the city from the sea. He often stopped to speak with acquaintances, from the elite of Portland society to the longshoremen on the harbor docks.[19]

As winter fastened its grip upon Maine that year, a letter from his granddaughter, eleven-year-old Rosamond, cheered Chamberlain. He replied, "How lovely and dear your letter to Gennie is! I shall keep it among my treasured things. You must come to me in the summer, with the birds and flowers, when all brown-eyed things are building their nests. We will build some too!" Rosamond was but one of his correspondents, for Chamberlain kept in touch with many old friends. From his Portland home on Christmas Day, 1909, Chamberlain wrote to a friend of his youth in Brewer, Manley Hardy:

Portland Tax Assessor's Office / Chris Church

Chamberlain home, Portland, Maine, c. 1924.

Chamberlain carriage house with Maltese crosses.

Your beautiful and generous tokens of remembrance came to my new winter-quarters here where I am just getting established, and wakened in me "thoughts that run before and after." I had just been looking over some old army papers and took up a little Testament which I had carried through the war on the first 'fly-leaf' of which was the inscription—Whitings' Hill Sunday School 1853.—What memories this brought up! Back over the surges of that great war rose the modest little school-house...where you and Joe Farrington and I used to meet the people of that forlorn region with lessons we meant to be loving and full of saving truth. Dear faces they were which answered my long & far gaze,—.... Life was all before us then & we knew not what was to come. And for us all three how full the years have been! I believe all as met our duties with faithfulness and not without honor.[20]

In 1909, Manley Hardy's daughter, Fanny Hardy Eckstorm, started several projects that honored Chamberlain in his home town. Her efforts saw a plaque placed in front of his birthplace, the cottage on Main Street in Brewer. And when the town's library expanded into new rooms, Mrs. Eckstorm requested a large photograph of Chamberlain for one of the reading rooms. He offered her a photograph that had just been done, in uniform and astride an impressively sturdy horse, taken on a hill near his home overlooking Back Bay. Sae eventually offered a plaster bust of Chamberlain to the Brewer Library. Having lost none of her willingness to offer candid opinions on likenesses of her brothers, she told Mrs. Eckstorm, "We have up in our attic a very poor bust—...of my brother, Gen. C—made some years ago by Charles Tefft...would it be better than none in some corner of our Public Library. It looks something like him!"[21]

In February 1910, Chamberlain returned to Brunswick to speak before Bowdoin's chapter of the Y.M.C.A. Late that night, he wrote to Sae, "Here I am after an evening with the Bowdoin Boys.... The boys came out in such numbers that we had to adjourn from the Lecture Room to the chapel.... The students received me with most marked & unusual courtesies. The entire assembly rose at my entrance & remained standing until I was seated, & the greeting was repeated with emphasis at the Conclusion of my address." He told Sae that the snow was two feet deep around his house and, unable to get the key, he had spent the night in a Brunswick hotel. "My house does not seem to have been disturbed in any way. How it will be when the snow melts on the roof & the rains come I do not know. I think I am pretty well, but dont like slippery walking."[22]

Wyllys joined his father at his house in Portland in 1910, and started the Chamberlain Electric Company, manufacturing batteries on Commercial St., just a few doors down from the Custom House. Lillian also became part of the Portland household, though her duties in these years became, more and more, that of nurse rather than housekeeper. Late that winter, Lasalle Pickett, Gen. Pickett's widow, spoke before a ladies' group in Portland, and she stayed at the Chamberlain home on Ocean Avenue. Mrs. Pickett was known both as a guardian of her husband's memory, and as a champion of reconciliation between the soldiers of the North and South. Though an accident had left her almost completely blind, she supported herself as a clerk in a Washington office and by her writing and speaking engagements. After returning to Washington, she sent Chamberlain a copy of her book, *Pickett and His Men*, with her wishes that "the memories of old, sad days which it may recall will not all be sorrowful and that they may come softened by the gentle influence of time and bringing with them a glint of pleasure with their sadness." A member of the household staff remembered that during her stay, Mrs. Pickett teasingly addressed Chamberlain as, "My dear enemy."[23]

A cold that Chamberlain had during Mrs. Pickett's visit deepened into serious illness as spring approached. News of his condition called forth all of Mary Clark's old desires to nurse her patient of so long ago. She had been a fast friend of the family ever since she had nursed Chamberlain at the Annapolis Hospital after he was wounded at Petersburg. In a letter addressed to "My beloved General," Mary asked questions about his health and suggested that he come to her summer cottage to convalesce. Expressing her wish to take care of him, Mary added effusively, "just as if you were the beautiful flower that you *are*—"[24]

Chamberlain regained his strength in the summer, and made another pilgrimage to Gettysburg. Before the year was out, another of the commanders at Little Round Top was gone. William C. Oates, at 75 years of age, died that fall.

Returning to Maine, Chamberlain spent a number of summer days sailing the coast of southern Maine on the *Pinafore*. But this rejuvenating period of good health and relaxation came to an abrupt end in the early fall. As he prepared Domhegan for a visit from Grace, he received word that she had a serious accident. He knew little, except that it involved an automobile. He wrote to Grace on October 13:

Wyllys told me of your accident and present condition last evening. I had not "dreamed" of this after your splendid mastery of the Gettysburg trip. I was sorry I had sent you a letter seeming peremptory in its demand for information about your time of arriving. I only wished to learn if I could get over to Bangor and back here before you could come. Now, I don't know how badly off you are; but presume pretty seriously disabled. I fear it, any way.[25]

Chamberlain assured her that he would keep the house open in Brunswick, in hopes that she would eventually be able to come:

Never mind! We will have our "good time" at the right time. I am pressed on all sides to make engagements just for these five days; but am not inclined to engage my self for any thing just now. We are holding the old house "in commission" as yet, and do not like to disturb its arrangements when it may yet be possible for you to come over in season to enjoy it. We have plenty of "wood and water" & coal there, if we should need to use them. But do not try to crowd your self to recover faster than "nature" will advise. We are really not dependent on almanacs. But I would much wish to know how you are—if not how you came so.

Grace, while out walking, had been caught between the wheel of an automobile and the corner of a stone wall, severely injuring her knee. It left her a semi-invalid for the rest of her life. Daughter Rosamond would say of her mother that she was "brave, like her father," but her sufferings and resulting disability must have caused her father much anguish.[26]

Chamberlain traveled to Massachusetts in December, and spent several days visiting with Mary Clark. There he received the loving sympathy of his old friend. His visit did Mary a world of good as well, for she wrote to him shortly before Christmas, telling him how much his visit had meant to her:

Your recent visit, though it gave me only two days of your dear presence, was a rare delight to me—You brought me love and joy and peace, and in parting, you left the sweetest and dearest of memories. How trying was the farewell! After you had gone, a sense of utter loneliness came over me, and continued, until I received your dear and beautiful letter, for which I thank you, and for the cheer and comfort it gave me—[27]

I must tell you, how you won <u>all</u> hearts, the evening we passed at Mrs. Rice's; and very proud I was of you—During the recital, I was so deeply moved I could not trust myself to look more than two or three times upon you, but each glance told me, my dear hero, was at his best— You can easily imagine how attentively I listened to every word So eloquently uttered, impassioned and inspired you seemed—[28]

To Chamberlain's protest that he had been made too much of that night, Mary responded, "You write dear, as if you *could* have been kept in the 'back-ground,' you can never be there, it is not your place, a man of too many and varied achievements for that...." And perhaps Chamberlain had expressed a weariness of his position in the limelight, for Mary continued:

...this is the reason of the constant "demand"—I do not like it or approve of, for you—I had not the slightest idea you would be led on, to rehearse all you so kindly did, you are too sensitive and magnetic for such an ordeal! The little company were so very eager to listen to every word you said, they never realized it was any strain upon you.... They listened to the past; I did at times, but was very near you in the present—after all, no one can know you quite as well as I do; and when you come to see me, I want to give you all I can of my love (the dearest) as well as of undisturbed rest....[29]

Mary described her disappointment that she was unaware of some affliction that had disturbed Chamberlain's sleep while he was her guest, and stated that she would have "watched over you, (something like the times of old, but now different)...." She added, "...this did not fall to my lot—But much, very much did, and, I was most happy and grateful to see you looking so well, and handsomer than ever; I can say this with safety, as you are not given to vanity...." It is not known when Mary's deep affection for Chamberlain turned to love. Now five years a widower, Chamberlain responded to Mary Clark's devotion and support. For Mary described a touching scene of two old friends, elderly and frail, but no less able to care deeply for one another:

Nor do I forget the dear "communion," the very happiest moments I have ever known—do you remember after we returned from Rockmoor...and our conversation? I will never forget you, as you sat by me, with your dear hand in mine, your face glowing with expression, and, told me, so tenderly, of all I most wished to know, your dear self—you know, the subject of this confidence and "communion" is the nearest and dearest to my heart, how can it be otherwise?

Mary worried about the pace Chamberlain had been keeping since his last illness in the spring. Though she knew he would keep working, she commented, "I trust it will be different now—Will you spare yourself, in this direction—please promise me—And are you careful to keep warm when you go out on the pier?"[30]

During Christmas 1910, Chamberlain sent greetings to another old friend, Ellis Spear. Replying that he had been ill since Thanksgiving, Spear told Chamberlain, "Your dear Christmas greeting helps, and gives me an impulse upward." Suggesting that Chamberlain come and visit them in Washington before he and his wife traveled to the South for the winter, Spear closed his letter with his own holiday wishes. "Many years & peaceful to you—You have seen enough of War—" Spear would recover in the next year and became president of the 20th Maine Association. It is hard to know what turned Spear away from his old friend in their last years. But this letter of caring expressions is the last evidence of his fond regard for his old commander.[31]

The damp cold of mid-winter invariably brought Chamberlain to his sickbed, and in January of 1911, he was once again down with an infection of his wound. And February brought terrible news. After several bouts of illness, Andy Webb died in New York. But once again, the approach of spring brought strength to Chamberlain, and by March of that year, he was able to travel to Boston and stay with Grace and her family. On returning to Portland, he wrote cheerfully to Grace that all at home had been "looking for me—especially Tibe." The large mongrel dubbed Tiberius Caesar was a favorite with Grace's family, and Chamberlain told her, "I did not forget to give him your greeting as you asked me to do."[32]

In April, describing the green sheen over the fields and the emerging crocus, he reported feeling uncommonly well. "Gardening begins now", he declared enthusiastically. But an old friend described that it was Lillian who put in the seeds and plants, with Chamberlain "hovering round, & giving good suggestions...." Despite his good spirits, Chamberlain made a revealing remark to Grace regarding an upcoming journey. "I suppose I shall have to go to Gettysburg in a week or so. Really do not want to go now. But by steam to Baltimore it may be not too hard a journey." He had survived another winter and another attack of his wound, but each one took its toll. Every year the number of his old comrades and friends was, as one old veteran said, "growing less on this side of the river."[33]

Pejepscot Historical Society

Joshua L. Chamberlain and Tiberius Caesar, c. 1900.

CHAPTER

26

"Looking On & Looking Back"

On Easter Sunday, 1911, though Chamberlain went out with Wyllys late in the afternoon to visit friends, he had chosen a quiet morning at home and a ramble in the fields surrounding his Portland home in favor of morning services. He wrote to Grace: "We were at home enjoying the Sunshine breaking through the mist that wrapped earth and sky at first. Nobody seemed to wish to go out to hear any other music but our birds." Their afternoon walk to a nearby brook included two four-footed friends, whom Chamberlain identified as "Tibe" and "Henry of Navarre."

That summer, with his health still precarious, Chamberlain's inclination for quiet introspection continued. When in Brunswick for Bowdoin's commencement, he reported that he received a warm greeting from the townspeople and graduates. But Chamberlain left a procession going into the First Parish Church to cross the street to his old home. He told Grace that he sat by the window, "looking on & looking back."[1]

It was well into summer before Chamberlain regained some of his usual vigor. One friend reported that he was looking better than he had for several years. But by early October, Chamberlain was seriously ill at Domhegan with what one newspaper called "acute indigestion." Grace came once again to help Lillian and Wyllys care for him. The illness proved to be relatively short but debilitating, and it prevented them from moving him from Domhegan to Brunswick for several days. A letter that Chamberlain wrote to a doctor friend later in the month reveals that he was treated with a tonic containing a mixture of strychnine and phosphorus. While it was commonly believed that such heavy metals were useful in treating indigestion, this mixture suggests that the "cure" might have turned a minor complaint into acute illness. At the end of October, Chamberlain made the trip to his Portland home, but an accidental fall in November further disabled him. It was December before he returned to his office.[2]

Before he resumed his duties at the Custom House, Chamberlain reported to Grace that on one mild December day he had "swung in the Balcony hammock for a couple of hours, after resting my spirit between the sun and the sea." And a visit from his granddaughters brightened his days. Near the end of his convalescence, Eleanor and Beatrice Allen went to Portland to visit "Gennie." Far from tiring him as Grace feared, he pronounced the girls "each lovely in her ways and words." Chamberlain declared the eldest, 18-year-old Eleanor, "a distinct and decided personality," not to be judged or treated by "general rules and conventional regulations." Sympathetic to Eleanor's frustration with anything that took her away from her studies, Chamberlain, in a rare offering of advice to Grace, suggested that Eleanor be allowed to go to a college, and one of her own choosing.[3]

Chamberlain received several heart-felt letters of advice from caring friends after his illness. Having admitted in a letter to Ira Evans that he must "avoid mistakes," in order to achieve a full recovery, Evans commented to Chamberlain: "These 'mistakes' are those of a great soul which has refused to recognize the limitations of the earthly temple in which it dwells." In less lofty prose, fellow veteran and ex-governor, Gen. Selden Connor, a miracle of survival in his own right, told Chamberlain that he thought it was about time for him to put a check on those energies that drove him to attempt to do so much. Yet friends encouraged him to continue with his writing. Thus, many days after returning from his office, the evenings were spent rewriting and dictating material for his book to the young woman, Catherine Zell, who assisted Lillian in household tasks and was secretary to Chamberlain. Young Catherine, whose spelling left something to be desired, received a dictionary from her employer that Christmas, inscribed with the words, "Remember and Go Forward."

Beyond the long sessions of dictation, Catherine also remembered family evenings when Lillian played the piano and Chamberlain, in a clear baritone, sang sentimental ballads from the Civil War. Family gatherings included spirited games of Twenty Questions or quieter evenings when Chamberlain read to the group gathered by the fire.[4]

Friends visited frequently in Portland, and one incident demonstrates that Chamberlain never lost his interest in politics and foreign affairs. During a visit from several old friends, he shared the details of a paper he was writing. It made a case that current discords in Europe would end in armed conflict. The comment of one skeptical listener, that Chamberlain was "playing at war," so exasperated him that he is said to have thrown his papers into the fire after they left. The ashes of his predictions were spread, as the household ashes always were, on the garden near the house where a profusion of flame-colored poppies grew, the flowers that became the symbol of the fast approaching First World War.[5]

Selden Connor, 1905.

In January 1912, Chamberlain unearthed a poem among his papers that he had written 47 years before, during his "feverish attempts to recover from the 'mortal wound'" he had received at Petersburg. He sent the verses to Henry Johnson, the curator of Bowdoin's art museum, in return for a poem on courage the professor had sent to him during his illness the previous year. Johnson was one of the few faculty members still at Bowdoin since Chamberlain's presidency. Pondering over what he called his "old idealized experiences," Chamberlain commented, "You will see what notions I had of what might be called courage—although I do not use the term." Adopting the voice of a cavalryman, Chamberlain called his poem, "The Trooper's Last Charge." Five of the original eleven stanzas are presented:[6]

Wrestlings of ages past
On this the crowning cast
Flames aloft across the vast
Man's measureless ideal
Imaging eternal right;
Lighting through darkest night
Charged with compelling might
Beckoning to the real.

Straight for the level flash!
Seething lead, and iron crash;
Right On! The Tempest's lash
And surge of men, too, breasting!
Archangels' trumpets ring;
Cannon hosannas sing;
This the sword Christ came to bring;—
Truth so stra[n]gely testing.

Close up! ye steadfast few!
Where the battering blast cut through
Rally! where your banner flew,—
Now drenched with strange caressing
Mortal sense is all in vain;
Deathless hearts, on you the strain
By such loss find life again;
Turning bane to blessing!

Ha! the cruel, crushing shot,
Through my life springs hissing hot:
Dark death-angel, beckon not
Until I see the glory.
High above joy or pain,
Deathless heart, ride still amain!
Body, bide the soul's disdain,
Firm-faced tho' pierced and gory.

It is done,—what was to do!
It is won,—what was the due!
Manhood's worth redeemed anew;
God's truth of siege and foray.
Clear above my swimming view
Gleams the guerdon glory:
Floats the flag with meaning true;
Starry white in heaven's blue;
Lanes of light leading thereto;
Deep-bordered red, the high way through
So runs my life's brief story![7]

Few other than Prof. Johnson ever saw these lines, written in 1864 on a bed of pain with an uncertain grasp on life. Looking at them again at 83 years of age, Chamberlain wondered at his own youthful perceptions and that hard to define quality, courage. But one friend of his offered testimony on that elusive characteristic, which he felt defined what made Chamberlain a great soldier. William Putnam recalled a conversation he once had with Gen. Charles Griffin, in which the General described young Chamberlain in battle. He remembered that "the peculiarity of Chamberlain was his absolute indifference to danger while in the field, all to such an extent that in the field his mind worked as deliberately and as quietly as it would in his own study." It is a quality that many, who bravely acknowledge their own fears, have puzzled over.[8]

General Morris Schaff, in his 1912 chronicle of the last days of the Civil War, *The Sunset of the Confederacy*, admired another of Chamberlain's qualities. Describing the surrender of the Army of Northern Virginia at Appomattox, he observed: "I believe the selection of Chamberlain to represent the Army of the Potomac was providential...that he, in the way he discharged his duty, represented the spiritually-real of this world. And by this I mean the lofty conceptions of what in human conduct, is manly and merciful, showing in daily life consideration for others, and on the battlefield, linking courage with magnanimity and sharing an honorable enemy's woes...when 'taps' shall sound for Chamberlain, I wish I could be in hearing...."[9]

During that year, one of Chamberlain's own works, "My Story of Fredericksburg," was published in *Cosmopolitan Magazine*, in that day, one of a number of literary journals that catered to the public demand for the reminiscences of the quickly vanishing veterans of the Civil War. While grounded on notes made years before, Chamberlain's prose resonates with the horror and emotion peculiar to that battle. His vivid recollections and depictions raise it beyond the scope of a simple eye-witness account. The enthusiastic reception of his article brought a demand for an article on Gettysburg. This proposition Chamberlain greeted with ambivalence in the first months of 1913, when a bout of bronchitis was followed by an attack of severe neuritis. He later quipped to Fanny Hardy Eckstorm that she probably had heard of "my practical extinction of February." With a candidness not seen in his younger years, he told her: "The pain was excruciating, and the disability attendant complete. I could do nothing but *scream*—....," to which he playfully added, "...with all my long habit of Indian stolidity at pain," teasing this recognized scholar on Maine Indians. Dr. Shaw had seen him every day, and though Grace came to be with him, the doctor insisted on providing him with attendants. Lillian, he wrote, "stood guard and kept them as much as possible 'in the outer court of the Gentiles.'" But for all his jests, during his attack of neuritis, he was unable to move his right arm. He admitted to Grace that when he tried to write to her, the resulting pain had sickened him.[10]

Forced to abandon ideas of completing any major writing for the Gettysburg article, he settled for what he called, "a condensed and 'de-natured' account." He managed to rework some of his old lectures by having Catherine Zell "watch for my 'lucid intervals'...." To his great surprise, the manuscript was accepted in mid-February, with the suggestion that an expanded version be published in book form. The acceptance of his article, however, brought little pleasure to Chamberlain, for he feared that the editors would cut out a good deal. At first, he consoled himself, telling Grace, "I dont care. I will make the '*book*' better."

Perhaps the $400 he received for his Gettysburg manuscript at this time eased other worries. Democrat Woodrow Wilson had claimed the White House that year, and whether it was benevolence or fear of a public outcry, Chamberlain was not displaced by a Democratic appointee. But when he returned to work at the Custom House at the end of the month, he knew that a reorganization of the Customs Service might eliminate his position. He reassured Grace, "I am not anxious. Prepared for anything." But within days, he again expressed anxiety over his article to Grace. He admitted that he wished it had been rejected so he could prepare it properly, and perhaps have it accepted by a more prestigious publication.

Beyond his writing and upheavals in the Customs Service, Chamberlain also admitted to Grace that his strength was strangely lessened, and that other trains of thought called for his attention. He was reading the philosophies of Henri Bergson and Rudolf Eukon, and he was looking into Boston's Emmanuel Movement and its "promise of healing power." This Boston ministry advocated a combination of basic physical and mental health with religious faith to combat the new stresses and tensions of life in the early 20th century. He told Grace he had some of his own ideas along these lines that he looked forward to discussing with her.[11]

Added to his cares that spring, Chamberlain was appointed a member of the commission to plan the celebration of the 50th anniversary of Gettysburg. He advised the commission that he was still not well, but in the style that had carried him through many years, he declared that he would be "right tomorrow." That month Chamberlain also tried to verify, by memory and his records, the claims made to Maine's adjutant general for the free passage to Gettysburg offered to veterans who fought there. Chamberlain explained the difficulties of establishing participation in the battle:

> *We had very hard marching two or three days before that battle, and during this time quite a number of men became exhausted or disabled. To such I gave permission to 'fall out' of the column of march with instructions to overtake us as soon as they were able.... Several of these men, I should say most of them did come up on the morning of July 2nd, at Gettysburg, and took their places in the ranks, and did their best, although by no means in perfect condition for duty. If they were in the battle under such circumstances, it would be a great wrong to bar them out of the privileges now offered to veterans of Gettysburg.*

Ellis Spear had been so disgusted years before at the number who claimed they had fought there, that when his granddaughter asked him about his role in the battle, Spear replied to little Mildred, "I was very much surprised to learn from your letter that you were not at the Battle of Gettysburg. So many people were there that I do not fully understand how you missed it!"[12]

In mid-May, Chamberlain traveled to Pennsylvania "under convoy" with Dr. Abner Shaw to meet with the planning commission. It was his last trip to Gettysburg. Returning home, he found a letter from *Hearst's Magazine*, which had a controlling interest in *Cosmopolitan*. A Hearst editor had taken charge of Chamberlain's manuscript and expressed the desire to shorten the article. Chamberlain sent the magnanimous reply, "I am far from being dissatisfied with any curtailments and improvements your good judgment has suggested." A letter from the artist who would illustrate the article gave Chamberlain encouragement concerning the integrity and intentions of the publisher. Anxious for advice on the battle flags carried by the 20th Maine at Gettysburg, the young artist confided that as a youngster he had read Theodore Gerrish's account of Little Round Top, "and I little thought when reading that story of the 20th Maine's fight, that I should have the honor of trying to illustrate their Colonel's story...."[13]

Chamberlain's article, "Through Blood and Fire at Gettysburg," appeared in *Hearst's Magazine* in June, just one month before the 50th anniversary of the battle. It is sufficient to say, as Chamberlain told a friend, that he felt Hearst's editors had "mutilated and 'corrected' my 'Gettysburg' so that I have not tried to get copies of their magazine in which it appears." Yet the last paragraphs of the piece bear the stamp of his thoughts and style and have become among the most admired of his words:

> *I went—it is not long ago—to stand again upon that crest whose one day's crown of fire has passed into the blazoned coronet of fame; to look again upon the rocks whereon were laid as on the altar the lives of Vincent and O'Rorke, of Weed and Hazlett—all the chief commanders. And farther on, where my own young heroes mounted to fall no more.... I sat alone, on the storied crest, till the sun went down as it did before over the misty hills, and the darkness crept up the slopes, till from all earthly sight I was buried as with those before. But oh, what radiant companionship rose around, what steadfast ranks of power, what bearing of heroic souls. Oh, the glory that beamed through those nights and days. Nobody will ever know it here!—I am sorry most of all for that. The proud young valor that rose above the mortal, and then at last was mortal after all; the chivalry of hand and heart that in other days and other lands would have sent their names ringing down in song and story!.... And so the Gettysburg hills which lifted up such splendid valor, and drank in such high heart's blood, shall hold the mighty secret in their bosom till the great day of revelation and recompense, when these heights shall flame again with transfigured light—they, too, have part in that adoption, which is the manifestation of the sons of God!*[14]

Within a month of publication, a letter from Ellis Spear entitled "The Left at Gettysburg," was published in the *National Tribune*, a well-known forum for veterans across the country. Under the heading, "The Men Themselves Started a Decisive Charge," Spear made public the belief he adopted in the years after the war. He claimed that no orders were given for the bayonet charge made by the 20th Maine at Little Round Top. Spear, who commanded the left wing of the regiment, asserted that he never received an order to go forward, but on seeing the men to his right advance, he joined the charge. Stating that the center of the 20th had also advanced without orders, he declared that "the men at the time and on the spot," were his source for this claim. These assertions of Spear's in 1913 are a puzzling contradiction to a wartime letter to the editor of a Portland newspaper attributed to Spear. The article, found pasted in the back of John Chamberlain's Gettysburg diary, beside which John wrote, "Capt. Spear's Letter," states: "...in the hottest part of the fight, when it was perhaps uncertain whether we should hold the place assigned us, the Colonel ordered a charge!" While opinions can change and memories grow dim, Spear's differences of opinion with his old commander in the coming months would sadly take on the appearances of a personal vendetta. Letters from Spear to Oliver Norton, whose book *The Attack and Defense of Little Round Top* would be published this year, and to Strong Vincent's brother, would grow more and more vitriolic, and would continue well after Chamberlain's death. The causes of the transformation from professed warm comradeship and mutual respect to bitter attacks on Chamberlain's veracity are buried with that apparently unhappy man.

The 50th anniversary of the battle was celebrated that summer of 1913. Neither Chamberlain nor Spear were well enough to travel to Gettysburg, but 63 veterans of the 20th Maine were among the 50,000 survivors of the war who met on the battlefield that July. Unable to bear the journey and the mid-summer heat of Pennsylvania, Chamberlain could do no more than go to Portland's Union Station to see his old comrades off.[15]

Chamberlain's condition was no better in the fall of 1913. Once again, he was down with the "old war way-layers" as he told a friend. In October, a letter to Wyllys indicates that Chamberlain suspected his son would soon have to make a go of it on his own. Wyllys, whose Portland battery factory closed sometime in 1911, moved to Boston in 1912, where he continued to pursue success with his electrical tinkering. He father wrote that all that was needed was to "get somebody to apply your inventions to actual use." Reassuring him that once this was accomplished, "...there is a good prospect ahead for you," he said, "You have worked hard, and bore up patiently; and deserve handsome rewards...." He observed, "Your attention has been absorbed in the inventions in which your brain is so fertile so that you have not got into the other stratum...of making money of it. That is the 'worldly way' of looking at things; but it has to [be] regarded." While offering his help, he commented on Wyllys' failed business, "...I want to help you to succeed in it. Anything but to undertake manufacturing in competition with established and commanding concerns. We tried that, with a good thing; but found it took too much money, in such times of concentrated capital as these."[16]

A visit from Grace that October cheered Chamberlain, but a letter to Sae in early November bore all the signs that he was feeling his age. A thought-provoking letter from Sae had prompted him to wish that they could get together and talk in his library at home in Brunswick. "But the 'world' is changing so fast & so much in these days, all old books are behind the times. It seems as if we were about to have a new creed of social ethics, found on 'natural law' instead of moral law,—which is now said to be the (imperfect) work of man. But all must admit that the revelation of God is still going on—in His Providence & in the minds of man." With an indecision and dependence that seems alien to his personality, shortly before Thanksgiving of 1913, he wrote to Grace: "I dont know whether we can come or not. Will ask Lillian & will look over my situation. We had been thinking that you might come here, and if not, we were going to stay quietly & thankfully as we could without you, in our little home, and take a rest." Tired and ill for months, he continued to revise his old war papers and write.[17]

Though pain from an infection of his old wound further weakened him in December, Chamberlain corresponded with the founders of a movement to place a Peace Monument at Gettysburg. Promoted as "a beacon light of Patriotism" and "the manifestation of peace and good will between the two sections" of the country, Chamberlain was asked to serve as one of two honorary presidents. He agreed. His Southern counterpart was Gen. Evander Law, the general who assumed command of the Confederate assault on the Union left at Gettysburg after the fall of Gen. Hood.[18]

Chamberlain's condition worsened during December. In the frigid days of early January 1914, it was feared that death was near. But he fought his way back in the middle of the month, easing anxieties to the point that Grace wrote an encouraging and cheerful letter to Eleanor, who was studying in Germany. "Gennie" was so improved, in fact, that Grace felt she could soon return to Boston. She confessed to Eleanor that she had grown so fat on Lillian's cooking that she was ashamed to go home to her friends, for they would surely think she had not been worried about "Gennie."[19]

As Lawrence rallied, he dictated a letter to Sae: "I am passing through deep waters! The Dr thinks I am going to land once more on this shore. I seem to be gaining deliverance from the particular disease which caused me such unspeakable agony, and gaining strength from the condition to which it reduced me." Telling Sae and her daughter that they need not come to help, he stated, "If the dear Lord has appointed me to live a little longer I am resolved it shall be of good to me and others. I am trying to get a little closer to God and to know him better." In early February, Lawrence sent word to Sae that he was still gaining, but it was "slow work. The bed and bed-side chair are still my habitual place."[20]

Dr. Abner Shaw still looked after Chamberlain, almost 50 years after that momentous day and night of Jun. 18, 1864. Grace reported: "The splendid old doctor we have had for him is the same one that sat up all night with him when all the others had given him up to die on the battlefield at Petersburg. He no doubt saved his life." But Dr. Shaw could not save him when he again began to sink in February. Grace had returned to Boston, but when he took a turn for the worse, she rushed back to Portland. The wound and pneumonia took his life just after 9:30 in the morning on Feb. 24, 1914. Grace was by his side at the end. Wyllys arrived in Portland from Boston several hours after his father's death, and could only share his sister's grief.[21]

Just before he died, Chamberlain had requested a simple funeral, in the style of the modest granite stone he had chosen to lie above him, that states: "Joshua Lawrence Chamberlain, 1828-1914." But the people of Maine were not willing to part with him on those terms. Though Grace and Wyllys honored their father's wishes as much as possible, they yielded to earnest pleas for public services to accommodate the many people who wished to pay their respects to their teacher, their governor, their college president, and their old soldier. Portland's City Hall Auditorium, then the largest facility of its kind in the state, was chosen for the first service, and a second was planned for the First Parish Church in Brunswick. Arrange-

Charles W. Plummer

Dr. Abner Shaw.

First Parish Church, Brunswick, Maine, c. 1900.

ments for the Portland service were left in the hands of Chamberlain's MOLLUS comrades. With the participation of the GAR and units of the state's military reserves, the funeral became distinctly military.[22]

At 9:00 a.m. on the morning of Feb. 27, the funeral cortege left Chamberlain's Ocean Avenue home. The horse-drawn hearse and carriages equipped with runners carried the family and honorary pallbearers through the snowy streets of the city. The procession, led by Portland's pride, Chandler's Band, slow marched to a dirge with the military honor guard. At city hall, 2,500 mourners waited outside in the cold, with an equal number waiting within. Sturdy young pallbearers carried the coffin into the crowded hall, serving for the old friends of Chamberlain who were the honorary pallbearers, including Dr. Shaw, Gen. Selden Connor and Lewis Pierce, now the last survivor of Chamberlain's Bowdoin Class of 1852. His sword was placed on the flag-draped casket. The few arrangements of flowers prompted one observer to describe the simplicity of the scene as almost severe. Chamberlain had requested that there be none of the elaborate floral displays of the time. Only the tributes of the Custom Service, the GAR, MOLLUS and one sent by Delia Chamberlain, John and Tom's widow, flanked the bier. The auditorium was dominated by the pipes of a magnificent organ, and among the selections that were played that morning was one requested by Chamberlain, *Death of Aase*. In its orchestral form, the solemn bowing of his favorite, the bass viol provided a thrilling ground for the solemn violin. After a heart-felt tribute was delivered by his friend, Portland minister Jesse Hill, the brief service came to a close. General Morris Schaff, the author of *The Sunset of the Confederacy*, was granted the wish he had so eloquently expressed in his book, and was present to hear taps played for Chamberlain. Members of the GAR and MOLLUS joined the procession as it made its way down Portland's main street, thronged with those who had come to pay their respects, moving toward the train that would take the family to Brunswick. It is said that until recently there were a few elderly residents of Portland who still remembered being there that day, and who, as small children, had wondered at seeing their grandfathers cry.[23]

The entire student body of Bowdoin met the funeral party at Brunswick's train station, and escorted them to the First Parish Church through the silent streets where all businesses had closed. The president of Bowdoin, William DeWitt Hyde, moved by the news of Chamberlain's passing, delivered an eloquent eulogy. On the board of trustees from his own presidency to his death, Chamberlain had told Hyde only months before how proud he was of the college Bowdoin had become. In the church, Chamberlain's favorite hymn, *Abide with Me* was sung, and with the solemn strains of a cello solo, Handel's *Largo*, Chamberlain's remains lay in state to allow his friends from the town and college to pay their respects. At last Lawrence was taken to Pine Grove Cemetery and laid to rest beside Fanny, to part no more.[24]

Endnotes

Abbreviations

BC	Special Collections Room, Hawthorne-Longellow Library, Bowdoin College, Brunswick, ME
CAA	Charlotte Amelia Adams
DGF	Deborah Folsom
DU	Special Collections Library, Duke University, Durham, NC
FCA	Frances Caroline Adams
GAD	George Eliashib Adams' Diaries, First Parish Church, Brunswick, ME
GDC	Grace Dupee Chamberlain
GEA	George Eliashib Adams
GNMP	Gettysburg National Military Park Library
HAD	Helen Root Adams' Diary
HWC	Harold Wyllys Chamberlain
JCC	John Calhoun Chamberlain
JCD	Transcription of John Chamberlain's Diary, Pejepscot Historical Soceity
JLC	Joshua Lawrence Chamberlain
JPN	John P. Nicholson, Gettysburg National Military Park Library
LC	Library of Congress, Washington, D.C.
MAGR	Maine Adjutant General's Report
MaHS	Ashur Adams Collection, Massachusetts Historical Society
MHS	Maine Historical Society, Portland, ME
MOLLUS	Military Order of the Loyal Legion of the United States
MSA	Maine State Archives, Augusta, ME
PHS	Pejepscot Historical Society, Brunswick, ME
RC	Chamberlain-Adams Collection, Arthur & Elizabeth Schlesinger Library, Radcliffe College, Harvard University, Cambridge, MA
SBC	Sarah Brastow Chamberlain Farrington
SDB	Sarah Dupee Brastow Chamberlain
TDC	Thomas Davee Chamberlain
UMO	Special Collections Department, Raymond H. Fogler Library, University of Maine, Orono, ME
YU	Manuscripts and Archives Library, Yale University, New Haven, Connecticut, Frost Family Papers unless otherwise indicated
WP	Writer's possession

Note: All materials in the above institutions are drawn from Chamberlain collections unless otherwise noted.

Chapter 1

1. GAD, Aug. 1850-Mar. 1851; Henry Wadsworth Longfellow, "My Lost Youth"; Annette Blaugrund, "The Evolution of American Artists' Studios, 1740-1860," *The Magazine Antiques*, January 1992: 216; George T. Edwards. *Music and Musicians of Maine* (Portland: Southworth Press, 1928) 81-86. The talented, but eccentric Prof. Crouch stayed but a few years in Portland, and was in Richmond, Virginia at the outbreak of the Civil War. Although he was in his mid- fifties, he enlisted in the First Regiment Richmond Grays and fought throughout the war.
2. To FCA, 22 Dec. [1850], RC; GAD, 1850; FCA to JLC, n.d. [Feb. 1857], RC; William B. Miller, "A New Review of the Career of Paul Aker, 1825-1861" *Colby Library Quarterly* Ser. 7, No. 5, (March, 1966) 227-255; Richard Cary, "The Misted Prism: Paul Akers and Elizabeth Akers Allen" *Colby Library Quarterly* Ser. 7, No. 5, (March, 1966) 193-198. Nathaniel Hawthorne acknowledged that he had had Aker's works, *The Pearl Diver*, and *John Milton* in mind when he described the statues created by his fictitious sculptor, Kenyon, in his novel, *The Marble Faun* .
3. FCA to JLC, n.d. [Feb. 1857], RC; Anna D. Davis to FCA, 10 Mar. 1852, MHS.
4. Andrew N. Adams, *A Genealogical History of Henry Adams of Braintree, Massachusetts and his Descendants* (Rutland, Vt.:Tuttle Co.,1898) 539, 595; Charlotte Adams to FCA, 10 Apr. 1846, PHS; Chamberlain Association, "Joshua Lawrence Chamberlain: A Sketch" 27; Eliashib Adams, *A Successful Life* (Bangor, Me.: Burr Printing Co., 1871) 5, 7, 9, 23, 30, 36-54; Ashur Adams to FCA, 3 Jun 1853, MaHS; Ashur Adams' family correspondence, 1830-60, RC.
5. Ashur Adams family correspondence, 1830-1860, RC; Ashur Adams to George W. Adams, 7 Apr. 1830, RC; Francis Wayland 23 June 1830, MaHS; Amelia [Emily] Adams to George W. Adams, 19 Feb. 1844, RC.
6. Charlotte Adams to FCA, 12 Mar. 1833, RC; Ashur Adams to FCA, 3 Jun. 1853, MaHS.
7. Louis R. Helmreich, *Our Town* (Brunswick: PHS, 1967) 26; Adams, Life 43-44, 52-53; "The Rev. George Adams" First Parish *Calendar* #1,068, 29 Dec.1929; Calvin M. Clark, *History of Bangor Seminary* (Boston: Pilgrim Press, 1916) 95-6; Louise Tallman, "Portsmouth Families" Portsmouth *Atheneum*, Portsmouth, New Hampshire
8. Anna D. Davis to FCA, 10 Mar. 1852, MHS; FCA to GEA, 29 Oct 1844, RC; Helmreich *Town* 26; Thompson E. Ashby, D.D., *History of the First Parish Church in Brunswick, Maine* (Brunswick, Me., 1969) 157; GAD, 20 Jan. 1853, and 1835-1850.
9. Ashby 271; GAD, 1839-1843.
10. GAD 1839-1843; FCA to GEA, n.d. [1830s], RC; George A. and Henry W. Wheeler, *History of Brunswick, Topsham, and Harpswell, Maine* (Boston: Alfred Mudge and Son, 1878) 479; See family correspondence 1838-1848, RC.
11. Amelia [Emily] Adams to FCA, 3 Apr. 1838, RC.
12. See family correspondence, 1840s and 1850s, RC; Amelia [Emily] Adams to FCA, 3 Apr. 1838, RC; FCA to Sarah Folsom Adams, 14 May 1842, RC; FCA to GEA, 29 Oct. 1844, RC; Amelia [Emily] & Ashur Adams to FCA, 19 Feb. 1844, RC; Charlotte Adams to FCA, 10 Sept. 1852, RC.
13. FCA to GEA, 31 Aug. 1838, RC; Ashur Adams to George W. Adams, 5 Mar. 1830, RC; See Ashur Adams family correspondence, RC; Amelia [Emily] Adams to FCA, 19 Feb. 1844, RC.
14. Wheeler 480; FCA to [Mr. Pike], 8 June 1843, RC.
15. GAD, 2 Jul. 1842, 25 Dec. 1843, 18 Jun. 1842, 2 Feb. 1844; Edwards 80; JLC to FCA, 21 May 1852, RC; GAD, 10 Oct. 1850.
16. See Family correspondence for 1830-1850, RC; FCA to GEA, 29 Oct. 1844, RC.
17. Clark 95; GAD 1839-1843; To FCA, 22 Dec. 1849, RC.
18. FCA to GEA, 29 Oct. 1844, 22 Sept. 1847, 31 Aug. 1838, RC; GAD, 1830-1850; Charlotte Adams to FCA, 21 Sep. 1845, RC.
19. Alice Rains Trulock, *In the Hands of Providence: Joshua Lawrence Chamberlain and the Civil War* (Chapel Hill:

University of No. Carolina Press, 1992) 44; Willard Wallace, *Soul of the Lion* (Gettysburg: Stan Clark Military Books, 1991 edition) 25-6; Rev. E.B. Mason "Mrs. Chamberlain's Funeral" Brunswick *Record*, Oct. 27, 1905, copy at BC; Frothingham, Richard, *A Tribute to Thomas Starr King* (Boston: Ticknor and Fields, 1865, 69. T. Starr King, a Unitarian minister and passionate advocate of the arts and poetry, lectured on the value of art to society. Neil Harris, *The Artist in American Society: the Formative Years 1790-1860* (New York: George Braziller, 1966) 306-7; JLC to FCA, n.d. [Jan. 1853], RC; FCA to JLC, n.d. [Jan. 1857], RC; Catherine Clinton, *The Other Civil War: American Women of the Nineteenth Century* (New York; Hill and Wang, 1984) 43.

20. GEA to FCA, 3 Oct. 1850, RC; GEA to FCA, 9 Jul. 1852, MHS; GAD, 1841-1855 and 24 Oct. 1841.
21. FCA to GEA, 29 Oct. 1844, RC; DGF to FCA, 17 Feb. 1853, MHS; Trulock 44; Wallace 26; See DGF to FCA correspondence, 1854, MHS; FCA to JLC, 22 Feb. 1854, and n.d. [Jan. 1857], RC; DGF to FCA, 30 Jul. 1853 and 18 Apr. [1861], RC; DGF to FCA, 22 Jun 1856, MHS.
22. To FCA, 22 Dec. 1849, RC; JLC *Early Memoirs*, BC, 69.

Chapter 2

1. Chamberlain Family Bible, Brewer Historical Society, Brewer, Maine.
2. "Address on the Incorporation of the Town of Orrington." *Bangor Historical Magazine* 1993 edition, VII-IX, 1,732; George T. Little, *Genealogical and Family History of the State of Maine* (New York: Lewis Historical Publishing Co., 1909) vol. 1, 133; JLC *Memoirs* 42-46; "Brastow Family." *Bangor Historical Magazine* 1993 edition, I, 365-367; Ronald Banks, *A History of Maine* (Dubuque: Kendall Hunt Publishing, 1876) 246-251.
3. *Historical Sketch of the First Congregational Church: Brewer, Maine*, 4; Banks 246-251.
4. JLC *Memoirs,* 41-2.
5. JLC *Memoirs* 51; *Congregational* 16, 24; "First Church Record Books," transcribed by Ethel Kenney Lord, 28 Jun. 1844, 23 Jun. 1845, First Congregational Church, Brewer, Maine; "Brastow Family." *Bangor Historical Magazine*, I, 366.
6. Lord "Record" 5-36; JLC *Memoirs* 57, 64; JLC to TDC, 4 Mar. 1861, BC.
7. JLC to Fanny Hardy Eckstorm, Apr. 26, 1909, Fanny Hardy Eckstorm Collection, UMO; Mildred Thayer and Mrs. Edward M. Ames Brewer, *Orrington, Holden, Eddington: History and Families* (Brewer, Maine, 1962) 244; JLC *Memoirs* 42-49, 53, 66; Chamberlain Association "Joshua Lawrence Chamberlain: a Sketch" 3-5; JLC to FCA, 8 Oct. 1854, RC.
8. JLC *Memoirs* 45-6, 63; "Gen. Chamberlains Speech" JLC Scrapbook, UMO; *Sketch* 3-4.
9. E. Anthony Rotundo, *American Manhood* (New York: Basic Books, 1993) 3; JLC *Memoirs* 56-7.
10. JLC *Memoirs* 41; Little 133. Two of Col. Chamberlain's ships were destroyed at his Orrington shipyard when the British came up the Penobscot River during the War of 1812. "The Star Spangled Life of Charles Jarvis Whiting" Ellsworth [Maine] *American* 14 Nov. 1974: Sect. II. 9. Major Whiting was a West Point graduate, class of 1835, who fought in the Seminole War, and served as a captain with the Second Cavalry during the Civil War. Louis Clinton Hatch, *Maine: A History* (New York: The American Historical Society, 1919) 72-79; "Representatives to the General Court of Massachusetts from Penobscot County." Bangor *Historical*, VII-IX, 1683-4. In Sept. 1814, the militia broke and ran during a skirmish with the British, downriver from Brewer in the town of Hampden. Then Major Joshua Chamberlain was one of three militia officers who were tried by court martial in Bangor. Though one of the officers was cashiered, Chamberlain was honorably acquitted. "Letter from Major Gen. Henry Sewall, of Augusta 1812." and "To Brigadier General Boyd, Commanding the Eastern Military District...." *Ibid.*, 1683-4; "The Aroostook War, and the Volunteer Troops Therein" *Ibid.*, I-III, 351-353.
11. Bangor *Historical* 133; JLC *Memoirs* 41; Sydney Ahlstrom, *A Religious History of the American People* (New Haven: Yale University Press, 1972) 1-7, 383; George M. Thomas, *Revivalism*

and Cultural Change: Christianity, Nation Building...* (Chicago: University of Chicago Press, 1989) 76-79.

12. *First Congregational*, 4, 10, 12-20, 38-9; Lord 3-4; JLC *Memoirs* 41-2.
13. Philip S. Wilder, *General Catalogue of Bowdoin College* (Portland: The Anthoensen Press, 1950) 89; *First Congregational* 16; JLC *Memoirs* 41, 57.
14. Rotundo 3.
15. Early documents, vault, Brewer Public Library, Brewer, Maine; Sketch 6-7; JLC to Sarah Shepard, 8 Feb. 1847, UMO. Sarah B. Shepard was the daughter of JLC's maternal aunt, Patty Brastow Shepard. While describing to Sarah the village in which he lived and the magnificent view of Mt. Katahdin to the north, he offered Byron's lines, "There is *too much* of *man* here, to look through, *With a fit mind the might which I behold.*"
16. JLC to Sarah Shepard, 8 Feb. 1847, UMO; JLC *Memoirs* 49-51; Ernst Christian Helmreich, *Religion at Bowdoin College: A History* (Brunswick: Bowdoin College, 1981) 1. 35-6, 99.
17. JLC *Memoirs* 50-51.
18. JLC *Memoirs* 51-52.
19. JLC *Memoirs* 52-53; Benjamin Galen Snow to JLC, 18 Mar. 1848, BC; BC 1847-48 Catalogue.
20. JLC to Nathan Dole, 5-8 May 1848, BC; JLC *Memoirs* 54-55; Benjamin Galen Snow to JLC, 18 Mar 1848, BC.
21. Benjamin Galen Snow to JLC, 18 Mar 1848, BC.
22. JLC to Nathan Dole, 5-8 May 1848, BC; Benjamin Galen Snow to JLC, 18 Mar 1848, BC; Helmreich *Religion* 52-55; JLC *Memoirs* 55.
23. JLC *Memoirs* 55-56, 60-61.
24. JLC *Memoirs* 61-63.
25. JLC *Memoirs* 61, 68.
26. JLC *Memoirs* 63-64.
27. JLC *Memoirs* 58-60, 64-65.
28. JLC *Memoirs* 65-66.
29. Helmreich *Religion* 114; Amelia [Emily] Adams to FCA, 19 Feb. 1844, RC. In 1844, Ashur Adams and family moved from Jamaica Plain to Roxbury, a town that became part of Boston proper as the city grew. CAA to FCA, Thanksgiving, 1847, BC; Mary O. Dunning to FCA, August 1848, RC.
30. GAD May 1850-March 1851; GAD 8, 14, and 16 Aug. and 11 Oct. 11, 1850; "Mrs. Chamberlain's Funeral," Brunswick *Record* 27 Oct. 1905; Smith "Soldier" 1.
31. JLC *Memoirs* 67-69.
32. *Ibid.*, 69.

Chapter 3

1. JLC to FCA, 21 May 1852, RC; JLC to FCA, 26 Jan. 1857, RC; "Mrs. Chamberlain's Funeral" Brunswick *Record* 2 Oct. 1905; Samuel S. Gardner to JLC, 1 Jan. 1856, RC; JLC to FCA, 14 Apr. 1853, RC; JLC to FCA, 17 May 1852, RC.
2. JLC to FCA, n.d. [mid-1852], MHS. Just after their engagement, Lawrence suggested that by the time they were married, "What'll you bet I shant be as old as you are, then? So you wont fuss about that any more."
3. JLC to FCA, n.d. [1851], RC.
4. *Ibid*; See JLC/FCA correspondence, 1851-1852, RC; FCA to JLC, 14 Jun. 1851, 23 Jun. 1853, RC; JLC to FCA, n.d. [summer 1853], RC; Stephen Allen to FCA, Jan. 9, 1852, RC.
5. FCA to JLC, 14 Jun. 1851, RC; JLC/FCA correspondence 1851-1852, RC; JLC to FCA, May 28, [1852], MHS; FCA to JLC, Feb. 22, 1854, RC; JLC to FCA, 17 May 1852, RC.
6. JLC *Memoirs* 69, 73; FCA to JLC, nd [late 1851] RC; JLC to FCA, 30 Dec. 1851, RC; JLC to FCA, Friday 22 Aug. 1852, RC.
7. GAD, 22 Jun. 1851-30 Dec. 1851, 7 Oct. 1965.
8. JLC to FCA, n.d. [1851], RC]; JLC to FCA, 30 Dec. 1851, RC.
9. JLC to FCA, 30 Dec. 1851, RC.
10. Stephen Allen to FCA, Jan. 9, 1852, RC; *The New-England Historical and Genealogical Register*(Boston: New England Historic Genealogical Society, 1894, XLVIII) 472-473. Stephen Allen [1819-1894], at seventeen, left his childhood home in Maine to establish himself in business in Boston and Roxbury while he attended school at night. Once successful in business, he attended Harvard Law School, receiving his LL.B. in 1846. Allen built the hydraulic canal at Niagara Falls and also invented one of the first methods of manufacturing paper from wool-fiber. In 1851, he was a member of the Massachusetts Legislature.

11. *Ibid.*
12. GAD, Dec. 31, 1851, Feb. 13 and 23, Mar. 23, 1852; DGF to FCA, 20 April [1853], RC; JLC to FCA, June 7th 1852, MHS.
13. JLC to FCA, 21 May 1852, RC.
14. Ahlstrom 390-399; Daniel W. Howe, *The Unitarian Conscience* (Cambridge: Harvard University Press, 1970) 6-7, 67; William G. McLouglin, Jr., *Modern Revivalism* (New York: The Ronald Press Company, 1959) 4, 30-31.
15. Howe 185-204; Ahlstrom 598-599; Neil Harris, *The Artist in American Society: the Formative Years 1790-1860* (New York: George Braziller, 1966) 175, 181; Barbara Novak, *American Painting of the 19th Century* (New York: Praeger Publishers, 1969) 62.
16. Novak *American* 22-23; Howe 90-96, 185-204; Ahlstrom 598-606; JLC to FCA n.d. [Jan. 1853 and 1853], RC; FCA to JLC, 22 Feb. 1854, RC; Barbara Novak, *Nineteenth -Century American Painting* (New York: Artabras, Abbeville Press, 1986); Novak *American* 97; The portrait artist, Jeremiah P. Hardy, with whom FCA studied in the early 1840s, is identified with the school of painting known as luminism, most associatied with the Transcendentalists. George S. Wardle to author, Nov. 18, 1996, WP. The First Congregational Church of Jamaica Plain, Ashur's Adams residence until 1844, was Congregational in name only and was in fact a member of the Unitarian fellowships. JLC to FCA n.d. [Jan. 1853] RC; JLC to FCA, 3 Jun. 1853, RC.
17. Helmreich *Religion* 90, 99; Ahlstrom 598; JLC to FCA, n.d., [1852 or 1853], RC. Ahlstrom, though pointing out the ambiguity of the term Transcendentalist, defined it as one who seeks, "the Good, the True, the Beautiful, the Divine," a description closely by echoed by Lawrence's description of Fanny's beliefs. JLC to Nathan Dole, 5-8 May 1848, BC; FCA to JLC, 14 Jun. 1851, RC; See JLC/FCA correspondence, 1851-1855, RC.
18. GAD 18 Apr. 1852; *Who's Who in America*, (1897-1942:I) 454; JLC to FCA, 16 May 1852, RC.
19. JLC to FCA, 17 May 1852, RC.
20. Trulock 43-4, 46-7, 51, 86, 420 n. 61; Wallace 25-27, 226-228; Michael Golay, *To Gettysburg and Beyond. The Parallel Lives of Joshua Lawrence Chamberlain and Edward Porter Alexander* (New York: Crown Publishers, 1994) 54, 311.

Chapter 4

1. JLC to FCA, 17 May 1852, RC; JLC to FCA, 28 May [1852], MHS; JLC to FCA, 7 Jun.1852, MHS; JLC to FCA, 20 May 1853, RC.
2. DGF to FCA, n.d. [Spring, 1852, RC]; GEA to FCA, n.d. [Summer, 1852], RC.
3. Helen Root Adams to JLC, Thanksgiving 1862, RC; GAD 1852.
4. JLC to FCA, 7 Jun.1852, MHS; Ashur Adams and family moved from Jamaica Plain to Roxbury in 1844.
5. JLC to FCA, 7 Jun.1852, MHS.
6. Anna Davis to FCA, 10 Mar. 1852, MHS.
7. JLC to FCA, 21 and 28 May 1852, RC.
8. GEA to FCA 9 July [1852], MHS; [JLC to FCA] fragment, n.d. [Jun. 1853], RC; DGF to FCA, 12 Jan. 1854, MHS.
9. GAD, 12 and 22 July 1852; JLC to FCA, n.d. [summer, 1852], RC; JLC to SDB, 6 Aug. 1852, UMO; DGF to FCA, n.d. [Spring, 1852], RC; GEA to FCA 9 July [1852], MHS.
10. JLC *Memoirs* 71.
11. GAD 29 Aug. 1852; JLC *Memoirs* 71.
12. JLC to FCA, 8 Oct. 1854, RC; CAA to FCA, 10 Sept. 1852, RC.
13. CAA to FCA, 10 Sept. 1852, RC; GAD 13 Oct. 1852; DGF to FCA, 9 Nov.1852, RC; DGF to FCA, 30 July 1853, RC; JLC to FCA, n.d. [Nov. 1852], RC; GAD, 25 Nov. 1852; GAD 11 and 18 Nov.,17 Dec. 1852.
14. JLC to FCA, 31 Oct. 1852, RC; JLC to FCA, 9 Nov. 1852, RC.
15. Abby Adams Edgarton Orme to FCA, 9 Dec. 1852, RC; "Milledgeville Female Academy" *Southern Recorder* 26 Oct. 1852; Anna Maria Green Cook, *History of Baldwin County Georgia* (Anderson, S.C.: Keys-Hearn Printing Co., 1925) 70, 425; James Bonner, *Journal of a Milledgeville Girl: 1861- 1867* (Athens, Ga.: Univ. of Georgia Press, 1964) 86; James Bonner, *Milledgeville: Georgia's Antebellum Capital*(Athens: Univ. of Georgia Press, 1978) 42, 93, 156, 182, 190-191; "John Orme" Macon *Telegraph* 2 Apr. 1912; Muster Roll of the Baldwin Blues, Co. H, 4th Reg. Geor-

gia Volunteers, 170. Abby Adams [1797-1869] was the daughter of Dr. John Adams, principal of Phillips Academy of Andover Massachusetts, and she was the former principal of the Midway Female Academy near Milledgeville. In 1842, the widowed Mrs. Abby Adams Edgarton married Richard McAlister Orme, a well-to-do land and slave owner, who was editor of the Milledgeville's newspaper, *Southern Recorder* . She is best remembered in Milledgeville for hiding her son-in-law, a Confederate officer, in the attic of her home while it was occupied by Capt. Henry Ward Beecher of Massachusetts, nephew of the New York divine, when 30,000 Union soldiers occupied Milledgeville during Sherman's March through Georgia. Though Mr. Orme's *Southern Recorder* did not support secession before the war, two of the Orme sons, Henry and John, served in the CSA. The Orme's home at 251 South Liberty Street, is still considered one of Milledgeville's most beautiful homes. The Presbyterian Church where FCA played the organ and lead the choir was founded by those families considered to be Milledgeville's elite in culture and learning, many of whom were originally from New England. GAD, 22 Dec. 1852; JLC to FCA, 22 Dec. 1852, Collection of Paul Loane.

16. Abby A. Orme to FCA, 9 Dec. 1852, RC; GAD 22 and 27 Dec. 1852.
17. GAD 27 Dec. 1852; Amelia Adams to FCA, Feb. 18, [1853] MaHS; FCA to CAA, 10 Jan. 1853, MHS.
18. Abby A. Orme to FCA, 9 Dec. 1852, RC; FCA to CAA, 10 Jan. 1853, MHS; Henry Chase and Charles Sanborn, *The North and the South; a Statistical View of the Condition of the Free and Slave States* (Boston: Jewett and Company, 1856) 15, 16, 103, 104; FCA to JLC, 1 and 6 April 1853, RC.
19. JLC to FCA, 6 Mar. 1853, RC.
20. *Ibid*; JLC/FCA correspondence, 1853-mid-1855, RC; Mary S. Hartman and Lois Banner, *Clio's Consciousness Raised: New Perspectives on the History of Women* (New York: Harper Torchbooks, 1974) 121-2; FCA to JLC, 1 and 6 April 1853, RC.
21. FCA to JLC, 1 and 6 April 1853, RC.
22. *Ibid.*
23. *Ibid.*
24. JLC to FCA, 20 May 1853, RC.
25. Fragment, JLC to [FCA] n.d. [late spring 1853], RC.
26. JLC/FCA correspondence, 1853-mid-1855, RC.

Chapter 5

1. JLC to FCA, n.d. [mid-October, 1852], RC. In this letter, written when Fanny was suffering with chilblains, Lawrence mischievously commented that "two or <u>three</u> things beginning with <u>ch</u> plague you, don't they?" The other two difficulties that he was likely referring to here were their opposing views on the church and children. FCA to JLC, 22 Feb. 1854, RC; GAD, 1840-1871.
2. Anna Davis to FCA, 10 Mar. 1852, MHS; JLC to FCA, Mar. 27, 1855, RC; Helmreich *Religion* 53; JLC to FCA, n.d. [mid-October, 1852] RC; JLC/FCA, June 1853-1855, RC. Herman Melville's *Typee*, published in 1846, shocked the American public with its graphic descriptions of native life on an island in the South Seas. It relates one tale of native awe for a missionary's wife turning to scorn when, overcome with curiousity, they upended the mysterious, bell-shaped person only to discover she had legs like everyone else.
3. JLC/FCA correspondence, 1853-1855, RC; JLC to FCA, 14 Apr. 1853, RC.
4. JLC to FCA, 14 and 20 Apr. 1853, RC.
5. JLC to FCA, n.d. [summer 1852], RC; JLC to FCA, n.d. [mid-summer, 1852] MHS; JLC to FCA, n.d. [summer 1852], RC.
6. JLC to FCA, n.d. [summer 1852], RC; JLC to FCA, n.d. [Jan. 1853],RC.
7. JLC to FCA, n.d. [late summer, 1852], MHS; JLC to FCA, 3 Jun. 1853, RC; JLC to FCA, 11 Apr. and 28 Sept. 1854, RC. In September 1854, Lawrence would remind Fanny "how much you were going to learn & do before the 'puddings' & 'two rooms.'" For information on mid-19th century contraception, see Linda Gordon, *Woman's Body, Woman's Right: A Social History of Birth Control in America* (New York: Grossman Publishers, 1976) 60-71.
8. Hartman 54-58; Susan Conrad, *Perish the Thought: Intellectual Women in*

Romantic America, 1830-1860 (New Jersey, Oxford University Press, 1976) 78. Hartman [22] presents evidence of increasing interest in or awareness of family limitation in the 19th century, and statistics of the average number of children born to white women surviving to menopause. The average declined from 7.04 in 1800 to 6.14 in 1840, to 4.24 in 1880, and finally to 3.56 in 1900.

9. Ellen K. Rothman, *Hand and Hearts: A History of Courtship in America* (New York: Basic Books, 1984) 132-133; JLC to FCA, n.d. [Jan. 1853],RC.
10. Rothman 132-133; Irene Sege "Love Letters" The Boston *Globe* 14 Feb. 1994: 34, 37; Hank Burns "Wanted: Heros for the 1990s" Portland *Press Herald* 28 Feb. 1994; FCA to JLC, nd [late 1851] RC; JLC to FCA, n.d. [summer 1852], RC; FCA to JLC, 22 Feb. 1854, RC; JLC to FCA, n.d. "evening edition" [late summer, 1852], MHS.
11. JLC/FCA correspondence, 1853-1855, RC; JLC to FCA, n.d. [Spring 1852] MHS; JLC to FCA, n.d. [Jan. 1853],RC; JLC to FCA, n.d. [Feb. 1853], RC.
12. Jane Thomas Bloomsbury, *Guides to English Literature: Victorian Literature, from 1830-1900* (London: Bloomsbury: 1994); 140-141; JLC to FCA, n.d. [Jan. 1853],RC. One of the most common books of this sort is a large volume by Matthew Hale Smith, *Sunshine and Shadow in New York* (District of Connecticut: J.B. Burr, 1869).
13. JLC to FCA, n.d. [mid-October, 1852], RC; JLC to FCA, 11 Jun. 1853, RC; JLC to FCA, 6 Mar. 1853, RC.
14. JLC/FCA correspondence, 1853-1855, RC; *Sketch* 8; JLC to FCA 20 May 1853, RC; JLC to FCA, 27 Apr. 1854, RC; JLC to FCA 3 Jun. 1853, RC; CAA to FCA, "Commencement day" 1851, RC. Fanny had apparently wanted a dog since childhood, and Lawrence agreed she should have one, though he showed a rather decided lack of enthusiasm by perversely teasing that she should also have a cage in the middle of the room to keep him in!
15. JLC to FCA 3 Jun. 1853, RC; FCA to JLC, 23 Jun. 1853, RC.
16. JLC to FCA 3 Jun. 1853, RC; JLC to FCA, fragment n.d., [Jun. 1853], RC.
17. JLC to FCA, fragment n.d., [Jun. 1853], RC. JLC also stated his intention to find a teaching position by the fall of 1854 in his letter of 3 Jun. 1853 [RC], but he added the comment, "... We don't know what is in store for us, it is best to be prepared for every thing."
18. FCA to JLC, 23 Jun. 1853, RC.
19. *Ibid*; JLC to FCA, n.d. [summer 1853], RC.
20. JLC to FCA, n.d. [summer 1853], RC.
21. JLC/FCA correspondence, 1853-1855; JLC to FCA, 14 Apr. 1853, RC; JLC to FCA, 11 Jun. 1853.
22. FCA to JLC, 23 Jun. 1853, RC; JLC to FCA, 1 Jul. 1853, RC; JLC Diary, Jun. 4, 1853- Sept. 8, 1853, BC; Chamberlain Family Bible, Brewer Historical Society, Brewer, Maine. The uncle JLC refers to is Jefferson Chamberlain, his father's younger brother. "Annie" is Jefferson's 21 year old daughter, Hannah B. Chamberlain. Their residence, at 12 Bower in Bangor, is a short walk from the Bangor Theological Seminary.
23. JLC to FCA, 1 Jul. 1853, RC.
24. *Ibid.*
25. Calvin Clark, *History of Bangor Theological Seminary* (Boston: Pilgrim Press, 1916) 131; JLC to FCA, 14 Mar [1854]; RC; JLC to FCA 6 Apr. 1855, RC; JLC *Memoirs* 41.
26. Clark 127-129, 174, 386-7; JLC *Memoirs* 71-72.
27. JLC Diary, Jun. 4, 1853- Sept. 8, 1853, BC; JLC to FCA, Jun. 1853, RC.
28. JLC to FCA, fragment, n.d. [June 1853], RC; Ashur Adams to FCA, 3 Jun. 1853, MaHS; Amelia [Emily] Adams to FCA, 26 Dec. 1853, MaHS; DGF to FCA, 17 Feb. 1853, MHS; DGF to FCA, 20 Apr. 1853, RC; DGF to FCA, 30 Jul. 1853, RC.
29. DGF to FCA, 30 Jul, 1853, RC; DGF to FCA, 30 Jul. 1853, RC; DGF to FCA, 17 Feb. 1853, MHS; DGF to FCA, 30 Jul. 1853, RC.
30. GAD 6 Feb. 1854. Rev. George Adams' sister, Eliza Adams Crosby, wife of James C. Crosby of Bangor, apparently paid Deborah Folsom for her share of the Brunswick house, at which time the house was deeded to Eliza. GAD, Jan.-Mar. 1853; DGF to FCA, 4 Mar. 1854, MHS; GAD 1853; GAD 13 and 24, 1853.

Chapter 6

1. Abby A. Orme to FCA, 9 Dec. 1852, RC; DGF to FCA, 12 Jan. 1854, MHS; Mrs. J. L. Beeson, *Historical Sketch of the First Presbyterian Church of Milledgeville, Georgia* (privately published, 1953); DGF to FCA, [27 or 29] Mar. [1854], MHS; Bonner *Journal* 43; Bonner *Milledgeville* 157; Lillian Henderson, *Roster of the Confederate Soldiers of Georgia: 1861-1865* vol. VI, 488; *Memoirs of Georgia* (Atlanta: Southern Historical Association, 1895: II) 242. Dr. Samuel Gore White [1824-1877] would not only support Georgia's secession, but was considered a "fire-eater." In 1861, he accepted a commission as surgeon in Cobb's Legion of Georgia Cavalry, and he also served with the 64th Georgia in 1863. Though he survived the war, it is said that his health was broken. Dr. White's residence on Jefferson St., a half block north of the Statehouse Square, was razed in 1958 and the site is occupied by the Georgia Power Company building. FCA to JLC, 22 Feb. 1854, RC; Ashur Adams to FCA, Feb. 8, 1855, MaHS. JLC informed Ashur Adams that more than half of his letters to FCA had "miscarried."
2. DGF to FCA, 12 Jan. 1854, MHS.
3. FCA to JLC, 22 Feb. 1854, RC.
4. *Ibid*; JLC to FCA, n.d. [1853], RC; JLC/FCA correspondence, 1852-1855, RC. JLC often referred to FCA as his little bird, girl, or child. JLC to FCA, 10 Mar. 1854, RC; JLC to FCA, Mar. 14 [1854] RC.
5. FCA to JLC, 22 Feb. 1854, RC.
6. *Ibid.*
7. *Ibid.*
8. *Ibid*; JLC to FCA, 10 Mar. 1854, RC.
9. JLC to FCA, 14 Mar. [1854], RC.
10. *Ibid*; JLC to FCA [fragment] n.d. [Jun. 1853], RC.
11. JLC to FCA, 10 Mar. 1854, RC.
12. DGF to FCA, [27 or 29] Mar. 1854, MHS.
13. JLC to FCA, 11 Apr. 1854, RC.
14. *Ibid.*
15. JLC to FCA, 27 Apr. 1854, RC; Charles Funk, *Heavens to Betsy and Other Curious Sayings* (New York: Harper and Rowe, 1986) 154-5. "'Working for a dead horse' is reported to be an English phrase that dates back to the 17th century, meaning performance of work for which payment has already been made."
16. Ashur Adams to FCA, 5 Jun. 1854, MaHS; JLC to FCA, 30 May 1854, RC.
17. *Ibid.*
18. Catherine Adams Lombard to FCA, 26 Jun. 1854, MaHS; GEA to FCA, 12 Jul. 1854, MaHS.
19. DGF to FCA, 30 Jul. 1853, RC; DGF to FCA, [27 or 29] Mar. 1854, MHS; DGF to FCA, 7 July 1854, MHS; DGF to FCA, 23 Dec. 1854, MHS.
20. JLC to FCA, 30 Jul. 1854, RC.
21. *Ibid.*
22. *Ibid.*
23. Ashur Adams to FCA, 10 Aug. 1854, MaHS.
24. JLC to FCA, 8 Oct. 1854, RC; JLC to FCA, 28 Sept. 1854, RC; Bonner *Milledgeville* 24, 41; Beeson 48; Henderson II: 307, 1040. The home of Dr. Augustus Parke Williams, at the corner of Liberty and Washington Streets, was the site where Milledgeville companies were presented with their battle flags before leaving for the war. Augustus Williams, and his brothers, Charles and William Williams, all served in the Confederate army. JLC to FCA, 28 Sept. 1854, RC.
25. JLC to FCA, 28 Sept. 1854, RC.
26. GAD 21 Jan. and 6 Sept., 1854; DGF to FCA, 7 July 1854, MHS; Ashur Adams to FCA, 5 Jun. 1854, MaHS. There are four American towns with the name of Galena, one in Kansas, Illinois, Maryland and Alaska, though it seems safe to rule out the last.
27. JLC to FCA, 8 Oct. 1854, RC; JLC to FCA, n.d. [17 Oct. 1854], RC.
28. *Ibid.*
29. *Ibid;* JLC *Memoirs* 72.
30. Ashur Adams to JLC, 14 Oct. 1854, RC; JLC to FCA, n.d. [17 Oct. 1854], RC.
31. FCA to JLC, n.d. first page, second page dated 27 Oct. [1854], RC; JLC to FCA, 31 Oct. 1854, RC.
32. JLC to FCA, 31 Oct. 1854, RC.
33. *Ibid;* JLC to FCA, "Warrantee Deed" 3 Nov. 1854, LC.
34. JLC to FCA, "Warrantee Deed" 3 Nov. 1854, LC.
35. JLC to FCA, 6 Mar. 1853, RC; JLC to FCA, 1 Jul. 1853, RC; JLC to FCA, n.d. [1853], RC; JLC to Hannah "Annie" Chamberlain, 10 Nov. 1854, RC.
36. *Ibid.*

37. Hannah "Annie" Chamberlain to JLC, 14 Nov. 1854, RC; *Lasell Female Seminary, at Auburndale, Massachusetts, 1854-5* (Boston: Bazin and Chandler, 1855); Donald J. Winslow Lasell: *A History of the First Junior College for Women* (Boston: Nimrod Press, 1987) ix. Lasell Female Seminary became the present day Lasell Junior College in Newton, Massachusetts.
38. Hannah "Annie" Chamberlain to JLC, n.d. [winter 1854-1855], RC.
39. JLC to FCA, 30 July 1854, RC; Hannah "Annie" Chamberlain to JLC, 14 Nov. 1854, RC.
40. JLC/FCA correspondence, 1853-1855; JLC to Hannah "Annie" Chamberlain, 10 Nov. 1854, RC.
41. DGF to FCA, 23 Dec. 1854, MHS; "Book of Ruth" 1:16.

Chapter 7

1. Ashur Adams to JLC, 8 Feb. 1855, MaHS; FCA to JLC, 12 Aug. 1855, RC; JLC to FCA 19 Jun. 1855, Paul Loane Collection.
2. DGF to FCA, 23 Dec. [1854], MHS; DGF to FCA, 19 Feb. 1855, MHS.
3. Ashur Adams to FCA, 8 Feb. 1855, MaHS.
4. Hannah "Annie" Chamberlain to JLC, n.d. [late 1855], RC; Hannah "Annie" Chamberlain to JLC, 27 Mar. 1855, RC; JLC to Martha Chamberlain, 5 Sept. 1855, RC. Martha Chamberlain was Jefferson and Ann Chamberlain's second daughter and Annie Chamberlain's younger sister. JLC to FCA, 27 Mar. 1855, RC.
5. JLC to FCA, 28 Sept. 1854, RC; JLC *Memoirs* 72.
6. Hannah "Annie" Chamberlain to JLC, 5 Apr. 1855, RC.
7. JLC to FCA, 6 Apr. 1855, RC; JLC to Manly Hardy, 25 Dec. 1909, First Congregational Church of Brewer, Maine. It is said that the Whiting Hill settlement where Lawrence and two of his friends ran a Sunday school, was home to a disreputable element, including prostitutes and the mistresses of local gentry and their progeny.
8. JLC to FCA 6 Apr. 1855, RC.
9. *Ibid.*
10. JLC to FCA, 19 Jun. 1855, Paul Loane's Collection; Lord 29. "Satin poets" are the poets of the 18th century.
11. *Ibid.*
12. GAD, 30 July 1855; FCA to JLC, 12 Aug. 1855, RC; JLC to FCA, 6 Apr. 1855, RC.
13. JLC *Memoirs* 72-73; FCA to JLC, 12 Aug. 1855, RC.
14. GAD 11 Aug. 1855; FCA to JLC, 12 Aug. 1855, RC; GAD, see October 1854, and 4 Apr. and 18 May, 1855.
15. FCA to JLC, 12 Aug. 1855, RC.
16. *Ibid.* Leonard Woods was Bowdoin's president from 1839 until 1866. Egbert Smyth was Bowdoin's professor of Rhetoric and Oratory.
17. JLC to Manly Hardy, 25 Dec. 1909, First Congregational Church of Brewer, Maine; 10th, 11th and 12th Annual Reports, Brewer Annual Reports: 1844-1874, Brewer City Hall, Brewer, Maine.
18. GAD 19, 22 and 23 Aug. 1855; GEA to JLC, n.d. [late summer, 1855], BC; Helmreich *Religion* 92.
19. GEA to JLC, n.d. [late summer, 1855], BC.
20. Wilder 98; JLC to Martha Chamberlain, 5 Sept. 1855, RC.
21. JLC *Memoirs* 73; GAD 28 Aug., 12 and 13 Sept, 1855; FCA to JLC, 20 Sept. 1855, RC.
22. DGF to FCA, 15 [Sept. 1855], MHS; FCA to JLC, 20 Sept. 1855, RC; FCA to JLC, 31 Jan. 1857, RC; Louis C. Hatch, *The History of Bowdoin College* (Portland, Maine: Loring, Short and Harmon, 1927) 214. FCA had previously notified JLC of a position that paid a starting salary of $1,500 a year. In comparison, by 1860, after having held a full professorship for three years at Bowdoin, JLC's salary was $1,100.
23. FCA to JLC 20 Sept. 1855, RC.
24. *Ibid*; Ashur Adams to FCA, 12 July 1854, MaHS. Harold Wyllys was FCA's birth mother's brother, who resided in Greenville, S. C. in the summer and Kingstree, S.C. in the winter. Ashur Adams described him as an eccentric but worthy gentleman. Until his extended visit with the Boston Adams in 1854 and 1855, the family had not heard from him since he went south 40 years before.
25. *Ibid.*
26. JLC to FCA, 21 Sept. 1855, RC.
27. *Ibid*; FCA to JLC, 2 Oct. 1855, RC.
28. SDC and SBC to JLC, 5 Oct. 1855, RC; Horace Chamberlain to JLC, 7 July 1858, RC; SDC to JCC, 5 Oct. 1855, RC.

29. GAD, 17 Oct. and 13 Nov. 1855; Hannah "Annie" Chamberlain to JLC, 24 Oct. 1855, RC.
30. DGF to FCA, 30 and 31 Oct. 1855, MHS; GAD 6, 7, 11 and 13 Nov. 1855.
31. DGF to FCA 3 Dec. 1855, MHS; GAD 6 Dec. 1855.
32. Sabbath students to JLC, 19 Nov. 1855, BC; *Catalogue of the Officers and Students of Bowdoin College...* (Brunswick: Joseph Griffin, Spring Term, 1856) 7.
33. GAD 22-29 Nov. 1855.
34. GAD 29 Nov.-7 Dec. 1855.
35. JLC to FCA, 1 Feb. 1856 [misdated, should be 1857], RC; Hannah "Annie" Chamberlain to JLC, 8 Dec. 1855, RC. A sad footnote to FCA and JLC's wedding day is a letter sent by Annie Chamberlain, in which she pleaded with him to come and see her once more before he married. It was written the day after their wedding.

Chapter 8

1. JLC to FCA, 1 Feb. 1856 [misdated, should be 1857], RC.
2. GAD 8 and 15 Dec. 1855; GEA to JLC, 14 Jan. 1856, RC; Samuel Springer Gardner to JLC, 1 Jan. 1856, RC; JLC to FCA, n.d. [Dec. 1852], RC.
3. GAD 23 Jan., 1 Feb. and 8 Mar. 1856.
4. JLC to Nehemiah Cleaveland, 14, Oct. 1859, BC; Edward Cutter to JLC, 18 Feb. 1856, RC; Hatch, *Bowdoin* 107. In 1856, Chamberlain reported that he had examined 1,100 themes. He also defended his theory that, in order to encourage and stimulate his students, it was warranted to avoid severe criticism of student efforts.
5. GAD 31 May- 4 Jun. 1856; DGF to FCA, 22 Jun. [1856], MHS; GAD 12 Sept. 1856; DGF to FCA, 21 Oct. 1856, MHS.
6. GAD 5 Aug. 56; Hannah "Annie" Chamberlain/JLC, see correspondence 1856, and 5 July, 1856, RC; *Historical Catalogue of Bangor Theological Seminary* (Bangor: Bangor Theological Seminary, 1964) 52. Peaselee Badger Chamberlain of Barre, Vermont was not a relative, though there seem to be distant ties between the Maine and Vermont Chamberlains. Though a number of Chamberlain family letters spell his name Peasley, references to his activities and movements consistently affirm that it is one and the same man.
7. To FCA, 17 Sept. [1856], RC.
8. Gordon 24; DGF to FCA, 21 Oct. 1856, MHS; GAD 26 Sept.-16 Oct. 1856; JLC *Memoirs* 73-74.
9. SDB to JLC and FCA, 21 Oct. 1856, RC.
10. *Ibid.*; SDB and SBC to JLC and JCC, 5 Oct. 1855, RC; JLC *Memoirs* 41.
11. GAD 25 Nov. 1856; DGF to FCA, 21 Oct. 1856, MHS; GAD 19 Nov. 1856.
12. GAD 28 Nov.-30 Dec. 1856.
13. FCA to JLC, n.d. [31 Jan. 1857] RC; Hannah "Annie" Chamberlain, 24 Jan. 1857, RC; GAD 24 Jan. 1857; Little 133; Chamberlain Family Bible, Brewer Historical Society, Brewer, Maine; Horace Chamberlain to JLC, 9 May 1858, RC.
14. JLC to FCA, 26 Jan. 1857, RC.
15. *Ibid.*; GAD Feb. 1857.
16. FCA to JLC, n.d. 31 Jan. 1857, RC; FCA to JLC, n.d. [Feb. 1857], RC.
17. JLC to FCA, 31 Jan. 1857, RC; FCA to JLC, n.d. [Feb. 1857], RC.
18. JLC to FCA, 1 Feb. 1856 [misdated, should be 1857], RC.
19. FCA to JLC, 5 Feb. 1857, RC.
20. JLC to FCA 8 Feb. 1857, RC.
21. FCA to JLC, n.d. [10 Feb. 1857], RC.
21. *Ibid.*
22. *Ibid.*
23. *Ibid*; Hannah "Annie" Chamberlain to JLC, 24 Jan. and 6 Mar. 1857, RC; Hannah "Annie" Chamberlain to FCA, "middle of May," [1857] RC.
24. JLC to FCA, 25 Feb. 1857, RC; JLC to FCA, n.d. [1851], RC.
25. FCA to JLC, 6 Mar. 1857, RC; JLC to FCA, 30 Mar. and 25 Feb. 1857, RC; FCA to JLC, 31 Jan. 1857, RC.
26. GAD 4 May 1857; Gordon 99, 109.
27. Ashur Adams to JLC, 8 May 1857, RC; GAD 11 May 1857; FCA to JLC, May and 17 May, 1857, RC; GAD 14 Oct. 1859; JLC to FCA, 26 Jan. 1857, RC.
28. FCA to JLC, May and 17 May 1857, RC.
29. JLC to FCA, 20 May 1857, MHS; GAD 27 May 1857; FCA to JLC, May 1857, RC.
30. JCC to Horace or TDC, 17 July 1857, BC; Little, 133; JCC to JLC, 18 Aug. [1857], RC; Horace Chamberlain to JCC, 14 Oct. 1857, RC; SDB and SBC to JLC, 5 Oct. 1855, RC; John M'Clintock, *Cyclopedia of Biblical, Theological, and Ecclesiastical Literature* (New York: Harper and Bros., 1891, X) 231.

31. GAD 19 Aug., and 1 Sept.-22 Sept., 1857; GAD 2 Nov. 1857.
32. HAD 5 Nov. 1857; GAD and HAD 19 Nov. 1857.
33. HAD 25 Nov. 1857; GAD 24 and 25 Nov. 1857; HAD and GAD 9 Dec. 1857.
34. Harriet Beecher Stowe, *Uncle Tom's Cabin* (New York: Penguin, Signet Classic Edition, 1981) 100-101.

Chapter 9

1. HAD 16 Jan. 1858; Horace Chamberlain to JLC, 30 Apr. 1858, UMO.
2. GAD Feb.-Apr. 1858; JLC to Horace Chamberlain, 30 Apr. 1858, UMO; GAD 2 May 1858.
3. JLC to Horace Chamberlain, 30 Apr. 1858, UMO; SBC to JLC, 7 Jul. 1858, RC; SBC to JLC, n.d. [August 1858], RC; GAD 15 Jul. 1858; JLC *Memoirs* 74-75.
4. Hatch *Bowdoin* 50, 92-92.
5. JLC to Nehemiah Cleaveland, 14 Oct. 1859, RC; Hatch *Bowdoin* 106.
6. Charles Calhoun, *A Small College in Maine* (Brunswick: Bowdoin College, 1993) 93-94; Hatch *Bowdoin* 103, 112-115; JLC *Memoirs* 74; JLC to Nehemiah Cleaveland, 14 Oct. 1859, RC.
7. *Ibid.*; Horace to JLC, 7 Jul. 1858, RC.
8. Horace to JLC, 9 May, 7 July, and August, 1858, RC; JCC and Horace Chamberlain to JLC, 8 Dec. 1858, RC; Chamberlain family Bible, Brewer Historical Society, Brewer, Maine; Mary Wheeler to JLC, 27 Mar. [1862], RC.
9. Horace to JLC, 9 May 1858, RC; JCC to JLC, 13 Aug. 1858, RC; SBC to JLC, 4 Sept. 1858, RC; Horace to JLC, 23 Jul. 1859, RC; SDB and SBC to JLC, 5 Oct. 1855, RC; Joshua Chamberlain, Jr. to JLC, 1 Sept. [1859], RC; SDB to JLC, n.d. [summer 1859], RC; SBC to TDC, 14 Apr. 1860, BC.
10. Joshua Chamberlain, Jr. to JLC 13 Feb. 1859, RC; GAD 25 Nov. 1858; Ashur Adams to JLC, 28 Jul. and 8 Nov., 1858, RC; Vital Records, Record of Deaths for the town of Jamaica Plain, Boston Public Library. Mary Webb Adams, age 53 years, died at 3 Bussy Place, Charlestown, on July 15, 1858 of consumption. DGF TO FCA, 21 Jun. 1859, RC; Joshua Chamberlain, Jr. to JLC, 3 Jan. 1858 [misdated, should be 1859], MHS; GAD 6, 17 and 25 Jan. 1859.
11. GAD 17 Jan. 1859; JLC to FCA, 25 Jan. 1859, RC; FCA to JLC, n.d. [late January 1859,], RC; JLC *Memoirs* 75.
12. FCA to JLC, n.d. [late January, 1859], RC; JLC *Memoirs* 74.
13. JLC to FCA, n.d. [late January, 1859], RC; JLC to FCA, 2 Feb. 1859, RC.
14. SBC and Horace Chamberlain to JLC and JCC, 14 Feb. 1859, RC; Joshua Chamberlain, Jr. to JLC, 13 Feb. 1859, RC; SBC to JLC, 6 May 1859 RC.
15. JLC *Memoirs* 75; GAD 22 Apr. 1859; SBC and Horace Chamberlain to JLC and JCC, 14 Feb. 1859, RC.
16. JLC *Memoirs* 75; Wheeler 715-716; GAD 26 Apr, 2 May, and 6 Jun. 1859.
17. SBC to JLC, 6 May 1859, RC; SDB to JLC, n.d. [summer 1859], RC; SBC to JLC, 6 May 1859, RC; GAD, 2 Aug. 1859.
18. DGF to FCA, 21 Jun. 1859, RC; Joshua Chamberlain, Jr. to JCC, 19 July 1859, BC; Chamberlain Family Bible, Brewer Historical Society, Brewer, Maine. Horace married Mary Wheeler on 11 May 1859. Horace to JLC, 23 July 1959, RC.
19. Samuel Gardner to JLC, 15 Sept. 1859, RC; SBC to JLC, 1 Sept. 1859, RC; Joshua Chamberlain, Jr. to JLC, 1 Sept. 1859, RC; SDB, Joshua Chamberlain, Jr. and JCC to JLC, 5 Dec. 1859, RC; JLC to JCC, 7 Nov. 1860, BC; JLC to Francis O. J. Smith, 1 Sept. 1859, BC.
20. SDB, Joshua Chamberlain, Jr. and JCC to JLC, 5 Dec. 1859, RC.
21. GAD 24 and 29 Sept., 3-30 Oct. 1859.
22. GAD 10-23 Dec.,1859; JLC to SDB, 31 Jan. 1860, BC; HAD 14 Jan. 1860.
23. JLC to SDB, 31 Jan. 1860, BC.
24. HAD 14, 27 and 29 Jan. 1860; GAD 17, 24 and 27 Jan., 9-18 Feb. 1860; DGF to GEA, 16 Jan. and 18 Feb. 1860, RC.
25. HAD Jan.-June 1860; GAD Jan.-June 1860; Dr. Frederick Hollick, *The Diseases of Woman* (New York: T. W. Strong, 1853) 40-42, 50, 53-54; Hartman 4; Judith Leavitt, *Brought to Bed: Childbearing in America, 1750-1950* (New York: Oxford University Press, 1986) 29-30; Gordon 68.
26. JLC to SBC, 30 Apr. 1860, BC.
27. SBC to JLC, 5 Jun. 1860, RC; SBC to TDC, 14 Apr. 1860, BC; JLC *Memoirs* 53.
28. SBC to JLC, 5 Jun. 1860, RC; Hannah "Annie" Chamberlain to JLC, 18 Jun. 1860, RC.

29. GAD 16-20 Jun. 1860; HAD 21 Jun. 1860; GAD 6 Nov. 1860; Ashur Adams to FCA, 8 Feb. 1855, MaHs.
30. GAD 23 and 26 Sept. 1860; JLC *Memoirs* 75; GAD 29 Nov. 1860.
31. Joshua Chamberlain, Jr. to JLC, 1 Oct. 1860, RC; SBC to JLC, 30 Dec. 1860, RC.
32. JLC to JCC, n.d. [early 1861], BC; JLC *Memoirs* 75; Horace Chamberlain to JLC, 9 May 1858, RC; JLC to SBC, 4 Feb. 1862, BC.

Chapter 10

1. Kennebec *Journal* 18 Jan. 1867, 2. During JLC's campaign for reelection as Maine Republican governor, this Augusta, Maine newspaper printed that JLC had been "brought up to the faith of the Democratic party by a father who still has the perversity to hold it...." Joshua Chamberlain, Jr. to Marcellus Emery, receipt for subscription to The Democrat from Aug. 1857-Aug. 1861, Box 9, folder 8, BC; R. H. Stanley and George O. Hall, *Eastern Maine and the Rebellion* (Bangor: R. H. Stanley and Co., 1887) 83- 98. In August of 1861, a mob of Bangor Unionists, enraged by the attacks of the editor of *The Democratic* on the government, destroyed his press. John Francis Sprague, "Hon. Thomas Davee" *Collections and Proceedings of the Maine Historical Society* (Portland: MHS, 1897, VIII) 331-336; "The Honorable Thomas Davee of Dover and Blanchard, Maine" *The Bangor Historical Magazine* (Camden: Picton Press, 1993, 7-9) 2120-21-22; Wallace 18-19, 317[fn22]; Hatch *Maine* 204-5, 209, 211-212, 213, 314; Irving H. Bartlett, *John C. Calhoun: A Biography* (New York: W. W. Norton and Co., 1993) 139-152.
2. Roger F. Duncan, *Coastal Maine: A Maritime History* (New York: W. W. Norton and Co., 1992) 257-277; Hatch *Maine* 72-73, 193-194, 204-205, 209, 211-213, 226, 314; Little 133; Bartlett 191-216, 231-238.
3. James M. McPerson, *Battle Cry of Freedom: The Civil War Era* (New York: Ballantine Books, 1988) 32-33; Hatch *Maine* 72-79; James H. Mundy, *Hard Times, Hard Men* (Scarborough, Maine: Harp Publications, 1990) 142, 167-168; Receipt for subscription to *The Democrat* from Aug. 1857-Aug. 1 1861, Box 9, folder 8, BC; Joshua Chamberlain, Jr. to JLC, n.d. [Fall 1862], RC; Hatch *Maine* 398-401, 533 fn.
4. GAD 1840s, 3 Nov. 1856, 6 Nov. 1860, 24 Oct. 1841, 20 Nov. 1861, 1861-65; Duncan 327-344; GAD 3 Sept. 1861. Rev. Adams visited Boston and noted in his diary that Captain Skolfield of the Brunswick ship, *Lydia Skolfield* had taken two nine-pounders aboard, as well as other arms as a defense against "pirates," as the captain referred to the Confederate raiders.
5. GAD 13 and 17 Jan. 1861; JLC to TDC, 4 Mar. 1861, BC.
6. SBC to JLC, 11 Mar. 1861, RC.
7. GAD 13 Apr. 1861; JLC to FCA, 22 Apr. 1861, RC.
8. SBC to JLC 28 Apr. 1861, RC.
9. DGF to FCA, 18 Apr. and 10 July 1861, RC.
10. GAD 8 May 1861; Hatch *Bowdoin* 117-119; John Minot, *Tales of Bowdoin* (Augusta, Maine: Press of Kennebec Journal, 1901) 261-272; Calhoun 170.
11. GAD 7 Aug. 1861; JLC to SBC, n.d. [August 1861], UMO.
12. GAD 19 Aug., 15 Sept., 5 Oct. 1861; HAD 5, 9 and 22 Oct. 1861; GAD and HAD, winter 1861-1862.
13. FCA to JLC, 2 and 6 Dec. 1861, RC; Little 133.
14. JLC to SBC, 4 Feb. 1862, BC; FCA to CAA, 10 Jan. 1853, MHS; HAD 3 Feb. 1862.
15. HAD 5, 18, and 22 Feb., 20 Mar. 1862; JLC to FCA, 3 Nov. 1862, LC.
16. JLC to SBC, 4 Feb. 1862, BC.
17. SBC to JLC, 23 Mar. 1862, RC; HAD 26 May 1862; Trulock 8-9, 76, 400 [fn13]; JLC *Memoirs* ; Golay 63; Catherine T. Smith "Brunswick's 'soldier statesman'" Brunswick *Times-Record* 7 Sept. 1976, 1 and 9. The 1976 interview with 86-year-old Catherine Smith, secretary to JLC from 1910-1914, is one evidence offered for FCA's disapproval of JLC's military service. Smith was not employed by the family until well after FCA's death, and her observations are based on her recollections and interpretations of her conversations with JLC. She stated, "She [FCA] was proud to be a professor's wife. But, he recalled, she hated his military and the short period of service

as governor of Maine." Untitled clipping, JLC scrapbook, n.d. [33rd anniversary of the 20th Maine's mustering in, 2 Sept. 1895], BC; JLC to Gen. Thomas T. Munford, 25 Oct. 1905, Munford-Ellis Papers, DU; JLC/FCA, wartime correspondence, RC and LC; Joshua Chamberlain, Jr. to JLC, n.d. [fall, 1862], RC; JLC *Memoirs*, 76.

18. A[mericus] Fuller to Charles H. Howard, 15 Jun. 1862, Oliver Howard Papers, BC; JLC to Gov. Israel Washburn, Jr., 14 July 1862, MSA; Jeff Hollingsworth, *Magnificent Mainers* (North Attleborough, Ma.: Covered Bridge Press,1995) 209-223. Israel Washburn was the oldest of seven remarkable brothers, three of whom served in the House of Representatives at the same time, representing Maine, Wisconsin and Illinois. Cadwallader Washburn also served in the war, achieving the rank of major general of volunteers. Elihu, who added a final "e" to the end of the family name, began his law career in Galena, Illinois. A close friend of both U. S. Grant and Abraham Lincoln, he would serve as President Grant's minister to France during the Franco-Prussian War. Three of the Washburn brothers were involved with the founding of the companies that would become Remington Typewriter, General Mills and Pillsbury Flour.
19. JLC to Gov. Israel Washburn, Jr., 17 and 22 July 1862, MSA; "War Meeting at Brunswick" Portland *Daily Advertiser* 22 July 1862.
20. *Ibid.*
21. Portland *Daily Advertiser* 21 and 22 July 1862; [Bangor] *Daily Whig and Courier* 22 and 23 July 1862; JLC to Gov. Israel Washburn, 22 July 1862, MSA.
22. TDC to JLC, 21 July 1862, RC.
23. Josiah Drummond to Gov. Israel Washburn, 21 July 1862, MSA; JLC *Memoirs* 76-77.
24. GAD 1 Aug. 1862; Gov. Israel Washburn to Edwin. M. Stanton, Secretary of War, 27 Sept. 27, 1863, William Henry Noble Papers, DU; Gov. Israel Washburn to JLC, 8 Aug. 1862, LC; JLC *Memoirs* 76; JLC to Gov. Israel Washburn, 8 Aug. 1862, MSA.
25. "Notes of my little speeches..." Box 5, BC; GAD and Family correspondence, 1860-1861, RC and BC; JLC to SBC, 3 Feb. 1862, BC; JLC to Nehemiah Cleaveland, 14 Oct. 1859, BC.
26. Index to the Greenville County, South Carolina General Sessions, Spring 1860, case #2322,408; See endnotes Ch. 6.

Chapter 11

1. HAD, 18-22, Aug. 1862; JLC to FCA, 24 July 1863, Don Troiani Collection.
2. John Pullen, *The Twentieth Maine: A Volunteer Regiment* (Dayton, Ohio: Morningside House, Inc., 1991) 1-3, 36; Blanche Butler Ames, *Chronicles from the Nineteenth Century: Family Letters of Blanche Butler and Adelbert Ames* (Privately published, 1957) 1.
3. Portland *Advertiser*, 1 Sept. 1862; John Furbish, *Facts About Brunswick, Maine* (Brunswick: Pejepscot Historical Society, facsimile edition) 9; Portland *Press*, JLC General Orders Book, PHS; William Livermore Diary, 5 Oct. 1863, Fogler Library Special Collections, University of Maine, Orono, Me. Livermore reported that JLC's beautiful gray mare had cost the people of Brunswick $900.
4. GAD, 1 Sept. 1862; [Portland]*Eastern Argus* , 3 Sept. 3, 1862.
5. MAGR 1864-1865, 82, 337; Sidenote to "History of Claimaint's Disability," TDC's Pension Record, NA; Joshua Chamberlain, Jr. to JLC, n.d. [Fall 1862], RC.
6. *Ibid.*; TDC to JLC, 21 July 1862, RC; Pullen 34; Ellis Spear to Gen. J. L. Hodsdon, 9 Mar. 1866, BC.
7. JLC to FCA, 17 Sept. 1862, Collection of Don Troiani. A number of the Chamberlains' letters have been withheld thus far from researchers by the developers of the Harrisburg Civil War Museum, while others have been sold to private collections.
8. JLC to FCA, 21 Sept 1862, The Pearce Civil War Documents Collection, Navarro College, Corsicana, Texas; Hyde, Thomas W. *Following the Greek Cross* (Boston, Houghton, Mifflin and Company, 1894); Wilder, 113-4, 117, 99-105. Thomas Worcester Hyde [BC 1861], a major at 21 years of age, was in command of the 7th Maine when the

regiment was ordered to make a suicidal charge by his drunken brigade commander at Antietam. Harlan Page Brown [BC 1860] was killed and William Lewis Haskell [BC 1860] died within a month. Haskell & Brown were both classmates of the 20th Maine's adjutant, "Mr. [John Marshall] Brown" [BC 1860]; Spear *Recollections* 12-13, 295; JLC to Gen. John Hodsdon, 15 Nov. 1865, and "Horses Shot Under Me" JLC Order Books PHS; Trulock 383; Wm. Livermore Diary, 20 Sept. 1862, UMO. Private Livermore remarked, that the "shells from our batteries would go so near our heads it seemed as though it would take the hair off from my head and some of our own burst overhead and wounded some of our own men."

9. JLC to Gen. John Hodsdon and "Army Correspondence," 23 Oct. 1862, 15 Nov. 1865, JLC Letterbook, PHS; Spear 12-13; JLC to FCA, 21 Sept. 1862, The Pearce Civil War Documents Collection, Navarro College, Corsicana, Texas.
10. JLC to FCA, 10 Oct. 1862, LC.
11. JLC to FCA, 26 Oct. 1862, LC.
12. *Ibid.*
13. Pullen 36; Holman Melcher to Nathaniel Melcher, 23 Oct. 1862 & 28 July, 1863, BC; Adelbert Ames to JLC, 18 Oct. 1864, LC; Ellis Spear, *The Civil War Recollections of General Ellis Spear* (Orono: University of Maine Press, 1997) 7, 10-11; Theodore Gerrish, *Army Life: A Private's Reminiscences of the Civil War* (Portland: Hoyt, Fogg and Dunham, 1882) 122; "Army Correspondence," 23 Oct. 1862, JLC Order Book, PHS; John Chamberlain Diary Transcription, PHS, 4; Powell, Wm. H. *The Fifth Army Corps* (New York: G.P. Putnam Sons, 1896) 301.
14. Pullen 37-39; Spear *Recollections* 14-15; TDC to JCC, 2 Feb. 1863, UMO.
15. JLC to FCA, 3 Nov. 1862, LC.
16. *Ibid.*; Wilder 113. John Marshall Brown [1838-1907] was a graduate of Bowdoin, class of 1860.
17. JLC to FCA, 3 Nov. 1862, LC.
18. *Ibid.*
19. JLC to FCA, 4 Nov. 1862, LC.
20. *Ibid.*
21. *Ibid.*
22. Wallace 24-27, 226-8; Golay 54; Trulock 86, 420 [fn61]. Wallace, who incorrectly proclaimed FCA an orphan, considered her, based upon her adoptive father's letters, spoiled, and prone to be moody & depressed if she did not get her way. Trulock made the case that FCA's alleged depression was a chronic disability, citing, as did Golay, evidence of FCA's "penchant for travel" as a "depressive reaction to life situations." It is a puzzling observation, apparently referring to FCA's two visits with her Boston family, each of about 3 weeks duration, in the six years of the Chamberlain's married life before the war. Trulock also cited the opinion of the Chamberlain's granddaughter, Rosamond Allen, born in 1898, who knew FCA only as a blind & feeble elderly woman. Trulock and Ms. Allen shared the view that a wartime photograph of FCA, showing what they felt was a sad expression, offered evidence of her state of mind.
23. FCA to JLC, 27 Nov. 1862, RC.
24. James McPherson, *Battle Cry of Freedom* (New York: Ballantine Books, 1989) 569-570; JLC "My Story of Fredericksburg," *Cosmopolitan Magazine* (January 1913) 150; JLC to FCA, 2 Dec. 1862, Collection of Don Troiani.
25. JLC to FCA, 2 Dec. 1862, Collection of Don Troiani.
26. *Ibid.*
27. Pullen 43.
28. GAD 11-16 Dec. 1862; JLC Order Book, PHS, 3. For JLC's accounts of his experiences of the battle, see "My Story of Fredericksburg." *Cosmopolitan Magazine* (January 1913): 148-159, and "The Last Night at Fredericksburg." *Camp-Fire Sketches* (Springfield, Ma.: King, Richardson and Company, 1889).
29. Noah Brooks, *Washington, D.C. in Lincoln's Time* (Athens: University of Georgia Press, 1989) 47; McPherson *Battle* 584; Gerrish 63-64.
30. Spear *Recollections* 199; GAD 10-13 Feb. 1863; HAD 15.
31. HAD 17 Feb. 1863; GAD 22 Feb. 1863; 20th Maine Consolidated Morning Reports, 23 Feb. 1863, MSA; Brooks 15-20.
32. Ellis Spear to Susie Spear, 15 Mar. 1863, MSA.
33. E. B. French to Conrad, 9 Apr. 1863, PHS; William Livermore Diary, April 1863, UMO; Robert E. Denney, *Civil War Medicine* (New York: Sterling Publishing, 1994) 7; Pullen, 76.

34. Spear *Recollections* 28; JLC to FCA 24 Apr. 1863, LC.
35. JLC *Memoirs* 75; JLC to FCA 24 Apr. 1863, LC.
36. *Ibid.*; Ames *Chronicles* 19 [fn1]. For a brief account of JLC and the 20th Maine during the Battle of Chancellorsville, see JLC Letterbook, PHS 44.
37. Katie [Catherine Adams Lombard] to JLC, 1 Jun. 1863, RC; FCA to DGF, 16 July 1863, WP.
38. SBC to TDC, 26 May 1863, RC.
39. FCA to DGF 16 July 1863, WP; Katie [Catherine Adams Lombard] to JLC, 29 Apr. 1863, RC; JLC to FCA 3 Nov. 1862, LC.
40. DGF to FCA, 3 Jun. 1863, RC.
41. Spear *Recollections* 29; JLC to DGF, 15 Jun. 1863, LC.
42. FCA to DGF 16 July 1863, WP; TDC to JCC, 2 Feb. 1863, UMO; JCC to JLC, 6 Mar. 1863, RC: For John Chamberlain's experiences in June & July, 1863, see JCD.
43. JLC to FCA, 4 July 1863, LC; For an examination of JLC and the 20th Maine's roles at Gettysburg, see Thomas Desjardin, *Stand Firm Ye Boys From Maine* (Gettysburg: Thomas Publications, 1995).
44. FCA to DGF 16 July 1863, WP. Daisy's "shaker" is likely a Shaker bonnet.
45. W. Johnson Quinn Collection, Hotel Card File, New York Historical Society, N.Y.C.; Adrian Cook, *The Armies of the Streets* (Lexington: University Press of Kentucky, 1974) 69-70, 91, 101, 103-104, 116-117, 143, 155, 162-163; *Mitchell's New General Atlas* (Philadelphia: J. Augustus Mitchell, Jr.,1865) 19.
46. JLC to FCA, 17 July, 1863, LC.
47. *Ibid.*; William C. Oates, *The War Between the Union and the Confederacy and Its Lost Opportunities* (New York: Neale Publishing Co., 1905) 771-772. For an account of JLC's encounter with Lt. Robert Wicker of the 15th Alabama, see JLC, "Through Blood and Fire at Gettysburg." *Hearst's Magazine,* June 1863, copy at BC, Box 5, folder 8; Bateman, L. C. "At Home with Gen. Joshua L. Chamberlain in Old Longfellow House, Brunswick." *Lewiston Journal Illustrated Magazine* (Aug. 1907). Second Lieutenant Robert Wicker remained a prisoner for the rest of the war. Wicker's pistol was one of JLC's most treasured relics of the war, and is now at the Maine State Museum in Augusta, Maine.
48. JLC to FCA, 17 July, 1863, LC; FCA to DGF 16 July 1863, WP.

Chapter 12

1. Spear 219-220; Homan Melcher to Nathaniel Melcher, 28 July 1863, BC; JLC Order Book, PHS, 44; JLC to FCA, 24 July 1863, Don Troiani Collection.
2. Spear *Recollections* 44-45, 220, 320-321; JLC to Lt. Jno. M. Clark, 30 July 1863, NA; JLC Medical Records, NA; GAD 30 July and 6 Aug. 1863. An indication that JLC's condition was physical exhaustion and an undefined illness can be found in the case of Winfield Scott Hancock, whose health broke down during the U.S. Army's arduous expedition against the Mormons in Utah prior to the Civil War. He also received the diagnosis "nervous prostration." Myra Hancock, *Reminiscences of Winfield Scott Hancock* (New York: Charles L. Webster and Co., 1887) 41; JLC Medical Record, 4 Aug. 1863, D.C. Reg. #526 Hos. # 2250, 83, NA. To further confuse the issue of JLC's diagnosis in August 1863, a page of JLC's medical record apparently surfaced at the National Archives in 1997 that had not been included in his records prior to that time. It states that JLC was diagnosed in Washington as suffering from "Endo Carditis" on August 4, 1863. It seems evident that this alarming diagnosis, by definition a dangerous inflammation of the heart valves or the membrane lining the heart, was incorrect.
3. HAD 12 Aug. 1863; affidavit of John D. Lincoln, M.D., 17 Aug. 1863, PHS; JLC Order Book, PHS, 39; James Rice to JLC 16 Aug. 1863, LC; JLC to the Maine Adjutant General and Gov. Abner Colburn, 25 Aug. 1863, MSA; JLC Service Record, NA.
4. Pullen 155-157; JLC to FCA, 31 Aug. 1863, LC.
5. *Ibid.*
6. Gen. James Barnes to JLC, 1 Sept. 1863, MSA; Gen. James Rice to Maine Adjutant General and Hon. Wm. Pitt Fessenden, 8 Sept. 1863, MSA; Copy

of Gen. Charles Griffin to Gen. S. Williams, 7 Oct. 1863, Wm. Henry Noble Collection; DU; Charles Gilmore to Gov. Abner Coburn, 8 Oct. 1863, MSA. A.A. Genl. C.B. Merriam sent a copy of Griffin's letter to JLC, "as the enclosed is the first endorsement of the kind General Griffin has ever made, I cannot resist sending you a copy 'sub rosa.'" Griffin's recommendation was also endorsed by Gen. George Sykes and Gen. George Meade, and Gen. O. O. Howard is reported to have sent his recommendation with Griffin's to the War Department. JLC to SDB 26 Oct. 1864, RC.

7. JLC "Address of Gen. Chamberlain" *Eastern Argus* 25 Apr. 1866; JLC "Blood" 37.
8. JLC to FCA, 12 Sept. 1863, LC.
9. *Ibid.*
10. The Index Project, 1 Oct. 1863, File numbers 11980, 11987, 111378; Spear *Recollections* 226-229; Surgeon's certificate, JLC to Lt. Col. Locke, 15 and 16 Nov. 1863, JLC Medical Records, NA; JLC Order Book 39.
11. DGF to JLC, 25 Oct. 1863, RC; Lt. William E. Donnell to FCA, 16 Nov. 1863, LC.
12. DGF to JLC, 25 Oct. 1863, RC; Jack Walsh, M.D., *Medical Histories of Union Generals* (Kent, Ohio: Kent State Press, 1996) 63; GAD 24 and 28 Nov. 1863; Medical Certificate, 28 Nov. 1863, JLC Medical Records, NA.
13. DGF to JLC, 25 Oct. 1863, RC; Wilder 17.
14. GAD 19 Dec.1863, 14 Jan. and 11 Feb. 1864; Medical Certificate, 28 Nov. 1863, JLC Medical Records; The Index Project, 1 Feb. 1864, case # 11303, 11372; JLC to DGF, 12 Mar. 1864, Noble Papers, DU. Grant was appointed Gen. in Chief on March 12, 1864, the same day that JLC wrote to Cousin Deborah of his impatience to return to the army.
15. FCA to DGF, 14 Apr. 1864, MHS; JLC "Blood" 36; JLC "Notes" BC.
16. FCA to JLC, 8 Mar. 1866, RC. One of the plays JLC and FCA saw in Washington was "Shylock" with Edwin Booth in the title role. JLC and FCA to DGF, 12 Mar. 1864, Noble Papers, DU; JLC to DGF, 14 Apr. 1864, MHS; JLC to Col. E. D. Townsend, 25 Apr. 1864, DU; FCA to DGF, n.d. [early May, 1864], MHS.
17. JLC to FCA, 7 May 1864, YU; JLC to Col. E.D. Townsend, 9 May 1864, NA; JLC Service Record, NA; Brooks 137-138.
18. Pullen 174; JLC Military Personal File, NA; JLC "The Charge at Fort Hell" William Henry Noble Collection, Special Collections, Duke University, 1.
19. JLC "Ft. Hell" 1-3, 8.
20. *Ibid.*, 9-12.
21. *Ibid* 12-13; JLC to FCA, 19 Jun. 1864, BC.
22. JLC "Ft. Hell" 14-16.
23. JLC "Ft. Hell" 16-17; Wilder 107; See Chamberlain correspondence, Mary Clark to JLC, RC & MHS.
24. SBC to JLC, 23 Jun. 1864, RC.
25. *Ibid.*; GAD 28 Jun. 1864.
26. Holman Melcher to [Chamberlain family], n.d. [summer 1864], RC.
27. JLC "Fort Hell" 17; Mary Clark to JLC, 11 July 1865, RC; JLC to Gov. Samuel Cony, 31 Aug. 1864, MSA.
28. A copy of George Files' report can be found in JLC Medical File, PHS.
29. *Ibid.*
30. JLC Medical Records, NA; JLC to SDB, 26 Oct. 1864, RC.
31. MAGR 1864-1865 323; SBC to JLC 26 Oct. 1864, RC, "Billings Brastow" JCD, PHS.
32. JLC Order Book 40, 46; GAD 29 Oct. 1864; JLC to SBC, n.d. [14 Dec. 1864], BC; TDC to SBC, 13 Dec. 1864, BC; JLC to JCC, 19 Dec. 1864, BC.
33. SDB to JLC, 1 Jan. 1865, RC.
34. Frances Jones to JLC, 15 Jan. 1865, RC; JLC Order Book, PHS, 41 and 46; GAD 16 and 20 Jan. 1865.
35. GAD Jan.-Feb. 1865; JLC to Joshua Chamberlain, Jr., 20 Feb. 1865, BC.
36. *Ibid.*; Doctor's statement, box 7, folder 10, BC; For an examination of the alienation soldiers experience on returning from war, see Gerald F. Linderman, *Embattled Courage* (New York: Collier Macmillan Publishers, 1987) 216-239.
37. JLC to Joshua Chamberlain, Jr., 20 Feb. 1865, BC.
38. JLC Order Book 41; GAD 21 Feb. 1865; JLC to SBC, 9 Mar. 1865, BC; Howard A. Kelly, *Dictionary of American Medical Biography* (Boston: Milford House, 1928) 934-937. It is not known whether Dr. Joseph Pancoast, a surgeon renowned for his innovative

techniques, or his talented son Dr. William Henry Pancoast, who served as Surgeon in Chief at the Sixth and Master Streets Military Hospital in Philadelphia, operated on JLC.

39. JLC to SBC, 9 Mar. 1865, BC.
40. JLC, *Passing of the Armies* (New York: Bantam, 1993) 35-40, 42-44; George Carleton to Farwell, 8 Jan. 1866, Collection 226, Box 1, YU; JLC to SBC, 9 Mar. 1865, BC.
41. JLC to FCA 19 Apr. 1865, PHS; GAD 3 Apr. and 8 Nov. 1865; Mrs. A. Lord to FCA, 17 May 1865, RC.
42. JLC *Passing* 178; For an account of JLC's role in the Army of the Potomac's last campaign, see JLC *Passing* 27-207.
43. R. H. Stanley & George O. Hall, *Eastern Maine and the Rebellion* (Bangor: R. H. Stanley & Co., 1887), 199; GAD 10 Apr. 1865.

Chapter 13

1. JLC *Passing* 186-187.
2. *Ibid.* 187-188.
3. *Ibid.* 194-196.
4. JLC to SBC, 13 Apr. 1865, BC.
5. *Ibid.;* JLC *Passing* 200-203. JLC wrote that when he approached Gen. Henry Wise, a former governor of Virginia, with the sentiment that "brave men may become good friends," he replied, "You're mistaken, sir....You may forgive us but we won't be forgiven. There is a rancor in our hearts which you little dream of. We hate you, sir." The discovery that JLC was the commander of the troops he faced at Quaker Road did little to sweeten his temper. Oates *War* 372, 376, 432. William Oates, who lost at arm at Petersburg, went on to command the 48th Alabama. Though he was on sick leave at the time of the Army of Northern Virginia's surrender, he cites information from the veterans that the 15th Alabama laid down 170 muskets at Appomattox.
6. JLC to FCA, 19 Apr. 1865, PHS.
7. JLC *Passing* 210-217; Holman Melcher to Nathaniel Melcher, 21 Apr. 1865, BC. Melcher wrote that there were a number in the Fifth Corps who wanted to burn the nearby town of Farmville in retaliation for a suspected conspiracy.
8. JLC Order Book, PHS, 46; JLC *Passing* 217-221.
9. *Ibid.*, 222-224.
10. *Ibid.* 225-229.
11. *Ibid.* 230-231.
12. *Ibid.* 236-239.
13. SBC to TDC, 7 May 1865, RC.
14. GAD 17-22 May 1865; Sheridan *Memoirs II* 208-228. Testimony of Meade's displeasure with Gen. Griffin can also be found in a letter from C. H. Morgan to Gen. G. K. Warren, 14 Mar. 1868, Warren Collection, New York State Library, Albany, New York.
15. JLC *Passing* 243-245; GAD 22 May 1865.
16. JLC *Passing* 248-250; GAD 23 May 1865.
17. Pullen 287-288; GAD 25 May 1865.
18. GAD Jan.-April, 22 and 26 May 1865.
19. JLC to SBC, 6 Jun. 1865, BC.
20. *Ibid.*
21. Mrs. A. Lord to FCA, 17 May 1865, RC; JLC to FCA, 19 Apr. 1865, PHS; Mary Clark to JLC, n.d. [late spring, 1865], RC; Jane "Jenny" Abbott to JLC, n.d. [Jan. 1865], RC.
22. JLC to Gen. Morris Schaff, n.d. [1905], YU; JLC to Charlton E. Lewis, 26 Jun. 1865, Charlton Lewis collection #981, YU.
23. JLC to Gen. L. Thomas, 6 July 1865, William Henry Noble Papers, DU.
24. Sheridan *Memoirs II* 214-217; TDC to SBC, 9 July 1865, BC; JLC Order Book, PHS, 45.
25. JCC to JLC, 12 July 1865, RC.
26. JLC Order Book, PHS, 46; JLC to Alexander Webb, 18 May 1893, Alexander Webb collection #684, YU; Stewart Sifakis, *Who Was Who in the Union* (New York: Facts on File, 1988) 136.
27. SBC to JLC, 30 July 1865, RC; "Commencement at Bowdoin" JLC Order Book, PHS; JLC to U.S. Grant, 31 July 1865, JLC Order Book, PHS, 36; Mary Bacon to FCA, August, 1865, RC.
28. "Commencement at Bowdoin" JLC Order Book, PHS.
29. *Ibid.*
30. "Commencement"; Hatch *Bowdoin* 116-117; GAD 2-3 Aug. 1865; Furbish 29.
31. "The Fifth Army Corps" JLC Order Book, PHS; Mary Clark, n.d. [summer, 1865], RC; Jane "Jenny" Abbott to JLC, 17 Aug. 1865, RC; GAD 15-17 Aug., 1 and 4 Sept., 1865; Maine Congressmen to Secretary of War, 20 Dec. 1865, LC; SBC to JLC, 1 Nov. 1865, RC.

32. GAD 18-22 Oct., 19 Dec. 1865; *Biographical Register of the Officers and Graduates of the U.S. Military Academy* (Boston: Houghton, Mifflin, Co., 1891). While Griffin awaited orders for a permanent assignment, he was given command of the District of Maine, with headquarters in Portland. JLC *Passing* 85, 93; to JLC, 15 Dec. 1865, LC; W. Terrell to JLC, Apr. 1868, LC; JLC to Hodsdon, 14 Nov. 1865, MSA.
33. A. Bedford to JLC, 15 Nov. 1865, collection of Dr. A. A. Warlam, copy at PHS; Eleanor Wyllys Allen to Pres. Howell, 21 Feb. 1978, BC; JLC to FCA, 12 Sept. 1863, LC.
34. Maine Congressmen to Secretary of War, 20 Dec. 1865, LC; A copy of George Files' research materials can be found in JLC Medical File, PHS.

Chapter 14

1. GAD December, 1865, January, 1866; FCA to JLC, 8 and 19 Mar. 1866, RC; SDB to JLC, 1 Jan. 1866, RC; *Who's Who in New England 1909* (Chicago: A. N. Marquis and Co.) 199.
2. SDB to JLC, 1 Jan. 1866, RC.
3. JLC "Loyalty" Box 5, folder 4, BC.
4. McPherson, *Ordeal By Fire* (New York: Alfred a. Knopf, 1982) 497-514; JLC "Loyalty."
5. JLC "Loyalty."
6. *Ibid.*
7. *Ibid.*
8. JLC to FCA, n.d. [7 Mar. 1866], MHS; SBC to JLC 18 Mar. 1866, RC; FCA to JLC, 8 Mar. 1866, RC; Smith *Sunshine* 281-282; William Smith, *A Smaller Classical Dictionary* (New York: Harper and Bors., 1895) 121. "Coladnus" is likely the children's stab at pronouncing Collatinus. Collatinus L. Tarquinius was one of the first Roman consuls, and though it may be an unusual name for a cat, it was one of a number of Chamberlain pets that would be named for historic personages, for example Charlemagne, Tiberius Caesar and Henry of Navarre.
9. FCA to JLC 8 Mar. 1866, RC; "General Affidavit," TDC's Pension Record, NA; FCA to JLC, 19 Mar. 1866, RC; G. Warren to JLC, 28 Aug. 1866, LC. No evidence of an offer from West Point was found, but JLC was eventually offered a colonelcy in the regular army.
10. Sarah Sampson to JLC, 22 Mar. 1866, RC; JLC to FCA, [illegible, 23 or 28?] Mar. 1866, RC.
11. SBC to JLC, 18 Mar. 1866, RC; FCA to JLC, 22 Mar. [1866], RC; JLC to FCA, 23 Mar. 1866, RC; JLC to FCA, [illegible, 23 or 28?] Mar. 1866, RC; JLC to FCA 7 Apr. 1866, RC.
12. JLC to FCA, 7 Apr. 1866, RC; JLC to FCA 7 Mar. 1866, MHS.
13. FCA to JLC, 15 Apr. 1866, RC; Barba Architecture and Preservation "Historic Structure Report for the Joshua L. Chamberlain House, Brunswick, Maine" 26 Apr. 1995, 2.
14. JLC "Address of Gen. Chamberlain" *Eastern Argus* 25 Apr. 1866, box 14, folder 5, BC.
15. *Ibid.*
16. *Ibid.*
17. *Ibid.*
18. FCA to JLC, 1 May 1866, RC.
19. *Ibid.*
20. JLC to FCA, 26 Oct. 1862, LC.
21. Hatch *Bowdoin* 533; "JLC to Hon. A. G. Jewett, 26 Jun. 1866" Bangor *Whig and Courier* 4 July 1866.
22. "What General Chamberlain Says" Bangor *Whig and Courier* 2 July 1866.
23. GAD 30 July, 2 and 28 Aug. 1866; Gouverneur Warren to JLC, 28 Aug. 1866, LC; Harry Coe, *Maine: A History* (New York: The Lewis Historical Publishing Co., 1928, I,175, and II, 810-811.
24. Chamberlain Bible, Brewer Historical Society, Brewer, Maine; GAD 16 Sept., 10 Oct., 7, 14 Nov. and 30 Dec. 1866; See GAD 1866-1867 for citations on Rev. Adams' deteriorating health; SBC to JLC, 25 Nov. 1866, RC.
25. D. A. Buehlen to JLC, 9 Aug. 1866, PHS; JLC to Board of Trustees, 13 Nov. 1866, BC. On this day the Trustees accepted JLC's resignation as Chair of the Department of Rhetoric and Oratory, and voted him full salary as acting college president.
26. JLC "Address of Governor Chamberlain to the Legislature of the State of Maine" January 1867, Maine Public Documents, 1867 (Augusta: Stevens and Sayward,1867) 3-41.
27. TDC to JLC, 10 and 14 Jan. 1867, RC; SBC and TDC to JLC, 16 Jan. 1867, MHS; GAD 21 Jan. 1867; SBC to JLC, 23 Apr. 1867, RC; Delia Jarvis and JCC to SBC, 23 Apr. 1867, BC.

28. MacPherson, *Ordeal* 522-528; Willian Frye "Report of the Attorney General" Maine Public Documents 1867 (Augusta: Stevens and Sayward) Appendix, 8; Chamberlain Bible, Brewer Historical Society, Brewer, Maine; SBC "Declaration" TDC's pension record, NA. John Chamberlain died so near midnight that, though the family Bible recorded his passing on the 10th of August, Sae's affadavit in Tom's pension record states that John died on Aug. 11. Deodat Brastow to SDB and Joshua Chamberlain, Jr., 24 Aug. 1867, BC; GAD 14 Aug. 1867.
29. Hatch *Bowdoin* 534-535; McPherson *Ordeal* 528-529; Sheridan *Memoirs II* 274-275; McPherson *Ordeal* 523. The Tenure of Office Act required Senate approval for the removal of federal officials, cabinet members and general of the army. It was designed to prevent President Johnson from removing from office those who were enforcing Congress' Reconstruction. See telegraphs to JLC, October 1867, DU; GAD 29 Oct. 1867; Sifalkis 166. JLC *Passing* 82; William L. Richter, *The ABC-CLIO Companion to American Reconstruction, 1862-1877* (Santa Barbara, Ca: ABC-CLIO, 1996) 212-215; Charles Griffin, as colonel of the 35th Infantry, found himself in a hornet's nest when he took up his duties in postwar Texas. Uncompromising Rebels dominated the state government and Indian hostility threatened the state's northwest frontier. Griffin took a bold stand against the unreconstructed Texans and enforced Congress' Reconstruction Acts to the letter and beyond, in an effort to protect the state's black population and white Unionists. When an epidemic of Yellow Fever swept Texas in the summer and fall of 1867, Griffin was given permission to move himself and his family away, but he refused to leave his post. The Griffin's little boy died a week before his father was struck with the disease. In less than three days, he was dead.
30. Smith "Soldier" 9; Wallace 226; Trulock 340; "Death of Mrs. Chamberlain" 20 Oct. 1905 Box 14 folder 17, BC; See letters from Jane "Jenny" Abbott to JLC, 1868-1872, RC; JLC to FCA, 20 Nov. 1868, YU.

Chapter 15

1. Wilder 55; See GAD 1848-1857; Francis G. Butler A History of Farmington (Farmington, Maine: Knowlton, McLeary and Co., 1885) 354-5; Hatch *Bowdoin* III, 827-828; Jane "Jenny" Abbott to JLC, n.d. [January 1865] and 17 Aug. 1865, RC; JLC to John L. Hodsdon, 11 Nov. 1865, MSA.
2. Jane "Jenny" Abbott to JLC, 6 Jan. 1866, n.d. [1868], 14 July 1869 and n.d. [July 1870], RC. Abbott/Chamberlain correspondence at RC covers a period from 1865-1873.
3. JLC "Address of Governor Chamberlain to the Legislature of the State of Maine, January, 1868" Maine Public Documents (Augusta: Stevens and Sayward1868) 3-46.
4. *Ibid.*
5. Hatch *Bowdoin* 534-536.
6. Godfrey Journal 14 Feb. 1868; "Lecture of Governor Chamberlain" *Whig and Courier* 17 Feb. 1868.
7. McPherson *Ordeal* 525-526, 530-533; Hatch *Bowdoin* 536-538; "Sketch" 18; William DeWitt Hyde's *Eulogy for JLC*, Box 14, BC.
8. Hatch *Bowdoin* 535; GAD 18 Apr. 1868.
9. GAD 18, 26 Mar., 5 Aug. 1868; Chamberlain Bible, Brewer Historical Society, Brewer, Maine; JLC to FCA, 11 Aug. 1868, MHS.
10. Hatch *Bowdoin* 540; Rev. George Loring, "Joshua L. Chamberlain—Maine Writer Recalls Interview with 'Hero of Little Round Top'," Lewiston *Journal*, n.d. [post-1914], copy at PHS; Henry E. Tremain, *Last Hours of Sheridan's Cavalry* (New York: Bonnell, Silver and Bowers, 1904) 11, 19-20, 79, 166-168. Gen. Tremain who served on both Gen. Daniel Sickle and Gen. Joseph Hooker's staff earlier in the war. Tremain has been mentioned as a possible candidate for "Historicus." This author of anonymous letters to the press after Gettysburg that attacked Gen. Meade and supported Gen. Sickle and the unauthorized advance of his corps on the second day of the battle.
11. William P. Frye "Report of the Attorney General of the State of Maine 1868" Maine Public Documents (Au-

gusta: Owen and Nash, 1868) 5-7. Edward Schriver "Reluctant Hangman: The State of Maine and Capital Punishment, 1820-1887" *New England Quarterly* LXIII,2,275-281.

12. JLC to FCA, 20 Nov. 1868, YU; GAD 15 Oct., 6, 11 and 26 Nov. 1868, 8 Jan. 1869, 24, 25 31 Mar. 1869. Miss Courlaender was a Brunswick teacher.
13. Justice Herbert T. Silsby to author, 14 Jan. 1995, WP. Judge Silsby, a retired justice of Maine's Supreme Court, cited the case of *Holyoke v. Holyoke*, Maine Law, 1886, 404-412, which describes Maine's 19th century divorce laws.
14. GAD 12 and 19 Dec. 1868; FCA to GDC, 25 June [1869], RC; JLC to GDC, 5 Nov. [1870], RC; FCA to GDC, n.d. [early 1870s], RC.
15. "About Executing Harris" Bangor *Whig and Courier* 16 Nov. 1868; Frye "Report 1868" 5-7.
16. JLC "Address of Governor Chamberlain to the Legislature of the State of Maine January 1869" (Augusta: Owen and Nash, 1869) 8-13.
17. *Ibid.*
18. *Ibid.*
19. Schriver 280; JLC to SDB, 27 Jan. 1868, BC; Joshua Chamberlain, Jr. to JLC, 30 Jan. 1869, RC.
20. GDC to HWC, 15 Feb. 1869, BC; FCA to JLC, 31 Jan. 1857, RC; Anne C. Rose, *Victorian America and the Civil War* (New York: Cambridge University Press, 1992) 164-166; SBC to JLC 7 Oct. 1867, RC.
21. Application for Invalid Army Pension" 26 Dec. 1868 and J.W. Toward, M.D. "Examining Surgeons Certificate" 19 Feb. 1869, JLC medical file, NA.
22. Eliza Quincy to JLC, 16 Mar. 1869, BC; Schriver 281; "Eleven Men Were Hanged in Maine and Most of Them Were Guilty" Maine *Times* 14 June 1974, copy at Bangor Public Library, Bangor, Maine.
23. JLC "The Old Flag" 4 Jan. 1878, JLC Scrapbook, UMO.
24. JLC *Passing* 219; TDC to SBC, 9 July 1865, BC; JCD 6.
25. JLC "Address of Governor Chamberlain to the Legislature of the State of Maine January 1869 (Augusta: Owen and Nash, 1869) 20-21; Godfrey III, 120. New Sweden, Maine was one of the towns founded by Maine's Scandanavian immigrants. Grateful for JLC's support, he was invited to attend the celebration of the 10th anniversary of the founding of New Sweden in July 1880.
26. Mundy 1-49, 136. The area bounded by 2nd, 3rd and Cedar Sts. near the Seminary in Bangor was known as "Paddy Hollow" or "Dublin." See Chamberlain family correspondence, RC; Joshua Chamberlain, Jr. to JLC, 13 Feb. 1859, RC; JCD 15-16. JCC noted that it was "Miss Bartly in her 'Confession of an Escaped Nun'" that had presented him with such a negative picture of the Sisters of Charity, before he observed their work at the battlefield and in the hospitals.

Chapter 16

1. JLC to GDC, 18 May 1869, RC; TDC to SBC, 2 Apr. 1869, BC; JLC to TDC, 5 Jun. 1869, MHS.
2. Hatch *Bowdoin* 560; FCA to GDC, 25 Jun. [1869], RC.
3. JLC "Army of the Potomac" JLC Scrapbook, UMO.
4. *Ibid.*
5. Hatch *Bowdoin* 560-562; FCA to GDC, 25 Jun. 1869, RC; Chamberlain Family Bible, Brewer Historical Society, Brewer, Maine. John Chamberlain Farrington [b. July 20, 1868] died Oct. 18, 1869. SDB to JLC Nov. [1869] RC; "Land for Sale" *Whig and Courier* 5 July 1869, 1. Joshua Chamberlain, Jr. placed an advertisement in a Bangor paper stating, "The undersigned having had his entire Home property and effects burnt up and carried off in the late fires, would like to sell his out lands as follows...."
6. SDB to JLC, Nov. [1869], RC; "Widow's Affidavit" TDC's Pension Record, NA. It is not known whether the marriage plans which SDB mentions refer to his future marriage to John's widow, Delia Jarvis Chamberlain on Dec. 14, 1870.
7. JLC to GDC, n.d. [November 1869], RC.
8. JLC to FCA, 31 Dec. 1869, RC.
9. JLC "Address of Governor Chamberlain to the Legislature of the State of Maine January, 1870" (Augusta: Sprague, Owen and Nash, 1870) 3-31.
10. *Ibid.*
11. Geroge M. Fredrickson, *The Inner Civil War: Northern Intellectuals and the*

Crisis of the Union (Harper and Row, 1965) 183, 193; McPherson *Ordeal* 547-548; JLC "Flag"; JLC "Ft. Hell." The page containing JLC's observations on Lincoln, interesting enough, was headed "not to be used"—an indication of JLC's unwillingness to publicly condemn Republican policy on Reconstruction.

12. GAD 1869-1870 and 10 Feb., 24 Jun., 15 Aug. 1870; JLC to FCA 20 Nov. 1868, YU.
13. JLC to GDC, 27 Apr. 1870, YU; Trulock 515, fn39.
14. Hatch *Bowdoin* 566-567.
15. John Gerow Gazley, *American Opinion of German Unification, 1848-1871*(New York: Columbia University, 1926) 175-319; JLC to William, King of Prussia, 20 July 1870, PHS.
16. Jane "Jenny" Abbott, n.d. [summer 1870], RC.
17. *Ibid.*
18. *Ibid.*
19. Hatch *Bowdoin* 568-569; Godfrey 4 and 18 Sept. 1870, II 24; H.M. [Haisted?] to JLC 21 Sept. 1870, PHS; Frederick Robie to George Gifford, 12 [Jan.] 1871, Gifford collection, DU; JLC to Hon. Henry W. Paine, 27 Dec. 1870, MHS.
20. GAD 23 and 25 Aug., 15 Sept 1870; JLC to Joshua Chamberlain, Jr. 26 Nov. 1870, BC; Charles O. Farrington to SBC, Aug.-Sept. 1870, BC.
21. JLC to Joshua Chamberlain, Jr., 26 Nov. 1870, BC; Jane "Jenny" Abbott to JLC, n.d. [summer 1870] and 20 Dec. 1870, RC.
22. Hatch *Bowdoin* 569; Joshua Chamberlain, Jr. to JLC, 21 Jan. 1871, RC; JLC to GDC, n.d. [early 1871], RC; "Widow's Affidavit" TDC Pension record, NA. Tom married John's widow, Delia Jarvis Chamberlain on Dec. 14, 1870 in Boston.
23. JLC to GDC, 18 Apr. 1871, RC; FCA to GDC, April [1871] RC; See family correspondence, 1870s, RC; Helen to JLC, June 1871, RC.
24. JLC to GDC, 28 Apr. 1871, RC.

Chapter 17

1. JLC to GDC, 28 Apr. 1871, RC; Calhoun 186-187; Helmreich *Religion* 93; W. A. Dillingham to George Gifford, 23 Feb. 1871, Gifford Collection, DU; JLC to SDB, 8 Sept. 1871, BC.
2. Waterville College [Colby] in Waterville, Bates College in Lewiston, and the Agricultural College in Orono. Hatch *Bowdoin* 156; Calhoun 189-191; Fannie Harlow Robinson D.A.R., Daniel Arthur Robinson (private printing, 1968) 39, copy at Bangor Public Library, Bangor, Maine.
3. Calhoun 189; JLC "The New Education" Box 5, folder 5, BC. Though JLC began his duties as president in the fall of 1871, his inauguration did not take place until Bowdoin's next commencement in the summer of 1872.
4. *Ibid.*
5. *Ibid.*
6. *Ibid.*
7. Jane "Jenny" Abbott to JLC 5 July 1871, RC; JLC to SDB, 8 Sept. 1871, BC; Butler to, 27 Apr. 1871, BC; Jane "Jenny" to JLC, 20 May 1872, RC.
8. Jane "Jenny" Abbott to JLC, 4 Oct. 1871, RC; Barba 5-6.
9. Barba 7, 13-16; L. Bateman "At Home with Gen. Joshua L. Chamberlain in Old Longfellow House, Brunswick" *Lewiston Journal Illustrated Magazine* 17-21 Aug. 1907.
10. Robinson 37-38.
11. McPherson 553, 568-571; "Sketch" 19. Horace Greeley, the founder of the New York *Tribune*, while clearly an outspoken opponent of slavery, had advocated a confusing succession of causes, including his temporary support for allowing the South to peacefully secede, while later advocating all out war and a negotiated peace.
12. JLC to Gov. Sydney Perham 18 May 1872, MSA; Hatch *Bowdoin* 127, 133, 345-347; Robinson 37.
13. HWC to Captain, 11 Apr. 1872, BC; JLC to GDC, 12 Feb. 1888, BC; GDC to JLC 24 July 1872, RC; GDC to JLC 8 Aug. [1872], RC; JLC to GDC, n.d. [late summer, 1872], RC.
14. Jane "Jenny" Abbott to JLC, 20 May and 22 Jun. 1872, RC.
15. JLC to GDC, n.d. [summer 1872], RC; JLC to Joshua Chamberlain, Jr., 25 July 1872, UMO; JLC to Joshua Chamberlain, Jr. 16 May 1873, PHS.
16. Helmreich *Religion* 128; C. F. Low to C. F. Brackett, M.D., 30 Sept. 1872, BC; JLC to C. F. Low, 9 Oct. 1872, BC; Calhoun 236.

17. McPherson *Ordeal* 571-572; JLC to Samuel Hersey, 20 Jan. 1873, PHS; 1870 and 1880 census; Ellen Bacon to Joshua, 24 Dec. 1872, RC.
18. JLC to Abner Coburn, Samuel Hersey, and J. W. Bradbury, 20 Jan. 1873, PHS; JLC to A. P. Gould, 7 Feb. 1873, PHS; JLC to Blake, 22 May 1873, PHS; Hatch *Bowdoin* 159; JLC to the Trustees and Overseers, 8 July 1873, MHS.
19. Hatch *Bowdoin* 159; Robinson 42.
20. JLC to Joshua Chamberlain, Jr., 16 May 1873, PHS.
21. HWC to JLC, 1 Sept. 1873, RC; Jane "Jenny" Abbott to JLC, 15 Sept. 1873, RC.
22. Hatch *Bowdoin* 131, 137.
23. Beda Simpson to Horace Allen, 7 Jun. 1874, BC; JLC to TDC, 28 Jan. 1874, BC; Minnie Northend to FCA 11 Jun. 1874, RC.
24. Hatch *Bowdoin* 137-139; Calhoun 193.
25. Hatch *Bowdoin* 134-142; Calhoun 193-195.
26. Hatch *Bowdoin* 143-144.
27. Hatch *Bowdoin* 160.
28. JLC to SDB, 4 July 1874, BC; Chamberlain Bible, Brewer Historical Society, Brewer, Maine; JLC to GDC, 1 Sept. 1874, BC.
29. JLC to GDC, 1 Sep 1874, BC; Beda Simpson to Horace Allen, 7 Jun. 1874, BC.

Chapter 18

1. Helmreich *Religion* 93; JLC to FCA, 2 May 1875, RC; Adelbert Ames to JLC, 22 Jan. 1875, LC.
2. McPherson *Ordeal* 593-395; Ralph Lowell Eckert, *John Brown Gordon: Soldier, Southerner, American* (Baton Rouge: Louisiana State University Press, 1989) 145-149, 164-165, 167.
3. Hatch *Bowdoin* 157, 179, Wilder 99; Robinson 52-53; *Encyclopedia Americana* 1989, XVII, 730; Little 139; Bateman.
4. Farrington 19; GEA to Mrs. H. C. Knight 24 Aug. 1875, YU; GAD 1870-1875; First Parish Church Calender #1,068, 29 Dec. 1929; Ashby 368.
5. Georgie O. Hutchins to JLC, 17 Nov.and 13 Dec. 1875, 7 Jan. and 14 Feb. 1876, BC; JLC to FCA, 2 May 1875, RC; Bangor City Directory 1875-1876 ; SBC to JLC and FCA, 5 Jan. 1876, RC.
6. FCA to GDC, 22 Mar. 1876, RC; C.H. Smith to JLC, 6 Apr. [1876], BC; GDC to Horace Allen, 5 Apr. 1876, BC; Helmreich *Religion* 115; Stephen Allen to JLC 26 Apr. 1876 LC; Dumas Malone, *Dictionary of American Biography* (Grinnell Hibbard, VIII) 99. Edward Everett Hale [1822-1909], minister of the Unitarians' South Congregational Church in Boston, is best remembered as the author of *The Man Without a Country*.
7. JLC to GDC, 29 May 1876, MHS.
8. *Ibid.*
9. Stephen Allen to JLC, 29 Apr. 1876, LC.
10. Hatch *Bowdoin* 548-557; Ari Hoogenboom, *Rutherford B. Hayes: Warrior and President* (Lawrence: University Press of Kansas, 1995) 261-265. The histories of Bowdoin College do not mention this proferred resignation, leaving some doubt as to whether JLC actually submitted it.
11. JLC to Trustees and Overseers of Bowdoin College, 26 Jun. 1876, MHS.
12. *Ibid.*; Robinson.
13. J.E.C. to JLC, 31 Jul. 1877, RC; Elbridge Chamberlain to Joshua Chamberlain, Jr., 23 Aug. 1876, BC.
14. McPherson *Ordeal* 598-603; Hoogenboom 277, 290-294; Eckert 181-184.
15. McPherson *Ordeal* 603-604.
16. Hatch 586-587; James G. Blaine, *Twenty Years in Congress from Lincoln to Garfield* 429-440.
17. JLC "Enthusiastic Rally in Faneuil Hall" JLC Scrapbook, UMO; See letters to JLC, August 1877, BC.
18. Hatch *Bowdoin* 148; James M. Larabee to JLC, 17 Oct. 1877, BC.
19. JLC to SDB, 27 Nov. 1877, UMO; Barba 7.
20. HWC to FCA, 10 Feb. 1878, RC; GDC to Horace Allen, n.d. [February 1878], RC; Hatch *Bowdoin* 169; JLC to Samuel H. Blake, 19 Feb. 1878, PHS.
21. JLC "The Old Flag: What was Surrendered? What was Won" JLC Scrapbook, UMO.
22. *Ibid.*
23. *Ibid.*
24. *Ibid.*
25. *Ibid.*
26. *Ibid.*

27. Hoogenboom 375-376; McPherson *Ordeal* 567.
28. JLC to FCA, 6 Mar. 1878, RC.
29. JLC to SDB and Joshua Chamberlain, Jr., 14 Jun. 1878, BC; Little 132; Farrington 19.
30. GDC to Horace Allen, 6 Aug. 1878, BC; GDC to Horace Allen, 28 Sept. 1878, YU.
31. Calhoun 193; Hatch *Bowdoin* 160-163.
32. Hatch *Bowdoin* 595; JLC to FCA, 15 Jan. 1880, BC.

Chapter 19

1. McPherson *Ordeal* 500, 571, 605-606.
2. *Ibid.* 606; JLC "The Heroes of the War" Lewiston *Evening Journal* 31 May 1879.
3. JLC "Heroes," Lewiston *Evening Journal* 31 May 1879.
4. *Ibid.*
5. *Ibid.*
6. *Ibid.*
7. Lewiston *Evening Journal* 31 May 1879; *Oxford Democrat* 10 Jun. 1879. The *Oxford Democrat*, despite its name, was a Republican newspaper.
8. Trulock 347; Registry of Deeds, 23 Aug. 1879, Book 461, 438; [JLC] "Domhegan" copy at PHS; Christopher Hibbert, *Gilbert and Sullivan and Their Victorian World* (New York: American Heritage Publishing, 1976) 103. *H.M.S. Pinafore* was first performed in London on May 25, 1878.
9. Nehemiah Cleveland, *History of Bowdoin College* (Boston: Pilgrim Press, 1916) 672; [JLC] "Twelve Days at Augusta, 1880" (Portland: Smith and Dale Printers, 1906) copy at PHS. Though no author is acknowledged, the very personal nature of the material in "Twelve Days..." indicates that it was endorsed, if not authored by JLC. Hatch *Maine* 601-606; James G. Blaine to JLC, 24 and 29 Dec. 1879, PHS.
10. *Twelve*; Hatch *Maine* 604-611; JLC to FCA, 7 and 9 Jan. 1880, RC.
11. *Twelve*; Hatch *Maine* 611; T.B. R.[eed] to George Gifford, 10 Jan. 1880, DU.
12. *Twelve*; See letters to JLC, Jan. 1880, PHS, LC, MHS and Rutherford B. Hayes Presidential Center, Fremont, Ohio, Chamberlain Collection, copies at PHS; F.B. Ward to JLC, 15 Jan. 1880, LC.
13. *Twelve*; Joseph Smith "General Order #2" 16 Jan. 1880, LC; JLC to James G. Blaine, n.d. [early Jan.], 14 and 16 Jan. 1880 PHS; Hatch *Maine* 608.
14. JLC to FCA, 15 Jan. 1880, LC; *Twelve*.
15. Hatch *Maine* 608; Coe I, 201; Daniel F. Davis to JLC, 17 Jan. 1880, MHS; *Twelve*; Horace Allen to GDC, 18 Jan. 1880, BC; clipping, JLC Scrapbook, UMO.
16. JLC to FCA, 11 May 1880, RC; Emerson Gifford Taylor, *Gouverneur Kemble Warren: The Life and Letters of an American Soldier* (Boston: Houghton Mifflin Co., 1932) 244-248; C. H. Morgan to Gen. G. K. Warren, 14 Mar. 1868, Warren Collection, N.Y. State Library.
17. JLC to FCA, 11 May 1880, RC; Thomas T. Munford, "Narrative of the Battle of Five Forks, 1 April 1865" Munford-Ellis Family Papers, DU, introduction and 15-16.
18. Munford 15-16; New York *Times* 6 Nov. 1880, clipping in Warren Collection, N.Y. State Library; Tremain 166-168; Sifakis 438-439.
19. George Mayer, *The Republican Party 1865-1966* (New York: Oxford University Press, 1967) 201-105; Hatch *Maine* 623.
20. Hatch *Bowdoin* 146, 162-163, 166, 214-215.
21. Chamberlain Family Bible, Brewer Historical Society, Brewer, Maine; JLC *Memoirs* 45-46.
22. Mayer 204-205; West Funk to Maine Legislature, October 1880, LC; JLC to Gen. G. W. Spaulding, 4 Oct. 1880, MHS; JLC to Capt. G. C. Goss, 4 Oct. 1880, MHS; See letters fall and winter, 1880, BC; Mary Clark to JLC, n.d. [1880], RC.
23. JLC to GDC, 14 Feb. 1881, PHS; May Bradbury to FCA, 8 Apr. 1881, RC; wedding invitation, 28 Apr. 1881, PHS; GDC to JLC 9 May 1881, RC; Horace Allen to GDC, 18 and 19 Jul. 1881, BC; Albert Nelson Marquis, *Who's Who in New England* (Chicago: A. N. Marquis and Company, 1909) 32. Horace Gwynne Allen, born in Jamaica Plain in 1855, received his LL.B. from Harvard in 1876 and practiced law in partnership with Nathan Morse in Boston. He was a member of Boston Common Council from 1888 to1891, and its president in 1889.

24. Mayer 206; Godfrey 3 Jul. 1881, III, 194.
25. Horace Allen to GDC, 18 and 19 July 1881, BC; JLC to GDC, 23 Dec. 1881, BC.

Chapter 20

1. J. Lester Dinkins, *Dunnellon: Boomtown of the 1890s* (St. Petersburg: Great Outdoors Publishing, 1969) 38-39; McPherson *Ordeal* 610-611.
2. Trulock 362; James Hoge "The Silver Springs, Ocala and Gulf: From Dream to Reality" At Home Inverness, Fla.: Citrus County Historical Society, Nov.-Dec. 1994, 3; "Florida Roster" 4th Florida, Co. G, 9th Florida Co. G; W. Horace Carter, *Nature's Masterpiece at Homosassa* (Tabor City, N.C.: Atlantic Publishing Co., 1981) 23; Boatner 326-327.
3. Carter 5, 12; JLC to SBC, 29 Jan. 1882, UMO.
4. JLC "Report to the Stockholders" 14 Apr. 1885, YU; McPherson *Ordeal* 610-611.
5. JLC to SBC, 29 Jan. 1882, UMO.
6. *Ibid.*
7. *Ibid.*
8. Hatch *Bowdoin* 149-150; "Sketch" 22; L. E. Bowers to JLC, 6 Mar 1882, BC.
9. Hatch *Bowdoin* 147-148, 150-152.
10. Joseph H. Warren, M.D. to JLC, 2 Mar. 1883, YU; Wilder 469. Dr. Joseph Huckins Warren [BC 1853 and 1882] practiced surgery in Boston from 1856 to 1891. JLC to FCA 19 Apr. 1883, BC; Portland *Transcript* 25 Apr. 1883, copy at PHS; GDC to FCA 19 Apr. 1883, BC.
11. J. J. Porter to JLC, 27 Jul. 1883, with New York *Times* clipping, YU, copy at PHS; [JLC] "Domhegan."
12. JLC to [Henry] Johnson, 6 Feb. 1884, BC; John Bigelow to JLC, April 1883, MHS; Ellis Spear to JLC, 25 Jun. 1883, YU; J.J. Porter to JLC, 27 Jul. 1883, with New York *Times* clipping, YU.
13. Hatch *Bowdoin* 163, 168, 172, 179-182.
14. JLC to [Henry] Johnson, 6 Feb. 1884, BC.
15. JLC to GDC, 1 Jan. 1884, BC; JLC, 1884 *Journal*, Jan.-Feb. 1884, PHS; SBC to FCA, 14 Jan. 1884, RC; Eckert 251; George Frederick Howe, *Chester A. Arthur: A Quarter Century of Machine Politics* (New York: Dodd, Mead and Co., 1934) 256; Eloise Robinson Ott, *Ocali Country, Kingdom of the Sun: A History of Marion County, Florida* (Ocala: Marion Publishers, 1966) 124; Dexter A. Hawkins to JLC, 1 Mar. 1884, YU; Dexter A. Hawkins to Chester Arthur, 1 Mar. 1884, YU; JLC to Chester Arthur, 4 Mar. 1884, copy, YU.
16. Mayer 209-211; JLC to Carl Schurz, 20 Feb. 1884, YU; Little 139.
17. Mayer 210-212; Richter 52.
18. JLC, 1884 Journal, PHS, 9 Sept. 1884; clipping from *Telegraph*, 24 July 1885, Domhegan folder, PHS; JLC "Report"; Hampton Dunn, *Back Home: A History of Citrus County, Florida* (Clearwater: Artcraft Printing, 1976) 94-95.
19. JLC "Report".
20. JLC to FCA 8 Aug. 1885, Maine State Museum, Augusta, Maine.
21. *Ibid.*
22. *Ibid.*
23. *Ibid.*
24. *Ibid.;* Hancock 178.
25. JLC to FCA, 20 Oct. 1885, BC.
26. *Ibid.*
27. *Ibid.*
28. *Ibid.*
29. SBC to JLC, 3 Jan. 1886, RC.
30. *Ibid.*
31. *Ibid.*
32. J.N. Wilson to Pennell, 15 Mar. 1886, BC; JLC "Report"; Carter 24.
33. JLC "Report"; HWC to GDC, 9 Aug. 1886, BC.
34. JLC to George Trowbridge, 2 Oct. 1886, BC; JLC to GDC, 13 Dec. 1886, BC.
35. JLC to GDC, 13 Dec. 1886, BC.

Chapter 21

1. JLC to GDC, 15 Feb. 1887, BC; Horace Allen to JLC, 4 Feb. 1887, YU.
2. Log book of the steamer *Mistletoe*, 19 Feb. 1887, in possession of Duncan MacRae, Homosassa, Florida; JLC to [George T.] Little, 28 Mar. 1887, BC; Mortgage, Homosassa Land and Improvement Co. of New Jersey to Francis S. Bangs, New York, George W. Morse, Boston, and Franklin A. Wilson, Bangor, Maine, 15 Oct. 1892, Filed 13 Feb., 1893, Mortgage Book 4, 74.
3. JLC to Charles Farrington, 24 Aug. 1887, BC; JLC to SDB, 8 Sept. 1887, BC.
4. JLC to GDC, 20 Oct. 1887, BC.

5. FCA to GDC, 8 Jan. 1888, RC.
6. JLC to GDC, 8 Apr. 1888, BC; Ott 130-132, 157.
7. JLC to GDC, 8 Apr. 1888, BC; HWC to JLC, 7 May 1888, YU; A.E. Willard to JLC, 18 July 1889, YU.
8. JLC to GDC, 13 July 1888, BC.
9. JLC to GDC, n.d. [fall 1888] BC.
10. Chamberlain Family Bible, Brewer Historical Society, Brewer, Maine.
11. JLC to GDC, 18 Jan. 1889, BC. Chauncey Depew was a brilliant and dramatic New York lawyer, and owner of the New York Central Railroad.
12. JLC to Prof. [George T.] Little, 22 Jan. 1889, BC; HWC to JLC, 22 Mar. 1889, BC; See Chamberlain and Henry Hill Boody Correspondence, 1889-1890, YU.
13. A.E. Willard to JLC, 18 July 1889, YU; John H. Jarvis to JLC, 9 Sept. 1889, YU; "Pension Declaration" 7 Dec. 1889, TDC Pension Records, NA.
14. John P. Nicholson, *Pennsylvania at Gettysburg* (Harrisburg: E. K.Meyers, 1893) 1098-1099.
15. JLC "Dedication of the Twentieth Maine Monuments at Gettysburg, Oct. 3, 1889" *Bayonet! Forward* (Gettysburg: Stan Clark Military Books, 1994) 184-202.
16. Eckert 324-328; Desjardin 128-129; JLC "Twentieth."
17. JLC "Twentieth." Holman Melcher, in his account, "Little Round Top," Lincoln County News, 13 Mar. 1885, stated, "...the time had come when it must be decided whether we should fall back and give up this key to the whole field of Gettysburg, or charge and try to throw off this foe, that were rapidly drawing the life-blood of our regiment by their deadly fire. It must not be the former; how can it be the latter? Col. Chamberlain decides it can only be the latter and gives the order to 'fix bayonets' and almost before he can say 'Charge!' the regiment, with a shout of desperation, leaps down the hill and close in with the foe...." While some of his comrades still insisted that Melcher conceived and initiated the charge, there were those who not only credited Chamberlain with its conception, but who also insisted that he had not only given the command for bayonets, but also ordered the charge. In the "Recollections of Nathan Clark, Co. H, 20th Maine" [29] at the Maine State Archives, Clark, whose company was two to the left of center of the regiment, recalled that Chamberlain ordered, "...Charge bayonets Charge and of[f] we went with a wild yell...."
18. *Ibid.*
19. *Ibid.*
20. *Ibid.*
21. Thomas Barker to JLC 26 Feb. 1887, BC; Allan Nevins, *Grover Cleveland: A Study in Courage* (New York: Dodd, Mead and Company, 1966) 330-335, 415-420; Albert Volwiler, *The Correspondence Between Benjamin Harrison and James G. Blaine, 1882-1893* (Philadelphia: The American Philosophical Society, 1940) 1.
22. JLC "Dedication of the Maine Monuments at Gettysburg" *Bayonet! Forward* 190-202.
23. *Ibid.* Chamberlain may, in part, have drawn his inspiration for these sentiments from Hebrews 11:13.
24. Jacob Hoke, *The Great Invasion of 1863: General Lee in Pennsylvania* (Dayton, Ohio: W. J. Shuey, 1887) 333-334; Pennsylvania 105; James C. Rice, clipping, JCD, PHS; Gen. George Sykes to Gen. Samuel Wylie Crawford, 17 Dec. 1863, Chamberlain personal papers , LC.
25. See Henry Hill Boody-JLC-Van Valdenburgh correspondence, July 1889-March 1890, YU. It appears that one of JLC's adversaries was Van Horne of the Canadian Pacific. E. W. Agnew to JLC, 6 Feb. 1889, BC; Dinkins 71, 110, 119-136; Ott 133; A. P. K. Safford to Albert E. Willard, 4 Dec. 1889, YU; Agreement between JLC and Isaac D. Guyer, 17 Feb. 1890, YU; Hoge 3.
26. C. G. Barth to JLC, 31 Jan. 1890, YU; "Stockholders Report, 1890" YU; Carter 12-13, 17.
27. HWC to JLC 7 May 1888, YU; HWC to JLC 22 Mar. 1889, BC; TDC Pension Record, NA; Charles Farrington to JLC, 28 Nov. 1890, PHS; JLC to Prof. [George] Little, 23 June. 1890, BC; Barba 1.
28. JLC to FCA, n.d. [early 1891], MHS.
29. *Ibid.;* John C. Leonard, *The Higher Spiritualism* (New York: Frederick Hitchcock, 1927) 70-71, 106, 263-264, 269-274; Andrew Jackson Davis, *The Great Harmonia* (Rochester, NY: The Austin Publishing Co., 1910 edition)

217-443. Slater Brown, *The Heyday of Spiritualism*(New York: Hawthorn Books, 1970) 115-245. "In Two Worlds," a phrase associated with Spiritualism, may indicate that the Chamberlains, like so many others at this time, were interested in some facet of the movement. Though mediums who claimed to communicate with the departed may be what most of us associate with the movement, Spiritualism encompassed a number of diverse interests and investigations into both physical and metaphysical disciplines.

30. HWC to FCA, n.d. [early 1891], MHS.
31. JLC to Ellis Spear, 15 Mar. 1891, PHS; JLC to Dodge 26 Sept 1891, PHS; John B. Gordon to JLC, 26 Feb. 1992, RBH; Eckert 246-247; 266-267, 293.
32. HWC to FCA, 5 Dec. 1891, RC.
33. JLC to GDC, 14 Feb. 1892, BC; HWC to JLC, 2 Nov. 1892, YU.
34. "Medical Referee's Instructions to the Examining Physician, March 1893, JLC Pension Records, NA; JLC to Pension Bureau, 6 Feb. 1893, NA.
35. Mayer 215, 224-236, 239; Volwiler x, 1-16.
36. Charles E. Russell, *Blaine of Maine: His Life and Times* (New York: Cosmopolitan Book Corporation, 1931) 426-430; Richter 52; Hoge Jan.-Feb. 1995, 6.
37. HWC to FCA, n.d. [early 1891], MHS.

Chapter 22

1. JLC to Bureau of Pensions, 6 Feb. 1893, JLC Pension Record, NA; Robert Holmes Greene, M.D. to Bureau of Pensions, JLC Pension Record, NA; Wilder 152. Dr. Robert Holmes Green [BC 1884, Harvard 1886] practiced urology in New York from 1886 to 1933. "Affidavit of Fitz John Porter to Bureau of Pension" JLC Pension Record, NA; Carswell McClellan to JLC, 22 May 1891, LC; Birney Sargent to Fitz John Porter, 13. Sept. 1889, LC. Fitz John Porter and JLC may well have become acquainted due to the common perception of JLC as a historian and defender of the 5th Corps. In May of 1871, Chamberlain was chosen, as president of the Society of the Fifth Army Corps, to present the organization's petition to reopen Fitz-John Porter's case to President Grant. Boatner 898; Alexander Webb to JLC, 4 Apr. 1892, LC. "Proceedings and Report of the Board of Army Officers Convened by Special Orders No. 78, Headquarters of the Army, Adjutant General's Office, Washington, Apr. 12, 1878, in the Case of Fitz-John Porter." Washington: GPO, 1879, I, 548.
2. JLC to Andrew Carnegie, 14 Feb. and 23 Mar. 1893, YU; JLC to, 23 Apr. 1893, MHS; Alexander Webb to Secretary Seward, 2 May 1893, LC.
3. JLC, "Impressives Services Held in Music Hall" 31 May 1893, JLC Scrapbook, UMO.
4. *Ibid.*
5. *Ibid.*
6. *Ibid.*
7. Boatner, 898; JLC to Alexander Webb, 18 May 1993, Alexander Webb Collection #684, YU; Fitz John Porter to the Secretary of War, 19 May 1893, NA.
8. SBC to FCA, 4 Dec. 1893, BC; JLC to Mott, 28 Jan. 1894, BC; JLC to FCA, 23 Jan. 1894, BC.
9. JLC to Prof. [George] Little, 20 Feb. 1894, BC; Wallace 281; JLC to Prof. [George] Little 16 Jun. and n.d., 1894, BC; JLC to FCA 23 Oct. 1894, BC; David S. Woodrow to JLC, 8 Dec. 1894, BC.
10. Clipping, n.d. or title, JLC scrapbook, BC; J.L. Smith to JLC, 22 Feb. 1896, BC; Survivors Association, *History of the Corn Exchange Regiment: 118th Pennsylvania Volunteers* (Phildelphia: J.L. Smith, 1888) vii-viii; C.E. Swinerton to JLC, 13 Jun. 1896, BC; Edwin March to JLC, June 1895, MHS; Francis A. Walker to JLC, 3 Apr. 1896, Alexander Webb Collection, #684, YU.
11. See JLC- Col. [Charles] Murphy-Merriam correspondence, June 1896, YU; Mayer 249-256.
12. JLC to FCA, n.d. [June 1896], RC.
13. JLC to FCA 30 Jun. 1896, BC; Ada and Frank Graham, *Kate Furbish and the Flora of Maine* (Gardiner, Maine: Tilbury House, 1995) 6, 144. Furbish's large collection of botanical watercolors were given to BC. TDC Pension Record, NA; TDC obituary, *Daily Whig and Courier* 13 Aug. 1896; JLC to GDC 29 Dec. 1896, RC. The MSA grave card states that TDC died of tuberculosis.
14. The Executive Committee, *Maine at Gettysburg* (reprint Gettyburg: Stan Clark Military Press, 1994) 249-289; Desjardin 129, 137; JLC to Ellis Spear,

27 Nov. 1896, Spear Collection, MSA; Spear to JLC, 25 Nov. 1896, Spear Collection, MSA.

15. A. G. Fernald to JLC, 25 Nov. 1896, BC; William C. Oates "Gettysburg-The Battle on the Right" *Southern Historical Society Papers* (1878, VI) 172-182; Dumas Malone, *Dictionary of American Biography* (New York: Charles Scribner's Sons, 1934, VII) 605; JLC to Hon. William C. Oates, 27 Feb. 1897, BC; JLC to William C. Oates 18 May 1905, GNMP; JLC to Ellis Spear, 27 Nov. 1896, Spear Collection, MSA.
16. JLC to Ellis Spear, 27 Nov. 1896, Spear Collection, MSA; Holman Melcher did not claim that he had conceived of and initiated the charge, for in his account of the battle, "The 20th Maine at Little Round Top," published in the *Lincoln County News*, Waldoboro, Maine, in March1885, Melcher wrote, "Colonel Chamberlain gave the order to 'fix bayonets' and almost before he could say 'charge!' the regiment leaped down the hill."
17. *Ibid.*
18. JLC to Hon. William C. Oates, 27 Feb. 1897, BC.
19. *Ibid.*
20. JLC to William C. Oates, 18 May 1905, GNMP; JLC to JPN, 14 Aug. 1903, GNMP; Wm. C. Oates to JLC, 8 Mar. 1897, Schoff Civil War Collection, William Clements Library, Univ. of Michigan. Oates would deny his correspondence with JLC before 1905. One of his letters however, as cited in this endnote, still exists.
21. JLC to GDC, 29 Dec. 1896, RC.
22. JLC to FCA 28 May 1897, RC.
23. Mayer 259-263; JLC notes on Cuba, box 5, folder 10, BC. JLC's notes in preparation for a speech indicate that, while JLC supported freeing the Cuban people from the rule of the Spanish monarchy, he did not feel they were ready for self-government. Feeling that Congress and the country's war fever had forced President McKinley to declare war, JLC felt that the majority of Americans had not wanted war. He nonetheless recommended that the war be pressed with a strong hand, or the United States would lose the respect of other nations.
24. JLC to Gov. Llewellyn Powers, April 1898, MSA; JLC to Sen. William P. Frye, 22 Apr. 1898, NA.
25. Secretary of War to JLC, 30 Apr. 1898, NA; A. H. Savage to JLC, 24 Apr. 1898, BC; *Who Was Who in America* (Chicago: A. N. Marquis Company, 1942, I) 909; Oates *War* 555-565. The outspoken Oates, angry when he did not receive command of the two white Alabama regiments he requested, condemned the Army's policy of abandoning organizing troops by state, stating: "organization was strictly in accord with the doctrines of the Republican party. It was intended as far as practicable to blot out State lines and State pride and to drill, mould, and fashion all volunteers as regulars, and to know no government but that of the Union. State pride is nauseating to Republican stomachs." Oates also had difficulty with his corps commander, Gen. Coppinger, whom he described as "far advanced in a state of senility" and "so inferior that he would not have made a good courier" for Oates' former commanders, Stonewall Jackson and Longstreet.
26. George O. Cutler to the Navy Dept., forwarded to Pres. McKinley,11 May 1898, NA; Stanley Karnow, *In Our Image: America's Empire in the Phillipines* (New York: Random House, 1989) 99-180; Mayer 265-269.
27. JLC to GDC, 4 Dec. 1898, MHS.
28. *Ibid.*
29. JLC to SBC, 4 Apr. 1899, LC; Davis, *The Great Harmonia* 278-286, 370-375, 443. The nature of FCA's "magnetic" treatment is unknown, and there were numerous practices at that time that would fall under that term, from hypnotism or mind over matter self-cures, to devices that applied battery-powered mild electrical charges to the afflicted area.
30. *Ibid.;* JLC to Frank A. Garnsey, 18 Jan. 1899, BC; Eckert 316-317; Frank A Garnsey to JLC 20 Jan. 1899, BC.
31. Francis Fessenden to JLC, 7 Mar. 1899, LC; JLC to Francis Fessenden, 9 Mar. 1899, LC; JLC to Alexander Webb, 18 May 1893, Alexander Webb Collection #684, YU.
32. William T. Livermore to JLC, 22 May 1899, MHS; JLC "Case of Andrew J. Tozier" application for Medal of Honor, 28 Mar. 1898, NA.

33. JLC to Charles Farrington, 2 Sept. 1899, BC; See correspondence Nov.-Dec., BC and MHS; Obituary Bangor *Daily News* 9 Aug. 1905, 2nd edition, 2; "Death of Mrs. Chamberlain" clipping, 20 Oct. 1905, Box 14, BC.

Chapter 23

1. JLC to SBC, 24 Dec. 1899, LC.
2. Thomas J. Carroll, *Blindness* (Boston: Little Brown and Co., 1961, 14,36,39-40, 44; Thomas Cutsforth, *The Blind in School and Society* (New York: American Foundation for the Blind, 1951) 103,124, 135; FCA Obituary Bangor *Daily News* 9 Aug. 1905, 2nd edition, 2; "Death of Mrs. Chamberlain" clipping, 20 Oct. 1905, Box 14, BC.
3. JLC to SBC, 24 Dec. 1899, LC; Ellis Spear to Hon. Amos Allen, 4 Dec. 1899, BC.
4. JLC to SBC, 24 Dec. 1899, LC; Amos L. Allen to G.M. Elliott, 12 Dec. 1899, RBH; Amos L. Allen to JLC, 12 Feb. 1900, RBH; JLC to John T. Richardson, 26 Dec. 1899, MHS; A.[bner] O. Shaw to JLC, 5 Dec. 1899, MHS; JLC to Dr. Dalton, 8 Mar. 1900, PHS.
5. JLC to John T. Richardson, 26 Dec. 1899, MHS; Sarah Sampson to JLC, 27 May 1900, MHS; JLC "The Loyal Legion" [12 Sept. 1901], Box 15, BC; JLC to Alexander Webb, 7 Dec. 1899, Alexander Webb Collection #684, YU; JLC to Hon. J.R. Hawley, 12 Jan. 1900, YU; JLC to Alexander Webb, 23, 24 and 28 Feb. 1900, Alexander Webb Collection #684, YU.
6. Treasury Dept. to JLC, 27 Mar. 1900, MHS; Wallace 293-294; See correspondence 1900-1913, RC; JLC to GDC, 18 Sept. 1900, RC; JLC to Secretary of the Treasury, [fall]1900, MHS; JLC to Secretary of State, n.d. [fall, 1900],YU; JLC to FCA "Warrantee deed" LC. At 72, JLC listed his height as 1 1/2 inches less than he was at age 26 in 1854.
7. Sarah Sampson to JLC, 2 Nov. 1900, MHS.
8. JLC to FCA, 6 Nov. 1900, BC.
9. GDC to FCA, 15 Nov. [1900], BC; "Welcome News" clipping of letter from JLC to A.L. Farnsworth, Deputy Collector of Customs, 7 Jan. 1901, PHS.
10. JLC to [FCA] n.d. [early 1901] fragment, LC; Bateman.
11. SBC to JLC, 12 Mar. 1901, RC; JLC to GDC, 11 Mar. 1901, RC; Bateman.
12. L.B. Eaton to JLC, 30 Jul. 1901, PHS; JLC to L.B. Eaton, 1 Aug. 1901, PHS; John W. Leonard, *Who's Who in America* (Chicago: A. N. Marquis, 1901-1902) 192. JLC "At the Lincoln Club" Portland *Daily Press* n.d. Box 14, BC.
13. Margaret Leech, *In the Days of McKinley* (New York: Harper and Brothers, 1959) 542-562. In the previous years, the Spanish premier, the French president and Empress Elizabeth of Austria had been assassinated. Mayer 266-270.
14. JLC "A Note of Warning" Box 14, folder 2, BC.
15. *Ibid.;* JLC "The Loyal Legion" 12 Sept. 1901, Box 15, BC.
16. JLC "Warning"; Mayer 271-272; Leech 562, 575-576, 587.
17. JLC to GDC, 9 Dec. 1901, RC.
18. *Ibid.;* JLC to HWC, 26 Dec. 1901, BC; Charles Farrington to HWC, 17 Jun. 1901, BC.
19. JLC to FCA, 13 May 1902, BC.
20. JLC to FCA, 1 Jul. 1902, RC.
21. JLC to FCA, 10 Jul. 1902, BC.
22. "Theodore Roosevelt" *Daily Eastern Argus* 27 Aug. 1902; "President Given Rousing Reception" and "Roosevelt's Speech" Portland *Evening Express* 26 Aug. 1902, last edition.
23. *Ibid.*
24. *Ibid.*
25. JLC to FCA, 11 Sept. 1902, BC; GDC to HWC, n.d. [October 1902], BC; JLC to GDC, n.d. [October 1902], RC.
26. Carroll 41, 44, 69; JLC to FCA, 14 Nov. [1902], BC; Cutsforth 103.
27. JLC to FCA, 11 Feb. 1903, BC.
28. JLC to FCA 21 Apr. 1903, BC; JLC to FCA, n.d. [1 Jun. 1903], BC.
29. JLC to GDC, 28 Jun. 1903, RC.
30. JLC to GDC, 3 Aug. 1903, RC.
31. *Ibid.*
32. *Ibid.;* JLC to FCA, 21 Aug. 1903, BC.
33. Coe II 801; JLC to FCA, 21 Apr. 1903, BC; See JLC Scrapbook, UMO; Charles F. McKenna to JLC, 1 Apr. 1903, BC; JLC to FCA, 1 Jun. 1903, BC; "Gen. Chamberlain in Oakland" JLC Scrapbook, UMO; "Last Campaign of the War" Brunswick *Record* 5 Feb. 1904, Box 14, BC.

34. clipping, 16 Oct. 1903, JLC Scrapbook, UMO; Annie Chamberlain Smiley "Private Witherell's Story" Folder 25, BC; Desjardin 163-166, 180. There were two privates named Witherell in the 20th Maine, Edwin S. and Robert A. Witherell; Eckert 337.

Chapter 24

1. JLC to John Nicholson, 17 Aug. 1903, GNMP; Max "Final Forward Given to General Chamberlain" *The Maine State Press and Turf, Farm and Home*, Box 14, BC; Myra Porter to JLC, 13 and 21 July, 11 Nov. and 22 Dec. 1904, MHS; Enlistment card for Willis M. Porter, MSA. Information provided by the Rockland County Historical Society, New York City, New York. Myra's work with disadvantaged children in New York City and Nyack on Hudson, a base for Orphan Train activities, suggests her connections with that organization.
2. John P. Nicholson to JLC, 6 Aug. 1903, GNMP; JLC to JPN, 14 Aug. 1903, GNMP; for Oates' earlier statements see Oates to JLC, 8 Mar. 1897, Schoff Collection, William Clements Library, Univ. of Michigan.
3. JLC to JPN, 14 Aug. 1903, GNMP; Oates "Battle"; William C. Oates to Elihu Root, 2 June 1903, LC.
4. JLC "Reminiscences of Petersburg and Appomattox, October 1903" *War Papers* (Portland: Lefavor-Tower Co., 1908, III).
5. JLC "On Old Fields" JLC Scrapbook, UMO; JLC "Loyal Legion" Box 14, BC; JLC "Last Campaign of the War, Brunswick *Record* 5 Feb. 1904, Box 14, BC.
6. JLC "Last Campaign."
7. JLC "Loyal." Chamberlain, inexplicably, wrote this piece as if his 1903 trip had been his first visit to Petersburg since the war. Though it was his first trip back to Appomattox, he had visited Petersburg in 1882, but may have taken this approach in his writing as a dramatic literary device.
8. JLC "Petersburg and Appomatox"; Spear 272. It is not known who JLC refered to as disputing his and the 1st Division's role at Appomattox, but Ellis Spear would not only belittle their part in the surrender, but eventually deny it, in spite of the fact that his own diary from 1865 recorded, "Our Brigade recd the arms of Gordon & Longstreets corps which included all the remains of the infantry force of the army of N. Vir[ginia]" Spears diary entry, however, indicates that he was either not present for, or unimpressed by the salutes that both Gordon and JLC claimed were exchanged by their troops, for he also recorded, "All passed off quietly without demonstration."
9. Eckert 341; "Final Foward"; JLC to T.R. Lounsbury, 17 Mar. 1904, T. R. Lounsbury Collection, #1231, YU. "Book of Admission for 1904" Eunice Frye Home [formely the Mary Brown Home], 37 Capisic St., Portland, Maine]; JLC to GDC, n.d. [June 1904], RC.
10. JLC to GDC, 16 Aug. 1904, RC; Myra Porter to JLC 22 Dec. 1903 and 11 Nov. 1904, MHS; Davis *Harmonia* 250; Leonard 263-269; JLC to FCA, 22 July 1902, BC; See Myra Porter/JLC correspondence, MHS; G. W. Hinckley "The Story of Good Will Farm" (Privately published pamphlet) copy at Bangor Public Library, Bangor, Maine.
11. JLC to GDC, 26 Dec. 1904, RC.
12. JLC to GDC, 27 Feb. 1905, RC; W. N. McNamara to JLC, 7 Feb. 1905, MHS; William C. Oates to JPN, 1 Mar. 1905, GNMP; Oates book, *The War Between the Union and the Confederacy, and Its Lost Opportunities* was published in this year.
13. JLC to JPN, 16 Mar. 1905, GNMP.
14. *Ibid.*
15. *Ibid.*
16. William C. Oates to JLC, 14 Apr. 1905, GNMP.
17. *Ibid.*
18. *Ibid.*
19. JLC to William C. Oates, 18 May 1905, GNMP.
20. *Ibid.*
21. Wm. C. Oates to JLC, 8 Mar. 1897, Schoff Civil War Collection, William Clements Lib., Univ. of Michigan; JLC to Wm. C. Oates, 18 May 1905, GNMP.
22. *Ibid.*
23. JLC to GDC, 23 June1905 RC.
24. JLC to FCA, 21 Aug. 1903, 1903, BC [on Domhegan House letterhead]; William T. Alexander, *Harpswell on Casco Bay* (Portland: The Print Shop) 135; Phinehas V. Stephens "Our Log" Box 10, folder 2, BC.

25. *Ibid.*
26. See Myra Porter/JLC correspondence, MHS; Hinckley. Porter's correspondence shows that a good part of her work as agent for the Good Will Farm involved obtaining funds for the orphanage's projects from a number of the prominent Portland benefactors who are acknowledged in Hinckley's pamphlet. Myra Porter to JLC, 8 July 1905, MHS.
27. Myra Porter to JLC, 19 and 22 July 1905, MHS.
28. Myra Porter to JLC, 22 July 1905, MHS; Myra Porter to JLC, n.d. [July 1905], MHS; Record of marriage, MSA.
29. Bangor *Daily News* 9 Aug. 1905, 2nd edition, 2; JLC to FCA, 12 Aug. 1905, RC.
30. JLC to Adelbert Ames, 2 Oct. 1905, DU; JLC to Alexander Webb 11 Oct. 1905, Alexander Webb Collection #684, YU.
31. JLC to Alexander Webb, 11 Oct. 1905, Alexander Webb Collection #684, YU.
32. Obituary, *Daily Eastern Argus* 19 Oct. 1905,1; "Death of Mrs. Chamberlain" 20 Oct. 1905, Box 14, BC; E.B. Mason "Mrs. Chamberlain's Funeral" Brunswick *Record* 27 Oct. 1905, Box 14, folder 17, BC.
33. Mason.
34. *Ibid.*
35. *Ibid.*
36. *Ibid.*
37. *Ibid.*

Chapter 25

1. Helen Adams to JLC, 26 Nov. 26, 1905, BC; James McKeen to JLC, 31 Oct. 1901, MHS; Bateman.
2. See family correspondence, 1908-1914, RC; James and Alice Trulock, "Rosamond Allen Interview" 5 Sept. 1983, PHS; Rosamond Allen "A Personal Memoir of Rosamond Allen—Granddaughter of Union General Joshua Chamberlain" *Blue and Gray Magazine* Dec.-Jan. 1983-1984: 16.
3. JLC to Gen. Thomas T. Munford, 25 Oct. and 10 Nov. 1905, Ellis-Munford Collection, DU; Gen. Thomas T. Munford "Narrative of the Battle of Five Forks, 1 Apr. 1865" Ellis-Munford Collection, DU.
4. JLC "Last Review of the Army of the Potomac, May 23 1865" *War Papers* (Portland: Lefavor-Tower, 1908, III) 315, 317-8.
5. JLC "Chamberlain's York Address Memorial Day" 31 May 1906, Box 14, BC; Larry Favinger "Enigma in Granite" [Portsmouth, NH] *Herald* 27 Aug. 1995.
6. Harold Raymond "Joshua Chamberlain's Retirement Bill" *Colby Library Quarterly* Dec. 1966, VII, 8, 341-354.
7. *Ibid.;* Boatner 363. Bvt. Brigadier Gen. Charles Henry Grosvenor, served in the west, and was elected a U.S. Congressman after the war. He was a "Chautauqua speaker and known as a "brilliant debater and spellbinding conversationalist."
8. *Ibid.;* JLC to Alexander Webb, 27 Feb. 1906, Alexander Webb Collection #684, YU.
9. "Sketch".
10. *Ibid.;* Elizabeth Upham to JLC, 29 Nov. 1906, BC.
11. L.M. Sturtevant's transcriptions of Sarah Sampson letters, PHS. "In Memoriam. John Marshall Brown" Mollus Commandery of the State of Maine, 1907, 243, copy at MSA.
12. A[urestus].S. Perham to JLC, 9 Sept. 1908, BC with transcription in JLC's hand of letter from Col. J.S. Mosby to Judge James Keith, Richmond Va.
13. JLC to SBC, 18 Oct. 1908, UMO.
14. George L. Lyon to JLC, May 1909, RC; JLC "Oration on the One Hundredth Anniversary of the Birth of Abraham Lincoln" 12 Feb. 1909 *Bayonet! Forward* (Gettysburg: Stan Clark Military Books, 1994) 244-261.
15. *Ibid.;* GDC to George T. Little, n.d. [post 1914], BC.
16. Alexander Webb to JLC, 12 Apr. and 7 May 1909, MHS; Selden Connor to JLC, 19 Mar. 1908, LC.
17. JLC to Fanny Hardy Eckstorm, 28 June 1909; JLC to GDC, 24 May 1909, RC.
18. JLC to Grace 14 Sept. 1909, RC; JLC to Robert E. Peary, 5 Oct. 1909, BC.
19. William Frye to JLC, 13 Dec. 1909, MHS; Joshua L. Chamberlain Civil War Round Table Newsletter Sept. 1995, X, 9, 8; JLC to SBC, 25 Feb. 1910, UMO; Elizabeth Copeland "Interview between Mrs. Paul Copeland and Mrs. Winfield Smith," PHS; Catherine Zell Smith "Brunswick's 'Soldier Statesman'" Brunswick *Times Record* 7 Sept. 1976, copy at PHS; Max.
20. JLC to Rosamond Allen, 27 Dec. 1909, PHS; JLC to Manley Hardy, 25 Dec.

1909, First Congregational Church of Brewer, Maine.
21. JLC/Eckstorm correspondence, 1909, UMO; SBC to Fanny Hardy Eckstorm, 11 Aug. 1911, UMO.
22. JLC to SBC, 25 Feb. 1910, UMO.
23. Portland Directory, 1910; JLC to Riley, 21 Apr. 1910, PHS; Lasalle Pickett to JLC, 25 Apr. 1910, BC; Frances E. Willard and Mary A. Livermore, *A Woman of the Century* (Detroit: Book Tower, 1967 edition) 570-571; Copeland.
24. [Mary Clark] to JLC, 24 Apr. 1910 [fragment], RC.
25. JLC to JPN, 19 Oct. 1910, source unknown, copy in Trulock Collection, PHS; Amy E. Blanchard to JLC, 1 Aug. 1910, RC; JLC to GDC, 13 Oct. 1910, RC.
26. *Ibid.;* Allen.
27. Mary Clark to JLC, 21 Dec. 1910, MHS.
28. *Ibid.*
29. *Ibid.*
30. *Ibid.*
31. Ellis Spear to JLC, 24 Dec. 1910, BC.
32. "Fear That Gen. Webb will Not Recover" New York *Times*, 12 Feb. 1911; JLC to GDC, 24 Mar. 1911, RC; Allen.
33. JLC to GDC, 26 Apr. 1911, RC; Dora to JLC, 5 May 1911, RC; Theodore Peck to JLC, 11 May 1911, BC.

Chapter 26

1. JLC to GDC, 17 May and 22 Jun. 1911, RC.
2. to JLC, 30 Jun. 1911, BC; Henry Burrage to JLC, 4 Oct. 1911, BC; Mary Kirchiner to JLC, 3 Oct. 1911, BC; A. M. Chamberlain to GDC, 3 Oct. 1911, BC; JLC to S. M. Chamberlain, 21 Oct. 1911, BC; JLC to Fanny Hardy Eckstorm, 29 Oct. 1911, UMO; JLC to Dr. [George T.] Little, 28 Nov. 1911, BC; JLC to L.B. Strout, 9 Dec. 1911, BC.
3. JLC to GDC, 9 Dec. 1911, RC.
4. Ira Evans to JLC, 23 Oct. 1911, BC; Selden Connor to JLC, 30 Dec. 1911, MHS; JLC to Fanny Hardy Eckstorm, 10 Feb. 1913, UMO; Smith "Soldier" 1, 9; Catherine Shen Hendley, "General Chamberlain-Does Anybody Remember?", copy at PHS; C.S.P. to JLC, 15 Apr. 1913, RC; JLC to GDC, 25 Apr. 1913, RC.
5. Smith "Soldier" 9.
6. JLC to Prof. Henry Johnson, 8 Jan. 1912, with "The Troopers Charge" BC; JLC to GDC, n.d. [early Feb.] 1913, RC.
7. *Ibid.*
8. William L. Putnam to President William DeWitt Hyde, 25 Feb. 1914, BC.
9. Morris Schaff, *The Sunset of the Confederacy* (Boston: John W. Luce and Co., 1912) 296, 299; JLC to Morris Schaff, n.d. [1912], YU. Despite the fact that Morris Schaff, graduate of West Point's class of 1862, had served as ADC to Gen. Warren, JLC and Schaff had never met.
10. JLC "My Story of Fredericksburg" *Cosmopolitan Magazine* Jan. 1913, LIC,2, 148-159; JLC to Fanny Hardy Eckstorm, 10 Feb. and 2 Mar. 1913, UMO; JLC to GDC, n.d. [late Feb. 1913], RC.
11. JLC to Fanny Hardy Eckstorm, 2 Mar. 1913, UMO; JLC to GDC, 28 Feb. 1913, RC; Frederic Boothby to JLC, 14 Feb. 1913, BC; JLC to GDC, 2 Mar. 1913, RC; E. Herman, *Eucken and Bergson* (London: James Clarke and Co., 1912) Henri Bergson was a French philosopher and writer whose major work examined the relationship between mind and body. Rudolf Eucken, a German professor of philosophy and winner of the 1908 Nobel Prize, rejected dogmatic theological values and maintained that there was not a conflict of theories in the world, but a conflict of hostile world powers. He wrote on man's relationship with nature, declaring naturalism and intellectualism rivals. Ellwood Worcester and Samuel McComb, *Body, Mind and Spirit* (Boston: Marshall Jones Co., 1931) v-vii, 194-97, 200-201.
12. JLC to GDC, 25 Apr. 1913, RC; JLC to AG of Maine, 25 Apr. 1913, MSA; Ellis Spear to Mildred, 1910, Spear Collection, MSA.
13. JLC to GDC, n.d. [early Feb.], 1913, RC; JLC to Perriton Maxwell, 22 May 1913, MHS; I.B. Hazelton to JLC, 18 Apr. 1913, BC; Desjardin 127-128. Oddly enough, Theodore Gerrish, author of *Reminiscences of the War*, was one of the soldiers JLC was agonizing over in drawing up his list of soldiers who had actually fought at Gettysburg. Though JLC had evidence that Gerrish was not there, he approved his transportation.
14. JLC to Fanny Hardy Eckstorm, 28 Aug. 1913, UMO; JLC "Through Blood and Fire and Gettysburg" *Hearst's Magazine* June 1913, 894-909.

15. Ellis Spear "The Left at Gettysburg" *National Tribune* 12 Jun. 1913; Spear *Recollections* 32-36, 215, 312-317; [Spear] "The 20th Maine at Gettysburg" JCD, PHS; JLC to Ellis Spear, 27 1896, MSA. JLC maintained that he "communicated" his intention to make a charge to Spear before Holman Melcher asked permission to advance. It is possible that Spear did not receive this verbal order. Spear also chooses to ignore the testimony that substantiates JLC's claims. For Nathan Clark and Holman Melcher's statement, see ch. 21, n. #17. Ellis Spear to Oliver Norton, 5 Jul and 19 Aug. 1913, 18 Jan. and 1 Feb. 1916, Clarke Historical Library, Central Michigan; Oliver Norton to Bishop Boyd Vincent, 5 and 12 Jan. 1916, Clarke Historical Library, Central Michigan; Ellis Spear to Rev. Boyd Vincent, 5 Jul. 1913, Clarke Historical Library, Central Michigan; It is obvious that Spear's article is an angry response to JLC's article in *Hearst's Magazine*. In his letters to Norton and Vincent, he declared that JLC's taking all the glory for himself, robbed Strong Vincent of the credit due him. Beyond what the Hearst editor may have cut and changed from JLC's article, the first pages of the article are dominated by a two page illustration of the death of Vincent. Andrew Cowan to JLC, 15 Dec. 1913, BC; "General Chamberlain Dies" Portland *Evening Express* 24 Feb. 1914, 6.
16. JLC to Fanny Hardy Eckstorm, 24 Sept. 1912, UMO; JLC to HWC, 18 Oct. 1913, MHS.
17. *Ibid.;* JLC to SBC, 7 Nov. 1913, LC. JLC to GDC, n.d. [Nov. 1913], RC.
18. Andrew Cowan to JLC, 15 and 19 Dec. 1913, BC.
19. "Maj. Gen. Joshua L. Chamberlain is Dead" *Evening Globe* 24 Feb. 1914, Box 14, BC; GDC to Eleanor Allen, n.d. [mid-January 1914], RC.
20. JLC to SBC, 20 Jan. 1914, UMO.
21. Grace to Eleanor Allen, n.d. [mid-January 1914], RC; "Maj. Gen."; Thomas H. Hubbard to JLC, 15 Feb. 1914, BC; "Grand Old Hero is Dead" *Daily Eastern Argus* 25 Feb. 1914; "Services City Hall Probable" Portland *Evening Express* 24 Feb. 1914.
22. "Simple Services" *Daily Eastern Argus* 26 Feb. 1914; "Services City Hall Probable" Portland *Evening Express* 24 Feb. 1914.
23. "For the Illustrious and Greatly Beloved" *Daily Argus* 28 Feb. 1914.
24. "Host Pays Tribute to Joshua L. Chamberlain at Funeral Held Here" Portland *Evening Express* 27 Feb. 1914; JLC to Wm. DeWitt Hyde, 3 Jun. 1913, BC.

Bibliography

Articles, Addresses, Reports, and Pamphlets

Allen, Rosamond. "A Personal Memoir of Rosamond Allen- Granddaughter of Union General Joshua Chamberlain." *Blue and Gray Magazine*. Dec.-Jan. 1983-84: 16.

Anonymous. "About Executing Harris." Bangor *Whig and Courier.* 16 Nov. 1868.

Anonymous. "Address on the Incorporation of the Town of Orrington." *Bangor Historical Magazine*. VII-IX, 1993: 1,732.

Anonymous. "The Aroostook War, and the Volunteer Troops Therein." *Bangor Historical Magazine.* I-III, 1993: 351-353.

Anonymous. "Brastow Family." *Bangor Historical Magazine.* I, 1993: 365-367.

Anonymous. "Eleven Men Were Hanged in Maine and Most of Them Were Guilty." Maine *Times*. 4 June 1974, copy of clipping at Bangor Public Library, Bangor, Maine.

Anonymous. "Farrington Memorial." Privately published. Copy at First Congregational Church in Brewer, Maine.

Anonymous. "Fear that Gen. Webb Will Not Recover." New York *Times.* 12 Feb. 1911.

Anonymous. First Parish Calendar. Dec. 29, 1929: #1,068, biography of the Rev. George E. Adams.

Anonymous. "For the Illustrious and Greatly Beloved." Portland *Daily Eastern Argus.* 28 Feb. 1914.

Anonymous. "General Chamberlain Dies." Portland *Evening Express.* 24 Feb. 1914.

Anonymous. "Grand Old Hero is Dead." Portland *Daily Eastern Argus.* 25 Feb. 1914.

Anonymous. "Historical Sketch of the First Congregational Church: Brewer, Maine." Privately published. Copy at Brewer Congregational Church, Brewer, Maine.

Anonymous. "The Honorable Thomas Davee of Dover and Blanchard, Maine." *Bangor Historical Magazine.* 7-9, 1993. reprinted by Camden, Maine: Picton Press.

Anonymous. "Host Pays Tribute to Joshua L. Chamberlain at Funeral Held Here." Portland *Evening Express.* 27 Feb. 1914.

Anonymous. "Letters to General Boyd." *Bangor Historical Magazine.* VII-IX, 1993: 1,683-4.

Anonymous. "Maj. Gen. Joshua L. Chamberlain is Dead." *Evening Globe* 24 Feb. 1914. Copy in Box 14, BC.

Anonymous. "Milledgeville Female Academy." Milledgeville, Ga., *Southern Recorder.* 26 Oct. 1852.

Anonymous. "Mrs. Chamberlain's Funeral." Brunswick *Record* 27 Oct. 1905. Box 14, folder 17, BC.

Anonymous. "President Given Rousing Reception." Portland *Evening Express.* 26 Aug. 1902, last edition.

Anonymous. "Representatives to the General Court of Massachusetts from Penobscot County." *Bangor Historical Magazine.* VII-IX, 1993: 1683-4.

Anonymous. "Services City Hall Probably." Portland *Evening Express.* 24 Feb. 1914.

Anonymous. "Simple Services." *Daily Eastern Argus.* 26 Feb. 1914.

Anonymous. "Theodore Roosevelt." *Daily Eastern Argus.* 27 Aug. 1902.

Anonymous. "The Twelve Days at Augusta, 1880." Portland: Smith and Sale, 1906. Copy at PHS.

Anonymous. "War Meeting at Brunswick." Portland *Daily Advertiser.* 22 July 1862.

Barba Architecture and Preservation. "Historic Structure Report for the Joshua L. Chamberlain House Brunswick, Maine." Apr. 26, 1995. Copies available PHS.

Bateman, L.C. "At Home with Gen. Joshua L. Chamberlain in Old Longfellow House, Brunswick." *Lewiston Journal Illustrated Magazine.* Aug. 1907.

Blaugrund, Annette. "The Evolution of the Artists' Studios, 1740-1860." *The Magazine Antique.* Jan. 1992: 215-225.

Burns, Hank. "Wanted: Heros for the 1990s." Portland *Press Herald.* 28 Feb. 1994.

Cary, Richard. "The Misted Prism: Paul Akers and Elizabeth Akers Allen." *Colby Library Quarterly.* March 1966:193-198.

JLC. "Address of Gen. Chamberlain." *Eastern Argus.* 25 Apr. 1866.

JLC. "Address of Governor Chamberlain to the Legislature of the State of Maine 1867." *Maine Public Documents 1867.* Augusta: Stevens and Sayward, 1867.

JLC. "Address of Governor Chamberlain to the Legislature of the State of Maine 1868." *Maine Public Documents 1868.* Augusta: Stevens and Sayward, 1868.

JLC. "Address of Governor Chamberlain to the Legislature of the State of Maine January 1869." Augusta: Owen and Nash, 1869.

JLC. "Address of Governor Chamberlain to the Legislature of the State of Maine January, 1870." Augusta: Sprague, Owen and Nash, 1870.

JLC. "At the Lincoln Club." Portland *Daily Press*, n.d., Box 14, BC.

JLC. "Dedication of the Maine Monuments at Gettysburg." *Bayonet! Forward.* Gettysburg: Stan Clark Military Books, 1994.

JLC. "The Heroes of the War." Lewiston *Evening Journal.* 31 May 1879.

JLC. Charles P. Mattocks and Seth C. Gordon. "In Memoriam. John Marshall Brown." *Military Order of the Loyal Legion.* 6, 1907: 243.

JLC. "Last Campaign of the War." Brunswick *Record* 5 Feb. 1904. Clipping, Box 14, BC.

JLC. "The Last Night at Fredericksburg." *Camp-Fire Sketches and Battle-Field Echos.* Springfield, Ma: King, Richardson and Company, 1889: 131-135.

JLC. "The Last Review of the Army of the Potomac." *War Papers.* Portland: Lefavor-Tower Co., 1908. III: 306-333.

JLC. "My Story of Fredericksburg." *Cosmopolitan Magazine.* January 1913: 148-159.

JLC. "Night on the Field at Fredericksburg." *Camp-Fire Sketches and Battle-Field Echos.* Springfield, Ma: King, Richardson and Company, 1889: 127-130.

JLC. "Oration on the One Hundredth Anniversary of the Birth of Abraham Lincoln." *Bayonet! Forward.* Gettysburg: Stan Clark Military Books, 1994.

JLC. "Reminiscences of Petersburg and Appomattox: October, 1903." *War Papers.* Portland: Lefavor-Tower, 1908: III.

JLC. "Through Blood and Fire at Gettysburg." *Hearst's Magazine.* June 1913. Copy at BC, Box 5, folder 8.

JLC. "What General Chamberlain Says." Bangor *Whig and Courier.* 2 July 1866.

Chamberlain Association. "Joshua Lawrence Chamberlain: A Sketch." Copy available at PHS.

Favinger, Edward. "Enigma in Granite." [Portsmouth, N.H.] *Herald.* 27 Aug. 1995.

Frye, William P. "Report of the Attorney General 1867." *Maine Public Documents 1867.* Augusta: Stevens and Sayward, 1867.

Frye, William P. "Report of the Attorney General 1868." *Maine Public Documents 1868.* Augusta: Owen and Nash, 1868.

Hatch, Francis W. "The Star Spangled Life of Charles Jarvis Whiting." Ellsworth [Maine] *American.* 14 Nov. 1974.

Hinckley, G. W. "The Story of Good Will Farm." Privately published. Copy at Bangor Public Library, Bangor, Maine.

Hoge, James C. "The Silver Springs, Ocala and Gulf: From Dream to Reality." *At Home.* Nov.-Dec. 1994, Jan.-Feb. 1995. Copies available from the Citrus County Historical Society, Inverness FL.

Lafantasie, Glenn. "Introduction." *Gettysburg.* New York: Bantam, 1992.

Lafantasie, Glenn. "The Other Man." *The Quarterly Journal of Military History.* Vol. 4, Summer 1993: 70-76.

Loring, George. "Joshua L. Chamberlain-Maine Writer Recalls Interview with 'Hero of Little Round Top'." Lewiston *Journal.* n.d., clipping at PHS.
Mason, Rev. E.B. "Mrs. Chamberlain's Funeral." Brunswick *Record.* 27 Oct. 1905. Copy at BC.
Max. "Final Forward Given to General Chamberlain." *The Maine State Press and Turf, Farm and Home.* Clipping, Box 14, BC.
Melcher, Holman. "The 20th Maine at Little Round Top." Waldoboro, Maine: *Lincoln County News.* 12 Mar. 1885.
Miller, William B. "A New Review of the Career of Paul Aker, 1825-1861." *Colby Library Quarterly.* March, 1966: 227-255.
William C. Oates. "Gettysburg- The Battle on the Right" *Southern Historical Society Papers.* Millwood, NY: Kraus Reprint Co. 1977: 172-182.
Raymond, Harold. "Joshua Chamberain's Retirement Bill." *Colby Library Quarterly.* VII, December 1966: 341-354.
Schriver, Edward. "Reluctant Hangman: The State of Maine and Capital Punishment, 1820-1887." *New England Quarterly.* LXIII, 2. June 1990: 271-287.
Sege, Irene. "Love Letters." *The Boston Globe.* 14 Feb. 1994: 34, 37.
Smith, Catherine Zell. "Brunswick's 'Soldier Statesman'." Brunswick *Times Record.* 7 Sept 1876, 1, 9. Copy at PHS.
Spear, Ellis. "The Left at Gettysburg." *National Tribune.* 12 Jun. 1913.
Sprague, John Francis. "Hon. Thomas Davee." *Collections and Proceedings of the Maine Historical Society.* Portland: MHS VIII, 1897.

Diaries

Adams, George E., PHS.
Adams, Helen, MHS.
Chamberlain, John C. PHS
JLC 1853 Journal, BC.
JLC 1884 Journal, PHS
Godfrey, John. *The Journals of John Edwards Godfrey.* Rockland: *Courier-Gazette*, 1979, 1984, 1985.
Livermore, William, Special collections, UMO

Unpublished Sources

Anonymous. "Commencement at Bowdoin." JLC Order Book, PHS.
Anonymous. "Death of Mrs. Chamberlain." 20 Oct. 1905, Box 14, BC.
Anonymous. "Florida Roster." 4th Florida, Co. G, 9th Florida, Co. G.
Anonymous. "General Chamberlain in Oakland." JLC Scrapbook, UMO.
Book of Admissions, Eunice Frye Home [formerly Mary Brown Home, 37 Capisic St., Portland, Maine.
Chamberlain Family Bible, Brewer Historical Society, Brewer, Maine.
JLC. "Army of the Potomac." JLC Scrapbook, UMO.

JLC. "Chamberlain's York Address Memorial Day." 31 May 1906. Box 14, BC.
JLC. "The Charge on Fort Hell." DU.
JLC. "Church and School." June 30, 1881, Box 14, folder 3, BC.
JLC. "Domhegan." [brochure], copy at PHS.
JLC. Early Memoirs. BC.
JLC. "Enthusiastic Rally in Faneuil Hall." JLC Scrapbook, UMO.
JLC. "Impressive Services Held in Music Hall." 31 May 1893, JLC Scrapbook, UMO.
JLC. "The Loyal Legion." [12 Sept. 1901]. Box 15, BC.
JLC. "Loyalty." Clipping, Box 5, folder 4, BC.
JLC. "The New Education." Box 5, folder 5, BC.
JLC. "A Note of Warning." clipping, Box 14, folder 2, BC.
JLC. "The Old Fields." JLC Scrapbook, UMO.
JLC. "The Old Flag: What was Surrendered? What was Won." JLC Scrapbook, UMO.
JLC. Order Book, PHS.
JLC. "Report to the Stockholders." 14 Apr. 1885, Collection #226, YU.
JLC. Scrapbook, UMO.
JLC. "The Troopers Charge." 1864, attached to JLC to Prof. Henry Johnson, Jan. 8, 1912. BC.
Files, George, M.D. Research on JLC's Petersburg wound, copy in JLC Medical File, PHS.
Hendley, Catherine Shen. "General Chamberlain-Does Anybody Remember?" Copy at PHS.
Hyde,William De Witt. Eulogy for JLC. Clipping, Box 14, BC.
Lord, Ethel Kenney. "First Church Record Books." Transcription, First Congregational Church, Brewer, Maine.
Munford, Thomas T. "Narrative of the Battle of Five Forks, April 1, 1865." Munford-Ellis Family Papers, DU.
Richardson, Capt. J. "Log Book of the steamer Mistletoe." In the possession of Duncan MacRae, Homosassa, Florida.
Smiley, Annie Chamberlain. "Private Witherell's Story." Folder 25, BC.
Spear, Ellis. "The 20th Maine at Gettysburg." Clipping, JCD, PHS.
Stephens, Phinehas V. "Our Log." Box 10, folder 2, BC.
"Stockholders Report, 1890." YU.
Tallman, Louise. "Portsmouth Families." Portsmouth *Atheneum*. Portsmouth, New Hampshire.
Trulock, James A. and Alice R. "Memories of Rosamond Allen Interview." PHS.

Books

Adams, Andrew N. *A Genealogical History of Henry Adams of Braintree, Massachusetts and his Descendants*. Rutland, VT: Tuttle Co., 1898.
Adams, Eliashib. *A Successful Life*. Bangor, Maine: Burr Printing Co., 1871.

Ahlstrom, Sydney. *A Religious History of the American People.* New Haven: Yale University Press, 1972.

Alexander, William T. *Harpswell on Casco Bay.* Portland: The Print Shop.

Ashby, Thomas E. *A History of the First Parish Church in Brunswick, Maine.* Brunswick: J. H. French and Son, 1969.

Banks, Ronald. *A History of Maine.* Dubuque: Kendall Hunt Publishing, 1876.

Bangor Theological Seminary. *Historical Catalogue of Bangor Theological Seminary.* Bangor: Bangor Theological Seminary, 1964.

Bartlett, Irving. *John C. Calhoun: A Biography.* New York: W.W. Norton and Co., 1993.

Beeson, Mrs. J. L. *Historical Sketch of the First Presbyterian Church of Milledgeville, Georgia.* Privately published, 1953.

Blaine, James G. *Twenty Years in Congress from Lincoln to Garfield.* Norwich, CT: Henry Bill Publishing, 1886.

Bonner, James C. *The Journal of a Milledgeville Girl: 1861-1867.* Athens, GA: University of Georgia Press, 1964.

Bonner, James C. *Milledgeville: Georgia's Antebellum Capital.* Athens: Univ. of Georgia Press, 1978.

Brooks, Noah. *Washington, D. C. in Lincoln's Time.* Athens: University of Georgia Press, 1989.

Brown, Slater. *The Heyday of Spiritualism.* New York: Hawthorn Books, 1970.

Butler, Blanche. *Chronicles from the Nineteenth Century: Family Letters of Blanche Butler and Adelbert Ames.* Privately published, 1957.

Butler, Frances G. *A History of Farmington.* Farmington, Maine: Knowlton, McLeary and Co., 1885.

Calhoun, Charles C. *A Small College in Maine, Two Hundred Years of Bowdoin.* Brunswick: Bowdoin College, 1993.

Carroll, Thomas J. *Blindness.* Boston: Little, Brown and Co., 1961.

Carter, W. Horace. *Nature's Masterpiece at Homosassa.* Tabor City, NC: Atlantic Publishing Co., 1981.

Chamberlain, Joshua L. *Bayonet! Forward.* Gettysburg: Stan Clark Military Books, 1994.

Chamberlain, Joshua L. *The Passing of the Armies.* New York: Bantam Books, 1993.

Chase, Henry and Charles Sanborn. *The North and the South: A Statistical View of the Condition of the Free and Slave States.* Boston: Jewett and Co., 1856.

Clark, Calvin. *History of Bangor Theological Seminary.* Boston: Pilgrim Press, 1916.

Cleaveland, Nehemiah. *History of Bowdoin College.* Boston: James Ripley Osgood and Co., 1882.

Clinton, Catherine. *The Other Civil War, American Women in the Nineteenth Century.* New York: Hill and Wang, 1984.

Coe, Harrie B. *Maine, Resources, a History*. New York: Lewis Historical Publishing, 1928.

Cook, Adrian. *The Armies of the Streets*. Lexington: University Press of Kentucky, 1974.

Cook, Anna Maria Green. *History of Baldwin County Georgia*. Anderson, SC: Keys-Hearn Printing Co., 1925.

Conrad, Susan P. *Perish the Thought, Intellectual Women in Romantic America, 1830-1860*. New Jersey: Citadel Press, 1978.

Cutsforth, Thomas. *The Blind in School and Society*. New York: American Foundation for the Blind, 1951.

Davis, Andrew Jackson. *The Great Harmonia*. Rochester, New York: The Austin Publishing Co., 1910 edition.

Davis, William Watson. *The Civil War and Reconstruction in Florida*. New York: Columbia Univ, 1913.

Denney, Robert E. *Civil War Medicine: A Day-by-day Chronicle of the Life of a Nation*. New York: Sterling Publishing, 1994.

Desjardin, Thomas. *Stand Firm Ye Boys From Maine*. Gettysburg: Thomas Publications, 1995.

Dinkins, J. Lester. *Dunnellon: Boomtown of the 1890's*. St. Petersburg: Great Outdoors Publishing, 1969.

Douglas, Marjory Stoneman. *Florida: the Long Frontier*. New York: Harper and Row, 1967.

Dunkin, Roger F. *Coastal Maine: A Maritime History*. New York: W.W. Norton and Co., 1992.

Dunn, Hampton. *Back Home: A History of Citrus County, Florida*. Clearwater: Artcraft Printing, 1976.

Eckert, Ralph Lowell. *John Brown Gordon: Soldier, Southerner, American*. Baton Rouge: Louisiana State University Press, 1989.

Edwards, George T. *Music and Musicians of Maine*. Portland: Southworth Press, 1928.

The Executive Committee. *Maine at Gettysburg*. Gettysburg: Stan Clark Military Books, 1994.

Fredrickson, George. *The Inner Civil War: Northern Intellectuals and the Crisis of the Union*. New York: Harper and Row, 1965.

Frothingham, Richard. *A Tribute to Thomas Starr King*. Boston: Ticknor and Fields, 1865.

Fuess, Claude Moore. *Carl Schurz: Reformer (1829-1906)*. New York: Dodd, Mead and Co., 1932.

Funk, Charles. *Heavens to Betsy and Other Curious Sayings*. New York: Harper and Rowe, 1986.

Furbish, John. *Facts About Brunswick, Maine*. Brunswick: Pejepscot Historical Society, facsimile edition.

Gazley, John Gerow. *American Opinion of German Unification,1848-1871*. New York: Columbia University, 1926.

Gerrish, Theodore. *Army Life: A Private's Reminiscences of the Civil War*. Portland: Hoyt, Fogg and Dunham, 1882.

Godfrey, John E. *The Journals of John Edwards Godfrey.* Rockland, ME: Courier-Gazette, 1979.

Golay, Michael. *To Gettysburg and Beyond: The Parallel Lives of Joshua Lawrence Chamberlain and Edward Porter Alexander.* New York: Crown Publishers, 1994.

Gordon, Linda. *Woman's Body, Woman's Right: A Social History of Birth Control in America.* New York: Grossman Publishers, 1976.

Graham, Ada and Frank. *Kate Furbish and the Flora of Maine.* Gardiner, Maine: Tilbury House, 1995.

Hancock, Almira. *Reminiscences of Winfield Scott Hancock.* New York: Charles L. Webster, 1887.

Hanna, Alfred and Kathryn. *Florida's Golden Sands.* New York: Bobbs-Merrill Co., 1950.

Harris, Neal. *The Artist in American Society: the Formative Years, 1790-1860.* New York: George Braziller, 1966.

Hartman, Mary S. and Lois Banner, eds. *Clio's Consciousness Raised: New Perspectives on the History of Women.* New York: Harper Torchbooks, 1974.

Hatch, Louis Clinton. *The History of Bowdoin College.* Portland: Loring, Short and Harmon, 1927.

Hatch, Louis Clinton. *Maine, a History.* New York: The American Historical Society, 1919.

Helmreich, Ernst C. *Religion at Bowdoin College: a History.* Brunswick: Bowdoin College, 1981.

Helmreich, Louis R. *Our Town.* Brunswick: Pejepscot Historical Society, 1967.

Henderson, Lillian. *Roster of the Confederate Soldiers of Georgia: 1861-1865.* VI.

Herman, E. *Eucken and Bergson.* London: James Clarke and Co., 1912.

Hibbert, Christopher. *Gilbert and Sullivan and Their Victorian World.* New York: American Heritage Publishing, 1976.

Hoke, Jacob. *The Great Invasion of 1863; or, General Lee in Pennsylvania.* Dayton, OH: W. J. Shuey, 1887.

Hollick, Frederick, M.D. *The Diseases of Woman.* New York: T.W. Strong, 1853.

Hollingsworth, Jeff. *Magnificent Mainers.* North Attleborough, MA: Covered Bridge Press, 1995.

Hoogenboom, Ari. *Rutherford B. Hayes: Warrior and President.* Lawrence, KS: Univ. Press of Kansas, 1995.

Howe, Daniel. *The Unitarian Conscience.* Cambridge: Harvard University Press, 1970.

Howe, George Frederick. *Chester A. Arthur: A Quarter Century of Machine Politics.* New York: Dodd, Mead and Co., 1934.

Hyde, Thomas W. *Following the Greek Cross.* Boston: Houghton, Mifflin & Co., 1894.

Jones, Eloise Knight. *Ocala Cavalcade, Through One Hundred Years.* Stephen F. McCready: 1946.

Karnow, Stanley. *In Our Image: America's Empire in the Philippines.* New York: Random House, 1989.

Kelly, Howard A. *Dictionary of American Medical Biography.* Boston: Milford House, 1928.

Ladd, David L. and Audrey J. Ladd, eds. *The Bachelder Papers: Gettysburg in Their Own Words.* Dayton, OH: Morningside, 1994.

Leavitt, Judith. *Brought to Bed: Childbearing in Amerca, 1750-1950.* NY: Oxford University Press, 1986.

Leech, Margaret. *In the Days of McKinley.* NY: Harper and Bros., 1959.

Leonard, John C. *The Higher Spiritualism.* NY: Frederick Hitchcock, 1927.

Linderman, Gerald F. *Embattled Courage: The Experience of Combat in the American Civil War.* NY: The Free Press, a division of Macmillan, Inc.,1987.

Little, George T. *Genealogical and Family History of the State of Maine.* NY: Lewis Historical Publishing Co., 1909.

Mayer, George H. *The Republican Party, 1854-1966.* NY: Oxford University Press, 1967. 2nd edition.

McLouglin, William G. *Modern Revivalism.* NY: The Ronald Press Co., 1959.

M'Clintock, John. *Cyclopedia of Biblical, Theological, and Ecclesiastical Literature.* NY: Harper and Bros., 1891.

McPherson, James M. *Battle Cry of Freedom: The Civil War Era.* NY: Ballantine Books, 1988.

McPherson, James M. *Ordeal By Fire: The Civil War and Reconstruction.* NY: Alfred A. Knopf, 1982.

Minot, John. *Tales of Bowdoin.* Augusta, ME: Press of Kennebec Journal, 1901.

Mundy, James H. *Hard Times, Hard Men.* Scarborough, ME: Harp Publications, 1990.

Nevins, Allan. *Grover Cleveland: A Study in Courage.* NY: Dodd, Mead and Company, 1966.

Novak, Barbara. *American Painting in the 19th Century.* NY: Praeger Publishers, 1969.

Oates, William C. *The War Between the Union and the Confederacy and Its Lost Opportunities.* NY: Neale Publishing Co., 1905.

Ott, Eloise Robinson. *Ocali Country, Kingdom of the Sun, a History of Marion County, Florida.* Ocala: Marion Publishers, 1966.

Pullen, John J. *The Twentieth Maine, a Volunteer Regiment in the Civil War.* Reprint. Dayton, OH: Morningside House, Inc., 1991.

Richter, William L. *The ABC-Clio Companion to American Reconstruction, 1862-1877.* Santa Barbara: ABC-CLIO, 1996.

Robinson, Fannie Harlow. *D.A.R., Daniel Arthur Robinson.* Privately printed, 1968.

Rose, Anne C. *Victorian America and the Civil War.* NY: Cambridge University Press, 1992.

Rothman, Ellen K. *Hand and Hearts: A History of Courtship in America.* NY: Basic Books, 1984.

Rotundo, Anthony. *American Manhood.* NY: Basic Books,1993.

Russell, Charles E. *Blaine of Maine: his Life and Times.* NY: Cosmopolitan Book Corp., 1931.

Schaff, Morris. *The Sunset of the Confederacy.* Boston: John W. Luce and Co., 1912.

Sheridan, Phillip. *Personal Memoirs of P. H. Sheridan.* 2 vols. NY: Webster and Co., 1888.

Sifakis, Stewart. *Who Was Who in the Union.* NY: Facts of File, 1988.

Smith, Matthew Hale. *Sunshine and Shadow in New York.* District of Connecticut: J. B. Burr and Co., 1869.

Southern Historical Association. *Memoirs of Georgia.* Atlanta: Southern Historical Associaton. II, 1895.

Spear, Ellis. *The Civil War Recollections of General Ellis Spear.* Orono, ME: University of Maine Press, 1997.

Stanley, R. H. and George O. Hall. *Eastern Maine and the Rebellion.* Bangor: R. H. Stanley and Company, 1887.

Stockbridge, Frank Parker. *Florida in the Making.* NY: The de Bower Publishing Co., 1926.

Stowe, Harriet Beecher. *Uncle Tom's Cabin.* NY: Penguin, Signet Classic Edition, 1981.

Taylor, Emerson Gifford. *Gouverneur Kemble Warren: The Life and Letters of an American Soldier.* Boston: Houghton Mifflin Co., 1932.

Thayer, Mildred and Mrs. Edward M. Ames. *Brewer, Orrington, Holden, Eddington: History and Families.* Brewer, ME: 1962.

Thomas, George M. *Revivalism and Cultural Change: Christianity, Nation Building....* Chicago: University of Chicago Press, 1989.

Thomas, Jane. *Bloomsbury Guides to English Literature: Victorian Literature, from 1830-1900.* London: Bloomsbury, 1994.

Tremain, Henry E. *Last Hours of Sheridan's Cavalry.* NY: Bonnell, Silver and Bowers, 1904. Reprint of Tremain's "War Memoranda."

Trulock, Alice Rains. *In the Hands of Providence, Joshua L. Chamberlain and the Civil War.* Chapel Hill: University of North Carolina, 1992.

U.S. Military Academy Biographical Register of the Officers and Graduates of the U.S. Military Academy. Boston: Houghton, Mifflin, Co., 1891.

Volwiler, Albert. *The Correspondence Between Benjamin Harrison and James G. Blaine, 1882-1893.* Philadelphia: The American Philosophical Society, 1940.

Verrill, A Hyatt. *Romantic and Historic Florida.* NY: Dodd, Mead and Co., 1935.

Wallace, Willard. *Soul of the Lion.* Gettysburg: Stan Clark Military Books, Thomas Nelson and Sons, 1991.

Walsh, Jack, M.D. *Medical Histories of Union Generals.* Kent, OH: Kent State Press, 1996.

Wheeler, George A. and Henry W. Wheeler. *History of Brunswick, Topsham and Harpswell*. Boston: Alfred Mudge and Son, 1878.

Wilder, Philip S., ed. *General Catalogue of Bowdoin College, 1794-1950*. Portland, ME: The Anthoensen Press, 1950.

Willard, Frances and Mary Livermore. *A Woman of the Century*. Detroit: Book Tower, 1967 edition.

Winslow, Donald. *Lasell: A History of the First Junior College for Women*. Boston: Nimrod Press, 1987.

Worcester, Ellwood and Samuel McComb. *Body, Mind and Spirit*. Boston: Marshall Jones, Co., 1931.

Index

About the Author

Diane Monroe Smith is a native of Maine. She received her degree in Human Development, the study of human relationships, from the University of Maine. Diane is a retired social worker, and currently tutors at Brewer High School in Brewer, Maine, Chamberlain's birthplace. Married with two sons, Robert and Alex. This book is the product of six years of research and writing.